FIRST LADIES

FIRST LADIES

The Ever-Changing Role, from Martha
Washington to Melania Trump

FIFTH EDITION

Betty Boyd Caroli

OXFORD
UNIVERSITY PRESS

Oxford University Press is a department of the University of Oxford.
It furthers the University's objective of excellence in research, scholarship,
and education by publishing worldwide. Oxford is a registered trade mark of
Oxford University Press in the UK and certain other countries.

Published in the United States of America by Oxford University Press
198 Madison Avenue, New York, NY 10016, United States of America.

Library of Congress Cataloging-in-Publication Data
Names: Caroli, Betty Boyd, author.
Title: First ladies : the ever-changing role, from Martha Washington to
Melania Trump / Betty Boyd Caroli.
Description: Fifth edition. | New York City : Oxford University Press, [2019]
| Includes bibliographical references and index.
Identifiers: LCCN 2019004676 | ISBN 9780190669133 (pbk. : alk. paper)
Subjects: LCSH: Presidents' spouses—United States—Biography.
Classification: LCC E176.2 .C37 2019 | DDC 973.09/9 [B]—dc23
LC record available at https://lccn.loc.gov/2019004676

1 3 5 7 9 8 6 4 2

Printed by Sheridan Books, Inc.
United States of America

FOR LIVIO

Contents

Photos follow pages 118, 182, and 262

Author's Note

I NEVER WANTED TO WRITE about women who became famous simply because of the men they married, and when an editor suggested I explore First Ladies, I interpreted what she was inviting me to do as presidential history. That was nearly forty years ago, and what I expected to be a one-time treatment of White House occupants turned into multiple editions, encompassing not only presidents but women's history, national politics, and the press.

The first Oxford University Press edition of *First Ladies* appeared in 1987, and the book grew as I added the records of four more First Ladies for subsequent OUP editions in 1995, 2003, and 2010. The last of these did not include two important chapters from the earlier editions: "First Ladies and the Press" and "The Women They Married." Readers delving into those topics should consult the earlier editions.

Book club editions of *First Ladies* came out in 1989, 1993, 1997, 2001, and 2009. In spite of having the same title as the OUP editions, the book club versions are very different, without source notes and lacking material on women's history and the press that I included in the OUP books.

Along with the different editions of *First Ladies* I produced two illustrated histories that enriched my appreciation of the subject: *America's First Ladies* and *Inside the White House*. Researching and writing about one presidential family (*The Roosevelt Women*, 1998) and one president's marriage (*Lady Bird and Lyndon: The Hidden Story of a Marriage That Made a President*, 2015) also altered my thinking.

I have profited from the insights and assistance of more individuals and institutions than I can possibly acknowledge here. Each edition of *First Ladies* carries its own list, and here, for the final edition, I am singling out persons and groups that have been particularly helpful these last few years. Topping the list is my literary agent, Susan Rabiner, whose sage advice and stalwart support has continued unabated since we first worked together on *Today's Immigrants, Their Stories.* Over the years, the team at Oxford University Press has changed but not their professionalism and collegial support. Tim Bent, currently Executive Editor, and his assistants have enthusiastically backed my work through this fifth edition.

New York City offers authors many congenial settings for exchanging ideas and networking. I have profited from several but want to thank particularly the members of the seminar, Women Writing Women's Lives, and two smaller groups: the Narrative Writing Group and the Gotham Book Group.

Livio Caroli initially found the label First Lady a curious designation, so unlike anything heard in his native Italy. But over time, he has become an ardent backer of my research, and, coincidentally, Italy has imported "First Lady" into its lexicon. He richly deserves the dedication.

New York City, October 1, 2018

Introduction

LIKE MANY HISTORIANS of women's records, I was not initially attracted to the prospect of writing a book on presidents' wives. (Hillary Rodham Clinton had not yet made the kind of headlines that encouraged serious discussion of the job of First Lady.) What value could there be in studying a group of women united only by the fact that their husbands had held the same job? The 1970s and 1980s had finally focused attention on women who achieved on their own—who, then, would want to read about women who owed their space in history books to the men they married? If presidents' wives had remained "footnotes to history," perhaps that was what they deserved.

My curiosity was piqued when I looked at what had been published on the subject. Even a cursory reading of the standard reference work on women revealed a striking pattern among presidents' wives.[1] Most of them came from social and economic backgrounds significantly superior to those of the men they married. Many of the women wed in spite of strenuous parental objection to their choices, and some of the men were younger than their brides. Recurring phrases hinted that the women assumed more control over their lives than I had imagined, and I began to wonder if I had mistakenly assigned them a free and easy ride alongside their prominent husbands. Several of the wives had eased the financial burdens of their households by managing family farms, teaching school, and working as secretaries after their marriages. Other information pointed to a pattern of early exposure to politics, and I was struck by the number of uncles, fathers, and grandfathers who had at one time held political office. Perhaps the women deserved a closer look.

As soon as I examined the women's unpublished letters, I was intrigued. Who could read Lucretia Garfield's poignant puzzlings in the 1850s about what being a wife meant and not then go on to learn how her marriage turned out? What about the indomitable Sarah Polk whose blunt letters and letters of others singled out as particularly opinionated and astute? Who would not want to read what the magazines of the 1840s said about her? Was the handwritten memorandum on the subject of Mary Lincoln's insanity trial to be believed? What about the mysterious Eliza Johnson who was much maligned as a hill woman of little education? Why did her son, then enrolled at Georgetown, write her a beautifully penned, grammatically perfect letter and ask her to "excuse the mistakes"? These and dozens of other questions arose.

I was encouraged by the amount of material available. Because of the prominence of their husbands, First Ladies left more complete records than most of their contemporaries. Evidence on mid-nineteenth-century presidents' wives is rather scant, but even the little-known Eliza Johnson, wife of the first president to be impeached, had her biographer (who went after information about Eliza like a detective intent on solving a crime). Several First Ladies, including Julia Grant, Helen Taft, Edith Wilson, and most of those who lived in the White House after 1963, published their memoirs. I was convinced that all this record keeping could help elucidate not only the First Ladies' lives but also the lives of their countrywomen. A few dozen examples from two centuries of American history cannot be taken to represent all women—no one would claim that they do—but where else could a researcher find so much material about women who moved consecutively through American history?

A handful of presidents' wives achieved great fame, of course, but others of equal or greater interest and significance have been allowed to drop into obscurity. Nearly 170 years before Jackie Kennedy charmed Paris, James Monroe's wife, Elizabeth, was dubbed "la belle américaine" in the French capital. Abigail Adams's injunction to John to "remember the ladies" became a familiar feminist refrain in the twentieth century, while her daughter-in-law, Louisa, wife of John Quincy Adams, was almost forgotten. Yet Louisa Adams showed considerable courage when she set out to travel alone from St. Petersburg to Paris during the Napoleonic Wars. Eleanor Roosevelt's break with precedents is well documented, especially her agreement to meet regularly with women reporters, but her predecessor, Lou Hoover, gained little credit for the feminist speeches she delivered on national radio or for the fortitude she showed in her personal life. Living in China during the Boxer Rebellion, she witnessed gun battles in front of her house but refused to show fright or to flee. Such courageous women surely deserved more attention than they had received.[2]

I was also fascinated by the evolution of the title "First Lady." In 1789, crowds accustomed to the pomp of royal persons heralded the wife of their new president as "Lady Washington." Usage soon changed, however, because in its adolescent decades, when the United States reaffirmed its democratic vows and "plain folks" politics, a "First Lady" made no sense at all. Presidential campaigns that boasted of candidates' humble origins, including log cabin births and little formal schooling, could hardly fasten noble-sounding titles on the wives of the winners. The women were addressed as "Presidentress" or "Mrs. President" or, as was frequently the case, not mentioned at all outside Washington.

Eventually the country's familiarity with its chief executive grew and expectations changed. Poverty and inexperience became somewhat less valuable stepping-stones to the highest office; railroads and mass circulation magazines made presidents more familiar figures across the continent. In response to a firm preference in the United States for married men at the political helm, wives began to travel with their husbands on official trips, and they assumed a popularity of their own. It is not insignificant that Lucy Hayes (1877–1881) accompanied her husband on the first trip a president ever took from the Atlantic coast to the Pacific and also heard herself heralded by a contemporary journalist, Mary Clemmer Ames, as the "first lady of the land."[3]

But the appearance of "first lady" in print predates both Ames and Lucy Hayes and was initially applied to a young woman who never married a president. Harriet Lane, the niece of bachelor President James Buchanan, became extremely popular when she acted as his White House hostess in the 1850s, and in 1860, when *Frank Leslie's Illustrated Newspaper* published a glowing account of her tenure, it dubbed her "first lady in the land."[4] By 1870, columnist Emily Briggs, under her pen name, "Olivia," was using the title for Julia Grant, who currently headed the president's household, scheduling social events and setting standards in style and etiquette. "Olivia" even applied the title to the nation's first presidential couple, noting that in spite of President Washington's attempt to practice "republican simplicity, courtly ways did creep in . . . [and] at Mrs. Washington's receptions in both New York and Philadelphia, the first lady in the land received precisely after the manner of Queen Charlotte's drawing room levées."[5] Even earlier, a British journalist traveling through the South during the Civil War reported overhearing a reference to Jefferson Davis's wife, Varina, as "first lady of the Confederacy."[6]

Dictionaries gradually began to include "First Lady" but only after the country's attention had been drawn to Washington.[7] Before the 1930s, city and county legislators voted on matters of immediate concern, and their names, rather than those of national leaders, appeared during debates over government services. Then the New Deal drew power to Washington, World War II added a large dose of unifying patriotism, and the media cemented the shift to Washington. Thanks to photograph-filled magazines, by the 1950s Americans knew more about Mamie Eisenhower's bangs, her recipe for fudge, and her preference for pastels than they did about their mayors or state representatives.

George E. Reedy, Lyndon Johnson's press secretary in the 1960s, underlined the changed focus when he recalled a trip to Washington D.C. he had taken in his youth. Although Calvin Coolidge was president, Reedy admitted he had not yet heard of him, and the only lasting memory young Reedy took away from that visit to the White House was of having viewed Grace Coolidge's portrait.[8] Reedy could not have ignored the fact that schoolchildren in the 1960s—even those who had never gone near the capital—recognized not only President Johnson but also his wife and daughters and perhaps even his dog, Little Beagle Johnson, all of whom had appeared on national television.

The use of "First Lady" seemed to flourish in spite of deeply felt, very logical objections to it. Women who held the title detested it, and Jackie Kennedy initially forebade her staff to use it.[9] Arthur Schlesinger, Jr., judged the term "deplorable" and began a search for a substitute.[10] As more women sought elective office for themselves, the question arose about what to call their husbands, and jests were made about "First Mate," "First Gentleman," or "First Spouse." None of these objections had any effect, however, and popular magazines continued to publish prominent articles about the current "First Lady," while television correspondents superimposed their own stamp of approval on the phrase.

The title seemed, in part, to reflect a continuing infatuation in the United States with royalty. Even after insisting they had rejected all the trappings of a monarchy, Americans continued to adopt royal terms, referring in the early decades of the republic to the president as "His Majesty," his residence as "the Palace," and his parties as "holding court." When such references disappeared from coverage of the president, they continued to be used for the women at the White House.

In the 1850s, Harriet Lane was praised as "our Democratic queen," and in the Republican administration that followed, Mary Lincoln became the "Republican queen." A century later, Abigail McCarthy, the writer and ex-wife of a presidential candidate, likened Jackie Kennedy's job to that of Princess Grace of Monaco,[11] and Margaret Mead, the anthropologist, was quoted as saying: "Kings and queens have always focused people's feelings and since we're not very far from a monarchy, the President's wife, whoever she is, has little choice but to serve as our queen."[12]

Aside from being there as a symbol, what is the role of a First Lady? The Constitution mentions no assignments for the chief executive's spouse, and yet she has become a prominent part of the presidency. Most Americans presumably know better than the 1920s immigrant who, when queried about who stood to succeed the president, responded "the president's wife." But anyone who watched television coverage of the 1985 Geneva Summit Conference might wonder why Nancy Reagan received so much attention or why President Reagan appeared in front of the United States Congress at the summit's end and thanked his wife for being "an outstanding ambassador of good will for us all."[13]

As though to lend importance to all the questions about White House wives, they have expanded their roles while the office of vice president continues to have a rather ill-defined and somewhat obscure profile, the subject of many jokes. For example, the nineteenth-century journalist Emily Briggs suggested in ironic jest that American women remained unenthusiastic about acquiring the vote because they feared they might be called on to act as vice president.[14]

Men who held the job have remarked on the uselessness of their assignment. John Adams, vice president under George Washington, declared his job "the most insignificant office that ever the invention of man contrived or his imagination conceived."[15] Thomas R. Marshall, Woodrow Wilson's vice president, jokingly compared the role of second-in-command to "a man in a cataleptic state; he cannot speak; he cannot move; he suffers no pain; and yet he is perfectly conscious of everything going on about him."[16]

Thomas Marshall did well to note the limitations of his job. Few people remember his name, while Edith Wilson acquired a reputation as one of the most powerful of all First Ladies. After Woodrow's stroke in 1919, she controlled the flow of communications between him and everyone else, thus prompting Massachusetts Senator Lodge to complain, "A regency was not contemplated in the Constitution."[17]

Regardless of such objections, the First Lady, with little public debate and no constitutional amendments, evolved a role of considerable power. Both outspoken Eleanor Roosevelt and reticent Bess Truman were named during their husbands' administrations as among the "most powerful people in Washington," while the vice presidents were conspicuously absent from such lists. President Ford, whose wife, Betty, explained that she resorted to "pillow talk" to convince her husband of her point of view, admitted that she was frequently successful. Her opinion had carried weight, he said, on some very controversial issues, including the pardon of Richard Nixon. Rosalynn Carter admitted that the enlistment of a president's wife in almost any project is of inestimable value. By 1986, Nancy Reagan was credited with elevating the job of First Lady to a kind of "Associate Presidency."[18] With the powerful Clinton duo in the White House, reporters routinely relayed the views of both the president and First Lady on important issues and appointments.

Since the institution of First Lady is an American one, it seems reasonable to ask what in the United States provided for such growth. Did a quirk in the presidential system nurture it? Or did it develop out of peculiarly American attitudes about leaders? The answer probably lies in both areas.

The United States' presidency, that unique assignment hammered out in the Constitutional Convention in 1787, includes two jobs that are performed by separate individuals in other types of representative governments: a head of state who presides over ceremonial functions, and a head of government who makes major appointments and takes a decisive role in legislation. The American president, charged with both tasks, frequently resorted to sending substitutes on ceremonial and other occasions when a mere physical presence was required. Members of the president's household made excellent surrogates— they signaled the president's approval and also his continued control of government. Martha Washington began what became a tradition when she attended a New York church service while George was ill,[19] and her example inspired her successors. Nearly two hundred years later, Nancy Reagan left her husband's hospital room to return to the White House and announce to guests assembled for a large reception that she was "the president's stand-in."[20] Political wives substituted in other ways for their spouses, sometimes maintaining a facade of civility while their husbands feuded. John Quincy Adams observed in 1824 that Andrew Jackson and William Crawford, contenders for the presidency, were avoiding each other socially but "the ladies have exchanged visits."[21]

The president's living arrangements also increased his wife's role. Once the decision had been made to combine the president's official residence with his private quarters, his spouse dealt with more than just guest lists at official dinners. With a husband who "worked at home," she could not, as John Quincy Adams's wife, Louisa, liked to point out, escape knowing something about his job—who supported him and who opposed.

The election process provided another push into prominence for candidates' wives. Although it was considered inappropriate for women to campaign openly until well into the twentieth century, the groundwork was laid much earlier. Since presidents must seek a popular mandate rather than the approval of their party caucus as a prime minister does, they cannot rely on the contacts and trust accrued from years of working with colleagues but must go to the population at large. A stand-in campaigner is always useful and enjoys some advantages over the candidate. Rosalynn Carter went off on her own in quest of votes for Jimmy fourteen months in advance of the 1976 nomination because she recognized the need to reach many voters. Lady Bird Johnson, confident that southern chivalry would accord her courtesies not granted her husband, campaigned on her own through several states in 1964. She called campaigning "one of the bills you have to pay for the job your husband has."[22]

The enlistment of presidents' spouses in prominent roles required the concurrence of the women, several of whom compiled remarkable records. Eleanor Roosevelt's unprecedented energy over twelve years raised the possibility of just what a president's wife could accomplish; Lady Bird Johnson moved the distaff side of the White House off the family pages of the country's newspapers and into the mainstream of her husband's "Great Society"; Betty Ford took public stands at odds with those of her husband; Rosalynn Carter attended cabinet meetings, defended her approach to mental health care in front of a Senate committee, and conducted talks of a "substantive" nature on a Latin American trip. During Ronald Reagan's convalescence in the summer of 1985, Washington watchers pointed to three people in control at the White House: the president, his chief of staff, and the First Lady. Hillary Rodham Clinton headed her husband's drive to reform health care, a reform he had set as central to his goals as president.

A few First Ladies marked watersheds in the history of the job. Dolley Madison's popularity does not stem solely, as many believe, from her having introduced ice cream to Americans. (That distinction belongs more likely to Thomas Jefferson who recorded in his own hand the preferred recipe for the cold dessert that he had liked so much in France.) But Dolley Madison did exert unusual influence. For almost half a century, she remained a central figure in the capital, showing an uncanny ability to use social occasions to her husband's political advantage. She had laid the foundation for her prominence in the Jefferson administration (1801–1809) when the widowed president turned to her to help him entertain. Later, when James Madison succeeded Thomas Jefferson, Dolley had two terms of her own (1809–1817) to solidify an important role for the president's consort. After her husband retired from office, she continued to act as unofficial tutor to young White House hostesses, making her last, very celebrated appearance at President Polk's party in 1849.

The two decades embracing the Lincoln (1861–1865) and Grant (1869–1877) administrations offered a similar turning point. For two generations preceding them, presidents' wives had made themselves nearly invisible in Washington. Some pled poor health or grief over family tragedies, but most felt justified in sending in substitutes to preside over social gatherings. Neither Mary Lincoln nor Julia Grant showed a similar reticence when confronted with the spotlight; both obliged photographers and reporters who requested pictures and information. The public appetite was whetted for trivia about important persons, and Jenkinsism (the nineteenth-century equivalent of what later came to be called paparazzi) had its day.

No member of a successful politician's family pushes too far beyond the accepted limits of the day. Lucy Hayes (1877–1881) was touted as the "New Woman" because of her college education and concern with issues outside her own family, but she and other presidents' wives in the last quarter of the nineteenth century stayed well within what had been defined as the "woman's sphere." Domesticity retained its high value and even the artistically inclined Caroline Harrison (1889–1892) was praised as the "best housekeeper" of them all. The intellectual Rose Cleveland, who assisted her bachelor brother Grover during his first year in office (1885), received less praise for the books she wrote than for her silk and lace dresses. Americans apparently preferred someone other than a "new woman" for their "first lady."

Nevertheless, some presidents' wives began expanding the job. While Theodore Roosevelt (1901–1909) took advantage of what he termed the "bully pulpit," his wife, Edith, streamlined the executive mansion and hired a staff for herself. Theodore officially renamed the mansion the "White House" and Edith helped transform it into an important national monument. Together they drew the nation's attention to the energetic young family residing at 1600 Pennsylvania Avenue and set the stage for the increased attention in the following decades.

The question of what name to use for women who happen to have married famous men remains a difficult one. American writers commonly refer to men by their last name alone (as in "Lincoln's Gettysburg Address" or "Washington's Farewell") so that wives, when they are mentioned at all, are left with the cumbersome combination of first and last names (Mary Lincoln) or the comparatively demeaning first name alone (Jackie and Nancy). The tacit agreement that women, even powerful ones, cannot be satisfactorily identified by surname only extends beyond the country's borders and into coverage of the highest ranks of government (as the records of "Indira" [Gandhi] and "Golda" [Meir] show), but that hardly justifies such usage.

Since famous couples are my subject here, I decided to treat both partners equally and to use given names wherever the text permits. Readers who cringe at seeing the father of their country referred to as "George" might want to consider why they had never reacted so strongly to seeing "Martha Dandridge Custis Washington" abbreviated to "Martha."

The few dozen women who shaped First Ladyship (counting is complicated by the fact that daughters, daughters-in-law, and sisters of presidents used the title) ranged in age from early twenties to late sixties, from superbly educated for their time to poorly schooled. Some showed themselves immensely courageous and adventuresome; others were emotionally unstable, withdrawn, and beset by enough personal tragedies to defeat even gargantuan wills. Each woman worked within a set of expectations for her time and place, often within the confines imposed by the special needs of marriage to a politician. In one sense, this book has become an inquiry into attitudes toward marriage.

No matter how they performed their jobs, First Ladies never lacked detractors. Critics pointed to their extravagance (Mary Lincoln), coarseness (Margaret Taylor), casual entertaining (Dolley Madison), elitism (Elizabeth Monroe), prudishness (Lucy Hayes), gaiety (Harriet Lane), excessive grief (Jane Pierce), advanced age (Martha Washington), and youth (Julia Tyler). When wives appeared to exert some influence on their husbands or on government, they were charged with exercising "petticoat government" (Edith Wilson), running their husbands' careers (Florence Harding), putting words into the president's mouth (Eleanor Roosevelt), "getting people fired" (Nancy Reagan), and making her husband look like a wimp (Hillary Rodham Clinton).

The reader who expects to find here a tightly argued thesis will be disappointed. None has emerged, except the unsurprising conclusion that individual First Ladies have reflected the status of American women of their time while helping shape expectations of what women can properly do. They extend our understanding of how women participated in government in ways other than simply voting and holding office.[23] Yet this book cannot substitute for a text on women's history or for the multitude of specific studies that have appeared in that field in the last few decades or are scheduled for future publication.

Partisans of individual First Ladies will be disappointed that material on their favorites has been abridged. Full biographies, when available, are indicated in the notes, but I have had to select and cut, as I sought to emphasize particular aspects of each woman's tenure. My focus has been the women—how each saw her place in her time and how others saw her. As much as possible, I have tried to quote the participants directly—not because I expected to demonstrate what was "true" but to illustrate a public perception or to document an explanation. Again and again, I skipped over important national events and presidential actions so that I could concentrate on fitting First Ladies into women's history. In cases where a great deal had already been written (on Eleanor Roosevelt and Abigail Adams, for example), I have intentionally limited my coverage so as to give more attention to the lesser known (such as Sarah Polk and Lou Hoover). I sought to illuminate all their records—not just those of a few exceptional individuals.

In the beginning, I considered writing a history of the institution of First Lady, a book that would have documented the decision-making process, the level of staff performance, and the rise in power on the distaff side of the White House. I abandoned that project when I realized that most readers would want more biographical information than that volume could have included. I was also persuaded by the need to wait for hundreds more boxes of White House materials to become available and then be carefully examined by several scholars.

Taking stock of the record of First Ladies at this point does not imply that their job will remain static. It will surely continue to change. If a married woman achieves the presidency, her husband will have to consider how to fit his life to the role. A woman whose husband becomes chief executive while she remains dedicated to a career of her own will have to formulate her own answers. Powerful couples who work in tandem may motivate Americans to legislate limits or to require accountability on the part of the spouse who, though unelected, behaves as though she (or he) were.

Whatever the future brings, it seems appropriate to look at presidents' wives over more than two centuries and see how the role of First Lady was transformed from ceremonial backdrop to substantive world figure. Each was given "a magic wand," it has been said,[24] with no instructions on its use—each woman had to figure that out for herself.

FIRST LADIES

1

Setting Precedents: The First Presidents' Wives (1789–1829)

ON A MAY MORNING in 1789, President Washington's barge docked at the southern tip of Manhattan and a short, matronly woman stepped ashore. After thirty years of marriage to the tall general beside her, Martha Washington was accustomed to fitting her life to his, but the direction of that accommodation was no longer clear. His role in this new government remained undefined, falling somewhere between monarch and commoner; her part was even less clear. If George would not be king, then she could not be queen; yet the thirteen-gun salute and shouts of "Long Live Lady Washington" suggested some kind of special prominence.

To deal with many problems, including some of the questions about her role, George Washington had preceded Martha to the new nation's temporary capital in New York,[1] and when he went over to New Jersey that morning to escort his wife into the city, he supplied the answer to at least one of those questions. Rather than let Martha Washington travel in a private conveyance, he brought her over in the presidential barge. Thus the two of them, the president and Martha, arrived to fanfare, signaling the beginning of what would become an American tradition—the presidential spouse had a public role in the ritual and ceremonial aspects of the presidency.

The crowds that lined the streets as the Washingtons made their way from the Battery to their rented house on Cherry Street were not the first that Martha had faced. On her trips to join George each winter during the Revolution, she had already responded to cheers for "Lady Washington." Those earlier outbursts had seemed almost part of the war mood and may have been directed as much to raising the morale of the spectators as to expressing tribute to the general's wife. When the shouts continued after the war ended, their meaning was less clear.

Other kinds of uncertainty surrounded much of the new government's activity in 1789. The Constitution writers, in their attempts to assign neither too much power to the chief executive nor too little, had debated the method of election of a president, the length of the term of office, the powers to be designated, and whether or not a single individual or a triumvirate might best serve the new nation's needs in the chief executive role. Even after weeks of discussion, however, they had not worked out many of the details and in the end chose to rely on the checks of the other branches and the good will of those who served in the first years to make the limits clear. No easy answers presented themselves. Complaints that presidents, such as "King Andrew" (Jackson), assumed royal prerogatives occurred all through the nineteenth century, giving way to charges that they assumed dictatorial powers in the twentieth. Accusations that their wives took on royal airs persisted even longer—with a 1982 cartoon depicting Nancy Reagan wearing a crown.[2]

The form of address for the chief executive was one of those details that had not been established in the Constitution, and as soon as George Washington arrived in New York he turned to a committee of Congress for advice.[3] The Senate had suggested "His Highness, the President of the United States and Protector of Liberties," but the more democratic House of Representatives would hear of nothing other than "Mr. President."[4] One newspaper editor argued vehemently for "His Excellency,"[5] and John Adams pointed out that a simple "Mr. President" showed too little deference and sounded like the officer of some local, insignificant association.[6] Suggestions of titles for the president's wife ranged all the way from "Marquise" and "Lady" down to a simple "Mrs."[7]

Titles became the subject of heated debate because of the consensus prevailing in the United States in 1789 that an important experiment in government was underway. The presidential system was quite daring, in that it placed in one individual—the chief executive—duties that would often be separated in other government systems. The president had to juggle the largely ceremonial obligations of a head of state with the more substantive, onerous duties of a head of government who runs the country. His success in the ceremonial role depended not only on how well he comported himself while entertaining foreign dignitaries—indeed, given the distance separating the United States from the great nations of Europe such obligations might be slim at best—but also on how well he expressed the needs and feelings of the people he governed.

Physical accessibility to leaders was no insignificant matter in the infant republic. A genuinely democratic spirit called for the president to open his doors to any caller anytime, and, initially, George Washington appears to have done just that. But the folly of this arrangement became clear when people arrived at all hours, leaving the president little time for work and permitting his household almost no privacy.

George Washington canvassed widely for advice, going to personal friends, a Supreme Court justice, congressmen, and his own vice president for counsel on how to balance the need for accessibility with the other demands of his job. Alexander Hamilton, an outspoken advocate of a powerful executive, advised his mentor to keep social contacts to a minimum, in order to preserve the dignity of the office. A president might issue invitations, Hamilton suggested, but not more often than once a week, and when he met his guests, he should spend very little time with them. As for visits to other people's homes, Hamilton thought these entirely inappropriate and he warned against them.[8] John Adams, who had never gained a reputation for catering to the masses, came out on the more liberal side in this discussion when he ventured that the president might call on close personal friends and hold as many as two parties a week.[9]

Finally George Washington took space in the local newspaper to announce his general calling hours: persons simply paying their respects should limit themselves to Tuesday and Friday afternoons between two and three o'clock, while those on business could come any time except Sunday, when the president wanted to see no one at all.[10]

George also resolved that he would host a reception for men only, called a "levée," each Tuesday afternoon and that Martha would preside on Friday evenings at another party, called a "drawing room" which both men and women could attend.[11] To mark this latter occasion as official but slightly less formal than the first, the president would attend but he would carry neither sword nor hat.[12]

Martha Washington had not even arrived in the capital for these discussions, so she could hardly have been consulted as to her views, but George's wide canvass for advice set the stage for his successors to admit that they included their wives in important presidential matters. Martha's acquiescence in her role is confirmed by the fact that immediately upon her arrival in New York she began performing tasks that had devolved on her simply by virtue of her husband's office. The first morning she awakened to face dozens of curious women who had directed their carriages to her Cherry Street house,[13] and that afternoon she sat down to dinner with guests whom George had previously invited. No mere social event, the dinner represented one of the president's first attempts at political brokerage, because although political parties had not yet developed, George had reasoned that congressmen from different parts of the country needed an opportunity to meet socially and work out possible differences.

The next day, a Friday, Martha held her first "drawing room,"[14] described by those who attended as a particularly "thick" party because it brought out New York's curious to evaluate the hostess's efforts to entertain graciously without seeming to carve a superior niche for herself. Whether or not Martha satisfied these competing claims to everyone's satisfaction remains unclear. But she certainly tried. While stewards "handed in" guests, she remained seated in queenly fashion and the president moved among those present, escorting them to the refreshment table and supplying introductions. When guests stood around uncertainly, not knowing how to end the party, Martha took control. Those present had wondered whether they should wait respectfully for the hostess to exit, as they would have done for royalty, or, in good democratic style, leave at whim. Martha's solution could hardly have offended or been interpreted as taking on airs. "The General always retires at nine," she stood and announced, "and I generally precede him." Then she walked out.[15]

While serving as hostess would often turn out to be an onerous, sometimes overwhelming part of the responsibilities assumed by presidents' wives, it is important to note that eighteenth-century America made fewer firm divisions than would the nineteenth century between men's and women's tasks.[16] George Washington, not Martha, for instance, had advertised for their housekeepers in Virginia. When he arrived in New York, he continued in his normal pattern, hiring a staff and supervising the renovation of their rented house. Tobias Lear, the Harvard-educated secretary who had worked for the Washingtons at Mt. Vernon, assumed responsibility for many household details, issuing the invitations and keeping the accounts, while Sam Fraunces, the West Indian tavern keeper who had impressed General Washington during the war, managed the fourteen servants.[17]

Curiosity about the chief executive's house continued to draw many callers to it, and despite the firm limits George set for himself, Martha reasoned that she should do otherwise. Custom dictated that a gracious lady, no matter what her husband's title, returned the calls of all women who had come to her door and left their calling cards, so Martha resolved to return each visit, and to accomplish this within three days of the original call.[18]

Even the vice president's wife, Abigail Adams, soon got caught up in this activity, noting in a letter that she had "returned 60 visits in

3 or 4 afternoons."[19] Following the Washingtons' lead, the Adamses invited all the congressmen and their wives to dine with them: "Indeed I have been fully employd," Abigail Adams wrote, "in entertaining company, in the first place all the Senators who had Ladies and families, then the remaining Senators, and this week we have begun with the House, and tho we have a room in which we dine 24 persons at a Time, I shall not get through them all, together with the publick Ministers for a month to come."[20]

When the house on Cherry Street failed to accommodate the guest lists that Tobias Lear assembled, the presidential entourage moved to larger quarters on Broadway.[21] But before settling completely into their new house, the Washingtons had to prepare to move again—this time to Philadelphia, where the nation's capital was transferred in the fall of 1790. The change pleased Martha in some ways—she thought the Market Street address afforded more privacy than she had found in New York—and by Christmas day, she was ready to open her house to local residents. A week later, many of them returned for her New Year's reception, a repeat performance of the party she had given the year before in New York. Her regular Friday drawing room occurred on January 1 in 1790, and George had postponed his Tuesday levée to coincide, thus beginning a tradition that the president and his wife would open their house on New Year's to all who wanted to come. Except in wartime or periods of mourning, the event was a regular feature of the president's schedule and eventually drew thousands, until it so taxed the energies of the hosts that the Hoovers stopped it in 1933.

By the time George Washington's two terms had been completed, some aspects of the president's role had been settled (although by no means all) and some of his wife's responsibilities had taken shape (although they would change.) In meeting the obligations of the two roles he had assumed—as head of state and head of government—the president would enlist his spouse's help openly in the first job but only covertly, if at all, in the second. Since the ceremonial side of the job required presenting a democratic image but also including enough formality to retain respect, a wife who was willing to do so could help maintain a balance. When her husband appeared pompous, she might stress humility; if he chose to move casually among guests, she could hold court in queenly fashion. Her calls at people's homes substituted for contacts that her husband's schedule did not permit.

George and Martha Washington thus set some precedents that would continue relatively undisturbed for more than a century, until gradually the job of president's wife changed to involve her more openly in the substantive part of the office. Martha gave no evidence of playing anything other than the hostess role—and George gave no evidence of ever requesting that she do more—but the role she filled should not be dismissed lightly. When he was too ill to attend church services, her presence was duly recorded, as though people in a pre-television age needed a glimpse of their leader for reassurance. When she made an appearance at the circus, she received the welcome of a special person.[22] She even helped her husband circumvent the prohibition against a president accepting gifts. When Pennsylvania offered her a costly carriage, George decided she could keep it since it had not actually been bestowed on him.[23] Had Martha Washington been less meek, and involved herself openly in the political debates of the day, or had she been more elitist and refused to call on everyone who called on her, she might have set a different tone for future presidents' wives.

But the next in line, Abigail Smith Adams, brought very different ideas to marriage and women's role in it—opinions that could not help but make themselves felt in how she handled the role of president's wife. Speaking out had always come naturally to her, and John's first admiring mention of her in his diary, when she was only fourteen, was as "a wit."[24] By the time she reached maturity, her sharp tongue and strong views had become more obviously part of her personality. When her husband ascended to the country's highest office in 1797, rumors multiplied concerning her influence. Rather than Lady Adams, she was dubbed "Mrs. President."

From very early in her husband's administration, Abigail Adams was accused of playing politics. When she spoke out on the split developing between Jeffersonian Republicans and Federalists, she had, in the opinion of many political figures, stepped beyond the proper bounds for her sex. Albert Gallatin, an Adams opponent, described in a letter to his wife that a friend had been at "the court" [the Adams house] and had "heard her majesty [Abigail Adams] as she was asking the names of different members of Congress and then pointing out which were 'our people'." Such partisanship in a woman offended Gallatin: "She is Mrs. President not of the United States but of a faction. . . . It is not right." More to his liking was his own apolitical spouse whom he saw as a model for all women as he assured her when he wrote: "Indeed my beloved, you are infinitely more lovely than politics."[25]

Abigail's two thousand extant letters leave no doubt that she held strong opinions on many matters and several leading political figures. In Alexander Hamilton's eyes she saw ". . . the very devil . . . lasciviousness itself."[26] She judged a Massachusetts congressman uninformed;

Albert Gallatin was dangerous, "sly, artfull . . . insidious . . . [leading a party of men who had so openly favored France that] the French have boasted of having more influence in the United States than our own government."[27] Against her husband's critics, she fought back, defending him against various charges, including that of giving preferential treatment to their son.

In seeking the reasons for Abigail's strong voice, her husband's support is not inconsequential. John's biographers found clear evidence that he discussed many important problems with her, engaged her help in drafting semi-official letters, and, in the words of historian Page Smith, treated her as "minister without portfolio."[28] It comes as no surprise that people who sought the president's approval sometimes went to his wife first. Nor did they hesitate to blame her when things went awry. After John Adams had made an unpopular appointment in his wife's absence, he wrote to inform her: "O how they lament Mrs. A's absence. . . . She is a good counsellor! If she had been here, Murray would never have been named or his mission instituted. This ought to gratify your vanity enough to cure you."[29]

To the minority who approved of opinionated women, Abigail Adams became something of a heroine. Henrietta Liston, wife of the British minister, wrote her uncle in 1797 that she was "much pleased with Mrs. Adams, [and hoped] to acquire [her] sort of spirit in time but the thing is new to me yet."[30] Albert Gallatin's kind of disapproval was the more common response, and Abigail found herself caricatured in both song and drawing. An English ballad of the time had popularized the story of an elderly married couple, "Darby and Joan," who were devoted to each other but woefully out of touch with their times, and Abigail was distressed to see herself and her husband referred to in print as America's "Darby and Joan."[31]

None of the criticism deterred Abigail in her efforts to help John in whatever way she could. During the early years of their marriage, when he absented himself for long periods, she eased his rise in politics by her willingness and ability to raise their children, run the family farm, and keep the household solvent. After John achieved high office, she turned her managerial abilities to promoting his success, relieving him of family responsibilities and training a careful eye on expenses. She had missed his inauguration in 1797 because she was nursing his sick mother in Massachusetts, and when he complained that he needed her with him, she replied she would come as soon as she could—she would not wait for "courting."

By the time Abigail arrived in Philadelphia in May 1797, inflation had so diminished the value of the chief executive's salary that

entertaining became a financial, as well as an emotional, burden. In
her diary she noted that for the Fourth of July reception that the president traditionally gave for representatives and senators, she would
have to supply "200 pounds of cake and two 1/4 casks of wine and
rum."[32] True to form, she managed to save part of the president's
salary while still fulfilling what she perceived as social obligations. Few
of her successors would be able to do so; her loud complaints indicate, however, that she had intended to save even more.[33]

Demands her husband's job imposed on her time became nearly as
objectionable as those on her purse. "I keep up my old Habit of rising
at an early hour," she wrote in May 1797, "[and] if I did not, I should
have little command of my Time. At 5 I rise. From that time till 8 I
have a few leisure hours. At 8 I breakfast, after which untill Eleven I
attend to my Family arrangements." The rest of the day was mostly
First Lady work. "From 12 untill two I receive company, sometimes
untill 3. We dine at that hour unless on company days which are tuesdays & thursdays. After dinner I usually ride out untill seven. I begin
to feel a little more at Home and less anxiety about the ceremonious
part of my duty tho by not having a drawing Room for the summer I
am obliged every day to devote two Hours for the purpose of seeing
company."[34]

Near the end of John Adams's single term, Abigail had to oversee
the transfer of the President's Palace, as it was still called by some
people, to the new capital on the banks of the Potomac. In letters to
her family she made little attempt to conceal her displeasure with the
unformed city that she found in December 1800. Streets remained
unfinished in Washington "which is [a city] only . . . in name," Abigail
wrote to her daughter, "[and as for neighboring Georgetown, it is] the
very dirtyest Hole I ever saw for a place of any trade, or respectability
of inhabitants . . . a quagmire after every rain."[35] Vacillating as usual
between wanting the president to live in comfort and frowning on too
much splendor, Congress had been stingy with appropriations for his
new permanent residence, and the Adamses arrived to find the house
unfinished. Not all the rooms had been plastered, "bells are wholly
wanting," Abigail complained, "and promises are all you can obtain."
When the time came for the requisite entertaining, Abigail herded
her guests into the one fully furnished hall, but, understanding the
political cost of appearing too critical of what had been provided, she
alerted her daughter, "When asked how I like it, say that I wrote you
the situation is beautiful."[36]

Abigail hardly had time to settle into the Washington house before
the results of the 1800 election signaled that she would have to move

out. Political parties had slowly coalesced around several themes, including matters of both domestic and international concern. Federalists tended to champion a strong central government at home and the rightness of the British cause over that of the French in the European war. Democratic-Republicans talked more about protecting the rights of the individual states and about the need to stand up for the French. In nominating John Adams for a second term, the Federalists had not been unanimous, and some of them hoped that Charles Cotesworth Pinckney of South Carolina, whom they had chosen as candidate for vice president, would top John Adams's votes and win the presidency, a possibility under a system that selected both officers on the same ballot. The opposition, zealously defending the common man and guarding states' rights against encroachment from the central government, ran Thomas Jefferson under the Democratic-Republican banner and selected Aaron Burr for the second spot.

The election went on for weeks because a tie in the electoral college between Jefferson and Burr threw the decision into the House of Representatives. Abigail Adams understood that her husband was out of the running but she could not bring herself to leave Washington until the final balloting on February 11, 1801, less than a month before the inauguration. Deeply disappointed but philosophical about Jefferson's victory which ended the administration she had frequently described as "ours," she wrote to her son: "The consequences to us personally is that we retire from public life, [and] . . . If I did not rise with dignity, I can at least fall with ease, which is the more difficult task."[37]

Nearly half a century would pass before Americans again voted into the presidency a man (James Polk) who appeared to hold such high regard for the counsel of his spouse as did John Adams. His, it should be noted, was respect resulting from experience. During their long marriage, Abigail showed both wisdom and strength, never permitting concern with domestic details to shut her off from important issues facing the country. When John was absent from Massachusetts, she kept him informed of political sentiment there, and she exchanged letters with many astute women, including Mercy Warren, the historian of the Revolution. Abigail's voicing of strong opinions after her husband became president represented no change in her behavior— she had always spoken her mind—and she demonstrated that a president's wife could, with her husband's support, move beyond a merely ceremonial role to involve herself in substantive issues.

The Adams administration also demonstrated, however, that a president would be criticized by the Gallatins of the time who preferred the model left by Martha Washington. Very early in her husband's career, Martha had set limits for herself well within the confines of domesticity. During visits to George at the front during the Revolution, she had darned the socks of other soldiers and carried them hot soup. Later, as the president's wife, she continued in a docile, supportive role. Which of the two examples became the pattern would be determined by those who followed.

Thomas Jefferson's two terms (1801–1809) offered an excellent opportunity to introduce different expectations for hostesses at the White House, as the president's residence was occasionally being called. Both Jefferson and his second-in-command, Aaron Burr, were widowers, and the new president's casual approach to etiquette suggested that little importance would be placed on entertaining. A staff could handle the mundane details, and Jefferson, extremely knowledgeable about food and wine, could evaluate their decisions. As for the ceremonial part of the office, the third president had quickly made clear that "pell mell" would prevail. He walked through the mud to his own inauguration and then returned to sit "far down" the boardinghouse table for his evening meal. Installed in the President's House (as he quickly renamed the residence), he insisted that seating be a matter of chance rather than protocol, thus diminishing the importance of rank. If both Martha Washington and Abigail Adams had voluntarily or out of a sense of loyalty to their spouses accepted a portion of the president's ceremonial tasks for themselves, Jefferson, by acting as the country's head host and protocol chief, seemed on his way to challenging the absolute necessity that a spouse be there to assume those duties.

As so often happens, a rigorously observed custom interfered. Etiquette dictated the presence of a hostess if women guests were to attend a dinner party. Showing no interest in breaking that tradition, President Jefferson asked his good friend, Dolley Madison, to "take care of the female guests expected."[38] His choice of Dolley came naturally. Jefferson's home, Monticello, was within a few miles of the Madisons' Virginia estate and in the first years of her marriage, when her husband's fame had drawn crowds of admirers, Dolley had frequently fled to the quiet of Jefferson's house to avoid the confusion at her own. James Madison's appointment as secretary of state in 1801 legitimatized her new prominence in Washington society, and she thoroughly enjoyed the elevation. She used Jefferson's two terms to assure a central role for whoever served as the president's hostess and to develop her own formidable reputation for adroitly mixing politics and parties. An older, less energetic, or more insecure woman in her place might have hesitated to assert herself, but Dolley Madison, at thirty-two, showed no reluctance.

Dolley Madison's emergence as a superior hostess is somewhat ironic since she was raised in the Society of Friends where frivolity and extravagance had little place. From a childhood among the "plain people," she grew to put great importance on what she wore and on having a good time, ordering her shawls and turbans from Paris and losing money at cards with considerable aplomb. Much of the change in her life can be attributed to her marriage, surely one of the most unusual unions in presidential history.

Dolley Payne Todd's marriage to James Madison had not been her first. Like Martha Washington and Martha Jefferson, she had been a widow when she wed a future president. The third-born child of failed shopkeepers in Philadelphia, Dolley had first married a young lawyer from her family's Quaker congregation. Within three years, both he and one of their young sons had died, leaving Dolley at age twenty-five to fend for herself and her remaining son. She moved back to her mother's to help run a boardinghouse. Within months, Aaron Burr introduced her to one of the most famous men in America—James Madison—who had passed age forty without taking a wife.[39] Because he was several inches shorter than she but of obvious intellect and even then of enormous reputation, she immediately dubbed him the "great little Madison."[40]

Shy, even sourish in public, he could be a wit in private and evidently admired a woman who could take her gaiety everywhere. Within months of their meeting and less than a year after her first husband's death, Dolley Payne Todd and James Madison were married. For the forty-odd years that they lived together, he complained if he had to be separated from his "Dolley" and she ran here and there in the service of the man she always called "Madison."

The first woman to witness her husband's swearing in, Dolley immediately indicated her intention to play a visible role by opening her Georgetown house for a reception following the inauguration ceremony. Perhaps because the event fell on a Saturday, larger than usual crowds had come to Washington and hundreds of people lined up to sample the Madisons' punch and cake.[41] The President's House would have accommodated a larger crowd, but ex-presidents did not vacate speedily in those days and Jefferson took a week to get his things together for the trip back to Monticello.

At the first inaugural ball, planned by Washington's Dancing Assembly for Long's Hotel that evening, Dolley continued to hold center stage. Heavy demand for tickets (only 400 were issued)[42] led to great confusion, and the room became so congested that someone had to break a window to provide ventilation. People stood on benches to catch a glimpse of the new president's wife, who behaved, one woman wrote glowingly, "with perfect propriety . . . dignity, sweetness and grace."[43] John Quincy Adams, who rarely enjoyed social gatherings and never shone at them, stood in the minority when he pronounced this party "excessive . . . oppressive and bad."[44]

The president's official residence remained unfinished at the beginning of the Madison administration. One young visitor from New York described its exterior as appallingly grim, more suitable for a "State Prison" than anything else.[45] Dolley insisted that improvements begin at once. When Congress appropriated $11,000, she spent almost one-quarter of the total on just the East Room (which Jefferson had neglected to furnish.)[46] For help in her selections, she turned to Benjamin Latrobe, the English-born architect who had become President Jefferson's surveyor of public buildings.[47] Fewer than eight weeks after the inauguration she was ready to show off the results at her first drawing room.

With the public's curiosity divided between the president and his wife, the weaknesses of one partner could be offset by the strengths of the other. James Madison, who could be appealing in private but appear disinterested around people he did not know, gained from Dolley's ability to charm almost everyone. Washington Irving, who attended a Madison reception soon after he arrived in the capital in 1811, captured the difference when he described Dolley as "a fine, portly buxom dame who has a smile and pleasant word for everybody . . . but as to Jemmy Madison, ah poor Jemmy—he is but a withered little applejohn."[48] The president preferred an inconspicuous seat at the dinner table so he could avoid having to play the host, and his guests frequently went away thinking he had not even noticed them. "He had no leisure for the ladies," one woman complained.[49]

With considerable skill, Dolley Madison could pick out guests who were uncomfortable and quickly put them at ease. One young man, so confused by the acrobatics of a president's party that he dropped his saucer and then, in desperation, stuffed his cup in his pocket, looked up to see a smiling Dolley Madison coming toward him. "The crowd is so great," she reassured him, "that no one can avoid being jostled."[50]

But Dolley's entertaining had its political side as well because she showed the skills of a candidate running for office, rarely forgetting a name or making an inappropriate comment. Aware of the criticism that had surrounded Abigail Adams, Dolley sought to avoid appearing an "active partisan,"[51] and she showered her husband's enemies with the same attention that she gave his friends. Frances Few, who visited the capital during Dolley's first season, pointed to her inscrutability when she wrote: "It is impossible to know what Mrs. Madison is thinking because she tried to be all things to all men."[52] Some critics claimed that Dolley paid too much attention to other men; one White House visitor reported that the president's wife had told an old bachelor that she was "no prude, and then held up her mouth for him to kiss."[53] A political opponent had hinted broadly during a campaign that James "had impaired" himself "by an unfortunate matrimonial connection,"[54] but such attacks were rare. Dolley Madison achieved a popularity that her successors would envy for decades to come.

The reputation resulted from more than the style of her parties. In delicate political maneuvering, she could soften a cruel dismissal. After her husband eased Robert Smith, secretary of state, out of his cabinet in 1811, she gave a dinner in Smith's honor. When Smith failed to appear, Dolley took her sister and "called twice," Smith wrote, "with professions of great affection."[55]

Dolley Madison's task became more difficult as the presidential election of 1812 approached. James Madison's first term had not been easy. Both the British and French had continued to interfere with American shipping on the Atlantic, and boundary disputes with Indians erupted frequently in the Great Lakes region. Yet James very much wanted another term and Dolley remained optimistic about his chances. As early as December 1811, she had observed that "the intrigues for President and Vice President [for the 1812 election] go on," but she correctly predicted victory: "I think it may terminate as the last did."[56]

In the summer of 1812, James Madison declared war on Great Britain, and the election a few months later became, in part, a referendum on the incumbent's decision to fight. Opposition Federalists in New England termed this "Mr. Madison's War" and prepared to ship their goods through Canada. In the election, they aligned with dissidents from the president's own Democratic-Republicans in an attempt to defeat him, and they nearly succeeded. When the results came in, James Madison had won but not by much. Had he failed to take one large state, such as Pennsylvania, his opponent, DeWitt Clinton, would have moved into the White House.

Dolley well understood the importance of keeping discontented congressmen in line so that they would not be tempted to vote for the opponent. Six months before the election, she wrote her sister that a large number of legislators were, "all offended [with Madison] and refused to dine with him," but a week later she had them there "in a large body."[57] James Blaine, who later tried for the presidency himself, credited Dolley with a large share in her husband's 1812 victory. Her cheerful impartiality brought the disenchanted around, Blaine wrote, and she convinced them to stick with the incumbent.[58]

James Blaine may have overstated the case (he was, of course, not an observer of the events he described), but historians who have carefully studied the Madison administration tend to agree that Dolley proved a valuable asset to her husband. In the continuing debate between a democratic chief executive and a regal one, she played both sides; and for every critic who thought she went too far on one side, she acquired an admirer on the other. One woman described approvingly how the Madisons maintained a royal setting at their parties where custom dictated that each female guest "courtesy [*sic*] to 'His Highness' [the President] and then find a seat,"[59] but a senator from Massachusetts stressed the egalitarianism at the Madisons' parties. For his tastes, Dolley went a bit too far in implementing democracy, mixing "all classes of people . . . from the Minister from Russia to under clerks of the post office and the printer of a paper—greasy boots and silk stockings . . . [with some of the women] giving the impression of 'high life below the stairs.' "[60] Such contrasting evaluations of Dolley Madison led one historian to conclude that she was "brilliant in the things she did not say or do."[61]

Moreover, the things she did do, even actions deemed inappropriate for her peers, merely earned her more accolades. Stained fingers left little doubt that she used snuff, not an acceptable habit for nineteenth-century ladies but one that was excused in her. "In her hands the snuffbox, seems only a gracious implement with which to charm," one woman offered in Dolley's defense,[62] and another admirer described the snuffbox as a "perfect security from hostility as bread and salt [are] among many savage tribes."[63] Some of Dolley's observers considered the possibility that she used cosmetics, with some deciding that she surely "painted," while others offered evidence that her heightened color resulted from natural enthusiasm. "I do not think it true [that she uses cosmetics]," one contemporary wrote, "I saw her color come and go at the naval ball."[64]

The desire to cultivate political support for her husband sent Dolley out visiting all the congressmen's families who moved to Washington. The fact that she called first was important—it signaled humility in the president's attitude toward legislators. But the number of congressmen and their aides had grown since the days of Martha Washington and Abigail Adams, and the congressional election of 1810 had brought to the capital a large, new group from the West.

The expectation that Dolley would not only call on each family but also invite them to the President's House imposed a large burden even on someone who thrived on playing the hostess. "We have members in abundance with their wives and daughters," Dolley wrote to friends in Paris, "[and] I have never felt the entertainment of company oppressive until now."[65] Although often perfunctory (with Dolley leaving her carriage only long enough to drop her card on the silver tray in the front hall), the calls took her from one end of Washington's unpaved streets to the other, consuming entire days so that she had only Sundays for herself. Yet tampering with tradition carried political risks that she understood all too well, since any family slighted might take revenge on her husband.

Dolley's successor, Elizabeth Monroe, was another story, however, and she acted to reduce dramatically the social obligations of all future First Ladies. The results of the 1816 election had hardly come in when it became clear that Elizabeth Monroe had no intention of allowing her daily schedule to be dictated by others, certainly not by the provincial wives of midwestern congressmen. Born to wealthy New Yorkers, she was acquainted with the courts of Europe, having accompanied her husband, James Monroe, when he held diplomatic posts in both Paris and London. She meant to guard her schedule against "democratic" encroachments.

If Dolley Madison was a First Lady of the people, Elizabeth Kortright Monroe was anything but. Extremely reticent, she preferred privacy and insisted on elegance. Parisians had dubbed her "la belle américaine" when she lived among them in the 1790s, and it was generally agreed that she had retained her spectacular beauty at age fifty-four when her husband became president. Portraits made of her at that time show a regal woman, dark and poised, flattered by the new fashions that exposed more arm and breast than had previously been considered proper. She preferred to order her dresses from France and reportedly paid $1,500 per costume for the privilege.[66] Her exquisite clothing, remarkable both for its design and workmanship, later added interest to the popular Smithsonian exhibition on First Ladies, but it produced a great deal of envy among her contemporaries.

Elizabeth Monroe's final indiscretion, in the eyes of many Washingtonians, was to appear much younger than her age. One indignant woman complained: "Mrs. Monroe [has] an appearance of youth which would induce a stranger to suppose her age to be 30, in lieu of which, she introduces them to her granddaughter 18 or 19 years old."[67] Fifty years old at the time, Elizabeth Monroe had one granddaughter, then age twelve. There was then some exaggeration in the statement, but it was generally agreed that she appeared much younger than her years. Since the use of cosmetics still carried the taint of wickedness, long debates ensued as to how much of her attractiveness resulted from nature and how much from "paint."[68]

Even while her husband served as secretary of state (1809–1817), Elizabeth Monroe had made clear that she expected to have little to do with the wives of other department heads, and, after seven years in the capital, she and her husband remained "perfect strangers," one social leader wrote, "not only to me but all citizens."[69] James's elevation to the presidency caused no deviation in the Monroes' custom. Some hope prevailed that invitations to the President's House would flow more freely after the mansion, destroyed in the 1814 burning of Washington by the British, had been rebuilt. However, Elizabeth's handling of her daughter's wedding ended that speculation.

In a "first" for a president's family, Maria, the younger of the two Monroe daughters, was married in 1820, and many Washingtonians expected to find their names on the wedding guest list. This was the chance, reasoned congressmen and diplomats, for the president to make them all one family, sharing the festivities associated with the nuptials. Dolley Madison would doubtless have complied, so dedicated she remained to maintaining political harmony, but Elizabeth Monroe had other ideas. She insisted that the wedding remain strictly private, and she invited only the family's closest friends. Later presidents' sons and especially their daughters, who chose to be married in small ceremonies even though their parents happened to reside at the White House, might well thank Elizabeth Monroe's stubbornness. She resisted all requests that she increase the number of guests invited, and when the diplomatic corps persisted, she dispatched the secretary of state to set them straight.

Such open refusal on the part of a president's wife to court public favor puzzled observers during the first Monroe administration; during her husband's second term, when Elizabeth put even more distance between herself and everyone else, the public reaction became severe. She stayed away from Washington for months at a time visiting her two married daughters. Such absences might have caused little more than speculation about her marital felicity, as happened when Jackie Kennedy took long vacations from the White House in the 1960s, but Elizabeth Monroe's behavior had more serious repercussions. The old rule still prevailed that no women guests came to the President's House in the absence of a hostess. This meant that wives and daughters who had accompanied congressmen to Washington had to keep their party dresses put away until Elizabeth

Monroe chose to make an appearance. Her absence caused, one Massachusetts senator wrote home, "no little mortification and disappointment [among the] ladies."[70] At the stag dinners of President Monroe, who had no reputation for conversational brilliance, long silences and early departures became the pattern.[71]

Left with much of the detail of running the White House, the president, rather than his wife, received the blame for mishandling furniture purchases. Just before James Monroe's inauguration in 1817, Congress had appropriated $20,000 for furnishing the rebuilt mansion and then two years later, another $30,000. Deeming furniture selection an official responsibility, he assigned the job jointly to his commissioner of public buildings, Colonel Lane, and to the auditor of the Treasury, William Lee. While the president waited impatiently for the new furniture to arrive from Europe, he offered the loan of his own fine pieces, acquired during his years in France.

The money exchanges that followed became so confused that Secretary of State John Quincy Adams expressed unqualified dismay. President Monroe accepted money from the furniture account, paid it back, then took it again.[72] When Colonel Lane died in 1823, his personal finances were so tangled, with so much public money missing, that Congressman John Cocke of Tennessee called for an investigation. In the end, stuffy John Quincy Adams concluded that the president had done nothing wrong but had, nevertheless, exposed himself to embarrassment "almost as incongruous to the station of a President of the United States as it would be to a blooming virgin to exhibit herself naked before a multitude."[73]

John Quincy Adams had considerable interest in James Monroe's behavior as president because he intended to claim the job for himself in the 1824 election. To that end he enlisted the aid of his wife, Louisa, who had already been caught up in the dispute over how accessible the wives of government leaders should be to other citizens. While John Quincy Adams served as James Monroe's secretary of state, Louisa had refused to make the initial call on the families of all legislators who arrived in the capital, causing Elizabeth Monroe to summon her for a conference. As John Quincy Adams explained in his diary: "All the ladies arriving here as strangers, it seems, expect to be visited by the wives of [Cabinet members] and even by the President's wife." It was an expectation they did not meekly renounce. John Quincy continued that Elizabeth Monroe, who offered poor health as the reason for not making the calls herself, had informed Louisa that "the ladies had taken offence at [Louisa's] not paying them the first visit. . . ." "My wife returns all visits," John Quincy Adams noted, "but [she] adopts the principle of not visiting first any stranger who arrives, and this is what the ladies have taken in dudgeon."[74]

When Elizabeth Monroe refused to go running all over Washington to court the favor of congressmen's wives, they retaliated by boycotting the few parties she did give. "The drawing room of the President was opened last night," one woman wrote in December, 1819, "to a beggarly row of empty chairs. . . . Only five females attended, three of whom were foreigners."[75] Louisa Adams received an equally severe reprimand; on one occasion, after inviting "a large party . . . only three came."[76]

Since offended congressmen figured in the results of the next election, this was no insignificant matter to John Quincy Adams, particularly when it spilled over into criticism of his own behavior. The wives' reluctance to pay visits had called attention to how the cabinet members handled their own social responsibilities, and the observation was made that insufficient attention had been shown to legislators. President Monroe called John Quincy in to discuss the "etiquette of the visits" and to relay the displeasure of senators who had complained "that the Secretary of State refuses to pay them the first visit." The President "mentioned it with much delicacy," John Quincy Adams wrote in his diary, "but observed that it occasioned uneasiness, heartburnings, and severe criticism."[77]

A cabinet meeting on the subject followed a few days later and when no agreement could be reached, John Quincy Adams wrote letters to both the president and vice president to outline his own position. The secretary of state evidently wrote in his usual pedantic style: one Washington woman, who gained access to the letters, described them as the work of "a bookworm and abstracted student [rather] than a man of the world."[78] But the letters served their purpose and settled the matter. Wives of cabinet members would not be expected to act as the Welcome Wagon to every legislator's family who moved to Washington, and the president's wife would similarly be relieved of the responsibility to call.

Elizabeth Monroe had won her point, but her ally, Louisa Adams, stood in quite a different position. James Monroe was already president but John Quincy Adams still had to capture the office and he had to rely on a caucus of congressmen to nominate him. Louisa recognized that she could ill afford to assert her independence in the matter of visits. "It is understood," she wrote sarcastically in her diary, "that a man who is ambitious to become President of the United States must make his wife visit the Ladies of the members of Congress first. Otherwise he is totally inefficient to fill so high an office."[79] Each morning her husband prepared a set of cards for her "as carefully as a commercial treaty," and she started on her hated rounds, going sometimes to as many as twenty-five different houses in one day even though it meant traveling from one end of the city to the other. "Oh these visits have made me sick many times," she wrote in her diary, "and I really sometimes think they will make me crazy."[80]

Nor did the visits end her responsibilities, because each time Congress convened, a new round of callers came to her door—representatives, their wives, relatives, and aides—to pay their respects to her husband. John Quincy made a meticulous accounting of the time thus consumed: "I have received in the course of this month two hundred and thirty-five visitors, which is an average of about eight a day. A half hour to each visitor occupies four hours a day; but that is short of the average. The interruption to business thus incessantly repeated is distressing, but unavoidable," he wrote in March 1824, as the date of the next presidential election approached.[81]

That John Quincy Adams performed so poorly on social occasions increased his dependence on his wife, who had a reputation for charming everyone. As part of the 1824 campaign, he decided that they should give a large party marking the anniversary of Andrew Jackson's great victory in 1815 at New Orleans. Though Louisa lacked enthusiasm for the idea, she bowed to her husband's conclusion that such a party could help win votes. "It was agreed this day," she wrote in December 1823, "that we should give a Ball to General Jackson on the 8th [of January]. I objected much to the plan but was overpowered by John's argument and the thing was settled."[82] She had less than three weeks to prepare. In addition to sending invitations, which went out by the hundreds up until the day before the event, she had to arrange that beds be folded up and furniture moved so that their house could accommodate the crowd. While preparations continued, she maintained a full social schedule, even giving a small party on January sixth.

The ball became the season's most spectacular social affair, singled out for years to come as the model of everything a party should be. Dolley Madison, then living in Montpelier, Virginia, could not attend but she received a glowing report from a good friend: "Mrs. Adams' reception on the 8th . . . was really a very brilliant party and admirably arranged. The ladies climbed on chairs and benches to see General Jackson and Mrs. A[dams] very gracefully took his arm and walked through the apartments with him, which gratified the general curiosity. It is said 1,400 cards [were] issued and about 800 [guests] present."[83]

From the hostess came a somewhat different report. She well understood the political implications of the evening, and when a lamp had fallen on her head and oil trickled down her back, she had joined in the joking about her "being anointed." But after the last guests left at 1:30 she concluded she was just glad to "have got so well through this business."[84] Louisa Adams had frequently remarked that "friends grow warmer as . . . Mr. A[dams] rises in popularity,"[85] and she saw the new attention focused on her as just one more example of the fickleness of politics.

In calling attention to the burdens of her ceremonial role in her husband's politicking, Louisa Adams echoed preceding presidents' wives, each of whom tackled the problem in a different way. Martha Washington had hardly arrived in New York when she informed her sister that she felt "more like a state prisoner than anything else. There [are] certain bounds set for me which I must not depart from and as I cannot do as I like I am obstinate and stay at home a great deal."[86] Later she confessed to her friend, the historian Mercy Warren, that a "younger, gayer woman" might have liked the job more. Only a stubbornness to make the best of things kept Martha trying, having "learned from experience," she wrote, "that the greater part of our happiness or misery depends upon our dispositions and not upon our circumstances."[87]

Energetic Abigail Adams had risen at five in the morning to take care of "family arrangements" so she could have the afternoons for First Lady work. Dolley Madison, who thrived on being the center of attention, wore herself out with a rigorous schedule of visits. Elizabeth Monroe protected her time and her privacy by staying away from Washington a great deal.

Contemporaries frequently commented that the women's health suffered from their heavy schedules. "Mrs. Monroe is in a very nervous way,"[88] Louisa Adams wrote late in 1820, and James Monroe admitted "the burdens and cares of my long public service have borne too heavily [on Mrs. Monroe]."[89] John Quincy Adams worried over his wife's sleepless nights, while friends concurred that she overexerted herself. "[Mrs. Adams' entertaining] keeps her ill half the time but she is a woman of great spirit and carries it through with a high hand," one senator wrote.[90] Louisa persisted in keeping social commitments even when she was ill. "Miserably sick," she wrote in her diary on New Year's, 1820, "but went to the President's to pay my respects."[91] All through her husband's administration, she made the President's House a center for the arts by playing the harp for her guests and encouraging them to perform in amateur musical and theatrical productions.[92]

Hard as she worked at her job, Louisa Johnson Adams did not win unanimous approval. She had been born in England and, although her father came from Baltimore, seemed a bit too foreign to suit some Americans, including her mother-in-law, Abigail Adams. Louisa did not set eyes on her husband's country until age twenty-six, when she arrived with John Quincy and their three-month-old son. The encounter was a disaster. "Had I stepped into Noah's Ark, I do not think I could have been more utterly astonished," she wrote, recognizing at once how unacceptable her husband's family found her. "Do what I would there was a conviction on the part of others that I could not suit . . . I was literally without knowing it a fine Lady."[93]

John Quincy offered little support to bolster his wife's confidence, and although she followed him back and forth, from Berlin to Massachusetts, then from Washington to St. Petersburg and Paris, she never ceased to complain about his insensitivity. In Russia, she became depressed because she regretted having left her two young sons back in Massachusetts with their grandparents. Her condition worsened in 1813 when her infant daughter died. She blamed herself for the baby's death, explaining in her diary, "Necessity alone induced me to wean her and in doing so I lost her."[94] Tutoring the one son who had come with her gave her some pleasure but she understood that her husband disdained her efforts. When time came to select a gift for her, he chose a book on "the diseases of the mind."[95] He refused to discuss anything relevant to his diplomatic work, although Louisa shrewdly pointed out that she could hardly remain ignorant of what went on around her. In commenting to her son many years later that the Adams men made poor husbands, she may well have had the St. Petersburg years in mind.

Louisa Adams's diary and unpublished autobiography, which she titled "Adventures of a Nobody," show evidence of a trained, inquisitive mind but one easily pushed into acquiescence. During the winter of 1812 to 1813 she noted that she had read more than twenty books, including many biographies and memoirs. The records of women, especially those attached to famous or powerful men, particularly interested her. After reading a biography of Diane de Poitiers, mistress of France's King Henry II, Louisa pondered how Diane's life had been shaped by others. "[This book] has convinced me," Louisa wrote, "how little we can do of ourselves."[96] Louisa had hoped to study astronomy but bowed to advice that it was too difficult for her,[97] and when warned away or kept ignorant of political intrigues, she showed a similar obeisance. "[I am] continuously told that I cannot by the Constitution have any share in the public honours of my husband," she wrote later after she had returned to the United States; when a congressman broached a political subject, "[I] was again forced to repeat that I had nothing to do with affairs of State."[98]

Politics formed the center of John Quincy Adams's life, but Louisa understood that he had effectively relegated her to the domestic sphere. "[Politics] is absolutely essential to [my husband's] existence," she wrote, "[but as for myself] I have since the first year of my marriage entered upon my great honours with tears and I do not recollect ever having lost them with regret. . . . I have nothing to do with the disposal of affairs and have never but once been consulted."[99]

At any public appearance, Louisa knew that she was carefully observed for some indication of her husband's position. "Trifling occurrences are turned into political machinery—even my countenance was watched at the Senate during Mr. Pinckney's speech as I was afterward informed by some of the gentlemen."[100] She had been among the first women to attend congressional debates during the Madison administration, but what had started out as a way to keep herself informed had turned into another opportunity to be scrutinized and evaluated.

In the early years of the republic, women shared their spouses' workloads—but from behind the scenes so that they received little public recognition. Thus they enjoyed a measure of latitude in some areas of their lives but found their autonomy firmly curtailed in other areas. That division had been obvious during the independence movement when women contributed in many ways but then attained no voice in the new government. Some wives fought alongside their men or took over for them when they were wounded. Others transported water and supplies. Housewives occasionally struck back at merchants who gouged customers on prices, as Abigail Adams explained when she related to John how one coffee merchant had fared. "[The women] seized him by the neck and tossed him into the cart," Abigail wrote. "[They] opened the warehouse, hoisted out the coffee themselves, put it on the trucks and drove off [while] a large concourse of men stood amazed, silent spectators of the whole transaction."[101] In Philadelphia, a group of women organized themselves to collect money for the colonial soldiers. The women originally planned to forward the collection to Martha Washington so that she could disperse it as they directed, but she had to return to Mount Vernon and they were forced to turn to George instead.[102]

Yet for all this hard work, women did not gain full political participation in the young American government. Abigail Adams had predicted as much. In 1776, when John was in Philadelphia helping to write the Declaration of Independence, she chided him: "I cannot say that I think you are very generous to the Ladies, for while you are proclaiming peace and good will to men, emancipating all Nations, you insist upon retaining an absolute power over Wives."[103]

Historian Mary Beth Norton has pointed out that American women increased control over their lives in the decades following the Revolution despite their failure to achieve suffrage. Norton recommended looking at women's private lives—their "familial organizations, personal aspirations, and self assessments."[104] The evidence showed, she wrote, new attitudes on courtship, spinsterhood, marriage, and bearing children.[105] Because the home took on new importance as a place for training "virtuous" citizens, wives and mothers assumed greater power. That this new autonomy remained in the home did not mean that it did not exist.

One prescription for how women should limit their governing to their own households shows up in the writings of Judith Sargent Murray. Under the pen name "Constantia," she achieved a reputation as a feminist in the 1790s because of her insistence that women deserved an education equal to that which men received. Yet she advised women to retain their "retiring sweetness" and "shun even the semblance of pedantry, rather question than assert," look on their partners' weaknesses "with pity's softest eye [and] praise the men's strengths." Mothers' role in government was confined to the home, where, she wrote, they would find pleasure in "viewing the smiles of their daughters and the sports of their sons."[106] "Constantia" would have approved of a popular magazine's advice to readers in 1787: "A kind look, or even a smile, often conquered Alexander, subdued Caesar and decided the fate of empires and of kingdoms."[107]

Not all American women accepted quietly the limitations placed on their participation in government. Some spoke out for a vote in both church and town.[108] For example, one Connecticut matron, who took the pen name "Female Advocate," suggested that the time had come to stop quoting St. Paul on how women should keep silence in the church and refrain from teaching men or preaching to them. "Female Advocate" pointed to other parts of the Bible that offered stronger models. The Old Testament's Deborah, for example, served her people as judge and helped deliver Israel from King Jabin.[109] If "Female Advocate's" view that women deserved full political rights had prevailed, other states would no doubt have followed New Jersey's lead and permitted women to vote along with "all free citizens." But "Female Advocate" spoke for only a minority, and even New Jersey narrowed its franchise in 1808 to white males only.

Except for Abigail Adams, for whom controversy came as naturally as breathing, the first presidents' wives fitted themselves into the contemporary model of womanliness. In public they were models of docility. Louisa Adams may have complained bitterly in private, and Dolley Madison confessed to great fatigue, but both maintained their sweet composure in front of others. Even Elizabeth Monroe, who contributed little to her husband's political success, hewed to the accepted "feminine" reticence. Visitors who stopped at Mount Vernon, including the famous Marquis de Lafayette, frequently mentioned Martha Washington's charming good nature,[110] and a young Dutchman wrote his mother that at the Washingtons' dinner table, George had ignored his guests but that Martha was so gracious she deserved an "exquisite" gift.[111]

Yet the records of all these women suggest a discrepancy between their public images and their private lives. Examination of each reveals how much spunk and courage lay behind the quiet voices and sweet smiles. Martha Washington provides an excellent example, although it is important to emphasize that the stories about her early years may be as apocryphal as those of George and the cherry tree. Accounts of her youth consistently describe her as a woman who had her own ideas. She slapped the face of an offensive suitor at a fashionable ball and rode her horse up the stairs of her uncle's house.[112] Later, after her first husband died, she found herself at twenty-six with two young children and one of the largest estates in Virginia. Writing to an English merchant, she outlined the conditions under which she would sell to him and her hopes that he would be fair. The many corrections in the manuscript draft indicate that she could not have found the task easy but the wording shows she could be firm: "It will be proper to continue this Account in the same manner as if [my husband] was living as most of the goods I shall send for will be for the good of the family." She signed herself simply, "Martha Custis."[113]

Martha showed fewer signs of that forcefulness in her later years. She managed her household well, and after George became famous and their home a mecca for visitors from all over the country, he commented to his mother that Martha ran Mount Vernon like a "well-resorted tavern."[114] Miniatures of her at midlife reveal stolid eyes, with no hint of either invention or merriment. They are the eyes of a woman unlikely to contradict her husband. Yet, in private, she continued to have a mind of her own. In a letter to her niece, written in 1794 while Martha was First Lady, she advised the younger woman to be "as independent as your circumstances will admit . . .; [because] dependence is, I think, a wrached [*sic*] state . . ."[115]

Abigail Adams's spunky vitality showed up throughout her life and is considered here only to emphasize that it was largely confined to the private sphere and best documented in letters to family members. During the years that John absented himself from home for first one patriotic duty and then another, she made the farm support the family, referring first to "your crops," then shifting to "our" and finally to "my."[116] Left to make decisions on her own about harvesting crops and buying land, she tried to keep John informed but made it clear that she was in charge: "You made no perticular [*sic*] agreement with Isaac," [the hired hand] so he insisted upon my paying him 13 [pounds], 6 [shillings] and 8 [pence]. I paid him 12, 18, and 8 and thought it sufficient."[117]

Abigail occasionally complained of the weight of her responsibilities, but her family appreciated her contribution to the men's careers. In 1776, nearly a century and a half before the publication of Virginia Woolf's *A Room of One's Own*, Abigail lamented the lack of time and space for herself: "I always had a fancy for a closet with a window which I could more peculiarly call my own."[118] Abigail's grandson may well have had her complaint in mind when he noted how her careful management had helped the Adamses escape the financial worries that plagued both Thomas Jefferson and James Monroe. In the introduction to his grandmother's letters, Charles Francis Adams wrote: "[She was] a farmer cultivating the land and discussing the weather and the crops; a merchant reporting prices current and the rates of exchange and directing the making up of invoices, a politician speculating upon the probabilities of war, and a mother . . . and in all she appears equally well."[119]

The active pen of Abigail and her descendants assured her a place in history, while Thomas Jefferson's wife, Martha Wayles Skelton Jefferson, left few traces. She had died in 1782, well before her husband became president. It is significant, however, that the single extant document in her hand is a letter, written in 1780 when her husband was governor of Virginia. She had been asked by Martha Washington to assist her "sisters of Pennsylvania" in gathering money for the soldiers. "I undertake with chearfulness [*sic*] the duty of furnishing to my countrywomen an opportunity of proving that they also participate of those virtuous feelings which gave birth [to the independence movement]," Martha Jefferson wrote.[120] In forwarding the "papers to be distributed" by women to women, she demonstrated once again how many matters of public concern were taken up in the domestic sphere.

Dolley Madison's vivacious personality guaranteed her fame, but in her most celebrated act, she performed as a wife engineering the transfer of her house's furnishings. That the item she arranged to save happened to be a portrait of George Washington rendered this a patriotic act. According to Dolley, British troops were approaching the capital in August 1814, and the president was out of town consulting with his military advisers. She had been warned that she should "be ready at a moment's warning to enter my carriage and leave the city; that the enemy seemed stronger than had at first been reported, and it might happen that they would reach the city with the intention of destroying it." Dolley insisted in a letter to her sister that she would not budge "until I see Mr. Madison safe so that he can accompany me." When a friend came to "hasten" her departure, she consented to go "as soon as the large picture of General Washington is secured. . . . I have ordered the frame to be broken and the canvas taken out."[121]

Elizabeth Monroe left very few records as First Lady, but her courage much earlier demonstrates another kind of "womanly" participation in public affairs. James Monroe had been named minister to France in 1794, not an easy assignment with France in the middle of a revolution. One of his first tasks required delicate negotiation. In the shifting of alliances that made factions of the French Revolution powerful one day and dead the next, America's old Revolutionary War friend, Marquis de Lafayette, had gotten caught. After denouncing the Jacobins in 1792, he fled the country but was soon captured and imprisoned near Vienna. His wife was first placed under house arrest back in France, but by the spring of 1794 when the Monroes arrived in Paris, she was being held in one of the city's prisons.[122] The French capital had become the site of bloody chaos and more than 1,500 people— including Mme. Lafayette's mother and other relatives—were led to the guillotine during a six-week period that summer.[123] The new American minister wanted to assist the wife of his country's old friend but understood the delicacy of the situation. Any foreign meddling in what was understood to be an internal matter could create a backlash and make the case against Marie-Adrienne Lafayette even worse.

The Monroes resolved to appeal to Parisians who might then convince the Committee on Public Safety, who decided such matters, to free the prisoner.[124] First, the Americans needed to draw attention to Mme. Lafayette and stir up sympathy for her plight. Because no private carriages were available for hire, the Monroes bought one and painted it so it would draw the curious. Then Elizabeth Monroe rode alone through the crowds that pressed in around her and demanded to know where she was going. They followed her to the prison gates, where a frightened and surprised Marie-Adrienne Lafayette came out to meet the American, and the two women chatted and embraced in full view of the crowds. Mme. Lafayette, who had feared she was heading for the guillotine when she was summoned that morning, could hardly conceal her delight at seeing Elizabeth Monroe instead. The crowds appeared every bit as moved as she, and their cheers had the intended result, or as James Monroe rather dryly summed up in his diary his wife's successful mission: "The sensibility of all the beholders was deeply excited" so that the Committee on Safety consented to Mme. Lafayette's release.[125]

Louisa Adams also revealed considerable courage but again in the role of wife and mother. While her husband was stationed in St. Petersburg in 1814, he was called to Ghent to work out the details of the peace treaty that ended the War of 1812. With that assignment finished, he wrote to Louisa, instructing her to sell everything and join him in Paris. Although it was the middle of winter and she would have to go through war-damaged areas, if not through actual fighting, she disposed of their belongings and prepared in a matter of weeks to begin the journey. For company she had only her eight-year-old son and three servants whom she hired the day she set out.

The account of Louisa's trip from St. Petersburg to Paris reads like a concocted adventure, filled with danger, intrigue, and murder. When her carriage sank into the snow she called "out the inhabitants . . . with pick axe and shovel to dig us out," she later wrote.[126] Warned that there had been a "dreadful murder" the night before on the "very road over which I was to pass," she refused to stop. Told that one of her servants had the reputation of a "desperate villain of the worst character" she had little alternative but to continue with him. Her informant begged her not to fire the man on the spot for fear he might uncover the source of her information and retaliate. Because she feared her servants might try to rob her, she carefully hid the gold she carried and then waved letters of credit in front of them so they would be misled into thinking that she picked up small amounts in cities along the way. When her servants deserted her, she hired others, and when impertinent border officials treated her rudely, she threatened to report them to their superiors. Her health was "dreadful," she later wrote, but she persevered, stopping to rest at houses where she knew no one. Sometimes she sat up all night because she feared for her life if she slept.

Although Louisa protested demurely that she could not attend the theater on a stopover in Königsberg, "unprotected by a gentleman," she dealt calmly with threats on her life. When crowds loyal to Napoleon surrounded her carriage and screamed "Kill them. They are Russians," she pulled out her American passport. Then when they cried "Vive les Américains," she obligingly responded, "Vive Napoléon," before moving on. Not far from Paris she learned that forty thousand men had gathered at the city's gates for battle and although "this news startled me very much," she resolved "on cool reflection . . . to persevere."[127]

When Louisa arrived in Paris on March 21, after weeks of difficult and dangerous travel, her husband was waiting at the Hotel du Nord "perfectly astonished at [her] adventures." His diary makes light of the whole trip, and he wrote matter-of-factly to his mother: "Mrs. A performed the journey from St. Petersburg in 40 days and it has been of essential service to her and Charles' health. She entered France precisely at the time when the revolution was taking place."[128] Although her maid needed two months of bed rest to recover, Louisa Adams, whom her family and historians portrayed as frail and sickly all her life, immediately resumed her regular schedule.

Abigail Adams could never match her daughter-in-law in European experience, but by the time her husband became president the older woman had lived in both France and England and had recorded her trials and triumphs in many letters home. She had joined John first in 1784 when for a few months the family rented a house in Auteuil outside of Paris. Because she could not speak French, although she read it, Abigail found dealing with servants difficult; dinner parties with non-English speakers made her uncomfortable. She worried about her clothes in a country where style obviously mattered. "To be out of fashion is more criminal than to be seen in a state of nature," she observed, "to which," she added primly, "Parisians are not averse."[129] But her curiosity and genuine interest in French ways proved more powerful than her complaints; and her own letters, as well as those of her daughter and husband, indicate these were some of the family's happiest times.

The French stay was cut short when John Adams was appointed Ambassador to the Court of St. James in 1785. It was an extremely awkward post since his presence served as a reminder to Britons that they had recently lost thirteen of their American colonies. Abigail found her reception icy, and she informed her sister: "I own that I have never felt myself in a more contemptible situation, than when I stood four hours together for a gracious smile from majesty."[130] She could not wait to leave England. When the queen was later reported as having her own worries, Abigail showed little sympathy: "Humiliation for Charlotte is no sorrow for me," she wrote her daughter, "[because she] richly deserves her full portion for the contempt and scorn which she took pains to discover."[131]

After five years in Europe, Abigail could not hide her nostalgia for home. "I have lived long enough and seen enough of the world," she wrote her friend Thomas Jefferson, "to bring my mind to my circumstances and retiring to our own little farm feeding my poultry and improving my garden has more charms for my fancy than residing at the Court of St. James where I seldom meet characters so inoffensive as my hens and chick[s] or minds so well improved as my garden. Heaven forgive me," she added, "if I think too hardly of them. I wish they had deserved better at my hands."[132]

In spite of their protests, the early First Ladies who lived for long periods in Europe profited from the experience—a preparation that few of their successors could boast. Not until a century later, during the Hoover administration of 1929 to 1933, would a First Lady's travels rival those of Abigail Adams, Elizabeth Monroe, or Louisa Adams, who acquired the reputation of the most traveled woman of her time. The Constitution had set very few requirements for election to the country's highest office and none at all in training or travel, but in the early years of the republic, when the psychological separation from Europe was not yet as complete as the physical one, international expertise rendered potential leaders more attractive. Four of the first six presidents (the two Adamses, Jefferson, and Monroe) spent several years in diplomatic service abroad and, except for the widowed Jefferson, had their families with them for at least part of the time, with their wives running large European households.

In one sense, the travel made up for the women's lack of formal education. Abigail Adams frequently complained that she had not had a single day of schooling in her entire life. Rules of grammar, spelling, and punctuation remained mysteries all her life, and in her letters, she made one mistake after another. Wide reading and long sessions with her Grandmother Quincy supplied her with her frequent references to the classics but did not prepare her, Abigail acknowledged, for knowing everything people expected her to know.

The other first presidents' wives came no better equipped. Dolley Madison had very little schooling, and during her husband's administration she admitted that she read infrequently. When a young man asked about the Don Quixote volume in her hand, she explained it was just a prop, carried to provide for awkward breaks in conversation. Martha Washington had so much difficulty with spelling that George finally took to writing out her letters for her and having her copy them; but even then she managed to botch the job, carelessly converting his "describe" to "discribe" and using her own quaint versions of "boath" and "occation."[133] Too little is known of Elizabeth Monroe to make a judgment on her education, but neither she nor any of the others made any move to improve women's education. Abigail Adams's one daughter had little more schooling than her mother, and Martha Washington raised her granddaughter much as she had been raised, putting more importance on the spinet than on spelling.

Small improvements in women's schooling in the late eighteenth century and early nineteenth did not result from the example or the cajoling of the presidents' wives. Some Americans argued that their sisters deserved education—it would make them better wives and better people. But the central argument was a practical one. As the country expanded westward, more teachers were needed. When the first girls' academies opened in the 1780s and 1790s, their founders claimed to offer instruction on the same level as boys' schools so that the graduates would be prepared to teach. Benjamin Rush, then professor of chemistry at the University of Pennsylvania and a leading advocate of better education for girls, explained in 1787 to the first class of the Young Ladies Academy in Philadelphia that they were there because of the country's needs. Since American girls married earlier and assumed more responsibility for tutoring their children than did their European counterparts, they ought to go beyond basic math and reading, Rush said, to learn world history and geography.[134] Elizabeth Monroe, Louisa Adams, and Abigail Adams learned their European history and geography first hand.

In assessing how each of the early First Ladies handled the responsibilities imposed on them when their husbands became president, it is safe to conclude that they reacted differently. Only Abigail Adams appears to have shaped the job more than it shaped her. She refused to be silenced, and, with her husband's encouragement, continued to air her opinions. Whether such activity constitutes "feminism" is beside the point—Abigail demonstrated very early in the republic that the opportunity existed for a substantive role (alongside the ceremonial role) for spouses who wanted it—provided, of course, they had the consent of the president. The others, despite objections and occasional rebellions, acquiesced in limiting themselves to a supportive role reflecting the predominant attitude about femininity.

In many ways, the early presidents' wives, along with their husbands, form a distinct group. Unlike those who followed them after 1829, the early chief executives are notable for their close personal connections and for their exceptional training. The wives also stand apart from their successors. In attempting to define just what demands their husbands' jobs imposed on them, they collectively built the foundation for those who followed, and they anticipated most of the problems. With one eye on the rules of protocol and another on their husbands' popularity, they sought (some more diligently than others) to find the middle ground. They worked to improve the President's House, which served as their home as well as a national monument, and they struggled with the publicity that focused on them as a result of their husbands' jobs. In the evident and continuing debate over just how much distance a president should keep between himself and the people, wives took an important part, striking a balance between commoner and queen.

2

Young Substitutes for First Ladies (1829–1869)

ANDREW JACKSON'S INAUGURATION in 1829 signaled a new mood in the country—one that would affect presidents' wives for decades to come. Crowds converged on the capital from all over the eastern seaboard, arriving in carriages and carts, wearing silk and homespun. Never one to disappoint crowds, the tall, white-haired war hero gave his speech, took the prescribed oath, kissed the Bible, and then in an immensely popular gesture bent in a low bow to the people. Word immediately went out that the President's House was now the People's House and open to all without distinction. Thousands headed toward it.

No precautions had been taken to protect the mansion's furnishings, but the unexpectedly large crowd would have rendered such measures ineffective anyway. Glasses shattered and furniture broke as the hungry and curious surged toward tables where food, prepared for hundreds, proved insufficient. People filled their pockets as well as their stomachs. When the president was nearly crushed, one Jackson admirer and staunch defender of "people's rule" decided this was going too far: "Ladies and gentlemen only had been expected at this Levée," Margaret Bayard Smith, a newspaper editor's wife, wrote, "not the people en masse. . . . Of all tyrants, they are the most ferocious, cruel and despotic."[1]

Margaret Bayard Smith rebelled against much more than the results of a single election. The 1820s and 1830s introduced changes that eventually altered the entire process by which Americans advanced to the top of the political ladder. Instead of looking to a small party caucus for nomination, anyone hoping to be president had to appeal to a convention of delegates, many of whom were strangers. Most states gradually changed the qualifications for voting so that all adult white males—rather than just property owners—had the suffrage. Old traditions of deference to the rich and the well educated weakened, paving the way for new ideas about who was qualified for high office.

Historians at first emphasized the democratic flavor of the changes and argued that the common man acquired great power, but later scholars concluded that candidates for high political office still came from wealthy backgrounds no matter how humbly they presented themselves.[2] Andrew Jackson, so frequently touted as defender and symbol of the common man, possessed enormous personal wealth, and most of the nineteenth-century presidents who claimed to have been born in log cabins actually came from much more prosperous beginnings.

Yet for all the shifting interpretations in American history, the fact remains that presidential styles changed after 1829 so that new importance was put on appearing "natural" rather than "cultured," and "good" rather than "learned." Heroes seemed to come from the ranks of the common folk rather than from the obvious elite. John Calhoun had commented in 1817 that the quality of congressmen had declined, a change he attributed to low salaries. Although that may have played some part, the addition of new western states was also relevant since frontier areas frequently elected representatives who had little formal education and even less regard for fixed class differences. Robert J. Hubbard, a congressman from upstate New York, reported with some shock to his wife in 1817 that his colleagues sat through legislative debates with their hats on, removing them only when they addressed the Speaker.[3]

Much more important than changes in etiquette, the new style in politics altered voters' ideas about who merited consideration for election to the highest office in the land. After 1829, presidents more frequently owed their elevation to military victories or to mundane political apprenticeships than to diplomatic service abroad or to years of leadership as statesmen. Their wives came to "the head of female society" with entirely different experiences from their predecessors. These later women had not had the opportunity to develop Elizabeth Monroe's familiarity with French philosophers or Louisa Adams's habit of sprinkling letters with Latin phrases. Nor had they had the pleasure, or pain, of having been presented at the Court of St. James as had Abigail Adams. Many had not ventured far from the town where they were born until they journeyed to Washington.

Thus, presidents' wives after 1829 lacked some of their predecessors' training in etiquette, a lack deemed important by a segment of

the Washington population that had taken upon itself the responsibility of formulating and enforcing rigid rules of protocol and style.
Called the "cave dwellers," because of their long and continued residence in Washington while elected officials and their families came
and went like "a kaleidoscope that changed every four years,"[4] the
locals did not shrink from claiming prerogatives. Sarah Pryor, wife of
a southern congressman and newspaper editor, explained how the
"cave dwellers" held themselves apart, separate from the "floating
population" of transients, reigning as a "fine society of old residents
who never bent the knee to Baal . . . sufficient to itself, never seeking
the new, while accepting it occasionally with discretion, reservations
and much discriminating care."[5] Presidents' wives always counted
among the "floaters," up for critical judgment by the entrenched
jury.[6]

In the middle four decades of the nineteenth century, presidents'
wives frequently chose to abdicate their public roles rather than risk
the censure of the "cave dwellers." Most First Ladies moved to Washington when their husbands were inaugurated, but they delegated
responsibility for official entertaining to someone else. From 1829 to
1869, it is the exceptional First Lady who carves out for herself a
public role. In the entire time, only Sarah Polk (1845–1849) and
Mary Todd Lincoln (1861–1865) achieved any kind of public recognition. The other administrations had stand-in chatelaines in charge
at the President's House.

Three presidents in the forty-year span had no choice but to rely on
substitutes. Andrew Jackson and Martin Van Buren were both widowers and James Buchanan never married. While they could have followed Thomas Jefferson's example and relied on the wife of a cabinet
member or on some other mature woman for official hostessing, each
chose, instead, a niece or daughter-in-law, all less than thirty years of
age. The other nine presidents in this period did have wives but six of
these women (Anna Harrison, Letitia Tyler, Margaret Taylor, Abigail
Fillmore, Jane Pierce, and Eliza Johnson) pled poor health or grief
and escaped performing the tasks that had come to be seen as traditional for a president's wife. They turned to daughters or daughters-in-law to serve in their stead. Elizabeth Monroe (1817–1825) had
taken a similar course, but what had been an exception during the
first few administrations became a pattern now. The long reign of
substitutes can hardly be explained away as mere coincidence.

Even the spirited Rachel Jackson, who died while preparing to
move to Washington, made arrangements for her niece to take over as
White House hostess. Earlier brushes with the "cave dwellers" had

soured Rachel on the capital, and she made no secret of her distaste for returning to live there. When word reached her of Andrew's victory in the 1828 election, she had explained, "I had rather be a doorkeeper in the house of my Lord than live in that palace in Washington."[7] "For Mr. Jackson's sake, I am glad, for my own part, I never wished it."[8]

Staying in Tennessee and not going near Washington would have been Rachel's preference, but she changed her mind after one of her husband's supporters informed her that everyone was watching to see what she did. John Eaton, who later became Andrew Jackson's secretary of war, wrote that if she failed to arrive she would not only disappoint her friends but also allow her "persecutors" to "chuckle" that they had scared her into staying away.[9] Whether unwilling to disappoint her fans or stubborn about facing down her critics, Rachel started packing and called in friends to help update her wardrobe. She understood she would have to face the same old charges once again.

Rachel's difficulties had begun many years before when she was just a teenager with more than her share of admirers around Harrodsburg, Kentucky. Described by a contemporary as of "medium height, [with a] beautifully moulded form, full red lips rippling with smiles and dimples,"[10] she could ride a horse as well as anyone her age, tell the best stories, and dance the fastest.[11] Among those who noticed her was Lewis Robards, and when she was eighteen, he married her. The couple went to live with his mother, who reigned as a kind of frontier aristocrat in that part of Kentucky. The elder Mrs. Robards got along well enough with Rachel but Lewis found fault with her every move. Abusive and jealous of even the slightest attention given her by other men, he soon sent her back to her mother. Attempts to patch up the marriage failed, and Rachel resolved to put as much distance as possible between herself and her husband. Neighbors said she feared bodily harm.

On her trip down the Mississippi to stay with relatives, Rachel had the company of two men—an elderly family friend and young Andrew Jackson, a boarder at her mother's and an open admirer of the daughter. After settling her in Natchez, Andrew returned to Nashville but before long was back at her side. Believing that Lewis Robards had secured a divorce, as he had announced he would do, Rachel and Andrew were married in August 1791.

The young couple had anticipated Robards by some years; after obtaining permission from the Virginia legislature to end his marriage, he had failed to follow through. Whether from simple negligence or from other, more sinister motives, Robards waited three years and then asked for a divorce on the grounds that his wife was then living with another man. As soon as they heard what had happened, the Jacksons promptly remarried, but their mistake furnished their enemies with ammunition for years.

Such legal snags occurred frequently on the frontier and Rachel seems to have troubled herself very little about this one, but Andrew kept his dueling pistols oiled for thirty-seven years. His widowed mother had advised him as a youth not to expect law courts to protect him when words were at issue but to "settle them cases yourself."[12] He may well have smarted from the charge that a gentleman would have verified his bride's divorce before marrying her; but whatever his reasons, his readiness to fight kept the subject alive long after gossip about it might have died out. In the process of defending his wife's reputation, he invited many quarrels and received a bullet which he carried in his shoulder for twenty years.[13]

Rachel's divorce was more than two decades old when she first accompanied Andrew to Washington in 1815 to celebrate his military victory at New Orleans. The Jackson marriage, although childless, appeared to be a happy one. That the capital gave Rachel such a cool welcome suggests that more than propriety was at issue. Her far bigger sin was her lack of both sophistication and education. As one social arbiter put it, "Mrs. Jackson is . . . totally uninformed in mind and manners," adding gratuitously, "although extremely civil in her way."[14]

Money was not the issue. Rachel's parents were of some means, and her father, John Donelson, had served several terms in the Virginia House of Burgesses. But Rachel was a child of the frontier. One of eleven children, she had moved with her family from western Virginia to Tennessee and then to Kentucky, where schools were scarce. Nobody claimed her husband had benefited from much education but he had acquitted himself on the battlefield, an opportunity his wife never had. The same qualities of naturalness and strength that had contributed to his immense popularity and had provided his nickname, "Old Hickory," became in his wife grounds for ridicule and exclusion. Women, especially the mature ones, were expected to represent culture, etiquette, and sophistication—not unstudied naturalness.

In no way did Rachel Jackson approach the accepted model of femininity. Nearing fifty by the time she made her first trip out of the Kentucky-Tennessee area, she had become set in her country ways. Tanned, leathery skin had replaced the creamy complexion of her youth. She preferred to ride a horse rather than sit in a carriage, and she cared little for fashions and cosmetics. Outside her family and friends, the Presbyterian church constituted her one interest, and a quiet evening at home smoking a pipe with Andrew remained her idea of a good time.

Rachel Jackson's additional transgression against prevailing standards of femininity was her stoutness. A miniature painted of her about 1815 shows a plump woman with dark curls under a lacy cap. Her eyes are placid and resigned rather than sharp or alert. She was, one observer noted, "fat, forty, but not fair."[15] Her girth had already provided a source of amusement in New Orleans, where Rachel had gone to help her husband celebrate his military victory. She had been dazzled by the sights of the city, but the local women had exhibited less enthusiasm for her and they had revived an old French saying to describe her: "She shows how far the skin can be stretched."[16] A cartoon made the rounds of New Orleans: it depicted Rachel being laced, without complete success, into a fashionably small-waisted dress. When she danced with Andrew, someone present described her as "a short, fat dumpling bobbing" opposite him.[17]

Hardly oblivious to the insults, Rachel preferred staying home. She reluctantly accompanied Andrew to Florida where he served as governor, but she caused him to turn down a subsequent appointment as ambassador to Mexico when she refused to go. Although she would have gladly confined herself to their Hermitage plantation the rest of her life, she braced herself for Washington and made her way there again in 1824 when Andrew took his Senate seat amid speculation that he stood next in line for the presidency.

At first, Rachel Jackson tried to keep to herself in the capital and, except for church twice a week, rarely left her rooms at Gadsby's Hotel. But on January 8, 1825, a party honoring her husband required her attendance. The hostess did little to make Rachel feel comfortable and the party became an ordeal for her. The other guests singled her out as "stout, vulgar, illiterate" and according to one who was present, they made "many repetitions of her ungrammatical speeches . . . the favorite form of spite."[18] Andrew Jackson later confessed that he had no idea his enemies would stoop so low as to treat "a woman in her declining years . . . [with such] wickedness."[19]

By the time of the 1828 presidential campaign, Rachel's fitness to occupy a conspicuous place had become a political issue. A North Carolina paper, admittedly hostile to Andrew Jackson, advised voters to consider carefully the wisdom of putting Rachel "at the head of the female society of the United States."[20] When rumors about her character multiplied, the Jackson camp sent out investigators to line up supporting evidence for its version of the divorce. Rachel understood that the attacks on her were politically motivated, but that hardly eased her discomfort. "The enemys of the Genls have dipt their arrows in wormwood and gall and sped them at me," she wrote, adding in her curious spelling, "thay had no rite to do [it]."[21]

Rachel Jackson died of a heart attack in December 1828, before her husband's inauguration in March. At sixty-one, she was older than any previous president's wife. Her decision just before her death to ask her niece, Emily Donelson, to substitute for her might have been based on her own failing health.

But that explanation fails to suffice when it becomes clear that Emily Donelson is only the beginning of a long list of youthful chatelaines. After Emily's untimely death at twenty-eight, another Jackson niece came from Tennessee to take her place; and in the subsequent administration, Angelica Van Buren, wife of Martin's son, played a similar role. She was followed by Jane Harrison (daughter-in-law of William), Priscilla Tyler (daughter-in-law of John), Bettie Bliss (daughter of Zachary Taylor), Mary Abigail Fillmore (daughter of Millard), Harriet Lane (niece of James Buchanan), and Martha Patterson (daughter of Andrew Johnson). They presented a stark contrast to the earlier White House chatelaines. All were sweet, young models of girlish innocence, and they fit well the mood of a nation that expected little more of prominent women than cheerful acquiescence.

Respect for age and experience had begun to fall away in America between 1790 and 1820. According to the historian David Hackett Fischer, men felt the effects of the emphasis on youth more than women did. In his book, *Growing Old in America,* Fischer dated the change before the advent of both industrialization and urbanization. Towns changed seating arrangements in the late eighteenth century so that the oldest residents no longer automatically received the choice seats at meetings but had to compete with everybody else in bidding for places. Some state constitutions added mandatory retirement ages so that officeholders, especially judges, had to step down at a prescribed age rather than serve for life as had been the practice. John Adams, for one, thought the age limitations despicable and fumed to Thomas Jefferson that he could "never forgive New York, Connecticut, or Maine for turning out venerable men."[22]

The new respect for youth enticed people to shave a few years off their real ages. "Rounding off" became common so that forty-five often translated into "early forties" and moving from the one decade to the next involved special reluctance. The temptation to remain thirty-nine rather than celebrate a fortieth birthday proved particularly irresistible.[23]

Concurrent developments in fashion reinforced the advantages of youth. The white wigs and powdered hair, favored by George Washington and Thomas Jefferson, disappeared. Knee breeches, which had flattered the older man by exposing his legs, often the last part of the anatomy to go, gave way to leg-concealing trousers. Men's jackets, which formerly featured a rather egg-shaped form with small shoulders and rounded middle, took on an entirely new outline which was considerably more difficult for the elderly man to wear: small-waisted with pronounced shoulders and a very straight, broad back.[24] The United States did not originate the mode—France already led in clothing design—but Americans enthusiastically adopted the new styles.

Women's fashion after 1800 also changed to feature first the straight-skirted, high-waisted line of the Empire style and then, the hoopskirt. Although it may be accurate, as David Hackett Fischer has argued, that women's clothes all through the nineteenth century reflected the subjection of the entire sex to men, it is also true that changes after 1800 gave new importance to a youthful figure. The large posterior and sagging bodice, styles of the late eighteenth century, accommodated more comfortably a matronly figure than did the high-waisted, slim-hipped styles of the early 1800s. Women's clothes in the early nineteenth century resembled children's frocks: thin muslin that clung to the body and shorter skirts that revealed the white stockings and flat slippers so often associated with little children.[25] The ribbons and curls of the 1820s and the hoopskirt and the simpler hairstyles of the 1830s all worked to the advantage of the young woman.

The English language also reflected a decreased respect for the elderly in the early nineteenth century. Words once flatteringly applied to older persons became pejorative or at least less complimentary. "Gaffer," formerly a contracted, but affectionate term for "Grandfather," changed to mean an old man deserving of contempt, and "fogy" went through a similar metamorphosis.

American writers joined in the praise of youth, and several of the transcendentalists commented bluntly on the uselessness of age. Henry David Thoreau wrote: "Age is no better, hardly so well, qualified for an instructor as youth, for it has not profited so much as it has lost. One may almost doubt if the wisest man has learned anything of absolute value by living. . . . Practically, the old have no very important advice to give to the young. . . . [The old] are only less young than they were."[26]

Among the many foreigners who commented on the new admiration for youth in America was the Frenchman Alexis de Tocqueville, who connected the change to democracy.[27] Others documented the existence of a youth cult but offered no explanation for its causes. Several European visitors thought the worship of youth had gotten completely out of hand, resulting in spoiled, although admittedly sometimes precocious, youngsters, but most outsiders wrote approvingly of Americans' infatuation with youth.[28]

Eventually the United States earned an international reputation for being "youth conscious," but the phenomenon began inconspicuously.[29] The president's residence, with its long string of youthful mistresses between 1829 and 1869, offers just one more example of the result.

Andrew Jackson's niece, Emily Donelson, was, in many ways, just a younger version of her Aunt Rachel. When she married at seventeen, Emily had traveled little and boasted no superior education. But when she arrived in Washington three years later, her age evidently excused her limitations.[30] Fanny Kemble, the British actress, described Emily approvingly as "a very pretty person . . . [with] simple and pleasant manners," and John R. Montgomery, a lawyer from Pennsylvania, wrote his daughter that he had found the young Emily Donelson "a very agreeable woman."[31] It is difficult to account for Emily's popularity in the same city that had so castigated her aunt, except by pointing to her youth. The very same adjectives ("sweet," "simple," "pleasant"), that had been directed at Rachel in sarcasm, became compliments for her young niece.

Andrew Jackson relinquished the White House in March 1837 to Martin Van Buren, the New York Democrat whose nomination for vice president Andrew had carefully engineered in 1832. In one term (1833–1837), Van Buren carefully groomed himself for the top office. A widower for many years, he maintained a mostly male preserve until his son's marriage in 1838. Then he quickly acted to install his son's bride as his hostess. Angelica Singleton Van Buren solicited the advice of her distant relative, Dolley Madison, whose word still carried a certain weight with the capital's social arbiters, and soon the president's parties livened up. After the 1839 New Year's reception, the *Boston Post* raved: "[Angelica Van Buren is a] lady of rare accomplishments, very modest yet perfectly easy and graceful in her manners and free and vivacious in her conversation . . . universally admired."[32] She left behind a revealing portrait of herself. Painted by Henry Inman, it shows a smiling woman in plumed headdress, her head tilted to one side, a model of the youth and obeisance in style for women of her time.[33]

Other men (to be discussed later in the chapter) would win the presidency before another came to office without a wife. Then, in 1856, James Buchanan, the only bachelor president (1857–1861), continued the tradition of installing young hostesses at the President's House by calling on his twenty-seven-year-old niece, Harriet Lane. At his inauguration, the press hailed her as the "Democratic Queen," and in many ways she performed like a member of royalty. A United States cutter was named for her, necklines went down in response to her fashion lead, and she became the first White House occupant to be credited with having had a song dedicated to her: "Listen to the Mockingbird."[34]

As a result of her popularity, Harriet was offered many gifts, which, although the president cautioned her not to accept the costly ones, she could not resist. One frequently repeated story had it that a wealthy young admirer of Harriet's had picked up some pebbles, fashioned them into a bracelet for her, and then increased the value of his gift by adding a few diamonds. Harriet very much wanted to keep the bracelet but she realized that her uncle would object if he knew the true worth. She waited until she found him in a particularly good mood and then asked if she could keep some "pebbles" she had been given. Buchanan replied offhandedly that she could. Later, when she told the story, she would remind her listeners, "Diamonds are pebbles, you know."[35]

Such stories of Harriet's girlish innocence and her insistence on having her own way caused the president some embarrassment, but the press and the public tended to indulge the ingénue at the "head of female society." Although campaigning for male relatives had not yet become acceptable for a "lady" in the 1850s, Harriet Lane met with an important Pennsylvania Democrat to promote her uncle's candidacy. Her youth, and perhaps her unmarried state, evidently rendered the meeting politically acceptable, and the Pennsylvanian pronounced himself much taken with her.[36] One contemporary judged Harriet the perfect combination of "deference and grace."[37]

Behind the innocent charm, Harriet Lane showed evidence of considerable exposure to Washington politics and to foreign courts. Buchanan, then a U.S. senator from Pennsylvania, had assumed her guardianship when she was ten years old and her mother (his sister) had died. He had sent his niece to the best Washington school, and later, when he served in James Polk's cabinet, he arranged for her to visit the White House. When he was appointed envoy to Great Britain in 1853, he took Harriet with him to London. Among her English admirers were Queen Victoria, who had accorded her the rank of minister's wife, and an elderly, titled gentleman who proposed marriage. Harriet rejected that offer and returned to the United States with her uncle, who, after many years in public office, finally won the presidency in 1856. By then, Harriet was prepared to leave her own mark on Washington. One southern congressman's wife saw in Harriet's White House management the "highest degree of elegance."[38] It was sometimes said that the capital had never been gayer than in the years of Harriet Lane, even if the possibility of civil war was on many people's minds.[39]

Harriet Lane was still a schoolgirl in Washington when Dolley Madison rounded out her long career as reigning social figure, but the lesson of the older woman was not lost on the younger. Harriet spared no effort in trying to complement her uncle's political success. "[Harriet was] always courteous, always in place, silent whenever it was possible to be silent, watchful and careful," one contemporary wrote of her in what might be considered a prescription for womanly success in the middle of the nineteenth century, and added: "She made no enemies, was betrayed into no entangling alliances and was involved in no contretemps of any kind."[40]

Further evidence for a more serious side to the publicly frivolous Harriet showed up in her reaction to requests she received. People who felt they lacked representation elsewhere sometimes appealed to her for help, and her papers indicate that she tried to comply. Indians who turned to her for assistance showed their gratitude by naming many of their daughters "Harriet."[41] She intervened to get jobs for friends and she interspersed artists with politicians at White House dinners to give more importance to cultural subjects.[42] Her genuine interest in art is attested to by the fact that she later provided that her own art collection, begun during the years she lived with her uncle, go to the Corcoran Gallery of Art. Eventually, after funds became available in 1920 and other donations of considerably more worth were added to it, it became the basis of the National Collection of Fine Arts at the Smithsonian.[43]

Harriet Lane's prominence and popularity led to rumors that she influenced the president, and according to one careful student of the correspondence between her and her uncle, people believed that he listened to her.[44] Sarah Agnes Pryor, wife of a Washington newspaperman, described Harriet as her uncle's "confidante in all matters political and personal."[45] She possessed political astuteness, Pryor noted, a trait of considerable value during the last months of the Buchanan administration when John Brown raided Harpers Ferry and war between the states seemed more likely than ever before.

In many ways, Harriet Lane is a transitional figure in the history of White House chatelaines. Although her age fits her into the string of youthful hostesses, her record indicates that she played a more substantial role. The historian Lloyd C. Taylor, Jr., singled her out as the "first of the modern First Ladies [because she] capture[d] the imagination of [her] contemporaries."[46] Indeed, her remarkable popularity, her experiment with campaigning, her response to individuals who sought access to the president through her, her mixing of artists and politicians at social functions, and her use of her position to promote American art all make her sound very much like a First Lady of the twentieth century.

The fact that youthful hostesses assisted Andrew Jackson, Martin Van Buren, and James Buchanan might not seem remarkable since none of these men had wives and each had to seek a substitute hostess somewhere. But the number of presidents' wives who relied on young surrogates to fulfill what had come to be considered their official responsibilities raises other questions. What explains why so many presidents' wives between 1829 and 1869 said they were too ill to take on the role of First Lady when such an explanation is quite rare before and after that period? Beginning with Anna Harrison in 1841 and ending with Eliza Johnson in 1869, there are only two exceptions to that curious pattern of invalidism.

Jacksonian America did not initiate illness among presidents' wives. Beginning with Martha Washington, whom George described as "scarce ever well,"[47] First Ladies recorded long and serious illnesses at one time or another. Abigail Adams became so sick in the summer of 1798 that John feared she would not survive.[48] Dolley Madison believed she was dying in the summer of 1805 and put herself in the care of one of Philadelphia's most prominent physicians, a man with the unlikely name of Dr. Physick.[49] Elizabeth Monroe's poor health had been the talk of Washington for years before her husband's retirement in 1825, when he cited the strain of politics on her. Louisa Adams's diary and that of her husband carry ample evidence that she frequently complained she was not well.

But none of these women, with the exception of Elizabeth Monroe, used their illnesses to excuse them from virtually all official tasks. Their successors did. From the distance of more than a century and without access to their medical records, it would be folly to attempt to assess the women's health. But the evidence extant does suggest that claims of illness easily relieved women from the responsibility of attempting tasks in which they had shown little interest.

Individuals can, of course, recover from sickness and live many more years, but Anna Harrison's longevity is intriguing. She cited illness as her reason for not going to Washington in 1841 for the inauguration of her husband, William Henry Harrison, but she survived another twenty-four years, outliving all but two of her nine children. Sixty-five years old at the time of William's nomination, she began the campaign enthusiastically enough, greeting the people who came to her North Bend, Ohio home to assess the candidate. Then in June of that year, one of her sons died, and she became despondent and refused to appear in public. Cincinnati newspapers began to describe her as an "invalid."[50]

When word came of William's victory, Anna had little inclination to accompany him to Washington. His friends had done him no favor by elevating him to high office, she pointed out, when he had been happy and contented in retirement. As for herself, she preferred to wait for milder weather to make the trip and sent her widowed daughter-in-law, Jane Harrison, to substitute for her in the capital. The younger woman had little opportunity beyond the inaugural festivities to establish her reputation because William Henry Harrison died one month after taking office, but contemporaries spoke approvingly, of the "attractive, young" daughter-in-law.[51]

Because no president had ever died in office, many people seemed to think none ever would. Congress debated what arrangements should be made for the widow, and the vice president, John Tyler, prepared to move to Washington. The entire Tyler household was thrown into confusion, but not more confusion than reigned among the Whigs who had put him on the ticket. They had chosen him for his balancing effect, not his potential as president. John Tyler was known to disagree with William Henry Harrison on just about every important issue—the question of whether or not the country should have a national bank, the ideal tariff, and how public lands should be distributed. Once John Tyler took office, the Whigs quickly abandoned him and he was dubbed the "president without a party."[52]

But John Tyler brought a large, supportive family with him to Washington and carried on the tradition of youthful hostesses at the President's House. His wife, Letitia, had suffered a stroke two years earlier and, although some evidence suggests that she had continued to oversee her large household in Virginia, she showed no inclination to participate in social life in the capital. Her actress daughter-in-law, Priscilla Cooper Tyler, twenty-five years old, appealed to a country infatuated with youth. "Here I am actually living in and what is more, presiding at the White House," Priscilla wrote to her sister in 1841, "and I look at myself like the little old woman and exclaim 'can this be I?' "[53]

Priscilla Cooper Tyler took great pleasure entertaining at other people's expense[54] and adding to her already large circle of admirers. "I am considered *'charmante'* by the Frenchmen, 'lovely' by the Americans and 'really quite nice, you know' by the English," she wrote with more than a little accuracy.[55] Priscilla had already made a name for herself when she toured the East Coast playing lead parts opposite her famous father, Thomas Cooper, and one French minister ridiculed a country where a woman could pass from being an actress to "what serves as a Republican throne."[56] But most of her guests thought she did her job well. John Quincy Adams, not an easy man to please, found "the courtesies of Mrs. Robert Tyler all that the most accomplished European court could have displayed,"[57] and the *New York True Sun* reported approvingly that Priscilla made "no enemies."[58]

Priscilla Cooper Tyler gave up her White House role in the spring of 1844 so that an even younger woman could take her place. In the fall of 1842, her mother-in-law, Letitia Tyler, became the first woman to die during her husband's presidency, and eighteen months later John Tyler remarried. At fifty-five, he selected a wealthy twenty-four-year-old New Yorker, Julia Gardiner, who had taken Washington by storm when she visited there with her family. Among the many marriage proposals offered the "Rose of Long Island," the president's evidently took precedence and in a very small ceremony at an Episcopal church in New York City, she became his bride on June 26, 1844.

A model of youthful exuberance and energy, Julia Gardiner Tyler served less than a year as First Lady but she worked hard to leave her mark. She initiated the custom of musicians greeting the president with "Hail to the Chief," and she engaged help to see that she received favorable publicity. The latter was an unnecessary gesture since she had always shown a knack for attracting attention. Before her marriage she had shocked her parents' socially conscious friends by posing for a department store advertisement at a time when ladies did not lend their likenesses to any commercial announcement. The Gardiners had whisked Julia off to Europe to save them all from further embarrassment.

Julia's impish, impetuous nature continued to gain her attention in the White House. Some people thought her extravagant to drive four horses, "finer horses than those of the Russian minister," and a bit self-centered when she "received [guests] seated, her large armchair on a slightly raised platform . . . three feathers in her hair and a long trained purple dress."[59] One woman compared Julia unfavorably to her predecessors and concluded: "Other Presidents' wives have taken their state more easily,"[60] but for the most part people indulged Julia. Her husband doted on her and the public watched approvingly one more young woman, not yet old enough to have to be serious, preside over the President's House.

The Tylers vacated the White House in March 1845, so that the hardworking Polks could move in for four years, a time in which Sarah Polk showed herself every bit as diligent in her role as her husband did in his. No substitutes would take her place, either in the limelight of executive mansion entertaining or in the close working relationship she had with her husband. Sarah Polk represents an exception, however, to be considered in the next chapter, and with her departure from Washington in 1849 the youthful substitutes tradition reappeared.

While Letitia Tyler's stroke and Anna Harrison's grief may seem plausible and sufficient reason for their retiring from First Lady duties, the cases of Margaret Taylor (1849–1850), Abigail Fillmore (1850–1853), Jane Pierce (1853–1857), and Eliza Johnson (1865–1869) are less convincing. Each maintained very low visibility throughout her husband's administration, with Margaret Taylor and Eliza Johnson so little known as to have their existences described as "mysterious." What remains undisputed about each one of the four women is her thorough dislike of the prospect of heading up Washington social life.

Margaret Mackall Smith Taylor, wife of the twelfth president, appeared to reject fashionable city life to marry Zachary Taylor. Educated in a New York City finishing school, she had to learn frontier ways as she followed her husband from one military post to another. While he built a military reputation (including acquiring the nickname "Old Rough and Ready" that extended beyond army life), she gave birth to five daughters and then finally to a son, when she was thirty-eight. By the time the Mexican-American War ended in 1848, she was looking forward to quiet retirement on their southern plantation, but a surge of popular sentiment pushed Zachary into political office. His admission that he had never cast a ballot in his life failed to quell enthusiasm for his candidacy. After he won the presidency in 1848, Margaret resigned herself to one more assignment with him— this time to the White House.

From the beginning, Margaret Taylor refused to have any part of the capital's social life and designated her daughter, Bettie Taylor Bliss, as her substitute. Only twenty-two years old and a recent bride, Bettie Bliss appealed to youth-conscious Washington while Margaret Taylor's vague explanations of having "delicate health" and being an "invalid"[61] sufficed as reason for her to stay upstairs at the White House and entertain her family and close friends there.[62]

Margaret Taylor's low visibility prompted many rumors about her, including the charge that she lacked sophistication.[63] One contemporary explained that Margaret did little more than knit in her room and smoke her pipe—a description that persisted well beyond her death in 1852. Forty years later, a writer for a popular magazine reported that Margaret had "moan[ed] to the accompaniment of her pipe,"[64] and other authors continued to refer to the pipe long after it became clear that she never touched one.

Family and close friends of Margaret Taylor pointed out that she had such a strong aversion to tobacco that no one who knew her smoked in her presence. As for resorting to moaning rather than talking intelligibly, she "ably bore her share in the conversation,"[65] according to guests who were present. Margaret's grandson, whom she raised, described her as a "strict disciplinarian . . . intolerant of the slightest breach of good manners."[66]

The Taylor administration ended abruptly in July 1850, when the president suddenly took sick and died. Margaret did not attend her husband's state funeral, such ordeals then considered beyond the capacity of widows. Two years later she died, so obscure that no likeness of her, either in painting or photograph, survives.[67] Her obituary in the *New York Times* did not even give her full name—referring to her only as "Mrs. General Taylor."

Abigail Fillmore, whose husband Millard Fillmore assumed the presidency at Taylor's death, followed her predecessor's example and turned to her eighteen-year-old daughter to substitute for her on official occasions. The daughter, Mary Abigail, had not yet had the chance to develop very clear ideas of her own, but the mother enjoyed a deserved reputation for erudition and wit. In the early years of her marriage, her large library and good conversation had made her home a gathering place for Buffalo's literati, and an insatiable curiosity and desire to learn continued to motivate her all through her life. As an adult she taught herself French and began studying piano. Thurlow Weed, Millard's political associate, reported that Millard always returned from business trips with books for Abigail because she was a "notable reader."[68] A Washington newspaperman described her as "tall, spare, and graceful with auburn hair, light blue eyes, a fair complexion—remarkably well informed."[69]

Throughout her marriage, Abigail followed the issues related to her husband's career and acted as a sounding board for him. She had a thorough understanding of pending legislation and could discuss knowledgeably current affairs.[70] Millard's respect for her opinions is well documented, including his admission that he never could destroy "even the little business notes she had sent him."[71] One of their friends described the great courtesy Millard always showed Abigail, "like that which a man usually bestows upon a guest," and went on to note that he often said that he "never took any important step without [Abigail's] counsel and advice."[72] In the spring of 1850 when he was vice president, Millard wrote to her after she had returned to Buffalo: "How lonesome this [hotel] room is in your absence. I can hardly bear to sit down. But you have scarcely been out of my mind since you left. . . . How I wish I could be with you!" After filling her in on the details of a Senate debate, over which he had presided, he ended the letter by outlining a political problem and then disclosing how he planned to resolve it.[73]

But Abigail Fillmore apparently had no interest at all in the social leadership role that went along with being the president's wife. She preferred an evening with a book rather than meeting strangers at a party, and she recognized that the "cave dwellers" found readers dull.[74] Although she attended weekly receptions and evening levées "health permitting," she followed the lead of her contemporaries, who "wearied with formal society . . . embraced the opportunity . . . to withdraw . . . more and more into the domestic circle . . . [and leave the parties to the] young women of the court."[75]

In her early fifties during her husband's term, Abigail Fillmore was by no means an invalid (although she complained of a weak ankle that sometimes required her staying a day in bed if she had to stand for hours in a receiving line). A lively conversationalist at small dinners for family and close friends on Saturday evenings, she "never accepted any invitations whatever and this custom was so rigidly observed that none was ever sent [the Fillmores.]"[76] Abigail fitted out a "cheerful room" on the second story of the White House, where her daughter "had her piano and harp . . . and here . . . surrounded by her books, spent the greater part of her time," a family friend reported.[77] Her one significant contribution as First Lady was the establishment of a White House library because she was disappointed to find that none existed.

That presidents' wives in the middle of the nineteenth century were wary of a public role is not remarkable. It was a time of significant change in women's lives. Industrialization took much of the work out of the home and put it in the factory, leaving wives who had supervised domestic production with less to do. The kind of operation that Martha Washington had managed at Mt. Vernon, or Abigail Adams at Quincy, was now altered or vanished. The division between women's work and that of men became clearer, and even the women who went out each day to work the machines aspired to the leisurely life and lack of responsibility that seemed to go with being a "lady."[78]

The nation was undergoing enormous geographic expansion at the same time. With just a few large acquisitions, the western boundary jumped to the Pacific Ocean by 1850. Behind the boasts about "manifest destiny" lay many problems, including how to distribute and govern the new land, how to service the people who settled there, and, most troubling of all, what role, if any, slave labor should play. The "stretch marks" of the rapid growth would prove disfiguring for decades to come, and it is not surprising that presidents' wives kept aloof from the major debates of their time.

Invalidism provided a convenient escape, and it was not an unusual one for that time. Catharine Beecher, a New Englander of considerable energy, noted that illness seemed particularly prevalent among the better-off married women. It was the exception, she wrote, to find a healthy one among the lot. "I am not able to recall," Beecher wrote in 1854, "in my immense circle of friends and acquaintances all over the Union so many as TEN married ladies born in this century and country, who are perfectly sound, healthy, and vigorous."[79] Foreigners underlined Beecher's observation. The British actress Fanny Kemble judged Americans "old and faded" at twenty-five. Other visitors noted "a delicacy of complexion and appearance amounting almost to sickness."[80] Young, single American women appeared more energetic and healthy than their European cousins, but they wilted after marriage into sickly matrons.

Women on both continents lacked the information to allow them to space, with any accuracy, the births of their children, so babies arrived one after the other more rapidly than the mother's health or inclination to sacrifice personal freedom would have indicated. Hannah Van Buren, who died almost two decades before her husband became the eighth president, remains one of history's shortest footnotes, but the small record she left points to the rigors of childbearing. Married at twenty-four, she gave birth to three (perhaps four) children in five years. Then after becoming ill, probably with tuberculosis, she gave birth to another son and died at age thirty-five.

Such experiences were becoming less common in Jacksonian America because women were having fewer children than had been the pattern and they were having their last child earlier.[81] Fewer births should have improved women's health, not worsened it. More important, it was not, Catharine Beecher and others noted, the women having the most children or performing the hardest labor who were the sickest. Middle-class and wealthy women complained the most. Poor women, compelled to go out to work to feed their families, may have concealed how they felt in order to earn, but the prevalence of illness among the economically advantaged women is striking.

Presidents' wives, examples of more privileged women, may be particularly relevant to Catharine Beecher's speculation that women used chronic illness to express unhappiness with the limitations on their lives.[82] A woman who sensed very little control over what happened to her could retreat behind invalidism to earn some autonomy, or at the very least to avoid unpleasant obligations. Beecher had other explanations, too. She admitted women's health would benefit if they avoided wearing tight corsets, but she stressed psychological factors, perhaps because she recognized their importance in her own life. As one of her biographers has pointed out, Beecher "consistently responded to external rebuffs by becoming unwell."[83] By retreating into illness, Beecher got a much-needed rest but, more importantly, she registered her own rebellion against contradictory signals that asked women to be both passive and strong.[84]

Women's magazines underscored contradictory models for readers, encouraging them to be retiring and submissive, while at the same time working to develop their minds. Catharine Beecher advocated increasing women's educational opportunities (because teachers were needed in the newly settled western territories), but she opposed enfranchisement as inappropriate. Abigail Powers Fillmore was about the same age as Beecher and from the same area of the country so the two women may have responded to contradictory signals in similar ways. As Millard rose from one political office to another, Abigail encountered a whole new world of ideas and action, but when he achieved the pinnacle of success, the presidency, she was left to look after seating arrangements at dinner parties. The wit and political savvy that had drawn admirers to her during Millard's tenure in less conspicuous offices earned her few friends in Washington. "Cave dwellers" preferred the innocence and the inexperience of her teenaged daughter. It is no wonder that Abigail Fillmore relied on a weak ankle to help keep her upstairs in her library at the White House.

Nineteenth-century America encouraged women to describe themselves as sick and frail. The languishing woman, who fainted frequently, epitomized femininity. Susan Sontag, the writer and critic, has documented how thin bodies, even those emaciated by tuberculosis, became equated with creativity, wealth, and good manners.[85] Although Sontag placed this development in both Western Europe and the United States, the latter took up the idea with greater zeal and applied it particularly to women. Foreign visitors frequently remarked on the great importance Americans placed on being thin. The Englishwoman Lady Isabella Bird reported in 1856: "The figures of the American ladies in youth are very sylph-like and elegant. . . . They are almost too slight for beauty. . . . Unfortunately a girl of 20 is too apt to look faded and haggard and a woman who with us would be in her bloom at 30 looks passé, wrinkled and old. It is then that the sylph-like form assumes an unpleasant angularity, suggestive of weariness and care."[86] The American fixation with slimness had its culmination in the twentieth-century maxim, attributed to various individuals, including the Baltimore-born Duchess of Windsor, "A woman cannot be too rich or too thin."[87]

It would be unfair to imply that all nineteenth-century American women who complained of illness feigned pain in order to appear more feminine or escape unpleasant assignments. Many of their complaints were no doubt genuine, made even worse by the inadequate or mistaken treatment which they received. Physicians frequently concentrated on the one organ peculiar to women, the uterus, and cauterized it or applied leeches, even though an entirely different part of the body might have been the origin of the complaint.

Presidents' wives, being such a small number of the total population, should never be thought of as a representative sample. Yet, with just a few exceptions, through the middle of the nineteenth century the women in the White House showed an amazing propensity for illness. What is perhaps more significant, the public accorded them enormous sympathy and wide latitude in refusing official responsibilities because of poor health or family tragedies.

Jane and Franklin Pierce, in the White House from 1853 to 1857, learned that such sympathy was reserved for women but denied their husbands. Just weeks before the Pierces moved into the White House, their young son, Bennie, was killed in a train accident in front of his parents' eyes. To Jane, who had doted on Bennie, the tragedy represented retribution for her husband's excessive political ambition—Franklin's capturing the presidency had somehow cost her their son—and the old hatred that she had always felt for Washington and politics revived in her with such force that she could not bring herself to attend the inauguration.

Jane Pierce had a long history—her entire adult life—of citing illness as a reason for doing very little. When she had married the Democratic Congressman in 1834 her prominent New England family had objected that he came from a different political party and that his family stood well below theirs in wealth and prestige. Whatever Jane's feelings about her husband, she never seemed to come to terms with his choice of careers. She accompanied him to Washington immediately after their marriage but begged off from the social engagements, saying she did not feel well enough to participate.[88] During Franklin's second year in Congress, Jane's pregnancy gave her a reason to stay with relatives in Massachusetts. When that son died, three days after birth in February 1836, Jane withdrew more and more from any kind of public role.[89] She insisted that Franklin sell their house in Hillsborough, another town she did not care for, while she remained in Lowell and submitted to leeching, the currently popular medical treatment.[90]

When Franklin Pierce's political reputation grew and he won election to the United States Senate, Jane reluctantly returned to Washington, but she made no attempt to hide her displeasure with the capital and rarely ventured out of the boardinghouse where they lived.[91] After giving birth to two more boys, one in 1839 when she was thirty-four and another in 1841, she became even more adamant in thinking that Washington would ruin her children as well as her husband. She thought the social scene encouraged Franklin to drink excessively, and she saw politics as a demeaning career that damaged the entire family. In 1842, when Franklin's Senate term ended, Jane prevailed on him to move back to New Hampshire.[92] To placate her, he refused an attorney generalship in the Polk administration, but the war with Mexico was another matter. He enlisted, achieved the status of local hero, and when the fighting ended, resumed his political career.

By 1852, when Franklin Pierce became a candidate for president, Jane's abhorrence of everything about the capital and politics was well established. When she heard that the Democrats had nominated him, she fainted. A messenger, who brought the news to the Pierces while they were out riding in their carriage, had thought to please by pronouncing her the next "Presidentess."[93] Jane fervently prayed for her husband's defeat because she could not bring herself to consider the alternative—his victory and her return to Washington, this time to the White House. If she had felt uncomfortable as a congressman's wife, she would surely suffer in the considerably more conspicuous and demanding role of First Lady.

Bennie's death in January 1853 relieved Jane Pierce of any obligation to attend her husband's inauguration two months later, even though her family, more favorably disposed to Franklin after he had become so famous, urged her to be strong. They understood that all through her marriage she had found excuses for avoiding unpleasant tasks, and they could only hope that national prominence would help her face up to her responsibilities. One cousin explained that Jane had always been "so depressed [and] now has such bitter cause [but we hope she will not become] a source of sorrow and anxiety [to her husband] when he needs strength and consolation."[94]

Although his grief may have equaled that of his wife, Franklin Pierce received little of the public sympathy offered to her. Bennie had planned to hear his father's inaugural speech, and Franklin was achingly aware of his absence as he stood before the crowds on a cold March 4.[95] The wife of a newspaper editor described Franklin Pierce as "the youngest and handsomest President we had ever elected, [but] . . . so sad." When he began his speech with a reference to Bennie's death, the audience was shocked: "The public does not tolerate the intrusion of a man's personal joys and griefs into his official life," Sarah Agnes Pryor observed, and some in the crowd pronounced Franklin's move a ploy to gain sympathy while others thought it an unseemly exposé of his private life. In any case, it was unacceptable: "To keep one's inner self in the background should be the instinct, and is surely the policy of every man and woman who aspires to popularity," Pryor warned.[96]

In Franklin's wife, however, grief was condoned and accepted as sufficient reason for avoiding official duties. Her widowed aunt stayed with her and became "virtually the lady of the White House," according to one guest.[97] The aunt shared Jane's "seclusion [because her son's death meant that] nothing of course will now be expected of her and wherever she is, she will be secluded from the world."[98] After the first few months when Jane saw no visitors and "seem[ed] to be bowed to the earth,"[99] she appeared at some public receptions but could not throw off her grief. Washingtonians dismissed her as an invalid and pronounced the President's House a gloomy place for the entire Pierce administration.

More than a decade would intervene between Jane Pierce's unhappy years in the White House and the arrival of the next "invalid" chatelaine.

In the meantime, Harriet Lane, niece of President Buchanan, enlivened the Washington social scene, and Mary Todd Lincoln—although she too grieved the loss of a son—refused to retreat into obscurity.

With Abraham Lincoln's assassination in April 1865, the newly inaugurated vice president, Andrew Johnson, assumed the presidency. The record of his wife, Eliza McCardle Johnson, lends credence to the theory that nineteenth-century women could easily withdraw from a public role by pleading illness or grief. In the case of a woman like Eliza, who had several reasons for not putting herself in a conspicuous role, the temptation may have proven understandably strong. Mary Lincoln had endured four years of almost unremitting criticism, and Eliza's husband had not exactly paved the way for her to enjoy a more favorable reception.

Andrew Johnson had distinguished himself at his vice presidential inauguration on March 4, 1865, by lurching forward to take his oath and slurring the lines of a long, rambling discourse. Word spread quickly through the audience that he was drunk. Eliza had not been on hand to nurse him through a bad cold, and when on the day of the ceremony he had fortified himself with alcohol, the dose had proven too strong. Abraham Lincoln defended his running mate by volunteering that "Andy ain't no drunkard," but Mary Lincoln was thoroughly annoyed. When the president was shot just weeks later, Andrew's performance was still fresh in people's minds, and they had not forgotten it when his family came to join him in Washington in June.

The fragile, blue-eyed Eliza Johnson had other reasons for delaying her arrival in the capital. She had visited the city only once before 1865,[100] but she understood how short she fell of possessing the social skill that "cave dwellers" assessed in each president's wife. Grief and poor health sapped her energy. She had tuberculosis before the Civil War; and family tragedies, including the deaths of a son and a son-in-law, had further weakened her. Her husband's political career had included few chances for her to develop self-confidence.

Eliza Johnson had not always lagged so far behind her husband, but like many political wives, she had watched the man she tutored outdistance her. Andrew had been a young, poorly educated tailor when she first saw him and it was partly her teaching and help that allowed him to move ahead. They had married while still in their teens, and as soon as he had mastered the three "r's" and put his tailoring business on a prosperous route, he arranged to have himself appointed a trustee of the local academy. He was, one wag had it, a self-made man, inclined to give too much credit to his maker.[101]

Certainly he gave little credit to his wife. While he progressed through a string of elective offices—state representative, U.S. congressman, governor of Tennessee, and finally U.S. senator—Eliza followed the example of many other political wives by staying home and setting her sights narrowly on her family.

Unlike Mary Lincoln, who had stubbornly claimed a prominent place in the capital's social life, Eliza Johnson insisted on remaining out of sight. Her invisibility was so complete that after four years in the capital, newspapers described her existence as "almost a myth."[102] She appeared briefly at only one dinner (but left after starting to cough),[103] and her only other recorded social activity was a children's party in December 1868, when she greeted her young guests by announcing that she was "an invalid."[104]

Her invisibility should not be taken for inactivity. One report that Eliza's influence over her husband was "boundless" no doubt exaggerated the case, but she did continue to keep remarkably informed during her life, reading many newspapers and magazines. During the White House years, she clipped articles she thought he should see, shrewdly separating the good news which she gave him at the end of each day, from the bad, which he got the next morning. One historian concluded that Andrew Johnson "may have consulted his wife and daughters more than he did any fellow statesman," leaving unclear how much he consulted anybody.[105]

Martha Johnson Patterson, who substituted for her mother at the president's table, could rely on the country's preference for youth to protect her from criticism. The Johnson daughter immediately disarmed potential detractors by announcing, "We are plain folks from Tennessee, called here by a national calamity. I hope not too much will be expected of us."[106] Then to lend credence to her claim, she covered the worn White House carpets with simple muslin and installed two Jersey cows on the lawn to provide fresh milk and butter. In an older woman, such decisions might have prompted ridicule or charges of bumpkin roughness, but in a younger woman, they apparently seemed refreshing. Margaret heard her sister and herself praised as assets to their father, "frank and unostentatious . . . [in a manner that has] gained for them the respect of all visitors."[107]

In 1868, the Johnson family found themselves in the unwelcome glare of the first presidential impeachment trial in American history. The House of Representatives, in a show of their own strength and their disapproval of the president's handling of a defeated South, had charged him with "high crimes and misdemeanors." For three months while the Senate tried the case, people flocked to witness the proceedings as though it were a carnival show rather than a national trial. Kate Chase, whose father presided as chief justice, appeared each day to watch his performance, while others competed for tickets to see her, one of the city's most popular young belles.

The Johnson women remained in the White House—the president's daughters keeping up a regular social schedule and Eliza staying upstairs and out of sight.[108] Each evening, a steward, delegated to attend the proceedings, reported on the day's events. Except for that contact, the Johnsons feigned disinterest in the trial. When acquittal came (by the margin of a single vote), Eliza insisted that she had correctly predicted her husband's vindication.

Several of the accounts of Eliza Johnson's life raise questions about whether or not she was physically able to assume a more active public role in the White House. Her grandchildren evidently enjoyed her company, and according to one witness they ran to her room as soon as they finished their lessons—hardly evidence that she was incapacitated. Often described as fragile or frail but never uncommunicative or disabled, she remained central to the family's life in the White House. After leaving Washington, she outlived her husband, and, when he died in 1875, she appeared healthy enough to have herself appointed his executrix under bond set at $200,000.[109]

Any conclusions about Eliza Johnson, however, are bound to be speculative because so little information remains. Her prospective biographer, Margaret Blanton, abandoned the project after years of work because she thought the subject impossible to know. Except for Eliza's loyalty to her husband, which was unquestioned, nothing was clear. "In the end I did not know," Blanton wrote, "whether she loved Andrew or hated him."[110]

Blanton did not definitely conclude that Eliza Johnson withdrew behind explanations of illness to avoid unwanted social duties. But Blanton did judge the entire Johnson family "not very clever [and] put in a position to which they were unequal."[111] If that is true and Eliza remained a frontier woman, pushed by circumstances far beyond her accustomed setting, then it is not surprising that she looked for an escape. By making herself invisible for four years, she avoided criticism. The country's acceptance of youthful substitutes provided a way out.

Illness as a permanent condition of First Ladies disappears with Eliza Johnson's departure from Washington in 1869 (except for Ida McKinley, who came to the White House much later). Other presidents' wives suffered serious and debilitating sicknesses but they remained inactive only temporarily. Helen Taft, after her stroke in 1909, delegated official responsibilities to her daughter and sister for much of the next year but then returned to resume a full and active role in Washington life. Florence Harding (1921–1923) and Lou Hoover (1929–1933) both suffered serious illnesses during their husbands' administrations but kept full schedules. Both Betty Ford (1974–1977) and Nancy Reagan (1981–1989) underwent surgery and other treatment for breast cancer but continued to make public appearances.

Nineteenth-century America's tolerance—indeed, solicitous sympathy—for women's withdrawal into illness and grief gave presidents' wives a convenient exit from what had become onerous, often unpleasant responsibilities. No written rules dictated the activities of White House chatelaines, leaving them free to react to public attitudes as well as to express their own frustrations and needs. Women who were bored by the role of hostess that so many of their predecessors had taken had another choice. Rather than face judgment by the "cave dwellers," they could take to their beds and install a young ingénue in their place, confident that any social lapses of the substitute would be tolerated and charged to inexperience.

Some exceptions (Sarah Polk and Mary Lincoln) broke the pattern, and they will be considered next. But for the most part, mid-nineteenth century America witnessed few mature or strong First Ladies. Youthful surrogates became a tradition because they evidently fit in with prevailing ideas about femininity. Womanliness could best be exemplified in obsequious, smiling mannequins who showed little evidence of thinking for themselves.

3

Three Exceptions: Sarah Childress Polk, Mary Todd Lincoln, and Julia Dent Grant

MOST HISTORICAL PATTERNS EXPOSE an exception—a conspicuous deviation from an otherwise straight, clear line. Presidents' wives are no different; and if in the middle half of the nineteenth century most preferred anonymity to exploring new possibilities in the job, a minority achieved prominence. Sarah Childress Polk (1845–1849) eschewed domestic details so that she could maintain a close working relationship with her husband. Mary Todd Lincoln (1861–1865) left observers unsure about whether or not she had any influence on important decisions, so that merchants, intent on catering to her, permitted her to run up enormous bills. Julia Dent Grant's activities (1869–1877) and those of her children received enough attention to qualify the Grants as the first "star" family in the White House. The three women totaled only a bit more than sixteen years in the White House, but they stand out in sharp contrast to the faceless First Ladies who preceded them.

All three had especially good educations for women of their time and place. The schooling itself was not so important, but it may have encouraged the women and those whom they encountered to give special weight to their judgments. Sarah Polk and Mary Lincoln had a long time to prepare for the White House. Their husbands had spent their entire adult lives in politics, and Mary Lincoln had never concealed her lifelong ambition to reach the top. That infatuation with the limelight and an acceptance of the careers their husbands had chosen characterize all three women.

In their forties when their husbands took on the presidency, the three exceptions may simply have had more energy than their older counterparts. At forty-one, Sarah was almost as young as Dolley Madison had been at her husband's inauguration. After James Polk had delivered his speech to a "large assemblage of umbrellas,"[1] Sarah had accepted the Bible used in the ceremony, tucked away a souvenir fan with its pictures of the first ten presidents, and ridden up Pennsylvania Avenue with her friends. The custom had not yet developed for the president's wife to accompany him to the White House, but in Sarah's case it would have been appropriate since she had played an important part in the career that took him there.

That Sarah Polk figured prominently in James's rise to power is less difficult to prove than the reasons, but from the beginning of their marriage she showed a mind of her own. On their wedding trip, following the nuptials on New Year's Day, 1824, Sarah impressed her husband's relatives as "display[ing] a great deal of spice and more independence of judgment than was fitting in one woman."[2] She might have been expected to defer to James, who was eight years her senior and a graduate of the University of North Carolina, but she showed little evidence of doing so.

Partly pampered and partly pushed into self-confidence, Sarah Childress Polk had grown up in very comfortable circumstances. Her parents, prosperous Tennessee planters and tavern keepers, had provided particularly good schooling for their children. In Sarah's case that meant beginning with a tutor at home, then continuing at a Nashville girls' school before enrolling at thirteen in the best girls' school in the South. Salem Female Academy in North Carolina, founded by Moravians who put great importance on girls' education, eventually drew students from all over the Eastern Seaboard.[3] When its reputation reached Tennessee, Sarah and her younger sister rode 200 miles on horseback to enroll. In addition to the usual academic subjects, the girls had to improve their needlepoint, practice the piano, and assist in cleaning the dormitory—all part of preparing them for assuming wifely responsibilities in adulthood. Sarah's stay at this exceptional school ended after less than a year when her father died and she was called home, but it is clear from her later statements and decisions that the academic part of Salem's program interested her far more than the domestic part.

From the very beginning of her marriage, Sarah Polk considered household tasks a peripheral part of being a wife, and if forced to choose between domestic chores and spending time with her husband, she almost always chose the latter. During the first year of James's term in Congress she remained in Tennessee, but the next session she accompanied him to Washington. In the style of the time, the Polks boarded—so Sarah had few housekeeping duties. James reportedly supported his wife's view of her role, because she explained that she had volunteered to stay in Tennessee and take care of the house but that he had chided her, "Why? If it burns down, we can live without it."[4]

With that kind of endorsement, Sarah evidently felt comfortable fitting herself into her husband's career. Whenever she could help him, she was there. Her skills as a hostess took on new importance as James became a more central figure in the capital. Under Andrew Jackson's protection, he was chosen Chairman of the House Committee on Foreign Relations and then Speaker of the House of Representatives in 1835. Rather than objecting to the inconvenience of dividing her life between two places, Sarah concentrated on the advantages of seeing the world beyond Tennessee. A detour to New York City or a stop in Pennsylvania to make political calls interested her as much as it did James. Physical danger in the form of overturned carriages and swollen streams failed to deter her.

When her presence in Washington might have complicated matters for James, as during the Peggy Eaton episode, she remained in Tennessee, offering vague explanations about wanting to economize. Her real motive was no doubt more political. She had every reason to want to avoid taking a position in favor of Peggy or against her. Peggy's husband, John Eaton, was a favorite of President Jackson but her own reputation, clouded by rumors of an affair with John while she was still married to another man, upset many of his colleagues and prompted their wives to refuse to socialize with her. Not until John Eaton left the cabinet in 1831 did the matter resolve itself and even then, harsh words, exchanged in anger, continued to echo and affect political careers.

Sarah Polk is sometimes credited with participating in her husband's career almost by default "because she had no children."[5] Congressmen's wives frequently complained about the difficulties of boarding a family in the capital; and if Sarah had been responsible for young children, she might have resisted moving them back and forth between Tennessee and Washington. But she remained childless throughout her twenty-five-year marriage. Unlike Rachel Jackson, who was evidently attracted to young people and surrounded herself with nieces and nephews to compensate for the children she never had, Sarah showed little feeling of loss in the letters she wrote.

They show, instead, overwhelming concern with her husband's health and his political career. Because the Polks were not often separated, their correspondence is not so voluminous as that of John and Abigail Adams. Many of the letters were written during campaigns, since the mores of her time did not permit a candidate's wife to campaign openly, and while James was out electioneering, Sarah had to content herself with reporting to him on local political maneuverings. She frequently began her letters with "nothing to report," but then always managed to find something. When the newspapers criticized James, with one editorial pouring out "a vial of wrath" against him, she passed the word along but predicted that the attack had "Too much of a flourish" to continue for long.[6] After the *Knoxville Argus* forecast an increased Democratic vote all over the state, "even in the strong Whig counties,"[7] Sarah wrote to James with a touch of glee, "The Whigs are dispirited. Good . . . Democrats are in extacies [*sic*]."[8]

While her husband went out looking for votes, Sarah worked quietly at home to promote "union and harmony [to] get . . . our own sort of men [elected]."[9] She did not always achieve the results she wanted, and once, after summoning politicos for a conference, she complained to James that she had accomplished little because many of the important men were out of town and "I have not much to opperate [*sic*] on."[10] She almost always included in her letters to James an admonition that he pay attention to his health. "It is only the hope that you can live through [the campaign] that gives me a prospect of enjoyment," she wrote in 1843 when he was running again for governor. "Let me beg and pray that you will take care of yourself and do not become to [*sic*] much excited."[11]

If Sarah regretted missing out on the excitement of the campaign trips, she kept up a good front and refused to crumble in self-pity. Temporarily disheartened by the lack of good news, she wrote James: "Do not think that I am down in the celler [*sic*] for as soon as I am done writing I am going to dress and go out visiting."[12] Only when compelled to play an entirely social role did she find herself completely out of sorts, and when she had to assume the part of the solicitous hostess for his visiting relatives she was really angry.[13]

In Washington, Sarah cultivated friendships with the city's strongest, most opinionated women, including Marcia Van Ness, the founder of the Orphan Asylum, Floride Calhoun, the outspoken wife of the South Carolina senator, and Josephine Seaton, a writer and wife of a newspaper editor. Even women whose husbands opposed James politically became Sarah's loyal friends. When the Polks announced that they would return to Tennessee in 1839 so that James could run for governor, Josephine Seaton volunteered that she did not mind seeing James go—he was her husband's political rival—but that she would miss Sarah.

In addition to a network of achieving women, Sarah maintained friendships with several important men. Andrew Jackson, who facilitated her husband's career, Franklin Pierce, who boarded near the Polks, and Supreme Court Justice Joseph Story all became her staunch supporters. In 1839, Justice Story published a farewell poem to Sarah, very unusual recognition for a living woman, particularly a congressman's wife:

> For I have listened to thy voice, and watched thy playful mind,
> Truth in its noblest sense thy choice, Yet gentle, graceful, kind.[14]

Her roster of friends indicates that Sarah Polk was one of the few nineteenth-century First Ladies to develop her own supporters—people who valued her abilities and judgment apart from her husband's. In that respect, she foreshadows a later development that saw its culmination in the campaign buttons, "Betty's husband for President."

Sarah claimed to have predicted her husband's winning the presidential election well before it happened in 1844, although historians have frequently singled this out as the first victory of a "dark horse." She had been exchanging letters with supporters who named James as "the best man" for the job,[15] and she appeared eager to see him nominated. State politics had begun to bore her, and she had tired of making do on a governor's meagre $2,000-a-year salary, although she received additional income from her Mississippi plantation.

The prospect of becoming First Lady carried all sorts of new possibilities, and Sarah meant to be more than a hostess. When someone threatened to support the opponent, Henry Clay, because his wife made good butter and knew how to look after a house, Sarah Polk reportedly countered, "If I get to the White House, I expect to live on $25,000 a year and I will neither keep house nor make butter."[16] Such a public disclaimer of domesticity was exceedingly rare in the nineteenth century; even in 1984, when the Democratic candidate for vice president, Geraldine Ferraro, was asked if she could bake a muffin, she replied, "I sure can."[17]

Keeping a clean house and making good butter appeared far less important to Sarah Polk than catering to voters. When news first reached the Polks of the 1844 victory, well-wishers flocked to their house and a friend of the family suggested it might be wise to keep them outside rather than let them dirty up the carpets. Sarah insisted they come in and the next day reported with satisfaction that the only marks they had left were those of respect.[18]

The affability that cloaked Sarah Polk's remarkable political interest satisfied observers who expected women to be merely pretty, social creatures. Had she broken the rules and dressed eccentrically or entertained inappropriately, she might have been criticized, but she did not. In appearance she reportedly combined the coloring and charm of a Spanish lady with the determination and strength of her frontier ancestors. Although few of her admirers thought her beautiful, most described her as "elegant" and "queenly." Henry Dilwood Gilpin, a good friend of Martin Van Buren's, reported he had been much impressed "with the good lady who is to preside at the [White House] . . . really a very superior person. Time has dealt kindly with her personal charms and if she is not handsome she is at least very prepossessing and graceful—dresses with taste—and is extremely affable as well as perfectly self possessed. If I am not mistaken she has both sagacity and decision that will make her a good counsellor in some emergencies."[19]

Vice president-elect George Dallas wrote his wife just before the 1845 inauguration that Sarah Polk "dresses rather too showy for my taste . . . but I go for the new lady all hollow [completely]." Dallas added fuel to rumors that the First Lady had the president under her thumb when he wrote: "She is certainly mistress of herself and I suspect of somebody else also."[20]

Sarah's many years of working alongside her husband had increased speculation that she controlled him. While still in her twenties, she had distinguished herself from other congressmen's wives by the forcefulness with which she stated her opinions. Senator Levi Woodbury had written his family in 1828 that only one of his fellow legislators appeared more under his wife's domination than did James Polk. Rudolph Bunner, a representative from upstate New York, reached a similar conclusion.[21]

In response to comments of this sort, Sarah explained that she was simply assisting her husband in order to protect his health. He had never been strong, and she recalled that she had once reprimanded him for keeping late hours. In reply, he had handed her a stack of papers to read for him.[22] Thus began what became standard practice in their relationship—she marked those portions she thought deserving of his attention, folded the papers so that he would not miss the important parts, and passed them back to him.

For two thinking persons to have agreed on everything would have been unusual, and James admitted that he and Sarah sometimes clashed. When the issue of a national bank divided the country, Congressman Polk stood firmly against it. On one of their many trips to Washington, he had asked his wife for money and she had turned first one trunk and then another inside out in the search. "Don't you see how troublesome it is to carry around gold and silver?" she chided him. "This is enough to show you how useful banks are."[23]

A strict Presbyterian, Sarah Polk had no use for dancing or the theater. She never attended a horse race, and although she liked music and resumed piano lessons as an adult, she thought music on Sunday inappropriate. James, who held less definite views on such matters, deferred to her. On their victory trip to Washington in early 1845, well-wishers came aboard their boat to play some festive tunes, but since it was a Sunday, Sarah insisted that the music stop. Someone turned to her husband to countermand her but James Polk replied: "She handles all domestic matters and she considers this domestic."[24] At the inaugural balls, dancing ceased when Sarah Polk entered the room, and she forebade such entertainment at the White House. Although some critics thought her rigid, many people admired her sincerity, and friends who did not want to be forced into attending church with her on Sunday morning learned to keep their distance that day.

Reading had been a habit of Sarah's since youth and in Washington she continued to order many books.[25] An Englishwoman visiting the White House found Sarah busy with several volumes, including one whose author was coming to dinner that evening. "I could not be so unkind," Sarah explained, "as to appear wholly ignorant and un-mindful of [the author's] gift."[26]

Sarah's intellectuality complemented the Polk administration's emphasis on hard work. James and Sarah had stayed at Coleman's Hotel in Washington five days before making a courtesy call at the White House, and when the Tylers gave a big final party (for which the candles reportedly cost $350), the Polks stayed away.[27] President Polk boasted that in his first year in office he rarely took an afternoon or evening off; and when he greeted guests every Tuesday and Friday, he did so as part of his job.[28]

All strong-minded people earn some enemies, and Sarah Polk was no exception. Anyone who criticized her husband raised Sarah's wrath, and she did not always conceal her displeasure. When Martin Van Buren's son, who held many unorthodox views, took issue with President Polk, Sarah banished him from the guest lists. When James had his secretary issue an invitation anyway, she burned it. "I was amused," James Polk noted in his diary, but he gave no hint of overrul-ing her.[29]

But Sarah rarely offended or took issue with anyone. Jessie Benton Frémont, then the young wife of the explorer John Frémont who later ran for president, pronounced Sarah a perfect model: "[an] admi-rable . . . erect, attentive, quietly gracious [woman who] . . . really did her part well."[30] Charles Sumner, the Massachusetts senator, wrote a friend: "Her sweetness of manner won me entirely."[31] One White House dinner guest startled Sarah by saying he had heard she had been "woed in the Bible." When called on to explain, he continued: "Doesn't it say in the Bible, 'woe unto him who has no enemies.'"[32]

Such apparently winning charm evidently excused Sarah from excessive attention to household management. Her old promise that if she got to the White House she would neither keep house nor make butter held true. An able staff took care of most of the domestic arrangements while she concentrated on more important matters. Food held little interest for her and she sometimes became so intent on discussions with her guests that she neglected to eat.[33] Rather than spending much energy on redecorating the mansion, she announced that whatever was good enough for the Tylers would do very well for her. She did install gas lights but in her very practical way insisted on retaining a chandelier of candles, and when the gas system failed during a dinner party, she earned her guests' applause by calling for the candles.[34]

James Polk is sometimes singled out as a particularly strong president because he accomplished in one term all four goals he had set for himself. Introductory history books find his administration very easy to describe. Before taking office, he promised that he would reduce the tariff, restore the independent Treasury, acquire California, and settle the boundary dispute in Oregon.[35] Four years later, he had accomplished all four of these goals, although not to universal approval of his methods. As part of the Southwest territorial question, the war with Mexico aroused great misgivings among people who saw the United States as bullying its smaller southern neighbor into acquiescence.

The Polk administration raises questions about how the forcefulness or success of the chief executive influences the public's judgment of the spouse. Will Americans more likely tolerate strong women if they move alongside decisive men? Can a wife stave off criticism by keeping a less prominent role for herself if her husband is viewed as a relatively ineffectual president? Does a weak president appear even less strong if he has an outspoken wife? Could Eleanor Roosevelt have broken so many precedents if Franklin had accomplished less? Did Rosalynn Carter's determination make Jimmy look less decisive?

Sarah Polk's record suggests no simple connection exists between a wife's public image and that of her husband. The most outspoken and politically involved wife since Abigail Adams, Sarah received a universally good press from both sides of the fence. Capital social arbiters who sized up her "feminine charms" could hardly fault her, and the more intellectually inclined, who wanted a thinking woman in the White House, apparently approved of her, too. Because she had the self-confidence to relegate much of her job as hostess to an insignificant chore—but not neglect it—she achieved remarkable success. The most prominent student of the Polk administration, Charles Sellers, pronounced Sarah "increasingly indispensable" to her husband as "secretary, political counselor, nurse and emotional resource."[36] It was, Sellers wrote, the combination of her "long experience in official circles and her social grace" that qualified her "superbly" to be an outstanding First Lady.

On the issue of feminism it is difficult to know what Sarah Polk thought, although she was living in the White House during the famous Seneca Falls convention in July 1848. Led by the pious Quaker from Philadelphia, Lucretia Mott, and the younger, more outspoken Elizabeth Cady Stanton, women gathered in that small upstate New York town to outline their hopes for better access to jobs, and the right to vote. Only on the franchise did the assembly split, with Lucretia Mott warning her friend, Stanton, that persevering on this matter would render the entire movement ridiculous.

Sarah Polk did not attend the Seneca Falls meeting, although one student of the Polk administration concluded that she encouraged James to address the group.[37] Perhaps she feared being included in the ridicule heaped on feminists at the time. Some newspapers called them "mannish women like hens that crow" and others implied that their unhappiness resulted from their inability to attract men.[38] Sarah doubtless had heard the opinion of some of her contemporaries who felt that childless women, like herself, with little to occupy their time, busied themselves with matters beyond their abilities. A fellow Tennessean may have had her in mind when he wrote to Martin Van Buren: "These women you know who do not breed must always be busy either in making matches or making and unmaking statesmen or some such things."[39]

Sarah spent the summer of the Seneca Falls meeting in tasks that had little relevance to the feminism discussed there. The Polks were building a new house for their retirement in Tennessee and she went to New York that summer to select the furnishings.[40] Portraits made of her at the time show little evidence that she associated with feminists who advocated less constraining clothing and simpler hairstyles. She appeared in elaborate, low-cut dresses and her hair was carefully arranged.

James Polk died in June 1849, three months after his presidency ended, but Sarah survived him by forty-two years. Although her name was briefly linked with that of the bachelor president, James Buchanan, she never remarried. At first her Mississippi plantation and slaves (whom she insisted on calling her "people") took much of her time; but in January 1860, as the Civil War approached, she sold her land and all her "people" for $30,000.[41] Although she explained that her husband would never have approved of secession, she could not conceal her strong sympathies for the South, with the result that her Polk Place in Tennessee remained neutral territory for the duration of the hostilities. Leaders from both sides visited her there and when the local historical society needed a safe place for depositing its holdings, it chose Sarah's residence.

Very popular when she left Washington in 1849, Sarah Polk had inspired a national publication, *Peterson's Magazine*, to take the unprecedented step of paying tribute to her in a poem that ended: "You are modest, yet all a queen should be."[42] Most magazines up to that time had chosen their heroines from classical examples or from lists of women long dead. The singling out of Sarah Polk for such a gesture indicates that she had attained unusual prominence.

Her popularity endured long after she left the capital. In 1881, when Congress debated giving a pension to Abraham Lincoln's widow, one man made his crucial vote dependent on including Sarah Polk.[43] On the state level, the Tennessee legislature planned annual pilgrimages to her house, and newspaper reporters continued to seek her opinions on political matters. The *Mt. Vernon Banner* reported that in her seventy-ninth year, she retained a "complexion as clear, . . . face as smooth and her eyes as bright as most ladies of 50."[44] In the election of 1884, she made comparisons to the one that had sent her husband to the White House forty years earlier. When she died in August 1891, an article in *American Magazine* described her mind as "undimmed to the end."[45]

Sarah Polk stands out in a period when most wives of public figures stayed home and out of sight. That she had excellent health, an inquiring and trained mind, a supportive husband and no children all increased her ability to participate in her husband's career. Reminiscent in many ways of Abigail Adams, Sarah Polk has remained lesser known, perhaps because she lacked some of Abigail's wit and sophistication. Both women considered themselves full partners in their husbands' political careers, opinions that their husbands shared. Yet neither woman showed much interest in reforms for women generally. It is interesting to speculate how they, with all opportunities being equal, would have done as presidents. Their interest in politics was genuine; and perhaps that explains, better than anything else, why they distinguished themselves at a time when most presidents' wives were absent, ill, or inactive during their husbands' administrations.

Compared to Sarah Polk, Mary Todd Lincoln's national prominence is on an entirely different level, more in the infamous category than the famous, more the result of her enemies' work than her admirers. Mary Lincoln's life included elements of unusual ambition and great personal tragedy, possibly explaining why she became one of the most written-about women in American history.[46] That she provoked unusual antagonisms and raised powerful defenses rendered her story all the more intriguing. It is no wonder that fact and fiction became so intertwined in accounts of her life that it is difficult to separate the two.[47] Unfortunately this woman who stubbornly insisted on staying in the limelight, even when criticism mounted, did not always record her motivation. Speculation about that must come from her associates.

A matronly mother of three by the time her husband became president, Mary Lincoln already had some experience with Washington. She had lived there during the winter of 1847–1848 when her husband served in Congress, but unhappy with the prospect of staying in a boardinghouse with her two young sons, she had returned to Illinois. Those few months had exposed her to the entrenched Washingtonians, but by 1861 she appeared to have forgotten how they operated. When her husband won the presidency, she prepared to return to the capital. Had she known the outcome, she might have reconsidered.

Even with her professed powers of premonition, she never predicted how miserable she would become in the next twenty years as she witnessed the deaths of her husband and two of her sons, found herself maligned on two continents, and was finally declared legally insane. A woman of many contradictions, Mary Lincoln may have stirred up controversy because of her enigmatic nature. Her husband called her his "child wife"[48] and "mother"[49]—neither term entirely inappropriate. He pampered her as a spoiled youngster, humored her when she veered toward fanaticism yet showed her enormous tenderness and affection. Although she had attended the best schools in Kentucky, indeed in the entire West, she dabbled in spiritualism throughout her life and persisted in believing in her own supernatural powers as well as those of others. Considerably better educated and socially more sophisticated than the man she married, she had become, by the time he was elected president, so unreliable and impetuous that he could not trust her judgment on any significant matter.

Part of the explanation for her contradictory nature no doubt lies in the particular circumstances of her childhood, which combined material comforts with considerable insecurity. When she was almost seven, Mary's mother died in giving birth to a seventh child, and a little more than a year later, Mary's father remarried. The new wife, Betsy Humphreys, came from a social stratum above that of the Todds and she did not hesitate to point that out. One of her favorite maxims had it that it took seven generations to make a lady and she indicated by her tone that in her family the requisite time had elapsed.[50] Betsy Humphreys Todd gave birth to eight children of her own, who added to her stepchildren made a brood of fifteen, too many for any one of them to claim much individual attention.

To distinguish herself from the rest, Mary competed in every possible way, becoming an ingenious prankster, an excellent student, a superb horsewoman, and a respectable seamstress.[51] Her good looks came naturally.[52] But behind the beauty and ingenuity, her contemporaries observed a very moody young lady, "much like an April day, sunning all over with laughter one moment, the next crying as though her heart would break."[53] She was frequently compared to her mercurial father, Robert Todd, much given to buying expensive clothes one day, then regretting his extravagance the next.[54]

But Todd, a leading businessman in Lexington, provided for every need of his large family and sent all his children, including the girls, to the best schools in the area. When she was eight, Mary entered the local academy, and at fourteen she enrolled in a boarding school outside Lexington. Taught French and social skills by a Paris-born couple,[55] Mary got tested when she went home for the weekends. Her step-grandmother Humphreys, one of Kentucky's grande dames, read French philosophers in the original and tutored the young women of her family in the social graces. To round out her very full education, Mary had the conversation of her father's friends, including the already famous Henry Clay. Young Mary Todd described herself as being much taken with the famous congressman and a "dedicated Whig."

That early interest in politics may help explain why Mary moved to Springfield, Illinois, when she was twenty-one to live with her sister. The older Todd daughter had married the son of the former territorial governor, and she counted many politicians among her friends and acquaintances. Mary's quick wit and beauty attracted several of Springfield's eligible young men, and according to two of her biographers, she was courted by two men who would run against each other in the 1860 presidential election.[56]

If that is true—and there is considerable doubt that it is because Mary's politics would hardly have put her in both their circles—then the short Stephen Douglas might have proven a more suitable match for her than the lanky Abraham Lincoln. Mary's brother-in-law had described Abraham as too "rough," and Mary sometimes joked about his lack of social graces. One story, perhaps as apocryphal as so many of the Lincoln stories were, had it that he had introduced himself to Mary by saying he wanted to dance with her "in the worst way" and then, she said, he did, "in the very worst."[57]

Whatever their reasons, Abraham and Mary were married in 1842, and their early years together were unremarkable. He built both an Illinois law practice and a national reputation, and she gave birth to four sons, including one who died at age four. The Lincolns prospered in the 1850s, partly due to Mary's small inheritances from her father and grandfather and to her reasonable management of the household. She often recalled these as the best times of her life, although people who knew her differed in evaluating her behavior. Some said that she kept up with what was happening in the country, frequently sharing her ideas with her husband; but others, less charitable toward her, saw her even then as a jealous, manipulative woman with few intellectual interests.[58]

Everyone agreed that she never lost her ambition to live in the White House—a prospect that increased in possibility when the Republicans, at their second convention in 1860, selected Illinois' favorite son as their candidate. The northern and southern states had by then become so divided over the issue of slavery and its extension into new areas that the Democratic convention could not agree on one candidate, with the result that the northern branch chose Stephen Douglas while the southerners went with John Breckinridge. To complicate matters, a fourth group, under the Constitutional Union banner, named John Bell, a Tennesseean who won not only his own state but also neighboring Kentucky and Virginia. When the results were in, Abraham Lincoln claimed victory, but with only 40 percent of the popular vote cast, his was a dubious victory. Uncertainty increased when it became apparent that the southerners' pique was not temporary. They refused to accept the results of the election, and additional states seceded from the Union. The capital grew somber as the indications of civil war multiplied.

Mary Lincoln stood squarely in the middle of the storm. Although she professed complete loyalty to the Union cause, several of her relatives enlisted on the side of the "rebels," as Mary and most northerners referred to those who favored formation of the Confederacy.[59] She presented an easy target for people who questioned how a woman could be dedicated to winning a war when her brothers were fighting for the enemy. As stories proliferated about spies in high places, the president's wife was named, sometimes by people whose statements could not be dismissed lightly. Thurlow Weed, a prominent New York supporter of Abraham Lincoln, reportedly announced that Mary had been banished from Washington because she was a "traitor."[60] That was, of course, untrue, but it indicates the kind of rumors that circulated.

Nor were the stories of Mary Lincoln's treachery confined to her lifetime. One poignant account of her husband's defense of her was originally printed in a Washington newspaper in 1905, then repeated many times even after it had been demonstrated to be untrue. It made its most recent appearance in a 1981 best-seller. According to the original source, an unnamed senator had recalled how President Lincoln had taken the unprecedented action of going before a Senate committee to defend Mary. Without mentioning her by name, the president had sworn that no "member of my family holds treasonable communication with the enemy." According to the senator's apocryphal account, the committee was so moved that it immediately and without discussion "dropped all considerations of the rumors that the wife of the President was betraying the Union."[61]

Even without a civil war, Mary's personal insecurities would have made her stay in Washington difficult. She understood that her education and social skill stood her well in the West where she had acquired them but might not satisfy the "cave dwellers." "The very fact of having grown up in the West subjects me to more searching observation," she explained to her seamstress, as though trying to justify why she spent so much money and effort on clothes.[62] Mary had stopped in New York on her way to Washington to purchase yardage for sixteen outfits, and she never let the seamstress catch up before placing more orders.[63]

In the early months of the Lincoln presidency, when the full horror of what would follow had not become clear, some national magazines described the Lincoln White House as though the war was confined to some distant country. *Leslie's Magazine* applauded Mary Lincoln's "exquisite taste" in redecorating the mansion, in entertaining, and in choosing her clothes.[64] "No European court or capital can compare with the President's circle and the society of Washington this winter in the freshness and beauty of its women," *Leslie's Magazine* reported, "and the dingy, sprawling city on the Potomac is bright with the blue of Northern eyes and the fresh rosy glow of Northern complexions."

The First Lady was described as "second in no respect . . . displaying the exquisitely moulded shoulders and arms of our fair 'Republican Queen.' . . . absolutely dazzling."[65]

But very quickly the reports changed. Hundreds of thousands of men took up arms for either the blue or the gray. Battlefield casualties climbed, and Mary Lincoln had her own personal grief in addition to concern for her relatives who were fighting for the "rebels." In February 1862, her eleven-year-old son, Will, died at the White House. Mary purchased costly mourning clothes and special mourning jewelry. Families who had lost sons and husbands in the war were dismayed by her extravagance, and they began to raise questions about the sincerity of her grief. How could she mourn her son and yet direct so much attention to spending money? But she had shown signs before of spending money as though that could help her forget her problems.

Stories began to spread that Mary threw tantrums to get her way, and because several of the accounts originated with her best friends, they could hardly be discounted. Julia Taft, a teenager who spent a great deal of time at the White House because her two younger brothers shared a tutor with the Lincoln boys, told how the First Lady had appropriated a part of another woman's hat for herself. At a concert one evening, Mary Lincoln had eyed the bonnet of Julia's mother and then asked for the ribbons from it. Mary explained that the fashionable French milliner whom both women patronized had been unable to find more of the black and white satin ribbon he had used on Mrs. Taft's hat and Mary wanted that ribbon for herself. In the end Mary got the ribbon, the milliner replaced Mrs. Taft's ties with some of a different color, and Julia concluded that "Mrs. Lincoln wanted what she wanted when she wanted it and no substitute! And as far as we know she always had it, including a President of the United States."[66]

Other stories had the First Lady threatening merchants who refused to humor her and deliver some item she demanded although it had already been bought by somebody else.[67] Mary Lincoln's dressmaker, who was devoted to her employer, described how the president's wife would kick and scream, sometimes lying on the floor, when costumes were not delivered on time or in quite the condition that she expected.[68] Julia Grant, wife of the general who commanded the Union troops after 1863, related other examples of Mary's irrational behavior. On one occasion Julia calmed Mary who insisted that another officer's wife was maneuvering to catch Abraham's interest. Mary became "annoyed" and could not "control her wrath," Julia reported, although there were no grounds for jealousy.[69]

These stories, added to those about her spending and the rumors of her southern loyalties, reached a peak during the reelection campaign in 1864, causing Mary considerable worry. She had neglected to share the extent of her extravagance with her husband and now she desperately needed him to win so she would not have to pay up. Merchants had extended credit, sometimes requesting her intercession with the president in return, and Mary had no illusions about how quickly her credit would be cut off if her husband lost the election. Reassured by the victory of November 1864, she quickly resumed her buying spree and spent in the first three months of 1865 several thousand dollars on non-essentials such as jewelry and silverware. She admitted to a friend that her unpaid clothing bills amounted at that time to $27,000[70]—more than her husband earned in a year—but she actually owed much more.[71]

Mary might have deflected some of the criticism by retreating to her room upstairs, as so many of her predecessors had done, but she refused all offers to substitute for her as hostess. Kate Chase, daughter of the secretary of the Treasury, coveted the White House for her father and would have relished a social leadership role for herself in the Lincoln administration. Other members of the cabinet volunteered to help, too, and when Prince Napoleon came for a visit, Secretary of State Seward offered to host a major event. But Mary Lincoln, proud of the French she had learned in Kentucky, insisted she could handle the arrangements herself; and at the end of the evening when "mostly French was spoken," she reported with some pride that the prince had turned to her and remarked with some surprise: "Paris is not all the world."[72]

If Mary Lincoln had diverted her attention from parties and clothes (subjects that appeared frivolous to many war-sufferers) and concentrated on appearing supportive and protective of her husband, she might have disarmed her critics. Instead, she badgered him more than she helped. According to one White House employee, she interrupted the president's work at the slightest whim,[73] and invited favor-seekers to meals without the president's knowledge. Then, when he appeared "sad and harrassed," she lobbied openly for whatever the guest had come to ask.[74] According to one of Mary's relatives, who had accompanied her to Washington, Mary was constantly being flattered by people who wanted to gain access to the president, and Abe's announcement that "women have no influence in this administration" did little to stop them.[75] With so many rumors of power on the distaff side of the White House, it is not surprising that Mary received an unusual gift from an anonymous donor. It made its point more clearly

than any words could—it was a bonnet with the president's photograph attached to each of the strings.[76]

Charges that a First Lady influenced her husband were nothing
novel—they went all the way back to the first Adams administration.
But Mary Lincoln's brand of self-centered manipulation appealed to
no one. People who championed strong women and respected their
opinions had found heroines in the partisan Abigail Adams and the
astute Sarah Polk, but Mary Lincoln's influence was negative—petty,
unpredictable, and self-serving.

Some of Mary's critics blamed her selfishness for exposing the president to danger, including that at Ford's Theater on April 14, 1865. The
president had been aware of the possibility of personal harm during his
entire first term, and special guards had been assigned to protect him.
Mary insisted, however, that her husband needed relaxation, too, and
she sometimes arranged for him to ride around the capital with her. On
the last day of his life, they had gone out driving and she later said that
she had rarely witnessed her husband so content as on that afternoon.
General Lee had just surrendered the armies and ended the long war.
Taking this move as initiating a new, more tranquil period for themselves personally, the Lincolns resolved to put behind them their grief
over their son Will's death and move on to better times.

That evening Abraham accompanied his wife to the theater and
she was seated beside him when the assassin struck. Mary, who never
attended funerals of any member of her family, did not go to this one
and delegated all the arrangements to her son Robert. Five weeks
later, she rallied enough to pack and leave the White House, thus beginning a long, tortured pilgrimage to find a place to spend the rest
of her life. She was forty-seven years old.

Of the two sons still living (of the four she had borne), Mary felt
closer to Tad, the youngest, than to Robert, then at Harvard Law
School. Tad required special attention because of learning problems
and a speech impediment that made him difficult to understand.[77]
Although generally cheerful, he could sometimes be hard to manage,
throwing tantrums until his mother had to have him removed from
the room. She had been indulgent with him, indeed with all the boys,
taking as her motto "Let the children have fun,"[78] but now she
determined to substitute strictness and to enroll Tad in a school in
Germany. Her motive held more than a little self-interest—she had
never traveled in Europe and believed she could live there more economically than in the United States.

Money so occupied Mary Lincoln's thoughts after 1865 that it may
well have been the most important consideration in her move to

Europe. Although her husband's estate left about $35,000 to her and to each of her sons, she thought the amount inadequate. Congress had traditionally paid a year's salary to the widow of any president who died in office, but Abraham Lincoln had been the first to be assassinated and Mary thought the wife of a martyr deserved more. Others agreed that the different circumstances somehow required a larger compensation for the family.

In a controversy that lasted until her death and beyond, Congress divided over the country's obligation to presidents' widows. As long as she lived, Mary Lincoln stayed at the center of the discussion, fueling it with exaggerations of her poverty. She arranged to auction her old clothes and jewelry in a New York hotel, and although she acted under an assumed name, word leaked out, increasing the suspicion that she was either poorer than anyone realized or slightly crazy.

The final blow in the long string of misfortunes that hammered away at Mary's natural instability came from her husband's old law partner, William Herndon. While the men worked together in the 1850s, Mary and Herndon made no secret of their dislike for each other. He had compared her dancing to that of a serpent, but her disapproval of him went beyond such tasteless but harmless comments. Herndon lacked the polish that Mary Lincoln required in her husband's associates, and she excluded him from her dinner parties. He retaliated by attributing Abraham's moodiness to pressures caused by Mary's unreasonableness.

After Abraham Lincoln's assassination in 1865, Herndon began a biography and requested interviews with anyone who had known the president. In the process of taking down notes, he gave currency to many stories that were patently false or enormously exaggerated. Although he did not publish his book until much later, his speeches on the subject received newspaper coverage, and his claims gained publicity in the works of other authors.

By far the most sensational of the Herndon material argued that Abraham Lincoln had never loved anyone but Ann Rutledge, a young woman who died before he met Mary. This was the first time that Mary Lincoln had heard the story, and although she had plenty of reason to doubt its truth, she was unprepared emotionally to deal with its implications. As headlines carried the news across the country, she became more and more distraught.

Herndon's evidence was shaky at best. Abraham knew Ann Rutledge but only as the young daughter of the boardinghouse keeper where he stayed. At the time the future president met her, Ann was already engaged to be married and gave no indication of breaking off the agreement when Abraham appeared on the scene. But evidence that the martyred president had never loved Mary appealed to people who wanted to believe the worst, and the Rutledge connection gained currency.

By going to Europe, Mary hoped to get away from the stories. She enrolled Tad in a Frankfurt school and went to take the waters at fashionable spas, never neglecting to follow news accounts of what was happening in the United States, particularly attempts in Congress to get her more money. Two other presidents' widows figured in the picture but each from a slightly different angle. Julia Tyler negotiated from a disadvantaged position since her husband had sided with the South in the Civil War; and Sarah Polk, who lived quietly in apparent comfort in Nashville, seemed in no great need.

After learning that Congress had granted her a pension of $3,000, Mary returned in the spring of 1871 to Illinois.[79] She thought it a niggardly sum but had decided to try living in her own country again. A few months later all her resolution fell away when Tad, her youngest son, died at eighteen. Of all her sorrows, she later said, this cut the deepest.

On all sides, Mary felt besieged. She continued to worry about money, although what she had was ample for her needs, and she was humiliated by the stories about her husband and Ann Rutledge. She felt estranged from her one remaining son, the rather cold and distant Robert, who had a promising government career. His marriage to the daughter of a prominent judge had not pleased Mary and the fact that the young couple named their daughter for her hardly evened things out.

By early 1875, Robert asked for a court decision on his mother's sanity. He knew she carried her life savings sewed into her clothes, and when suspicious-looking characters began calling on her, he feared she would lose everything. In May 1875, Mary Todd Lincoln sat quietly in an Illinois court and heard her son and old friends describe her erratic behavior.[80] Some talked of her heavy spending and others of her dabblings in spiritualism, a popular pastime involving supposed communication with dead relatives. The judge listened and then committed her to the care of Robert who promptly arranged for her to enter Bellevue. A private mental institution near Chicago, Bellevue catered to "a select class of lady patients of quiet and unexceptionable habits."[81] Mary, one of twenty patients, had freedom to wander about the grounds. Doctors prescribed very little medication, and she had a private room and her own attendant.

But confinement under the best of circumstances did not appeal to Mary Lincoln, and she became less cooperative as time passed.

Hospital records show that she would order one dish for breakfast, then change her mind and refuse to eat it; she requested a carriage and then would not get in it. Such "lying and deceit should be put down to insanity," a hospital attendant reported with considerable overstatement.[82]

Evidence pieced together later shows that Mary spent a good deal of her time plotting how to regain her freedom. When Robert came for one of his weekly visits, she discussed her wish to live with her sister, and when he left, she asked to accompany him into town in order to mail a letter. Hospital attendants, who agreed to the trip, later learned that she mailed several letters, including one to a former congressman and another to an attorney, asking for their assistance in securing her release. Both the congressman and the attorney came for visits. The latter, Myra Bradwell, the first woman to be admitted to the bar in Illinois, pronounced Mary Lincoln "no more insane than I am."[83]

Mary's older sister, with whom she had lived when she first arrived in Springfield as a young woman, was becoming less convinced that Mary belonged in an institution. The attendant publicity was certainly unpleasant. Joining forces, the sister, lawyer Bradwell, and Mary requested a new hearing. Without alerting hospital attendants, Bradwell arranged for a newspaper reporter to interview Mary, and after a two-hour talk, the reporter concluded that Mary showed "not a sign of weakness . . . of mind."[84] The efforts of the three women led to Mary's release in September 1875.

Still looking for a place to settle, Mary returned to Europe and made her headquarters in Pau, France, until a bad fall partially paralyzed her. Saddened and broken, she returned to America on the same ship that carried the famous actress Sarah Bernhardt. In terms as dramatic as the parts she played on stage, Bernhardt later described how she had saved Mary Lincoln from falling down a flight of stairs. The two women introduced themselves, and after they had talked, Bernhardt realized that she had done the one thing for Mary Lincoln that she should not have done—saved her life.[85] But not for long. Mary returned to her sister's house in Springfield, the same house where she had married, and she died there in 1882.

Except for her good education and remarkable spunk, Mary Todd Lincoln had everything against her. Geography made her suspect, both socially and politically. The competitiveness and insecurity she had shown as a young girl matured into a self-defeating combination. The loss of three sons and the assassination of her husband in front of her eyes broke her.

It is ironic that Mary Todd Lincoln would become so much discussed, more books and plays being written about her than any other
First Lady of the nineteenth century, because in all important ways
she was a failure. After the early years of her marriage (when she may
have helped Abraham develop socially and may have improved his
financial situation by her inheritances), she proved a hindrance to
him. Historians have generally dismissed her as unbalanced; and a
century after her death, a highly respected scholar, Henry Steele
Commager, described her as "a half-crazy woman."[86]

Yet for all her flaws, Mary Lincoln showed considerable determination throughout her life, particularly in her refusal to accept anonymity in Washington and later, in engineering her release from the
mental institution. She had a good excuse, especially after the death
of her son in 1862, to plead grief as a reason to avoid social life in the
capital. Or she could have fallen back on her recurring headaches
and refused any public role. Only her stubbornness lifted her out of
the obscurity that surrounds most nineteenth-century presidents'
wives. In a time when women had few constructive outlets for their
energy and talents, they sometimes selected destructive ones, directing their strong wills to insignificant, even damaging actions. Given
other choices, Mary Lincoln might have behaved differently.

Julia Dent Grant, the third woman to emerge from a long string of un-
noticed First Ladies, demonstrates how quickly circumstances change.
Wife of Ulysses S. Grant, one of the least prepared presidents in
American history (1869–1877), Julia spent a great deal of money but
escaped the criticism leveled at Mary Lincoln. Boasting none of Sarah
Polk's political savvy, Julia received equally favorable press notices.

Perhaps she profited from the optimism that surrounded her husband's first inauguration in 1869. The Federal City, as people still
called the capital, was cold and dark that day; but the rain held off and
thousands of people got the chance to see the man they trusted to
initiate "a reign of loyalty and truth and patriotism."[87] To signal their
determination to put both the Civil War and the bungled Johnson
administration that followed it behind them, supporters had traveled
many miles and paid high prices for seats to witness the Grant inauguration. About the new president's wife the crowd knew very little, but
in the next eight years they would hear a good deal. Julia Dent Grant
had never been one to stay in the background.

Born in 1826 to relatively wealthy Missouri slaveholders who
already had three sons, Julia had enjoyed more than her share of her
parents' attention. Even after the birth of another daughter, Julia

Dent remained her father's favorite. A cheerful, good-natured young-ster, she matured into a self-assured young woman who chose to marry against strong parental objection. Ulysses Grant showed little promise of success, and Julia's father thought she could do better—an opinion that did not change quickly. Ulysses performed well enough in the army as long as he was fighting against Mexico, but later assignments to Panama and then to a lonely outpost at Fort Vancouver, Washington, went less well. Rumor had it that his excessive drinking led to his resig-nation from the army. He tried selling real estate and farming before going to work in his father's Illinois harness shop. Although Julia later brushed aside hints that these had been trying times, as she tried to cope with her erratic husband and the four children born to them in twelve years, friends admitted she had been frequently unhappy.

Had the Civil War not rescued Ulysses from obscurity, he might well have ended up a stooped, soft-spoken, sloppy store clerk, who never excelled in anything. At West Point, he had been a mediocre student—riding was his best subject. But the war brought out new strengths in the middle-aged Ulysses and he managed to get himself appointed head of the twenty-first Illinois Volunteers. Then in one battle after another he showed he could be both ruthless and tena-cious. His insistence on the enemy's "unconditional surrender" earned him the nickname "butcher," and provided a new explanation for his initials "U.S." Through all the criticism, President Lincoln defended his victorious general. His determination to fight to the bloody end repelled many people, Abraham Lincoln admitted, but it achieved the desired results.

By the time Ulysses Grant met Robert E. Lee at war's end at Appo-mattox, he had become a national figure and soon there was talk of nominating him for president. He won in the 1868 election, just two months after Mary Lincoln, who had vowed to leave the country if "that butcher" ever became president, had sailed for Europe.

The Grant family appeared particularly healthy and appealing oc-cupants of the White House after the tragedies associated with the Lincolns and the difficulties encountered by the Andrew Johnsons. The two older sons, Frederick and Ulysses, Jr., spent most of the first years of their father's tenure away at college, but teenager Nellie and mischievous Jesse, the baby of the family, made up for their absences. Nellie's participation added a youthful touch to official parties that had tended to become stiff and predictable. Her White House wed-ding in 1874 became a national celebration.

Twelve-year-old Jesse Grant, whom his mother described as "never at a loss for an answer,"[88] kept several reporters busy with his antics and his gossip about other family members, especially his two grand-fathers who often stayed at the White House. Frederick Dent, Julia's father, and Jesse Grant, Ulysses's father, did not get along, according to young Jesse, and sometimes they would refuse to communicate with each other except through Julia. In the presence of the elder Grant, Frederick Dent would instruct Julia to "take better care of that old gentleman [Grant]. He is feeble and deaf as a post and yet you permit him to wander all over Washington alone." Overhearing the remark as he had been meant to do, Grandfather Grant would retort to young Jesse: "Did you hear him? I hope I shall not live to become as old and infirm as your Grandfather Dent."[89]

Accounts of such harmless family squabbles entertained a public that had become accustomed to a more somber White House, and the Grants' extravagant spending increased their attractiveness. In what came to be called the Gilded Age, large price tags were less objection-able than they had been during the Lincoln war years, and no one seemed to care what Julia bought. No expense appeared in bad taste, no shine too bright. The newly rich vied with each other for the title of bigger spender, with the prize placed squarely on quantity of pur-chase rather than quality. In such an atmosphere, the White House hostess could hardly overspend, and an approving nation watched as Julia served dinners of twenty-nine courses, accompanied by high-priced French wines.

On more significant matters, she evidently understood very little. By her own admission, she once came out both for and against a par-ticular piece of legislation. She explained that she had been in New York on a shopping trip when she was approached by both propo-nents and critics of the bill, wanting her to influence the president in their behalf. Since she knew nothing about the bill at that time, she cheerfully implied agreement with both sides.

Back in Washington, she confronted Ulysses and asked that he explain the bill and its possible effects. When he had finished, she urged him to veto it. "I always flattered myself," she wrote, "that I had rendered my husband and the country a very great service in advising the President to veto the all-important Finance Bill that was almost convulsing the country . . . but I find I had more than one rival in that honor. . . . To tell the truth, I think the President knew his duty quite well and would have fulfilled his duty in any case."[90]

Ulysses made no secret of the fact that he liked the women around him dependent, and Julia usually humored him by appearing docile and agreeable. She never quite hid, however, a stubborn, willful streak. She once signaled her independence by refusing to sign the necessary papers for the sale of their Washington house. As president-elect, Ulysses had arranged the sale without consulting his wife, and to underscore her objection, she refused to go along. Ulysses was thus forced to back out of the deal with no other explanation than that his wife would not cooperate. The next time he located a prospective buyer, he discussed the offer with Julia, and this time she reported that she cheerfully signed, having made her point.[91]

Julia Grant prolonged her tenure in the public eye by accompanying her husband on a trip around the world after his second term ended in 1877. She would have preferred a third term in the White House but Ulysses did not consult her on the matter.[92]

In the twenty-eight-month journey, Julia was treated more like a reigning monarch than like the wife of an ex-president, and she thrived on the attention she received. The Grants dined with royalty at Windsor Castle, breakfasted with "London literati," and drank with English workingmen. After more banquets and honors on the continent, they sailed for the Far East. Governments along the way competed for title of biggest giver, the Japanese distinguishing themselves only slightly more than the others by offering the ex-president the furnishings of an entire room.[93]

The Grants returned to settle in New York, and Ulysses set about writing his memoirs. He was already ill with a spreading throat cancer and just days after he completed the work, he died. He had feared he would not finish in time and had sketched in the important parts first, knowing he could go back and fill in the details if time permitted. What later became a standard exercise for ex-presidents—the writing and selling of their memoirs for large sums—began with Ulysses Grant, and it did not spring so much from his own ego as from a desire to provide an income for his family.

The book earned half a million dollars in royalties,[94] so that Julia was encouraged to write her own autobiography—the first by an ex-president's wife. Memoirs of Abigail Adams and Dolley Madison had already been published but heirs had spliced them together out of the women's letters. Unfortunately, Julia's work failed to interest a publisher until nearly three quarters of a century after her death, and it was not published until 1975.

Less than one-tenth of her book deals with Julia's eight years as First Lady and in those few pages, she concentrates on describing her social accomplishments and defending Ulysses. His own autobiography had ignored rumors about his malfeasance in office, and Julia determined to set the record straight. Several of her relatives took jobs on the public payroll but that hardly constituted corruption.

"There was that dreadful Black Friday," she admitted, referring to a scheme drafted by the financiers Jim Fisk and Jay Gould early in the Grant administration to "corner" the New York gold market and make themselves millions richer. They enlisted the help of President Grant's brother-in-law and believed—incorrectly as it turned out—that they had secured the president's assurance that the federal Treasury would cooperate and not release gold. On "Black Friday" in September 1869, the plot reached its culmination. While businessmen watched helplessly, Gould and Fisk bid gold prices up and out of reach. Then the federal Treasury moved in and filled the vacuum by releasing its funds. Questions remained about the president's complicity. Had he intended to participate or been misread?

Julia's account of her husband's role predictably concurred with that of historians who later decided Ulysses was naïve and a poor judge of character but not dishonest. As for her own part, she explained: "The papers seemed to say I knew something of [the Fisk and Gould scheme] but I did not; only this." The president had instructed her to add in a letter she was sending to his sister: "If you have any influence with your husband, tell him to have nothing whatever to do with [Fisk and Gould.] If he does, he will be ruined for come what may, [Ulysses] will do his duty to the country and the trusts in his keeping."[95] Thus Julia added, for what it was worth, her own account of her husband's honesty.

Ulysses Grant's two terms as president were also marred by reports that members of his family and some of his closest advisers were involved in plots to defraud the government; and in each case Julia's account portrays her husband as naïve and misunderstood rather than dishonest. The Whiskey Ring involved Orville E. Babcock, the president's secretary. Contrived as a kickback system in which federal taxes on alcohol production were not collected if distillers paid off the inspectors, the scheme would have enriched the Republican Party and Babcock. Julia explained that Babcock had always been "civil and obliging and never officious,"[96] and she urged the president to assist him at his trial. When Babcock was acquitted in the courtroom, but not in the public's mind, Julia encouraged the president to replace him at the White House.[97]

In the case of the cabinet member William Belknap, Julia extended the same tolerance for poor judgment and bad luck that she had offered her husband. Belknap had entered into agreements with prospective traders in the Indian Territories but the agreements appeared to line Belknap's pockets more than they provided needed items to the Territories. When evidence mounted against him, Belknap went to the president and resigned, thus protecting himself from a worse fate. He was impeached but the Senate would not convict since members believed his resignation removed him from their jurisdiction. In spite of a great deal of concrete evidence to the contrary, Julia accepted Belknap's plea of innocence and she continued to see the Belknaps socially.[98]

Julia reported that she felt "much injured by [Ulysses'] neglect to inform me on . . . important matters,"[99] but the press and public showed her more attention. She recalled how she had been "followed by a crowd of idle, curious loungers, which was anything but pleasant." When she requested that the White House grounds be shut off to the public so that she and her children would have some privacy, she observed a "ripple of comment [that] followed [about] the Grants . . . getting too exclusive." The objections had little effect on her, however, and Julia got her way. Later she looked back on the White House years and remembered: "The children and I had that beautiful lawn for eight years, and I assure you we enjoyed it."[100]

Rather than an exception in a long line of faceless presidents' wives, Julia Grant represents an important turning point. Her predecessors had acted as local figures, judged by the capital "cave dwellers" but little known to the rest of the nation. Julia marked the beginning of a new phase in which the First Lady would eventually become a national leader, widely recognized, frequently criticized, and often emulated. Julia's energetic clan and her own vivacious personality appealed to reporters who were increasingly focusing their attention on Washington.[101] The media played only one part in the change. Julia's cross-country travel, her long journey around the world, and her memoir writing all hint at the kind of activities that would become more common for presidents' wives who followed her. Like Sarah Polk and Mary Lincoln, she expended considerable energy on a public role for herself, and thus helped set the stage for First Ladies who came later.

4

The Limited Promise of the
"New Woman" (1877–1901)

ALTHOUGH THE IMAGE of the First Lady as nothing other than the nation's chief wife, head hostess, and leading fashion plate seemed firmly in place under Julia Grant, history had shown that an individual woman might, if she chose, do more in that role. Lucy Hayes (1877–1881) appeared to be just such a woman. The first college graduate to preside over the White House, she was widely heralded as introducing the era of a "New Woman."[1] An even more intellectually inclined Lucretia Garfield followed. After James Garfield was assassinated, a widower, Chester Arthur, took over the presidency, and he was succeeded by Grover Cleveland, a bachelor. If the nation could ever be diverted from its need for a purely social creature "at the head of female society," the decade after 1877 was surely the time to try to divert it. Two thinking women and then two vacancies on the distaff side of the White House ought to have had some effect.

Events outside the executive mansion indicated change, too, because the generation of women who came of age in the late 1870s were less inclined than their mothers to marry, or at least to see marriage as their only choice.[2] More and more colleges and universities, including some medical and theological schools, had opened their doors to women, and several states permitted women to practice law. Even the justices of the United States Supreme Court finally capitulated in 1879 and admitted a woman to practice before them.[3] M. Carey Thomas, who later became president of Bryn Mawr, joined other women barred from advanced training in the United States and traveled to Europe for graduate work that would help them compete with men for professorships.[4]

Much of the impetus for change had come out of the Civil War, which, although a national tragedy, had encouraged many women to give their first speech, organize their first club, or take their initial trip out of home territory. Mary Livermore, a Chicago mother of four who reportedly became the most successful woman speaker of her time,[5] explained how the war had started her on the road to fame: "It was not of my seeking. But my acceptance of an active membership in [a Civil War relief organization] carried me inevitably into methods of work different from any that I had known before. . . . I could not avoid it."[6]

The large number of woman-run organizations formed after the war indicates the extent to which women were redefining their lives to reach beyond their own families. Sorosis, a woman's club founded in 1868, announced in its charter an intention to help women by encouraging "useful relations among [them] . . . the discussion of principles [which would aid them] . . . the establishing of an order which would render [them] helpful to each other and actively benevolent in the world."[7] One of the club's founding members, Jennie June Croly, had acted out of anger at being treated shabbily by the New York Press Club. Although a syndicated columnist, she had been denied the opportunity to hear Charles Dickens speak at the Press Club. When she and other women protested, the decision was altered—on condition that they sit behind a curtain and out of sight of the lecturer. Croly responded by starting a club for women only to supply them with a network of their own.

Hundreds of other clubs followed. Some, such as the National Council of Jewish Women and the National Association of Colored Women's Clubs, had ethnic bases, while others, such as the PTA and the Sunshine Club, reached out to a broader membership, but all shared the objective of encouraging women to join together and take a more activist role in the world.

Unlike the local organizations of pre–Civil War days, these new organizations were national in scope, with branches in many states. One of the largest, the Women's Christian Temperance Union, was formed in 1874 just before Lucy Hayes entered the White House. Frances Willard, the Union's president for twenty years, repeatedly stressed how the WCTU joined together women from different sections of the country, and she used a chain metaphor to describe the result: "The voice of God called to [members of the WCTU] from the lips of his prophet: 'Make a chain for the land is full of bloody crimes and the city is full of violence' and so in every town and village we are forming these chains of light and loving helpfulness."[8]

Because support for women's right to vote was still weak, Victoria Woodhull's campaign for president in 1872 was more principled than practical, but women did register other political gains at just about this time. Some won local elections and others gained appointive positions in government. Samuel Tilden, the New York governor (who unsuccessfully ran against Rutherford Hayes for president in 1876), named Josephine Shaw Lowell, a young widow with a child, to sit that same year on the State Board of Charities.[9] The suffrage movement gathered force, and even some anti-suffragists argued that working women deserved better wages.

The woman who became involved in these kinds of endeavors—running an organization, carving out a career for herself, or speaking out on public issues—was vaguely referred to as a "new woman." Eventually that appellation came to have many meanings, including the woman who dressed daringly, or the one who flaunted her nonconformity by taking up residence in a bohemian enclave. But in references to Lucy Hayes and other presidents' wives of the late nineteenth century, "new woman" meant a serious woman concerned with substantive matters such as reform rather than with empty party-giving. It meant having opinions and an identity of one's own.

Reporters' coverage of the Hayes inauguration signaled the change represented in Lucy Hayes. Mary Clemmer Ames, in her "Woman's Letter from Washington," announced that she had "never seen such a face reign in the White House." Lucy's conservative hairstyle and "eyes which we have come to associate with the Madonna" suggested to Ames a seriousness of purpose at odds with that of many of Lucy's predecessors. How would the public react? And how would magazines treat her? Ames pondered particularly about the fashion magazines such as *Vanity Fair:* "Will [it] friz that hair? powder that face? . . . bare those shoulders? shorten those sleeves? hide John Wesley's discipline out of sight, as it poses and minces before 'the first lady of the land?' "[10]

This serious image was not a pose assumed for the inaugural stand. Lucy Webb Hayes's Ohio family had a long history of enthusiastically pursuing many of the reforms of their time. Her parents, moved by the evangelical fervor that swept America in the 1830s and 1840s, had joined the Methodist church. Drawn into the abolitionist camp, Lucy's father went to Kentucky to arrange for the manumission of some slaves he had inherited, but he became ill with cholera and died there.[11] Lucy's mother, dependent on the generosity of her family for her support and that of her three small children, nonetheless made no concessions to her reduced circumstances and dedicated the rest of her life to seeing that her two sons and Lucy received the best education available.

It is doubtful that Lucy's mother would have uprooted her family so frequently had the education of girls been involved, but she had no qualms about moving around to obtain quality schooling for her sons. Lucy benefited in the process. When her brothers enrolled at Ohio Wesleyan, a Methodist college, she became the school's first woman student. Later, when the Webb boys chose medical school in Cincinnati, the family moved again and Lucy enrolled at Wesleyan Female College.

During her early years, Lucy had been exposed not only to abolitionists and reformers in education and religion, but also to the arguments of the emerging feminist movement in which two of her aunts participated.[12] In college, she had confronted the question of whether or not women's intellectual abilities equaled men's and had concluded, "Woman's mind is as strong as man's . . . equal in all things and his superior in some."[13] After her marriage to Rutherford B. Hayes in 1852, her exposure to feminism continued when his older sister, Fanny, took Lucy to hear famous speakers on the subject. One of Lucy Stone's lectures, on improving women's wages, so moved Lucy Webb Hayes that she wrote to her husband defending "violent methods" if necessary to achieve change.[14]

All this reform interest in her early years might have indicated to observers that Lucy would exert special influence in the White House. Her prominence gave her word exceptional weight, and why should she not use her popularity on behalf of her sex? Feminists, who had made the vote for women their central objective, decided to enlist the president's wife in their cause. The Citizens' Suffrage Association of Philadelphia appealed to her, and her Aunt Phebe made a personal plea: "There is but one cause in which my whole soul is engaged," she wrote to her famous niece in 1877, "and that is Woman Suffrage and if my influence is of any avail it will be in that cause."[15]

The groundwork was thus laid in the Hayes administration for what would become an important controversy surrounding presidents' wives: how much of the influence they held because of their marriages to famous men would they be willing to use on the side of women's causes? And which causes? "New woman" advocates, including reporters and suffragists, would encourage presidents' wives to break out of old traditional forms while other, more powerful voices would insist that First Ladies remain supportive, opinionless backdrops to their husbands.

Lucy had already tempered her youthful enthusiasm for reform well before she had to face up to defining just how she would handle the First Lady role. As soon as Rutherford had entered politics, she transferred her own energies there, too. She had some experience with election campaigns because her uncle had served in the state legislature, and now she turned attention from what might have become a feminist crusade and directed it toward her husband's career and to the victories of other Republicans.[16] In 1856, she had attended a rally in support of John Frémont for president, and she wrote her mother at that time that she hoped he would win. When Frémont's defeat became clear, Rutherford informed his Uncle Birchard that Lucy "takes it to heart a good deal. . . . She still clings to the hope that the next election will bring it all right."[17]

By the late 1850s, Lucy's world pretty much centered on her husband's career and her family. She gave birth to eight children in twenty years, but in reacting to the often competing demands of being a good mother or being a valuable wife, it appears that she chose to make herself an extension of Rutherford. He suggested that she would have liked to have enlisted on the Union side in the Civil War but had to content herself with sending him and then joining him whenever possible. "Lucy enjoys [the action]," Rutherford wrote his uncle, "and wishes she had been in Fort Sumter with a garrison of women."[18] Sometimes she left her young children with relatives and other times she took them along to their father's army camp. In June 1863, during one of her visits, the youngest Hayes son died. Although Lucy described that time as the "bitterest hour" of her life, she shipped the boy's body back to Ohio for burial while she remained at her husband's side.[19]

During the war years Lucy became a great favorite with her husband's comrades and she began then to achieve what eventually became an almost legendary reputation for kindness and simplicity. One story had it that several of the soldiers had decided to embarrass a new recruit by convincing him to take his mending to the "sewing lady" down at the colonel's cabin. Shirts in hand, the youth knocked at Hayes's cabin door and when he announced his purpose, Lucy Hayes got out her needle. When he returned to the others, they were waiting for their laugh but learned, to their disappointment, that he had accomplished his mission. When the other soldiers pointed out that the "sewing lady" was the colonel's wife, he stuck to his initial judgment that whoever she was she had treated him kindly.[20] Years later when she was living in the White House, a Civil War veteran came to be photographed and, so that he would have the appropriate insignia on his uniform, First Lady Lucy Hayes sewed it on for him.[21]

Close behind the stories of Lucy's kindness were those illustrating her dedication to her husband's welfare. During one wartime separation she had received a telegram informing her that he had been wounded near Washington, D.C. Although she lacked specific details on his whereabouts, she left her three children, including one she had been nursing, and set off to find Rutherford. Her search took five days, but when she located him, she took charge of his care and then escorted him and several of his comrades back to Ohio to recuperate.[22]

By the time the Civil War ended, Rutherford B. Hayes had been elected to represent his Ohio district in the U.S. House of Representatives, and Lucy left her children with relatives in Ohio so she could join her husband in Washington. Her strong abolitionist views had led her to favor a punishing reconstruction policy for the South, and she became an avid observer of congressional debates on the subject. When she returned to Ohio, Rutherford wrote that he missed seeing her "checkered shawl" in the gallery, and she replied that he should send her more details of the debates.[23] He had already informed his mother that "Lucy finds politics very pleasant in all respects."[24]

With the elevation of her husband to the Ohio governorship in 1868, Lucy assumed a more active role. Although her children were still young (the last to survive was born in 1871), she traveled around the state with her husband to visit prisons and mental hospitals. When the Democratic legislature refused to appropriate money to start a home for children orphaned by the war, Lucy worked with others to collect voluntary contributions. Then, when the home had been started, she lobbied friends in the legislature to have the state assume financial responsibility for its operation. Lucy appeared to be occupied on many fronts, and Rutherford wrote his brother-in-law: "Lucy employs herself about the soldiers' orphans . . . about the decoration of soldiers' graves and about the deaf and dumb pupils at the Reform Farm for boys."[25]

Each time Rutherford registered a political success, Lucy's excitement grew, although she recognized that her enthusiasm was not shared by her children.[26] As speculation grew that Rutherford would be nominated for the presidency, Lucy gleefully reported that even the family cook was caught up with the prospect of moving to "the top of the ladder."[27]

As soon as the 1876 presidential campaign began, reporters zeroed in on the sober Lucy Hayes and contrasted her with the fun-loving Julia Grant whom she meant to replace. Some accounts still concentrated on appearances and the *New York Herald* described Lucy as "singularly youthful" and "a most attractive and lovable woman."[28] But as the campaign went on, the *National Union* speculated in its column "Gossip About Women": "Mrs. Hayes is said to be a student of politics and to talk intelligently upon their [*sic*] changing phases."[29] Few people could recall similar claims for a prospective First Lady since Sarah Polk moved into the White House in 1845.

The results of the 1876 election could hardly be called a victory for anyone since the count was so contested that a commission had to decide who had won, but on March 5, 1877, simply dressed Lucy stood in a prominent place at Rutherford's public inauguration.[30] In this first appearance in her new role, she signaled that she would neither compete with fashion models nor disappear—as many of her predecessors had done. Public approval was overwhelming in the next few months, and even the politically unfriendly *Philadelphia Times* reported: "Mrs. Hayes deserves the thanks of every true woman for the stand she has taken against extravagance in dress."[31] Six months later the same paper reported that the White House showed "a refreshing absence of pretension and formality."[32] Employees at the executive mansion underlined these glowing reports with their own compliments, noting that Lucy remembered each employee with an individually selected Christmas gift and invited employees to the family's Thanksgiving table.

The saintly image was not effortlessly achieved. Although the Hayeses spent freely from their own considerable personal fortune, Lucy fostered a reputation for being economy-minded. She carefully preserved her clothing receipts to prove her frugality,[33] and when Congress refused to appropriate funds for refurbishing the executive mansion, she searched attic and cellar for old pieces of furniture to put back into service. She relegated the billiard table to the basement and used the space it had occupied for a conservatory to produce the fresh flowers that she liked to dispense to sick friends, lonely orphans, and journalists who wrote kind things about her. One White House steward, who had served every president since Abraham Lincoln, reported that Lucy Hayes brought a "new atmosphere" to the executive mansion.[34]

This was not exactly the change that the phrase "New Woman" promised. Rather than exemplifying strength and independence, Lucy's model stressed demureness and solicitous attention to those around her. Instead of emphasizing her college education, she operated entirely within the definition of "wife" as that word had been used since colonial days when it was, as a matter of course, combined with "good" to mean a woman "obedient to her husband, loving to her children, kind to her neighbors, [and] dutiful to her servants."[35] If Lucy Hayes failed to portray exactly the innocent youthfulness that had been so favored in the White House in the 1830s and 1840s, it was a difference of style, not substance. Hers was only a matronly version of the "goodness" of Emily Donelson and Angelica Van Buren who had so charmed Jacksonian America.

Such an image did not fail to find rewards. Even women reporters who had begun to work in the capital could not praise Lucy Hayes enough. Mary Clemmer Ames, one of those favored with Lucy's flowers because of a kind story she had written about the First Lady, responded in a sugary description of Lucy that might have pleased the White House but could only have brought consternation to feminists who urged more autonomy for women:

> The state of womanhood star-like doth shine,
> Regina, reigning at Love's holiest shrine.[36]

Lucy Hayes, the same woman who had once defended "violent" measures to achieve equal pay for women, now worked very hard for no pay at all. She oversaw large receptions and on nights when she had nothing scheduled, she received callers. Perhaps she considered her overwhelming popularity adequate recompense. Hers became the most familiar woman's face in America. Advertisers used her picture, without her approval, to promote household products,[37] and popular magazines carried photographs of her, often with her children or flowers or animals. Longfellow, Whittier, and Oliver Wendell Holmes toasted her in words.[38] Ben Perley Poore, a famous Washington reporter at the time, judged that she had become more influential than any president's wife since Dolley Madison.

Even her husband, who suffered from charges of having attained the office unfairly and heard himself taunted as "His Fraudulency," admitted that Lucy had become extremely popular: "It is very gratifying to see," he wrote in his diary in May 1879, "the heartiness and warmth of friendship for Lucy. Her large warm heart and lively sympathy for or with all around her, with a fair share of beauty and talents, have made her wonderfully popular."[39] If he had not entirely decided what guaranteed approval for a president, he at least recognized the value of a popular wife.

Some Americans, including Washington's more sophisticated set, found the Hayeses impossibly dull, and they singled out Lucy as a tight-lipped moralizer. The family's decisions to attend the unfashionable Foundry Methodist Church, hold prayer meetings each morning, and sing hymns with their friends on Sunday evening were generally attributed to her influence. Lucy's storytelling and mimicry may have delighted her family, but the diplomatic corps and more traveled Washingtonians were not amused. In a short story, "Pandora," which

Henry James published in 1884 and which was generally understood to refer to the Hayes administration, a witty, sophisticated character says: "Hang it, there's only a month left: let us be vulgar and have some fun. Let us invite the President."[40]

Henry Adams's novel *Democracy*, written at the end of the Hayes administration, drew an unflattering picture of "the President's wife" who remained unnamed but whose likeness to Lucy was clear. Midwestern in origin and rigid in her views, the First Lady in *Democracy* lashed out at anyone who did not share her opinions. She insisted that "in her town in Indiana, a young woman who was seen on the street in such clothes [as were then worn in Washington] wouldn't be spoken to," and when a woman guest in the story mildly criticized the president, his wife became furious and vowed, "See if I don't reform you yet, you jade!"[41]

Even people who did not share the tastes of Henry James and Henry Adams objected to the Hayeses' ban on alcohol. Rutherford had not always abstained from strong drink. In his youth, he had enjoyed a glass or two of wine with his friends at the Literary Club,[42] and he never advocated state prohibition of the sale of alcohol.[43] His presidency coincided, however, with a powerful surge in temperance sentiment and both he and Lucy realized that refusing to serve alcohol in the White House could win votes without causing any personal inconvenience. Lucy had the example of her parents who had pledged never to touch alcohol, and both she and Rutherford found repulsive the drunkenness they sometimes witnessed at Washington parties. "The exclusion of wine from the list of refreshments has turned out exceedingly well," the president explained. "There is a good deal of dissipation here . . . disgraceful things were done by young men made reckless by too much wine. Hence the necessity for our course is obvious and is commended in unexpected quarters. . . . We shall stick to it."[44] As he prepared to leave office in early 1881, he elaborated in his diary that the decision was right: it was favored by friends in the temperance movement and it helped keep votes in the Republican column.[45]

The suspicion that political expedience, as well as personal preference, figured in Lucy Hayes's ban on alcohol in the White House emerges from evidence of several kinds. Lucy actually served wine at her first White House dinner, honoring two Russian dukes, and then responded to the outburst of criticism by changing her course. Her failure to participate in the Women's Christian Temperance Union, the most important voice in urging a ban on liquor, is even more revealing. Lucy Hayes never joined the WCTU, an omission that cannot be explained on the grounds that she steered clear of all such organizations since she accepted a national office in the Women's Home Missionary Society. Lucy's biographer, Emily Apt Geer, concluded that although Lucy did not drink alcohol, she was "not adamant" about abstinence in others. A chance remark to this effect, overheard by temperance advocates, so angered them that they changed plans and did not name their Washington chapter for her.[46] The WCTU's reputation for militance displeased Lucy, and Rutherford evidently encouraged her to keep a distance from the WCTU president, Frances Willard. On one of Lucy's trips to Chicago where she expected to meet Willard, Rutherford had counseled her to "smother [Willard] with politeness but promise her nothing."[47]

Whether or not alcohol was served in spite of the ban remains uncertain. The reporter Ben Perley Poore insisted that state dinners included a course, called "Life Saving Station" by those in the know, that provided alcohol to anyone who requested it "with the strongest mixture going to those needing it most."[48] President Hayes countered that the joke was on the tellers. He had given orders, he said, that flavoring be added to the punch and some people had mistaken the extract for the real thing.

Whether it was Lucy or the president who stood more firmly behind the ban remains unclear but she clearly took the blame.[49] To taunts about her "dry dinners" and nicknames of "Lemonade Lucy," she replied in terms particularly revealing about how she viewed her role: "It is true I shall violate a precedent; but I shall not violate the Constitution, which is all that, through my husband, I have taken the oath to obey."[50]

Because temperance was an immensely popular cause in the 1870s, Lucy gained many friends for her stand. When she accompanied her husband on a seventy-one-day trip to California, temperance supporters flocked to her train to obtain her autograph and cheer her on. The crowds became so thick at one point that her youngest son, traveling with her, mingled with the others and got his mother to sign his album several times before she noticed him.[51] At one stop, women held up a silk banner imprinted with the biblical quotation, "She hath done what she could."[52]

Except for her well-publicized refusal to serve liquor, Lucy Hayes remained silent on every important issue, her absence particularly noted on the suffrage front. The stand she had taken earlier when she spoke out on the equality of the sexes did not lead her to conclude that women should vote. When Susan B. Anthony and Elizabeth Stanton came to discuss the issue with the president, he received them alone, and Lucy appeared only at the conclusion of the interview for the housewifely duty of showing the visitors around the mansion. Her Aunt Phebe McKell, who continued to urge Lucy to speak out for woman's suffrage after she had become First Lady, had no effect. Lucy either did not see voting as an appropriate activity for women or she perceived it (correctly) as a politically unpopular cause. Perhaps she agreed with Rutherford who had written in his diary before he became president: "My point on [suffrage] is that the proper discharge of the functions of maternity is inconsistent with the like discharge of the duties of citizenship."[53]

The president's wife had always been seen as an avenue to the president, but the Hayes administration marked a new level of appeals for her help. Lucy's travel across the continent and the appearance of her picture in advertisements and magazines made her one of the most famous women in America, and people who lacked advocates elsewhere looked to her. One member of the Church of Jesus Christ of Latter-Day Saints couched her request in woman-to-woman terms when she wrote "Mrs. President Hayes," asking that she help defend plural marriage. "Having been informed through friends of the goodness of your heart," Elizabeth Davis wrote, "and your sympathetic nature toward those of your sex who appeal to you for aid, I determined to approach you by letter in behalf of myself and my sisters."[54]

Such entreaties, along with those of the suffragists and the leaders of the temperance movement (which had become dominated by women in the late nineteenth century), show that something new had happened to the role of First Lady, as the president's wife was now being called. Women throughout the country approached her as their special representative. Those who saw themselves as traditional homemakers would seek her endorsement of their view, while those who sought a more active role in public affairs would want to make her their champion. The old conflicts were still present. Some Americans would expect the president's wife to represent the taste of the majority while others wanted to see in her the epitome of sophistication and high culture (like the characters in Henry Adams's novel.) Never an easy job to fill, the role of the president's wife now became even more complex.

The interest in describing the role was just beginning when Lucy Hayes left the White House. In the 1881 edition of *Ladies of the White House,* Laura Holloway divided her subjects into three groups. From Martha Washington to Louisa Adams, they had been strong women, Holloway wrote, "appropriate to the needs of a young country," but those who followed (1839–1877) had reigned as "social queens, nothing more." Lucy Hayes initiated the third period: "her strong, healthful influence gives the world assurances of what the next century's women will be."[55]

If Holloway's readers understood her to be introducing a champion of independent thinking and careers for women, they were wrong. Lucy Hayes had played an important part in her husband's political career, Holloway concluded, "and she so freely identified herself with [his] administration that it can never be remembered apart from her," but she knew her limits. "The highest place for a woman in a republic is beside the man," Holloway wrote, "performing the pleasant duties of hostess of the Executive Mansion." As for influence on legislation, Lucy "has had no more power in the White House than in Ohio. . . . She did not impose taxes upon [the President] or make him pay tribute to her rank as wife."[56]

Holloway's enthusiastic support of Lucy Hayes has not stood the test of time, and history has tended to write her off as narrow-minded "Lemonade Lucy." Whatever her failures—and since so many sought her help, she was bound to disappoint some of them—Lucy Hayes did mark an important change. She played the part of First Lady as an adult role, rather than in the childlike mode of some of her predecessors, and her popularity shows that for many Americans she was the ideal First Lady. If her feminist contemporaries could not stomach her docility and her devotion to her husband's career rather than her own, they would certainly have noticed that they stood in a minority.

Lucretia Rudolph Garfield, who followed her sister Ohioan, Lucy Hayes, into the White House in 1881, provides another, far more poignant example of a political wife who learned to fit her own ambitions into her husband's career. Her diaries, although not nearly so complete as those of her husband, show real evidence of an intellectually alert, capable, feminist-inclined young woman who was nearly erased into nothingness. Her transformation does not divide into neat parts, and it might have followed a similar pattern had she married a businessman, minister, or member of any of the other professions that include a wife's contribution as part of the husband's job. But the Garfields matured in a period of history that took its name from Queen Victoria, when strong pressures pushed wives to conform to accepted standards and heavy sanctions awaited those who did not. Dress reformers, "free love" advocates and even suffragists found themselves the object of reproach and ridicule, and even a tentative word favoring reform was interpreted as taking an extreme position.

It is almost inconceivable that a man could have reached the presidency in the nineteenth century had his wife publicly advocated any feminist cause. Although effect does not neatly follow cause in Lucretia Garfield's case, her increasing docility parallels James Garfield's political success.

The woman who became the wife of the twentieth president of the United States had attended Ohio's Eclectic Institute (later renamed Hiram College), a school her parents and other members of the Disciples of Christ Church had helped found. James Garfield also began his studies there in the early 1850s but he quickly transferred to the considerably more prestigious Williams College in Massachusetts, where his good looks and charm earned him immediate popularity. His prowess in debate attracted many women friends and even he seemed unsure why he continued an almost dutiful courtship to a serious and shy Lucretia Rudolph back in Ohio.

James's first mention of Lucretia in his diary indicates that her abilities first attracted him. While both were still at the Eclectic Institute, they had been selected to speak at a school ceremony, and James judged his own performance poor; but Miss Rudolph's speech, he wrote, was "full of good, practical, sound commonsense and elegantly and eloquently expressed."[57]

About a year later, after he had broken off a romance with another woman, James's thoughts turned again to Lucretia, whom he alternately praised and criticized. She had, he admitted, "a well balanced mind, not of the deepest and most extensive kind but logical and precise." Yet he could not deny that he found her dull and he concluded that she "is either studiously concealing [her social nature] or she does not possess it." Her views on women's rights alarmed him: "There are some of her notions concerning the relation between the sexes which, if I understand, I do not like."[58]

Until James and Lucretia married in 1858, their courtship never followed a smooth line and they both showed real doubts. When they were separated, James raised his expectations of what she meant to him and then found himself disappointed when they met. One vacation went so badly that James seemed ready to terminate the courtship—until she showed him her diary where she had expressed her strong feelings about him, thus convincing him she had "depths of affection that I had never before known that she possessed."[59] After he returned to Williams, her correspondence became full-blown love letters in which she wrote of "walking in the warm sunlight of your love" and he responded that he looked forward to the time when "I will have you in my arms again."[60]

James Garfield confessed at one point in the courtship that he did not feel about Lucretia as he thought a bridegroom should but then abruptly, in the fall of 1858, when Lucretia was twenty-six and employed as a teacher, he told her to proceed with plans for their simple marriage rites. She had her own doubts and right up to the time of the ceremony worried about losing the autonomy she had enjoyed—earning her own money and making her own decisions. Just weeks before the wedding, Lucretia warned James: "My heart is not yet schooled to an entire submission to that destiny which will make me the wife of one who marries me." She determined to try her best, even though her "heart almost broke," she wrote, "with the cruel thought that our marriage is based upon the cold, stern word duty."[61]

In the first years of her marriage, Lucretia continued to live almost as a single woman. She kept her teaching job, and since she and James boarded with another family, she had few housekeeping chores. Her husband's election to the state legislature a year after their marriage meant that he was frequently absent from home, and when the Civil War started, he enlisted. James made very clear that he considered their marriage a mistake, and although Lucretia accepted much of the blame, she thought him "a little hard."[62] While his letters were often brusque and judgmental, hers repeatedly promised to attempt to conform to his demands and become the submissive helper he required: "I am going to try harder than ever before to be the best little wife possible," Lucretia wrote in March 1860. "You need not be a bit afraid of my introducing one of those long talks [that strike in you] such a terror . . . ever again."[63]

On their fourth wedding anniversary James coolly appraised their time together as unsatisfactory but concluded that both partners deserved credit for trying. Lucretia, who had become aware of his attentions to a New York widow and confronted him on the matter, learned in late 1862 that James did not wish to continue with his wife "any[thing] other than a business correspondence."[64] After four and one-half years of marriage, Lucretia calculated that she and James had spent less than five months together.[65] They both understood that the separation was partly voluntary and that theirs was a troubled union.

Had something not affected the course of this marriage, it is unlikely that James Garfield's political career would have proceeded as it did, but Lucretia became increasingly docile in the 1860s and her husband's attitude toward the family changed. In part the alteration may have resulted from grief. Within a few months of each other, two of their children died—their first daughter at age three and then, only weeks later, an infant. In 1867 Lucretia and James went to Europe, a kind of second honeymoon,[66] and soon after their return she convinced him that they should move the family, now numbering three children, to Washington. The house they built at Thirteen and I Streets became their residence for much of the year.

Two more children were born to the Garfields, and James began to take greater interest in his older sons' education, drilling them in Latin and Greek and urging Lucretia to brush up on her knowledge of languages so that she could help, too. He did not lose interest in other women and even had to make a special trip to New York to retrieve compromising letters he had sent to a woman friend there, but more and more of his time centered on family activities. In 1873, after fifteen years of marriage, he wrote to his wife, "The tyranny of our love is sweet. We waited long for his coming but he has come to stay."[67]

Whatever James Garfield meant in that letter, his actions did not show that he considered his wife an important part of his social life in the capital. Between 1872 and 1874, his diary records that he accepted dozens of invitations, only three of which involved Lucretia.[68] The Garfields rarely invited people to their home, and Lucretia understood that Washingtonians found her dull. One man wrote his daughter after an evening with the Ohio congressman and his wife that they were probably "very good people . . . but a plainer, stiffer set of village people I never met."[69]

By the time James Garfield won the Republican party's nomination for president in 1880, Lucretia had become a seasoned political wife in the nineteenth-century meaning of the term. She avoided all controversy and kept her opinions to herself. Newspapers extolled the Garfields' exemplary family life, and Republican party literature bragged that its candidate, born in a log cabin, had made a "fortunate marriage [to] a farmer's daughter . . . refined, intelligent [and] affectionate. [She] shared his thirst for knowledge and his ambition for culture," but, the Republican party emphasized, she was no bluestocking: "[She has] the domestic tastes and talents which fitted her equally to preside over the home of a poor college president and that of a famous statesman."[70] In that brief but telling description of Lucretia Garfield, nothing remained of the young bride who had described herself twenty-two years earlier as in no mood for "submission."

Unfortunately Lucretia Garfield, who had been ill with malaria and absent from the capital, had only a few weeks in the White House before her husband was shot on July 2, 1881. Most of her record as

First Lady comes from the weeks she kept vigil at her husband's side until his death nearly three months after the assassination attack. The entire country monitored the president's condition through frequent medical bulletins and newspaper accounts that made a stoic martyr of Lucretia. "The wife of the President is the bravest woman in the universe," one newspaper reported.[71]

On September 19, 1881, when James Garfield succumbed to the infection that gathered around the bullet lodged in his spine, he became the second president to be killed by an assassin, and this less than twenty years after the first. Talk of senseless "martyrdom" encouraged an outpouring of sympathy to the widow and children, whose pictures had become familiar to people all over the country. School youngsters, summoned to special memorial programs, heard how "poor Mollie Garfield" (the President's daughter) let "a tear [roll] down her cheek."[72] Congregations listened as ministers chronicled how James Garfield's family had figured in his meteoric rise from poor boy to president. Individual, unsolicited contributions to Lucretia and her children eventually amounted to more than $360,000 or about seven times the chief executive's annual salary.[73]

For the first time in history, the presidential widow participated in her husband's public memorial services. William Henry Harrison, Zachary Taylor, and Abraham Lincoln had all died in office but, in the style of the time, their widows deemed the public ceremonies too trying to attend. Lucretia Garfield assumed a prominent part in the funeral and made a point of letting the crowds see her, even insisting that the curtains be left open in her railroad car, much as Jacqueline Kennedy, eighty-two years later, kept on a blood-stained suit so the people "can see what they have done."[74]

During the brief time that Lucretia Garfield served as First Lady, she kept a White House diary that shows that she could deal firmly with critics. A newspaper correspondent who came to complain about some of the president's advisers got nowhere with Lucretia. "I made her understand," Lucretia wrote in her diary, "the President knew not only the men around him but also knows what he is about."[75] When a writer on etiquette insisted on a "special appointment" with the president's wife, Lucretia treated her severely, and later, after the two women had talked, Lucretia decided that she had been seen as "wax in the [etiquette writer's] hands." "This is only the beginning," Lucretia complained in her diary, "of the petty criticism which might worry me, if I would let it."[76] When a temperance advocate came to request a continued ban on alcohol in the White House, Lucretia pointed out that "drinking wine at a respectable dinner was so small a factor in bringing about the intemperance of the country that I felt there was great inconsistency in giving it so much importance."[77]

The former schoolteacher who had liked having her own money stopped short of advocating the vote for women, and her husband phrased his own disapproval in rather strong terms. When Elizabeth Stanton had invited him to address the 1872 suffrage convention, he refused: "While I heartily sympathize with all efforts that will elevate woman and better her condition, I do not believe suffrage will accomplish that result. Had I no other reason for this opinion, the recent [radical] tendencies of the suffrage movement in this country would confirm me in the correctness of my conclusion."[78] James Garfield insisted that political differences between husband and wife would lead to divorce: "The suffrage movement is atheistic in a great measure and it must logically result in the utter annihilation of marriage and family."[79]

Although Lucretia Garfield appeared to share her husband's view of suffrage, she showed a great deal more understanding than he of the particular problems of her sex, and she sometimes tempered the pettiness and moralizing that characterized his thinking. The contrast between the two is obvious in an exchange of letters concerning the conduct of a Maine senator. A rumor circulated in Washington in 1875 to the effect that James G. Blaine, a Republican contender for the presidency, had many years earlier become a father only six months after his wedding date. "How does this story strike you?" James Garfield wrote his wife. "If it is true, should it have weight with the people in the Presidential campaign?"[80]

Lucretia replied that she had previously heard something similar but she had not given the story much importance. "If it is true, it ought not to affect the voters very much unless it should have been considered more honorable by the majority to have abandoned the woman—seduced. My opinion of Mr. Blaine would be rather heightened than otherwise by the truth of such a story for it would show him not entirely selfish and heartless."[81]

Lucretia frequently based her judgment of men on how they treated women. As for Roscoe Conkling, the New York senator who openly courted a married woman, Lucretia objected that he had acted improperly on two counts, compromising the reputation of the woman in question and neglecting his own wife: "History will write him down for just what he is—a peacock."[82]

Not yet fifty years old at the time her husband was murdered, Lucretia lived another thirty-six years, dedicating most of that time to his memory. She supervised the preservation of his papers, one of the most extensive and complete of any set left by a president, and although she had plenty of opportunity to destroy documents illustrating the troubled phase of her marriage, she never did so. Not until the 1960s, more than forty years after her death, did her family consent to placing those revealing letters between Lucretia and James Garfield in the presidential collection.[83] That correspondence reveals a very different woman from the one described in her husband's diary or in accounts published during her lifetime. The letters show an intelligent, capable woman who reluctantly relinquished her own autonomy in favor of her husband's career. She had not started out that way, but she became, as one of her contemporaries pointed out was frequently the case with politicians' wives, a "quiet and noncommittal little moon revolving around a great luminary."[84]

Despite the "little moons" epitomizing traditional femininity in the White House, women outside were enlarging their sphere of activity in the late nineteenth century. Spurred on by better education, the power of unity in their national organizations, and their greater acceptance in the professions, they branched out into new fields. Some women even earned high fees for speaking in public. Anna Dickinson, a Philadelphia Quaker, became a popular lecturer in the 1870s when she addressed more than one hundred audiences in one year and earned more than the president of the United States.[85] Since women had only recently been accepted as speakers to audiences that included men, some of her popularity may have resulted from curiosity. Many subjects were still considered beyond her grasp or appropriate awareness. When she lectured on immigration, she was often heckled, and when she discussed prostitution, critics pronounced it one subject that a young unmarried woman (such as Dickinson) should know nothing about.[86]

That women could now speak up in public (and get paid for it) suggests that ideas about womanliness were shifting in late nineteenth-century America. Models took more substantial forms than had been the case in the antebellum period. The old emphasis on youth had not entirely disappeared but the most admired woman was now taller, more rounded, and more imposing than the shy, innocent, emaciated maiden so fashionable a few decades earlier. Advertisements pictured stout women, often "of a certain age" to tout their household appliances and beauty aids. The bustle, with its emphasis on a large posterior, returned, and the preferred dress fabrics were weighty and ornate, so heavy that only a large woman could manage them easily, England's Queen Victoria, whose name came to apply to much of the furniture and clothing of her time, was in her seventh decade by 1880 and the solidness and rectitude that she exemplified seemed embodied best in a mature woman. This new vogue was underlined by what happened in the White House in the 1880s—two presidents who had no wives installed their serious, mature sisters as substitute hostesses rather than choosing ingénues.

Chester Arthur, the widower who became president at the death of James Garfield, had almost an entire term to serve. His one daughter was much too young to take on any social responsibilities and his teenaged son was not old enough to take a wife. President Arthur could have relegated much of the First Lady work to a staff, leaving for himself final decisions on matters that had political implications. He had always shown considerable interest in living well (having brought along with him from New York his own chef and valet, the latter a "first" for the White House) and could have been expected to want to implement some of his own ideas about entertaining.

Chester Arthur's attention to detail, especially in his surroundings, had become evident when he had surveyed the White House and then announced that he could not possibly live in a place that looked like that. He promptly arranged for Louis Tiffany, the famous New Yorker, to design changes, but the president kept a close check on the progress, going by each evening to see the results of the day's work. When Tiffany finished, the house had a "robin egg" blue room and a red room full of eagles and flags, but much less furniture than had been there when he began because the president arranged that twenty-four wagonloads be removed and auctioned off.[87] The redecorated executive mansion had its critics, but the president pronounced it an improvement over the "badly kept barracks" he had found when he arrived.[88]

In spite of his apparent willingness to oversee many of the details formerly handled by the president's wife, Chester Arthur imported his sister, Mary McElroy, to act as his official hostess. He occasionally hosted dinners for men who were either single or had not brought their families to Washington, but for the formal events, he relied on his sister to even out the numbers so that guests could go to the table in two's, like animals entering Noah's ark. Then in her forties and the mother of four, McElroy had followed her schooling at the progressive Emma Willard's with a completely conventional marriage. The daughter of a minister, she had married a minister, and when her brother moved to the White House, she temporarily left her own family to help him during the capital's social season.

As though to underline the country's new preference for older, more mature women, Chester Arthur's successor, the bachelor Grover Cleveland, also enlisted his sister as White House hostess. Rose Cleveland, the most intellectual woman to preside over the White House up to that time, had graduated from the Houghton Academy and then gone to head an institute in Indiana.[89] She had read widely, studied several languages, including Greek, and had completed a book-length manuscript on George Eliot. Her reputation as a lecturer on women's rights was well established. Yet her entire adult life had been shaped around the needs of her mother and her brother, and when he summoned her to Washington, she dutifully abandoned her own career to assist him in his.

The new respect for seriousness in models of femininity did not extend to scholarly types—at least not in the press's treatment of Rose Cleveland. In spite of her many intellectual achievements, reporters preferred to concentrate on what she wore. Her "Spanish lace over black silk" and "rose colored silk" both made the first page of a major newspaper,[90] while a review of her book was relegated to the inside section and treated with condescension. The *New York Times* noted in 1885 that Rose Cleveland shared numerous writing faults "with many brilliant women and not a few men . . . [but she] may well be congratulated on her first book, [because although] its trappings may offend the taste of some of the fastidious, its heart beats warm and womanly."[91]

Rose Cleveland's boredom with her White House social obligations, although not explicitly stated, can be inferred from her confession that she occupied herself in reception lines by silently conjugating difficult Greek verbs.[92] When her brother announced that he would marry, Rose left Washington and resumed her own life. She edited a literary magazine in Chicago for a while and taught history in New York City before moving to Italy, where she died in 1918 while caring for people stricken in an influenza epidemic.

Rose Cleveland relinquished her role of White House hostess in June 1886, when her brother married twenty-one-year-old Frances Folsom. Speculation about his marital plans had surrounded Grover Cleveland since his inauguration and several suggestions had been offered about the ideal First Lady. Various candidates' names appeared in print, and reporters appraised each White House guest list for a potential bride. By the time more positive evidence leaked to the press in May 1886, many readers refused to take it seriously, believing this just another unsubstantiated bit of gossip.

But the bachelor Cleveland really did mean to marry and he had chosen the young daughter of his former law partner. The president had known Frances Folsom since she was born. He had bought her first baby carriage, and according to accounts of his fellow club members, had led "chubby Frankie" around by the hand when she was a youngster. After her father's death, when she was eleven, Grover became in effect, although not in law, her guardian and played a role in her upbringing. As governor of New York, he invited her and her mother to be his guests in Albany and later they came to the White House. Anyone observing Grover's attentiveness to Frances over the years might have guessed at his intentions had not the twenty-seven-year difference in their ages made marriage seem unlikely. Gossip centered more on Frances's mother as the subject of the courtship than on the daughter.

Nothing in either the appearance of the young bride or in her actions resembled the ingénue stance of Julia Tyler, the only preceding president's bride. Frances was all seriousness. A graduate of Wells College in 1885, she was taller than average and full-figured, and she carried herself with such authority and confidence that she might have been mistaken for a much older woman. Advertisers who freely appropriated her picture to sell their own products portrayed her as a mature individual. Flimsy, virginal white dresses had been the typical costume of young women in antebellum America, but the vogue now was the matronly shape, even for twenty-one-year-old Frances Cleveland.

The young bride became one of the most popular First Ladies of the century. Women imitated her hair style and lined up by the thousands to catch a glimpse of her at White House receptions.[93] Presidents' wives would hear her singled out for years to come, alongside Dolley Madison, as one to imitate.[94] The president had attempted to divert some of the attention from Frances and provide a refuge for them both by setting up a second Washington home. The possibility of the president dividing his time between an official residence and a private one had been debated since the earliest days of the republic, but the Clevelands were the first to work out the details very successfully. At the time of his marriage, Grover informed his sister: "I shall buy or rent a house near here where I can be away from this cursed, constant grind."[95] "Red Top," as reporters dubbed the house, offered the Clevelands a retreat, with a magnificent view of the Potomac, and except during the busiest part of the White House social season, they could live there and arrange for the president to commute to his office.[96]

Frances Cleveland received many requests that she champion one reform or another, but she refused to associate her name with any cause. An advocate of temperance (she had toasted her own marriage with mineral water), she would not impose her beliefs on others and blithely served wine at all White House functions. Temperance advocates could hardly reprove her since she reportedly had her own wine glasses removed at the start of the meal. Although her receptions were frequently described as elegant, she offset possible charges of elitism by scheduling regular events for Saturday afternoon so that working women could attend.[97]

The image of Frances as a sweet, gracious lady contrasted sharply with her husband's reputation as boorish and morally corrupt. During his first campaign for the presidency in 1884, rumors had spread when he acknowledged that he supported a child whose mother he had never married. During the reelection campaign of 1888, stories circulated that the president physically abused his young wife.[98] When a Worcester, Massachusetts, woman wrote asking Frances Cleveland if the reports were true, the First Lady felt obliged to issue a disclaimer unique in American history. These were "wicked and heartless lies" aimed at Grover, Frances wrote, and "I can wish the women of our country no greater blessing than that their homes and lives may be as happy and their husbands may be as kind, attentive, considerate and affectionate as mine."[99]

The voters may have taken her word on that matter but many of them faulted Grover in other areas. His attempt to make a lower tariff the central issue of the 1888 presidential campaign backfired, as so often happens when a complex issue is injected into a popular election. Grover had not been generous with veterans' pensions, and, as the first Democratic president since the Civil War, he was vulnerable to charges of having treated southerners too kindly. When the votes came in, the incumbent lost to Benjamin Harrison in the electoral college, although not in the popular vote.

Frances packed up to leave the White House but she instructed the servants to take good care of all the furnishings because she expected to be back in exactly four years. When history proved her right and the Clevelands returned to Washington in 1893, they brought a young daughter with them, and again they rented a separate residence to protect the family from excessive attention.

This second Cleveland administration was marred by a devastating economic downturn, perhaps the worst of the century. Thousands of businesses collapsed, and serious unemployment in the cities was exacerbated by depression on the farms. In the end, the president

turned to a Wall Street syndicate to help him borrow the gold needed
(for a commission, of course) and sell the bonds that would restore
faith in the Treasury.

It was during this second term that a second daughter, Esther, was
born to the Clevelands—the first to be born to a president in the
White House. By the time the Clevelands left Washington to settle in
Princeton, New Jersey, they had a third daughter, and later they had
two sons. Grover Cleveland did not live, however, to see them all
mature, because he died in 1908 at age seventy-one.

Five years later his widow remarried, thus testing for the first time
the perquisites that had been assigned to presidents' widows. It had
never been quite clear whether the franking privilege and the pension, both generally accorded all former First Ladies who requested
them, constituted a reward for services each had rendered or represented some sort of recompense for her husband's work. Frances
Cleveland had not sought a pension after Grover's death, but she
continued to avail herself of the franking privilege, even after her
remarriage, adding only a final surname "Preston" to her signature of
"Frances Cleveland."[100] Before she died in 1947, she had amassed a
string of firsts—the first to marry a president in the White House (the
Tylers had married in New York City), the first presidential wife to
serve two noncontinuous terms, and the first presidential widow to
remarry after her husband's death. Perhaps because she was a young
bride, the public tolerated her doing what several of her predecessors
had unsuccessfully attempted—keeping a distance between the president's private residence and the White House.

What stands out most about Frances Cleveland, however, is the
extent to which she underscores a change in style for First Ladies.
Coming almost exactly forty years after Julia Tyler, Frances made no
attempt to imitate the other woman's immaturity and almost childlike
egotism. Rather than sitting on a raised platform to receive her guests
in imitation of royalty as Julia Tyler had done, Frances was the model
of simplicity and maturity, even though she was still in her twenties.

The serious model continued in the White House with Caroline
Scott Harrison (1889–1892) but once again it was the seriousness associated with domesticity rather than with scholarship, public action,
or a career of her own. In her youth, she had shown exceptional talent
in both music and art, and after graduating from the Oxford Female
Institute in Ohio, she had taught music in Kentucky. After her marriage to Benjamin Harrison in 1853, those interests gradually lost out
to the demands of her husband's career. She enlisted in the appropriate women's organizations, and after her husband's election to the

United States Senate, she dutifully moved the entire family to a rented suite in Washington.[101] Although her mother had described Caroline in her young years as showing no interest at all in domestic chores, she was singled out by contemporaries as the "best housekeeper the White House has ever known,"[102] and characterized by her biographer as "by nature strongly domestic . . . [choosing] to remain in the background."[103]

Every administration refurbished the White House but Caroline Harrison wanted to make major structural changes, a course long overdue for a building whose cornerstone had been laid almost a century earlier and not rebuilt since 1818. Architects went to work on plans and came up with two. The first outlined minor alterations, and the second, which the First Lady favored, projected a whole new look, including the addition of a large office wing on one side and a "historic wing" on the other, with conservatories for plants and flowers stretching across the grounds to give the enclave the look of a European palace.[104]

Congress drew back from supporting such luxury and the Harrisons had to settle for much less. Caroline ordered the vermin exterminated, the floors repaired, and the furniture fixed. After she had arranged in the spring of 1891 to have electricity installed, she began a renovation program to replace the open fireplaces and spits that had been used for cooking.[105] In modernizing the President's House, the First Lady was following, rather than setting, the national style. Electric appliances were being heralded as introducing a new age and some people even hinted at an eventual "servantless kitchen." "Perfectly controllable cooking," easy laundry, and effortless cleaning were all in the near future, one home economist argued, for wives who mastered the elements of scientific management.[106]

Part of the new emphasis on household management, apparent in the table of contents of the nation's women's magazines, resulted from a change in immigration patterns. Irish and Swedish daughters had willingly taken jobs in other people's homes during the middle of the nineteenth century, but their numbers had fallen off by the 1890s, to be replaced by Italian and Jewish women who shunned domestic work. Caroline Harrison had grown up in a home where Irish maids did all the work,[107] but she found fewer of them available for hire in her own home. The servantless kitchen, and how to manage it, developed into a major topic for debate.

When it became clear that household appliances could not substitute for physical labor, a campaign began to make paid housework more attractive. Even middle-class women, the argument went, could be drawn into other women's kitchens if the job offered enough advantages. Much of the discussion resembled that which surrounded the enlisting of women to teach school in the preceding decades—it concentrated on pay, which reportedly equaled that of any other job available to women, and on the opportunity to learn skills that a woman could use after she started her own family. *Good Housekeeping* even hinted that college graduates might like to try domestic work since many of them evidently had nothing better to do after picking up their diplomas than return to live with their parents. One survey at Vassar College found that only one in four of the graduating class had plans for work or travel.[108]

Basic to the articles encouraging women to accept paid domestic work was the view that housework should satisfy any woman, no matter how intellectually inclined or well educated. Indeed, the woman who took a job outside her home, when economic necessity did not dictate the move, was "a snob because she wanted more material things than otherwise she would have."[109] It was bad enough that young single women were being enticed into the job market but "the case is still more serious," *Ladies' Home Journal* advised in 1887, "when a married woman, dissatisfied with a moderate living of her husband's providing, or tempted by some real or fancied ability for business, endeavors to combine domestic duties and some money-making employment . . . [The result is] too often the sad spectacle of a husband rendered contemptible and his own spark of manliness extinguished by the greater, unnatural and unnecessary prominence of a selfishly energetic business wife."[110]

In the face of such high praise for domesticity, politicians' wives did well to emphasize their homemaking abilities. *Good Housekeeping* singled out Pennsylvania Governor Pennypacker's wife for admiring notice because she was "most domestic in her tastes and habits. Home is to her the acme of happiness." The wife of Iowa's Governor was described as "perfect" because she directed all her attention to domestic chores.[111] In the most conspicuous position of all stood the president's wife, and although one Washington journalist discounted as "absurd the stories that Mrs. Harrison spends half her time in the kitchen, actually taking part in the preparation of the food, . . . she knows about every detail of the household and . . . the servants adore her."[112] Caroline Harrison gained considerable attention when she designed the cornstalk-and-flower border for the china used during her husband's administration and then began the White House collection of china patterns that had been chosen by the preceding presidents and their families.

Caroline Harrison became ill with tuberculosis during the last year of her husband's term. She died just weeks before the 1892 election. The death of Letitia Tyler, the only preceding First Lady to die in the White House, had occurred half a century earlier but accounts of the two women's lives varied little. Both had directed their energies to family concerns, and only a hint of the "new woman" breaks that pattern in the latter's record. At the time of the founding of the Johns Hopkins Medical School in 1890, Caroline Harrison agreed to help in fundraising on the condition that women be admitted to study on the same basis as men.[113] It is ironic that she should be remembered for two such different achievements—starting the White House china collection and helping make one of the country's major medical schools coeducational. Only she could have said which of the two she considered the more appropriate memorial, but it is a sign of her times that her contemporaries gave considerably more attention to the plates.

Soon after Caroline Harrison's death, her husband lost the presidential election to Grover Cleveland and Frances Cleveland returned to the White House. By the time that administration ended, some important changes were underway. National magazines had begun to give considerable coverage to wives of presidential candidates—something unheard of in the early part of the century. Changes in transportation and communication account for part of the difference, with railroads offering presidents' wives the opportunity to travel across the continent so that voters from New York to California could see them. Women's magazines covered White House activities in detail so that readers from Minnesota to Louisiana could follow the antics of the president's children and grandchildren. Before the Civil War, people outside the capital and the president's home state rarely saw his family, but by the end of the century a national audience was beginning to develop.

This widened exposure did not necessarily enlarge a First Lady's opportunities for autonomy since there is little evidence that intelligent, strong women fitted in with voters' notions of femininity. Reporters of both sexes who covered the capital typically praised sweetness and docility over independence, and in no case is this better illustrated than in the comparisons of Ida Saxton McKinley, wife of the successful Republican candidate for president in 1896 and 1900, and Mary Baird Bryan, wife of the Democratic loser. The first, frail and sick, insisted on all the attention that Mary Lincoln had wanted, but received little of the criticism. Mary Bryan, who attended the same law school as her husband and was known to research, write (and type) his speeches, gained little favorable comment for her efforts. It is significant that *Notable American Women,* the most complete reference work on the subject, includes no entry for the remarkable Mary Bryan but devotes a page to each president's wife, including the ineffectual Ida McKinley.

By all accounts Ida had been a vigorous young woman whose physical and mental condition deteriorated rapidly in the first years of her marriage. In just three years' time, she had lost her mother, with whom she had been very close, and two young daughters. She never recovered her strength or came out of the depression that followed these tragedies.

Although accurate medical opinion on Ida McKinley is difficult to find, there is every indication that her illness was very real. After the delivery of her second child, she may have suffered from phlebitis, making unassisted walking difficult, and she also had seizures, resembling epilepsy (although the name for the disease, still so misunderstood in the nineteenth century, does not appear in newspaper coverage of her). Even in the McKinley household, the nature of Ida's illness remained outside the bounds of acceptable discussion. Her niece, who spent considerable time with Ida, remarked after her death that she had first heard "epilepsy" in connection with her aunt in a political campaign and she had assumed it was part of the opponents' plot to discredit William McKinley.[114]

The grief and limitations Ida experienced in her adult years represented a big change from her youth. In Canton, Ohio, where she grew up, her family had been prominent for two generations and one of her grandfathers had started the town's major newspaper.[115] Nurturing bigger ideas for her schooling than Canton could satisfy, Ida enrolled first in an academy in Delhi, New York, then in a Cleveland academy before finishing at Brook Hill Seminary outside Philadelphia.[116] To round out her education, she went off to Europe with her sister on an eight-month tour. The teacher who chaperoned the girls later complained that she had found Ida so obstreperous that she had contemplated abandoning her charges and going off on her own.[117]

Back in Canton, Ida continued in her independent ways by going to work in her father's bank at a time when middle class young women eschewed paid labor,[118] By some accounts Ida even managed a branch, but whatever her official title, she had taken it not out of necessity but because she wanted a job. Young William McKinley, new in town and from much less advantaged circumstances than hers, appealed to young Ida so much that she vowed to marry him. Her parents made an imposing Canton house their wedding present and the young couple appeared started on a fairy-tale marriage—until the deaths of both their children and the onset of Ida's illness.

While the loss of her daughters appears to have precipitated Ida into depression and disability, her husband rushed into politics, making his first run for Congress in 1876. For the rest of their marriage, as he progressed through several terms in the legislature, to the governorship of Ohio and finally the presidency, Ida developed a reputation as one of the most demanding invalids in American history. Unlike many of her predecessors who had relied on their poor health to excuse them from unwanted official tasks, she insisted on a central position for herself at every public event.[119] She frequently summoned her husband from important meetings in order to ask his opinion on ribbons for a new dress or some other trivial matter. During his governorship, the McKinleys lived in a hotel across from his office in Columbus and each morning when he went to work, he turned and waved to Ida from the street. Then precisely at three in the afternoon, he stopped whatever he was doing to signal her again and wait for her to respond with a swish of white lace.

In the White House, Ida continued to insist on occupying center stage even though she was too ill to be more than just physically present. Each time the president left Washington, Ida was at his side, waiting to be escorted out on the train platform to acknowledge crowds at every stop. Wherever she went in Washington, a special exit route had to be prepared in advance so that she could be removed quickly in case she had one of her seizures.

The seating arrangement at formal dinners was adjusted so that the president could always sit near her. At the slightest sign of one of her attacks, he would take a white handkerchief that he carried especially for this purpose and throw it over her face. William Howard Taft, a guest on one occasion, reported hearing a hissing sound while he was talking to the president and before anyone knew what had happened, the president had shrouded his wife's face from view. While William McKinley continued his conversation as though nothing unusual had happened, Ida remained rigid in her chair and then when the seizure had passed, she removed the handkerchief and resumed her conversation.

William McKinley's solicitous attention to his wife earned him the reputation of a saint. A brochure in 1895, later expanded into a kind of publicity release, predicted that he would go down in American history among the country's greatest heroes. "It was an example," *Century* magazine wrote effusively after his death, "which even sin respects and the criminal can admire. . . . Knowledge of this exceptional domestic relationship . . . passed . . . beyond our geographical boundaries and reached even the people and the courts of Europe."[120]

Others thought William McKinley went too far. They pointed out that for twenty years he had renounced almost all pleasures, except work, in order to nurse his wife. The one diversion he still permitted himself—smoking several cigars a day—had to be enjoyed away from home because Ida did not care for the odor. The magazine *Nation,* at odds with President McKinley over the Spanish-American War, noted a few months before his death that he was "likely to be known as the mildest mannered President that ever suffered long and was kind in the White House," but *Nation* wondered if "flabby good nature" was what the country needed.[121] William made no attempt to control Ida's outbursts of bad manners, and she frequently snapped back at people. One White House guest was amazed when Ida pointed a finger at a startled woman and announced: "There's somebody who would like to be in my place and I know who it is."[122]

Popular magazines included many formal, posed pictures of Ida McKinley in the 1890s but failed to prepare people for how ill she seemed in the flesh. Rows of delicate, expensive lace and lots of diamonds, her favorite jewel, gave her a doll-like appearance, and one young congressman's wife, meeting Ida McKinley for the first time, described her in terms more fitting an inanimate object than a person: "The first glimpse [of Ida McKinley] . . . made me ashamed of coming. . . . She sat propped with pillows in a high armchair with her back to the light. Her color was ghastly, and it was wicked to have dressed her in bright blue velvet with a front of hard white satin spangled with gold. Her poor relaxed hands, holding some pitiful knitting, rested on her lap as if too weak to lift their weight of diamond rings, and her pretty gray hair is cut short as if she had had typhoid fever. She shook hands with us lightly, but didn't speak."[123]

Ida's one demonstration of strength and stamina came after her husband's assassination in the summer of 1901. She had accompanied the president to Buffalo but had not gone with him to the exposition where he was shot as he stood greeting admirers. As the dying president was being carried away, his thoughts ran to his wife ("Be careful how you tell her").[124] Escorted to his bedside, Ida amazed everyone by appearing much stronger than she had been for some time. At first she begged to die with him, then composed herself and accompanied his body back to Ohio for burial. Before her death six years later, she oversaw the building of his mausoleum and planned for the dedication of his monument.

Ida McKinley's tenure as First Lady raises more questions about the country than about her. Sick and depressed by the deaths of three of the people closest to her, she could hardly be expected to exemplify the "new woman" (although her youth, when she worked in her father's bank, showed evidence that she had a mind of her own). What is more interesting is the public's easy acceptance of an invalid as First Lady—a role which seemed to demand no more than a doll-like figure propped up against some cushions.

Mary Baird Bryan, whose husband lost to William McKinley in the elections of 1896 and 1900, made a far larger intellectual contribution than Ida to her husband's career and would have brought an entirely different outlook to the job of First Lady. Only thirty-six and barely old enough to meet the constitutional requirements for the presidency, William Jennings Bryan was nominated by the Democrats in 1896. He had already achieved a reputation as the "boy orator" from Nebraska, The McKinley-Bryan campaigns raised large questions about the direction of the country, about the continued political dominance of the rural areas over the cities and about how to finance a national government that was assuming more and more responsibilities. An economic downturn in the first half of the 1890s made change imperative, and William McKinley, with his proposed higher tariff, appealed to some voters, while William Jennings Bryan moved others with his pleas for "free silver."

When Bryan delivered his famous "cross of gold" oration to the 1896 Democratic convention, his wife of twelve years was sitting in the gallery. Mary Baird Bryan had more than a casual interest in the response because she had helped research the speech. Since her marriage, she had tailored her intellectual interests and most of her energy to Will's career, and it was to assist him that she had entered law school, where she placed third in the class. Neither housekeeping, nor clothes, nor social affairs held much interest for her, and she frequently admitted that she was happiest while checking references for her husband at the National Library. A career of her own had never appealed but she thought his "a mind . . . worth working with and working for . . . [so that I was] willing to plod through heavy books in order to give him the leading thoughts, and help form for him a background of erudition which he was too busy to acquire unaided."[125]

Three times nominated and three times defeated for the presidency, William Jennings Bryan stood as a major figure in American politics for more than three decades, but his wife, whom most of his biographers consider a major force in his success, remains almost unknown. From the time the two met in Jacksonville, Illinois, in 1879 until Will's death at the conclusion of the Scopes trial in Tennessee in 1925, the Bryans formed a partnership, and no one who knew them well assigned Mary an insignificant role. A Washington newspaper in 1892 commented on her "excellent" judgment and on her skill in revising her husband's speeches.[126] An early Bryan biographer thought Mary's mind "more analytical" than Will's,[127] and later students have concurred. Political historian Louis Koenig described Mary as a shrewd judge of people and her husband's "chief aide and counselor."[128] Louise M. Young, in a biographical sketch of the elder Bryan daughter, Ruth, who made history herself, described Mary as a "remarkable woman who left a strong imprint on [Ruth's] character . . . [and was] far abler than [William Jennings Bryan] in intellect and judgment."[129]

A spunky young woman, Mary Baird had not immediately taken a liking to young Will Bryan, but when she learned that he did not drink, smoke, or swear and that at college he regularly carried a Bible around under his arm, she decided: "I preferred marrying a man who was too good rather than one who was not quite good enough."[130] The courtship proceeded with difficulty since her school, affectionately known as "Angels' Jail," did not permit its students to socialize with the local college men. Elaborate subterfuges had to be worked out for the young couple to meet at the home of a cooperative faculty member or during one of Mary's purported visits to a "sick mother." When the deception was uncovered, Mary was expelled from school but she did not alter her resolve to marry Will. Mary's mind, once made up, rarely changed on anything, and she reminded Will before they were married that she expected him to respect her views. "So NOW I want you to understand that I mean . . . what I say."[131]

After their marriage in 1884, Will struggled to start a law practice, first in Illinois and then in Nebraska, while Mary began her legal studies and helped start a Sorosis chapter. She made no secret of her lack of interest in domesticity, explaining matter-of-factly, "[I] naturally do not like housework."[132] When he proposed running for Congress in 1890, she countered that their short residence in the state and the needs of their three children made a wait prudent. When he ran anyway and won, she packed up the children, ranging in age from nine months to six years, and moved them to Washington. For the next four years, the Bryans boarded with a family across from the National Library so that Mary could divide her time between the children and the book stacks. On the days Will was scheduled to speak in the House, she stationed herself in the gallery, ready to nod an approval or signal caution with a frown.[133]

The contrast between Ida McKinley and Mary Bryan could hardly have been more marked, as *Harper's Bazaar* pointed out in the campaign of 1900. Although not openly taking sides, the magazine implied a certain criticism of Mary Bryan when it described Ida as "a gentle sedative to the typical woman of today who aims to do too much . . . an inspiration to all women . . . a revelation of the glory of the woman at home . . . and a First Lady who exalts mere womanliness above anything that women dare to do." Mary Bryan's competence was noted: "[She is a] woman of action, a successful woman, a full-fledged lawyer . . . whose mind is a storehouse of information on all subjects that pertain to her husband's duties and ambitions." Such activities evidently rendered Mary less feminine, although her contribution to her husband's success was clear: "It was said that the speech in Congress which first brought Mr. Bryan into national prominence was written by his wife, [and if he wins] she will bring an intellectual character . . . even perhaps a salon [to the White House and will] compel women to think about issues of the day."[134]

The Bryans lost that election and again in 1908, but their working partnership continued. They started a periodical, the *Commoner*, in 1901 and continued to speak out on a variety of causes, including woman's suffrage which Mary had publicly favored in the 1890s when only a very small minority of women and virtually no politicians' wives admitted to such views. Even after Mary became crippled by arthritis and was eventually confined to a wheelchair, she continued to work hard to advance Will's career. In 1911 she accompanied her husband to Princeton to meet Ellen and Woodrow Wilson,[135] and she appealed (unsuccessfully) to Florence Harding for a place for Will on the U.S. Peace Commission.[136] After he died in 1925, she used the remaining five years of her life to edit his *Memoirs*.

Comparison of Mary Bryan and Ida McKinley might seem unfair. The former was fourteen years younger and had matured with more examples of strong, independent women to guide her. Mary had a far better education and came out of the frontier tradition that accepted large and responsible roles for women in family decisions. No string of tragedies of the magnitude of Ida's had deterred her. Why then, one might ask, did she prefer to funnel her remarkable energy and talent into her husband's career rather than develop one of her own?

Mary Bryan may have judged her time as premature for a woman to pursue her own career and left that for her daughter's generation. In any case, she lived to see her elder daughter, Ruth, make a remarkable name for herself and constitute the sole entry for the family's distaff side in the history books. Unlike her mother, who married a man she "could work for," Ruth Bryan married three men, none of whom she worked for, and she developed her own reputation as speaker, politician, and diplomat. Born in 1885, she was only five years old when her father won his first election to Congress but she grew up listening to him debate the tariff and campaign all across the nation.[137] Those experiences no doubt influenced her as an adult and she became the first congresswoman elected from the South (Florida in 1928) and then the first American woman to win appointment to a major diplomatic post (envoy extraordinary and minister plenipotentiary to Denmark, 1933).

But the century ended and time "turned over" in 1900 with Ruth Bryan's string of "firsts" far in the future. Women could vote in only four states (Wyoming, Idaho, Colorado, and Utah), and most women who desired elective office chose to attach themselves to their husbands' careers. Despite all that women had done to speak out in public, form chains of national organizations, and break down some of the barriers that kept them out of the professions, ideas about femininity had not altered. Wives who took an activist role in the world outside their families were criticized for attempting "too much."

First Ladies of the late nineteenth century fit easily into their times. Most had attended college (Lucy Hayes, Lucretia Garfield, Mary Arthur McElroy, Rose Cleveland, Frances Cleveland, and Caroline Harrison), but their degrees were in the typical "women's" fields of art and teaching. Even those who had shown a hint of independence in their youth seemed to mature into models of domestic acquiescence. A small minority of the country might appeal to them to speak out on women's issues but a majority still held for the homey hostess. The nation's Head Housekeeper might present a more serious, mature image but she was not really a "New Woman."

Martha Washington, as portrayed by Charles Wilson Peale in 1776, about thirteen years before she became First Lady. Courtesy of The Mount Vernon Ladies' Association.

Although Abigail Adams lived nearly eighteen years after leaving Washington, she died before her son was inaugurated President of the United States in 1825. Courtesy of the Library of Congress.

Dolley Madison as she appeared in one of her famous turbans in 1817, about the time she ended her two terms as First Lady. Formerly attributed to Ezra Ames, this portrait is now considered to be the work of Otis Bass. Courtesy of The New-York Historical Society.

Stylish Elizabeth Monroe, dubbed "la belle Américaine" in Paris, aroused considerable envy among her peers in Washington. Courtesy of the Library of Congress.

Louisa Adams boasted many talents, as shown in this Smithsonian exhibit, which includes her harp, music stand, and music in front of a portrait of her. Courtesy of the Division of Political History, the Smithsonian Institution, Photo No. 41487-A.

Angelica Van Buren (left),
daughter-in-law of widower
Martin Van Buren, and
Julia Tyler (below), young
bride of John Tyler, both fit
into a long line of youthful
White House hostesses.
Courtesy of the Library of
Congress.

Before taking on the duties of White House hostess for her widowed father-in-law, Priscilla Cooper Tyler won fame for her stage appearances opposite her father, thus prompting comments about a country in which a woman could pass from being an actress to "what serves as a Republican throne." Courtesy of the Library of Congress.

Sarah Polk as she was portrayed by George Dury in the 1840s. Courtesy of the Library of Congress.

Harriet Lane, as she appeared during the presidency of her bachelor uncle, James Buchanan. Courtesy of the Library of Congress.

Mary Todd Lincoln wore an elaborate gown to her husband's inauguration, and she continued to spend extravagantly on clothes. Courtesy of the Library of Congress.

For family pictures, Julia Grant, shown here with her husband and son Jesse, liked to face away from the camera to conceal her slightly crossed eyes. Courtesy of the Library of Congress.

Lucretia Garfield lived only a few weeks in the White House before she became ill and her husband was assassinated. Photo courtesy of the Library of Congress.

In this advertisement, carried in *Harper's Weekly*, May 15, 1878, the President and First Lady appear to endorse a household appliance. Courtesy of the Rutherford B. Hayes Presidential Library & Museums.

Caroline Harrison, the second wife of a president to die in the White House, was noted for starting the White House china collection and for helping to make a medical school coeducational. Courtesy of the Library of Congress.

At age twenty-one, Frances Folsom became the first woman to have married a president in a White House ceremony. Courtesy of the Library of Congress.

Grover Cleveland's admitted association with a Buffalo woman resulted in many cartoons such as this one. Courtesy of the Library of Congress.

Ida McKinley, weak and ill during most of her White House stay, managed to symbolize the kind of femininity that many Americans found attractive. Courtesy of the Library of Congress

5

The Office of First Lady: A Twentieth-Century Development

AS THE TWENTIETH CENTURY began, the sickly, self-centered Ida McKinley still sat in the White House. Before many more administrations had ended, however, evidence would show that the job of First Lady was changing. Gradually, presidents' wives began to hire separate staffs of their own, take more public roles in policy and personnel decisions, and lead important reform movements. Although still unpaid, the job was quasi-institutionalized. Edith Wilson (1915–1921), Woodrow's second wife, received most of the publicity associated with this shift and heard herself criticized for exercising "petticoat government," but she should be seen as part of a trend rather than an anomaly. Each First Lady between 1901 and 1921, even the most insecure, left her mark. Together, they guaranteed that their successors would never find an easy retreat from a public role.

It is no accident that a new and stronger role for the president's wife coincides with the United States' growing importance in the world and the executive branch's ascendancy over the legislature. Theodore Roosevelt (1901–1909), William Howard Taft (1909–1913), and Woodrow Wilson (1913–1921) all possessed much greater knowledge and experience in the field of foreign affairs than had most of their immediate predecessors, and Theodore and Woodrow held definite ideas about a president's preeminent role. Theodore Roosevelt's attempt to engineer a peace settlement between Russia and Japan in 1905 and Woodrow Wilson's vigorous activity at the Versailles Peace Conference in 1919 are only examples of how the two men put their ideas into action, causing the rest of the world to focus more attention on the United States and, in particular, its presidents. Press coverage of chief executives increased dramatically, and some of the new attention focused on the president's family. When Theodore

Roosevelt described the presidency as a "bully pulpit," he might have also noted the increased opportunities for a First Lady.

For almost a dozen years (September 1901 to March 1913), either Edith Carow Roosevelt or Helen Herron Taft presided over the White House. With their husbands at the top of the Republican party, their paths crossed many times, and that they did not particularly like each other is a matter of record. Edith's step-daughter, Alice, revealed at least part of the reason when she wrote of Helen Taft: "Her ideas were rather grander than ours."[1] Helen, who in 1914 became the first ex-president's wife to publish her own memoirs, implied that Edith did not excel at household management and had left the executive mansion depleted of linens and china.[2]

Although the two women bore an uncanny resemblance to each other in the bare facts of their lives, they differed markedly in their views of their places in the world. Born in 1861, they married within six months of each other and each died in her eighties. Yet beneath these irrelevant similarities lay sharp differences. Edith Roosevelt always appeared supremely confident, in command of herself and often, it seemed, of those around her—while Helen Taft's ambition pushed her to try for more. No achievement sufficed, and even a very large prize, like residence in the White House, never quite equaled her expectations.

Portraits of the two women underline the contrast. Edith Roosevelt sits regally, chin up and arm gracefully arched as though she never meant to move, apparently unconcerned about the stray wisp or two that falls on her face. Helen Taft is perfectly coiffed, leaning forward as though ready to pounce into action.[3]

Edith Carow Roosevelt traced her American roots all the way back to the 1630s, through a line of illustrious men and women that included the prominent Puritan Jonathan Edwards. She grew up in New York City in the same Union Square neighborhood where the Roosevelts lived, and Corinne, Theodore's sister, became Edith's best friend. Theodore's relationship with Edith is less clear. Although he was three years older than she, they moved in the same circles, and before he enrolled in Harvard the two may have reached an agreement to marry.[4] Edith later explained that Theodore had proposed but that she had refused, presumably influenced by her family's opinion that she was too young to accept. In any case, Theodore's path in Cambridge intersected with that of an exceptionally beautiful young woman, Alice Lee, and as soon as he graduated, he married her. Four years later she died of Bright's disease on the same day that

Theodore's mother died of typhoid fever. He was inconsolable and left his New York State Assembly seat for a period of reflection and strenuous exercise on a North Dakota ranch. Rejuvenated, he returned to run (unsuccessfully) for mayor of New York City in 1886. A few weeks later, in an unheralded ceremony, he married Edith Carow in London.

In addition to Theodore's daughter, Alice, product of his first marriage, Edith raised five children born to her and Theodore. Frequently she implied that she considered her husband a sixth. While he rough-housed with them and encouraged them in all kinds of shenanigans, she remained aloof, neither participating nor intervening. Once, while she was preparing to return to their Sagamore Hill home on Long Island, someone suggested that she wait until Theodore could accompany her, but she laughingly dismissed the offer, saying that she already had her hands full.

Whether hurt by being second choice or because of some other inclination, Edith showed an almost complete detachment from everything around her, an attitude described by one historian as almost "Oriental."[5] She was one of those rare women with such a strong sense of her own self that neither a large family nor a conspicuous place in the country's capital could disconcert her or shake her certainty that she knew what was appropriate.

This exceptional confidence helped Edith Roosevelt initiate changes in the executive mansion that a more insecure woman would have hesitated to risk. In slightly less than eight years, she solved the old problem of how to separate the president's personal residence from his official home, developed a new model for dealing with the insatiable demand for information about the president's family, removed herself from decisions about official entertaining by turning to professional caterers, and hired a secretary to handle her official correspondence, thus institutionalizing the job in a way that had not been done before.

Part of Edith's managerial ability resulted from years of running a large household and overseeing its transfer from one city to another. In the fifteen years between her marriage to Theodore and his ascendancy to the presidency, he had progressed rapidly through several important offices, including president of the New York City Police Board (1896–1897), assistant secretary of the Navy in Washington (1897–1898), and governor of New York State (1899–1901). Although the governorship had lasted only two years, it provided Edith, just as it did Theodore, with valuable experience in administration. The family's house on Long Island became an extension of the governor's mansion, with political associates and foreign dignitaries visiting the Roosevelts there.[6]

Edith opposed Theodore's run for vice president in 1900, just as she had previously objected to his attempts to win other elective offices, because she understood that the financial drain would be considerable. When the Republican ticket won and William McKinley was assassinated only months later, she had to face the prospect of moving her family to Washington. At his inauguration in 1901, Theodore was the youngest yet to take that oath of office. Edith, who had just turned forty, had to solve the problem of how to spread a president's salary to cover the costs of her brood of six and yet meet all the other obligations of her husband's job.

The rambunctious children reinforced the image of a vibrant, energetic man in the White House. Ranging in age from debutante Alice down to four-year-old Quentin, they had already gained national attention for their antics in the New York governor's mansion. On one occasion, widely and gleefully reported in magazines, they caused an official party to end abruptly when the windows of the reception room were opened and smells unmistakenly those of a barnyard wafted in from the children's basement menagerie.[7]

The White House provided new opportunities for their imaginative minds, and no corner remained long unexplored. The children slid down bannisters, tried their stilts in the Red Room, and repeatedly startled dinner guests by introducing pets at unexpected moments. Jacob Riis, the famous journalist, reported that he had been breakfasting with the Roosevelts when the president apologized for not being able to show him the children's kangaroo rat. Young Kermit Roosevelt immediately obliged by taking the rat from his pocket and demonstrating how it could hop, first on two legs and then on three, across the dining room table.[8]

Such a young and active family acted like a magnet for the curious, and Edith resolved to handle the publicity more successfully than her predecessors had managed. Frances Cleveland had assumed that she could bar reporters from the White House lives of her children, but she found that the lack of access resulted in wild rumors that they were deformed or ill. An older and wiser Edith Roosevelt, aware that she could not deny the public's curiosity, decided to satisfy it on her terms. Raised in a society that dictated that a lady's name should appear in print only at her birth, her marriage, and her death, she had to cope with being a First Lady whose activities the public wanted to see in print every day. By supplying posed photographs of herself and her children, she solved most of the problem. *McClure's, Harper's*

Bazaar, Harper's Weekly, and *Review of Reviews*[9] all ran pictures of the Roosevelt family but gave little information. Edith appeared on the cover of the *Ladies' Home Journal* and alongside articles that featured her husband but had nothing to do with her.[10] When the time came for Alice Roosevelt's wedding to Nicholas Longworth and for Edith's daughter's debut, photographers and reporters were included in the preparations so that the uncontrolled snooping that had marred the Cleveland wedding would not be repeated.

Anyone who thought the formal, posed photographs of the White House family represented increased access was wrong, because Edith Roosevelt instituted changes to increase, not lessen, the distance between her brood and the public. In Albany, she had learned that a bouquet of flowers, firmly held, relieved her of the duty of shaking hands in a reception line, and she continued this practice in Washington. After Theodore obligingly greeted 8,538 people on New Year's Day, 1909, one writer in a national magazine asked readers if anyone could blame Edith for clutching her bouquet of orchids.[11]

Extensive renovation of the mansion during the summer of 1902 made possible a greater division between the family's quarters and those set aside for official events. While the Roosevelts stayed at another house on Lafayette Square, the architectural firm of McKim, Mead and White supervised the enlarging of the White House.[12] The conservatories came down and were replaced by an office wing. Many First Ladies had wanted a separate residence for the family, at a distance from the official duties of the president. Edith Roosevelt settled for one house but engineered a clearer division between its two functions. The family's quarters were upstairs and off-limits to the president's staff and to people invited to the public areas down below.

In many ways, Edith acted as top commander. The secretary she hired, Belle Hagner, oversaw many details, and one of the other aides reported he was "simply astonished at [Hagner's] executive ability. She really is the chief factor at the White House."[13] To control the information that went out concerning official entertaining, Edith enjoined her children not to talk to reporters but arranged for Hagner to release details. All presidents have attempted to some extent to control the reports concerning their administrations, but Edith showed that presidents' wives could learn from the same book. Her stepdaughter, Alice, explained how Edith was not above "managing" the news. She would wear the same dress several times but instruct reporters to describe it as "green" one evening and "blue" the next.[14]

In a further move to establish command over Washington social life, Edith scheduled weekly meetings with the wives of cabinet members. On Tuesdays, while their husbands conferred on one side of the White House, the women met on the other. Archibald Butt, an aide to the president, reported that the women did nothing more than take tea and compare crochet patterns, but Helen Taft, wife of the secretary of war, attended and supplied a different version when she explained: "This was not a social affair."[15]

Indeed, they were planning conferences engineered by Edith to set the limits on entertaining and help keep expenses down. Even with a presidential salary of $50,000 and an equivalent allowance for running the household, she needed to economize. Simply cutting costs would not accomplish her purpose. She could not risk having the president's parties judged inferior to those of cabinet members. The other wives would naturally be tempted, she understood, to compete among themselves unless she set boundaries for them all. By announcing just what she planned to serve or wear or how she would decorate or entertain for a particular reception or dinner, she restrained exuberant hostesses and reassured the insecure ones who feared falling behind.[16] Rumor had it that she also used the gatherings of cabinet wives to issue ultimata on behavior and that on one occasion she warned a married woman to break off her romantic involvement with a foreign diplomat or else find herself banned from the capital's social events.[17]

The institutionalization of the job of First Lady is underlined by Edith's delegating to specialists the responsibility of preparing food for official dinners, rather than burdening herself with small details. Though the caterers were expensive, charging $7.50 per person per guest (the average woman clerk did not earn that amount in a week), the arrangement shielded Edith from some public criticism and saved her a great deal of work. To ensure that her own contribution and that of other First Ladies would not be forgotten, she continued the presidential china collection, begun by Caroline Harrison, and she initiated a portrait gallery so that all presidents' wives, "myself included," she said, could have memorials. Haphazard and incomplete before Edith Roosevelt, the series gained regular additions after her tenure because every administration arranged for an official portrait of the wife, as well as the president, to stay behind when residence in the White House ended.

When Edith Roosevelt vacated the White House after nearly eight years, opinion was almost unanimous in her favor. Archibald Butt judged that she left the job "without making a mistake."[18] Columnists marveled at her stamina, and a leading women's magazine, in an article entitled, "Why Mrs. Roosevelt Has Not Broken Down," attributed her good health to exercise.[19] That was far less important, however, than the shield of self-confidence that seemed to insulate her against criticism that had worried some other presidents' wives. When a famous woman was quoted in a national magazine as saying Edith Roosevelt "dresses on 300 dollars a year and looks it," Edith proudly clipped the column for her scrapbook.[20]

Her most celebrated brush with public opinion resulted from a disagreement over her right to remove a piece of furniture from the White House, and she wisely abandoned her fight rather than pursue it. The question arose when she left the White House and wanted to take with her a small settee that she had purchased for $40 during the refurbishing of the mansion. It had come to symbolize for her the years in Washington and she wanted to have it reproduced, at her own expense, and take the original back to Sagamore Hill. Word leaked out and the press treated the settee as though it were a national treasure that the First Lady was trying to purloin. Edith surrendered, saying that she would not have the settee even if it were given to her because of the unpleasant associations it now carried for her.[21]

Edith Roosevelt never went beyond classes at New York's Comstock School, but the erudite setting in which she was raised provided a complete education. If she failed to flaunt this, as her husband sometimes did his intellectual prowess, it was because of a difference in their styles. Theodore confessed that Edith's education was really much broader than his own and that he often got credit for her ideas. "She is better read," Theodore told a friend, "and her value of literary merit is better than mine. I have tremendous admiration for her judgment. She is not only cultured but scholarly. I sometimes fear she has a good natured contempt for my literary criticism and I know she scorns secretly my general knowledge of literature."[22]

Edith's shrewdness extended to politics, and she told a friend she could not understand why, in 1904, Theodore made a premature public promise not to run again in 1908.[23] Her strong streak of practicality and good sense helped moderate her husband's view of the world and his chances in it, and she was one of the few people who did not hesitate to set him straight. When Theodore ventured into crowds, evidently oblivious to possible physical danger, she kept tabs on his guards and encouraged them to disregard his requests for less surveillance.[24] His plans to wear a fancy colonel's uniform on a post-presidential tour of Europe received a veto from Edith, who pointed out that he would be ridiculed by his countrymen. When he toyed with the idea of trying for an unprecedented third term in 1912, she advised him to "put it out of your mind. You will never be President again."[25]

Political differences with the Democratic Roosevelts enticed Edith to take an uncharacteristically public role in the presidential campaign that pitted Franklin Roosevelt against Republican Herbert Hoover. Though Franklin's wife, Eleanor, was Theodore Roosevelt's niece, she had campaigned against Theodore, Junior, in the New York State election in 1928. Edith, therefore, felt justified in speaking out against Eleanor's husband in the 1932 election. Her endorsement of Herbert Hoover made the front pages of the country's newspapers in August 1932. Her appearance at a large Madison Square Garden Republican rally in October received similar notice.

Edith could not always control contacts between the two branches of Roosevelts, as her daughter-in-law pointed out. In the Philippines in 1933, Theodore, Junior, was asked by a reporter why his younger brother was yachting with Franklin Roosevelt back in New York when it was well known that the two sides of the family were political foes. Theodore, Junior, hesitated, uncertain how to answer, but Edith spoke up from across the room: "Because his mother wasn't there."[26]

For the most part she lived quietly the years between her husband's death in 1919 and her own death in 1948. Rather than write the memoirs of her marriage or of her years in the White House, she teamed up with her son Kermit to produce a volume on her illustrious ancestors.[27] When her children decided to publish a book on travel, she contributed a chapter in which she suggested that at least one woman who seemed fully occupied in the jobs that marriage had given her recognized what she had missed. "Women who marry," Edith wrote, "pass their best and happiest years in giving life and fostering it . . . and those born with the wanderfoot are sometimes irked by the weight of the always beloved shackles."[28] By diplomatically refusing to cite which of the shackles she connected with her job as First Lady, Edith Roosevelt added a final enigmatic note to a remarkably successful tenure in the White House. Like many presidents' wives who preceded her and others who would follow, she decided that the job required a little distance between herself and everybody else. Few of the others had her self-confidence to make that work.

Helen Herron Taft, who succeeded Edith Roosevelt in 1909 when William Howard Taft became president, lacked Edith's quiet control but greatly outdistanced her in personal ambition. Born in southern Ohio in 1861, Helen (known as "Nellie" to family and close friends) had determined very early to escape that region, not only because of a desire for adventure but because of the narrow limits she perceived for herself if she remained there.

Being a woman complicated the escape, she realized, and she fretted over her lack of options. At age eighteen she wrote in her diary that she doubted she would ever marry, and at twenty-two, she explained why: "I have thought that a woman should be independent and not regard matrimony as the only thing to be desired in life."[29] Helen tried teaching, one of the few jobs open to middle-class women like herself and one that many used to leave home, but she found that an imperfect solution. "I do not dislike teaching when the boys behave themselves," she wrote, implying that much of the time they did not.[30] Her mother, more content with the routine of life in southern Ohio, counseled her daughter not to attempt too much.[31] Helen knew she had musical talent but not of the magnitude to justify planning a career around it, and church work did not appeal. Depressed by the lack of alternatives, she admitted that she cried a lot.[32]

With the purposefulness that marked her entire adult life, Helen Herron enlisted the help of two of her friends to start a Sunday afternoon "salon" where "specifically invited" young people could "engage in what we considered brilliant discussion of topics intellectual and economic. . . . We were bent on improving our minds."[33] Showing an unusual ability to predict who in Cincinnati would eventually achieve most success, Helen invited the two Taft brothers: William Howard, who would later become the first man to serve as both his country's president and chief justice, and his younger brother Horace, who founded the Taft School in Connecticut.[34]

The young attorney, whom she called Will Taft, was soon squiring Helen to Cincinnati social gatherings, including the then popular "German" dancing party.[35] His letters literally begged for her attention and approval, and when she complained that he did not put high enough value on her opinions, he tried to reassure her: "I know no one who attributes more weight to [your opinions] or who more admires your powers of reasoning than [I.]"[36] Bouquets of flowers arrived at Helen's house with Will's cards, some of them asking forgiveness for "inconsiderate words and conduct" and others declaring, often in German, his love for her.[37]

Years of insecurity about her appearance and social skills made Helen Herron wary of all compliments, no matter how genuine, and she demanded reassurances. Her diary shows ample evidence of self-criticism, and she repeatedly judged that she had behaved like "a goose" or failed to invent a witty rejoinder. When she accused Will of "reasoning" himself into loving her, he replied patiently in his careful script that he was genuinely attracted to her "high character . . . sweet womanly qualities and . . . intellectual superiority over any woman I know."[38]

Helen Herron refused Will Taft's proposal for marriage at least twice before accepting in 1886 when she was twenty-five. A three-month European honeymoon, with a $1,000 price tag, was her idea, although he worried they could ill afford it and finally rebelled when she filled their itinerary with too many visits to the opera.[39]

Back in Cincinnati, William practiced law and Helen attempted to settle into quiet wifedom. She gave birth to three children and helped start the city's Orchestra Association but made no secret of her unwillingness to continue such a monotonous life indefinitely. William's appointment to solicitor general in 1890 and to a federal circuit judgeship in 1892 raised the dreaded prospect that she might pass her entire adult life as the unnoticed wife of an unimportant judge.

For an ambitious woman who had decided to pursue a vicarious career through her husband, the need to intervene in his decisions was obvious. In the case of Helen and William Taft, the choice to enter elective politics appears more hers than his. Her father and maternal grandfather had both served in Congress and, unlike her husband who preferred the law, she enjoyed the excitement of a campaign. The prospect of putting herself forward as the candidate apparently held no interest for her, although William laughingly predicted early in their marriage that if they ever got to Washington, it would be because of an appointment for her. Even after he had won election to the presidency, he wrote that he felt a little uncomfortable in the new office but "as my wife is the politician . . . she will be able to meet all the issues [and] perhaps we can keep a stiff upper lip."[40]

Women of Helen Taft's generation exercised few political rights on their own. In the four states that had provided for female suffrage before 1910, popular prejudice against women in high office was almost as great a barrier as were discriminatory laws. The lower echelon offices that women sometimes captured, such as justice of the peace or sheriff, did not appeal to Helen Taft. When she was seventeen, she had gone with her parents to visit their friends in the White House, fellow Ohio Republicans, Rutherford and Lucy Hayes, and Helen had stayed for a few days. She later admitted that she had been impressed and that she had set her sights at that time on becoming First Lady.[41]

An opportunity to move closer to her dream came in 1900 when President William McKinley selected William Taft to head a commission to the Philippines. Even the nominee was surprised by the offer and said the president might just as well have "told me that he wanted me to take a flying machine."[42] When her husband hesitated, unsure about what the job entailed, Helen urged him to accept, although her ideas were no clearer than his. "It was an invitation from the big world," she later wrote, "and I was willing to accept it at once and investigate its possible complications afterwards."[43] While some of her friends and relatives worried about unknown diseases and other dangers for the Taft children, she packed them up and moved them halfway around the world. Her only regret in leaving Cincinnati, she later wrote, was relinquishing the reins of the city's Orchestra Association.[44]

Helen Taft's decision to seek status and power through her husband's career is in marked contrast to other women, also born in the 1860s, who made names for themselves on their own. A sampling of a few of Helen's contemporaries indicates a variety of routes to public prominence, but few of them involved conventional marriages. Jane Addams (born 1860) rejected marriage entirely in order to concentrate on her own work in settlement houses, reform, and peace; Mary Kingsbury Simkhovitch (born 1867) waited until age thirty-two to marry and, after giving birth to two children, tried to integrate them into her career of settlement house director; Charlotte Perkins Gilman (born 1860) risked criticism by divorcing her first husband and giving him custody of their daughter so she could pursue her own career as speaker and writer.

Helen Herron Taft lacked none of the drive of these contemporaries of hers, but she chose the older route to the top—through her husband's career. The Philippine assignment, which lasted four years and eventually led to governorship of the islands, marked an important step for both of them. William gained administrative experience, and Helen learned to manage a large staff of servants who, she frequently pointed out, did not always follow her orders but appeared more valuable to her after she no longer had their services. When she published her autobiography in 1914, she used more than half of its 395 pages to describe the four years she spent in the Philippines and only a fraction to discuss an equivalent length of residence in the White House.[45]

As the consort of the Philippines governor, Helen lived more luxuriously than she ever had before or would afterwards, but her insistence on perfection in every detail resulted in a nervous exhaustion that sent her to Europe for rest.[46] In 1904 when the invitation came from Washington for William to return to the United States to enter the cabinet, she worried privately how they could live on a secretary of war's salary. President Roosevelt's chiding her that Edith "never minded not having champagne" did little to cheer her up.[47]

William Howard Taft accepted the chance to become secretary of war, and Helen faced up to a different set of wifely duties when she returned to Washington. Cabinet wives still engaged in the leaving of cards, and Helen was expected to call on the spouses of other cabinet members and set aside one day each week to receive them at home. It all added up to a routine she described as "monotonous stress."[48] Holding less than first rank annoyed Helen, who clearly had become accustomed to the deference accorded the top of the foreign community in the Philippines, and even the prospect of accompanying her husband on official missions abroad did not make up for the loss.

Helen bided her time in Washington as patiently as she could, always ready to speak up when she thought she could advance her husband's ascent to the presidency. That he might receive a lifetime appointment to the Supreme Court appeared one of the obstacles she faced, and she had already made clear her opposition to that. While the Tafts were still in the Philippines, President Roosevelt had held up the possibility of a Supreme Court appointment for William Taft, but both Helen and William's mother urged him to refuse. By 1906 when another vacancy on the court revived the prospect of putting the scholarly William Taft on the country's highest court, Helen was back in Washington and could speak more directly on the subject.

President Roosevelt put great importance on his judicial nominations, declaring on one occasion: "The President and the Congress are all very well in their way. They can say what they think they think but it rests with the Supreme Court to decide what they have really thought."[49] Helen saw things differently, especially by 1906 when a Taft-for-President movement was growing outside the family. William explained in his diary that he had told the president that Helen was "bitterly opposed to my accepting the [court] position and that she telephoned me this morning to say that if I did, I would make the biggest mistake of my life." Who scheduled the resulting meeting between Helen Taft and President Roosevelt remains unclear, but afterwards the president wrote to William Taft that after "a half hour's talk with your dear wife," he understood why the court appointment was not desired.[50]

In 1908 when William was nominated to run on the Republican ticket for president, Helen finally saw victory in sight. William appeared less enthusiastic. "I didn't think I was going to be foolish enough to run for the presidency," he jested on one occasion, and another time: "I was engaged in the respectable business of trying to administer justice [but] I have fallen from that state now, and am engaged in running for the presidency."[51]

After defeating the Democrat nominee, William Jennings Bryan, in November 1908, William Taft dallied in making appointments. He sought advice, appeared to dangle cabinet jobs and then withdraw them, then seek advice again. Ten weeks after being elected, he confessed to a reporter that cabinet-making was not easy, and he waited until after his inauguration to reveal his choices.

Helen went about preparing for the inauguration with more determination, sending her dress to the Philippines to be embroidered and confidently outlining her plans for the White House. "I had been a member of Washington's official family for five years," she later wrote, "and I knew as well as need be the various phases of the position I was about to assume."[52]

On the day of the inauguration, Helen Taft signaled publicly her intention to play an important role in her husband's administration—she took the unprecedented step of riding back to the White House with him. Theodore Roosevelt had decided to leave Washington immediately after the ceremony and so could not accompany his successor. Helen was determined that she, rather than some insignificant member of the inaugural committee, should claim the vacant place of honor.[53] The solution was worked out almost a week before the inauguration but kept a secret, and Helen had to rush down from her seat in the gallery before her husband had finished his speech to make sure she arrived ahead of all usurpers. Her innovation did not go unobserved. Ike Hoover, a White House steward, noted "severe criticism" of Helen's adding a new ceremonial role to those already accepted for First Ladies.[54] She felt obliged to defend herself: "Of course there was objection . . . but I had my way and in spite of protests took my place at my husband's side."[55]

Only the servants and a few friends were on hand to greet the Tafts when they arrived at the White House, but their accounts emphasized that the new president and his wife reacted very differently. Helen remembered that as soon as her eyes lit on the presidential seal, she immediately thought, "and now that meant my husband."[56] William was more sanguine, and according to separate accounts of two of the servants, he threw himself into a chair and said, "I'm President now and tired of being kicked around."[57]

William Howard Taft's discomfort in high political office and Helen's zeal to achieve perfection in her role had an effect on both their lives, more disastrous for her than for him. His weight, always on the rise when he was feeling dissatisfied with himself, rose to 340 pounds, the highest in his life, and necessitated the installation of a new bathtub. Helen, then forty-seven years old, suffered a stroke two months after the inauguration, impairing her speech so severely that she had to work for the next year to relearn how to form sounds. Newspapers described Helen as suffering from a "nervous breakdown,"[58] which kept her away from the White House during the summer of 1909. For several months after she returned to Washington in October, she made only token appearances that did not require her to speak.

Missing the social events constituted the least of Helen's regrets—she could rely on her sisters or her college-aged daughter to substitute for her—but her illness necessitated her absence from important decisions of her husband's administration. One Taft biographer, who admitted to assuming "speculative privilege," pointed to the irony of the situation. "Seven months after the election, it was [Helen] not her husband who proved unable to handle the stress . . . [and] the dramatic ironies multiply when it is remarked that she—his prod, his alter ego, his voice—lost the power of speech and became totally silent just when he needed her most."[59] Judith Icke Anderson concluded that Helen's absence gave William a chance to be "his own man" and that he acquitted himself remarkably well. Although he feared that historians would judge his a "humdrum" administration, he believed he had performed well enough. When the split within the Republican party promised to end his presidency after only one term, he wrote to his wife that he was content to retire "with the consciousness that I have done the best I could. . . . I think you and I can look back with some pleasure in having done something for the benefit of the public weal."[60]

President Taft's inclusion of his wife's accomplishment along with his own is not remarkable. Well before he took on the country's highest political office, national magazines had spoken openly of her influence on her husband. In its March 1909 issue, the *Ladies' Home Journal* informed its readers that the new First Lady had a touch of domesticity and a healthy respect for the arts but was most remarkable because of the mentor role she played for her husband. Her "intense ambition" had helped propel him into the job and she remained his "close confidante." "Had it not been for his wife," the *Journal* readers learned, "Mr. Taft would never have entered the Presidential race."[61] In the beginning of his term, she sat in on important discussions, justifying her presence by claiming to keep him awake. She accompanied him on political forays and golf outings. One acquaintance characterized their relationship as resembling that of "two men who are intimate chums." Helen's demurral that her "active participation in [her] husband's career came to an end when he became President" rings a little false in light of so many descriptions to the contrary.[62]

Helen lost little time in taking charge at the White House. Unlike Edith Roosevelt, she did not care for the company of women and she dispensed with the meetings of cabinet wives. If given the choice, and as First Lady she was given her choice on many things, she preferred staying close to the center of power rather than being shunted off on a peripheral social mission. She had frequently complained that on campaign trips her husband was "taken in charge and escorted everywhere with honor while I am usually sent with a lot of uninteresting women through some side street to wait for him at some tea or luncheon."[63]

While Edith Roosevelt had proceeded as confident administrator, keeping herself aloof from the details of White House management, Helen involved herself in every tiny matter. She insisted that her vigilance could save money. The Roosevelts had attempted economizing but had judged it inappropriate to try saving anything from the president's salary or living allowances. Helen Taft harbored no such reservations. Since the chief executive's salary had just been increased from $50,000 to $75,000, she resolved to budget carefully so that $25,000 could go into the family's personal bank account. Like most of the objectives she set for herself, she succeeded in this one and accumulated $100,000 dollars during the four-year term. Her zeal during the first two years alone resulted in an $80,000 nest egg which the president bragged to his aide was a "pretty good sum."[64]

New economies were effected by revolutionizing the running of the White House. A housekeeper replaced the steward because Helen decided that "no man, expert steward though he might be, would ever recognize [what needed to be done]."[65] Elizabeth Jaffray, the woman hired, insisted that she had not set out to obtain the White House job, but "this rather outspoken, determined [Helen Taft]" was very convincing and Jaffray found herself "swept into the position."[66] Later, Jaffray had further opportunities to witness the First Lady's commanding presence when orders came down for comparison shopping to economize and for the scrutiny of every expenditure.

The celebration of their silver wedding anniversary in 1911 gave the Tafts another opportunity to appreciate a material gain. Helen dispatched invitations to four or five thousand people (she could not recall the exact number), and although some of her friends thought gifts inappropriate, she saw no reason to discourage generosity. The response was overwhelming. One White House employee confessed that he had not known so much silver existed in the world. The head of U.S. Steel, Judge Elbert Gary, who hardly knew the president, sent a silver tureen reputedly two hundred years old and worth $8,000. A congressman's wife described the rather bizarre party scene in which one guest, Alice Roosevelt Longworth, took center stage in her "electric blue suit, flesh colored stockings and gold slippers, [kicking about and moving her body] sinuously like a shining leopard cat," while other guests made "*sotto voce* inquiries" about how much each had "put up" for a gift.[67] The president attempted to head off criticism by ordering that none of the gifts go on display, but Helen showed much less embarrassment and treated the presents as money in the bank: later she attempted to have the Taft monogram erased on one piece so that she could recycle the silver as a gift for someone else.[68]

While Edith Roosevelt's influence on her husband had been quiet and private, Helen Taft's was rather publicly documented. Early in their marriage he had called her his "dearest and best critic . . . worth so much to me in stirring me up to best endeavor,"[69] a description she took every bit as seriously as he. Her contemporaries commented repeatedly on her competitive nature, and one biographer later reinforced their conclusion that "without her ambitions, [William Taft] would probably never have become President."[70] Although she did not include cabinet meetings in those she attended (as Rosalynn Carter would later do), she stayed close by the president's side whenever political discussions occurred in social settings. One aide reported that Helen supplied her husband with names and numbers he forgot, and during parties, whenever "some important politician took the President aside for a private talk, they would always be joined by Mrs. Taft as soon as she realized the situation."[71] Helen made no secret of her differences with the president, and she announced that she would serve wine at White House dinners although "Mr. Taft does not drink."[72]

Personnel decisions interested her particularly and she frequently based her judgments on subjective or irrelevant considerations. One visitor overheard her countermanding her husband on an important nomination, because she found the individual in question "perfectly awful and his family are even worse. I won't even talk of it."[73] She engineered the recall of an American ambassador to France, a man judged by Theodore Roosevelt as the most capable in the service,[74] because he had slighted her on her honeymoon in London more than twenty years earlier. Easygoing William Taft confided to his friends that he would have forgotten the whole matter and let the man remain at his post but Helen proved less forgiving.

The complexity of Helen Taft's association with her husband's administration is hinted at in her memoirs where she refers to William as "Mr. Taft," except in the presidential years when she frequently switches to "my husband." She did not relinquish the White House power base without a fight. Suspecting that Theodore Roosevelt wanted to reclaim the presidency in 1912, she pushed her husband to fight hard for the party's nomination.[75] When Theodore Roosevelt accepted the nomination of the Progressives, thus splitting the Republicans and guaranteeing a Democratic victory, William Taft noted that Helen was too pleased with her correct evaluation of Theodore's motive to worry much over losing the election.

Thus, Helen Taft's stint as First Lady ended after only one term. Her illness had rendered her far less effective than she had planned and her one permanent contribution to the capital was a cosmetic one, although not insignificant. During the years she spent in the Orient, she had become fond of Japanese cherry trees and she saw no reason why they could not survive in Washington's climate. She arranged for the planting of several thousand, thus providing for one of the capital's biggest tourist attractions, the annual spring blossoms.

Helen Taft had engineered her flight from Ohio many years earlier and she had no intention of going back just because her husband had lost an election. After a period in New Haven where William taught classes at Yale Law School, the Tafts returned to Washington in 1921 when he was appointed chief justice of the Supreme Court. Even after his death in 1930, she remained in the capital. When she died in 1943, she was buried beside him in Arlington National Cemetery, the only First Lady to be interred there at the time.

In escaping the limitations imposed on the wife of an Ohio judge, Helen Herron Taft journeyed around the world more than once and to a place at his side at the top of American political power. However, she never put much effort into helping other women engineer easier escapes. Like other First Ladies before her, she refused to take a public stand in favor of woman's suffrage and never supported reforms for her sex in general. In 1912, President Taft appointed Julia Lathrop to head the newly formed Children's Bureau, but there is no evidence that Helen influenced this first appointment of a woman to such a post.[76]

The only Taft daughter, Helen Taft Manning, compiled an entirely different record. Raised partly in the Philippines and in Washington where she received considerable attention as a cabinet member's daughter, the younger Helen chose the privacy of an academic life and the satisfaction of a career of her own rather than a share in her husband's. After being graduated from Bryn Mawr, she earned a doctorate at Yale and then published in the field of British colonial history before taking a job at her alma mater, first as dean and then as history professor. She expended considerable energy in achieving female suffrage, and while her mother had complained of being isolated with "a lot of uninteresting women," Helen Taft Manning worked most of her life in a women's college.

The women whom the elder Helen Taft sought to avoid may have been considerably less schooled and less stimulating than the ones whom her daughter met a generation later. Education and leadership opportunities had begun to widen, and more women felt confident to voice their own opinions. First Lady Taft's role in that change should not be neglected because, for all her faults, she introduced a stronger model in the White House. She made no additions to the First Lady's staff, but by abolishing the cabinet wives' meeting and inserting herself in more substantive discussions, she showed her disapproval of a limited "woman's sphere." If her influence was sometimes petty and unfair, it should be pointed out that she, like other women of her time, had often been confined to taking control over small matters. She worked with what she had.

The degree to which a more substantive, less purely social role for the president's wife was becoming common rather than exceptional is apparent in the brief tenure of Woodrow Wilson's first wife, Ellen Axson Wilson (1913–1914). Although she lived little more than a year in the White House and was seriously ill much of that time, she took a prominent leadership position in housing reform and had her name attached to the slum clearance bill that Congress passed at the time of her death. That such a reticent woman, who admitted she was more interested in painting than in politics, should have been drawn into a major reform effort suggests that it would be difficult for any woman in her place to withdraw completely from a public role.

Woodrow Wilson's presidency (1913–1921) coincided with the dropping of many barriers against women in politics. In 1912, the summer his fellow Democrats chose him as their standard-bearer, Jane Addams, the settlement leader, stood up at the rebellious Bull Moose Convention to second Theodore Roosevelt's nomination for a third term. In 1917, Jeannette Rankin, a thirty-seven-year-old former teacher and social worker from Montana, broke Congress's old tradition of no women members when she took her seat in the U.S. House of Representatives. In August 1920, near the end of Woodrow Wilson's second term, Tennessee ratified the nineteenth amendment. Overnight millions of American women acquired exactly the same power at the ballot box as their husbands and brothers.

Such an assault on the old male monopoly of politics perplexed Woodrow Wilson, the first president since Andrew Johnson to have been born in the South. Although Woodrow eventually came out in favor of the suffrage amendment, he acted reluctantly, moved less by conviction than by the realization that he could not arrest change. He had, after all, been raised in a Presbyterian manse where he was accustomed to hearing the male head of the household speak not only for the family but also for God, and he did not easily transfer authority to women. Few men outdid Woodrow Wilson in appearing to like women, but rather than treating them as intellectual equals, he expected them to supply his support system: bolster his ego and laugh at his jokes.

Beautiful women who knew how to conceal their brains beneath adoring glances and innocent repartee were especially welcome in his presence. Youth did not necessarily attract him—indeed, he called all the women he liked, even the middle-aged ones, "My little girl"—and he exacted from all those who wished to be counted as his friends a juvenile obeisance to his views and an unquestioned acceptance of his courtesies. In the list his daughter compiled of the women he admired most, southerners predominated.[77]

His first wife, Ellen Axson of tiny Rome, Georgia, might not at first glance appear a likely candidate for Woodrow's attention. Like her husband, she grew up in a Presbyterian manse and in her case, both grandfathers had also been men of the cloth. Ellen showed little interest, however, in following the examples of her mother and grandmothers. Her father pronounced her as a youngster too "obstreperous and independent" for her own good,[78] and she dreamed of going to New York to study art as her teacher had done.[79] That plan was deferred, however, while Ellen attended a local women's college. Then her mother died, leaving Ellen, the oldest of four children, to help raise the younger ones. Just as she was finally working out the possibility of combining serious art study and family responsibilities, young Woodrow Wilson came through her town and imposed another complication. He renamed her "Eileen," and pursued her with what one historian called "among the greatest love letters in the English language."[80]

Ellen put Woodrow off, pleading first that her family needed her and then pointing out that he could hardly think of supporting a family on his income. Both her excuses ring a little hollow, however, because when Ellen, at age twenty-four, inherited some money of her own after her father's death, she left the brothers and sister and headed north—not to Baltimore where Woodrow had gone to pursue a doctorate in political science, but to a boardinghouse on New York City's West Eleventh Street and art classes nearby.

Like many presidents' wives, Ellen Axson showed a streak of independence in her youth that her husband lacked. While he picked his schools carefully from among the most prestigious (Princeton, University of Virginia, and Johns Hopkins), Ellen enrolled in the infant New York Art Students' League.[81] Inexpensive and student-run, the League admitted both men and women,[82] and its constitution mandated equal representation of both sexes on its governing board. The League hewed to the mores of the time, however, by segregating drawing sessions that included nude models—women attended in the afternoons and the men went in the evenings.[83]

Not yet known as Greenwich Village when Ellen Axson arrived there, the area around West Eleventh Street already attracted a wide variety of people moving into the city. The 1880s marked the largest single decade of that century for population shift to the cities, and New York drew more than its share—not just immigrants from Europe but men and women from farms and small towns across the United States. The aspiring painter from Rome, Georgia, was not unique in her complaints of loneliness. To fill her time and help her feel more useful, she joined a reading club[84] and volunteered to teach two nights a week in a "missionary school."[85]

Since Ellen Axson had evidently already decided to marry Woodrow Wilson, her assertion of independence is remarkable, particularly in light of Woodrow's disapproval. From Baltimore he wrote that he did not like the idea of her going out alone in the evening, although he hastened to add that she had every right to develop her own talents. In any case, he considered this show of independence on Ellen's part a temporary aberration because he was convinced, and assumed she agreed, that a woman found completeness only through marriage and a family.[86] Ellen showed only temporary ambivalence between accepting the excitement of art classes in New York City and the staid life of a professor's wife. She wrote to Woodrow in strangely biblical terms: "I was indeed meant for you—that I may do you good and not evil all the days of my life."[87]

Ellen Axson's flirtation with the artist's life may have grown out of several considerations, including the inspiration of contemporaries who had achieved national and even international reputations. Mary Cassatt, the Philadelphia painter, had been exhibiting in Paris since the 1870s, and Harriet Hosmer, the Boston sculptor, had earned wide acclaim and considerable personal wealth. Several women had exhibited at the Philadelphia Centennial in 1876 and two of them had won medals.[88] Even women of lesser promise than these might have seen advantages in an art career. Preparation and study often occurred in private, without the necessity of enrolling at an established institution, and the work itself was performed at home, so that like a writer, an artist did not have to travel to some central place of employment.

But Ellen Axson must have also noticed that women artists who boasted large reputations had not combined their careers with marriage. Neither Cassatt nor Emily Sartain (the medal winner at the Philadelphia Centennial) nor Hosmer ever married, and Hosmer had explicitly stated her reasons. "An artist has no business to marry," she wrote. "For a man, it may be well enough but for a woman on whom matrimonial duties and cares weigh more heavily, it is a moral wrong, I think, for she must neglect her profession or her family becoming neither a good wife and mother nor a good artist. My ambition is to become the latter, so I wage an eternal feud with the consolidating knot."[89] There is no evidence that Ellen Axson knew of Hosmer's pronouncements, but her study at the Art Students' League stopped after one year.

In June 1885, Woodrow completed his course work for the doctorate at Johns Hopkins, and Ellen accepted his calculations that two could live "as cheaply as one and one-half." Since Woodrow's beginning salary at Bryn Mawr was only $1,500, he and his bride had to pay careful attention to finances. They boarded the first year with another family, and Ellen did her part in economizing by putting her painting easel away and traveling into Philadelphia twice a week to take a course in home economics. The next year the Wilsons were able to rent a house of their own and bring Ellen's younger brother and sister to live with them.

The move came none too quickly because Ellen gave birth to two daughters, Margaret and Jessie, within twenty-five months. When she bore still a third daughter two years later, Woodrow concealed rather poorly his disappointment—he had written his wife that he was "glad—almost as at the thought of having a boy."[90] The future president now headed a family of four females, and under his tutelage they could also become adoring.

For a man who showed little appreciation of brainy women, Bryn Mawr was a mistake, and Ellen had her own reservations about his going there. When Woodrow was considering whether or not to take the job, he had informed Ellen that he found women speakers "manly," giving him a "chilled scandalized feeling."[91] She replied as though she thought all women moved in an intellectual realm well below his: "Do you think there is much reputation to be made in a girl's school—a 'Woman's College?' . . . Can you be content to serve that sort of an institution?" Although Ellen had studied art in a coeducational school, she placed Woodrow on a pedestal far above women, and the idea that he would consider working as a subordinate to a woman was dismaying. She begged him to consider: "Can you with all your heart cooperate with the strong-minded person who conducts [the college]? The 'Dean!' how ridiculous! If they are going to have 'prudes for proctors, dowagers for deans,' it would be more consistent . . . to exclude men altogether. . . . Seriously dear, I fear you would find it very unpleasant to serve, as it were, under a *woman!* . . . [It would be] so unnatural, so jarring to one's sense of the fitness of things, so absurd . . . beneath you."[92]

In spite of his own and Ellen's misgivings, Woodrow took the job as the best of his offers and soon he was complaining that his boss, M. Carey Thomas, was younger than he, forgetting that it was a question of five days and that both were only twenty-eight. After three years at Bryn Mawr, Woodrow confessed he had been "for a long time hungry for a class of men,"[93] and he escaped with relief to Wesleyan College where he became an enthusiastic sports booster. An alumnus recalled years later that Professor Wilson ran up and down the sidelines at football games, exhorting Wesleyan players to victory.[94] In 1890 Woodrow moved on to the better known Princeton.

Frances Wright Saunders, in a carefully researched biography of Ellen Axson Wilson, portrays the rest of the Wilson marriage as a partnership, with Ellen playing an important, background role in Woodrow's success while, at the same time, pursuing her own interest in art. More than a skilled hostess, she translated German texts for Woodrow[95] and worked out administrative arrangements which he, when he became president of Princeton, offered to the faculty for their acceptance.[96] She traveled on her own and continued to paint and sell her work.

That view of Ellen Wilson fails to give adequate weight to the evidence that shows her repeatedly sacrificing her own time and energy so that Woodrow could have more pleasure and rest. When he received an invitation to travel, she encouraged him to go while she stayed home with the children. He explored the Chicago Exposition in 1893 and then she made the trip later.[97] He traveled through Europe twice on his own and then she went with one of their daughters. As a student of government and an advocate of the parliamentary system, he was drawn to Britain, but Ellen headed for Italy's art treasures.[98]

Although Ellen knew that one of Woodrow's trips was financed by a "wealthy widow around the corner"[99] and that other journeys involved meetings with women, she refused to appear jealous. Frances Wright Saunders concluded, after an examination of the letters between Woodrow and his wife, that Ellen knew of her husband's long involvement with a divorcée, Mary Hulbert Peck, but rather than feed gossip and harm Woodrow's political chances, she treated Mary as a family friend.[100] Woodrow indicated that he regretted his relationship with Mary Peck as a "contemptible error, . . . a madness of a few months, . . . [that left him] stained and unworthy,"[101] but he continued to correspond with Mary until his wife's death.

The youngest Wilson daughter, Eleanor, wrote two books about her parents, and she described a considerably more self-sacrificing Ellen Wilson than did Saunders. Eleanor saw her mother as accepting the fact that she could not provide sufficient gaiety and laughter for Woodrow. He remained the center of the family—a loving, funny clown who could recite more senseless verses and perform more facial contortions than anyone else she knew. Even her adoring account indicates, however, that he divided his life into compartments, with women confined to the audience. His daughters, all of whom favored woman's suffrage before he did, failed to change his mind. When time came for them to enter college, he rejected more intellectual settings, which, as a Princeton professor and president he could certainly have arranged, and sent the older two to the nearby Woman's College of Baltimore (later renamed Goucher College) and the youngest to St. Mary's in North Carolina where, he hoped, she could unlearn her Yankee accent.[102]

Plans to make southern belles of his three daughters had obviously failed by the time the Wilsons moved into the White House because all three had chosen careers. Margaret, the eldest, worked hard to become a concert singer and while her father was in office she found opportunities to perform more plentiful than they would ever be again. Jessie, the dreamer and Phi Beta Kappa key-holder, had abandoned plans for foreign missionary work in favor of work in a Philadelphia settlement house. Eleanor, the youngest, reflected some of her mother's interest in art and enrolled in Philadelphia's Academy of Fine Arts to study commercial illustrating.[103]

Although they had been exposed to publicity when their father had served as New Jersey's governor, the Wilson daughters were unprepared for the attention focused on them after he became president. Magazines took such an interest in them that one congressman's wife confessed she was sick of reading about them. "They are more

before the public than any other White House family I have known,"
Ellen Slayden wrote. "T[heodore] R[oosevelt] personally never let
the public forget him, but the ladies of his household—until Alice
took center stage—preserved a well-bred privacy."[104] Even Woodrow
complained that he might be a public figure, fair game for all reporters, but he did not think his wife and daughters fell into the same
category.

Ellen Axson Wilson received particularly close scrutiny. A month
after the inauguration, the *Ladies' Home Journal* published two of her
landscapes in full-color pages and noted that one painting had been
exhibited at the Pennsylvania Academy of Fine Arts and that others had
been shown in Chicago and Indianapolis.[105] *Good Housekeeping*[106] and
Current Opinion[107] carried similar stories. Ellen's domestic interests and
abilities were not ignored and there were the usual speculations about
the cost of her wardrobe. She felt moved to defend herself when one
newspaper reported that on one of her shopping trips she had bought
seven new gowns ranging in cost from $200 to $300 each. The actual
amount spent had been much less, as she proved with the receipts
which showed two gowns, one hat, one "waist," two pairs of gloves, and
some fabric to repair old clothes—all for a total of $140.84.[108]

The intricate political maneuvering that had appealed to Helen
Taft held little interest for Ellen Wilson, but she was not opposed to
acting as an intermediary to promote Woodrow's career. He was out of
town in March 1911 when William Jennings Bryan, three times nominated to head the Democratic ticket, came to speak at Princeton.
Ellen had to make her own decision about what to do. She invited the
Bryans to dinner and then wired Woodrow to get back in time. When
questioned later about her motives, Ellen replied that she had thought
it the kind thing to do, but historians have seen it differently and have
emphasized the importance of Bryan's support in Woodrow's attain-
ing the 1912 nomination.[109]

Ellen Wilson edged toward advocating the vote for women but
refused to take a public stand on the issue. The experience of her
middle daughter in Philadelphia's slums had influenced her and she
was quoted as saying in March 1913: "The arguments of my Jessie
incline me to believe in the suffrage for the working women."[110] Such
a statement left unclear Ellen's opinion on votes for nonworking
women or on just how the change should be effected—so that it could
not possibly have embarrassed the president who had not yet come
out for suffrage on the national level.

Much safer than suffrage as a "cause" for the president's wife was
housing, and in the same month as her husband's inauguration, Ellen

Wilson started her own investigation of Washington's slums. While enlarging the electorate might be controversial, amelioriating housing was more acceptable, because the fallout from slums hurt everyone, resulting in epidemics, increased infant mortality, and absenteeism. The very reforms that had first been advocated to improve housing had in fact worsened conditions in many cities by razing dilapidated buildings without providing replacements. By the beginning of the twentieth century, housing had become a major reform movement throughout Europe and the United States.

Washington's slums, hidden away from view because many of them were in the back alleys where only local residents passed, needed stricter law enforcement and more funds if they were to be improved. The thousands who lived there, mostly blacks and recent immigrants, lacked the political clout to act for themselves but their poor health and high mortality rates left little doubt of their need. Ellen Wilson's first scheduled visit had to be postponed because of a smallpox out-break.[111] When she finally saw the dilapidated and filthy housing, she was appalled and became determined to work for congressional ap-propriations to provide clearance money. A White House maid, well acquainted with the poverty of the capital's black neighborhoods, went home after meeting Ellen Wilson for the first time and told her daughter that she thought they had "an angel in the White House—she's talking about helping the poor and improving housing."[112]

The First Lady's reputation for caring about the problems of black neighborhoods contrasted with the president's poor record in that area (although it may well be, as their middle daughter charged, that Ellen Wilson's support for segregation of the races was stronger than Woodrow's). During his first administration, the president either con-doned or encouraged the introduction of segregation in government departments where it had formerly not been the rule—in offices, rest-rooms, and lunchrooms of the Post Office Department, the Treasury Department, and the Bureau of Printing and Engraving where large numbers of blacks and whites had worked together. After visiting the capital in the summer of 1913, Booker T. Washington wrote to Oswald Garrison Villard, a leader in the National Association for the Advance-ment of Colored People, that he had "never seen the colored people so discouraged and bitter as they are at the present time."[113]

While President Wilson responded to these criticisms by arguing that segregation would serve the interests of blacks, Ellen Wilson set out to improve their living conditions. She designated a White House car for touring alleys and arranged a reception so that housing reformers could present their case directly to congressmen. Ellen

Wilson's involvement in slum clearance gave the topic a respectability and urgency that it had not had, and one co-worker jokingly remarked that no one could move in polite society without a thorough understanding of alley housing.[114] By February 1914, the relevant legislation, known as Ellen Wilson's bill, had been introduced in Congress.

Had she come into the White House half a century earlier, Ellen Wilson would almost certainly have stayed in the background, hidden as much from public view as the slums that she now worked to publicize. She had suffered the usual initial qualms about becoming First Lady and had tried to bolster her ego by outfitting herself for the inauguration in "the most wonderful gown I've ever had."[115] Her apprehension that she would not measure up had increased after she arrived in Washington, and before setting out for the traditional pre-inaugural visit to the White House, she burst into tears. Her youngest daughter, observing her mother's discomfort, predicted then that the White House would "kill her."[116]

Family responsibilities piled on top of official ones when two of the Wilson daughters had White House weddings within six months of each other. Not long after Jessie's big ceremony in November 1913, Ellen's health began to fail. She had spent the entire summer of 1913 in New Hampshire, but a few weeks back in Washington wiped out all the gains she had made. A kidney disease, later diagnosed as Bright's disease, debilitated her and, although she seemed to rally at the time of her daughter Eleanor's marriage in May 1914, she soon worsened. By August 1914, it was clear to everyone except her husband that she was dying.

The housing bill that she had championed still lay in congressional committee where there was unanimity on the abysmal quality of alley residences but little agreement on who should pay for improvements. After word of Ellen Wilson's deteriorating health reached Capitol Hill, the Senate quickly approved the measure so that she could be told before she died. The House of Representatives acted the next month on this, the first piece of legislation to be passed with such direct and public assistance from a president's wife. Other First Ladies had acted behind the scenes—Ellen Wilson's influence made headlines, and at least one major newspaper concluded that a demanding schedule had figured in her death. She had died, the *New York Times* reported, of Bright's disease, "aggravated by a nervous breakdown, attributed to the exactions of social duties and her active interest in philanthropy and betterment work."[117]

Until her death on August 6, 1914, Ellen Wilson insisted that her only objective in life had been to make life more comfortable for her husband and daughters, but her record is more complex. Naturally shy, she shooed away photographers and refused to appear on the platform with Woodrow. Yet she was often there to support her husband on public occasions. When he broke tradition and addressed Congress directly, she and her daughters set their own precedent by seating themselves prominently in the gallery to hear him.[118] Only a little of the rebellious young artist from Rome, Georgia, remained in the White House Ellen Wilson, but she permitted her paintings to be exhibited, sometimes under the name "E. A. Wilson" so as to disguise the origin of the work, and when they sold, she donated the proceeds to charity. Nonpolitical and insecure, she showed that even a very reticent First Lady can make a difference.

Other presidents' wives had died in office but none for almost twenty years and none so early in a chief executive's term. Caroline Harrison had succumbed only months before her husband's administration ended, but Woodrow Wilson had almost three years to serve when Ellen died. Because his daughters were all busy with their own families or careers, he asked his cousin, Helen Bones, who had helped Ellen as social secretary, to assist him in running the White House. It was Helen who invited her friend Edith Bolling Galt to the White House one March afternoon in 1915, thus setting the stage for Woodrow's remarriage.

The first meeting between the president and the attractive, forty-three-year-old widow was entirely accidental, Helen Bones later wrote. She had not reckoned with the possibility that the same rainy weather that forced her inside that day, with her friend Edith in tow, would also terminate the president's golf game. As they all sat down to take tea together, Helen Bones observed the almost immediate attraction between her cousin Woodrow and her friend Edith. After months of gloom, the president finally laughed.

Edith Bolling Galt combined a good measure of exuberant independence with sufficient amounts of the subservience that Woodrow Wilson found essential in all women. A bit more stylish and sophisticated than most of the women Woodrow liked, she was accustomed to ordering her clothes from a top Paris designer and creating a stir when she drove herself around the capital in her own little electric runabout. She reported that policemen learned to halt traffic at Fifteenth Street so she could maneuver through.[119] At a time when most matrons shunned close association with "business," Edith helped manage her own jewelry store. Yet she resembled other independent women in seeing such activities as somehow unique to herself. Working to increase opportunities for other women evidently held no interest for her. Before meeting Woodrow, she had paid no attention to politics and she admitted that during his victorious 1912 campaign she could not have named the candidates.[120]

The path to Edith Galt's financial independence had been cut by accident, although she should not be deprived of the credit for picking her way across it. In 1896 when she was twenty-four, she had married a cousin of her sister's husband. Older men had always appealed to her, she admitted, and although she "did not want to marry anyone," Norman Galt, part-owner of the capital's most prestigious jewelry store, pursued her "[until] his patience and persistence overcame [her]."[121] Their one child did not survive infancy, and when Norman Galt died in 1908, Edith was left with considerable personal and financial freedom. While keeping some control over the jewelry business, she made several trips to Europe.

The only president to possess a doctorate at the time of his election, Woodrow Wilson fell in love with a woman whose education was very limited. One of eleven children born to a Virginia judge and his wife, she received most of her instruction at home, then enrolled for two years at Virginia finishing schools. At least one historian concluded that, even as an adult, she wrote a "primitive . . . almost illegible" scrawl.[122] Much more relevant to her place in history, however, was the self-confidence that allowed her to act without constant reinforcement from those around her. Years of making her own decisions had prepared her to handle new ones with relative ease, and if she ever felt the inadequacy that had troubled Ellen Wilson, she kept it to herself. While Ellen Wilson had agonized over details, including whether or not to purchase a particular piece of clothing, Edith showed little hint of caring what people thought of her or of the amounts she spent on clothing. She never offered to show her bills to an inquisitive public.

Only two presidents before Wilson had married in office and each had approached courtship differently. John Tyler wed Julia Gardiner before reporters learned the intrusion tactics that they later mastered, and Grover Cleveland avoided detection by using the mails. Woodrow Wilson and Edith Galt had to conduct their nine-month courtship in the full glare of curious reporters, at first concealing their meetings under cover of Edith's friendship with Helen Bones and with the Wilson daughters.

Whatever inconvenience the burdens of his office imposed (and they were, no doubt, considerable, since much of Europe stood embroiled in World War I), the president's courtship progressed rapidly. When Woodrow vacationed in New Hampshire in June 1915,

Edith was there, ostensibly as Helen Bones's guest. But a postcard written during that visit testifies to the fact that Edith's romance with Woodrow had already matured into commitment only two months after their first meeting. Dated June 29, 1915, on the "West Porch," the card conveys the same kind of subservience that Ellen Axson had promised Woodrow thirty years earlier in a similar situation. Edith Galt pledged ". . . with all my heart absolutely to trust and accept my loved Lord and unite my life with his without doubts or misgivings."[123]

Even after having sworn such devotion, Edith shied away from marriage to the president for two reasons. Her own explanation was that she had lived in the capital too long to have missed the public's fascination with whoever happened to occupy the White House. Early in her acquaintance with Woodrow, she discovered that he shared her disdain for the snooping that had become a part of Washington life and for the vigor with which tourists hounded the president's family, but she knew that the two of them together could not change those habits. Much more important, however, was the matter of allowing an appropriate interval to elapse after Ellen Wilson's death. Woodrow was so in love he refused to acknowledge the consequences, but his advisers warned that a quick remarriage would hurt his chances for reelection in 1916. Such considerations became all the more important when rumors began to circulate that the courtship had begun before Ellen's death.

In spite of all these objections, the marriage took place in Edith's Washington home on December 18, 1915. The third bride of a president in more than a century, she attracted enormous attention. At five feet nine, she wore her fashionable French clothes well and, for a touch of the exotic, she explained to reporters that she could trace her ancestry back through nine generations to Pocahontas and John Rolfe. After months of dreariness, the White House came alive again under her direction as she entertained, sat devotedly at the side of a contented-looking president, and even learned to ride a bicycle.[124] Elizabeth Jaffray, who worked more than seventeen years as the mansion's head housekeeper, judged Edith's first two years there the best of all.[125]

By the time of the 1916 election, Americans had more on their minds than the circumstances of the president's remarriage and whether or not he now slept in a double bed. The war in Europe threatened to involve the United States, and many voters believed a victory for the Republican candidate Charles Evans Hughes, who was reputedly under the influence of Theodore Roosevelt, would increase the chances of the United States' entry. On the other hand, Wilson's campaign slogan, "He Kept Us Out Of War," implied a continuation he never actually promised.

Advocates of woman's suffrage changed their tactics by 1916 and superimposed a new element on the election. The young minds that Woodrow had so disparaged at Bryn Mawr had matured, and many of them had joined the professorial ranks themselves. Along with their students, they were encouraged by reports from London where the woman's suffrage movement had taken a decidedly radical turn. Alice Paul, a Quaker, had concluded after witnessing the tactics of English suffragists that American women would have to increase their visibility if they ever expected to vote. She gathered like-minded thinkers around her and ironically used President Wilson's own political philosophy to justify an attack on him.

Woodrow Wilson had achieved his scholarly reputation with a doctoral dissertation, published as *Congressional Government*, which argued the superiority of a parliamentary system over a presidential one. The former provided for assigning accountability, Woodrow Wilson wrote, because the majority party and its leader could be blamed for inaction or inferior legislation. The American presidential system, with lawmaking divided between the Congress and the chief executive, made it more difficult to assign blame. Woodrow Wilson had urged that the president act as head of his party, fully responsible for its failures, and now that he was in the driver's seat himself, he had to juggle his own prescription with the reality. President Wilson's Democratic party held large majorities in both houses of Congress during his first two years in office, but he refused to use that leverage on the side of those who sought a constitutional amendment guaranteeing women's suffrage.

Alice Paul and her followers had already gained national attention in March 1913, when they had secured from Congress a special resolution directing that Pennsylvania Avenue be kept clear for them during the inaugural parade. According to one major newspaper, "Crowds broke through the barriers and formed a solid mass [so that] many persons [were] injured."[126] In response to multiple eye-witness accounts charging the police assigned to that area with negligence, the Senate called for a complete investigation, including an explanation from the Superintendent of Police as to why his men failed to control the mobs. According to one witness, the police had joined in beating the demonstrators. Such an assault on defenseless women prompted many people, who had never previously considered carefully the justice of the suffrage argument, to rethink their position.

The attention focused on her in 1913 contributed to Alice Paul's drive during the mid-term election in 1914, and by 1916 she hoped to bring about President Wilson's defeat. Under the rubric of the National Woman's Party, Paul's followers urged people sympathetic to their cause to use their vote in 1916 for one issue only—suffrage. Nine states had already enfranchised women, and a tenth, Illinois, allowed them to vote in presidential elections. Added together, these states totaled eighty-four electoral votes, a significant chunk out of the total of 531, especially in a close election. Both major parties had written suffrage planks into their 1916 platforms but had left action up to the states even though some southern states showed no evidence of budging, and, in fact, Mississippi did not ratify the 19th amendment until 1984. Only the Socialist Party favored the passage of a federal amendment in 1916, and the Woman's Party leaders thought the time had come to put pressure on both major parties.

Women who could vote in November 1916 evidently responded more to the peace promises of the Wilson camp than to Alice Paul's advice, and the incumbent took all but two of the equal suffrage states. Yet Woodrow Wilson could hardly miss the message—that he had garnered only twenty-three electoral votes more than his Republican opponent who had personally advocated a suffrage amendment. Women's power, if they chose to use it, was no longer insignificant. To underline their point, suffragists stepped up their campaign in January 1917, when they placed twenty-four pickets outside the White House fence. The president, raised to believe that chivalry always wins, sent his secretary to invite the picketers in for tea, and he was visibly upset when they refused.[127]

After the United States entered the war in April 1917, the woman suffrage movement divided even its most ardent supporters from one another. In a country at war, some women argued, wisdom dictated putting aside the suffrage fight to concentrate on military victory. Anna Howard Shaw, former president of the Woman Suffrage Association, shelved her pro-vote lectures to devote full time to the war effort, and she could not understand why other suffragists continued with their picketing activities, defending them as an exercise in free speech. The demonstrators exhibited little subtlety in attacking the president, and one of their gold and white lettered signs read: "An Autocrat at home is a Poor Champion of Democracy Abroad."[128]

Edith Wilson showed no sympathy at all for the demonstrators. After her husband had the picketers arrested and imprisoned, she referred to them disparagingly as "those devils in the workhouse," and she opposed his decision to pardon them a few weeks later.[129] Edith's position in this phase of the Wilson administration makes an interesting footnote to her much publicized role after Woodrow became incapacitated. In neither case did she express the slightest interest in providing for or setting an example for strong and independent women. In both instances, her concern centered on how the issue affected her husband's well-being—not the issue itself.

By January 1918, the woman's suffrage cause seemed poised for victory. New York State had finally passed its own amendment, and the United States' war ally, Great Britain, prepared to extend the vote to its women. If enough states followed suit, any serious candidate for election in November 1918 would be advised to board the bandwagon. After the House committee gave its nod of approval, a group of Democrats met with the president on January 9, 1918, and announced, as they left the White House, that he now favored a federal amendment on suffrage. The president's shift was termed "a surprise" by the *New York Times,* "despite some indications of change."[130] He had been persuaded, he explained, by the need to reward women for their work in the war effort. He could hardly have done less. Two of his Cabinet members, Treasury Secretary McAdoo and Navy Secretary Daniels, had already announced their support for a federal amendment. With many Republicans already on record in favor, passage seemed likely.[131]

It is true that many women, including those in the president's family, had participated on various levels in the war effort. His daughter Margaret announced that she would donate all the proceeds from her singing to the Red Cross, and Eleanor, now married to the secretary of the Treasury, went six mornings a week to supervise a Red Cross storeroom. She left at noon only because she was scheduled to preside at meetings of the Women's Liberty Loan Committee.

Edith Wilson outdid them all by converting the White House into a model of wartime sacrifice. She announced that she would observe meatless days just like everybody else, and to save the cost of cutting the lawn, she borrowed a flock of Shropshire sheep from a Virginia farm. When time came to shear them, she donated the wool, totaling ninety-eight pounds, to the forty-eight states for auctioning, the proceeds designated for the war effort. In Kansas one zealous bidder bought two pounds of White House wool for $5,000 each, and the total sold in all the states brought more than $50,000.[132] With less publicity, the First Lady knitted sweaters for soldiers and arranged for a White House car to take furloughed men around Washington. When time came to christen warships, the only First Lady to claim Indian ancestry selected Indian names.[133]

At the war's end in November 1918, President Wilson announced that he would go to Europe to work personally on the details of the peace agreement. The first American president to engage in such an international overture, Woodrow gained enormous attention, and Edith, who accompanied him, also received considerable notice. Florence Harriman, another American present in Versailles, reported that Edith "then, as always, was a First Lady to be proud of."[134] When the Wilsons traveled to Italy after the peace conference, an American army captain compared Edith to the Italian queen and concluded, "I don't think the Italians have got anything on us."[135]

It remained for Edith's return to the United States, however, for her to achieve lasting prominence in the history of presidents' wives. Woodrow had decided to appeal directly to the people for support of his peace plan—a measure necessitated, in part, by the opposition to it in the Senate. On September 26, 1919, while traveling through Pueblo, Colorado, he suffered a paralytic stroke and then returned to Washington. For several weeks his condition remained uncertain, and his doctor refused to say specifically what ailed him or even how severely disabled he was. Rumors spread.

Woodrow's trusted friend and physician, Cary Grayson, had impressed Edith with the importance of keeping all business from the patient but she hardly needed convincing of the seriousness of his affliction. His trembling hands, gray color, and halting speech told her that, and she resolved to spare him all unnecessary stress. If anyone mentioned that Woodrow ought to relinquish his office to his vice president, the suggestion was quickly discarded, on the grounds that fighting to get back in shape would prove the best medicine. Edith isolated Woodrow from everyone except his doctors, so that even his secretary did not see him for weeks. Any communication that reached the president went first to the president's wife. "So began my stewardship," Edith later wrote. "I studied every paper [but] I myself never made a single decision regarding the disposition of public affairs."[136]

Observers had no way of knowing who made decisions in the White House, and when she issued memos, signed Edith Galt Wilson, curiosity grew. On papers requiring the president's signature, Woodrow's name bore so little resemblance to what it had looked like before his illness that charges of forgery were raised. Edith explained the discrepancy by saying that the bedridden president lacked a hard surface for writing but that his handwriting improved as soon as she provided him with a board.

Word spread that Edith Wilson was running the government. Housekeeper Jaffray referred to Edith as the "Assistant President,"[137] and at a Foreign Relations Committee meeting, one senator stormed that the country was under a "petticoat government."[138] Requests to the president frequently began "Dear Mrs. Wilson," indicating that the writers recognized her as controlling access to the president if not actually making all decisions. Popular magazines reinforced this impression by reporting that Edith "came close to carrying the burden of the First Man."[139]

Rumors multiplied until finally New Mexico's Republican Senator Albert Fall and a more sympathetic Nebraska Democrat, Gilbert Hitchcock, were delegated to call on the president, ostensibly to inquire about the handling of a foreign policy matter but actually to ascertain the president's physical condition and ability to preside. Woodrow appeared surprisingly alert, propped up in bed so that his right arm could shake their hands and retrieve relevant papers which were conveniently placed nearby. Edith sat holding a pen, poised to take notes but pointedly unprepared to shake hands with the men whom she detested as traitors because they had come to check up on her husband. The senators were surprised by the president's quick retort to Albert Fall, who had insisted, "We are praying for you," and the president had answered, "Which way?"[140]

The cabinet looked for precedents about what to do when a president became seriously incapacitated but refused to relinquish the office. In the one case that seemed relevant, James Garfield had lingered for almost three months in 1881 but the vice president had not taken over. The Constitution left unclear who should decide that a president was no longer able to discharge the powers and duties of the office. In the vacuum that developed, the president's wife was permitted to enter center stage. She did not have to risk the charge that an ambitious politician might have feared of using the president's illness to advance her own career.

Edith Wilson's relationship with her husband during the winter of 1919–1920 falls into a familiar pattern of activity for First Ladies. Married to men in demanding, stressful jobs, the women attempted to protect their husbands. That marital concern, however, should not be confused with any great personal interest in politics or in government. The theme of First Lady as protector of her husband's well-being runs through the memoirs of several twentieth-century First Ladies, with Lady Bird Johnson putting it eloquently when she explained to an interviewer: "[Every First Lady] feels first primarily the obligation of trying to make a comfortable area, an island of peace, if you will, a setting in which her husband can do his best work."[141]

Nancy Reagan's role during her husband's campaigns and presidency was described in similar terms: she saw her jobs as protecting him from overwork, inadequate staff, and poor scheduling. If Ronald Reagan had been a used car salesman, one wag had it, Nancy would have been dusting the interiors. This particular view of the role of a president's wife had very little to do with kind of work he did, and it should not be confused with the blatantly political roles that other women (Helen Taft, Sarah Polk, Abigail Adams, and Rosalynn Carter) took in their husbands' administrations.

Evidence mounts on several sides that Edith Wilson's influence in her husband's administration has been greatly overrated. Edith had never shown any interest in politics, although in the romantic early days of their marriage, she had sat alongside him while he studied official communications. After his death, she refused political involvement, and when Eleanor Roosevelt appealed to her for a statement in support of a woman candidate, Edith cited her forty-year record of obliviousness to politics.[142]

Most telling of all, in assessing Edith Wilson's influence, is the nature of the criticism leveled at her. Her alleged dominance occurred only during Woodrow's illness, from September 1919 until early 1920. A time of great tumult in the United States, this period included a miners' strike and a government injunction against mine leaders, a steel strike, the continuation of the fight over the peace treaty, and the deportation of aliens. Yet through all these difficulties, the complaint leveled at the White House was a lack of direction, an unwillingness to act—hardly evidence of a powerful leader. When the attorney general, Mitchell Palmer, began his wholesale attack on people he suspected of being disloyal, the president's secretary futilely begged Edith to see that her husband acted.[143]

Edith had married a man who rarely listened to women on any substantive issue, and only his debilitating stroke placed him in a dependent position so that rumors could thrive about his wife running the country. Her memoirs describe how during his illness she abandoned ideas that differed with his rather than risk upsetting him. When the fight over the League of Nations became particularly acrimonious, for example, she reported that she had suggested to Woodrow that he compromise rather than hold out for what might be a losing proposition. She quickly reversed herself, however, when he accused her of deserting him.[144] At least one student of the Wilson administration concluded that Ellen Wilson, had she lived, might have exerted strong influence on a sick president and possibly convinced him to accept Senator Lodge's amendments concerning the

League of Nations.[145] Such a judgment reinforces the interpretation of Edith Wilson as nonpolitical, interested only in Woodrow's health and happiness. It is ironic that Edith should have gone down in history as the "Mrs. Wilson [who] virtually took over the reins of the White House,"[146] while Ellen Axson Wilson has been almost forgotten except by researchers who resurrect evidence of her strength and talent.

Edith Bolling Galt Wilson survived her husband by thirty-eight years, and when she died in 1961, she was buried beside the president, a tradition begun by Martha Washington. Every widow who had remarried and become First Lady had chosen burial beside her second husband rather than by her first. Edith had lived only eight of her nearly eighty years as Woodrow's wife, but those few years brought enormous publicity. Two full-length biographies[147] detailed the influence she supposedly exerted in the White House and virtually all accounts of her husband's life assessed her role. She had been called "Gatekeeper Extraordinary"[148] and "surrogate President."[149] Yet the consensus is that she described her role as accurately as anyone when she wrote that she simply looked out for her husband's health.

Her role during Woodrow's illness demonstrated another potential trouble sport in the presidential system, whose weaknesses Woodrow had studiously pointed out. In a parliamentary government, which he had favored, the prime minister functioned as head of his party, more dependent on other party members than was a president who won power in a popular election. The prime minister's term of office is more flexible, and elections take place in response to current needs and problems, while the president's term is a fixed four years. Woodrow Wilson's second term had almost eighteen months to run when he became ill, and members of his family thus had the opportunity to make decisions that in other government systems would have been handled by fellow party members. Not until the passage of the twenty-fifth amendment in 1967 was that power vacuum officially filled. Under that amendment, Congress could designate some "body [other than the Vice President and the Cabinet]" whose judgment of a president's incapacity could be used to relieve him of his official duties. Although not explicitly mentioned in the amendment, the president's spouse was understood by some people to be able to participate in that decision.

Edith Wilson's prominent tenure as First Lady capped the institutional changes made by Edith Roosevelt, the public and influential participation of Helen Taft, and the acknowledged reform leadership of Ellen Wilson. Together, the four women altered the meaning of the title they held. What had been unusual before 1900—the contribution of significant work of their own—became common among presidents' wives in the next two decades: three of them wrote books about themselves or their families, and the fourth, Ellen Wilson, left a sizeable collection of her own paintings.

To comprehend their cumulative impact, it is necessary only to ask what if they had acted otherwise. What if Edith Roosevelt had refused to acknowledge White House mail directed to her and had not hired a secretary to handle it? What if she had confined herself to family matters and delegated all First Lady mail to her husband's staff? What if Helen Taft had not admitted to an important role in shaping her husband's career, keeping him off the Supreme Court until he had a chance to be president? What if Ellen Wilson had not used a deathbed wish to encourage passage of a slum clearance bill that carried her name? What if Edith Wilson had not controlled access to a sick president? What if she had failed to write her account of that period? The answer is that the job of First Lady would have retained its nineteenth-century character rather than taking on the marks of the twentieth.

6

The Paradoxical 1920s

THE MOST POPULAR BOOK on the 1920s emphasizes enormous contradictions in the American scene. At the same time that individuals experienced great strides in their personal lives, the nation took one giant step backward into "normalcy." A country tired of sacrificing for war and weary of high-minded slogans about "making the world safe for democracy" reverted to old ways that emphasized personal comfort and national isolation.[1]

Nowhere is the contradiction more apparent than in accounts of women's lives. The view of the 1920s as "roaring" gives only half the picture. It is true that contraception and cosmetics became more available and acceptable; Freud and flapper fashions offered new freedoms. Electric appliances promised to diminish the time required for housework (if standards of acceptable cleanliness did not rise concurrently) and old barriers that had stood between the sexes, in matters such as smoking in public, dropped. Women increased their percentage of the labor force, and 450,000 of the new jobs were in the professions.[2]

But the decade had a less exuberant side, one that showed disillusionment and restraint. Some women approached their new opportunities with suspicion, while others refused to change or did so only reluctantly. Reliable contraception information and equipment did not reach all women who would have used it, and only a small percentage of women eligible went out to vote in 1920.[3] The number of female physicians actually declined in the decade as did women's share of college enrollment, and three out of every four women who earned college degrees went into fields commonly considered "women's work"—teaching and nursing.[4]

This paradox of apparent freedom circumscribed by old, strong traditions shows up in the lives of the three First Ladies of the 1920s.

Warren Harding's landslide victory over James Cox in 1920 brought into the White House Florence Kling Harding, considerably more conscious of the value of good public relations than any of her predecessors but, at the same time, extremely narrow in her outlook. At Warren Harding's death in 1923, charming Grace Goodhue Coolidge captured the nation's attention. With her dropped waistlines and raised hemlines, she epitomized current flapper style. Not until she had left Washington did she reveal her considerably more serious side in the poetry she published. After Calvin Coolidge chose "not to run" in 1928, an erudite, well-traveled Lou Henry Hoover became First Lady, and for all her demurrals about merely "forming a backdrop for Bertie,"[5] she gave some remarkably feminist speeches. All three of the presidents' wives who moved into the White House in the 1920s sought to present themselves—their educations, marital arrangements, participation in their husbands' careers, and views on women's roles—in ways that reflected contemporary standards without offending those whose views remained less modern. Together they set the stage for many of the innovations for which Eleanor Roosevelt gained credit in the 1930s and 1940s.

None of the three was young by the time her husband took the presidential oath. Florence Kling Harding, at sixty-one, was the oldest woman yet to assume the job of First Lady. She made a point, however, of appearing energetic and youthful, and in the 1920 campaign, she seemed every bit as up-to-date as the twenty-nine-year-old wife of Warren's Democratic opponent. Both major parties had looked to pivotal Ohio for names to head their tickets that year and both had settled on former newspapermen who had moved on to politics, James M. Cox to the governor's seat and Warren Harding to the U.S. Senate. The men's parallel careers had not, however, included similar wives.

In a campaign interview with a New York reporter, James Cox's young wife sounded as sweet and docile as an antebellum matron, concerned only about her children and the "price to pay" if her husband won the 1920 election. Florence Harding at least appeared more in control of her life as she insisted that victory would not affect her marriage (which was later rumored to have contained a great deal of discord) and that nothing could "disturb our serenity and happiness." Margaret Blair Cox, who had graduated from an elite eastern girls' school, described her interest in gardening and canning while Florence ignored the domestic side of her life and stressed her part in her husband's career. "Some people in Ohio will tell you she is the better politician of the two," the reporter Ann O'Hagan wrote, adding that even Warren admitted that his automobile was the only thing he possessed that "Florence did not have a desire to run."[6]

The new acceptability of cosmetics assisted Florence considerably in her determination to appear young and vigorous. Married for almost thirty years to a man five years her junior, she had grown adept at camouflaging the difference, and even her enemies agreed that she usually succeeded in looking younger than her years. She employed lace inserts and wide velvet ribbons, often studded with a bauble, to cover neck wrinkles. Instead of accepting the comfort of flat shoes, she wedged her feet into the then fashionable pointed toes with tooth-pick heels. Daily appointments with a hairdresser kept every gray hair marcelled tightly in place, and liberal applications of rouge suggested, at least from a distance, the rosy glow of youth.

The 1920s rewarded a different kind of youthfulness than had been the vogue in the first half of the nineteenth century. Instead of the innocent, ingénue stance of the antebellum period, the preferred model in the 1920s suggested adventure, glamor, and sophistication. Movie stars and aviators had replaced sober reformers as the "most admired women in America,"[7] and all three of the 1920s First Ladies reflected that change. Even the scholarly Lou Hoover released a formal photograph of herself, swathed in white fur and peeking almost flirtatiously from behind a fan.[8] Florence Harding's wardrobe of plumed hats and pearl-studded satin gowns could have competed with those of a Hollywood starlet.[9]

By far the most successful of the three in conveying energy and glamor was the youngest, Grace Coolidge, who at forty-four showed some of the fun-loving rebelliousness for which she had been known in her teens. A sorority member at the University of Vermont, enthusiastic dancer, and Boston Red Sox fan, she was among the first to arrive at parties and the last to leave. She longed to try whatever was new, from smoking a cigarette to bobbing her hair and traveling in an airplane. That she recognized her marriage to a successful politician limited her opportunities is clear from a statement she made soon after moving into the White House. "Being wife to a government worker," she wrote, "is a very confining position."[10]

Grace's description of herself should not obscure the fact that, unlike any of her predecessors, she had attended a coeducational university and prepared for a career of her own. Although Lucy Hayes (1877–1881) is often credited with being the first president's wife to have graduated from college, hers was a women's academy that did not offer the same curriculum that would have been offered to men students. Grace Coolidge earned a bachelor's degree at the University of Vermont and then went on for additional training so that she could teach the deaf. Many nineteenth-century presidents' wives had taught school, but only temporarily, in order to earn some money and perhaps put some distance between themselves and their parents. Their letters convey little sense of education as a career or lifelong interest. Grace Coolidge worked only three years between her college graduation in 1902 and her marriage in 1905, but she maintained a permanent interest in training the deaf. After her husband's political career ended, she served on several boards and committees dedicated to improving conditions for the hearing-impaired.

Lou Henry Hoover's degree in geology also came from a coeducational university, Stanford, where she studied with the same professors who had taught her husband. Of the three, only Florence Harding followed a traditional woman's course of study, but her training at the Cincinnati Conservatory of Music equipped her for the time when she had to support herself and young son. Any American young woman searching for a model in the 1920s had three examples of presidents' wives who had prepared to take care of themselves. That each chose to join forces with a politically ambitious husband is another matter.

Divorce statistics suggest that Americans ended their marriages in the "roaring twenties" more often than in any preceding decade,[11] and here, too, examples stood at the top of political life. Short-memoried reporters, who seemed to imply in 1952 and 1956 that Adlai Stevenson was the first divorced man to win the presidential nomination of a major party, would have profited from a close look at the 1920 election. Both Florence Harding, whose husband headed the Republican ticket, and James Cox, the Democratic hopeful, had been divorced from their previous spouses. Florence had sued her first husband for desertion in the 1880s, and Cox had split with the mother of his three children in 1911.[12] Neither breakup received much attention in the 1920 campaign, however, perhaps because each side considered restraint advisable in light of its own vulnerability.[13] The divorces may have seemed irrelevant since both had occurred well in the past and, at the time of the campaign, all the principals had either remarried or died. A prominent woman journalist, who interviewed both candidates' wives for an article in a popular magazine, wrote the entire piece without mentioning either divorce.[14]

By the time she became First Lady, Florence Harding had been married to Warren for nearly thirty years—time in which she had shown two powerful traits which her enemies and supporters agreed she excelled in: willfulness and determination. While still enrolled in the Cincinnati Conservatory, her energies had turned more to play than to the piano, and she had joined in with a hometown group of young people known as the "rough set" because they took up among other sports the new fad of roller-skating. One of their number, Henry A. De Wolfe, was particularly attractive to her, perhaps because her father detested his heavy drinking and playboy attitude. When Amos Kling, Florence's father, forbade her seeing Henry, she promptly married him and six months later gave birth to a son.[15]

The young couple's attempt to run a roller-skating rink in nearby Galion failed, and Henry quickly tired of the responsibilities attached to being head of a family. Before their son had reached two years of age, he deserted Florence who had little choice but to return to Marion. The story persisted for years that she had taken her son and slept in an abandoned house the first night back rather than humble herself by appealing to her father for help.[16] Her in-laws supplied some money; Florence gave piano lessons; and eventually her father came to her rescue, but she had learned an important lesson about the costliness of dependence and never allowed herself to become quite so defenseless again. After her divorce, she let her father adopt and raise her son while she set out to try again.

In a city of 4,000 people, an ambitious young piano teacher could not have remained long unaware of the charming, handsome newcomer who had just bought part ownership in one of Marion's newspapers. The publisher, Warren G. Harding, had a sister who studied piano with Florence, and soon teacher and newspaperman met. That Amos Kling vehemently opposed his daughter's having anything to do with Warren increased his attractiveness immensely.

By the 1880s the Hardings ranked below the Klings in Marion's hierarchy, although a few years earlier that would not have been the case. In 1860 when Florence was born, her family lived in an apartment over their hardware store, but circumstances changed as Amos Kling prospered in real estate and business. By the time Warren began to court Florence Kling, her father was one of the most important men in town. Warren's parents both practiced medicine and his mother later acquired midwife certification, but their specialty, homeopathy, paid none too well. Warren, who had prospered during his first few years with the *Marion Star*, had bought out his partners and built himself a handsome house on one of the town's best streets. Such considerations mattered far less to Amos Kling than the persistent rumor around town that Warren had Negro ancestry. Marion, Ohio, was not integrated in the 1880s, and racial prejudice was strong. In such a setting, the ancestry of a new, young man in town became the subject of considerable speculation. Some of the locals insisted they detected Negro features in Warren.

Continuing a long tradition, the future First Lady married against strenuous parental objection, and in this particular case, the objection remained so strong that Amos Kling did not speak to his daughter for seven years. The small ceremony at Warren's new house in 1891 united a divorcée, one week short of celebrating her thirty-first birthday, with a promising businessman, then twenty-five. Some of their friends detected a mother-son relationship in the match and they pointed out that Warren had always been very attentive to his mother, taking her fresh flowers every Sunday or, if he could not go, arranging for someone else to make the delivery. Now he transferred that filial devotion to his wife, making her his conscience, bookkeeper, and monitor. For the fun part of his life he evidently went elsewhere—at least two women friends left accounts of the time they spent with Warren, and his poker-playing friends supplied their own recollections of his participation in their games.[17]

Florence had her own reasons for entering the marriage—she came from the same generation that had produced many women who insisted on independence. Born in the same decade as First Ladies Helen Taft and Ellen Wilson, Florence Harding kept her rebellions closer home than they had—she married local young men whom her father detested and then worked hard to prove him wrong.

Florence devoted herself to Warren's career as though her own reputation were at stake. His mother, Phoebe Dickerson Harding, who was something of a career woman herself, had warned Florence to keep the icebox full and both eyes on Warren. Florence lost no time stopping at the *Star* office to see how the business—and Warren—operated. She remained for fourteen years, first streamlining the bookkeeping system and then organizing a home delivery service to boost circulation. One of the carriers whom she hired ran for president himself later, and he recalled how she had taken over the *Star*. "She was a woman of very narrow mentality and range of interest or understanding," Norman Thomas wrote, "but of strong will and within a certain area of genuine kindness. . . . It was her energy and her business sense which made the *Star*." According to Norman Thomas, Florence complemented her husband's enormous affability by overseeing the advertising and circulation while Warren supplied "the front . . . a joiner . . . popular."[18]

As for the other part of her mother-in-law's advice, Florence dutifully pedalled her bicycle home to cook Warren's dinner, but her domesticity did not extend to maternity. She showed little interest in the son from her first marriage, and by Warren she remained childless even though one of his women friends reported that he would have very much liked to have a child. It was "Florence [who] would not hear of it," he said, and he explained that she took "tiny white pills" to avoid conceiving.[19]

The control over her own life that had been so conspicuously absent from Florence's first marriage showed up in other ways in her second marriage. She involved herself in each of Warren's campaigns: from state senator he moved to lieutenant governor and then, after losing a bid for governor in 1910, to the United States Senate in 1915. In the early days, she accompanied him on the lecture tour, impressing some of his managers as "meanly accurate in calculating expenses."[20] By the time Florence arrived in Washington, one politically active woman observed in her a "ruthless ambition to become First Lady" as she "constantly worked and made Warren work toward that end."[21] Florence once confided to Norman Thomas's wife that Warren got into a lot of trouble when she was not around so she limited those opportunities whenever possible. During his Senate days, she encouraged him to give his interviews at home so that she could participate, and she kept up with the issues so that eventually Warren's campaign manager pronounced her "one of the best informed women in the country."[22]

When, as the wife of an Ohio senator, Florence first arrived in Washington in 1915, she lacked the celebrity status that she might have liked. But she could prepare for success. Alice Roosevelt Longworth who, with her husband Nicholas, socialized with the Hardings in their Senate days, reported that Florence kept a little red book with the names of people she meant to get even with when she got the chance. In the meantime, the handsome senator from Ohio appeared on many guest lists and even Alice included him at her poker table. She waited until he was dead to write: "He was not a bad man, just a slob."[23]

Florence had spent too much time around the newspaper office to remain unaware of the value of good publicity, and she added some dash to her own image by associating with the capital's wealthy, risk-taking social leaders. One of Florence's closest friends became the legendary Evalyn Walsh McLean, when Evalyn was looking around for some "serious" cause to "save," as she put it, her husband, Edward, from "dissipation."[24] Dabbling in politics and associating with politicians would divert him, she thought, from his playboy ways. The daughter of an Irish immigrant who made his fortune in Colorado mining and then spent the remainder of his life enjoying the money and spoiling his children, Evalyn had married a man every bit as fun-loving as she. On their European honeymoon, $200,000 proved insufficient to pay the bills. Back in Washington he concentrated on running the *Washington Post*, which he owned, and she engineered a highly publicized social life for them and spent money as though it would never run out. On one shopping trip, conducted comfortably from her chauffeured Rolls Royce, she admitted to paying $5,000 for a St. Bernard dog for her daughter (although the girl had requested a poodle).[25] On another day, Evalyn purchased the famous Hope diamond, reputed to bring tragedy to whoever owned it, and then attempted to negate the curse by having a priest bless the gem.[26]

Such extravagance fascinated small-town Florence Harding, and Evalyn admitted that she grew fond of Florence, who could be haughty and nagging, "her mouth a revelation of discontent."[27] The unusual friendship between the two very different women continued until Florence's death. Evalyn, who rarely admitted to caring what anybody thought about her, confessed she was flattered to have an important politician's wife seek her advice.[28] Florence knew where to place herself when the cameras started rolling, but she knew where to draw the line, too, and on one occasion, when she feared being photographed beside a cigarette-smoking Evalyn, she knocked the offending article from her friend's mouth.

The careful housewife's dependence on the flamboyant Evalyn McLean represents one of several inconsistencies in Florence Harding's life. When Warren's name came up for consideration for president in the 1920 campaign, she intensely wanted the glory of victory but she feared the disastrous exposures that a national campaign could bring. Warren had already been linked romantically with at least two women, and one of them, a Marion housewife, had frequently vacationed with her husband and the Hardings. Because the woman's husband was in poor health, he removed himself from the scene for long recuperative jaunts to the West Coast, and Florence, who had had one kidney removed in 1905, was often ill. Their absences left their spouses considerable freedom, causing speculation in Marion about what they did in their time together.[29]

Warren Harding's other reported romance involved a much younger woman who had developed a crush on the senator while she was still a high school student and had first aroused Florence's suspicions. Nan Britton later published a book about her involvement with Warren Harding and thus became the first (but not the last) to divulge the details of her own sexual liaison with a president. Like her latter-day counterparts, Judith Exner (who publicized her relationship with

President John F. Kennedy)[30] and Kay Summersby (who described the time she spent with then-General Dwight Eisenhower during World War II), Britten waited until the other principal was dead before going public.[31]

Britten titled her account *The President's Daughter*, although at the time of her daughter's birth, Warren was still a senator. The book details how Warren helped young Britten move from Marion to New York City and find a job. On trips the two took together, Warren registered her in hotels as his niece. With that record and that visibility, her relationship with Warren could hardly have escaped sharp-eyed Florence or his colleagues, and Florence had good reason to fear the close scrutiny of a national campaign.

Even if fear of exposure of her husband's active extramarital sex life had not deterred Florence, she had other misgivings. While she would have liked to think that matters of life and death did not depend on such things as the stars, she could not free herself from the belief that they did. A medium whom she frequently consulted had predicted that Warren would win the presidency but that disaster would follow: Warren would die in office and Florence, soon afterward. When he won the nomination, Florence was widely quoted as saying she saw only tragedy in his future.[32]

Her own poor health also concerned Florence. Her one remaining kidney frequently became infected, swelling to several times its normal size and causing great pain. She had barely escaped death once when she had chosen to rely on her Marion homeopath rather than on other doctors who had advised surgery, and she understood that her luck might not hold the next time.

In spite of these misgivings, Florence put her best effort into getting Warren nominated and elected. Early in the primary campaign when his determination flagged, she stymied his attempt to drop out by seizing the telephone from him and shouting to his campaign manager on the other end that they were in the race until "hell freezes over."[33] When people came to Marion to assess the candidate, she was unfailingly courteous to all, smiling agreeably when they ran over the hedge and trampled the grass so thoroughly that the yard had to be graveled. On questions of politics she curbed her inclination to speak out and deferred to Warren, even though more than one of her friends thought she found it trying to learn at her age to appear submissive.

Florence held strong ideas about when to use the press and when to keep quiet. When a Wooster College professor published pamphlets outlining Warren's black ancestry, Warren and his campaign advisers were uncertain how to react. The candidate wanted to go public with the explanation he had already given his friends—that the story persisted because of his family's record of giving aid to slaves escaping on the underground railroad. Florence decreed otherwise and ordered a cancellation of the denial that Warren's staff had drafted.[34] Some charges, if treated as unworthy of response, would eventually die down, she reasoned, and no statement on the matter came out.

Warren Harding won the 1920 election (garnering sixteen million popular votes to Cox's nine million), and preparations began for an inaugural celebration to outshine all previous ones. Edward McLean, who headed the inaugural ball committee, planned a party that would combine, his wife wrote, "the liveliness of ten July fourth celebrations with the ending of a victorious war."[35] The Republican National Committee, having a more modest celebration in mind, balked at spending that kind of money and dropped sponsorship of the official inaugural ball so that the McLeans hosted their own party at their Friendship estate outside Washington.

The expensive, private initiation of the Harding administration set the tone for what followed, and the Hardings persisted in acting as though they operated above and apart from the rules governing other people. In spite of a constitutional amendment prohibiting the "manufacture, sale or transportation of intoxicating liquors" the Hardings kept a well-stocked bar in the private quarters of the White House. While official "dry" receptions were held downstairs, the president would be upstairs, Alice Roosevelt Longworth reported, surrounded by his friends and all brands of whisky, playing cards, and poker chips, thus presenting an atmosphere more appropriate to a saloon than to the residence of a head of state.[36] The First Lady was left to move between the two worlds, adding a touch of schoolteacher rectitude while keeping the drinks fresh.

In honing a public image as a nonimbiber, Florence reflected typical First Lady behavior, not restricted to the prohibition years. Until Betty Ford's post–White House confession that she was an alcoholic, presidents' wives regularly objected to accounts that they consumed alcoholic beverages and to photos showing them with drink in hand. The temperance movement itself rarely caught their fancy, however, and except for Lucy Hayes, no First Lady became an outspoken advocate of the cause.

To ensure the most favorable publicity possible, Florence carefully honed her relationship with reporters—the men became "my boys" to her and the women "the girls." One Washington veteran recalled that

Florence invited newspaperwomen to cruise down the Potomac with her on the presidential yacht and then startled the group by slapping one of them on the back and exclaiming, "Well here we are, all girls together."[37] She even invited women reporters to interview her and then, wearing a rose-colored negligee, she spoke with them in her bedroom.[38] Although Ohioan Jane Dixon of the *New York Telegram* was a personal favorite with Florence, she never showed her preferences and reporters responded by treating her well. Although some of them found her haughty,[39] much of what they wrote was not unflattering. Her claim that she gave them important, newsworthy information is difficult to substantiate because she said she asked them not to name her as a source, and none of them did.[40]

The intentional management of the press extended to virtually every area of Florence's life. Rather than divulge just how precarious her health was, she attributed frequent and sometimes lengthy absences to food poisoning, thus giving the public a picture of a much healthier First Lady than was actually fact. A life-threatening attack of nephritis, which she suffered in August 1922, was not reported for several weeks and then not in detail.[41] Her two grandchildren did not visit her in the White House so that photographers had no opportunity to catch her in grandmotherly poses that might focus attention on her age.[42] Mindful of the anti-German sentiment that lingered in America after World War I, Florence tailored her ancestors accordingly. Although a prominent historian has concluded that Florence was descended from German Mennonites,[43] she carefully credited her "French grandmother" with teaching her excellent posture and good taste in clothes.[44]

In spite of her expertise in public relations, Florence showed little skill at managing the White House. Nor did she seem to care. The 1920s did not place the same importance on domestic skills as had been the case at the turn of the century, and none of the First Ladies of the 1920s spent much time honing her domestic image. Florence had managed only modest-sized houses in Marion and Washington, and she lacked the preparation for taking on an establishment as large and complex as the executive mansion. On first meeting with its staff, she seemed unsure of herself, saying first that she would find a new housekeeper and then that she would retain the old one. Ex-president William Howard Taft, who stopped by the Harding White House to offer advice, judged her completely unprepared for that side of the job.[45] She did make one innovation in the staff, adding a Secret Service agent to the usual retinue of housekeepers, maids, and stewards, and then assigning him sundry tasks that had little or nothing to do with her safety. The surveillance that Eleanor Roosevelt so disliked began in the Harding administration when Florence decided she could use extra help to chauffeur her clairvoyant or keep watch on Warren.

Florence tempered her feminism so that it either fit accepted standards or remained very private. Photographers snapped her voting alongside Warren in November 1920,[46] but a surprisingly feminist letter that she composed in the White House remained unmailed. A woman had solicited Florence's views on careers for women, and the First Lady replied that one career was about all any couple could manage. "If the career is the husband's," Florence wrote in 1922, "the wife can merge her own with it, if it is to be the wife's as it undoubtedly will be in an increasing proportion of cases, then the husband may, with no sacrifice of self respect or of recognition by the community, permit himself to be the less prominent and distinguished member of the combination."[47]

In line with her view that the White House belonged to everybody, Florence worked hard to make it (and herself) available to visitors. One of the maids recalled how Florence would run down the steps to greet tourists,[48] and on New Year's Day she stood to shake hands with thousands of guests even though she needed two days in bed to store up strength for the ordeal and two days to recuperate.[49] Her prediction to Evalyn McLean that being First Lady meant "nothing but work, work, work"[50] proved accurate, and she insisted on expending considerable energy on the job, even when she was seriously ill.

In the end, the calculated secrecy that Florence used in dealing with the press worked against her. Neither she nor her husband (who had a long history of high blood pressure and symptoms of heart disease)[51] had supplied accurate health information, and the public had little preparation for their deaths. On the fatal western trip in the summer of 1923, Warren's doctor had issued a bulletin citing food poisoning resulting from eating bad crabs when in fact none had been consumed. When the president died on August 2, many people questioned the cause and some even suggested foul play with Florence as the culprit.[52]

The affable, charming man who had attracted Florence had continued to exert his strong magnetism all the way to the White House. He had himself noted a major personal weakness when he laughingly told a group of reporters that his father had been grateful Warren was not born a girl or he would have been "in the family way all the time." He could "not say no."[53] On the political level, this inordinate desire to please showed itself in a zigzag course of appointments and actions.

Although his cabinet included some of the best minds of the time, it also included some crooks, because Warren Harding had never learned to tell one from the other. One wag of the time had it that the difference between the first president and the current one was that while George Washington could not tell a lie, Warren Harding could not tell a liar.[54] The value of having the experienced Charles Evans Hughes as secretary of state and the hardworking Herbert Hoover as secretary of commerce was offset by two others who later went to prison: Albert Fall, secretary of interior, and Warren Harding's old friend, Attorney General Harry Daugherty.

The extent of scandal in President Harding's administration had not yet become public when he died in August 1923, and his last recorded activity was listening to Florence read from the *Saturday Evening Post* a glowing account of his presidency. The train carrying his body across the country for burial passed the largest crowds seen since Abraham Lincoln's death, with a million and a half people gathering in Chicago alone to pay their respects.[55]

Florence made the cross-country trip with her husband's corpse, attended memorial services in the capital, and then traveled to Ohio for the burial. It was during the stop at the White House that she made her famous nocturnal visit to the president's bier. Evalyn McLean, who had stayed with her friend, reported that Florence had gone down in the middle of the night to the coffin in the East Room and had stood for a long time talking to it. She sounded more like a mother addressing a dead child when she finished: "They can't hurt you now."[56]

With very little time to live, Florence stayed for a while at the Willard Hotel in Washington and then returned to Marion. She had neither forgotten nor discounted the fortune-teller's prediction about her own death and she recognized the signs of further deterioration in her health. Her trusted homeopath died in the summer of 1924, and the following September, when Evalyn McLean came through Ohio in her private railroad car, Florence announced that this would be their last visit. Weeks later, fifteen months after Warren's death, she was dead.

The sum of Florence Kling Harding's influence on her husband's political career remains difficult to assess, partly because she destroyed much of the physical evidence that could have helped define it. Of the 350,000 documents that survive of the Harding administration, few relate to her political views or activities although hundreds of thank-you notes addressed to her suggest that she was not idle. She contributed to the enigma of her role by juxtaposing strong and blatant claims of her own power alongside demure self-effacement. She smiled obligingly when her husband's friends called her "Duchess" in a not altogether complimentary tone. She seems to have held strong opinions and expressed them freely. Some historians who have evaluated the evidence have concluded that Florence's influence on her husband has been exaggerated, but most of her contemporaries insisted it was real, and many of them offered specific instances to support that point of view.

Harry Daugherty, the campaign manager who later served in the Harding cabinet, reported being summoned to the White House one evening to referee an argument between the Hardings on the wording of a presidential address. In the end, Florence got her way.[57] Secretary of State Hughes called Florence "her husband's most faithful counselor."[58]

Nicholas Murray Butler, a guest at the White House during a discussion about accepting a mansion as a residence for the vice president, reported that it was Florence Harding who applied the veto. Senator John Henderson's widow had offered to donate her house on Sixteenth Street for the use of the vice president, but Florence Harding would not hear of accepting the gift. "Not a bit of it," she fumed, according to Butler, "I am going to have that bill defeated. Do you think I am going to have those Coolidges living in a house like that? A hotel apartment is plenty good enough for them."[59] Whatever the reasons, Congress turned down the gift and the vice president remained without a permanent official residence for forty more years.

To the widespread view that politicians' wives should form a social backdrop, Florence Kling Harding, as she always signed herself, offered a notable exception. Early in her White House tenure, she had reportedly inquired of a senator whom he judged the most successful First Lady in history. When he replied, "Dolley Madison or Frances Cleveland," Florence Harding retorted, in what might be considered a slogan of her mature years: "Watch me!"[60] She only partly concealed her partnership in her husband's political decisions and yet she received little of the criticism leveled at her predecessor, Edith Wilson. For a woman whose husband admitted her influence, she died popular with the nation, although not with those who worked closely with her. Few of the Hardings' friends would contest the view that she imposed a strong discipline on herself and that she showed exceptional determination throughout her life.

Unfortunately, the "narrow mentality" that Norman Thomas had identified years earlier prepared her poorly for strong leadership. Her tendency to judge issues in terms of the people involved and how they treated her was also a fault. Poorly educated in matters of government but richly endowed with ambition, she determined, like many women of her generation, to hitch her own career to her husband's because the time had not yet come, as she predicted it would, when a couple might profitably choose to put their combined energies into the wife's career.

No one ever accused Grace Goodhue Coolidge, who followed Florence Harding into the White House, of exerting influence on her husband's political decisions. Not long after her marriage, she had prepared to go hear her husband speak but he had stopped her with a laconic "Better not," and that separation between politics and family continued for the rest of their time together. While he progressed from state representative to mayor of Northampton, then state senator, lieutenant governor and governor of Massachusetts, Grace and her two sons remained in half of a house they rented in Northampton. After his work took him to Boston, Calvin commuted home on weekends. "I knew nothing of the conducting of [political] affairs," Grace later wrote, "considering that they lay outside my province. If I had manifested any particular interest, I feel sure that I should have been put properly in my place."[61]

Calvin Coolidge had made clear his contempt for his wife's general education when, early in their marriage, he quizzed her on Martin Luther and her answers did not satisfy him.[62] He gave no indication that he ever consulted her on any important question. She had to learn from friends of his decision not to run in 1928 because he had not bothered to tell her. By her own admission, her monthly meetings with wives of cabinet members did not go beyond social schedules and the "insoluble problems which have confronted Cabinet hostesses since Martha Washington's day."[63]

It would be wrong, however, to conclude that Grace played no part in Calvin's success. He had announced that "the business of America is business," and he proceeded to act as though government were an arm of business. In his appointments and in his actions on tax and tariff matters, he paid careful attention to the needs of the business community. Having a wife who did not divulge her opinions on any important matter fitted in with his image of the president as corporate head.

But she was hardly inconspicuous, and Calvin profited from her visibility. For a politician who found it very difficult to show interest in the people around him, having a wife who charmed everyone she met was a decided advantage. Grace was frequently photographed hugging children or playing with her pet racoon or her dog, Rob Roy. Florence Harriman, who was acquainted with several presidents, pronounced Grace's "vivacity and savoir faire . . . the administration's greatest success."[64] Grace characterized her role as Calvin's "safety valve."[65] A 1926 *New Yorker* profile described her as his "psychological frame" and after offering the supreme accolade—a comparison with Dolley Madison—concluded: "Few White House chatelaines have been so genuinely popular in Washington."[66] *Good Housekeeping* included Grace on its list of most admired women, the only one without a profession of her own, and the *Pictorial Review* praised her for complementing her husband's personality and giving him "the light touch."[67]

Visitors to the White House who had a chance to see Grace Coolidge in action reinforced this view with their own stories. When their son John brought his fiancée to dinner, she was noticeably nervous and, although the daughter of a governor and accustomed to meeting important people, she could not quite manage her plate of fish. A large piece plopped on her lap. The president broke the ensuing silence with his New England twang: "Miss Connecticut has spilled on her lovely gown," and it remained for a thoughtful First Lady to provide the talcum powder.[68]

At official receptions, the president curtly nodded to people and quickly passed from one obligatory handshake to the next while Grace's exceptional memory for names and her genuine concern for guests' comfort made them feel at ease. People meeting her for the first time reported they liked her immediately. A tourist who managed to get an invitation to one of the twice-weekly receptions confessed that she felt awkward and feared she would do something wrong, but the president's wife assured her that would only make her more interesting.

The sharp contrast between charming Grace Coolidge and taciturn Calvin mystified many of their closest friends. The only child of a Vermont engineer and his wife, Grace showed such irrepressible humor and outgoing personality all the way through the local schools and the state university that nobody, least of all her mother, could see what attracted her to the rather eccentric lawyer whom she married. Not long after their wedding, the Coolidges attended his tenth reunion of the Amherst Class of '95, and another young wife remarked to her husband that she could not see "how that sulky, red-haired little man ever won that pretty, charming woman." Dwight Morrow, whose wife had made the comment, offered his own opinion that they would all hear one day from the sulky little man, and his wife replied, "Yes, but through [Grace]."[69] Like many First Ladies, Grace apparently recognized somewhat sooner than others the potential for success in the man she married.

Many stories emphasize the impish sense of humor that Grace and Calvin Coolidge shared, and that trait may explain their attraction to each other more than any other. That they perceived incongruity and humor in diverse ways increased the magnetism. She had been watering flowers at Clarke Institute for the deaf where she taught when she happened to look up one morning and see a man shaving himself near the window.[70] What drew Grace's attention was the felt hat he had planted firmly on his head when his only other garments were his underwear. Grace laughed so loudly that he noticed her and very soon he arranged a meeting to explain to the slim, dark haired teacher that he anchored the hat on his dampened hair in order to help control an unruly lock of hair.

Although Calvin's taciturnity is well established, evidence that he possessed a sense of humor is less easily assembled. Yet Will Rogers, who should have known, applauded the Vermonter's joviality but pronounced it too subtle for most people to appreciate. Calvin never played for the big laugh but rather for the slow, long reaction, Rogers pointed out, and he offered this example to illustrate his point. Once Rogers had invited the president to hear him and then added, as an after-thought, that an excellent quartet would be singing too. Calvin Coolidge, who had sat silently through the invitation, perked up at the mention of music and said, "Yes, I like singing."[71]

About his wife's cooking, Calvin Coolidge was merciless. He delighted in dropping one of her freshly baked biscuits on the floor and stomping his foot loudly at the same time to emphasize its lack of delicacy, and he suggested that her pie crust recipe should go to the road commissioner as a substitute for the paving material currently used. Grace, who had no illusions about her ability as a cook, took this as well as his other ego-deflaters in the same imperturbable way. Sometimes she came back with some of her own, frequently zeroing in on his reputation as a man of few words. On one of their weekend cruises on the Potomac, Calvin had sat silently through an entire meal without so much as acknowledging the two women seated beside him. The next morning, one of the women entered the dining room as Calvin was inquiring of Grace where the two guests were and heard Grace explain that they were resting because they had been "exhausted by your conversation last evening."[72] Calvin's refusal to say very much led to many stories, including one about two men discussing the Coolidges. The first man pointed out that Grace had taught the deaf to speak, and the second responded, "So why didn't she teach Cal?"[73]

Grace Coolidge appeared to accept with equanimity this quirk in her husband as well as his frugality, which she had encountered very early in her marriage. When they returned from a one-week honeymoon in Montreal, cut short so Calvin could campaign for election to the local school board, they moved into a hotel suite in Northampton, Massachusetts. A few months later, they rented the quarters which they continued to occupy until Calvin won national office. When the local hotel went out of business, the Coolidges purchased the supplies so that for years their linens and silverware carried the marking "Norwood Hotel."[74] Grace told the joke on herself of how Calvin, soon after their marriage, had presented her with socks to be darned. Since there were fifty-two pairs of them, she decided that he must have been saving them for some time, and she inquired if that was the reason he had married her. "No," he had answered, "but I find it mighty handy."[75]

On only one subject did Calvin forget his frugality. In purchasing clothing for Grace, he could be extravagant. Nothing was too good for her. When he saw a particularly striking dress or hat, he brought it home for her to try and she cooperated by wearing his selections even when her friends pronounced the colors too flamboyant or the styles inappropriate. While he was still a struggling lawyer, saving postage costs by sending his secretary out on foot to deliver bills, he paid $19.98 for a rose picture hat for Grace and no one recalled his regretting the expenditure.[76] In the White House, he pouted if she wore the same gown twice, causing her secretary to conclude that she had never seen a man who took more interest in his wife's clothes than did Calvin Coolidge.[77]

Grace's natural dignity and determination to remain just what she was earned her the praise and the satisfaction that no clothing extravagance could have matched. She arrived in Washington, conspicuous as the wife of the vice president, but with little experience outside small towns. Rather than try to compete with other, more sophisticated women, she relaxed in what she was, and later confessed that she could not remember a single embarrassing moment. She recalled that at her first big party, she had stood in a "simple gown by a village dressmaker" and received guests alongside the hostess "resplendent in a gorgeous creation of brocaded white satin by Worth. . . . It was all very gay and I had a wonderful time."[78]

Grace Coolidge's ingenuousness was as complete as Florence Harding's artifice and stood her well in the paradoxical 1920s. Rather than making her seem stupid, her casualness appeared refreshing to Washingtonians accustomed to formality and pretentiousness in First

Ladies. As wife of the vice president, Grace presided capably over meetings of Senate wives but she rarely missed a chance to play the comic. On one occasion when someone stood up to thank her for providing ham and potatoes, she banged a fork on the table and reminded the group: "Don't forget I brought a cake too."[79]

Although Calvin Coolidge permitted his wife to give no interviews while she was in the White House, her exuberance generated so many stories that the public felt an acquaintance with her as with few other First Ladies. On shopping trips to the local department stores, she was often recognized. When a salesclerk remarked on her resemblance to the First Lady and suggested that she must often be mistaken for her, Grace murmured, "Sometimes I am," and continued her shopping.[80]

Her husband laid down strict rules for Grace's White House tenure, and she followed them in the manner of an obedient child. Once when she had decided that the White House stables provided an excellent opportunity, she secretly outfitted herself and went out with a riding instructor. The next day Washington papers carried prominent headlines: "Mrs. Coolidge Learns to Ride." At breakfast the president read the item and then turned to his wife: "I think," he said, "you will find that you will get along at this job fully as well if you do not try anything new."[81]

That dictum continued to limit her activities for the rest of her husband's term. When she appeared one day in a stylish culotte outfit, Calvin suggested that none of the Coolidges had ever worn anything like that and she returned it. He bragged that no photographer had ever caught him with a cigar in his mouth, although he chewed one frequently, and she carefully confined her smoking to private places.[82] On one of the rare occasions when Grace found herself out dancing and having a good time at a party, someone volunteered, "I wish your husband could have been here." Grace replied quickly, "If he were, I wouldn't be."[83]

In explaining her White House years, Grace Coolidge projected the same detachment that later characterized Eleanor Roosevelt's statements. Grace wrote, "This was I and yet not I—this was the wife of the President of the United States and she took precedence over me; my personal likes and dislikes must be subordinated to the consideration of those things which were required of her."[84] Not until her husband's presidential term had ended would she express herself more fully.

The most extensive remodeling of the White House since the turn of the century was done during the Coolidge administration but Grace had little choice in undertaking her part in it. The Office of Public

Parks and Buildings had informed the Coolidges in 1923 that the mansion had deteriorated badly and needed extensive renovation, but work did not begin until early 1927.[85] The president's family moved to a house on Dupont Circle and then took an extended summer vacation in South Dakota. When Grace returned to Washington, she obtained Congress's permission to accept period pieces to furnish the White House, but Americans were not in a generous mood and few gifts arrived. Her own offering was a coverlet which she had crocheted, one small square per month, for the Lincoln bedroom.

The Coolidge sons, John (born 1906) and Calvin, Jr. (born 1908), absorbed some of Grace's view that politicians' families should remain in the background. When Calvin, Jr., received a letter addressed to "First Boy of the Land," he responded: "You are mistaken in calling me the First Boy of the Land since I have done nothing. It is my father who is President. Rather the First Boy of the Land would be some boy who had distinguished himself through his own actions."[86]

This particular anecdote was recalled by Grace Coolidge after Calvin, Jr.'s death. In the summer of 1924 when his father was about to be nominated to run for a term of his own, Calvin, Jr., got a blister on his toe. He left it unattended, developed blood poisoning, and died within days. Whatever ideas the Coolidges had about preserving privacy in the White House, this tragedy thrust them even more into the national spotlight, and hundreds of thousands of messages poured into Washington. The president's wife wore black and tempered her usual gaiety, but she resumed a full schedule within weeks.

A woman with Grace's spirit might have brought a new dimension to the job of president's wife but she chose to accede to the wishes of her husband and limit her activities to those her predecessors had made traditional—working with the Girl Scouts and giving receptions. When prevailed upon to give a speech, she injected a note of humor by using sign language which she had learned in her work with the deaf, a language which no one else in the room understood. She remained the most uncontrolling of individuals, never seeming to mind how many guests showed up unannounced for lunch or when she would learn what Calvin expected of her next. When White House staff inquired about her travel plans, she frequently replied that they should inform her as soon as they learned the answer from the president.

If observers perceived her as mysterious, they were mistaken—she simply waited until she left the White House to "come back to myself."[87] In 1930, the year after Calvin's term in Washington ended, she published a poem, "Watch Fires" which began:[88]

Love was not given the human heart
  for careless dealing.
Its spark was lit that man might know
  Divine revealing.

After her husband's death in 1933, Grace gave interviews and published an article, "The Real Calvin Coolidge" in which she revealed a
great deal about herself. In the nearly quarter of a century that she
survived her husband, she matured beyond the childlike woman who
had been First Lady and began to speak out on such issues as early intervention in World War II. She sold the house she had shared with
Calvin (and the furniture in it), toured Europe, and then went to live
with a friend in Northampton. When the WAVES came to train at Smith
College, she offered them the use of her house.[89] Her work to win
better education for the deaf continued until her death in July 1957.

Calvin's choice of a political career almost certainly limited his wife's
actions. Her writing and other activities after his death indicate that she
might have thought more than people gave her credit for, but she kept
well within the traditional boundaries that Calvin had set. What she
might have done in other circumstances, without the constraints imposed
by marriage to the president, remains unknowable, but she herself
related an anecdote which lends interest to the question. A painter came
to the White House to do her portrait, in which he rendered her uncharacteristically solemn. When Grace's son asked why, the painter replied:
"Because I once saw in your mother's face a look of resignation."[90]

That kind of acceptance is not apparent in portraits of Lou Henry
Hoover, who replaced Grace Coolidge in the White House in 1929;
and in other ways, the two women differed. Rather than reflect the
comic-serious split of Grace Coolidge, Lou Hoover showed many of the
same contradictions that marked interpretations of Herbert Hoover's
record.[91] Historians have continued to debate whether President
Hoover remained stubbornly tied to the past in evaluating possible
solutions for the Great Depression or anticipated many of Franklin
Roosevelt's answers. Did those four years under Herbert Hoover show
excessive reliance on volunteerism to end hardship or did they introduce a steady increase in the role of centralized government? Was
Herbert Hoover efficiently hardnosed or was he deeply involved in
and responsive to people's suffering? Lou Hoover's record remains
just as paradoxical, because in many ways she helped make way for an
activist and modern First Lady while remaining, herself, very much a
retiring gentlewoman of the nineteenth century.

Undoubtedly, the Hoover presidency suffered from the economic problems well advanced (but little recognized) before he took office. Descent into serious depression came rapidly. Although the Hoovers moved into the White House in March 1929, confident and optimistic about their chances for success, the president lost his halo within months. The stock market crash in October 1929, multiple business failures, and rising unemployment all added to his problems. Before his term ended, the Bureau of Labor Statistics would report that one in four Americans was jobless, lending credence to the judgment that this was the most devastating depression in the country's history. While its causes were numerous, its solution appeared unclear, and the president reluctantly reexamined his own views about the role of government.

"It is not the function of government," he liked to say, "to relieve individuals of their responsibilities to their neighbors or relieve institutions of their responsibilities to the public,"[92] but in his first year in office he set up the Federal Farm Board with half a billion dollars at its disposal to assist farmers with their surpluses. Later he approved creation of the Reconstruction Finance Corporation to lend money to banks and businesses. When asked about her own interests and accomplishments, Lou's pronouncements were just as puzzling and incomplete: "My chief hobbies are my husband and my children," she explained in 1921,[93] failing to note that she had given speeches on two continents in behalf of a long list of causes and that her translation into English of a Latin mining text had won an important professional award.

The remarkably parallel lives of Lou Henry and Herbert Hoover began the same year (1874) in small Iowa towns less than one hundred miles apart but did not intersect until twenty years later when they met in California. Lou's youthful interests had run closer to those of boys than of most girls. With only one sister, eight years younger than she, and a sickly mother, Lou's energy drew her to her father who introduced her to the pleasures of camping, horseback riding, and hiking. When time came for college, she chose first a normal school that boasted "the best gymnasium west of the Mississippi"[94] and then switched to a teacher's college from which she earned a certificate in 1893. Neither of those schools nor a clerking job in her father's bank satisfied Lou, and not until she had a chance encounter with geology did she find her direction. A public lecture by a Stanford professor led her to enroll in the university as the only woman majoring in geology.

Herbert Hoover's route to the same department in the same university had been more direct, and during Lou's freshman term, he was already a senior. Shy and awkward, he had a reputation as a minor campus leader—a reputation resulting more from diligence than from charisma. That tenacity paid off when he looked for employment. He started out at the Reward Mine Company in Nevada City, California, pushing a cart for $2.00 a day, ten hours a day, seven days a week, but never felt, he later wrote, "like a downtrodden wage slave."[95] Perhaps he understood, even at twenty-one, that his Stanford degree would soon separate him from his co-workers who were mostly unschooled foreigners. Carefully saving some of his earnings, he returned to San Francisco and took an office job where he surprised his employers by demonstrating modest typing skills. When an offer came to supervise an Australian mine for $600 a month, he took it, and by the time he was twenty-four, he was earning, by his own calculation, about $40,000 a year.[96]

Lou Henry learned that a Stanford degree in geology, when earned by a woman, got fewer job offers, and she taught school for a few months before Herbert wired his proposal from Australia. He wanted to accept an invitation to head China's mine program if she would go along as his wife. Almost from their first meeting, the Hoover partnership had a particularly international and ecumenical quality. In order to catch a ship for China the next day, they rushed their marriage ceremony, and because they could locate neither a Quaker minister (Herbert's religion) nor an Episcopalian (Lou's faith), they settled for a civil ceremony performed by a family friend who happened to be a Catholic priest.[97] With little time to pack for their honeymoon, they filled their suitcases with books on Chinese history and culture, so that they had plenty to read on the long trip to Tientsin.

Within months of arriving in China, the Hoovers found themselves in the middle of an attack, supported by the dowager Empress Tzu Hsi, to rid the country of all foreigners. In late 1899, a secret society, called I Ho Chuan [literally, The Harmonious Fists but always referred to by Westerners as the "Boxers"], began to launch violent attacks on the parts of the international community that had an influence on the local economy and culture, such as railroad construction, missionary work, and mining. The Hoovers quickly decided that expeditions into the country's interior were too perilous for Lou, although she had originally intended to go, and by June 1900, Herbert called in all his workers.

To protect themselves, Tientsin's foreigners barricaded themselves in their homes along the edge of the city behind a wall fashioned out of bags of sugar and grain. Then they watched their numbers multiply as Chinese nationals, who had aligned with outsiders by converting to

Christianity or taking jobs with international companies, asked for refuge. Supplies became scarce as days stretched into weeks. A herd of dairy cattle furnished milk and meat, but the closest water source lay outside the barricade and residents had to sneak out at night with buckets. With only two physicians to tend the wounded, Lou Hoover volunteered to help, even though that required dodging bullets to ride her bicycle to the makeshift hospital.[98]

Because their own house at the edge of the settlement seemed particularly vulnerable, the Hoovers moved to a friend's residence at the center of the compound but then returned just before their area came under attack. An American journalist, who had taken refuge in the Hoovers' house, told how Lou had run to the door at the first shelling to see where it had hit. A big hole in the backyard told her the answer. Expecting other shellings to follow, she sat down in the living room and dealt herself a game of solitaire. Even though a Japanese soldier in front of her house was blown to bits and the post of the stairway behind her splintered, she continued turning over the cards.[99]

Although she lived in Tientsin for less than two years, Lou developed a lifelong interest in China, particularly in porcelains of the Ming and K'ang Hsi periods. She added Mandarin to the other languages she spoke fluently—an achievement her husband never matched—and after they left China she kept his very limited Chinese vocabulary usable by relying on Mandarin whenever she needed to communicate privately with him in the presence of others.

With their usefulness in China ended, the Hoovers moved to London, the world's mining capital during what Herbert called "the golden age of mining." Herbert became a partner in Bewick, Moreing and Company and until 1908, when the partnership ended, their "Red Roof" house served as home base for their family and as a gathering place for London's foreign community. Herbert had undergone no social metamorphosis since college. Conversational awkwardness still marked him in all discussions but those of mining—one woman described him as "the rudest man in London"[100]—but his wife's charm compensated and drew guests to their table.

Lou's balancing of household management and travel in the first decade of her marriage invites comparison with Louisa Adams a century earlier. When two sons were born to the Hoovers (1903 and 1907), Lou took them on the road almost immediately: Herbert, Jr., left London to go to Australia when he was five weeks old and his brother, Allan, began his first trip to Burma at the same young age. The parents, after circling the globe more than once with their sons, insisted that infants traveled more easily than adults. After 1908, the family moved less, but Herbert still ran mining consulting offices around the world from San Francisco to Petrograd. In one year (1910) his wife and sons joined him in the British Isles, France, Russia, Burma, Korea, and Japan.[101]

While her children were still toddlers, Lou Hoover undertook her one enduring intellectual achievement—the translation into English of a sixteenth-century text on metals. *Agricola's De Re Metallica* offered a significant challenge because its German author, George Bauer, had coined some of the terms when he published the work in Latin in 1556. Finding English equivalents required extensive knowledge of both science and language—an unlikely combination in one person, as reviewers pointed out when the Hoovers finally finished the task after five years.[102] When the work was privately printed in 1912, with both Hoovers sharing equal billing in its translation, it won the Mining and Metallurgical Society's gold award and considerable attention from the scholarly community.[103]

When war broke out in Europe in the summer of 1914, the Hoovers were in London preparing to return to California, but Herbert delayed his trip to assist stranded Americans find sailings home.[104] Just a week before he was finally scheduled to leave, he undertook the job of overseeing food distribution to Belgium and northern France. Under German occupation, most Belgian cities were near starvation, and farmers, who made up only about one-fifth of the population, fared almost as poorly. Herbert Hoover accepted the job without pay, a generosity he could well afford, because, as he later wrote, "My aggregate income from professional activities in various countries probably exceeded that of any other American engineer."[105] In any case, he did not expect the job to last long. The knowledge that it would extend to "four years . . . a billion dollars, [and] five million tons of concentrated food . . . was mercifully hidden from us," he wrote after the war was over.[106]

While her husband earned a reputation as an efficient food administrator in Europe, Lou Hoover traveled with less fanfare back and forth between England and the United States. In London she worked with the American Women's Committee to set up canteens, maintain a war hospital, and operate a fleet of Red Cross ambulances.[107] She even helped start a knitting factory to assist unemployed women.[108] In the United States, she gave speeches to attract money for her European activities, raising $100,000 in the San Francisco Bay area alone.[109] At the invitation of the Stanford faculty, she spoke to them about unrestricted German submarine warfare.[110]

When the United States entered the war in the spring of 1917, Herbert returned to Washington to serve as Food Administrator, and Lou complemented his role by publicizing strategies for food conservation. She invited reporters into her home to show how she achieved "wheatless and meatless days" and cut sugar consumption below the suggested limits. The same woman who would later cringe and refuse when reporters sought interviews with her in the White House allowed the *Ladies' Home Journal* to publish "Dining with the Hoovers" in March 1918 and include information on what she fed her family.[111] Besides acting the part of public model housewife, Lou helped start a club, a cafeteria,[112] and a residence, all for young women who had come to Washington to work during the war.[113]

After 1921 when her husband entered President Harding's Cabinet as secretary of commerce, Lou Hoover continued her public, activist role. The time seemed right to finish what Elizabeth Monroe and Louisa Adams had begun a century earlier, and Lou resolved to stop the mindless "leaving of cards" that had been traditional for cabinet wives since the beginning of the republic. She "rebelled at spending four or five afternoons a week at this fruitless job," Herbert explained, and "secured an agreement among the Cabinet Ladies to an announcement that it would not be done any more." Herbert may have exaggerated Lou's role, but the visits ended.[114]

Nothing about Lou Hoover in the early 1920s suggests she would retreat from active leadership, especially of women and young people. In 1924, in the wake of revelations about the Teapot Dome scandal of the Harding administration, she called a special conference to emphasize women's responsibility to speak out on the dangers of dishonesty in government.[115] She persuaded the National Amateur Athletic Association, on whose board she served as the only woman, to form an advisory council of athletic directors to encourage physical education for women "in every institution" in the country.[116] When invited to speak to a convention of teenagers, she used the opportunity to exhort the girls to plan to combine marriage with a career, and she volunteered her own opinion that anyone who fell back on children as an excuse for not working outside the home was "lazy."[117]

Lou, who had started married life with a staff of six and worked her way up, might easily have underestimated the hours of work needed to run a household, even with the new appliances available in the 1920s. But she was not unique in expecting that wives could have careers, too. More married women were working outside their homes than ever before, the percentage rising from twenty-three to twenty-nine in the 1920s.[118] Although "glamorous" new jobs in decorating and copy-writing were opening up to women, most women still found their jobs in low-paid drudgery—laundry, domestic, and agricultural sectors—but they were not the focus of Lou Hoover's discussion. For her, work had brought personal satisfaction, and she seemed to assume that other wives and mothers would profit as she had done. Just how they would balance cooking, cleaning, laundry, and child care with their jobs remained unclear.

Increased discussion of wives' roles in general may explain why the candidates' spouses received so much attention in the 1928 contest between Herbert Hoover and Al Smith. The cosmopolitan Lou Hoover, in her subdued blues and grays and her crown of queenly white hair, contrasted sharply with Catherine (Katie) Smith, a product, like her husband, of New York's Lower East Side. Katie's Roman Catholicism, her city speech, and reputed weakness for excessive imbibing reinforced her husband's unpopularity in areas of the country intolerant of such habits and beliefs. Jokes spread that if she got to Washington, she would present a vulgar model of American womanhood to the rest of the world.[119] "Can you imagine," one Texas Republican woman reportedly asked a public meeting, "Mrs. Smith dealing with foreign dignitaries? One of them might say, 'That's a nice hat,' and she would answer, 'You said a mouthful.' "[120]

The Democrats became so concerned with Catherine Smith's effect on votes that the party's Women's Division organized speaking trips through the South. Frances Perkins paired with the wife of Charles Dana Gibson on one such assignment, and the two of them went from luncheon to tea, insisting that their good friend Katie would do perfectly well running the White House. She had a natural dignity, they argued, that would appeal to anyone who met her. As for the rumors about her drinking, they had never seen her touch a drop "even in her own house."[121]

In spite of the work of Perkins and other Democratic women, some national periodicals reported the Hoover victory with sighs of relief. Finally the sophistication that had disappeared under the untraveled Florence Harding and Grace Coolidge could be restored, one magazine suggested. Frederick Collins, writing in *Woman's Home Companion* the month of Herbert Hoover's inauguration, stressed Lou's "serenity . . . and . . . cosmopolitan background,"[122] while novelist Mary Roberts Rinehart, in *World's Work,* pointed to Lou's strength. Recent First Ladies had suffered under the pressures of the job—Ellen Wilson and Florence Harding had collapsed—but the athletic Lou would prove stronger, Rinehart predicted.[123]

Between 1992 and 2008, the First Ladies exhibit at the Smithsonian highlighted the women's roles in the nation's political history and social reform movements. The current exhibit features their dresses and china. Courtesy of the Division of Political History, National Museum of American History, Smithsonian Institution.

Regal Edith Roosevelt reportedly never made a mistake. Courtesy of the Library of Congress.

Helen Taft (also seen below) raised many eyebrows when she broke precedent and rode with her husband to the White House after his inauguration. Courtesy of the Library of Congress.

Painter Ellen Wilson kept a low profile in her own work and in her efforts to improve Washington's slums. Courtesy of the Library of Congress.

Edith Wilson showed none of her predecessor's reticence. She thrived on the attention she received as First Lady. Courtesy of the Library of Congress.

Although one of the
oldest First Ladies,
Florence Harding
made every effort
to appear vital
and energetic as
she greeted White
House visitors.
Courtesy of the
Library of Congress.

Popular Grace
Coolidge kept
several pets
and was often
photographed with
her dogs or her
raccoon, Rebecca.
Courtesy of the
Library of
Congress.

Lou Hoover, the first president's wife to broadcast from the White House, was an enthusiastic promoter of the Girl Scouts and fitness training for young women. Courtesy of the Library of Congress.

Called "Our Flying First Lady," Eleanor Roosevelt chose air travel when most Americans refused to try it. Here she is pictured in Dallas, Texas, just weeks after becoming First Lady. Courtesy of the Franklin D. Roosevelt Library.

Before her marriage, Bess Truman (shown fourth from left) was considered one of the best tennis players in Independence. Courtesy of the Harry S. Truman Library.

Mamie Eisenhower made hostessing and fashion her chief White House interests and, in doing so, reflected the predominant American view of femininity in the 1950s. Source unknown, provided by the Dwight D. Eisenhower Library.

Sizing up the White House as though it were just another of the many residences where she would make a "backdrop for Bertie," Lou pronounced it "as bleak as a New England barn."[124] She quickly rearranged virtually every piece of furniture in it and added some of her own things from California. Within three months, nothing moveable remained where the Coolidges had left it, causing one house employee to quip that Lou would next reverse the positions of the elevator and the spiral staircase. Of more permanent importance, Lou organized a systematic cataloging of the mansion's furnishings and assigned her friend and secretary, Dare Stark, to write a book about the White House. Although Stark did not complete that project, she did publish articles calling attention to the dearth of reliable information about the house and its furnishings.[125]

Unlike other presidents' wives who felt motivated by their new visibility to make themselves over, Lou Hoover seemed to retreat even from the accomplishments she had. Learning a new language, high on the agendas of many First Ladies, held little urgency—she already spoke five—but when questioned about her ability, she equivocated. Other White House chatelaines had embarked on ambitious buying trips to outfit themselves beyond criticism, but Lou, whose bank account would have allowed for any extravagance, paid little attention to clothes. Rather than attempting to slice a couple of years off her age, she seemed to take pleasure, one maid decided, in looking like the grandmother she was.[126]

The White House staff found the new First Lady a contradictory mix of international customs and small-town America. At Christmas, when she arranged for the family to trek through a darkened house, the girls and women ringing handbells and the men and boys carrying candles, the staff dismissed it as "ghostly" and "another of Mrs. Hoover's ideas." Although she had a reputation for liking to talk (servants called it "broadcasting"), she relied on hand signals during official parties to communicate with employees.[127] Each dropped handkerchief or raised finger carried a specific command: move the guests more quickly through the reception line, or more slowly; replenish the punch.

What Lou had concocted as an efficient innovation—or perhaps a variation on the dressage exercises she learned as a rider—appeared to the staff as dehumanizing and complicated. They had trouble "reading" her, they complained, and sometimes waited carefully for a particular signal and then missed it because of the subtlety with which it was delivered. Nor did they like her instruction that they stay out of sight. Bells rang to announce the president and his wife when they passed through the halls of the private quarters, warning employees to dart into the closest nook or hiding place. After four years in the Hoover White House, some employees could count on one hand the number of times they had actually encountered face to face either the president or his wife.

More than one disgruntled White House employee complained in print about the Hoovers' uncaring treatment. The housekeeper, Ava Long, described how "company, company, company," often arrived on such short notice that she had to contrive out of leftovers enough servings for dozens of people. On one occasion she had shopped for six, only to learn at 12:30 that forty would arrive for lunch at one. She instructed the cook to grind up all the icebox's contents and serve the result as a croquette with mushroom sauce. When one guest requested the recipe, Long dubbed it, with a touch of sarcasm, "White House Surprise Supreme."[128] The Hoovers liked company so much, the housekeeper reported, that they dined alone only once a year, evidently oblivious to the work they imposed on their employees. Eventually Long quit the job, and her colleague, the head usher, singled out the Hoovers as among the least likeable of his bosses when he published *Forty-Two Years at the White House.*[129]

Other observers praised Lou Hoover's interest in people as her greatest asset. She was indefatigable, they said, in her willingness to welcome groups to the White House, and in her busiest year (1932), she gave forty teas and received eighty organizations.[130] Camp Rapidan, the Hoover retreat in the Shenandoah Mountains, became an extension of the capital when Lou Hoover invited representatives of the Girl Scouts to accompany her there or used the camp as a setting to speak by radio to the country's youth. Much of her generosity, including funds for a school for poor children near Camp Rapidan, was supported by her own pocketbook.

A very deep prejudice against publicizing her personal life kept secret from most Americans the more appealing side of Lou Hoover. She shared with her husband a deep resentment, he later wrote, "of the intrusion of the press and public into our family life."[131] Even he did not know, until after his wife died in 1944 and he was settling her estate, how many people benefited from her largesse. Some of those whom she had supported regularly for years wrote when their checks stopped, wanting to know what had happened. A desire to protect the privacy of people she had helped contributed to the decision to keep her papers closed until forty years after her death.[132]

What makes Lou Hoover's attitude toward publicity more intriguing is her willingness to take a public role as First Lady. Recognizing the value of radio, which had begun to carry inauguration ceremonies in

1925, she arranged to speak to a nationwide audience. She even set up a lab on the second floor of the White House to "test" her performances and "improve [her] talkie technique."[133] A speech professor who later analyzed recordings of the talks judged Lou's voice "tinny" but admitted that the equipment was poorly adjusted for women's voices since so few of them had the opportunity to use it.[134]

Unimaginative in phrasing, Lou's radio speeches to young people had a definitely feminist slant. On a Saturday evening in June 1929, when she spoke from Camp Rapidan to a group of 4-H club members, the National Broadcasting Company carried the message coast to coast. After praising the joys of camping, Lou urged her listeners to help make their homes more attractive places, a responsibility, she said, "as much the work of boys as of girls. . . . Just stop a second to think what home is to you. Is it just a place where mother and the girls drudge a good part of the day in order that father and the boys may have a place to come to eat and sleep? [Everybody should help] with dishes, sweeping. . . . Boys, remember you are just as great factors in the home making of the family as are the girls."[135]

In other ways, Lou Hoover exerted a surprisingly modern and liberated influence on her husband's administration. She invited noticeably pregnant women (who had traditionally been excluded) to join her in reception lines,[136] and she encouraged women to pursue individual careers. When her husband issued Executive Order 5984 in December 1932, it amended the Civil Service Rule VII to require nominations "without regard to sex," unless the duties to be performed could be satisfactorily performed by only men or women. At least one careful student of the Hoover record believes that Lou influenced her husband's decisions in this and other matters.[137] In his single term, President Hoover named seven women to positions requiring Senate approval, bringing the total up to twenty, double what it had been in 1920.[138]

A woman of such intellectual bent and feminist persuasion might be expected to take a dim view of the requirement that a First Lady had to greet anyone who wanted to visit her, and Lou did. After shaking the hands of more than four thousand people at one New Year's reception, she abandoned the ritual that had originated with Martha Washington. Her husband explained that her "rigid sense of duty" stopped her from abolishing other receptions: "To her it was part of the job."[139]

On matters delicate to the Washington political community, Lou Hoover preferred to increase her work load rather than offend anyone. She knew she was there to "help Bert." When a protocol feud erupted between Dolly Gann, prominent sister of the vice president, and Alice Roosevelt Longworth, longtime leader in capital society, Lou gave two parties so that neither would be assigned precedence over the other. Such a solution caused one *New York Times* reporter to announce "a particularly Quaker victory."[140]

When time came to entertain wives of congressmen, Lou Hoover had to decide what to do with the wife of Chicago congressman Oscar DePriest, the first Negro to serve in the legislature since Reconstruction. No black had been a guest at the White House since Theodore Roosevelt dined with Booker T. Washington in 1901, and Lou Hoover understood that an invitation to Jessie DePriest could bring unpleasant repercussions. She sounded out a few of the other wives, found twelve who would not embarrass the congressman's wife, and then gave a separate tea for them.

When word of the invitation got out, several Southern publications objected that Lou Hoover had "defiled" the White House, and the *Mobile Alabama Press* reacted bitterly: "Mrs. Herbert Hoover offered to the South and to the nation an arrogant insult yesterday when she entertained a negro [*sic*] woman at a White House tea. She has harmed Mr. Hoover to a serious extent. Social admixture of the negro and the white is sought by neither race. The negro is entitled to a social life but that the two races should intermingle at afternoon teas or other functions is inadmissible."[141]

Lou Hoover's decision to follow through with the DePriest tea, in spite of criticism, reinforced her reputation as extremely egalitarian. She drove herself around Washington and invited a wide variety of people to dinner, causing one reporter to note: "She does not keep the rules, [but] mixes the great and the near-great with the obscure and the near obscure."[142]

A woman willing to brave so much controversy might have been expected to open up to the press, but she was far less open with reporters in the White House than she had been in her early days in Washington. She refused to permit either interviews or casual photographs. Her grandchildren, who resided in the White House for a few months while their father recuperated in the South, were strictly off-limits to journalists. The formal, posed studio portraits that she released, showing a perfectly coiffed, distant matron, did little to render her human or compassionate.

The Hoover White House provided such a dry spell for thirsty reporters that one of them, Bess Furman of the Washington AP, contrived to enter the family quarters by passing herself off as a Girl Scout Christmas caroler. Dressed in the traditional uniform, hair tucked under her cap, Furman went in "as one of the taller girls" and moved undetected within arm's reach of people who encountered her every-day as a reporter. During the carols that she could not sing, Furman kept her face down, furtively taking in details so she could write an account of how a president's family celebrated Christmas. In a burst of bravado, Furman sent a copy of the article to the First Lady, who marked it "nice story," without ever discovering who supplied the details.[143]

Lou Hoover's reticence in the White House extended to policy matters as well as publicity, thus underlining the traditional side of her view of a wife's role. If she differed with Herbert on any significant matter, she kept the difference to herself. She tailored her own suggestions for economic recovery to fit her husband's remedies, and her public pronouncements on how to end the Great Depression reinforced her husband's reputation for relying on volunteerism. In March 1931, when the country edged toward the trough of unemployment, she went on radio to thank American women for their donations of food and clothing. The First Lady urged women to volunteer in one of three ways: by identifying people in need and determining how they could be helped, by working in hospitals and visiting-nurse programs, and by setting up recreation opportunities for unemployed young people.[144] Even after Herbert lost the 1932 election (and Lou heard that one indignant mother had changed her young son's name from Herbert Hoover Jones to Franklin Roosevelt Jones), she took to the airwaves to encourage "every woman in America . . . to consider herself a volunteer associate member of the National Women's Committee of Welfare and Relief Mobilization . . . [because if people cooperate there is] ample food and clothing for us all."[145]

More than most of her predecessors, Lou Hoover had exceptional ability and training for leadership, but she failed to win the country's approval or its interest. She foreshadowed Eleanor Roosevelt in her formidable energy and active participation in her husband's presidency. Alice Roosevelt Longworth (who was never particularly charitable to her famous cousin) credited Lou with being the first president's wife "to take a public part on her own."[146] But Lou's natural reticence unfortunately isolated her, so that, while she set the stage for Eleanor's accomplishments, she came nowhere close to equalling them.

Lou also lacked Eleanor's willingness to take risks. While Eleanor did not hesitate to disagree with her husband or introduce guests who would question his ideas, Lou preferred a safer course. She protected Herbert by inviting guests for his pleasure rather than for his growth, and then she diverted conversation from difficult topics. While other presidents' wives sought to watch out for their husbands' health, Lou gave the impression of standing guard against challenges to Herbert's thinking—challenges that might have moved him in other directions than those he took.

The contrast between the two women is underlined in the letter that Lou Hoover wrote to her sons and husband not long before her death in 1944. It is a message that could not have come from Eleanor's hand. Even from Lou, it startles. The woman who started out camping and fishing like a boy, and then proceeded to earn a geology degree equal to her husband's, ended up describing her life as entirely peripheral to him and their sons: "I have been lucky," she wrote, "to have my trail move alongside that of such exceptional men and boys."[147]

Together, the three First Ladies of the 1920s reflect that decade well since they present contradictions and inconsistencies rather than one clear line of development. But they also form a bridge to the period that followed, and it is difficult to imagine Eleanor Roosevelt initiating the changes she did without the foundations laid by her immediate predecessors—in experimenting with the press, speaking out on important issues, and extending women's rights and opportunities.

7

Breaking Precedents and Reaffirming Old Ones (1933–1961)

EVEN BEFORE THE 1932 presidential election, Eleanor Roosevelt (1933–1945) made clear that she meant to break some precedents if her husband won. Just how much she was responding to the special urgency of the Great Depression remains unclear. Perhaps she would have been just as active and innovative a First Lady if her husband had presided over a prosperous nation. But most Americans in 1933 were neither prosperous nor optimistic. The previous summer, midwestern farmers, disgusted by the low prices they were receiving, dumped their milk. Then thousands of jobless veterans marched to Washington and set up camps of shacks and tents, dubbed Hoovervilles. By the time Franklin Roosevelt took his oath of office in March 1933, many of the country's banks had closed and business halted. Young children in the largest cities learned to walk past furniture, sidewalk-stored, of their dispossessed neighbors and to expect that one day they would return from school to find their own things there.

Surely such times called out for new approaches, and Eleanor Roosevelt complied on several fronts. She had hinted during the campaign that she and Franklin sometimes disagreed, but the real shocker was her announcement that she meant to keep—even if she became First Lady—the job she had held while Franklin had served as New York's governor. During his four years in the Albany state house, Eleanor had traveled down to New York City to teach three days a week at her school on East Eightieth Street, and she saw no reason why his transfer to Washington should alter her schedule or stop her from doing what she "enjoyed more than anything I have ever done."[1]

Such independence came late to Eleanor Roosevelt, after a childhood notable for its loneliness and lack of strong female models, and a marriage dominated for many years by her mother-in-law. The only daughter of an exceptionally beautiful woman, Eleanor had suffered greatly as a child when she heard herself described as an unattractive "Granny." Nor did her confidence grow after her mother's death when she and her younger brother, Hall, came under the control of a stern and distant grandmother. Only the erratic attentions of her *bon vivant* father saved that period from becoming, for Eleanor, an uninterrupted bad memory. Much later in her life, after she had married and had children of her own, she singled out the times spent with her father as the best of her life.[2]

When his excessive drinking and playboy lifestyle led to an early death, those pleasant interludes abruptly ended and strict Grandmother Hall took an even larger role in Eleanor's life until, at age fifteen, she was enrolled in a boarding school in England. There she met a strong, thinking, caring Parisian, Marie Souvestre, who had a powerful impact on her young student.[3] "She gave me an intellectual curiosity and a standard of living which have never left me," Eleanor wrote years later. "[On trips across Europe,] she did all the things that in a vague way you had always felt you wanted to do, enjoying the food and being comfortable but at the same time seeing how the people lived."[4]

Three years with Mademoiselle Souvestre could hardly cancel out the fifteen years that went before, and Eleanor returned to New York to do the expected: make her début and marry at the first opportunity. Although she later admitted that at the time of her marriage, she had little idea of what loving or being a wife and mother meant, she quietly accepted the mold that had been cast for women of her class and time.

Urbane and handsome Franklin Delano Roosevelt could not have seen beauty or sophistication or confidence in his bride in 1905, but like many of the men who later became president, he made an advantageous marriage. In this respect he illustrates a remarkable pattern evident in presidents' lives. Most of the men who later achieved the country's highest office married up into socially or economically superior strata of American society, while the women married into more adventure, travel, or risk than they had found in their parents' home. Franklin's choice of his distant cousin was hardly social climbing, but the marriage helped him in two ways. As Joseph Lash, the Roosevelts' biographer noted, young Franklin's "dissemblings contrasted with Eleanor's scrupulousness." Lash concluded: "Perhaps she appealed to Franklin because he needed someone to temper his fun-loving, easygoing, frivolous side."[5] Another motive may have been working, at least subconsciously. Eleanor's uncle, Theodore Roosevelt, then resided at the White House, and a politically ambitious young man—even one who intended to align with the Democrats—could do worse than marry the favorite niece of an immensely popular Republican president.

For her part, Eleanor recognized the difficulty of fitting into Franklin's world. His mother, with whom the couple lived, imperiously controlled the household; and Franklin's friends, with their cigarette smoking and quick wit, made Eleanor so painfully aware of her rigid views and conversational inadequacies that she often begged to stay behind when he went out partying.

Six pregnancies between 1906 and 1916 left Eleanor little time to gain confidence or acquire control over her life. Even the nurses she hired for her children intimidated her and made her feel inadequate. She tried to improve her French and German but found such study unrewarding, and when she ventured down to the Lower East Side to teach in a settlement house, her mother-in-law advised her to stop because of her fear that Eleanor might bring home diseases.

If Eleanor had shared her husband's interest in politics, she might have found a way to break out of her mold earlier but on that subject she lacked both knowledge and curiosity. The intricacies of government remained a mystery to her, and she later admitted that at the time of her marriage she could not have explained the difference between state and national legislatures.[6] At the 1912 Democratic convention in Baltimore, she found the confusion and noise so objectionable that she left early and joined her children at the family's summer retreat on Campobello. When Franklin's jubilant telegram arrived later to announce Woodrow Wilson's nomination, she failed to comprehend the reason for his excitement. Her husband's support of woman's suffrage about the same time shocked Eleanor, and she realized that she had never given the matter serious thought, although it had been the central objective of the feminist movement for more than half a century.[7]

About 1917, the shy and insecure Eleanor Roosevelt began a metamorphosis so enormous in its consequences that historians have debated its causes. By then in her thirties, she had already managed a partial escape from her domineering mother-in-law when Franklin's appointment as assistant secretary of the Navy took them to Washington in 1913. Sara Roosevelt still came down to rearrange the furniture, but as soon as she left, Eleanor could put it back. And put it back she did. More important, Eleanor had the examples of other Washington wives who were breaking away from old traditions and accomplishing something on their own.

In part, they were drawn out by the exigencies of war, just as women in the 1860s had been impelled by the Civil War to make speeches, collect money, and put their energies into national organizations to aid in victory and to ease suffering. In Washington, as in other American cities, the entry of the country into World War I created shortages of male workers so that women ran streetcars, delivered mail, and took other jobs that under peacetime conditions they would not have gotten. Eleanor Roosevelt joined with wives of other government officials to open canteens for servicemen stationed in the capital and to visit wounded and sick men. This was the kind of activism and involvement that she had so admired in Mademoiselle Souvestre, and Eleanor could hardly conceal her enthusiasm: "I loved it," she wrote later, "I simply ate it up."[8] Her cousin, Alice Roosevelt Longworth, singled out the war years as the time when Eleanor went "public."[9]

About the same time that Eleanor found reasons outside her home to draw her out, she found others inside to push her in the same direction. She had opened by mistake a letter to Franklin and found irrefutable evidence that he was having an affair with Eleanor's former social secretary, Lucy Mercer. He refused Eleanor's offer to divorce him, and the marriage continued until his death. But the union became a formal one, the distance between the two partners rather formally defined and rigidly observed. She frequently referred to him in the manner of a trusted employee discussing a superior, waiting for "my regular time to see him."[10] When he announced he would run for governor, she learned of his decision by radio, along with other New York voters.[11]

In writing about her life, Eleanor acknowledged that she began to change some of her attitudes before 1920, but she avoided marital problems in detailing the reasons. Her Grandmother Hall had died in 1918, Eleanor explained, causing her to wonder whether that woman's life and those of her children might not have been happier had she developed her own interests rather than attempting to live vicariously through others. Grandmother Hall had shown artistic talent in her youth but had died without developing her ability to paint, and Eleanor resolved not to miss such opportunities for herself.[12]

Most of the credit for Eleanor's increased self-confidence went, by her own account, not to negative examples but to positive ones. The League of Women Voters exposed her to the excitement of political participation, and the Women's Trade Union League reawakened her old interest in helping others. She owed a large debt, she often said, to settlement house leaders such as Mary Simkhovitch and to League workers such as Elizabeth Read and Esther Lape.[13] By helping her understand politics and social movements, they built her confidence in herself. Eleanor failed to note what her friends saw so clearly—that the public activities gave new meaning to her life and close friendships that substituted for the lack of warmth in her marriage. The same activities also helped fill the emptiness Eleanor had found in the performance of upper-class social forms. The "leaving of cards" had ceased among Washington wives during World War I, and when the war ended, the ritual was not resumed. The women turned instead to political and benevolent organizations. Eleanor took typing lessons, a definite change from the language classes she had chosen earlier.

To one tutor Eleanor Roosevelt gave particular credit. Louis Howe, the wizened newspaperman who took her husband as his protegé, recognized during Franklin's 1920 run for vice president that Eleanor had the potential to campaign and speak out on issues, but not until Franklin's bout with polio in 1921 and subsequent paralysis did the necessity of developing her skills become clear. If Franklin meant to pursue politics, he needed an exceptionally active and supportive spouse. Louis Howe urged Eleanor to take speaking lessons to increase her self-confidence and lower her high pitch. When she balked at facing crowds, he cajoled her into trying until eventually she could speak comfortably and effectively to large groups.

Eleanor's energy and confidence grew rapidly in the 1920s, inspired by the support of other women, cheered on by Howe, and persuaded by the necessity of her husband's career. The exuberance of her colleagues who felt they could accomplish whatever they set out to do also affected her. She formed two business partnerships with other women: one to operate a school in New York City and the other to manufacture furniture at Hyde Park. As though bursting with long-stored energy, she became involved in New York State politics and served on the Platform Committee at the 1926 state Democratic convention.[14] In 1928, the *New York Post* referred to Eleanor's new prominence when it ran a headline, "Roosevelt's Wife is His Colonel House." Buoyed by her new success, Eleanor began publishing magazine articles, some of them advising other wives how to run their households and care for their children. The shy bride who had retreated from managing her own family had matured into a confident teacher of others.

In August 1930, *Good Housekeeping* singled out the prolific wife of New York's governor as the "ideal modern wife." In an interview with the author, M. K. Wisehart, Eleanor outlined what she thought being a wife meant. It still combined the three roles, as it always had, but she explained that the relative importance of each had shifted. While women had formerly put most emphasis on motherhood, they now stressed being full partners to their husbands. "Everything else depends upon the success of wife and husband in their personal relation," Eleanor was quoted as saying. "Partnership. Companionship. It is a major requirement for modern marriage."[15] But this was not a partnership weighted on one side—Eleanor urged wives to develop interests of their own so they would not smother their children with excessive attention or depend too heavily on their husbands' careers for their own sense of achievement.

Her own definition of marriage evidently guided Eleanor in the White House, which she had entered reluctantly. "I never wanted to be a President's wife and I don't want it now," she told her good friend Lorena Hickok in 1932. "You don't believe that. Very likely no one would except some woman who has had the job."[16] But now that she had the job, Eleanor showed that she meant to use it—on the side of causes she believed in—rather than let it use her.

All through the 1930s, Eleanor's letters reveal uncertainty as to how to combine her own private concerns with the demands of her public role as wife of the president. When Hickok attempted to distinguish between Eleanor, the "person" whom she preferred, and Eleanor, the separate public "personage," Eleanor wrote back: "I think the personage is an accident and I only like the part of life in which I am a person."[17] It was a dichotomy not easily dismissed, however, and Joseph Lash reported that it became an "old discussion" among her friends as to whether she gained prominence as a "result of being the President's wife" or because of her personal skill in using the "opportunities afforded her as First Lady."[18] Lash's own conclusion was that the person and personage eventually merged into one,[19] but that Eleanor insisted on dividing them: "I drove up [to northern New York State] in the capacity of ER," she wrote in 1933, "and only on arriving became FDR's wife."[20]

Many decisions called for working out the competing claims of the two roles. Eleanor arranged for a leave of absence from her teaching, but she stubbornly continued her other professional activities, including lecturing and writing. When the question of doing radio broadcasts came up, Eleanor wavered, first refusing and then reversing herself. To counter criticism that the president's wife had no right to a profitable career of her own, she donated much of her income to organizations such as the Women's Trade Union League and the Red Cross. After seven years as First Lady she explained to reporters that she had earned a "great deal," but that she had "not one cent more of principal or of investment" than in 1932. "I have the feeling that every penny I have made should be in circulation."[21]

The earning of money, not the spending of it, appealed to Eleanor because it was money that resulted from her own efforts. She liked the feeling of having funds apart from the trust income she had inherited from her family and the allotment she got from her husband. Her paycheck was hers "to do a lot of things [with], just things that give me fun."[22] Often that meant gifts for her family and friends but rarely an extravagance for herself. Clothes held no interest at all and a friend observed that Eleanor frequently wore dresses in the $10 range.[23]

Having felt the satisfaction of making her own money, Eleanor was particularly sensitive to attempts to curtail other women's opportunities to earn. During the Great Depression, when as many as one in four workers could not find jobs, public sentiment held that wives of employed men should renounce jobs of their own and stay home. In fact, a 1936 Gallup Poll concluded that 82 percent of Americans held that view,[24] which rested, in part, on the mistaken assumption that women worked for "pin money" to buy luxuries. In many families, wives' earnings made the difference between real hardship and comfort, but the evidence was not often forthcoming since it reflected on men's earning abilities. Even in cases where a second income was not essential to a family's budget, the woman's job might play an important part in her sense of worth, as it had for Eleanor.

The president's wife acted on more than one level to combat prejudice against married women working. She encouraged Ettie Rheiner Garner, who had worked as her husband's secretary for many years and did not want to stop when he became vice president in 1933, to continue.[25] On a public level, the First Lady teamed up with Molly Dewson, then prominent in the Women's Division of the Democratic National party, to denounce the Economy Act of 1933, which permitted firing women in civil service if their husbands also had government employment.[26] Her news conferences, which she had begun immediately upon becoming First Lady,[27] served as forums for Eleanor to speak out on wives' right to work if they wanted to (although she carefully noted that each woman should make up her own mind about whether to work outside the home or not). When individual states sought to enact laws that would have permitted firing working wives, Eleanor used her conferences with women reporters to fight back: "It is of great moment to us [women] not to let this happen."[28]

Multiple biographies of Eleanor Roosevelt make clear that her concerns extended beyond women's rights and well-being, but she broke precedent in putting the power of First Ladyship to work on the side of women—both married and single. When the Civilian Conservation Corps offered jobless young men the chance to get out of cities and earn money, Eleanor worked with the Labor secretary, Frances Perkins, to gain equivalent opportunities for young women. The Federal Emergency Relief Administration responded by setting up camps for women,[29] and although the number enrolled totaled only about eight thousand, compared to two and a half million men in the CCC, this victory marked another small strike against the double standard.[30]

In her attempt to influence New Deal legislation, Eleanor worked through every channel she could find. Before moving into the White House, she had helped her friend Molly Dewson obtain leadership of the Women's Division of the Democratic National Committee, a post from which Dewson could effect the appointment of other women to party jobs in the various states and in federal agencies. One of Dewson's early victories was the naming of Frances Perkins as secretary of labor in 1933, the first woman to serve in a president's cabinet. Dewson also orchestrated a remarkable increase in women campaign workers, from 73,000 in 1936 to 109,000 by 1940.[31] It was this kind of pyramiding that made Eleanor Roosevelt such an effective proponent—she carefully laid the groundwork for change and made way for women at the lower echelons in government and politics so that they could prepare for the bigger jobs. Her efforts achieved remarkable results. In slightly more than twelve years, the number of women holding jobs requiring Senate confirmation doubled, and countless lesser jobs were filled through her influence. Lois Banner, the historian, credits Eleanor with helping achieve the appointment of four thousand women to post office jobs.[32]

Always sensitive to charges that she held inordinate power, Eleanor frequently issued disclaimers. "I never tried to influence [Franklin] on anything he ever did," she announced at one press conference, "and I certainly have never known him to try to influence me."[33] When the *New York Times* credited the president's wife with achieving the appointment of a particular woman to attend an international conference, Eleanor wrote to Secretary of the Interior Ickes, who had made the selection, that she had been merely passing along the president's thoughts when she informed Ickes of the woman's qualifications. "There is such a concerted effort being made," Eleanor wrote, "to make it appear that I dictate to FDR that I don't want people who should know the truth to have any misunderstanding about it. I wouldn't dream of doing more than passing along requests or suggestions that come to me."[34] When one man publicly credited Eleanor with obtaining a job for him in Washington, she reprimanded him, pointing out that he had put her "in a very embarrassing position by having made it appear that I had used my influence."[35]

At the very same time she was issuing these disclaimers, Eleanor Roosevelt made other statements, sometimes very privately, that indicate she was not unaware of her influence. When Jerre Mangione, a young author who worked as national coordinating editor for the Federal Writers' Project in the late 1930s, visited the White House, Eleanor told him that she had argued with the president late into the night on a particular matter and then had been surprised when the next day he presented her opinion as his own to the British ambassador. "I was so astonished," Eleanor told Jerre Mangione, "that I almost dropped the teapot."[36]

Eleanor peppered her letters to friends with references to her attempts to influence both legislation and appointments, and she discussed powerful Washington figures as colleagues rather than superiors. After meeting with Postmaster General James Farley and his aides to "start them off on patronage for women,"[37] she judged both Harry Hopkins and Secretary of Interior Harold Ickes "good to work with;"[38] and when Hopkins came through with improvements in school lunches, she upgraded her estimate of him to "swell."[39] She admitted that she used the occasion of a dinner for senators to "throw bombshells about federal controls and setting minimum standards,"[40] and when she invited the Rexford Tugwells and Harry Hopkins to the White House, she confessed that she hoped "we'll have a real talk of some ideas I think we should work on."[41]

Her own children offered rather different descriptions of Eleanor's influence with Franklin. James Roosevelt, who acted as his father's secretary, assigned her a significant role, even "if he didn't always sympathize with her causes" and called her part of the "kitchen cabinet."[42] His sister Anna, who lived at the White House for several years, described her parents' lives as very separate and Franklin as so intolerant of Eleanor's primness and shrillness that he sometimes barred her from his study when he entertained his friends. Anna thought her mother often miscalculated people's moods and tried to bring up serious matters when everyone wished to relax and be frivolous. Whenever Eleanor joined Franklin for a pre-dinner cocktail, Anna recalled, she usually planned to use the occasion to make an appeal.[43]

Eleanor's persistence in trying to get what she thought was necessary or right became almost legendary, and one example, related by Joseph Lash (who was present), indicates that other members of her family did not always appreciate her efforts. According to Lash, the Roosevelt clan was gathered at Hyde Park a few days before the 1941 inauguration, and Eleanor sought some assurance from Franklin that a recent appointee to supervise housing construction would look out for the needs of the poor rather than bow to real estate interests. Franklin's mother, who noted her son's reluctance to discuss this particular matter right then, called for the butler and the wheelchair, and only by physically removing the president from the room was she able to cut off Eleanor's appeal.[44]

Often Eleanor's lobbying was more genial, and she herself explained how she had acted to win Franklin's endorsement of the National Youth Administration, a program to employ young people and offer financial aid to those who could not be employed. On May 17, 1933, she met with an assistant to Harry Hopkins and reported that "they have a good youth programme ready to submit to FDR I think."[45] As she explained in her autobiography, she went to Franklin that evening just before he went to sleep and described "the whole idea" to him.[46] The next day, she was optimistic about success: "I think we are going to get a youth programme started & one for artists far more far reaching than I dared hope."[47] Often Eleanor's role involved merely providing access to the president at some social occasion. Molly Dewson explained that whenever she wanted some help from the president, "Mrs. Roosevelt gave me the opportunity to sit by [him] at dinner and the matter was settled before we finished our soup."[48]

Although much of her influence remained private, Eleanor Roosevelt became increasingly outspoken on controversial subjects during her twelve years as First Lady. Early in her husband's first administration she had announced that she would not comment on pending legislation, but she gradually changed her own rules.[49] Her magazine articles, which had in the beginning stuck to innocuous topics such as family camping trips and baby care, gradually took on such matters as the president's plan to enlarge the Supreme Court, the correct level of preparedness for war, and a war referendum amendment.[50] Beginning in 1936, she also wrote a newspaper column, "My Day," in which she offered her own pithy judgments of people and policies. In 1939 she used the syndicated column to publicize her resignation from the Daughters of the American Revolution because of the organization's refusal to permit Marian Anderson to sing in Constitution Hall, thus causing *Time* to describe her as "increasingly vocal these days."[51]

Such a visible and unconventional First Lady raised many eyebrows and she became almost immediately the subject of caricatures. Within months of the 1933 inauguration, a national magazine carried a much-repeated cartoon showing a group of miners deep under the ground, one turning to the next and announcing, "Gosh, here's Mrs. Roosevelt."[52] By 1940, the criticism appeared on campaign buttons,

"And we don't want Eleanor either." But the First Lady took it all as part of the job. On entering the White House, she had told Lorena Hickok, "I shall very likely be criticized, but I cannot help it,"[53] and there is little evidence that she changed her mind. One reporter, who preserved shorthand notes of many of Eleanor's news conferences, observed that she responded cordially to all questions, even those clearly hostile to her, except when she "took on an edge to her voice when asked an unwelcome question about one of her children."[54]

Eleanor could pass off much of her activity as helping Franklin, and he shrewdly saw the advantages of having a visible, politically involved wife who was known to disagree with him. When asked if her liberal views might not taint him for the more conservative voters, he could answer, "Well, that's my wife, and I can't be expected to do anything about her." Yet at the same time, he gained support from those who saw Eleanor as their own champion. She simply served as "his eyes and ears," it was sometimes said, when she inspected mines, toured slums, interviewed families of the urban poor and then relayed her impressions to him. She did show an unusual knack for catching the poignant detail, and once at a White House dinner party, she told about visiting a poor Appalachian family. They had all appeared shy about greeting such a famous visitor, but as she was about to leave, a small boy brought his pet rabbit to the door to bid her goodbye. The boy's sister looked at the president's wife with a "glint in her eye" and said, "He thinks we're not going to eat [that rabbit] but we are." With that, Eleanor recalled, "the boy went running down the road, rabbit clutched to his chest." At least one of Eleanor's guests felt moved to mail a check "to help keep the rabbit alive."[55]

But Eleanor Roosevelt also used her considerable influence in behalf of her own friends and projects. When the congressional committee headed by Martin Dies summoned several Youth Congress members to testify in 1939 about possible connections to communism, she went to witness their treatment. Later, she described how she had silently intervened: "At one point, when the questioning seemed to me to be particularly harsh, I asked to go over and sit at the press table. I took a pencil and a piece of paper, and the tone of the questions changed immediately. Just what the questioner thought I was going to do I do not know, but my action had the effect I desired."[56]

Eleanor Roosevelt's multitude of activities in the 1930s led reporters to describe the Roosevelts as a team. Arthur Krock suggested that Eleanor might try to succeed her husband in 1940,[57] and in 1941 Raymond Clapper, a syndicated journalist, selected Eleanor as one of the ten most powerful people in Washington, along with John L. Lewis and General George C. Marshall. "She has had," Clapper wrote, "almost the importance of a cabinet minister without portfolio. She deserves credit for many humanitarian projects of the administration, including the National Youth Administration, nursery schools, slum clearance and others. For eight years she had been the traveling ears and eyes of the President. Now her influence is stronger than ever. Count Mrs. Roosevelt not only the most influential woman of our time but also a most active force in public affairs."[58]

Such popularity required many adjustments, and Eleanor's childhood had not prepared her for being on a first-name basis with the rest of the world. She tried to adapt. When her husband asked her to go to the Pacific in World War II, she was taken aback in Guadalcanal to hear a young serviceman say loudly, "There's Eleanor," but she decided to accept it as a compliment and respond with a wave and a smile.[59]

The confidence she gained in her mature years led Eleanor Roosevelt to adventures she would not have attempted in her youth and encouraged her to break out of the old limits imposed on women of her time. She flew in a plane piloted by the famous Amelia Earhart who, for that occasion, wore a long evening dress while she sat at the controls.[60] Eleanor told reporters that she would "love to cross the Atlantic by plane" well before she had the opportunity, and when the time came for her to go to Europe and to the Pacific, she flew. In 1933, *Good Housekeeping* dubbed her "our flying First Lady," and in 1939, she titled one of her own articles "Flying is Fun."[61] At a time when most Americans still thought flying too dangerous to try, Eleanor Roosevelt delighted in leading the way. She was photographed alongside planes and interviewed inside, doing more for the aviation industry, it was sometimes said, than anyone since Charles Lindbergh.

As the 1940 election approached and speculation grew that Eleanor might like a political office for herself, she insisted, "Nothing under heaven could ever persuade [me to run]."[62] That did not mean, however, that the subject of women in politics was far from her mind. The same month that Eleanor renounced a political career for herself, she began a three-part piece in *Good Housekeeping* by noting the gains women had made in the twenty years since obtaining the vote. The number serving in state legislatures had actually declined, Eleanor noted, from a peak of 149 in 1929 to 129 a decade later, but she judged this a temporary phenomenon. The presidency would never go to a woman, Eleanor predicted, until women had first established themselves in prominent business and government positions.[63]

Eleanor Roosevelt's feminism hewed more closely to the lines of the conservative branch of the movement in the 1930s and 1940s than to the radical wing, which, under the rubric of the National Woman's Party, sought the elimination of all discrimination on the basis of sex. Since the suffrage victory in 1920, the feminists had divided, with one branch defending protective legislation for women while the Woman's Party attacked such approaches, pointing out that women could not expect equity in pay and promotions if they insisted on superior, protected treatment. Since 1923, the Woman's Party had advocated an Equal Rights Amendment to the Constitution to bar discrimination on the basis of sex, but Eleanor and her friends on the other side defended the hardearned legislation that shielded women workers from night shifts, heavy loads, and other dangerous assignments. To give up these protections for a potentially unenforceable Equal Rights Amendment made little sense to her; and even in her friendly conversations with women reporters, many of whom stood on the other side, Eleanor stuck by her position. This intransigence prompted the journalist Ruby Black to say, "She talks like a social worker and acts like a feminist."[64]

The point has been made that, even without an influential First Lady, women would have increased their share of important federal jobs in the 1930s because the government moved into the kinds of social welfare areas that had traditionally been associated with home and family.[65] Perkins's apprenticeship in the Consumers' League and in the (New York) State Factory Investigating Commission prepared her to head the country's Labor Department. Molly Dewson's directorship of the parole department of Massachusett's State Industrial School for Girls and her involvement in minimum wage legislation equipped her for active participation in the New Deal. Whatever the routes to their new jobs, Perkins, Dewson, and many others, such as Mary McLeod Bethune, who headed the Negro affairs division of the National Youth Administration, held important decision-making positions which affected the entire nation; and they held those jobs in unprecedented numbers. Other appointments of women in the 1930s, such as those in foreign service, were unrelated to welfare issues. Franklin Roosevelt selected Ruth Bryan Owen as the country's first woman minister when he named her to represent the United States in Denmark in 1933. In 1939, Florence Jaffray Harriman was appointed minister to Norway.

Eleanor also used her influence in the cause of achieving civil rights for black Americans. Her years as First Lady coincided with events that emphasized very old, strong traditions of racism in

American culture: the Depression, the continued migration of blacks out of the South and into northern and western cities, and a renewed reliance on lynching, which had long served in the South to help maintain white dominance. She reacted by involving herself in the campaign for equal rights as no other president's wife had ever done. In this respect she led, rather than followed her husband, and she earned the permanent admiration of many Americans. Her resignation from the DAR over their treatment of Marian Anderson was only her most publicized stand. She also worked for the appointment of blacks to high office, appealed directly to officials to remove disabilities faced by black workers on their jobs, and served as go-between when civil rights advocates sought the ear of the president. Only the threat of harming Franklin's chances prohibited her from doing more, and she once confessed, "I frequently was more careful than I might otherwise have been."[66]

Whatever Eleanor's direct influence in these and other appointments, she could not have acted on so many fronts had not her incredible energy level permitted her to pack into one day more than most people could do in a week. In a typical day, she breakfasted with guests, read several newspapers, attended a conference, returned to the White House to hold her own press conference, made a radio broadcast, and dictated her own column—all before lunch. In the afternoon she saw callers, attended a five-cent dinner to learn how people on WPA wages managed, met with her husband and then worked on her mail until three in the morning.[67] And she managed all this activity with a tiny staff. Only her personal secretary, Malvina Thompson, was a regular, full-time employee, assisted by various White House staffers who worked on temporary assignments. Eleanor admitted she had the benefit of a very healthy body and insisted that she never permitted herself to feel hurried. If anything kept her awake once she had gone to bed, she never admitted it.

Such an energetic and independent national figure might have been expected to influence her daughter and granddaughters to move in the same direction, but courage to break new ground did not go with the genes. Eleanor's formal education had ended at the English boarding school, and her daughter, Anna, bowed to her grandmother Sara Delano Roosevelt's opinions on the proper training for her sex and did not go to college. Anna's daughter, also named Eleanor, spent considerable time with her grandparents both at the White House and Hyde Park, but she later defined her own youth as a time of very narrow opportunities for girls: "I thought of being a teacher," Eleanor Seagraves told a 1984 audience in Grand Rapids, Michigan, "or maybe a librarian, but those were really the only two options open to me."[68]

Even if she had little effect on the thinking of her daughter and granddaughter, Eleanor Roosevelt set a new standard against which all later First Ladies would be measured. Much of what she did simply extended the activities of her predecessors. Called the president's political confidante and counselor, she repeated what Abigail Adams had done. Described as the president's eyes and ears, she functioned as Sarah Polk had. Identified as the humane side of the presidency, its conscience and link with the underdog, she continued a long tradition associated with First Ladies since Martha Washington. Eleanor Roosevelt's unique contribution lay in braving criticism by opening up to the press and using her influence as a force separate from the president's, especially in extending opportunities for women and others lacking equal chances. In the process she helped destroy some old, strong prejudices against combining substantive political action with "ladylike" behavior.

That a woman raised in one of New York's oldest families, when considerable attention went to learning to curtsey to one's elders, would turn up her collar and cuffs and go down in the mines to see conditions for herself or off to the Pacific to inspect military operations for her husband, surprised many people and marked a new level of performance by a president's wife. Eleanor's letters show that by the time she occupied the White House, she had become bored by the kind of activities that still concerned her wealthy relatives. After visiting a cousin in Rhode Island in 1933, she wrote "Newport is so smug,"[69] and after seeing her mother-in-law off on a European trip, Eleanor noted how far she had moved from the older woman's world: "I did not want to go in the least. She's staying at the Embassy in London, going to stay with the King and Queen. . . . Lord I would hate it & how she will love it."[70] Only when royalty had ideas worth discussing did Eleanor appreciate conversing with them. "I talked to the Queen [Wilhelmina]," the First Lady wrote during one of the Dutch monarch's visits to Hyde Park, "and I like her. She has quality when you talk to her seriously."[71]

Talking seriously—regardless of the status of the person on the other end of the conversation—became so important to Eleanor that she paid little attention to old ideas about what was proper for a lady, particularly a First Lady. On a car trip between Washington and New York, she picked up a hitchhiker, one of the many jobless wanderers known as "hoboes" or "tramps" in the 1930s, and she offered him a card with her New York address so that he could go there for a meal.

Her old reservations about the propriety of smoking evidently had disappeared in the 1930s, and she broke precedent in the White House by having cigarettes offered to women guests at the conclusion of White House dinners. The young wife who had objected to her husband's friends because they smoked now counted among her best friends cigar-smoking women reporters and she occasionally lit up a cigarette herself just to make her strike against the double standard. Perhaps she, too, had recognized in herself the merging of the "person" and the "personage."

When Franklin died suddenly on April 12, 1945, just eighty-two days into his fourth presidential term, Eleanor, then sixty-one years old, had to work out whether she still existed as a private "person" apart from the "personage" who was Franklin's wife. She had always objected to the "fishbowl" aspect of living in the White House (although she would insist until her death that there were compensations),[72] and she prepared to take up residence in a rented apartment on Washington Square in New York City. Reporters who met her train as she arrived in Pennsylvania Station got from her a terse, "The story is over,"[73] but of course it was not.

Until her death on November 7, 1962, Eleanor Roosevelt continued an active public life, representing her country at the United Nations, where she surprised both her American colleagues and her Russian counterparts by showing firmness in the drafting of the Universal Declaration of Human Rights. In December 1948, when the Declaration passed the General Assembly and the other delegates rose to applaud Eleanor Roosevelt, one of her old political adversaries, Michigan Senator Arthur Vandenberg, conceded publicly what many people were thinking privately: "I want to say that I take back everything I ever said about her and believe me, it's been plenty."[74] Her final appointment came in 1961 when President John Kennedy named her to head the Commission on the Status of Women.

In the seventeen years that she survived her husband, Eleanor Roosevelt achieved recognition as "First Lady of the World"—a status that would have been impossible to attain without the springboard of the White House. Living there longer than any of her predecessors, she had experimented with the role of president's wife and changed it, opening up what had been hidden and breaking down barriers that had stood firm for a century and a half.

To those searching for some explanation of why the apparently shy and insecure young woman matured into a precedent-breaking First Lady, Eleanor offered few clues. Examples of politically shrewd, risk-taking ancestors may have moved her—relatives sometimes noted that she resembled her Uncle Theodore, her father's brother, more than any of his own children did. Eleanor herself pointed out that her Uncle Theodore often included his two sisters in discussions during his governorship and presidency. The older sister, whom Eleanor called "Auntie Bye," lived in Washington, and Eleanor recalled, "There was never a serious subject that came up while [Theodore] was President that he didn't go to her home on N Street and discuss with her, that was well known by all the family. He may have made his own decisions, but talking with her seemed to clarify things for him."[75]

Eleanor's loneliness in her own marriage may have encouraged her to look to public service for a sense of worth, especially after her children were grown. Perhaps as helpful as any explanation is one offered by Joseph Lash, her biographer and friend. Lash reported that Eleanor divided women into the "Marthas" and the "Marys," after the biblical sisters who defined their lives in such different ways. Martha was "devoted, feminine, fun-loving, frivolous," while Mary preferred the world of ideas and action. "[Eleanor Roosevelt] knew that she never could be the admiring female," Lash wrote, "and while she accepted the fact that men sought their Marthas as well as their Marys, she insisted there would be only one 'First Lady' in the White House."[76] For 1600 Pennsylvania Avenue—and for the nation—that represented a courageous redefinition of womanliness.

Whether Eleanor Roosevelt placed her successor among the Marthas or the Marys is not clear—she might have lacked the information on which to judge—because Elizabeth Virginia ("Bess") Wallace Truman (1945–1953) moved into the White House an unknown quantity. In more than twelve years of the Roosevelt administration, journalists had depended so heavily on Eleanor that they had paid little attention to those waiting in the wings, and Bess Furman, of the Associated Press, admitted that she and her colleagues had been caught with "their pencils down."[77]

Harry Truman had served less than three months as vice president when Franklin Roosevelt died. Although Harry had served in Congress and lived with his family in Washington since 1935, none of the Trumans had attracted much notice. Other Senate wives could offer little insight into Bess because she reportedly stopped attending their meetings when she found them boring.[78] Even the Democratic Party lacked accurate biographical information on the wife of the new president and erroneously reported that she had once taught school.[79]

Margaret Truman called her mother the "least understood" member of the family.[80] Bess's deep desire for privacy evolved out of her view that publicity was undignified and unbecoming a lady, a bias that guaranteed her a different relationship with the American public than her predecessor had cultivated. Neither Eleanor Roosevelt nor any other First Lady exceeded Bess in her commitment to help her husband but she wavered on just what that meant. At first she had agreed to have Eleanor introduce her to reporters; but then on the train back to Washington after the Hyde Park funeral, she had sounded out Frances Perkins on the subject. "I'm not used to this awful public life," Bess explained, and Perkins consoled her and assured her that Eleanor was unique in thriving on the exchange with reporters. When Bess learned that no other president's wife had held regular press conferences, she promptly cancelled hers and never scheduled another one.[81]

Ceremonial appearances could not so easily be avoided, much as Bess would have liked to limit them. Her hands perspired profusely at White House receptions even when things went smoothly,[82] and when some mishap occurred, Bess detested being at the center of attention. One of her least pleasant public appearances, permanently recorded on film, occurred only weeks after Harry's inauguration. Scheduled to christen two hospital planes, she approached the first one and swung the champagne bottle in a way she hoped would befit a lady but also break the bottle. Neither that strike nor the eight others that followed had any effect and finally an exasperated Bess turned to a military aide for help. His four swings failed because no one had scored the bottle first.

Margaret Truman, who accompanied her mother that day, found the spectacle amusing, but Bess was nonplussed as she moved on to the second plane. This time the bottle had been prepared too well and her first strike showered her with champagne. The navy lieutenant in charge of the ceremony suggested that reporters describe it as though it had gone perfectly but they preferred the real version and gleefully relayed all the details. Harry Truman tried to make a joke of it all by teasing his wife about losing the tennis champion's arm of her youth, but she refused to be placated and retorted that she would have liked to have cracked the bottle on his head.[83]

Although Bess Truman and Eleanor Roosevelt were born within months of each other, Bess remained very much a private, introspective woman of the nineteenth century while Eleanor pushed farther and farther outside herself and into the twentieth. Eleanor found traveling by plane efficient and invigorating; Bess thought it too fast to be dignified—she took the train.[84] Eleanor struggled with public speaking and eventually mastered it while Bess refused to try.

Eleanor thought women would continue to make gains in politics until one of them eventually won the presidency but Bess believed that "would never happen."[85] Eleanor went out on her own, apparently unconcerned about criticism, while Bess kept carefully in her husband's shadow because she feared looking foolish. On a 1948 trip to Cuba, she would not even attempt speaking Spanish, a language she had studied, because she feared an error might be reported in the newspapers.

Such low public visibility should not obscure a very important part for Bess in the Truman administration. Margaret Truman noted that her mother felt shut out of some decisions during the White House years and became a spectator, but it was only a relative exclusion. (Harry later composed a significant epitaph for her: "First Lady, the United States of America, 1945–1953.) Eleanor Roosevelt, who strongly supported her successor's desire to do the job her own way, might well have noticed that the Truman marriage was much closer than her own to the partnership of respecting equals that she herself had described as ideal. Servants and neighbors, visiting royalty and newsmen, all agreed that the Trumans were the closest family they ever saw in the White House. With their daughter, a senior in college when Harry became president, they were dubbed by their staff the Three Musketeers. All of them laughed a lot, but particularly Bess who, one maid observed, acted as though she had invented laughter.[86]

Neither Bess nor Harry concealed the fact that their partnership extended to his work. Her family connections in politics had helped launch his career. In 1944, when a reporter asked what role she would have in Harry's campaign for vice president, Bess replied that she would make no speeches but would help him write his "because we've done that so long, it's a habit."[87] When it was revealed that she had been on his Senate payroll, Harry defended hiring her: "She's a clerk in my office and does much of my clerical work. I need her there and that's the reason I've got her there. I never make a report or deliver a speech without her editing it."[88]

A lifetime of correspondence between Harry Truman and his wife reveals how much he valued her judgment and how often he conferred with her on important matters. Not all the letters survived, as their daughter pointed out. After he had become president, Harry found Bess burning some papers and inquired what they were. "They're your letters to me," she said, and he responded, "Well, why are you burning them? Think of history." "I have," she replied and kept on burning.[89] Enough were saved, however, to make more than one book, and in 1983, hundreds of Harry's letters, written to his wife over half a century, were published in *Dear Bess*.

The correspondence shows a continued sharing of thoughts with so much background information missing that the writer must have assumed no need to repeat it. In September 1941, for example, Harry wrote from his hotel in Kansas City that he had spent hours with various Democratic Party leaders. After naming some of them, he concluded: "My, what a difference from last year . . . and what a kick there is in it. They all . . . wonder what I am going to do for the poor old 'Party'. What should I do?"[90]

In his breezy accounts of meetings with Joseph Stalin and Winston Churchill at the end of World War II, he summarized in the manner of one associate updating another. From Berlin he wrote on July 25, 1945: "We have accomplished a very great deal in spite of all the talk. Set up a council of ministers to negotiate peace with Italy, Rumania, Bulgaria, Hungary, Finland and Austria. We have discussed a free waterway program for Europe, making the Black Sea straits, the Danube, the Rhine, and the Kiel Canal free to everyone. We have a setup for the government of Germany and we hope we are in sight of agreement on reparations."[91]

Harry Truman continued to defend his confidence in Bess's opinions long after he left office. In a 1963 interview with the Washington reporter Marianne Means, he explained that he had talked over with his wife the use of the atomic bomb, the Marshall Plan and post-war rebuilding, and the Korean military action: "I discussed all of them with her. Why not? Her judgment was always good." The Trumans' daughter later underlined her mother's impact on the administration by crediting her with obtaining increased funding for the National Institute of Health and with arranging for theater groups to tour the world under the auspices of the State Department.[92]

The foundation for strong mutual respect between Bess and Harry was established when they were very young. His family had left their Missouri farm when he was six and moved into Independence so that he and his brother could get a "town" education. The Trumans owned hundreds of acres but like many farmers, they had borrowed heavily in order to buy. They always owed money, Harry once said, to somebody. First in Sunday school and then in the Independence elementary school, the bespectacled Harry was permanently smitten by a blond, blue-eyed classmate (whose family rarely owed money to anyone). Almost sixty years later he wrote her from the White House, "You are still on the pedestal where I placed you that day in Sunday School in 1890."[93]

Bess Wallace's maternal grandfather, George Gates, had moved to Independence from Vermont in the 1850s and had established a profitable milling business that produced the nationally famous "Queen of the Pantry" flour. For his wife and three daughters, he built a seventeen-room Victorian mansion that was still impressive when it became the summer White House almost a century later. It was, one reporter wrote, a residence that "in any city anywhere . . . would command respect."[94]

When one of Gates's daughters, Madge, the "queenliest woman" Independence ever produced,[95] married David Wallace, the son of the town's first mayor, it seemed a perfect match. But neighbors later concluded that Madge's egotism made her a less than sensitive wife. One story that made the rounds of Independence had it that Madge had her dress splattered by a cantering horse, and she had immediately registered her surprise. "Doesn't he know who I am?" she asked, leaving it unclear whether she referred to the rider or the horse.[96]

Whatever his reasons, David Wallace put a gun to his head and took his life when he was forty-three, leaving Madge with four children. Bess, the oldest, was just eighteen, and according to Margaret Truman, this tragedy, more than any other single event, produced Bess's unusually great insistence on privacy.[97] Widow Wallace moved her family back into her father's house on North Delaware Street but she never quite recovered from the shock. Bess, the dutiful daughter, did not go away to college, but remained in Independence and commuted to Barstow Finishing School in nearby Kansas City. Thus, she could begin a long correspondence with Harry Truman who was working his parents' farm ten miles out of town.

Harry, the most faithful of writers, constantly chided Bess about owing him a letter and reported his own activities with a combination of self-doubt and braggadocio. He insisted that if she married him he would try to provide the same level of luxury she had in the Gates mansion or, failing that, he would supply equivalent prestige. "How does it feel being engaged to a clodhopper who has ambitions to be Governor of Montana and Chief Executive of U.S.?" Harry wrote in 1913, but continued, "He'll do well if he gets to be a retired farmer . . . but I intend to keep peggin' away and I suppose I'll arrive at something. You'll never be sorry if you take me for better or for worse because I'll always try to make it better."[98]

The combination of blundering ambition and great determination evidently appealed to Bess and, although she admitted she found him an enigma, she appreciated his devotion. He repeatedly offered to buy tickets for whatever show she would consider seeing with him.

Aware of her tennis prowess, he constructed a playing court at the Truman farm to tempt her to come visit him on Sundays.

Whatever Harry could offer her, he never seemed to think it enough, and while he tried first one scheme and then another, he compiled the longest courtship record of any president. He later complained that he never understood why she made him wait fifteen years to marry her. Bess's mother, the hard-to-please Madge Wallace, judged a farmer like Harry unworthy of her only daughter, but Harry was partly to blame, too, because he wanted to make good first. When the farm did not produce as he hoped, he turned to mining and then to drilling for oil. In 1917 he enlisted in the Army and opened a canteen.

Fighting in France evidently tempered Harry's expectations about what he should be able to offer his bride or changed Bess's ideas about how long she wanted to wait. They had announced their engagement before he sailed and when the war ended, he could not conceal his eagerness. She rejected his suggestion that she meet him in New York so that they could marry there, and their wedding took place in Bess's hometown church with the appropriate number of attendants on June 28, 1919. Madge Wallace continued to doubt that the bride-groom would ever amount to much. He had shown up for the wedding in a Shepard plaid suit, she noted disapprovingly, when solid linen would have been more appropriate.[99]

Harry's mother-in-law was not the only one surprised by the marriage. The bride and groom, both in their mid-thirties, differed so much from each other that even their daughter, born when her parents were almost forty, marveled at the contrast. Bess, an athletic young woman who developed into a controlled and very private woman, made Harry look particularly bookish and impetuous. As a child, he stuck to his books because he feared breaking his spectacles, and he never did learn to mask his sharp temper. While he became widely read in American history, she liked a good murder mystery. He delighted in winning small stakes at poker, but she preferred bridge. Theirs was, apparently, one of those unions of sharply different partners who chose to team up in maturity after both had developed very separate identities.

Harry did not immediately set out to win political office. After he failed at running a men's store, opened in partnership with an army buddy, he accepted the invitation of another army friend, James Pendergast, nephew of Jackson County's political boss, and tried for a judgeship. When Harry Truman assumed that office in January 1923, he began a government career that lasted, with the exception of two years, for three decades. Bess reluctantly faced the prospect of being a political wife.

Unlike Eleanor Roosevelt, who seemed intent on carving out her own niche in Washington, Bess merged her identity with Harry's. In 1945, when questioned about her past, Bess replied: "I have been in politics for more than 25 years."[100] But it was a subtle participation, quite unlike that of Eleanor who had combined her public and private lives into one seamless whole. For Bess, the two parts remained separate—her public role consisted of keeping quiet and making sure her hat was on straight. Her private life was her own business, although it was understood in Washington that she did not lack opinions.[101]

This apparent contradiction led to considerable confusion. Although *Good Housekeeping* named Bess Truman one of Washington's ten most powerful women in 1949, the public knew little about her because she refused to tell much. After nine months in the White House, she went Christmas shopping alone and unnoticed.[102] When the *New York Times* published a feature article on her in June 1946, the headline read, "The Independent Lady from Independence,"[103] and three years later readers of *Collier's* learned that Bess was "still a riddle."[104]

All information about the First Lady came from her two secretaries: Reathel Odum, who had formerly worked for Harry, and Edith Helm, whose White House experience went back to the Wilson years. Reporters soon learned to expect from Odum and Helm only the barest facts, none of them very informative about the Trumans. After much badgering, Bess finally consented to respond to reporters' written questions but even then she used "No comment" for nearly one third of their queries. She revealed that she thought the two most important characteristics for a First Lady were good health and a strong sense of humor but, she added, a course in public speaking would also be helpful.[105] Perhaps her most telling response came to the question of whether she had wanted her husband to be president. "Definitely did not," she wrote, underlining "definitely."

In the absence of other information, reporters wrote about her comings and goings, her housekeeping, which was "excellent," and her "mind of her own about menus."[106] Her refusal to speak out on matters of public concern gave readers the impression she knew less than she did and that she was the "Martha" type who contented herself with "minding her knitting."[107]

Much of the information was simply wrong. One national news magazine reported that Bess Truman "neither drinks nor smokes."[108] Another ran a photograph of her refusing a glass of wine, with the caption: "No prohibitionist, Mrs. Truman just doesn't like the taste of the stuff."[109] When Bess and daughter Margaret chose orange juice over cocktails at a New York dinner, they made the *New York Times* and received an approving letter from a Binghamton (New York) Methodist church. Bess politely thanked her supporters but failed to enlighten them about her drinking preferences.[110]

White House employees made clear in their published memoirs that the Trumans liked a cocktail before dinner. In fact, they had definite preferences in how their drinks were mixed, something the staff had to learn. According to J. B. West, who worked many years in the White House, Bess rang for the butler her first night there and ordered old-fashioneds for herself and the president. Since the butler had once worked as a barman, he took considerable pride in his mixing abilities, and he confidently added fruit slices and bitters to the drinks before serving them. Bess made no comment about the fruit slices but pronounced her drink too sweet. The next evening an identical order received even greater attention from the butler but the same reaction from the First Lady. Finally on the third night an exasperated butler poured straight bourdon into the glasses. This time Bess smiled. "That," she said, "is the way we like our old-fashioneds."[111]

That such stories became known only after the Trumans left the White House resulted from Bess's refusal to talk rather than from her adjusting her behavior to fit what the public wanted. In fact, what endeared her to many people was her insistence on remaining unchanged by her prominence. She invited the entire membership of her hometown bridge club to stay at the White House and see Washington from the top. Each time she returned to Missouri she made clear that she wanted no fuss from her neighbors and that she expected to be treated like everyone else. In spite of heavy commitments as the president's wife, she kept her mother with her until Madge Wallace died in December 1952. Bess's brothers had volunteered to help but she insisted that it was a daughter's duty.

Beyond the household management and the ceremonial appearances, Bess Truman spent much of her time answering about one hundred letters a day. It was a far less demanding schedule than Eleanor had kept, but one congressman thought she ought to be compensated. Calling her job the "only case of involuntary servitude in the USA," Representative James G. Fulton (Republican, Pennsylvania) proposed giving the president's wife an annual salary of $10,000. The country provided for widows of presidents, Fulton said, but did little "for wives who are in there working on their job every day."[112] The proposal was quickly dropped as not being authorized by law,[113] and Bess continued working as presidents' wives had before her—for nothing.

Unlike Eleanor Roosevelt, Bess Truman had never shown any interest in earning money on her own. She had spent the twelve years between graduation and marriage at home, improving her tennis and learning how to run a household. When Harry opened the men's clothing store, she assisted in keeping the books, and when he needed her in the Senate office, she helped out, but her income came from her husband.

To encourage women to break out of that kind of dependence, the 1944 Democratic Convention ran a campaign school to help women improve their public speaking skills and understand economics and foreign policy. Teachers included Helen Gahagan Douglas, a candidate for Congress from California, and Florence Jaffray Harriman, former minister to Norway, who demonstrated how to capture the attention of a street-corner audience. Bess Truman, who accompanied Harry to the 1944 convention which selected him to run for vice president, took no part in the women's school, and when reporters approached her and the wife of the current vice president, Henry Wallace, and asked for a statement, both women begged off. Bess "shrank from comment" according to the *New York Times,* and insisted she was primarily a homemaker.[114]

The shyness that marked Bess Truman in public led people meeting her for the first time to characterize her as formal and cold, but the household staff held quite a different view. One maid who served almost thirty years in the White House, following her mother who served an equivalent time, concluded that "Bess was best."[115] When John Kennedy invited the Trumans back to the White House in the early 1960s, he commented on how exuberantly the older staff members greeted them.

Much of Bess's value lay in her tempering influence on her husband. When his salty language and fiery temper got him into trouble, she reprimanded. Her frequent "You didn't have to say that" became a joke with the White House staff.[116] Liz Carpenter, later press secretary to Lady Bird Johnson, remembered seeing Bess take her husband by the collar and back him into a hotel room when she thought it unwise for him to go out.[117] Harry's most noted outburst of indignation—the fiery letter he sent to Paul Hume, music critic of the *Washington Post* who had disparaged Margaret Truman's singing ability—appeared in print because the president wrote it and mailed it himself rather than checking it out with Bess or the usual White House channels that were equipped to save him from his own excesses.

Harry repaid his wife with frequent vows of devotion and swift attacks on her critics. When Washington reporters hinted that she lacked style, being "dull, dumpy and distant,"[118] Harry retorted that she looked just the way a woman of her age ought to look. Leonard Lyons, the columnist, remembered that he had driven past a billboard with Harry and had noted the advertisement, "Gentlemen Prefer Blonds." Harry had sniffed and said that "real gentlemen prefer gray."[119]

In defining just what a First Lady should do, Harry and Bess Truman apparently agreed that Bess's activities, except for ceremonial appearances, were her own business. He liked to remind reporters that he had been the candidate and if something in the Truman household did not please, he would take the blame.

For her part, Bess acted as though she could go where she pleased regardless of her husband's job. When she attended a reception of the Daughters of the American Revolution after that organization had refused to permit a black pianist to perform in its Constitution Hall, her critics were many and loud. The pianist, Hazel Scott, was married to a New York congressman, Adam Clayton Powell, who quickly dubbed Bess "Last Lady of the Land." The president retaliated by barring Powell from the White House along with Clare Booth Luce, who had nicknamed the president's wife "Payroll Bess" because of her Senate office job. So willing to confront criticism of himself, Harry Truman would not tolerate derogatory remarks about his wife or daughter.

In Bess's definition of a lady, especially a First Lady, taking sides in public controversy did not appear. She went ahead with her plan to attend a play starring Ingrid Bergman, even though she had to cross a picket line protesting George Washington University's exclusion of Negroes from the audience.[120] Except for an occasional appeal that people buy savings bonds or contribute to the March of Dimes and the Girl Scouts, she rarely issued public statements; her announcement in 1949 that she hoped Congress would repair the old White House rather than taking the cheaper option of constructing an entirely new mansion was an exception. She publicized a drive to prevent waste of food by inviting one thousand War Hospitality volunteers to a garden party and then did not serve refreshments,[121] but when mothers appealed to her in early 1951 to oppose the draft for eighteen-year-olds, she answered that she could not help. On the matter of extending women's rights, she showed little interest, and the number of women holding high presidential appointments did not register big gains during her husband's two administrations.

In one of her more revealing statements, reported in *McCall's* in 1949, Bess chose the Monroe administration as the period in American history that she found "interesting."[122] She did not explain whether it was the lack of party rivalry that drew her to the early nineteenth century or the reputed skill with which Elizabeth Monroe shunned the public's curiosity about her. Perhaps Bess felt a special sympathy for Elizabeth Monroe, who followed the popular Dolley Madison into the White House and had to redefine the limits of being a president's wife. Like Elizabeth Monroe, Bess Truman realized how different her own training and inclinations were from those of her predecessor, and she insisted on working with what she had and letting those who followed do the same.

That tolerance for difference served Bess Truman well when the time came to introduce her successor to the White House. After giving Mamie Doud Eisenhower (1953–1961) the traditional tour, Bess turned to one of the domestic staff and predicted a "lot of pink" in the years ahead. That maid had reason to recall those words later as she watched Mamie Eisenhower add "fluffy, fussy" touches everywhere, from the pink furniture in her bedroom[123] down to pastel cloth covers on her lipstick holders.[124] The First Lady's favorite color fit well America's mood in the 1950s when femininity meant opinionless dependence. Pink was, after all, the insignia of baby girls.

Mamie Eisenhower did not invent that model of femininity, but she represented it well, making clear by her every public utterance that she thought a wife's role entirely secondary and supportive. Her thirty-six years of marriage had been a series of moves, averaging almost one per year, as she trailed her army husband from one assignment to another. When he went to Panama or the Philippines or Paris, she followed, and when she could not, as in the war years, she settled down in Washington to wait. When he took her along on tours of historic battlefields, she tried not to yawn, and when he relaxed on long golf trips where there was nothing to interest her, she improved her mah-jongg and canasta, becoming a "demon" player.[125] To the reporters who inquired in 1952 how she felt about her life, she replied she was "thankful for the privilege of tagging along by [Ike's] side."[126]

Even a magazine named *Independent Woman* accepted this concept of the perfect wife and put Mamie on its January 1953 cover. The new First Lady had adapted to each change in her husband's career, Lenore Hailparn wrote, quickly rearranging successive new homes for his comfort. Mamie even carried swatches of her favorite colors to save time in the redecorating. A large part of an army wife's job involved fitting in, the *Independent Woman* writer explained, and never distinguishing oneself or staying apart from the other spouses.[127] Mamie had met that test well, and Hailparn predicted that similar behavior would assure her success in the White House.

Eleanor Roosevelt had made her first name familiar because of her ubiquitous presence and constant writing on behalf of one cause or another, but "Mamie" became a trademark for a certain style or taste. In addition to "Mamie's Fudge," there was "Mamie pink" and the famed "Mamie bangs." Americans' penchant for associating First Ladies with such matters went back to the nineteenth century, when women wore their hair à la Cleveland, but television and mass circulation magazines in the 1950s made Mamie familiar in a way that her predecessors had not achieved.

Public recognition of General Eisenhower's wife ("Mrs. Ike") had developed during World War II, when he was catapulted to fame as Supreme Allied Commander in Europe and she was singled out by reporters for both her breezy manner and her example of the patient wife. "Eisenhower's Wife Finds Wait Tough" the armed forces' newspaper, *Stars and Stripes,* reported in an article later carried in the *New York Times.*[128] Part of the public's interest in her personal life caused her great discomfort—especially the reports that her husband was romantically involved with his Irish driver, Kay Summersby. While Mamie waited in Washington, she could not fail to hear speculation about the two, who were frequently photographed together. Summersby, a willowy ex-model, young enough to be Mamie's daughter, had first been assigned to drive Ike around England. Later she followed him to Africa, and after the death of her financé in 1943, speculation increased about the relationship between her and her boss.

Evidence of just what happened between Summersby and Dwight Eisenhower is not easily assembled. Years later, Summersby wrote her own account, raising doubts about the general's ability to perform sexually at the time she knew him. "For years I never thought of making love," he reportedly told Kay, "and then when I did . . . I failed."[129] The Eisenhowers' surviving son published his father's wartime letters to Mamie to bolster claims of Ike's devotion to his wife.[130]

Harry Truman, in an interview with author Merle Miller for *Plain Speaking,* added as much fuel to the gossip as anyone when he recounted how Dwight Eisenhower had written to his superior, General George C. Marshall, after the war ended to announce that he intended to divorce Mamie and marry Kay.[131] According to Truman, Marshall threatened to end Ike's career if he went ahead with his plan, and the matter ended there. This exchange of letters was never made public for reasons not entirely clear. Summersby admitted that she had no hint that Ike had written to Marshall until she read Truman's account,[132] and Marshall's biographer doubts that the exchange of letters ever took place.[133]

Whether or not the relationship threatened the Eisenhowers' marriage, reports of it circulated freely and continued to be part of Washington gossip even after Ike became president.[134] Mamie kept up a cheerful front, maintaining in *Look* magazine that there could have been nothing improper between her husband and Summersby because "I know Ike."[135]

Between 1945 and 1952, when Dwight Eisenhower served first as Chief of Staff, then as president of Columbia University, and finally in Paris as Commander of NATO forces, Mamie perfected her skill at entertaining large groups of important people. She paid close attention to centerpieces, menu selections, and seating arrangements, giving reporters every reason to believe that being a good hostess would continue to be her focus in the White House. In contrast to Eleanor Roosevelt and Bess Truman, who both disliked that part of the job, Mamie insisted she enjoyed it, and at her first press conference she read a projected schedule for herself, listing what one reporter described as "tea by inexorable tea."[136]

One group after another descended on the executive mansion for a personal greeting from the president's wife, and she tried to satisfy as many requests as possible. When she could not manage to receive 1600 members of the Federation of Women's Clubs who wanted to come by for tea on short notice, she went down to their convention center to soothe hurt feelings.[137] During the 1952 campaign she shook hands with thousands of people, averaging more than 700 in a day, and managed, her admirers said, to make each greeting individual and different.[138] Rather than complaining, she gave the impression, *Time* reported, of being a "happy household manager."[139]

What her husband called her "unaffected manner" made Mamie's choices for the White House a reflection of popular taste rather than a showcase of high culture. She liked to call on Fred Waring or on male quartets to entertain her guests,[140] one of whom reported that Mamie's favorite number was "Bless This House."[141] Her publicized preference for gladioli (flowers her successor, Jackie Kennedy, reportedly detested)[142] and for taking her dinners off TV trays (just-as many Americans learned to do in the 1950s) rendered her a familiar, friendly figure. She made the White House "livable and comfortable," her husband said, and therefore "meaningful for the people who came in."[143]

Behind the scenes, the staff gave a different picture—one that reflected Mamie's "spit and polish" army background. She checked for cleanliness by running a white glove over window sills as she passed through rooms, one of the staff reported, and she insisted that vacuum cleaners be run frequently to erase evidence that anyone had walked on the plush carpets.[144] To one maid who had seen many presidents' wives come and go, Mamie's possessiveness about her temporary domain grated, particularly her references to "my sofa" and "my rugs" as though they belonged to her personally.[145] J. B. West, assistant chief usher, argued that Mamie was simply establishing her command, having developed in her years as an army officer's wife a "spine of steel" and a complete understanding of how a large household worked. "She could give orders," West wrote, "staccato crisp, detailed and final, as if it were she who had been a five-star General."[146]

Americans less acquainted with the running of the White House saw only Mamie's "softer" side and they found her as charming as a pretty little girl accepting compliments at a family reunion. For a woman who spent much of her energy on how she looked, there could be no headier reward than a bevy of ubiquitous photographers. She obliged them cheerfully. In 1952 she had accompanied Ike on the campaign train and she posed with him even if that meant getting up in the middle of the night to satisfy well-wishers who had waited for hours to catch a glimpse of the famous general. On one occasion she had gone out on the platform in her bathrobe; when some photographers, who had missed the shot, asked for a replay she gamely acquiesced even though it meant putting her hair back in curlers.[147]

The Eisenhower White House presented its occupants as a typical family with Mamie as familiar and folksy as the woman next door. She insisted that reporters call her Mamie "because it's so much friendlier,"[148] and her close associates revealed that she greeted them with "girls" or "kiddo," regardless of their ages and that she signed her letters "Bless you, Mamie E."[149] She announced that she often bought clothes off the rack, and that once, after having spotted a $17.95 dress in a store window during a campaign, she had mailed off an order for it. Instead of expensive jewelry, she wore costume pieces and had a costume jeweler design a set of pearls and rhinestones for the inaugural ball.[150]

In spite of her protests that she spent no more than most women on clothes, Mamie Eisenhower made the Dress Institute's roster of Best Dressed Women, a list enlarged in 1952 beyond the usual ten to accommodate two from the world of politics: Mamie and Oveta Culp Hobby, later named Secretary of Health, Education and Welfare. Both women had started out slowly in the polling, the Institute announced, but had ended up tying for eleventh place.[151] The wardrobes of presidents' wives had been a recurring topic of conversation since the earliest days of the republic, and Mamie's popularity promised that she could affect cash registers. One major newspaper put it this way: her "taste in garb [will] give a lift to the fashion industry . . . [because she always wears her clothes] with an air."[152]

Mamie's claim to fashion fame relied less on line than on coordination of color. She favored full skirts and small hats that clung to her head and showed off the bangs she had worn for years to conceal a high forehead. Young ladies (and their mothers) all across America imitated her and matched their accessories in the pastel pinks and greens that she preferred. Mollie Parnis, who designed many of Mamie's clothes, explained that the First Lady had very little fashion sense but relied on others to "bring all the accessories she would need . . . to make sure Mamie would be put together correctly."[153]

In a decade that put more stress on women's youthfulness than on their intelligence, Mamie became a national heroine. Reporters frequently noted that she looked younger than her years, and she herself admitted that she hated "old lady clothes."[154] Pink strapless evening dresses that she chose for White House parties differed little from those selected by high-school seniors for their proms.[155] Because she felt "too young to be a grandmother," she urged her grandchildren to call her "Mimi,"[156] and to maintain a figure in line with that image of herself, she made frequent trips to an Arizona spa.

Mamie contributed to the 1950s maxim, so well illustrated in the movies of Marilyn Monroe and Judy Holliday, that intellect and femininity did not mix. A national women's magazine described her as "no bluestocking feminist,"[157] and she announced that, like Bess Truman, she preferred mysteries for reading matter.[158] She cheerfully admitted that she had no ear for languages, and although she had lived all over the world, in Panama, the Philippines, and France, she spoke little Spanish or French. Language classes with Bess Truman and other Washington women had been mostly for laughs, Mamie admitted: "None of us ever really studied."[159] When St. Joseph College in Emmitsburg, Maryland, conferred an honorary degree on her in March 1959; she had such a case of "mike fright" that she called on Ike to relay her thanks.[160] Anyone suggesting that she might enjoy writing her memoirs was reminded that she did not like to work.

Such breezy, nonintellectual femininity satisfied so well the predominant mood of the 1950s that when *Better Homes and Gardens* published a series on how to raise children, it suggested Mamie's background as perfect for producing a First Lady.[161] Born in Boone,

Iowa, to a couple who quickly accumulated enough money to live comfortably the rest of their lives, Mamie resembled in many ways her Swedish mother, Elivera Carlson Doud, who at age sixteen married a man considerably her senior. Before she was twenty-two, Elivera had borne him four daughters and in many ways acted as a fifth. When the family moved to Denver for the benefit of the health of one of the girls, Elivera made their house on Lafayette Street a gathering place for the neighborhood. The red carpet that lined the front porch steps served as seating for whoever came by and distinguished the rather ordinary structure from others on the street. A staff of four performed all domestic chores while the woman of the house ran around Denver in her Rausch and Lang electric auto, an extravagance that reportedly cost her husband $4,800 in 1910.[162]

On one of the Doud family's winter trips to San Antonio, Mamie met young second lieutenant Eisenhower, who came from a family of seven boys and had received none of the pampering that Mamie and her sisters had. Ike had supported one brother through college, then gotten himself an appointment to West Point so that he could attend free. His pacifist mother had overlooked the implications of his going to a military academy, he said, because of her determination to see all her sons through college. Mamie's parents, who paid no attention to cost, put far less importance on schooling for their daughters, and Mamie stopped after one year of finishing school. That was quite enough, *Better Homes and Gardens* reminded its readers: "Neither [Mamie's mother] nor Mamie had attempted to become an intellectual yet both have been outstandingly successful as wives of their well-educated husbands."[163]

Partly to preserve her youthful appearance and partly because of poor health, Mamie Eisenhower spent much of her White House day in bed. After being served a tray at 8:00 or 8:30, she sat in her pink bed jacket, a pink ribbon holding back her hair, and went over the day's schedule with head usher Howell Crim and his assistant, J. B. West.[164] Then came sessions with Mary Jane McCaffree, her social secretary, and with the housekeeper, Mabel Walker, a holdover from the Trumans. Mamie spent so much time in bed, one maid reported, that the staff nicknamed her "Sleeping Beauty."[165]

For additional rests, Mamie sometimes went off to her mother's house in Denver or to the Gettysburg farm that the Eisenhowers had bought, the only home they used for any length of time during their entire marriage. To speculation that these trips were really drying-out spells for her alcoholism, Mamie never gave a reply during the White House years, but in 1973, she admitted in an interview that she was aware the stories had circulated. They had begun, she said, because of the effect of a condition, carotid sinus, which put excessive pressure on her inner ear and upset her sense of balance. So severe was the disequilibrium that she was frequently covered with bruises because she collided with objects, but since her condition had no cure, she had learned to live with it.[166]

Mamie's equilibrium had become a matter of discussion almost from the time her husband entered politics. In 1952 a Republican delegate from Nebraska confronted Ike directly: "We hear [Mamie's] a drunk." Ike waited a bit, one witness reported, and then replied, "Well, I know that story has gone around, but the truth of the matter is that I don't think Mamie's had a drink for something like 18 months."[167] Later, White House staff would back up Ike's claim. If Mamie had a drinking problem earlier when she was an army wife, she showed no signs of it as First Lady.[168]

All her adult life Mamie had suffered poor health, and one illness had figured in the central tragedy of her life. In the winter of 1920 to 1921, her first-born son, then three years old, had become sick and been hospitalized. Mamie, suffering herself from a respiratory infection, was not permitted to go near him. Weeks later, when he died, her grief was multiplied because of her sense of helplessness. Ike called his first son's death "the greatest disappointment and disaster in my life."[169] For Mamie, the loss was at least as traumatic. Even after the birth of a second son in 1923, she did not appear completely recovered from the tragic loss suffered earlier.

By the time Ike was assigned to the Philippines for a four-year stint (1935–1939), Mamie was already spending much of her time in bed.[170] A weak heart and respiratory problems caused doctors to forbid her to fly and then when they permitted her to go up in planes, they suggested she not exceed five thousand feet.[171] Her first term in the White House showed no decline in her health and in some ways she seemed better, but her physical condition again became an issue in the 1956 campaign. The Republican national chairman Butler referred indirectly to Mamie when he ventured that the incumbent would probably not run for reelection because of a "personal situation in the Eisenhower household."[172] The reference was not quite indirect enough, and the president and his supporters denounced Butler for bringing up Mamie's health. James Reston, the widely read columnist, objected: "To drag a President's wife into the political bear pit is a dubious maneuver. It has been tried before but never with notable success."[173] Mamie's mother had fueled the speculation by declaring that her daughter could not stand another four years in the White House.[174]

By the time of renomination in the summer of 1956, the country's attention focused more on the president's health than on that of his wife. In September 1955, while visiting Mamie's family in Denver, the president had suffered a coronary thrombosis, and the first reports from Denver indicated that the entire family had united to urge him not to try for another term.[175] John Eisenhower later reported it had been Mamie, aware of the consequences for Ike if he was forced into inactivity, who encouraged him to run again. The final decision was the president's, of course, and he announced at a news conference, in response to a reporter's question about family influence, that he had made up his own mind and the family had gone along in good military fashion.[176]

Although reporters went into considerable detail explaining the president's medical condition, they evidently considered details of the First Lady's health inappropriate copy. When Mamie entered Walter Reed Army Medical Center in August 1957, James Hagerty, the president's press secretary, told newsmen she had undergone a "two hour operation by a gynecologist . . . similar to those that many women undergo in middle age." When a reporter asked if that had been a hysterectomy, Hagerty replied that he could "not go beyond [my] original statement."[177]

This reticence in discussions of health, reticence so often associated with femininity and propriety, still extended to political campaigning in the 1950s. Even Eleanor Roosevelt had once questioned the wisdom of campaigning for her husband, and in 1932 she had spoken up—not for Franklin but for Herbert Lehman who was running for New York State governor. "I don't think it would be proper," she explained, "for the wife of a candidate to appeal to voters on his behalf . . . and I'm not going to mention [Franklin] in any speech I make."[178] Joseph Lash attributed Eleanor's reluctance to "her clear concept of what was fitting in a democracy for a public official's wife," and he concluded that she struggled with that concept all through Franklin's career. In Mamie Eisenhower's case, the decision came more easily. She apparently had little interest in the political process, and Republican strategists in both 1952 and 1956 limited her campaigning to posing alongside Ike and to permitting an occasional article to be published under her name. "Vote for my husband or for Governor Stevenson, but please vote," Mamie's article in *Good Housekeeping* began.[179]

In showing little interest in politics, Mamie reinforced the very low profile of women in public affairs in the 1950s. Several women held elective and appointive office during that decade, but when the National Federation of Business and Professional Women's Clubs decided to honor women in government at its 1957 spring luncheon, it selected vice president Richard Nixon as the speaker. On the day he appeared, fifteen women served in the House of Representatives, one in the Senate, and one sat on the cabinet, but he ignored them and talked instead about Hungarian refugees and Communists in government.[180] If the Business and Professional Women's Clubs had no objection to having the accomplishments of their sisters ignored, the president's wife could hardly be faulted for keeping in step.

After eight years, Mamie Eisenhower left the job of First Lady as she had found it, except for one small, tentative change. The *Congressional Directory* of March 1953 acknowledged for the first time the distaff side of the Executive Office when it listed Mary McCaffree, "Acting Secretary to the President's wife." Mamie's name did not appear, but the foundation was laid for a much expanded staff under her successors.

In nearly three decades (1933–1961) only three women presided over the White House, and their unprecedented longevity meant that more than one generation of Americans grew to maturity with these three models. The last First Ladies to have been born in the nineteenth century, they illustrate more variety than similarity and prove once again that while some presidents' wives build on precedents, almost nothing is binding. Eleanor Roosevelt had little patience for discussing clothes and flower arrangements, while Mamie Eisenhower talked of little else. Bess Truman dedicated her energies to serving as private sounding board for her husband's ideas, while Eleanor Roosevelt went out on her own to develop projects. Bess and Mamie stuck closely to the definitions of "lady" taught them by their genteel mothers, while Eleanor added a whole new dimension to the word, especially when preceded by "first."

After 1960, expectations for presidents' wives would change rapidly, and few candidates' spouses would dismiss campaigning for their husbands as not "proper." In fact, campaigning on her own would become the accepted—even expected route to First Lady. The old conflict between private "person" and public "personage" would continue to trouble all who took the job, and a new feminist movement would raise other expectations for each of them. Curiously enough, it was Mamie Eisenhower, generally perceived as the least shrewd of the three, who pointed out in 1977 how completely the job of First Lady had changed since she left Washington. Reticence and a place on the list of "Most Admired Women" no longer sufficed, she acknowledged when she met Rosalynn Carter and explained, "I stayed busy all the time and loved being in the White House but I was never expected to do all the things you have to do."[181]

8

The Turbulent Sixties

IN FEBRUARY 1960, WHEN the field of likely nominees for that year's presidential election had narrowed to five, *Newsweek* compared the men's wives and predicted that one of them would preside over the White House in the next four years. As it turned out, two of them did; and before the decade ended, three of the five had served as First Lady. With very different personalities and priorities, each carved out an individual response to a turbulent period in American history—one of exhilaration, then questioning and delusion as attention turned from space exploration and the Peace Corps to John Kennedy's assassination and then to Vietnam. In less than a decade, the style of First Ladies changed too, so that campaigning became a requirement instead of an option. Acting as White House hostess dropped as a priority; spearheading substantive reforms rose. In short, the president's wife moved out of the society columns and on to the front page.

Of the five singled out by *Newsweek* before the major parties convened to choose their candidates, only Evelyn Symington fell from national prominence. Muriel Humphrey, the most traditional of the five and the one who described herself as a "mother of an ordinary family," never lived in the White House, but she saw her husband take the vice presidency in 1965, and after his death she served briefly as a United States senator from Minnesota. The remaining three in *Newsweek*'s list, Pat Nixon, the disciplined "super-duper" wife of the vice president, Lady Bird Johnson, the "human-dynamo business-woman," and Jacqueline Kennedy, the youthful, "stunning egghead," all got a chance to preside over the White House.[1]

As soon as the two major parties made their nominations in 1960, attention focused on Thelma ("Pat") Ryan Nixon and Jacqueline

Bouvier Kennedy, whom the *New York Times* described as "fantastically chic." Beginning what became almost unqualified adulation of everything the Kennedys said or did, the *Times* announced in mid-July that Jackie had already captured "fashion's high vote" by showing an interest in clothes that paralleled her husband's approach to politics: both the Kennedys combined "confidence, individuality, a mind of [their] own and a knowledge of issues."[2] Photogenic Pat Nixon, already a familiar face since her husband had just completed eight years as vice president, fared less well in the *Times*, but crowds came out to see her campaign for the Republicans.

This prominent role for candidates' wives marked a new development, fostered by the proliferation of television sets. By 1960, nearly 90 percent of American homes boasted at least one set. (The figure had been less than 50 percent when the Trumans left Washington in 1953.) Mamie Eisenhower had not ignored the medium—she had chatted amiably with Edward R. Murrow on "See It Now," but the aging military wife lacked the charisma of a star. Both candidates' spouses tried to do better in 1960, and one major newspaper emphasized how they had broken precedents: "Never before have the wives of both candidates been so active. . . . Mrs. Nixon sits in on strategic councils with her husband, travels extensively, and follows a busy schedule of press conferences."[3] Not many years had passed since Eleanor Roosevelt had deemed campaigning for one's husband to be in poor taste—a view that Bess Truman and Mamie Eisenhower apparently shared.

Neither Jackie Kennedy nor Pat Nixon took real pleasure in the political game but each had learned, with varying degrees of success, to disguise her feelings. Pat Nixon insisted she found handshaking invigorating and the difference in crowds "interesting," while the less experienced wife of the Massachusetts senator fought to curb her tongue on the subject. She had already angered reporters with her flip answers about wearing sable underclothing. Her lack of enthusiasm for the long hours of handshaking and small talk that went with winning primaries showed up in several ways. In the Midwest, she had reportedly baffled one audience by suggesting that everybody join in singing "Southie is my Hometown," a song virtually unknown west of Massachusetts.[4]

Jackie Kennedy's pregnancy (announced soon after her husband's nomination) allowed her to retire to Hyannisport for the rest of the campaign, an absence generally interpreted as her best contribution to victory. Some wags suggested that the impending birth had been contrived to keep her home, and one story labeled the pregnancy a hoax: John Kennedy would wait for the election returns to come in and then turn to his wife and say, "Okay you can take out the pillow now."[5]

Although Jackie's political interest remained very low, she evidently had known the goal of John Kennedy's ambitions before she married him in 1953. According to her cousin, John Davis, she had initially dismissed John as "quixotic because . . . he intended to be President."[6] John Davis concluded that Jackie found the "unity and spirit" of the Kennedy clan appealing after the "dissipation and squabbling" in her own family, but that she never completely disguised her boredom with politics—or her preference for discussing art and artists.[7]

If the woman whose husband would be president did not enjoy going to the people, she could perfect another campaign style which made them come to her. By remaining aloof—but glamorous and confident in her aloofness—she stirred up more interest than if she had mingled with the crowds and hugged every child in sight. Jackie Kennedy had the uncanny knack of intriguing a nation, partly because her personal history read like a fairy-tale with more than its share of sophistication, money, and villains.

Born on Long Island in 1929 to a stockbroker and his society-conscious wife, Jackie Bouvier attended the fashionable Chapin School in New York and then the prestigious Miss Porter's in Connecticut. After her parents divorced and her mother was remarried, this time to Hugh Auchincloss, who was considerably wealthier and more successful than Jack Bouvier, Jackie and her younger sister Lee divided their time between Merrywood, the Auchincloss estate outside Washington, and Hammersmith Farm in Newport, Rhode Island. When time came for college, she took two years at Vassar and a year in Paris before finishing at George Washington University. Her stepfather arranged through a family friend for her to go to work for a Washington newspaper and soon she had her own byline for a column, "Inquiring Photographer."

Although many other young women in the 1950s compiled similar records of international travel, multilingual competence, and careers of their own, none of the others topped off their accomplishments with marriage to a senator who seven years later won the presidency. Jackie's youth (she was only thirty-one when she became First Lady), her wit (she had joked with reporters about the meaning of "egghead"), and her flair for fashion all put her in sharp contrast to her immediate predecessors. She would have aroused curiosity even if she had done nothing more than play the White House hostess, but she resolved to do more.

Just weeks after John Kennedy's victory over Richard Nixon, Jackie gave birth to a son, and within days, she was announcing through her social secretary, Letitia Baldrige, "sweeping changes [so the White House would become] a showcase of American art and history."[8] Following this precedent-breaking, pre-inaugural announcement, Jackie assembled a large staff, until eventually Baldrige reported that she had "forty people . . . in the First Lady's Secretariat."[9] Not all of them could boast the credentials of Baldrige, who came well prepared for the job. The daughter of a congressman, she was a veteran of American embassies in both Rome and Paris, and she had been on the Kennedy staff since the summer of 1960, well before the outcome of the election was clear.

Astute observers did not fail to note how the wife of the president-elect tailored her public statements to complement his upbeat, energetic approach to the office. While John Kennedy incorporated phrases about a "new frontier," his wife talked of "new beginnings" and the "best" of everything. The *New Yorker*, in an amusing article entitled "Mrs. Kennedy's Cabinet," underlined the parallels when it compared the Kennedys' appointments. Both John and Jackie had included Republicans (Letitia Baldrige and Douglas Dillon), the *New Yorker* pointed out, and both had rewarded early boosters (in her case, the hairdresser Kenneth). Their most important selections, however, had come slowly, with both Kennedys announcing on the same day the designer of her inaugural wardrobe (Oleg Cassini) and his secretary of state (Dean Rusk). Both Cassini and Rusk had been, the *New Yorker* explained, "rather dark horses."[10]

As soon as her husband was sworn in, the new First Lady moved to leave her imprint on his administration. Old tensions about whether a president's wife should stress humility in order to appeal to the people or set herself apart at a royal distance went all the way back to the Monroe administration. Jackie Kennedy quickly took her place in the elitist camp. Within a week of the inauguration, she had begun her campaign to upgrade the taste of the nation. On January 25, she met with an old friend, the artist William Walton, and experts from the Commission of Fine Arts and the National Gallery to discuss plans for restoring to the White House its original furnishings.[11] That same afternoon she took tea with George Balanchine, the Russian choreographer who then headed the New York City Ballet. By the end of her first week on the job, she had made clear that although she had listed her priorities in the same order as had Bess Truman and Mamie Eisenhower, placing husband and children first, she meant to perform in a very different way.

For a start, she meant to gain notice, and she began in what had traditionally been the province of presidential wives. Each White House family had enjoyed considerable freedom to choose what to bring into the mansion and what to throw out. Over the years many valuable pieces had simply disappeared—sold at auction or carted off as junk. Presidents did not usually involve themselves in the decisions (James Monroe and Chester Arthur were the notable exceptions), and wives could choose to reflect their own personal preferences or treat the mansion as a museum of the country's treasures. Following structural renovations in the 1920s, Grace Coolidge had prevailed on Congress to pass legislation permitting the president to accept appropriate antiques, but so few were forthcoming that the law had little effect. Lou Hoover had attempted to stimulate interest in the White House by asking a secretary-friend to write a book on the subject, but depression times were hardly conducive to attracting donations of the Federal or Early Empire styles.

The early 1960s found Americans in a more giving mood, especially when a popular First Lady and new tax laws encouraged them in their generosity. Television did its part by making Jackie Kennedy a celebrity. During her first year in the White House, two networks produced documentaries, showing how she had popularized the pillbox hat, bouffant hairstyles, and the name "Jacqueline" for baby girls. No one could explain exactly why she had achieved such instant stardom, but one commentator suggested that she appealed to the country's fascination with youth. The youngest First Lady since the 1890s, she underlined her youth by being frequently photographed with her two little children. More subtly, however, Jackie Kennedy offered a new model of womanliness. Here was a First Lady who seemed acquainted with Europe, informed about literature and the arts, yet attractive enough to compete with movie actresses and sex symbols. The "dumb blond" stereotypes of the 1950s appeared curiously dated, and NBC concluded its adulatory program on Jackie Kennedy with the question: "Whatever became of Brigitte Bardot?"[12]

This enormous popularity helped promote the campaign to furnish the White House with authentic antiques. The First Lady prevailed on wealthy individuals to contribute, assembled a professional staff to oversee the collection, and engaged scholars to give guidance and advice.[13] To insure that her efforts could not be cancelled by a successor with different tastes, she secured passage of legislation making the furnishings of the White House of "historic or artistic interest . . . to be inalienable and the property of the White House."[14] John Kennedy feared that she might be criticized for extravagance, so it was arranged that the sale of White House guidebooks, which began July 4, 1962, would help finance the project.

Jackie Kennedy's efforts to restore the White House (she did not like the term redecorate) received considerable publicity, including a one-hour special on national television during which millions of viewers watched her move through the mansion and describe the provenance and significance of the furnishings and artworks. Jack Gould, television reviewer for the *New York Times*, pronounced her an extremely able historian, art critic, and narrator, but even such an admirer as he could not fail to notice that she sidestepped the substantive questions. When narrator Charles Collingswood asked her what relationship the federal government should have with the arts, she thought it too "complicated" to answer but she reiterated her view that the White House deserved "only the best."[15]

But something besides Jackie Kennedy's interest in art came through that night. In escorting television cameras around the White House, she projected the image of a little girl, her breathy and hesitant, Marilyn Monroe–type voice moving over a very narrow pitch range. For those viewers who had seen Jackie at her television debut on the Edward R. Murrow "Person-to-Person" program in 1953, this appearance marked some progress. A new bride at that time (the program was entitled "Senator John Kennedy and His Bride"), she had said very little, and her incongruous holding of a football during the time she was on screen caused some viewers to wonder if she had anything to say.

Her participation in the televised tour of the White House in early 1962 was more than a personal milestone. Harry Truman had escorted television crews around the renovated White House in his administration, and Tricia Nixon would later perform this task for her father. Jackie did not come across as exactly professorial, but she did inject a somewhat worldly note, and she signalled the possibility that a president's wife could bring some of her own interests to the job of First Lady, at least as long as those interests remained traditionally feminine. As a *New York Times* reporter observed: "It is now all right for a woman to be a bit brainy or cultured as long as she tempers her intelligence with a 't'rific' girlish rhetoric."[16] This was a small beginning in altering attitudes about what constituted femininity, but it marked a change from Mamie Eisenhower's unwillingness to show that she could think and Bess Truman's reluctance to be seen.

Jackie rationed her appearances—even those at family gatherings. Her cousin John Davis explained how a group of Bouviers and Auchincloses proceeded to the White House after the inaugural parade, but the new First Lady would not come downstairs to see them, even after her mother went to intercede. True, the schedule of a president's wife at inauguration time is packed, and Jackie had given birth by Caesarean section only two months earlier, but her relatives were understandably bewildered by her treatment—to them, she was, according to Davis, "just Jackie."[17]

Most Americans remained oblivious, of course, to tensions within the Bouvier-Auchincloss clan, but they could read in any newspaper that the new president's wife had little time for the luncheons and teas that typically filled a First Lady's calendar. Citing obligations to her children, Jackie Kennedy simply refused to go. Sometimes she sent her husband or her secretary or enlisted the vice president's wife, but she adamantly preserved most of her time for herself. Her refusals to appear caused considerable embarrassment to those left with the task of inventing excuses for her. Katie Louchheim, an active Democratic Party regular, acknowledged that she could not persuade Jackie to meet even briefly with the consort of an important South American, although the visitor was such an ardent admirer of the American First Lady that she had brought a piece of her wedding silver as a gift.[18]

Although reporters later grumbled about Jackie's failure to cooperate with them, they continued to turn out flattering copy. Even Margaret Mead, the anthropologist who wrote regularly for *Redbook*, climbed aboard the press's pro-Kennedy bandwagon and suggested that the new First Lady had managed to alter Americans' ideas about White House occupants. Allowed little freedom to voice their own opinions or expose their own tastes, most First Ladies had attempted to remain discreetly unobtrusive, but not Jackie Kennedy, who, Mead explained, had "gladdened the eye" and awakened Americans to their cultural heritage.[19]

Mead's analysis, stated in such general terms, missed an important point about the Kennedy years. Several of Jackie's predecessors, especially the young ones such as Julia Tyler and Frances Cleveland, had "gladdened the eyes" of their countrymen and women, but none had done so in quite the same way. Many of the others had contented themselves with echoing the administration line and staying close to home. Jackie Kennedy insisted on being her own person—breaking all kinds of precedents for First Ladies by going off on her own extended vacations. Previous presidents' wives had limited themselves to dutiful family trips (such as Bess Truman's summers with her mother and daughter in Independence) or to serious, fact-finding missions (such as Eleanor Roosevelt's car trips to both the East and

West coasts) but none gained the attention of Jackie's luxury-packed international forays. She often vacationed away from Washington without her husband, yachting one time in the Mediterranean with Aristotle Onassis and friends, another time riding elephants in India with her sister, still another summer introducing her daughter Caroline to the sights of Italy.

Jackie evidently gave considerable attention to leaving her mark as First Lady—her correspondence with Eleanor Roosevelt on the topic and her determined effort to restore the White House would argue that she meant to be no slouch—but she refused to include subservient wifeliness in her definition of First Lady. For those political wives who sacrificed all individuality in order to fit themselves into a faceless mold, she showed considerable contempt, and her reported comment that Lady Bird Johnson would crawl down Pennsylvania Avenue on broken glass for Lyndon reveals more about the speaker than the subject.[20]

Not surprisingly, her record involved many contradictions. Although she was sometimes pictured as a rather spoiled princess, she persisted with projects she considered worthwhile, such as the White House restoration which she had been "warned, begged and practically threatened," she said, not to undertake.[21] Aloof and unapproachable in a country that stressed friendly casualness in its leaders, she managed to remain much admired. Even the country's historians got caught up in the contradictions in her appeal. Long after she had left the White House, one hundred American professors rated her sixth among all twentieth-century First Ladies, but in "integrity," that supposed *sine qua non* of government, they rated her last.[22]

Even her femininity involved contradictions. Soft-spoken, yet assertive, she refused to concern herself with important national or international issues although she appeared intelligent enough to do so. Both John and Robert Kennedy underlined this interpretation of her role. Robert, the attorney general, noted approvingly that she was the kind of wife who would not worry her husband at the end of a long day with, "What's new in Laos?" John Kennedy made the same point when he said, "I don't have to fight the day's political battles over again at night."[23]

Like many politically ambitious men of his generation, John Kennedy had trouble taking women seriously, a trait possibly influenced by his parents' distinction between the education of sons and daughters. The boys had the best preparatory training and Ivy League schools while the girls were enrolled in intellectually less rigorous women's schools.[24] In other important ways, the parents had set distinctly different models for their children. While Rose Kennedy had her children's respect, she never received the homage they paid their father, whose brashness, blatant ambition, and separation of wife and family from other romantic interests contrasted sharply with Rose's piety and dependence.[25]

Later revelations of John Kennedy's sexual activities in the White House would titillate readers and inspire television programs, but little was published on the subject before his death. Even the most casual White House observer could see, however, that a different model of wifeliness accompanied Camelot. Jackie Kennedy's decision to play something other than the loyal wife may have resulted from John's decision not to play dutiful husband; but regardless of the causes, it paved the way for future First Ladies to act on their own. Eleanor Roosevelt had been perceived as separate from Franklin, with her own friends and interests, but Franklin's physical incapacity partly excused the deviation. John Kennedy was not disabled, but Jackie struck out anyway, thus helping prepare the way for her successors to maintain their own individuality.

The Kennedy administration ended before the feminist movement of the 1960s got its full start, and most women's magazines continued to present a model that included the old combination of kitchen, kids, and kindness to all. Diamonds and hope chests still dominated the thinking of most young women, while graduate schools cooperated by setting firm quotas to hold the line against female applicants. First-rate medical schools accepted only a handful of women in each class.

The description of the Kennedy years as a kind of Camleot came from Jackie Kennedy in speaking to the writer T. H. White a few days after the assassination. Although she no doubt intended to make a different point, her description aptly fitted the mentality of the young president and his circle of close advisers who resembled chivalrous and energetic knights eager to do battle. John Kennedy named no women to his cabinet—although Dwight Eisenhower had—and none to any highly visible, powerful post although Janet Travell served as one of his personal physicians. Of all his appointments requiring Senate approval, less than 3 percent went to women, about the same as in the Eisenhower and Truman administrations.[26]

India Edwards, a longtime Democratic Party regular, blamed the president's "Irish Mafia" for excluding women from power, and she suggested John Kennedy viewed women as "nothing but sex objects."[27] Nan Dickerson, television correspondent and Kennedy friend, pronounced John Kennedy "the complete male chauvinist . . . and he thought it ridiculous to pay them the same as men."[28] Lady Barbara

Ward, the British economist, told an interviewer after John Kennedy's death: "[He] had little empathy for the trained, intelligent woman— he may have, but my impression is he hadn't."[29]

John Kennedy's appointment of the Commission on the Status of Women is often singled out as an important step in beginning the federal government's move into guaranteeing women's rights, but in light of his total record, his motives seem suspect. The impetus for that move came from Esther Peterson, a former lobbyist who had known John Kennedy in his Senate days. She worked for him in the 1960 campaign and then prevailed on him to take some action on women's rights, which he did in spite of his own reluctance.[30] By appointing the commission, John Kennedy deflected pressure to do something more substantive.

Whether or not that record on women's issues would have changed in a second Kennedy term remains unknowable. The First Lady had just returned from a vacation in Greece when she consented to make one of her rare political trips with her husband. Partly to mend Democratic fences in preparation for the 1964 election, the president and vice president went together to Dallas, where, with the assassin's bullet, the Kennedy administration ended. Thus it happened that Lyndon Johnson, unlike other vice presidents in similar circumstances, was there to be sworn into office on the afternoon of November 22, 1963, just ninety-nine minutes after John Kennedy died.

The quickly improvised ceremony aboard Air Force One was delayed until Jackie Kennedy arrived; photographs of the inauguration show her standing, in a pink suit stained with her husband's blood, alongside the grim-faced Johnsons. This marked an unprecedented appearance of an ex–First Lady, as though her presence might help confer legitimacy on the transition even though the details of the assassination—who killed John Kennedy and why—remained unclear. No woman widowed as First Lady had ever been present for the inauguration of her husband's successor—even Eleanor Roosevelt did not attend Harry Truman's inauguration in 1945 although she was still in the White House at the time.

In planning for John Kennedy's funeral, Jackie assumed a far more prominent, publicized role than had any of her predecessors in similar circumstances. Presidential widows had attended their husbands' funerals since 1881, and both Florence Harding and Eleanor Roosevelt had made important decisions about the services, but none of them provided quite the drama Jackie Kennedy did.

Six years earlier when her father died, she had amazed her relatives with her decisive orchestration of his funeral. She oversaw the flower arrangements, located a particularly appealing photograph, and insisted that the obituary be hand-delivered to the *New York Times*.[31] Now turning that same determination and confident taste to her husband's funeral, she chose the smaller St. Matthew's rather than the huge Shrine of the Immaculate Conception. It was within walking distance of the White House so mourners could move toward it in a procession that combined the spirit of a western town at "High Noon" with the ritual of a Mediterranean village. Few from among millions of television viewers who watched the veiled, black-clad Jackie Kennedy walk behind her husband's coffin would ever forget the sight. After the funeral, she stood to accept the condolences of leaders who had come from all over the world; and then, as though to assure a permanent reminder of her residence in the White House, she arranged for a plaque to be placed over the bedroom mantel recording the number of days that "John F. Kennedy and his wife Jacqueline" had lived there. This last effort proved unnecessary, because she had stimulated such great interest in the White House and its occupants that no future First Lady could ignore her example.

Certainly the immediate successor, Lady Bird Johnson, could not dismiss Jacqueline's popularity as inconsequential. Later the First Lady from Texas wrote that she doubted "anyone else is a star when Mrs. Kennedy is present,"[32] but she set out, nevertheless, to make a record for herself. Claudia Alta ("Lady Bird") Taylor Johnson (1963–1969) had already served a long Washington apprenticeship, having arrived there as a bride in 1934. Except for two years (1935–1937), she had spent at least part of every year in Washington while Lyndon progressed from being secretary to a congressman to congressman himself (1937–1949) and then U.S. senator (1949–1961) and majority leader (1955–1961). Despite that long acquaintance with the capital, she apparently never expected to live in the White House, and in November 1963, she described herself as feeling as though she were "suddenly on stage for a part I never rehearsed." She may well have been the "political wife" who told Abigail McCarthy "in confidence": "If I had known that this was going to happen to me, I would have changed my nose and my nickname."[33]

Although the nickname was typically traced back to a nursemaid who pronounced the young Claudia "pretty as a ladybird," the truth is more complicated. In interviews late in life, Lady Bird Johnson admitted that in East Texas, where she was born in 1912, her early playmates were children of her family's African American employees, and it was they, with names like "Stuff" and "Doodlebug," who conferred "Lady Bird" on her.[34] Later, when she met and married Lyndon Baines

Johnson, he seized on the coincidence of their initials and proceeded to extend it to every possession or offspring—daughters, dogs, and ranches. Lady Bird confessed she had come to live with her name (friends and family called her "Bird") although she had suffered some embarrassment when, traveling through Europe with her husband, she heard the nobility-conscious ask, "Lady Who?"

When Lady Bird Taylor was five, her mother died. Although she later insisted that her childhood was never lonely, many students of the Johnson record have concluded otherwise. A sickly, unmarried aunt assumed responsibility for much of Lady Bird's upbringing, and although she initiated her niece into the pleasures of literature and nature, she left other areas untouched. "She never taught me how to dress or dance," Lady Bird later remembered, and her weakness and frailty presented a model of what to avoid, rather than what to attempt. Although the aunt had genuinely poor health, Lady Bird suspected "that some of it must have been psychosomatic. She was completely mild and unaggressive, and . . . because I saw how inhibiting it was to her life to be so weak and full of illnesses. . . . I set my sights on being more like my father, who was one of the most physically strong people I have ever known."[35]

Bright and quick, Lady Bird finished high school at fifteen but arranged to rank third in her class, one-half percentage point behind second place, because she feared giving the graduation speech required of the top two students. Still not ready to consider large universities, she enrolled for two years at a small Episcopal boarding school in Dallas. The choice was hers, not her father's. He had not been impressed with the school but bowed to her wishes, showing a faith in a fifteen-year-old's judgment, she later said, that she hoped she extended to her own daughters.[36]

Later, when she enrolled in the University of Texas, Lady Bird had more than the average student. She drove her own car, had an unlimited expense account at Neiman-Marcus, and a checkbook that required only that she fill in the numbers. Yet hers was neither a glamorous nor luxurious life. She wore her aunt's cast-off coats and never emerged as a belle at parties, showing early evidence of both the shyness and spending habits that she retained through adulthood. She continued to shop for "seconds" in linens long after she became a multimillionaire. For John Kennedy's funeral, she reportedly borrowed rather than bought the requisite black attire.[37] Although she liked to characterize herself as "careful [with money] only to the point of not liking to see waste,"[38] even her kindest supporters used stronger terms. Nan Dickerson, the news correspondent, described her friend Lady Bird as "both very rich and very frugal."[39]

This carefulness extended beyond money to other areas of young Lady Bird's life. Having completed requirements for her liberal arts degree at the University of Texas, she remained another year to earn a journalism degree as well, and just to make sure that she had prepared for all contingencies, she perfected her typing and steno- graphic skills. It would be difficult to contrive an education for an American woman in the 1930s that prepared for more eventualities than the one that she worked out for herself. She had hoped to become a newspaper reporter but carefully enrolled in courses that would qualify her for a teaching certificate, not because she ever wanted to teach but because she hoped to go to some faraway place "like Alaska or Hawaii."[40]

A woman as careful as that might be expected to proceed very cau- tiously in choosing a husband, but after years of plotting to get herself out of small-town Texas, Lady Bird Taylor made the most important decision of her life in uncharacteristic haste. Following a two-month courtship, carried on mostly by mail and telephone between her home and Washington where Lyndon Johnson worked, she married the tall, overpowering Texan who, she later admitted, resembled her father in many ways.[41]

Twenty-six-year-old Lyndon, then employed as Congressman Kleberg's secretary, had been visiting his home state when a friend introduced him to Lady Bird and he immediately engaged in a courtship which she her- self described as "whirlwind."[42] He arranged a date with her at the earliest possible moment, which happened to be breakfast the next day, and then regaled her with every detail of his life story: how he had come from a poor family, worked his way through Southwest State Teachers College, taught briefly, and then taken a job in Washington. He even told her how much life insurance he carried. Lady Bird admitted she was impressed. "I knew I had met something remarkable," she later said, "but I didn't know quite what."[43]

Two months after that first encounter, Lyndon returned from Wash- ington to marry her and, even though she remained unconvinced, he loaded her in his car, told her "now or never" and started off toward San Antonio. Her Aunt Effie had counseled caution, but Lady Bird's father had warmed immediately, telling his daughter: "This time you brought home a man."[44] In spite of the fact that her aunt "was scared to death" for Lady Bird, the marriage took place on November 17, 1934. Even the bride conceded it was "kind of whacky. You know some man comes in and wants to marry you, and you've only known him two months."[45]

After a short honeymoon, the Johnsons settled in Washington and Lady Bird, at twenty-two, began what she later described as her education in politics. She had not previously shown any interest in the subject but Lyndon proved a persuasive teacher. He brought home a list and told his bride: "I want you to learn the names of all these counties— . . . [the ones] my boss, Congressman Kleberg, represents. These are the county seats. These are the principal communities in each county and one or two leaders in each. Whenever you travel around with me; when we get to this town, you want to know. . . ."[46]

At home, Lady Bird learned that a political wife had other responsibilities as well. Their small Washington apartment became "open house" for any of Lyndon's political friends—and for those he hoped to bring into that category. For a woman who had never cooked a meal, she learned fast, not only to prepare food for her husband but also for whatever number he brought with him unannounced. And she did it all on a minuscule budget. When Lyndon's salary totaled only $265 a month, he took $100 for his car, insurance, and other personal expenses, leaving her $165 to pay for everything else, including an $18.75 savings bond every month.[47]

When a Texas congressman died in 1937, leaving his seat vacant, Lyndon decided to try for it. Lady Bird borrowed against her inheritance, still under her father's control, to stake him to the race. Although Robert Caro, one of Lyndon's biographers, later concluded that the campaign cost many times the $10,000 that Lady Bird put up for it,[48] she took much of the credit for financing it, and she admitted that she carried with her the relevant bank withdrawal slip until it became too faded to decipher. Lyndon's campaign manager later recalled how Lady Bird had attempted to use her financial support as leverage to influence how that first political race was run: "She came and told me that she was helping pay for this campaign and she wanted her husband to be a gentleman. She didn't want him to [speak out against the other candidates.]"[49]

In the end it was more than Lyndon's victory in 1937 that drew Lady Bird to politics. She found her husband more vibrant and exciting during that first difficult race for Congress than ever before or after, and she loved being part of it all, if only from a back seat. She lacked both the confidence and the inclination to campaign openly and such participation would have been highly unorthodox in Texas at that time. Although the state had elected a woman governor in 1924, she had been a stand-in for her husband, who had been impeached, convicted, and removed from the same office.[50] Candidates' wives still stayed in the background in the 1930s and 1940s, and one senator's wife pretty much set the standard. When asked if she campaigned for her husband, she replied: "No, indeed. . . . I just go along with Mr. George and sit on the platform to show them I don't have a cleft foot."[51]

Lady Bird Johnson might never have moved beyond such a definition of her role had not the war intervened. Lyndon Johnson had represented Texas's 10th Congressional District a little more than four years when Japan attacked Pearl Harbor in December 1941. Within hours, he asked to be assigned to active duty, at an officer's pay which was one-third what a congressman earned. Lady Bird took charge of his office and managed it without compensation until he was called back, along with other congressmen, a few months later. She frequently singled out this period as a turning point in her life, because it helped her understand her husband better, but more importantly, it gave her confidence that she could do things on her own. She attended to the needs of Lyndon's constituents (a word written with a capital "C," she sometimes said) as though they were her own, providing detailed answers to their inquiries and escorting those who came to the capital to see the tourist sites. Although she never showed an interest in holding office herself, one aide judged that she could have defeated Lyndon in an election for his job.[52]

Rather than setting out on her own, Lady Bird played the supportive wife—a designation that in this case involved financial support. Her own modest inheritance would never have financed Lyndon to the top of the political ladder, and elective office itself paid little. The Johnsons then set out to make the money that would support them during his career in government. When an almost bankrupt Austin radio station went up for sale in late 1942, Lady Bird took more of her inheritance, borrowed an additional $10,000 from the bank, and bought the station. The former journalism student explained that she and her husband had always wanted to own a newspaper but could never afford to buy one so they settled for a radio station instead. She moved to Austin for half a year to oversee staff changes and help select programming, and by the time she returned to Washington, the station showed a small profit. When time came to license a television station in Austin, her KTBC was the only applicant, a situation later students of the subject found intriguing. Hard evidence that federal agencies favored the Johnsons over competitors is difficult to assemble, but David Susskind later voiced the objections that many people shared with him when he queried Jack Valenti on the matter, "If you wanted a station in Austin and you knew that a Senator's wife wanted one too, wouldn't that be enough to kind of scare you off?"[53]

As television gained popularity and technical sophistication, the revenues of Lady Bird's Texas Broadcasting Corporation skyrocketed and the market reached beyond Austin. When asked about her phenomenal success, Lady Bird attributed it to timing and a good staff, saying her family had entered the field just as the industry underwent great expansion and they had profited from the work of an exceptionally astute group of employees. She suggested that her own role in management of the stations had been exaggerated,[54] and evidence suggests that Lyndon maintained a close, protective eye on what happened to the corporation, even after he became Senate Majority Leader.[55]

It would be wrong, however, to conclude that she functioned merely as a figurehead for the empire-building of her husband, whose political aspirations made too close identification with the company unwise. She continued to review weekly packets of information on the corporation all her Washington years (until the presidential period when the holdings were placed in trust),[56] and after Lyndon's death, she resumed an active role in the corporation. The family ranch was turned over to the National Park Service before Lyndon's death, because he apparently decided that his wife would not want to manage it, but the considerably more valuable broadcasting empire remained under family control. After 1977, when her business manager died, Lady Bird increased her role, and when an interviewer asked how it felt to be "back as a business-woman," Lady Bird answered that it had happened in a way that she had not anticipated, but that she was "enjoying it."[57] Her daughter Luci remarked in 1984 that she had never appreciated her mother's business acumen until she sat with her on corporation boards and understood how hard she had worked "to build up a family business for us all."[58]

While marriage to Lyndon may have pushed Lady Bird to meet new challenges, such as buying a radio station, it had its trying side as well. He frequently berated his wife in front of others, criticizing her clothes or her makeup, but when he chided her, "You don't sell for what you're worth," she chose to hear the compliment in the remark rather than the censure.[59] Robert Caro, in his book on Lyndon, reported that the criticism started as soon as the marriage ceremony had ended. On the first day of their honeymoon, the Johnsons stopped to visit old friends, and as soon as they sat down to talk, Lyndon noticed a run in Lady Bird's stocking and told her to go change. When she hesitated, evidently embarrassed, he insisted that she leave the room immediately.[60]

Later Lyndon's list of "Don'ts" included full skirts and T-strap shoes because he thought they made her look fat. She dieted and exercised because he made no secret of his preference for svelte women, and she wore the reds and yellows he liked and struggled with high heels even though she admitted she "hated them [and] always felt I was going to fall down and that . . . people weren't really meant to wear high heels, the Lord didn't fix the foot that way."[61] Rather than complaining, she insisted, in the manner of a diligent student defending the excesses of an overzealous teacher, that his likes were her likes: "What pleases Lyndon pleases me."[62] She pointed out that she grew because of his demands, and she later told an interviewer: "I think we were a whole lot better together than we were separate."[63]

The petite woman who had, one friend said, the "touch of velvet and the stamina of steel,"[64] found few critics except those who disdained her unfailing loyalty to her husband. Even Lady Bird once admitted that her view of her role might be too traditional for some tastes: "I really wanted to serve my husband and serve the country, and if that sounds—geesy, well . . ."[65]

This was no easy assignment she set for herself, and reporters marveled at how she managed. Lyndon Johnson could be exceptionally coarse; one journalist reported how Lady Bird had sat through a 1960 press conference, head held high and appearing not to hear a word, while Lyndon announced to the assembled group that his sleep the night before had been interrupted by some "vigorous activity." He winked to underline his meaning and then suggested that dubious reporters could check with Lady Bird.[66] Her silence should not be mistaken for approval or acquiescence, and she later told an interviewer: "I thought his jokes were—his language was too—it did not please me."[67]

Lady Bird learned to accept Lyndon's raucousness and his chiding as well as his continuing use of their home as an extension of the office. Marvella Bayh, the spunky wife of the Indiana senator, recalled that Vice President Johnson had taken her and her husband to The Elms, the Johnson home in 1963, soon after the Bayhs arrived in Washington. "He went from room to room, opening doors and calling out," Bayh wrote in her autobiography, "and then finally he opened a door and there was Luci in her bathrobe with her hair in rollers. "She greeted us with a big smile," Bayh wrote, "as if she were accustomed to having her bedroom door thrust open to admit strangers."[68] Nan Dickerson remembered that Lyndon once called Lady Bird from an Austin airport saying that he was bringing home nine reporters for the weekend. When they arrived an hour later, everything was prepared for their comfort.[69]

More than household management was involved in Lady Bird Johnson's political education. After Lyndon accepted second spot on the Democratic ticket in 1960, she took speech lessons and then traveled 35,000 miles in two months to speak to voters.[70] Before 1960, Lady Bird's work for Lyndon had been within the traditional woman's sphere—telephoning, stuffing envelopes, and shaking hands at tea parties—but her new role, as wife of the vice president, imposed other demands. Because Jackie Kennedy frequently refused to appear on ceremonial or political occasions, Lady Bird substituted, and one Democratic party official pronounced her "more than generous" with her time.[71] Sometimes this meant preparing in only a few hours to speak to large audiences; when Lady Bird filled in for Jackie on national television, one reporter deemed her "Washington's Number 1 pinch-hitter."[72]

In November 1963, when Lyndon became president, Lady Bird's opportunities for action increased, and she proceeded to alter the public's expectations of what a First Lady might do. Much of what she did is detailed in her book, *A White House Diary*, which resulted from the tapes she made during her husband's presidency. It was the most complete record of a First Lady's tenure since Eleanor Roosevelt turned out her daily columns.

Comparisons between the two women came quickly, with many observers noting that both grew along with their husbands' political successes to personalities of their own. The fact that both women began their marriages as shy, supportive helpmates should not obscure, however, important differences between them. Unlike Eleanor Roosevelt, Lady Bird did not thrive on the controversies inherent in politics, and she disapproved of First Ladies who involved themselves in issues that might divide the country.[73] Lady Bird kept her views on civil rights and Vietnam to herself, and she never sought an individual constituency for herself. Nor did she pursue a political or diplomatic career in her own right. After her husband's death, she withdrew from public life and ventured out only when her son-in-law, Charles Robb, sought help. It had all been fun, she said, and she had learned a lot but "Politics was Lyndon's life, [not mine and] 38 years were enough."[74]

While Lyndon lived, his ambitions always came first with Lady Bird, and she put all her energies into helping him. He could have won the 1964 election without carrying states below the Mason-Dixon line, but his wife volunteered to campaign there because she did not want to lose those states "by default."[75] Many southerners had vigorously opposed President Johnson's stand on civil rights and any move by him to change their minds seemed doomed to failure, but his wife's campaigning was something else. On a train dubbed the "Lady Bird Special," she wound her way out of Washington into the Carolinas and over to New Orleans, giving forty-seven speeches along the way.[76] Assisted by daughter Lynda for the first two days and then by Luci, she enticed local politicos to join her (although many of them would have balked at being photographed with the president.) Because they could pass off an appearance at Lady Bird's side as simple chivalry, one after another recalcitrant Democrat climbed aboard. Some of the holdouts sent their wives.

Lady Bird did not meet individuals to bargain on specific matters— her husband's staff had come along to perform that task—but in her deep Texan accent she pleaded with crowds of southerners to understand that her husband was one of them. When hecklers tried to outshout her, she waited a moment and then said, "Now you've had your say. Will you give me mine?" "There will always be somebody in the audience," she later pointed out, "who will say, 'that's fair.'"[77] For a woman who had always hated giving speeches, she did remarkably well. When the trip ended, just about everybody agreed that she had helped win votes for Lyndon—the disagreement came over how many. Making the president's wife appear all the more courageous, her Republican counterpart in that election took only a traditional handshaking role.

After Lyndon Johnson achieved his own clear victory in 1964 and held the presidency in his own right, Lady Bird resolved to do more for the success of the administration. The history of presidents' wives taking on causes for themselves went back almost ninety years to Lucy Hayes's temperance stand. Ellen Wilson had lent her name to a housing bill, and Eleanor Roosevelt had assisted artists, women, blacks, and other groups she judged in need of her attention. Most First Ladies had contented themselves, however, with supporting noncontroversial charities. Lou Hoover had become publicly associated with the Girl Scouts, and Bess Truman spoke up in behalf of the Cancer Society. Jackie Kennedy's White House restoration had attracted so much favorable publicity that Lady Bird perceived a public expectation that she should do more than sit in the White House, and she set out to find a cause of her own.

Choosing an area in which she held a deep and lifelong interest and one in which her staff believed Lyndon would not interfere, Lady Bird Johnson launched her "beautification" project. The interest went back to childhood and lasted into retirement so it was not contrived for the moment. She frequently said that she enjoyed most those hours of the day just before sunset when she drove around the family ranch. After Lyndon's death, she spent most of her energy on wild-flower preservation. It was a devotion, her daughters noted with some exasperation, that had not been passed on to them—"It did not come with the genes."[78]

The early 1960s offered a propitious time for encouraging Americans to care more for their environment. Rachel Carson's book, describing a "silent spring" when birds could not sing and trees could not green because of the effects of harmful chemicals, was published in 1962, the year before Lyndon became president. The First Lady's campaign to capitalize on that concern was named "beautification," even though she disliked the term and called it "cosmetic and trivial [sounding] . . . and . . . prissy, [but] try as we would we couldn't come up with anything better."[79] First Ladies had traditionally concerned themselves with the appearance of the capital, but Lady Bird went further than the others. Unlike Helen Taft, who arranged for the planting of the cherry trees, Lady Bird persisted in linking natural beauty with the quality of life, and she attributed problems of crime and juvenile delinquency, in part, to the ugliness in which people lived. Contests sponsored by her Committee for a More Beautiful Capital rewarded neighborhood participation, and she lauded historic preservation that linked people with their past.[80] Her beautification efforts did not stop in Washington—she went national—and in thousands of miles of traveling around the country, she planted trees, shot rapids, and urged people to care more about the world they would pass on to their children. Headstart, an education program for preschool children that Congress initiated in February 1965, stayed on her agenda and she became its Honorary Chairman, but for most Americans she was permanently associated with environmental concerns.

Some issues, perceived by the public as "soft" because they directly touch people's lives—matters such as aging, care of foster children, education, the arts and the environment—are often relegated to insignificant spots on the president's agenda. Deep concern and caring, not commonly associated with strength and power in American politics, tend to fall more within the responsibility of a surrogate of the president, often a wife or daughter. When visiting orphanages and homes for the aged, planting trees, and sitting in on kindergarten classes cannot command high priority on the president's schedule, a spouse can substitute, and each First Lady since 1963 has chosen a project from within these categories. Foreign policy questions, defense strategies, labor reforms, and banking practices are not likely choices for presidents' wives' projects.

To conclude, however, that the "soft" issues are trivial would be wrong. In many cases, they concern people more directly than do international confrontations and bureaucratic regulations. Before writing off Lady Bird Johnson's efforts as a contrived publicity stunt or as innocuous garden-club-lady work, it is important to remember that she appropriated for herself one of the few areas of the administration in which she would have been permitted a significant role of her own. Her husband gave no evidence of consulting with her on troop buildups, harbor mining, or bombings in Cambodia. But even Lyndon Johnson would have agreed that a successful administration had many parts and that people could not think about Vietnam all the time (although by 1968, it may have seemed to him that they did). Sometimes their minds moved to the polluted streams and the need to improve classrooms for their children—areas in which an additional spokesperson for the administration could be of help.

Lady Bird Johnson was particularly suited for this role because she appeared naturally more concerned about people's feelings than he was. When it came time to defend her friends, she sometimes acted on her own without clearing the matter with Lyndon. Her public announcement in behalf of Walter Jenkins is a case in point, although some accounts of this episode have her seeking the president's approval. Jenkins, who had worked for the Johnsons since the 1940s and whose wife and children were close to the Johnson family, was arrested in a Washington men's room on a morals charge just weeks before the 1964 election. The president, in New York for a speech, remained silent until he could assess his options and the possible consequences, but Lady Bird responded immediately. J. Russell Wiggins, then of the *Washington Post,* recalled her decisiveness: "All other times she would have followed Lyndon to the guillotine if it were necessary [but this time she acted on her own, summoning me to the White House] and in [she] came. My God, she was like a vessel under full sail. She came into that room, and she issued a statement declaring full loyalty to Walter Jenkins. She read it, and she said she wondered if we'd print it."[81]

When Lady Bird turned that same decisiveness to environmental issues, she knew she would not find unanimity on a solution. On a factfinding trip with friends outside the capital, she had been appalled by a "tunnel of filling stations, billboards, neon signs and dilapidated little buildings." Yet she understood they had a purpose and a right to be there: "These enterprises are conveniences for people and this is private enterprise. What is the answer?" she pondered in her diary.[82] Although few Americans would stand up to defend large billboards and junkyards that lined the highways, little agreement appeared on who should pay for their removal. What constituted "fair" compensation for billboards erected many years earlier, and what was the role of the federal government in dictating to the states in such matters?

The highway beautification program was promoted on many fronts. Federally sponsored conferences on the subject began in early 1965, and regional meetings were scheduled to involve governors and city officials. The administration prepared drafts of several bills on the subject, and Lady Bird went to work lobbying. She telephoned congressmen and urged her friends to do the same. Guest lists for White House dinners and receptions reflected an interest in enlisting votes, and when Lady Bird spoke to members of the Associated Press, she encouraged editorials on the subject. Reporters who followed her suggestion received a personal thank-you. Liz Carpenter recalled that she had put on her "best perfume and [gone] to Capitol Hill to call on members of Congress I knew. We needed every vote we could get, for the billboard lobby was active and well-heeled."[83]

The president pressured the House Rules committee to report the measure out (which it did by a seven to six vote) and then he urged the House to act during a night session on October 7. Notwithstanding some grumbling about the measure being a present for Lady Bird, the Highway Beautification Act became law in October 1965. It provided federal money for states that controlled billboards and junkyards along noncommercial highways. States that failed to comply with the new law within two years risked losing 10 percent of their federal allotments. Three-quarters of the compensation to billboard and junkyard owners would come from Washington. Additional money was authorized for landscaping and roadside development, but it would come from the Treasury instead of the Highway Trust Fund so as not to jeopardize new road building. Neither the president nor the First Lady conceded that the law went as far as they would have liked, but it marked a beginning.

Lady Bird's association with the Highway Beautification Act was not unprecedented—and the reaction was predictable. Cartoons featured her as they had once pointed to Eleanor Roosevelt's activities—one picture showing a maze of highways running through a forest, with the caption, "Impeach Lady Bird." Criticism remained light-hearted, however, and she wrote in her diary, "Imagine me keeping company with Chief Justice Warren! [whose impeachment had been sought by some right wing groups.]"[84]

The busy First Lady was everywhere. In addition to the more than 700 various appearances, she gave 164 speeches while her husband was president.[85] Nineteen "women-doer" luncheons recognized other achievers, and it was during one of these luncheons that the singer Eartha Kitt made her much publicized attack on Lady Bird because of the president's failure to wind down the war in Vietnam. Kitt waited until Lyndon had made a brief appearance and then left before she lashed out at Lady Bird. Young Americans understandably turned to crime, according to Kitt, because they felt hopeless about their future in a country that offered few jobs but drafted young men for war. Only Kitt knows whether her attack on the president's wife resulted from her perception that power was shared in the White House or from an entirely different conclusion that Lady Bird was weaker and more vulnerable than the president. Regardless of the motivation, Kitt's outburst put the president's wife on the spot, requiring her to reply in a situation that was widely reported. Thus she was drawn into a controversial area whether she wanted to be there or not.[86]

Lady Bird underlined her prominence by appointing a larger and better-trained staff than any previously seen in the East Wing of the White House. Liz Carpenter, a Texas newspaperwoman who had arrived in Washington about the same time as Lady Bird, served as press secretary. The social secretary, Bess Abell, daughter of Kentucky senator and wife of the assistant postmaster general, could hardly be expected to run her operation without directing a seasoned eye to the political implications. The First Lady's press section of six full-time employees, under the direction of an experienced Washington reporter, represented quite a change from the preceding administration. A team of four handled details of the social secretary's office, and another four answered correspondence. Two staff members dealt only with beautification issues, and even this entourage did not complete the team since others came from the president's wing to work on temporary assignments.[87]

Expertise became as much a mark of the East Wing as of the West. Unlike Jackie Kennedy who liked to scrawl long memos on legal pads, Lady Bird was a remarkably well-organized businesswoman and ran her side of the White House in the manner of a chairman of a large corporation. One aide, who worked for both her and Lyndon, judged her wing more efficient than the president's.[88] Leaving details of flower arrangements and menus to assistants, she was tutored on the issues by the best advisers available, including McGeorge Bundy and members of the Council of Economic Advisers.[89]

The successful combination of energy, organization, and experience won Lady Bird many admirers. Within two years of moving into the White House, observers pointed out that she had altered the job.

"What Lady Bird Johnson has done," Meg Greenfield wrote in the *Reporter*, "is to integrate the traditionally frivolous and routine aspects of the East Wing life into the overall purposes of the administration and to enlist the peculiar assets of First Ladyhood itself in the administration's behalf. They are assets no one fully understood until Mrs. Johnson moved into the White House—or at least no one fully understood their potential political clout."[90]

By the time Lady Bird prepared to leave Washington in early 1969, James Reston, the syndicated columnist, pronounced her "probably the most remarkable woman who has presided over the White House in this century."[91] Shana Alexander called Lady Bird "quite possibly the best First Lady we have ever had."[92] The same historians who rated Jackie Kennedy eighth among all First Ladies placed Lady Bird Johnson third—right behind the formidable Eleanor Roosevelt and Abigail Adams.[93] Lady Bird may well have found her predecessor's example daunting but it never paralyzed her.

Presidents' wives traditionally refuse to admit they have models, and they give little credit to their predecessors. Perhaps a fear of being judged inferior to the ideal explains this ahistorical approach, or maybe it results from a lack of information. Lady Bird Johnson insisted that she never patterned herself on anyone else—she engineered her own ways to help Lyndon, but she did see some parallels between herself and her predecessors. They had all concentrated on their husbands' well-being first, she noted, and tried to provide a setting in which the men could do a good job. "But from then on," she wrote, "it's just whatever makes your heart sing. What do you know about? What do you care about? What can you do to make this a better administration?"[94]

By 1968, Lyndon Johnson had to face up to his own questions about his administration because he encountered problems on several sides. The country's monetary system appeared in trouble, and several of the nation's cities had suffered outbreaks of violence and destruction. In the summer of 1967, National Guardsmen had been called out to restore order when rioting erupted in New York City, Rochester, Birmingham, Alabama, and New Britain, Connecticut.

The president from Texas had not ignored the fact that black and white Americans still faced very different opportunities a century after the Civil War ended. In July 1964 he signed a Civil Rights Act, often deemed the most significant legislation of that kind since Reconstruction. It outlawed discrimination in public places, including restaurants, theaters, and hotels, and it attempted to provide for Negroes to take jobs alongside white workers regardless of the prejudices of employers and union officials. The Voting Rights Act, passed in 1965, placed the registration of voters under federal scrutiny so that the right to cast a ballot would not depend on race. But for all these words on paper, equal opportunity was not yet a reality, and several inner cities seemed poised to explode with anger and frustration.

The subject that eventually dominated the 1968 presidential election, however, was the war in Vietnam. The United States' involvement there in the 1950s had attracted little notice, and even at the end of the Kennedy administration when 15,000 American "advisers" served in Southeast Asia, the men and women at home paid little attention. But by the middle of Lyndon Johnson's full term as president, the Vietnam War represented a major drain on the country's public purse and morale. Eventually, nearly nine million Americans would serve in the conflict, and more than 47,000 would die. Televised reports of the fighting brought it very close, and in 1968, talk of a new draft system, based on a kind of lottery, threatened to involve many American homes where enlistment had not been considered. Young people redefined their career plans or left the country to avoid participating in or supporting a war they could neither understand nor justify. The president's own advisers split over whether or not to continue support of South Vietnam against its northern neighbor and over what level that support should reach.

Still, most Americans expected Lyndon Johnson to seek a second term of his own, and he surprised them by announcing in March 1968, that he would not. The Minnesota senator Eugene McCarthy, outspoken critic of the American policy in Southeast Asia, had already demonstrated the potency of anti-war sentiment; and Robert Kennedy, seen by many as his brother's rightful political heir, threatened to erode Lyndon Johnson's support in other quarters. Neither of these challengers managed to capture the party's nomination, one being stopped by an assassin and the other beaten at the party's convention by the incumbent vice president Hubert Humphrey. In November, when the Democrat proved unable to put enough distance between himself and the less popular aspects of the Johnson record, the Republicans took thirty-two of the fifty states. Richard Nixon, who had appeared to renounce politics after his 1962 gubernatorial defeat in California, reemerged as a national leader.

Pat Nixon, who had thrived on those few years of private life, dutifully returned to full-time volunteer work for the administration, but she had to reconcile her old ideas about the job with the new models popularized by her immediate predecessors. Her entire Washington apprenticeship had been served under First Ladies Truman and Eisenhower, neither of whom moved beyond ceremonial appearances and social leadership. But styles had changed by 1969, and many Americans expected a more activist White House consort, one who employed a large staff of her own and involved herself in issues and causes.

Showing that she understood the shift, Pat Nixon tried to attach herself to a cause that would complement her husband's agenda for social welfare measures. Before the election, she had announced that she would concentrate on adult education and job training.[95] After the inauguration, she turned to volunteerism but except for one short trip to the West Coast in the summer of 1969, her efforts received little public notice. She then announced, through the Education Office, that she would spearhead a "Right to Read" program,[96] and when that project produced little, she spoke of becoming "more active in the environment field."[97] The next year she widened her horizons to "improve the quality of life."[98]

Some of Pat's critics blamed her husband for her failure to identify with any one project,[99] but other observers pointed out that she brought her own disabilities to the job. To ignite the country's enthusiasm, any one of these projects needed a crowd pleaser—someone who spoke easily to large groups. Yet Pat Nixon, who could charm individuals, stiffened in front of large audiences. It was her misfortune to come into the White House at a time when leaders faced the nation through television, a medium that made her uncomfortable and one that never flattered her.

Her two immediate predecessors had often been described as distant (Lady Bird) or uncaring (Jackie) in personal encounters, but both blossomed in public appearances. Jackie Kennedy, in particular, was singled out for her icy treatment of reporters and political visitors, and Bess Truman remarked after a visit to the Kennedy White House that it was as though a "veil came down" over Jackie's face during conversations. Yet she dazzled millions of television viewers as she conducted them on a White House tour. Pat Nixon's veil was of a different weave—and she lowered it on public, rather than private, occasions, causing observers to characterize her as cold and unfeeling. White House aides reported that Lady Bird Johnson, even in posing with a muscular dystrophy poster child, questioned her staff on the disease, its causes and treatment, while Pat Nixon stuck to light conversation and contented herself with hugging the child and complimenting her on her dress or her smile.[100]

Pat Nixon's youth, truncated like that of several First Ladies by the death of a parent, may explain some of the restraint in her personal style. For most Americans, she was quintessential Irish, because so much had been made of her name and her birth just hours before the dawn of St. Patrick's Day in 1912. Few people realized that her mother had immigrated from Germany and was a miner's widow with two young children when she met and married William Ryan. Later she bore him two sons and a daughter, Pat. Like many of the Europeans who immigrated to the United States around the turn of the century, Kate Halberstadt Bender Ryan never lived to see her adopted country deliver on its promises. But before she died of cancer in her early forties, she had convinced her second husband to give up the dangers of mining for a more healthful, but never prosperous, small farm outside Los Angeles.

Even with the housekeeping chores that Pat assumed after her mother's death, she continued to excel in school. She caught up, in grade level, with her two older brothers and, at the same time, took part in many extracurricular activities. When she won election to vice president of her class and secretary of the entire student body, she impressed those she worked with as masking a "strong personality" behind a "very quiet" exterior.[101] "It was only after I worked with her for a while that I understood what she was doing," the student body president later explained. "You wouldn't know what was hitting you because it hit so suddenly. I know we'd be conducting meetings [of the student body] and I was supposed to be conducting them but it wound up that she was taking over."[102]

Pat's father died (of tuberculosis) about the time she graduated from high school. Orphaned and with little money, she earned her way by sweeping floors and working as a teller in a local bank. When the chance came to drive an elderly couple to New York, she took it, although superhighways had not yet, in 1932, smoothed the hills or straightened the curves across the continent. The couple's old Packard performed imperfectly and she was, at twenty, she later told an interviewer, "driver, nurse, mechanic and scared."[103]

For two years Pat Ryan worked in New York as an X-ray technician, and by the time she returned to Los Angeles, she had saved enough money to enroll at the University of Southern California. Before she was graduated in 1937 she had prepared herself for several careers, having earned a merchandising degree and two traditional back-ups—a teacher's certificate and secretarial skills. She had even found work as a movie extra, but full-time jobs were scarce in the Depression years, and in the end she accepted an offer to teach commercial subjects at Whittier High School.

Little about Pat Ryan up to that time suggested the stiff, robot figure whom Americans would later caricature. Her students found her so lively and likable that they selected her to advise the Pep Committee, organized to arouse school enthusiasm.[104] Robert C. Pierpoint, who later covered the White House as a correspondent for CBS, was a member of the Pep Committee, and he remembered Miss Ryan of his Whittier student days as "approachable, friendly and outgoing. She was happy, enthusiastic, sprightly. Her disposition was sunny, not intermittently but all the time. . . . We liked her enormously."[105]

Since Whittier encouraged its teachers to take part in community activities, the new commercial subjects instructor went down to try out for a production of the local drama club. A young lawyer, back in his hometown after graduating from Duke (where his glumness had earned him the nickname Gloomy Gus),[106] auditioned the same night and his attraction to the new teacher was so immediate and immense that he proposed marriage that same evening. "I thought he was nuts or something," Pat later recalled.[107] He was ten months younger than she and not yet established in his profession but he pursued her with the same diligence he turned to just about everything he did. Two years later, when she was twenty-eight years old, she accepted.

The arsenal of skills that Richard Nixon's wife had carefully accumulated now went to develop his career. While he served in the Navy during World War II, she worked in a San Francisco bank, and when he got the chance to run for Congress in 1945, her savings helped finance the campaign.[108] She contributed her considerable secretarial skills to winning that election and then to running the congressman's office, all without a paycheck of her own.

Whenever Pat Nixon was questioned about her use of time, she emphasized (some thought excessively) her domesticity. Until 1952, when her husband ran for vice president, she did her own housework, and she once confided to reporters that whenever she had a free evening, she took down her husband's suits and pressed them.[109] Rather than talking about what she read or her views on national issues, she shared her thoughts on sewing dresses for her daughters and stitching up draperies on her home machine. Her husband emphasized the same helpmate quality in Pat when in the famous "Checkers" speech, he referred to her as a "wonderful stenographer."

Pat Nixon retreated farther and farther from the vivacity of her youth as her husband moved up in politics. She performed as energetically as anyone on the campaign trail, but she showed more stoic determination than real pleasure, and her distaste for politics grew as the races became dirtier. In 1950, when Richard Nixon ran for U.S. senator from California against Helen Gahagan Douglas, he accused his opponent of being pro-communist and called her "Pink Lady" at a time when such a charge was particularly vicious. Douglas replied in kind, pronouncing Congressman Nixon a "pipsqueak" for whom she had "utter scorn."[110] This campaign prompted the pro-Douglas *Independent Review* to come up with a nickname that stuck: "Tricky Dick."[111]

In 1952, when Pat Nixon watched Dwight Eisenhower abandon her husband as running mate—until he could go on national television and convince viewers that he had properly handled campaign funds—her disillusionment with politics grew. Although she encouraged Richard to make the speech that could clear him, she resented the humiliation of having to bare the family's finances for the entire nation. As her husband put it in his *Memoirs*, she "lost zeal in 1952 for politics."[112] By the mid-1950s she so strongly wanted her husband out of office that she obtained a written promise from him not to run again, but after signing the pledge, he broke it four times: 1960, 1962, 1968, and 1972.[113]

Instead of retreating (as her nineteenth-century predecessors often did) or publicly pouting, Par Nixon dutifully accompanied her husband on every trip where her presence was requested. When Dwight Eisenhower sent his vice president on all kinds of international missions and advised him to "take Pat," she went. In Caracas, where the Nixons were spat on, had their car stoned and the windows broken, they feared for their lives. Other trips proved less dangerous but very tiring, requiring that the Nixons leave their two young daughters for weeks at a time. Pat later estimated that she spent only a fraction of her time at home.

During her husband's vice presidential years, Pat evolved for the public, at least, a stiff, fixed smile and perfectly coiffed hair and she began to keep herself what was frequently described as "painfully thin." If she could not control many parts of her life, she would concentrate on those she could, and in the process she obliterated the lively high school teacher who had charmed her students. Robert Pierpoint, who had not seen her since the days of the school Pep Committee, could not believe the change. He found her tense, nervous, and drawn. Off camera, she could still be caring and warm but on film she became a "marionette," he wrote, "playing a politician's wife."[114] Foreign reporters came to a similar conclusion. "She chatters, answers questions, smiles and smiles, all with a doll's terrifying poise," a London newspaper reported in 1958 after she had visited there, "[but] there is too little comprehension. Like a doll she would still be smiling while the world broke. . . . One grey hair, one hint of fear, one golden tea-cup overturned on the Persian carpet and one could have loved her."[115]

By the time of Nixon's presidency, the robot had become a popular image to describe wives who erased all spontaneity to please their husbands. Ira Levin's novel (and later movie) *The Stepford Wives* (1972) was only one of several attempts to treat this theme. In this particular account, mechanical figures substitute for human beings with no one the wiser because the women had repressed so completely all individuality.

Stepford husbands were successful businessmen who thought they required personality-free spouses, but politicians' wives began to apply the robot image to themselves. When Betty Ford learned of her husband's elevation to the vice presidency, someone asked what she planned to do. "Just wind me up and point me in the right direction," she answered, "and I'll be there."[116] Angelina Alioto, wife of San Francisco's mayor, disappeared for seventeen days and returned to explain: "I'm nobody's robot."[117] Marion Javits, who abandoned her own career because of criticism that it conflicted with her husband's Senate work, put the matter only somewhat more subtly: "No one knows better than the woman who accompanies the man who shakes the hands how faceless one can be."[118]

Pat Nixon did not employ the robot image, but her husband's cousin, Jessamyn West, hinted at it when she reported that Pat insisted she was "never tired," something she had in common, West pointed out, with God and machines.[119] Pat included subservience as an essential part of being a good wife when she told a reporter: "A man has a right to make his own decision about his career and a woman should support that decision."[120]

Richard Nixon underlined his wife's facelessness by giving no evidence that he considered her opinions when framing his own. A longtime aide to the president admitted that he had never once heard Pat's name mentioned.[121] In his books, Richard refers to his wife's looks or to her courage and patience but not to her ideas. When questioned by the press on whether he tried out a particular speech on her, Pat replied: "He never tries anything out on me."[122] Researchers who later sought information on her White House years were likely to receive the curtest of all refusals from Richard Nixon's office.[123]

There is a long, documented record of Richard Nixon leaving his wife out of significant decisions. According to one biographer, Pat thought she had convinced her husband to refuse the second spot on the Republican ticket in 1952, but then learned while watching television that he had accepted.[124] The dilemma of whether or not to try again for the presidency in 1968 was resolved on a trip he made alone, and according to one magazine writer, Pat did not receive notice of his decision for several days.[125]

In the White House, the president's staff quickly picked up and exaggerated for their own reasons Richard Nixon's evaluation of Pat's insignificance. Jealousy between the East Wing and the president's side is a staple of White House history, especially since the First Lady's role has become more visible and her staff larger and more astute politically. Careers on both sides are quickly made and destroyed in the high-pressure atmosphere of the executive branch, and a constant jockeying for position reminds all participants how high the stakes are. However strong the president's advisers believe themselves to be, they understand that the president's wife enjoys a unique position, and part of preserving their power involves limiting hers.

The staff assembled by Pat Nixon complained of condescension from the West Wingers, especially H. R. Haldeman. The First Lady and the chief of staff made no secret of their dislike for each other— he called her "Thelma" behind her back,[126] and she objected to his puritanical views on smoking and drinking and to his hypocrisy in other matters.

Helen McCain Smith, an aide to Pat Nixon throughout the White House Years, reported that Haldeman was "always pushing, pushing, pushing the President to keep [Pat Nixon] away from the public, to dump her, advising [the President] not to take her on trips because he would do better on his own."[127] "I couldn't believe that Haldeman could be that stupid," Smith continued, "He simply did not realize her potential and her very significant assets. . . . Many times we would receive staff memos from Haldeman informing us that the President was about to go somewhere and we would see that the First Lady was not included."[128] Pat's assignments were sometimes treated a jokes. Rather than building a significant spot for her in some project that would complement her husband's work, John Ehrlichman explained that he had sent her off to "do the Indians" (visit a reservation) in order to keep her quiet and get her out of sight.[129]

Had she been stupid or behaved in a way that would have embarrassed the president, such treatment might be understandable, but many Washington reporters liked Pat Nixon. One of their number later wrote: "[We] found that the tense, guarded campaign wife with the rehearsed smile was in relaxed moments a warm and peppy person."[130] Another veteran of the Washington scene put it more bluntly, perhaps because she was speaking off the record. "Mrs. Nixon had these ideas, but [the President] wouldn't let her do anything about them. Each time she set out to try, her side of the White House would check with his, and by the time the answer came back, it was too late."[131] For Pat Nixon's staff, the explanation for being excluded lay in the attitudes of the president's staff: "You wouldn't believe the sexist attitude of some of those guys," one of Pat Nixon's aides told a writer, "and Haldeman was the worst of the lot."[132]

Pat Nixon was thus forced to turn her most productive efforts inward—to the White House where West Wingers apparently allowed her a free hand. Helen McCain Smith noted that Pat's contributions lay in two areas: she made the mansion more accessible (by arranging special tours for disabled and blind persons, preparing a booklet on the gardens, adding exterior lighting, and changing the guards' uniforms to less imposing blazers); and she restored authentic antiques to the state rooms. Many of Jackie Kennedy's acquisitions had been copies, Smith noted, and the total effect was more "frenchified" than some people would have like. Pat Nixon managed to bring in, without congressional appropriation of any kind, chairs that had once belonged to the Monroes, Duncan Phyfe pieces, and other authentic American furniture. She also restored the Map Room and arranged for the transfer, either by gift or on loan, of several important paintings of presidents and First Ladies.[133] Pat, always a modest woman, played down this particular aspect of her tenure, and when television cameras came to tour the White House, Tricia provided the commentary.

Pat's supporters noted evidence of her democratic appeal. Americans flocked to the White House and during her second year, the number of visitors broke all records.[134] She chatted endlessly and tirelessly with hundreds of people, one observer noted, and "had more ways to say someone had a pretty hat than anyone I ever knew."[135] Her concern with those she called "the little guys" as opposed to the "big shots" led her to pay careful attention to the mail she received, and she insisted on an individual reply to each letter. She refused to use a facsimile of her signature, even in the face of staff arguments that no one could tell the difference. For four or five hours a day, she looked over responses that had been prepared, sending back for revisions those she deemed in need of improvement. She followed up on some of the requests herself, helping an immigrant woman, for example, with her citizenship problem. Right up to her husband's resignation, when the White House seemed in disarray and confusion, Pat Nixon persevered with her mountain of mail, causing one writer to conclude that she had "abdicated" her First Lady role to her daughter Julie.[136] Pat's critics ridiculed her dedication as misplaced martyrdom, while her supporters thought it substantiated her promise to help the "little guys."

Popular magazines failed to spread the word of the Nixon acquisitions, just as they played down Pat Nixon's travel. Her daughter Julie later pointed out that her mother was the most widely traveled First Lady (eighty-three nations).[137] She crisscrossed the United States many times. These could be gruelling trips, as one reporter noted when she chronicled one western visit. Pat Nixon was "pelted by rain, sleet, snow and hail [then] sat serenely through sheets of rain in an outdoor amphitheater" before proceeding on to another city where she dedicated a new industrial arts building and addressed a crowd of 5,000 young people, most of whom were not old enough to vote.[138] "I do or I die," Pat Nixon was frequently quoted as saying, "I never cancel out."

Her White House residence ended in 1974, after a series of events connected with Watergate. President Nixon had arranged to record what went on in his Oval Office so that he would have a full account of his administration, and when he was accused of being involved in a break in at the National Democratic Party headquarters, the contents of the tapes gained importance. The burglary at the apartment building complex, known as Watergate, occurred in the summer of 1972; but not until two years later, after several of the president's aides had been implicated, did attention turn directly and unremittingly to the Oval Office. A House Committee, appointed to decide whether sufficient evidence existed for a bill of impeachment, heard testimony in nationally televised sessions. Then opinion turned increasingly against the president. Experts testified that the tapes had been altered, and a lengthy blank spot could not be adequately justified, although the president's loyal secretary tried to assign the blame to her own clumsy foot on the erase pedal of her office machine. By August 1974, the president's options had narrowed to one, and he became the first president in American history to resign from office.

In his final speech as president, Richard Nixon refused to accept personal responsibility for the Watergate debacle, and he subsequently insisted he had not obstructed justice. But in a televised interview with British journalist David Frost in May 1977, he admitted he had shown bad judgment and let many people down. He had hinted earlier that he would have fared better had he destroyed the tapes before their contents were revealed. His lawyers had convinced him, he said, not to destroy evidence.

Pat Nixon, whose counsel the president apparently rejected or never sought, had reasoned otherwise, and reportedly told her friend, Helene Drown, "I would have burned or destroyed [the tapes] because they were like a private diary, not public property."[139] The First Lady's press secretary gave corroborating evidence: "Very early, before they had become the subject of litigation, [Pat] urged him to destroy them but he did not listen. . . . [She] believed the whole idea of the tapes was ridiculous. They simply never should have been done."[140] Pat evidently concluded that public service did not extend to providing the material for one's own indictment.

That she felt she had failed in this, as well as in other parts of her husband's administration, is hinted at in statements Pat made. She frequently said that she wanted to be remembered only as the "wife of the President" but when Jessamyn West asked her how she differed from Dolley Madison or Grace Coolidge, she replied, "Does it matter?"[141] On that hot August morning in 1974, when the television crews gathered at the White House to record Richard Nixon's last words as president, she stood behind him, apparently struggling to hold back tears. In a speech so rambling that it frightened some listeners, he spoke warmly and at length about his mother whom he called "a real saint," but about his wife, he had not one word. As the Nixons walked with the Fords, who would replace them, to the helicopter that would take them on the first leg of their trip to retirement at San Clemente, Betty Ford, seeking to make conversation, remarked on the red carpet that had been rolled out. No longer impressed by red carpets, Pat Nixon replied: "You'll see so many of those . . . , you'll get so you hate them."[142]

The woman who had humbly stated how she hoped to be remembered showed in her announcements about volunteerism, literacy, and the environment, that she would have preferred to do more than play the hostess. That she failed is no doubt due to her own uneasiness in a public role and to the limited value which the president's wing placed on her contributions. It may not be true (as reported in the *Atlantic Monthly*) that a White House aide overheard Pat tell her husband, "You have ruined my life,"[143] but it is certainly accurate to say that reporters "observed with alarm [his] coldness."[144]

The Nixon years serve as a reminder that every First Lady relies on the president to set parameters of her power and effectiveness. If he refuses to involve her in any important decisions or show that he regards her seriously, she is forced into an insignificant role no matter what her own inclinations may have been. Even the greatest ambition cannot override a veto from the Oval Office. According to Letitia Baldrige, John Kennedy "never interfered" with his wife's White House restoration project,[145] and Lyndon Johnson's active support of the beautification project is well documented. Richard Nixon relied on his wife and daughters to help in campaigning, but their roles apparently ended—except for ceremonial appearances—as soon as the votes were counted.[146] Julie Nixon Eisenhower, who insists her parents were closer than people thought, could offer only one instance of her mother's attempting to influence policy. According to Julie, Pat encouraged her husband to appoint a woman to the Supreme Court.[147]

Pat Nixon finished off the turbulent 1960s—a decade in which three very different First Ladies presided over the White House. Even in fiction, it would be difficult to create a more diverse trio. In the 1960 election, a patrician horsewoman from the East was pitted against a miner's daughter from California; and the two women whose husbands shared the Democratic ticket that same year stood, if possible, even farther apart: the frugal, but rich, Texan, whose loyalty to her husband went beyond the usual bounds, and the young mother who spent considerable energy examining (on approval) expensive jewelry and paintings.

But the three women shared a great deal, too, possibly of more significance than what divided them. Each had come through a troubled youth, having lost at least one parent through death or, in Jackie's case, divorce. They had all shown exceptional self-discipline in shaping their early lives, a control that persisted into adulthood and through their marriages. While philandering and insensitivity became part of the public records of their husbands, the wives stoically carved out their own niches, and refused to disappear into obscurity or relinquish their own dignity. All very much women of their century (Mamie Eisenhower had been the last First Lady to be born in the nineteenth), they had graduated from major universities and each had worked (or prepared to do so) before her marriage, unlike their three immediate predecessors whose formal education had stopped with boarding or finishing school and who never held jobs before their marriages.

First Ladies of the 1960s were hardly isolated from what went on around them. They had come of age when more married women than ever before were working outside their homes. The White House years of Jackie Kennedy, Lady Bird Johnson, and Patricia Nixon coincided with the beginning of a new feminist movement that redefined objectives for many women and made them less tolerant of their sisters who continued to see themselves solely in terms of their husbands' accomplishments. A widening political consciousness, as shown in increased attention to international issues and to the method of selecting presidential candidates, helped restructure campaign strategies and draw entire families into the process of winning an election and then helping win history's favorable account of an administration.

Perhaps most important in the redefinition of the job of the president's wife were the new federal programs. The "New Frontier" and the "War on Poverty" extended the federal government's role in such areas as housing and transportation (both of which gained cabinet status in the 1960s). Subjects that had once been the concern of local politicians were now discussed on the national level. When something did not suit, voters found it easy to make the capital the center of their discontent. Chartered buses headed toward the Potomac with thousands of Americans ready to demonstrate in behalf of one point of view or another. Men and women who could not volunteer their congressman's name knew very well the address of the White House and the face of each occupant.

Television increased recognition of presidential wives and pulled them into the public arena. Jackie Kenndy's clamorous reception in Paris caused her husband to introduce himself as the "man who had accompanied her." Lady Bird Johnson learned to factor in demonstrators on any trip she took, and she went to sleep in the White House to the chants from anti-war protesters outside:

Hey/Hey/Hey
L./B./J./
How many kids/
Did you kill today?

Later Pat Nixon learned to walk coolly through showers of confetti, accompanied by jeers of, "If this was napalm, you'd be dead." The job of First Lady was no longer private and ceremonial—it had moved into the public arena of matters affecting the nation's prestige abroad and of issues seriously dividing the country at home.

9

New Dimensions to the Job of First Lady (1974–1993)

AS THOUGH TO ACCELERATE the trend begun in the 1960s toward strong, more activist First Ladies, a quartette of particularly determined, energetic women passed through the White House in the 1970s and 1980s. What had once been a daring exception, much commented on in the press, became commonplace. Elizabeth ("Betty") Bloomer Warren Ford, in the job less than a full term (August 1974 to January 1977), spoke with such candor about subjects that had formerly been taboo that she introduced an entirely new style; and her support of women's rights made headlines. Rosalynn Smith Carter (1977–1981) continued Betty Ford's example of using First Ladyhood as a platform for women's issues; but she added a new component by going off on international missions, which the White House billed as "substantive," and then testifying in front of a congressional committee on a mental health program. Nancy Davis Reagan began her Washington tenure in 1981 by insisting that she had little say in presidential decisions. But by July 1985, when Ronald Reagan underwent surgery for cancer, she displaced the vice president from the front pages of the country's newspapers and announced herself at a White House reception as "the President's standin."[1] Barbara Pierce Bush (1989–1993) chose to stay in the background on matters of public policy, but she was widely believed to hold strong views of her own on abortion and gun control. Unlike Edith Wilson, who had faced charges of "petticoat government" and "rule by regency," these four encountered only the mildest criticism.

Betty Ford appeared particularly eager to make her own mark, and she apparently had her husband's support. While Pat Nixon had described Richard as unwilling to confer with her about anything, Betty Ford often spoke of the "pillow talk" that she used to bring

Gerald around to her point of view. President Ford publicly acknowledged that he valued her opinions and admitted that in one of his
most criticized moves, the pardon of Richard Nixon, she had exerted
considerable influence. "Betty and I talked [the Nixon pardon] over,"
Gerald Ford told an aide. "We felt we were ready. This [uncertainty
over Nixon's treatment] just has to stop; it's tearing the country to
pieces."[2] On another occasion, Gerald Ford volunteered to an interviewer: "[Betty] obviously has a great deal of influence."[3]

That special partnership had begun twenty-six years before it reached
the White House when, within three weeks in 1948, Gerald Ford of
Michigan made two significant changes in his life. He married Betty
Bloomer Warren, a young divorcée, and won his first election to Congress. The thirty-five-year-old lawyer had not included a Washington
career in his proposal, and his wife admitted many years later that she
had lacked preparation to "be a political wife."[4] From the moment he
arrived late for their marriage ceremony because of a campaign appearance, she began learning the long and sometimes painful lesson that
Gerald Ford's family frequently came second to his work.

During his time in Congress, she dutifully joined the appropriate
wives' clubs, taught Sunday school, and saw to most of the details of
raising the three boys and one girl born to them in the first seven
years of their marriage. As her husband's ambitions grew to include
Speaker of the House, so too did his absences from home, but these
were not the campaign trips that aspiring presidential candidates
make with spouse in tow. Gerald Ford appeared in his Republican
colleagues' home districts to bolster their election chances—and in
such contests, his wife played no part.

While Gerald Ford accepted as many as two hundred speaking invitations in one year, Betty became so accustomed to chauffeuring
their sons to the emergency room of the local hospital after minor
injuries that she laughingly suggested that the family car could make
the trip on its own. Single parenting produced its strains, causing her
to reply rather petulantly to questions about her role. When asked
who in her life had influenced her most, she answered, "my mother,"
and added that her children should reply the same way because "their
father's always away."[5]

Friction resulting from conflicting demands of career and family is
by no means unique to political marriages—it marks many marriages
in which work takes so much time and energy that little is left
for home. Yet autobiographies of Washington wives underline the
multiple demands and stresses that politicians' families feel. Marvella
Bayh described in *Marvella* how she relied on prescribed drugs to get

through the exhilarating and hectic schedule of a conspicuous senator's wife.[6] Ellen Proxmire subtitled her book on Washington living: *Perilous Life of a Senator's Wife*.[7] Abigail McCarthy, more reticent than most of her colleagues but also more eloquent, explained the circumstances that led her husband, Minnesota's Senator Eugene McCarthy, to "leave our home in August, 1969," after she had coped for many years with the pressures of being a political spouse. Not only did Abigail McCarthy perform seemingly endless unpaid tasks in support of her husband's career, she also acted, she wrote, "as den mother to the inevitable strays who attach themselves to campaigns."[8]

In addition to the strains documented by other wives, Betty Ford suffered from a pinched nerve and arthritis. Finally, in 1970, she sought professional help, and as a result of several months of counseling, she resolved to keep more time for herself and to persuade her husband to leave Washington after his congressional term ended in 1976.[9] Those plans abruptly changed in late 1973 when vice president Spiro Agnew resigned and Gerald Ford was named to that job. Instead of preparing to end her Washington residence as the unknown spouse of a Michigan congressman, Betty Ford moved into the center of national attention. The stock-taking begun in the therapy sessions served her well, however, and she resolved to guard part of her time and to continue to be "just me."

Maintaining her equilibrium was not easy when, within a year, Richard Nixon resigned the presidency, and Gerald Ford moved up to that office. The entire Ford family, none of whom had ever campaigned in a constituency larger than half a million people, became the focus of more scrutiny than they had ever imagined possible. Magazines profiled the four Ford children, and Betty Ford, the woman *Good Housekeeping* said "nobody knows,"[10] quickly became someone whom everybody sought to meet.

Having arrived in Washington when Bess Truman was First Lady, Betty Ford had come to admire (as many other Washington wives had) the way Bess combined being in the spotlight with staying "so humble." Bess's example guided her, she wrote.[11] Perhaps Betty Ford felt particular sympathy for another Midwesterner, who like herself had moved without much warning or preparation into the White House. Certainly the two women shared little in their attitudes toward privacy or in their views about whether presidential wives should take sides on controversial issues. While Bess Truman refused to speak up on any matter more divisive than that of restoring the White House, Betty Ford appeared willing to talk about almost anything.

Jacqueline Kennedy made a pleasure trip to India with her sister, and in traveling without the president, she helped make the American First Lady an international figure. Courtesy of the Library of Congress.

Jacqueline Kennedy made a poignant appearance at the inauguration of Lyndon Johnson aboard Air Force One less than two hours after her husband's death. Courtesy of the Lyndon Baines Johnson Library.

Newlyweds Lyndon and Lady Bird Johnson appear to be tourists in the capital, but already in 1934, they had come to Washington to stay. Courtesy of the Lyndon Baines Johnson Library.

Pat Nixon visited the Great Wall of China during the Nixons' historic tour of China in 1972. Courtesy of the Library of Congress.

When Gerald Ford's voice gave out on election night in 1976, Betty Ford read his concession speech. Courtesy of the Gerald R. Ford Library.

Three First Ladies were represented at the National Women's Conference in Houston in November 1977: from left, Liz Carpenter, press secretary to Lady Bird Johnson, is shown with Rosalynn Carter and Betty Ford. Courtesy of the Carter Presidential Library.

After her first White House year, Nancy Reagan increased her involvement in programs to combat use of illegal drugs. Courtesy of the Ronald Reagan Library.

Although she frequently poked fun at her own appearance, Barbara Bush oversaw a White House that released very flattering photographs of her and her family. Courtesy of the George H. W. Bush Presidential Library and Museum.

Hillary Clinton frequently felt the need to emphasize her domestic side during her time in the White House. Courtesy of the William J. Clinton Presidential Library.

Laura Bush maintained high popularity ratings while her husband's poll numbers sank. Courtesy of First Lady Laura Bush's office.

As First Lady, Michelle Obama billed herself as mom in chief to two young daughters, but many Americans focused on her fashionable wardrobe and her athleticism. Courtesy of the White House website, www.whitehouse.gov.

As the first naturalized citizen to preside over the East Wing of the White House, Melania Trump aroused considerable interest in her wardrobe and style. Courtesy of the White House website, www.whitehouse.gov.

The country's disillusionment with government influenced the new First Lady. The United States' recent military involvement in Vietnam and the rumors of doctored casualty reports and other concealments, Spiro Agnew's "nolo contendere" response to charges that he had accepted bribes, and Richard Nixon's alleged complicity in the Watergate crimes committed during his 1972 campaign all added to a consensus that honesty had value but that in government it was rare. Betty Ford explained that she felt a need to be open: "I tried to be honest," she later wrote. "I tried not to dodge subjects. I felt the people had a right to know where I stood."[12]

In discussions with reporters, she spoke with disarming frankness about her children, her own health problems, and how she felt about being a political wife. When she hired a press secretary, she gave her two assignments, one of which was to provide "honest answers."[13] This was no new guise contrived to "sell" a First Lady. Betty Ford had always had a reputation for candor, and she had already shocked reporters when, as wife of the vice president, she gave as explanation for her drowsiness: "I take a Valium every day."[14] In the fishbowl at 1600 Pennsylvania Avenue, her announcements simply received more attention, and rather than rendering her gauche or stupid, they made her enormously popular. In short order, Betty Ford made honesty something chic—and reticence, passé. Helen Thomas, veteran UPI reporter, echoed her colleagues when she pronounced Betty Ford a "real friend" of the press,[15] and Rosalynn Carter, who succeeded Betty, credited her with "making it easier to talk."[16]

This new approach became immediately evident when Betty Ford scheduled her first press conference less than a month after Gerald's swearing in. Helen McCain Smith, press secretary to Pat Nixon, had stayed on to help in the transition, but this event in no way resembled Pat's encounters with the fourth estate. One hundred and fifty reporters heard a slightly nervous Betty Ford announce that she intended to work for substantive changes, especially in the campaign for ratification of the Equal Rights Amendment. This was quite a different exchange than the one in March 1933, when fewer than three dozen reporters attended Eleanor Roosevelt's first press conference and heard her promise to avoid substantive issues and never comment on pending legislation. In Betty Ford, feminists finally had a First Lady who worked for them openly, rather than discreetly behind the scenes.

Surprises continued when a reporter asked how the new First Lady stood on abortion, and she described her position as "definitely closer" to that of Nelson Rockefeller, who supported the Supreme Court's decision leaving the matter up to the woman and her physician, than to that of Senator James Buckley who thought the Court had gone too far. Reporters could hardly fail to notice that Gerald Ford would have answered differently.[17] In Alabama, a a few days later, Betty Ford spoke to the fears of many American mothers when she speculated that her children had probably experimented with marijuana.[18] Later, she raised some eyebrows when she confessed that she had often been "tempted to split" her ticket.[19]

For the rest of her time in the White House, Betty Ford showed no signs of abandoning the stands she took in those first few weeks, and she became closely identified with the Equal Rights Amendment. First introduced in Congress in 1923, the version approved in 1972 was short and simple: "Equality of rights under the law shall not be denied or abridged by the United States or by any State on account of sex." Pat Nixon, First Lady at the time Congress acted, kept a good distance from the amendment, insisting that she favored equal rights and equal pay but that she saw no need for federal action to guarantee either one.[20] Pat Nixon's view had, in fact, been the common one before about 1970; even some self-identified feminists had opposed the amendment because of the fear that it would wipe out the hard-won protective legislation for women workers—laws that shielded women from having to lift heavy loads, work night shifts, and undertake hazardous tasks.

By 1970, however, the situation had changed because federal courts had begun to void those state laws as discriminatory. Working against the ERA while claiming to protect women's interests no longer made sense. The anti-ERA movement, increasingly visible and vocal in the 1970s under the direction of Phyllis Schlafly, used different arguments, including the charge that such an amendment was unnecessary (since several states had passed their own equal rights measures) or unwise (because women would then be expected to move into dangerous or unpleasant areas—including the armed forces and unisex toilets). Feminists responded to the opposition by making the Equal Rights Amendment the focus of their campaign, just as their grandmothers had singled out suffrage.

By the time Betty Ford turned the weight of her position to the issue, the amendment stood before the states, waiting for the final three to ratify (of the thirty-eight necessary). When time came for votes in states considered likely to approve the amendment (Illinois, Missouri, North Dakota, Georgia, Nevada, and Arizona), the president's wife got on the telephone and lobbied wavering legislators for their votes. Her press secretary, Sheila Rabb Weidenfeld, reported that Betty used a very gentle approach, but that she could be persuasive. "I realize you're under a lot of pressure from the voters today," she told one woman legislator from a rural district in Missouri, "but I'm just calling to let you know that the President and I are considerably interested. . . . I think the ERA is so important."[21] The president's wife installed a separate telephone line in the White House for her lobbying because, as she later explained, "there's a law or something about that sort of thing."[22]

First Ladies had been twisting arms since Abigail Adams went after funds for furnishing the White House, but never before had the action been quite so open, so widely reported, or directed at a decidedly feminist cause. When questioned about the propriety of intruding in state politics, Betty's press secretary insisted this was a national issue since an amendment to the Constitution was at stake. To those who thought such activism inappropriate, Betty Ford replied: "[I] will stick to my guns,"[23] and she did, even when mail ran three to one against her[24] and pickets marched in front of the White House waving "Stop ERA" signs.[25] She appeared undaunted by letters to the editors of major newspapers charging her with "arm twisting tactics . . . [which are] unseemly at best,"[26] or by more dramatic objections, such as that of a group of black-clad figures who paraded in front of the White House and then were shown on evening television, chanting in unison: "Betty Ford is trying to press a second-rate manhood on American women."[27]

In spite of her efforts, the Equal Rights Amendment failed ratification by the requisite number of states, and Betty Ford directed the remainder of her work on behalf of women to getting them appointed to important jobs. It is impossible to calculate exactly her influence; but in light of the president's own pronouncements, his record is interesting. In his abbreviated presidency, he named twenty-one women to posts requiring Senate approval. Another forty-five selected by his predecessors remained in their jobs, bringing the total to sixty-six, far higher than it had ever been.[28] Some of the Ford appointments were at high levels, including several commission heads, important judgeships, and a cabinet member: Carla Anderson Hills, as secretary of Housing and Urban Development after March 10, 1975. Betty did not have the pleasure of seeing her husband appoint the first woman to the Supreme Court. Gerald Ford filled only one vacancy on the high tribunal and that went to John Paul Stevens in December 1975.

In addition to her work on women's issues, Betty Ford devoted considerable attention to the arts, especially dance. She had begun dancing when she was eight years old and during two summers she had studied with Martha Graham at Bennington College. After graduating from high school, she had rejected college and Grand Rapids in favor of New York City and more dance. Although she never made Graham's top troupe and had to support herself partly by modeling for the John Powers Agency, she retained a lifelong interest in dance. In middle age, when she was advised by a psychotherapist to take time for something she enjoyed, she chose dance.

Art enthusiasts welcomed an advocate in the White House and predicted she would help them,[29] but First Lady Ford gave less to the arts in the next few years than she got from her association with them. Innumerable photographs of her attending dance programs and meeting with artists gave the public an image of a healthy, active president's wife involved in a noncontroversial area. In fact, her association with dance far outshadowed much of her other hard work. When she accompanied the president to China, she had wanted to avoid the "peeking in the kitchen pots" coverage that Pat Nixon had received in 1972, and she consulted with Chinese specialists so she would be informed. What television crews preferred to catch, however, was her visit to a school, where the Ford team had coached the children. Betty, whom the *New York Times* described as "Not a Robot at All," delighted them all by clapping her hands and dancing with them.[30]

That kind of coverage, publicizing an attractive, energetic First Lady, achieved immediate rewards, and in 1975, the National Academy of Design named Betty Ford a Fellow, the first president's wife to be so honored since the group singled out Eleanor Roosevelt in 1934. In making the award, the photographer Ansel Adams called Betty "the most refreshing character we've had in public life for sometime," (and he significantly did not limit the field to women).[31]

In many ways a very traditional wife, Betty Ford crossed lines to appeal to feminists and to less independent-minded housewives. In conversations, she frequently emphasized her traditional values, telling a legislator on one occasion that she was no "wild-eyed Liberal" and that she enjoyed "being a wife and mother as much as anyone." "But," she would continue, "that is not the point . . . women should have equal opportunities."[32] She refused to bow to Phyllis Schlafly's claims of being chief protector of mothers' interests and would point out that Phyllis's six children outnumbered her own brood by only two. In describing "liberation" as "inwardly happy," she found friends in both the feminist and more traditional camps. Her whole life history spoke to the experience of women who, like herself, had never worked a day outside their own homes after their marriages. But her outspoken support of women's issues gained approval from others who could not imagine adulthood without careers of their own. Her candor in dealing with her own experiences—drug dependence, cancer surgery, psychotherapy, and her children's experimentation with illegal drugs—won the admiration of women who were tired of hearing about "super perfect" families in the White House.

Before she had held the job six months, Betty Ford's hope that she would be remembered "in a very kind way as a constructive wife of the President"[33] was assured. Her unfortunate bout with cancer aroused admiration for her courage, and her popularity cut across social and economic lines. She played a cameo role on the Mary Tyler Moore show and topped the Gallup Poll of "Most Admired Women"[34] (although *Good Housekeeping* readers had rated her less favorably, causing a spokesperson for the magazine to explain early in the Ford administration that "feminist types" did not appeal to all Americans.)[35] Betty Ford also led a list compiled by five "opinionmakers" as "best epitomizing the word 'class,'"—outranking old-timers Princess Grace of Monaco, Fred Astaire, Cary Grant, and Katharine Hepburn. The woman almost unknown to the public three years earlier had made large strides, and 1976 campaign buttons supporting "Betty's husband for President" showed just how valuable an active presidential wife could be.

Betty Ford's Democratic counterpart in the 1976 election proved a formidable opponent, but unlike Betty (or any of the preceding four First Ladies), Rosalynn Smith Carter was a newcomer to Washington. Had she trained at the center of national politics, she might have formed a loyal support system among reporters and other oldtimers, but her apprenticeship had been limited to the Georgia governor's mansion and to a long campaign across the nation.

That background did not stop her, however, from compiling a remarkable list of accomplishments in just four years, and she did it as the most traditional of wives. "Jimmy and I were always partners," she would announce, and then proceed to act in such a way that historians would describe her as "surrogate, confidante, and joint policymaker."[36] Abigail McCarthy, the perceptive observer of political wives, attributed Rosalynn Carter's special combination of supportive wifeliness and independent strength to her southern roots, and she had much in common, McCarthy pointed out, with the heroine of Ellen Glasgow's novel, *The Vein of Iron.*[37]

Rosalynn was fifty years old at the time of Jimmy's inauguration in January 1977. Her life up to that point had been divided roughly into thirds, with the initial segment ending at age thirteen when her father died. Like most of her immediate predecessors, she experienced the death of a parent before she had reached adulthood, and for her the loss was traumatic. "He thought I could do anything," she later recalled;[38] and since she was the oldest of his four children, she took his deathbed request to "look after Mother for me" more to heart than did the others.[39] Her mother added to Rosalynn's sense of responsibility by relying on her almost as another adult. "I was devastated," Rosalynn wrote. "My childhood really ended at that moment."[40]

Her education, however, was just beginning. A seventh grade teacher who was "young" and "beautiful" and "[who] I thought knew more than anyone I had ever met . . . was extremely interested in current events and prodded us to read the newspapers and listen to the radio, to stretch our minds about our country and the world. . . . I began . . . to discover a world of interesting people and faraway places."[41] High school graduation came first—with Rosalynn delivering the valedictory for her class of eleven—and then two years at a nearby junior college. Her real education began, however, when at eighteen, she married the local boy who had already distinguished himself by being nominated to the U.S. Naval Academy. Jimmy Carter, ready for his first naval assignment, was her ticket out of Georgia.

For a curious and energetic young wife, having a husband whose assignments took them to Norfolk, Virginia, then Hawaii, and finally Connecticut offered opportunities that she could only have dreamed of in tiny Plains, Georgia. While Jimmy was frequently on duty at sea for days or even weeks at a time, Rosalynn managed a household that eventually included three sons born within five years. When her husband came home, she worked with him through courses in the "Great Books" and in classical music. She learned the hula in Hawaii and memorized Shakespeare in Virginia, but most importantly she developed confidence that she could do things for herself. "[Jimmy] assumed that I could manage well and always made me feel he was proud of me. So I was forced to discover that I could do the things that had to be done."[42]

The absence of close friends increased Rosalynn's emotional dependence on her husband. Plains had "literally no other girls . . . my age," she told an interviewer,[43] and the naval assignments, each lasting only a few years, gave little opportunity to forge strong friendships. Her days were filled with housekeeping. "I was the total wife and mother," she later wrote, washing, ironing, cooking and mopping floors, but she was doing it all on her own, without the supervision of either mother or mother-in-law. The new independence suited her, and she recalled, "I was more content than I had been in years."[44]

The third (but first political) segment of Rosalynn Carter's life began inauspiciously when she reluctantly returned to live in Georgia. In 1953, her father-in-law died, and Jimmy decided that his younger brother Billy, still in high school, needed help running the family businesses. Rosalynn disliked relinquishing the independence that she had gained but in "the only major disagreement" of their marriage, she lost. Or in the short run, it seemed that she had. She returned to Plains with Jimmy and their three sons. Very quickly she realized that the town had not changed but she had. With the confidence she had acquired away from home, she set out to explore the opportunities she had not recognized before. She played golf, took dancing lessons, and went off with friends on a trip to New Orleans. Even she had to admit she was "enjoying this life."[45]

More significantly, she became involved in some of the issues that affected the small town—issues that often had direct and personal implications but on the local level seemed solvable. Jimmy's appointment to the school board put the Carters in the middle of the integration struggle, or, as Rosalynn described their position, off to a minority side of it. "Though we were both raised in the South and had accepted segregation as children," she wrote, "Jimmy and I had traveled enough to see a different way of life . . . [and] I could count . . . on two hands, [the people] with whom Jimmy and I could talk openly about the issue."[46]

The Carters' work in their church and other local organizations led them into politics, but it was Jimmy who took the lead. On his thirty-eighth birthday, he announced his candidacy for the state Senate.[47] Rosalynn had already taken over the bookkeeping at the family's peanut warehouse, and she could evaluate, just by checking the accounts, which sections of the business made money and which lost. While Jimmy spent more time at legislative sessions in the state capital, she had to make more business decisions. Her own public service was very limited—the idea of delivering speeches made her physically ill, and when Jimmy first ran for governor in 1966, she and her sons did nothing more than pass out brochures and smile for photographs in front of a vehicle marked "Carter Family."

Jimmy Carter lost that election, but in his next try in 1970, the entire family resolved to work harder. For Rosalynn, that meant conquering her fear of public speaking. Jimmy encouraged her to stop memorizing her script so she could speak extemporaneously from notecards, and the results surprised even her: "It was easy. [People] were listening attentively, and when I got through they wanted to hear more. . . . It was a wonderful feeling and quite a breakthrough for me."[48]

Successful in that second gubernatorial race, the Carters moved into the spotlight of the state capital. It was a larger transition, she frequently said, than that she later made from Georgia to the White House.[49] Other presidents' wives (including Edith Roosevelt and Eleanor Roosevelt in Albany and Ellen Wilson in Trenton) had pointed to their husbands' governorship years as times of growth, and Rosalynn also reported that she used those years to gain confidence in her social and administrative abilities. Travels around the state exposed her to problems in mental health, education, and care for the aged, and she developed a new appreciation of what government could do to make individuals' lives better. By the time Jimmy prepared to run for president in 1976, she showed almost none of her old reticence about taking a public role for herself. By January 20, 1977, when she strode down Pennsylvania Avenue toward Number 1600, little remained of the tentative teenager who had left Plains, Georgia, thirty years earlier.

Much of the confidence developed during her fourteen months on the road before Jimmy won the 1976 nomination. It was a campaign unequaled among politicians' wives. Victory must have seemed an impossible dream at the beginning when few Americans outside Georgia had heard of Jimmy Carter. Even Jimmy's mother, the indefatigable Lillian Carter, was rumored to have responded to her son's announcement that he was running for president with the question "President of what?" Rosalynn became accustomed to similar replies when she first went out to speak for Jimmy.

The Carters had reasoned that in this difficult, uphill campaign, they could cover more ground if they traveled separately, and when she set out on her first out-of-state appearance to nearby Florida, she was accompanied only by one good friend. Guided by a Florida road map and a slightly outdated list of Democratic party officials, the two women stopped wherever they spotted a radio transmitter or found somebody willing to gather a few friends together. Rosalynn would make her speech about why Jimmy should be president, answer any questions, and then prepare to speed on to the next town.[50]

Rosalynn later graduated to commercial airlines and then to her own private plane but her schedule never lightened. She described campaigning as "a job, a very demanding job, with pressures and deadlines . . . constant studying and cramming . . . being able to stay cool under fire."[51] From Monday to Friday, she was on the road, and then on the weekend she returned to Plains to rest up, eat "a square meal," confer with her husband and see the rest of the family, including their daughter, Amy, who was not yet ten years old. "It was not a vocation I would want to pursue for a life," Rosalynn wrote when it was all over, "but it was essential."[52]

Like all successful campaigners, Rosalynn Carter had to decide what to do with victory, and no woman ever entered the White House with a clearer agenda for herself. Nor a longer one. She ticked off her causes in order of importance: she would continue to be active in mental health, because that was what she knew best, and she would work for the ratification of the Equal Rights Amendment which still needed the approval of three states. She also expected to help the aging and to encourage volunteerism on the local level. To assist her, she appointed a staff of eighteen, headed by Press Secretary and East Wing coordinator, Mary Finch Hoyt, a veteran of the Muskie and McGovern races. Eventually Rosalynn had a staff of twenty-one, not so large as she would have liked but larger than any East Wing staff in history.[53]

Even before the inauguration, Rosalynn Carter was off and running on her new job. In December 1976, she attended (although not in an official capacity) the inauguration of Mexico's new President, and then she returned to preside over a mental health conference in Philadelphia. After Jimmy took office, she increased momentum and within months had announced a precedent-breaking trip to Central and South America.

While other presidential wives had typically represented their husbands on ceremonial and fact-finding international missions, none had claimed to work out policy. Eleanor Roosevelt's trips across both the Atlantic and the Pacific during the war and Lady Bird Johnson's attendance at the funeral of Greece's king had underlined the surrogate role some First Ladies took, but neither had claimed to make decisions. Rosalynn Carter's trip to seven Central and South American countries in the spring of 1977 was billed by the president's office as "substantive,"[54] and she encouraged that interpretation by revealing that she had prepared by studying Spanish and by briefings with members of the State Department and the National Security Council.[55] She planned to deliver in each country a "summary of the administration's foreign policy approach," and then go on to discuss more specific problems of local interest.

In Costa Rica she listened to complaints that the United States was restricting that country's trade, in Ecuador to objections that her husband should not have vetoed the sale of Israeli jets, and in Peru to an explanation for that country's arms buildup. When she returned to Washington, she reported to the Senate Foreign Relations Committee on what she had seen and heard.[56]

The trip brought mixed returns. Heads of state who met with the American First Lady appeared uncertain as to how they should react, and while some Latins applauded her enthusiasm for learning their language, others expressed discomfort about receiving a United States representative who had been neither elected nor appointed. Reporters in Jamaica questioned whether she had the right to speak for her husband, and when she got home, the discussion continued. Meg Greenfield, in an article entitled, "Mrs. President," explored the implications of the First Lady's trip and concluded that if Rosalynn wanted a role in diplomacy, she should find a way to make herself accountable for her actions.[57] A State Department official attempted to blunt some of the criticism by describing Rosalynn's trip as "mainly questioning."[58]

The fact that all her later international travel fell within the older, more traditional bounds for presidents' wives indicates that the Carters may have judged the South American venture not entirely successful, although Rosalynn explained the lack of additional trips by saying that Jimmy was "able to go himself."[59] She continued to signal her significant role in her husband's administration but in other ways—in announcements that she met regularly with him for "working" lunches and that she attended meetings of his closest advisers, including the cabinet.

Most of her energies were concentrated on the projects she had named early in the administration, especially mental health. Because she could not legally serve as actual chair of the President's Council on Mental Health, she took an honorary (but working) title and then accepted invitations to speak on the subject in Canada and in Europe.[60] On February 7, 1979, she went before the Senate Resource subcommittee to testify in favor of increased federal spending for mental health programs, and there she tangled with Chairman Edward Kennedy over what constituted a satisfactory federal health budget.

As Rosalynn continued to follow her Mental Health Systems Act through the various committees, she made history of two kinds.[61] Not only was she the first presidential wife to testify before a congressional committee since Eleanor Roosevelt appeared in the 1940s, but in this case the chairman of the Senate committee was a strong contender for her husband's job.[62] "I had to swallow some pride—for the cause," she later wrote, because during the early stages of the 1980 campaign when it was not yet clear who would win the Democratic nomination, "Senator Kennedy one day would be on the stump making one of his statements, such as 'President Carter is making the poor eat cat food' and the next day would be saying to me, 'Mrs. Carter, the committee is completing work on the Mental Health Systems Act.' "[63]

Although the act did not provide for a national health insurance program, it did outline three goals: to help move mental health patients with chronic problems to smaller community facilities, to incorporate mental health care into the nation's health care system, and to increase services to the poor. The Act finally passed in September 1980, but the Carter celebration was brief because within weeks Ronald Reagan had won election. "The funding for our legislation was killed," Rosalynn wrote, "by the philosophy of a new President. It was a bitter loss."[64]

Not all Rosalynn's White House time went to revising the mental health program. In addition to the average of two meetings per month that she attended on that subject, she also met with groups concerned about women's issues and with people working on problems of the elderly.[65] In November 1979, she journeyed to Thailand to inspect refugee camps, and on her return to Washington, she added another cause to her agenda.

Comparisons of Rosalynn Carter and Eleanor Roosevelt arose inevitably. Jimmy occasionally pointed out that Rosalynn's long-forgotten first name was Eleanor and that he liked to call her his Eleanor.[66] William Shannon, writing in the *New York Times,* judged her the "most influential First Lady since Eleanor Roosevelt,"[67] and Jimmy underlined this perception of Rosalynn's importance by pronouncing her a "political partner" with whom he discussed domestic and foreign policy issues.[68]

When President Carter invited Middle Eastern leaders to a meeting at Camp David in September 1978, he involved Rosalynn in a special way, thus demonstrating once more how the elasticity in the American presidency opens the way for including spouses in substantive decisions. Not since Theodore Roosevelt mediated between two foreign powers to end the Russo-Japanese War in 1905 had an American chief executive attempted quite what Jimmy Carter did. Theodore had absented himself, however, from much of the discussion while Jimmy insisted on participating in each segment of the bargaining process.[69] His aim was not to settle all the disputes in the Middle East but to bring the two principal leaders of the opposing sides—Israeli Prime Minister Menachem Begin and Egyptian President Anwar Sadat—to an agreement that could then be recommended to all parties in the conflict. It was a risky venture, not only for the American president, who stood to lose face if he failed, but also for Begin and Sadat who invited, by their participation, charges from home that they had given up too much. Terrorist attacks threatened to undermine the talks and *Pravda* denounced the meeting.

In his invitations to both Middle Eastern leaders, Jimmy Carter had pointedly included their wives, telling Rosalynn: "There are going to be a lot of hard feelings and tough fights [and] the atmosphere will be more congenial if all of you are there."[70]

Rosalynn's role at the Camp David summit extended, however, beyond providing a hospitable setting for the talks and companion-ship for the wives. Jimmy briefed Rosalynn, she later wrote, "[because] he wanted me to understand the issues as well as the nuances of cer-tain words and phrases. What we called the West Bank, for example, was Judea and Samaria to Begin. . . ."[71] Although she lost her chance to sit in on the first meeting of the three leaders because the other two wives were delayed in arriving, she began immediately to keep a record of what she observed and what her husband told her. By the end of the twelve-day meeting, she had "almost 200 pages of typed notes" which eventually became the basis for one chapter in her autobiography.[72]

Previous presidential wives had played down their influence— Helen Taft insisted her advice stopped when her husband became president; Edith Wilson maintained that she never made any decision; Eleanor Roosevelt patiently reiterated to dubious listeners that she never tried to steer Franklin to any particular course of action. Rosalynn Carter took no credit, of course, for conducting the Camp David talks but she did not minimize her role. It had been her enthu-siastic support for the idea that had convinced Jimmy to try for the peace agreement, she wrote, and she went with him through a "see-saw" of emotions during the long negotiations.

Rosalynn played more than one role at the Camp David talks. Partly, she served as the president's cover, returning to the White House to substitute for him at events that had been previously scheduled. No-body had expected the summit to continue so long, and the president had agreed to meet with leaders of the Italian-American and Hispanic communities and to host a concert for the world-famous cellist, Mstis-lav Rostropovich. "One of us had to be there," Rosalynn explained, "and it was obviously going to be me,"[73] so she helicoptered back to the White House, making every effort to give no premature indica-tions of how the talks were going. Her subsequent description of the summit earned her high marks, and one reviewer wrote that Rosalynn was a better and franker writer "hands down" than her husband, and that in describing the Camp David summit and other events of the Carter administration, she had written "what may turn out to be the best human account . . . that we are likely to get."[74]

Such a prominent First Lady exposed herself to many judgments. Some critics declared her too programmed and disciplined, while others noted that she lacked the eloquence of Lady Bird Johnson and the zaniness and candor of Betty Ford. Jimmy's aides frequently commented that her ambition exceeded his, but perhaps they would have found any evident ambition excessive in a woman. The *New York Times* reporter Judy Klemesrud had dubbed her a "steel magnolia blossom" early in the campaign and the term had stuck, rather to Rosalynn's chagrin.[75] She gamely pointed out that she did not mind being thought strong because she admired strength but she objected to the calculating connotation in the characterization because it obscured her compassion and caring.

Although Rosalynn Carter has described as "considerable" the time she spent on ceremonial appearances,[76] she gave the impression of being much more involved in the substantive aspects of her husband's administration than in the hostess part. She never selected a china pattern for the White House collection and did not even spend the full amount of money allotted for refurbishing the family's quarters in the mansion. The chapter in her autobiography entitled "People, Parties and Protocol" is one of the shortest in the book (twenty pages), and researchers who hope to find there descriptions of her clothing, menus, and flower arrangements will be disappointed. Julia Grant's *Memoirs,* which were written (but not published) almost exactly one century before Rosalynn's, contained little but social details on the White House years, but Rosalynn correctly realized that expectations for First Ladies had changed. "Cave dwellers" still influenced Washington's social life, but they held little sway in the Carter White House.

The preceding century had altered (among other things) women's chances for education, employment, and political participation, and Rosalynn Carter followed Betty Ford's example of using her influence to make further changes. She lobbied state legislators to vote for the Equal Rights Amendment and she attended the International Woman's Year meeting in Houston in November 1977. But while Betty spoke of the need for women to "feel liberated whatever their jobs or family situation," Rosalynn emphasized the justice of equal pay for equal work. That kind of feminism showed a "working class bias," one writer pointed out,[77] but it was a bias that many Americans shared. Rosalynn proudly listed her husband's appointments of women to important positions: three cabinet secretaries (out of a total of six in history) and forty-one federal judges. "It was always understood between us," she wrote, "that a woman would be appointed if a vacancy occurred [on the Supreme Court.]"[78]

Jimmy Carter's record with feminists was hardly duplicated in other areas, and he had to defend that record in the 1980 election. This time the Carters could not present themselves as Washington outsiders ready to do battle for efficiency and integrity—they had to account for what they had done. Double-digit inflation, an oil crisis, and the holding of American hostages in Iran contributed to feelings of national helplessness and to a demand for change. When Republican Ronald Reagan talked in soothing tones about tax cuts and strong defense, he had a winning combination. Rosalynn Carter returned to Plains just a few hours before the voting began, but she already knew that the election was lost.[79]

Rosalynn's partnership with her husband combined competence with unquestioned loyalty, but it never won her the popularity enjoyed by several of her less risk-taking predecessors. She failed to dominate the lists of "most admired women" (as had Mamie Eisenhower and Pat Nixon) or to inspire a following equal to that of the glamorous Jackie Kennedy. A natural reticence restrained her from engaging in the kind of candid interchange that had endeared Betty Ford to reporters, and because she had never developed many friendships with other powerful women, as had Eleanor Roosevelt, she lacked a supportive network outside her family to advise and promote her. The First Lady's staff, although large and competent, did not compensate for the lack of friendships with powerful women.

Yet her four years in the White House helped extend the job of president's wife beyond what it had ever been. Her husband was not physically disabled, as Eleanor Roosevelt's had been, and she did not have three terms in the White House or the double calamity of a great depression and a major war to push her into prominence. On her own, and with her husband's concurrence, she took a portion of his quest for her own—campaigning full-time and putting her best efforts into making the administration a success.

In the process, Rosalynn Carter joined that list of remarkable women generally judged more successful than their husbands in the White House. The same historians who ranked Jimmy Carter next to last among all twentieth-century presidents put Rosalynn in third place, behind Eleanor Roosevelt and Lady Bird Johnson.[80] The disparity raises questions about how much a First Lady depends on her husband's success for her own place in history. Could Eleanor Roosevelt have fared so well had she been the spouse of Herbert Hoover? What if the highly ranked Lady Bird, Rosalynn, and Betty had been wives of more successful presidents? What kind of public careers might the women have compiled on their own, had they not married at all? What differences in opportunities and expectations resulted in such different records within one presidential family?

For her part, Rosalynn was pleased with her demanding role. Once presidents' wives had been confined to "official hostess" and "private helpmeet," she wrote, [but] "Nowadays, the public expectation is just the opposite, and there is a general presumption that the projects of a First Lady will be substantive, highly publicized, and closely scrutinized. I am thankful for the change."[81]

The success of Ronald Reagan's 1980 presidential campaign, emphasizing traditional values and smaller government, might have encouraged his wife to view the example of her outspokenly feminist predecessors as outdated models. Nancy Davis Reagan was old enough to remember the popularity of Mamie Eisenhower who had stuck with the "home-maker" image. Perhaps more to the point, Jackie Kennedy's emphasis on elegance and style, which had gained her so many permanent admirers, coincided with Nancy's own inclinations. She saw nothing wrong with putting "the best of everything" in the White House, and she underscored her point by inviting Letitia Baldrige, social secretary in the Kennedy years, to return to Washington to make sure things were done correctly.

This elitist approach to living in the executive mansion was not unique to the 1980s, but it contrasted markedly with the Carters' reputation for carrying their own luggage and entertaining informally. Although it would be difficult to calculate the amount of time each First Lady devoted to her own wardrobe and guests, Nancy Reagan gave every indication that she meant to develop a public image very different from that of Rosalynn Carter. While the First Lady from Georgia had projected herself as a full-time serious worker who chaired conferences on mental health and testified in front of Senate committees, Nancy Reagan appeared to concentrate her time on china patterns and luncheons for her glamorous friends. Both Rosalynn and Betty Ford had used their prominence to help solve important problems and improve the status of women, but a *Washington Monthly* reporter declared that the coterie surrounding Nancy Reagen considered it a "divine mission" to make such serious women "look tacky."[82]

Old discussions about the proper role of a First Lady were revived. Traditionalists, who preferred the helpmate, voted solidly for Nancy Reagan. Washington caterers, whose business in caviar and other imported delicacies increased overnight, and dress designers, whose creations in the four-figure range became *de rigueur* at White House parties, applauded the change. But there were dissenters. Washington reporters who had cooperated in making a heroine of Jackie Kennedy treated Nancy Reagan as though she bought her wardrobe out of public funds. Feminists and other women, who refused that label but shared the goals, entered that very old debate about what kind of model the country needed "at the head of female society."

The alternatives had shifted considerably but were as hotly discussed as during the days of Rachel Jackson, and it was a contemporary of Nancy Reagan's at Smith College who received most credit for outlining the current situation. In 1963, Betty Friedan (who graduated from Smith College one year ahead of Nancy), had published *The Feminine Mystique*, which indicted wives who defined themselves entirely in terms of husbands and children.[83] Friedan had set out to write about her Smith classmates and what had happened to them in the fifteen years following graduation so she may well have had women like Nancy Reagan in mind. When Friedan found many unhappy women, some so dissatisfied with their lives that they were seeking help in therapy or turning to alcohol and drugs, she enlarged her focus to include all American women. For Friedan, the problem was an outmoded model of femininity, one that severely limited women's options, and she termed this "feminine mystique" that kept women from developing as much as they might have, the "problem that has no name."

Friedan had her own recommendations for change and she argued for them forcefully in this and later books. Women needed to pattern their lives the way men did, working out a "life plan" or agenda of what they hoped to accomplish. No one argued that the turning of the calender would bring each goal easily into reach, but list-making itself would impose direction. Friedan offered other suggestions as well, some of them involving an infusion of federal funds to equalize educational opportunities, much as the federal government had footed the bill for training war veterans. Such suggestions were hardly radical. They offered no attack on traditional family structure or on the economic system. They simply suggested a different division of the American pie of good schools and good jobs so that women got a bigger share.

But there were problems, and Friedan later confessed that she had not foreseen all the difficulties that arose when women entered the professions in much larger numbers. Her sharpest critics pointed out that she had not dealt at all with the problems of working-class women, who, like their fathers, brothers, and husbands, had never had much control over their lives. Forced to earn at a young age, they could hardly make a "life plan" in the manner urged by Friedan. Low family income, illness, monotonous and unrewarding jobs kept them on a treadmill that offered few opportunities to pause for reevaluation. While Friedan seemed to see a job as liberating, most working-class women saw it as something to escape, and they retained dependence and luxury as their ultimate goals.

One popular statement of the anti-Friedan position came in Marabel Morgan's book, *The Total Woman,* which described a route to happiness that centered on a husband.[84] Morgan urged the suspension of all critical faculties in order to become a "total woman." She advised her readers to make a list of their husbands' faults and strengths, then throw away the first list and refer frequently to the second. The definition of "Wife" became for "Total Woman" advocates an attractive but unthinking supportive robot, whose value lay in pleasing others, particularly her husband.

Nancy Davis Reagan would not have described herself as "unthinking" but at least one journalist thought she epitomized the *Total Woman.* Gloria Steinem entitled an article in *Ms* magazine, "Finally, a Total Woman in the White House."[85] Nancy Reagan had announced on more than one occasion that her "life began when I met my husband" and that seeing to his well-being was her one career.[86] She had gladly let an MGM movie contract expire at the end of seven years in order to dedicate her total energy to her husband and children. Ronald had not pushed her—it was what she had always wanted, she said, and on the questionnaire she completed when she arrived in Hollywood, she had listed as her ambition in life: "to have a successful, happy marriage."[87]

Biographers frequently point to the lack of security and permanence in Nancy's childhood as the reason for her putting great emphasis on her marriage. Born to an actress who soon left her daughter with relatives in order to pursue her career and to an auto salesman who left both of them, Nancy Davis Reagan spent her early years (as Anne Frances Robbins) living in Baltimore with an aunt. When her mother remarried, this time choosing a more settled mate, and took her daughter to live in Chicago, the new husband adopted the girl, providing the name she later used in movies—Nancy Davis. Her stepfather had a son from a previous marriage but Nancy was the only daughter of this successful neurosurgeon and he made the rest of her growing up protected and secure: a debut, four years at Smith where she majored in drama, and then a try, with help from family friends, at Hollywood.

Feminists and liberal critics would later charge that Nancy went too far in her devotion to her husband, and one reporter dubbed Nancy's loving focus on Ronald during his speeches "the gaze."[88] Such ridicule should not obscure, however, the important part she played in Ronald's political ascent. Several of her husband's advisers, even those who had suffered expressions of her displeasure, agreed on her value. Michael Deaver, close adviser to the Reagans over many years, said she deserved "as much responsibility for [Ronald Reagan's] success as he."[89] Historians, who initially gave her a very low rating as First Lady, admitted she had been a valuable asset to her husband.[90]

Part of Nancy's value resulted from the unorthodox path her husband took to the top. National politics had shown a tendency in the 1960s and 1970s to open up to the outside. While most high offices had typically been gained by working up a ladder of lesser jobs, some of the most visible posts began to go to people who had achieved a reputation in one field and then transferred that popularity to government. Astronauts, athletes, and actors turned up as candidates for high office.

Such a horizontal entry into politics at the top (Ronald Reagan took his first political office as governor of California in 1967 when he was almost fifty-six years old) involved considerable money and a support staff that could play a variety of roles. A "Total Woman" spouse who could be endlessly amiable and pleasant to prospective contributors was no small asset. Nancy Reagan lunched with wives, and she gamely shared long private plane rides with people she had just met.

Nancy Reagan gave every indication of wanting to transfer this supportive wife-style to Washington, and she began by refurbishing the White House. The routine appropriation of $50,000 that Congress allotted each new president was entirely inadequate for her plans, which included a decorator who usually put that much into a single room (art and antiques were additional).[91] To raise the $900,000 she needed, she turned to private donors. Some of the contributions came from old Hollywood friends, well-heeled and cheerful givers, but critics were not so sure about the provenance of the rest. President Reagan had ended the remaining price controls on domestic oil and gasoline as soon as he took office, several months before the controls were slated to come off; when names of some who had apparently profited from the move showed up on the list of White House donors, suspicion grew that the largess was not motivated solely by patriotism.[92] Whatever their reasons for giving, the contributors had received tax deductions, and since many of them paid federal levies at the rate of 50 percent, the government was footing half the bill.

Considerably more unsettling to many critics was the nearly simultaneous announcement of cuts in federal programs for the poorest

Americans: those who used subsidized day-care centers, food and nutrition programs, job training centers, and family planning services. Rumors of planned cuts in social security benefits frightened other Americans. Jackie Kennedy's spending two decades earlier had hardly been modest, but most Americans had closed an eye—perhaps because reporters had encouraged them to do so. When upbeat talk about progress and "putting a man on the moon in this decade" dominated presidential addresses, few people stopped to worry about who would pay the bill. Two decades later, the rhetoric had turned to pruning the national budget and cutting back, and people caught outside the "safety net," that Ronald Reagan insisted would always be there for the neediest, questioned why they had been cut when so many other people seemed to be doing so well. Nancy Regan's penchant for expensive items may have had a long history, but she was not so visible then nor so close to decisions affecting others who lived on considerably less. Her timing was off—an announcement about $200,000 for new china came one day before the administration publicized a plan to decrease nutrition standards for school lunch programs. The new guidelines would have permitted, according to some interpretations, catsup to be classified as a "vegetable." Although the president later blamed an Agriculture Department official for needlessly stirring up the catsup controversy, the harm had been done.[93]

Nancy Reagan's first year in Washington was not a good one. In addition to facing up to the fact that returning elegance to the White House was not going to win her the same permanent admiration that Jackie Kennedy received, she had to deal with one of the worst experiences of her life—the attempted assassination of her husband in March 1981. For months afterwards, she could not even refer to the incident more directly than "that thing that happened," and, during a televised interview much later, she broke into tears when describing her reaction. She had announced early in the administration that she would continue with a Foster Grandparents program that she had worked with in California, but the effects of the assassination attempt left her little energy, and public perception of her association with the program was weak at best.

Identification came, instead, as part of "millionaires on parade," and she was singled out as the "administration's number-one public relations problem."[94] Feminists ridiculed a woman whose "two-china policy" dealt with dishes, and historians rated her among the worst of all First Ladies, just below the ineffectual Jane Pierce and superior only to Ida McKinley, Florence Harding, and Mary Lincoln.[95] References were made to "Queen Nancy," and even her loyal friend Michael Deaver admitted she had a problem.[96]

In 1982, the highly effective Reagan staff turned its attention to Nancy and set out to temper her elitist image. Her secretary announced that the designer clothes received as gifts would be donated to museums.[97] Nancy Reagan learned to make jokes about herself. She quipped that she would never wear a crown, because it would mess her hair, and when time came for the Gridiron Dinner on March 29, 1982, the First Lady appeared in old, ill-assorted clothing and sang a ditty about wearing "second-hand clothes."[98]

By the middle of the first Reagan administration, it had become clear that Nancy needed to do more. In what one major newspaper described as the "Washingtonization of Nancy Reagan," she began to devote more time to serious problems, particularly drug abuse. She visited facilities, headed up a series of community-based endeavors billed on television as the "Chemical People," made a cameo appearance with Gary Coleman on "Diff'rent Strokes," and invited the wives of other countries' leaders to meet with her in Washington to discuss drug problems. The First Ladies Conference in April 1985, received front-page coverage across the country.[99] The perception was not so much that a president's wife could end drug abuse—no one, least of all, Nancy Reagan, would have expected she could do that—but that she was concerned about unglamorous, public problems.

Whatever the reasons for Nancy Reagan's changed approach to her job, it immediately paid off. She had occasionally explained that drug abuse had always been a top priority for her but that she had been warned away from it by advisers who judged it too "downbeat." Whether she was listening to new advisers or they had changed their counsel remained unclear, but her popularity immediately improved. One pollster reported a twenty-point increase in her approval rating, a change he attributed to the perception that her involvement in rehabilitation programs was both genuine and significant.[100]

As the country's economy improved, the president's popularity rose even higher. This show of confidence along with the security of having entered into a second—and presumably last—presidential term in January 1985 encouraged Nancy Reagan to take an even more prominent part in the administration. The Reagans had always played down or laughed off accounts that Nancy exerted clout in Ronald's political decisions, and to some extent, this pose continued. An NBC special on the First Lady, broadcast in June 1985, showed her laughingly dismissing accounts of her political expertise and interest, but only the naïve believed. Too much evidence to the contrary came from high White House sources who publicly described her as "indispensable," "a savvy adviser," and important on political matters, such as "getting the Russians to a summit," personnel decisions, such as removing Alexander Haig from the cabinet, and procedures, such as preparing her husband for debates against Walter Mondale during the 1984 campaign.[101] When important people played musical chairs in the executive branch, it was generally conceded that she had a part in calling the tune.

What happened in the summer of 1985 added fuel to that speculation. Immediately following President Reagan's surgery for cancer in July, Nancy returned to the White House to receive foreign dignitaries.[102] As soon as it became clear that the president's surgery would require him to work on a reduced schedule, broadcasters speculated on who was "in charge in the White House." Consensus settled on a triumvirate: the president, his chief of staff (Donald Regan), and the First Lady.[103]

Ronald Reagan lent weight to this interpretation when, in a radio address following his surgery, he spoke about the contributions of First Ladies who, he said, "aren't elected and they don't receive a salary. . . . They've mostly been private persons forced to live public lives, and in my book they've all been heroes. . . . Abigail Adams helped invent America. Dolley Madison helped protect it. Eleanor Roosevelt was F.D.R.'s eyes and ears." Then, as though to stake out a place for his wife on the Mount Rushmore of First Ladies, he added: "Nancy is my everything. When I look back on these days, Nancy, I'll remember your radiance and your strength, your support and for taking part in the business of the nation. I say to myself, but also on behalf of the nation, 'Thank you, partner. Thanks for everything.' " [104]

No wonder the *New York Times* chose to describe Nancy Reagan as having "expanded the role of First Lady into a sort of Associate Presidency."[105] The change was not that the president's wife played a part in important decisions but that her participation was taken as a matter of course. Spouses had often acted in unusual ways in times of illness or other crisis, but in the White House that role had often been camouflaged or, as in the case of Edith Wilson, denigrated. By 1985, Americans had become so accustomed to acknowledgments of power on the distaff side of the White House that Nancy Reagan's prominence caused little comment. After Betty Ford, who openly disagreed with her husband on a whole list of important national issues, and Rosalynn Carter, who sat in on cabinet meetings and represented Jimmy in substantive talks with leaders in Latin America, Nancy Reagan's stepping forth seemed unremarkable. That perception of the change had become international is suggested by a duo of telephone calls made from the Philippines to Washington in February 1986, as the ruling Marcos family decided whether or not to flee. Ferdinand Marcos sought advice by telephone from Senator Paul Laxalt, a close friend of President Reagan's; Imelda Marcos called Nancy.[106]

White House insiders underscored Nancy Reagan's clout when they wrote their memoirs: Former Chief of Staff Donald Regan's *For the Record* got special attention for its disclosure that the First Lady had intervened in the president's scheduling of important trips and news conferences, and that she had done so after consulting with a California astrologist. Nancy had kept the president convalescing too long after surgery, Regan complained, and the delay hurt. "Mrs. Reagan's concern for her husband's health was understandable, even admirable," Regan wrote, "but it seemed to me excessive, particularly since the president himself did not seem to think that there was any need for him to slow down to the point where he was lying dead in the water." [107] Rather than apologize, Nancy explained that she had simply been doing what First Ladies had done since the beginning of the Republic—looking out for their husbands' health and well-being.

Soon after leaving Washington, Nancy Reagan got the chance to explain her position more carefully in her own autobiography. Rather petulantly, she titled it *My Turn* and then pointedly dedicated it to "Ronnie who always understood. And to my children, who I hope will understand." She thus alluded to strained family relationships that had been the subject of numerous articles and daughter Patti's thinly veiled fiction.

Like Betty Ford, Nancy chose to work with an editor, and she selected William Novak who had already had his name on Lee Iacocca's best-selling story. Nancy's *My Turn* dealt with the low times of her White House tenure—the assassination attempt, the president's various illnesses, her own mastectomy, and the death of her mother. But she also admitted to having had some influence in the Oval Office: "For eight years I was sleeping with the president, and if that doesn't give you special access, I don't know what does." Even that power had bounds, she explained: "Believe me, if I really were the dragon lady that [Donald Regan] described in his book, he would have been out the door many months earlier."[108]

In January 1989, she showed no reluctance to return to California (except for leaving behind the perks of 1600 Pennsylvania Avenue). For her successor, she had little advice, except to reiterate the point made many times before that the job of First Lady was one "you can never get used to."[109]

For eight years, Barbara Bush had been preparing for the job from the vantage point of the vice president's house. Ascent of the second-in-command was by no means assured in American political history. Not since the 1830s, when Martin Van Buren moved up, had a sitting vice president won election to chief executive, and several Republicans worked to keep that tradition alive a bit longer. Conservative Representative from New York Jack Kemp, television evangelist Pat Robertson, and Senate Republican leader Robert Dole all made spirited runs for the nomination in 1988. But George Bush had not merely bided his time, since losing out to Ronald Reagan in 1980; he had worked hard to cement support among key Republicans and raise the funds to make a strong presidential run.[110]

During the course of the 1988 campaign, both George and Barbara Bush became considerably better known to voters. Like so many of her predecessors in the White House, she boasted more than one ancestor who had served in public life. Her father Marvin Pierce was distantly related to the fourteenth president of the United States, Franklin Pierce, and her mother Pauline Robinson Pierce was the daughter of an Ohio Supreme Court Justice.[111] Like many presidential spouses, she had grown up in circumstances very similar to her husband's.

Born on June 8, 1925 in the affluent New York suburb of Rye, Barbara was the third of four children of businessman Pierce whose job at the McCall Corporation in New York City, where he started as an assistant to the publisher and then worked up to become president in 1946, provided a comfortable life for his family. Full-time household help allowed Barbara's mother to devote her days to gardening and volunteer work, two interests that her daughter would later take on as her own.

The Pierce children could choose from among the best public and private schools, and after attending the local public school through the sixth grade, Barbara enrolled in the Rye Country Day School for four years before transferring to Ashley Hall in Charleston, South Carolina, for her final two years.[112] Her attractive older sister Martha had preceded her to Ashley Hall so Barbara could not have been surprised that the boarding school placed as much emphasis on the social graces as it did on the classics. Nothing about her stay there—or any of her education—suggests that she was more than an average student. Like most females of her generation, she considered school a waiting game until she could make the same kind of marriage that her mother had made—to a man who would provide her with a good life.

During Christmas vacation of her junior year, Barbara met a likely candidate—George Herbert Walker Bush. Introduced at a party, the two apparently were attracted to each other immediately, and Barbara later joked that she had married the first man she ever kissed.[113] Since she was only sixteen at the meeting and he scarcely a year older, the marriage had to wait until both finished school, a wait lengthened by the events of World War II.

On his eighteenth birthday, George enlisted in the navy and went to fight in the Pacific while she returned to Ashley Hall to complete her senior year. Still waiting his return, she enrolled at Smith College, just missing Nancy Davis (later Reagan) who had graduated a few months earlier. Barbara remained little more than one year. Within weeks of beginning her sophomore year, she dropped out to prepare for a Christmas wedding, scheduled to coincide with her fiancé's return. He was delayed and the nuptials had to be rescheduled, but on January 6, 1945, Barbara Pierce married George Bush. She was nineteen years old, one of only four teenage brides in the history of First Ladies.[114]

After the war ended in 1945, George and Barbara Bush prepared for his return to civilian life and college education. When he enrolled at Yale, to work toward a degree in economics, she settled into being a student's wife. Such arrangements were common at the time when the government provided GI benefits to returning veterans, and the men, unwilling to postpone marriage any longer, squeezed their families into crowded housing. Everyone learned to juggle babies' night feedings around typing term papers and studying for examinations. Money was often tight, and like many other wives, Barbara worked at a college cooperative until the birth of her first child in July 1946. Except for a summer job during her high school years, this was the only paid employment that she ever had, and she never returned to complete the college education that she had dropped after little more than one year at Smith.

As soon as George collected his degree in 1948, his young family moved to Texas where he hoped to make his own way without either the help or hindrance of family connections in the East. The work in a burgeoning oil business was hard, involving frequent uprooting and moves from one assignment to another. The names of those towns often blurred in Barbara's mind and only her husband's later prominence would provide for sorting them out: Odessa, Texas, then several towns in California, and back to Midland, Texas.[115] Since some of these stays ended before the unpacking, the number of Bush family residences resists computation, but by the time she moved into the

White House, Barbara counted 28 homes in 17 different cities in 44 years of marriage.

Barbara's life centered on running a home efficiently and looking after her children, three of whom were born within the first eight years of her marriage. It was soon after the birth of the third, son Jeb in early 1953, that the Bushes encountered what they would later single out as an event that changed their lives forever. Their three-year-old daughter Robin was diagnosed as having leukemia and the local doctor advised them that nothing they could do would save her life. He counseled them to tell no one, make the child's last days as comfortable and happy as possible, and in three weeks she would be dead.

As Barbara told an interviewer in 1988, she and George rejected this advice entirely. Within twenty-four hours, everyone in town knew about Robin's illness, and the entire Bush family drew on every resource they could muster to get her the best medical help.[116] Trips back and forth between Texas and New York's Sloan-Kettering Hospital resulted in only temporary remission for the child and enormous stress on the rest of the family. Eight months later, she was dead.

Barbara often singled out this period of her child's illness and the inevitable grieving that followed her death as one of the most difficult in her life, and it was at this time that her hair began to turn prematurely white. She felt the need to return to her normal workload and the mothering of her two young sons, but had trouble finding the inner strength to pull herself out of her depression. Son George, then seven, was credited with inadvertently helping in his mother's recovery. She had overheard him telling a young friend that his mother was "so unhappy."[117] Her husband got even more credit—he simply made her get on with her life, she said.

In the next few years, Barbara settled into the routine of a traditional wife and mother while George devoted his time to an increasingly successful oil business. She gave birth to three more children (two boys and a girl), making a total of five, whose needs filled her days and took most of her energy. Little League games, parent conferences with teachers, and unscheduled trips to the hospital emergency room kept her busy, but they hardly engaged her full potential, "This was a period for me, of long days and short years, of diapers, runny noses, earaches," she told an audience at the American University in 1985. While George was out "having an exciting time," she was "sitting home with these absolutely brilliant children who say one thing a week of interest."[118]

But these apparently mundane household management chores gave her time to develop a confidence that she could do things well on her own, and she realized she could juggle tasks so that all the important ones got attention. Neighbors reported that she not only looked after her own lawn—she also mowed theirs when they were away—and they thought her inordinately well organized. Her son Jeb later suggested that if born in a later generation, she would have made an excellent CEO.

After George's election to the House of Representatives in 1966 (the first Republican to represent Houston in Congress), Barbara enrolled in the unofficial quick course that many candidates' wives find useful. She conquered her fear of public speaking and memorized the names of political contributors and opponents—while keeping her own household running smoothly. That role changed little when George's job took them to New York where he served as Permanent U.S. Representative to the United Nations, then to Washington, D.C., where he chaired the Republican National Committee, and to Beijing, China where he headed the U.S. Liaison Office.

The Bushes' return to Washington in late 1975 caused Barbara to reconsider, perhaps for the first time in her life, the choices she had made.[119] The feminist movement, reaching a peak with its talk of consciousness raising and self-fulfillment, appeared to have its sharp arrows aimed at precisely the kind of life that Barbara Bush, then aged 50, had led. Her children, now grown to adulthood or nearly so, needed her less, and her husband's job at the Central Intelligence Agency did not permit his sharing many work problems with her. Like other women of her generation, she began to reexamine her past and think about what to do with the rest of her life.

Volunteer work, the female version of public service that had attracted generations of American women before her, became Barbara's focus. She later said that she considered several different alternatives before selecting literacy as her chief interest. Having struggled with the problems of a dyslexic son, she had gained a new appreciation for the problems related to a lack of literacy, and she tended to connect many of society's ills, including homelessness and drug abuse, to the lack of power that springs from inability to read. Although she failed to make the connection, others noted that literacy was a "safe" and acceptable project for the wife of an ambitious politician. In fact, her involvement in the literacy campaign coincides with George's first full-fledged attempt to win the Republican nomination for president.

When the 1980 run failed and George Bush settled for second place on a Reagan ticket, Barbara Bush faced the prospect of eight years in close proximity to the White House. Much of her energy went to promoting literacy. She volunteered at dozens of events that advanced the cause, organized a public broadcasting project focused on the need to raise reading levels, and after publishing a book about the family dog, C. Fred, donated the proceeds to literacy groups. By the time her husband took on the presidency in 1989, she had geared up for the job of First Lady as she saw it: engage an experienced staff who would guard her interests, employ a self-deprecating wit that would win her popularity, and keep a tight lip so as not to go on public record as disagreeing with her husband.

As First Lady, Barbara Bush exuded self-confidence, perhaps because of her preparation and her age. At 63, she was the oldest woman ever to take on the job. (Anna Symmes Harrison, wife of the seventh president, had been 66 at the time he was elected but she never moved to the capital.) Barbara had managed homes from California to New York to Beijing. She also appeared blessed by a healthy constitution and a "centered" personality that thrived on doing whatever the day brought her to do.

Unlike many of her younger, more timid predecessors, she expected no great changes in her life as a result of her husband's high office. Lady Bird Johnson had used Lyndon's presidency (and his prodding and cajoling) as an incentive to lose weight and dress more stylishly. Rosalynn Carter felt pushed by the focus put on her in the White House to study Spanish and tutor with experts in economics and world affairs. Pat Nixon turned to wardrobe consultants. Indeed, most First Ladies approached the job as though their husbands' election imposed some kind of giant mandate to do bigger and better things with their lives now that they stood at the center of national attention.

Barbara Bush took a different tack. She appeared enthusiastic at the prospect of her husband's elevation to the presidency, and she promised to work hard at the job of First Lady. But in the seventh decade of her life, she knew who she was and apparently had no intention of changing. She would do anything asked of her, she sometimes was quoted as saying, except dye her halo of white hair into a "more youthful" color or go on a diet to diminish her size fourteen figure. Hers was no easy announcement since jokes punctuated the 1988 campaign about her looking more like George's mother than his wife.[120] But many Americans evidently applauded her approach. Her mail told her, she said, that "a lot of fat, white-haired, wrinkled ladies are tickled pink."[121]

Much about the Bush agenda played on differences with the Reagans, and the contrast was especially pronounced on the First Lady's side.

Barbara Bush joked with reporters that one of her thighs would just about equal Nancy's size four silhouette, and she warned photographers that they would have a hard time catching her in one of the expensive dresses or elaborate hair styles that Nancy favored. When reporters queried Barbara on the reason for wearing a three-stranded faux pearl choker, she cheerfully replied that it covered some wrinkles. Such candor contrasted with actress Nancy Reagan's acceptance of aging—she had shaved two years off her birth date when she went to Hollywood and then found difficulty putting them back on when she moved to Washington. Advertisers immediately seized on the different styles of the two women and boasted that they sold "Nancy Reagan merchandise at Barbara Bush prices."

In fact, the Bushes had not known the frugal life for some time. He had sold the family's share in Zapata Oil for more than one million dollars, and she was thoroughly familiar with the price tags of Arnold Scaasi dresses and Hermès handbags. But her relaxed attitude toward style and appearance appealed to Americans who agreed that a wise woman spent her time on other matters. She cheerfully converted Nancy's exercise-beauty-salon in the White House into a birthing room for the family dog.

During her first year at 1600 Pennsylvania Avenue, Barbara Bush, was diagnosed as having Graves's disease, a disorder of the thyroid that causes severe weight loss, requires long-term medication, and produces considerable discomfort, including red itchy eyes.[122] Rather than withdraw from public appearances, she maintained a full schedule, promoting literacy and fighting against prejudice aimed at those infected with AIDS. A widely circulated photo showing her holding a baby born with AIDS was credited with helping reduce fear about how easily the disease could be transmitted.

The First Lady's large, professional staff was carefully balanced to include minority women. Anna Perez, the first African-American woman to serve in a prominent East Wing position, held the title of press secretary to the First Lady.[123] Other staff members, under the direction of Susan Porter Rose, carefully culled from the many invitations proffered so that Barbara Bush would appear at those events designed to increase her popularity and that of her husband.[124] Requests for photographs of events inside the residence portion of the White House went routinely to the East Wing.

Barbara Bush made her own First Lady history when she put together *Millie's Book as Dictated to Barbara Bush,* a collection of photographs and purported musings of the family dog who divided her time among three homes—the White House, Camp David, and

Kennebunkport, Maine—meeting famous people, cavorting with the president's grandchildren, and preening in the Blue Room. When the book became a best seller, earning nearly $800,000 in royalties in 1991, the First Lady donated the net proceeds to the Barbara Bush Foundation for Family Literacy, an organization she had helped establish as soon as she moved into the White House. Had she not given the money away, she would have earned far more than her husband that year and a great deal more than any previous president's spouse had earned while in the White House.

Unlike her Republican predecessor Betty Ford, who had publicly differed with her husband on important public issues, and Nancy Reagan, who was widely reported to take a hand in her husband's personnel decisions and scheduling, Barbara Bush kept her views to herself. She had briefly flirted with the dangers of sarcasm in the 1984 election when she had described the Democratic candidate for vice president Geraldine Ferraro as "a 4-million dollar . . . I can't say it but it rhymes with rich."[125] Barbara Bush's phoned apology to Ferraro failed to obliterate the remark from the public record, and her disclaimer that she had meant "witch," rather than a stronger term commonly applied to forceful women, found few believers. Opponents took this outburst as evidence of a small nasty streak in an otherwise kindly genteel front.

The White House years showed no public repetitions of this lapse, and Barbara Bush stuck to noncontroversial topics related to her family and her hostessing duties whenever she gave an interview. Not since Bess Truman had the nation witnessed in a First Lady such a combination of self-confidence in herself and "hands off" national issues. Other presidents' wives, including Mamie Eisenhower and Jacqueline Kennedy, had not forayed into the political thicket but they had not been seen as holding strong opinions of their own on such topics. Barbara Bush was widely believed to differ with her husband on gun control laws and on a woman's right to terminate a pregnancy, but she skillfully skirted attempts to put those views on public record.

By the 1990s, such a traditional approach to the job of First Lady had many critics, and some of them surfaced during the debate over whether Barbara Bush was the appropriate commencement speaker at Wellesley College. The invitation had been offered by administration officials without consulting students, who, when they learned of it, got up a petition against her appearance that more than 150 students signed. They objected that she boasted no achievement of her own—her fame resulted entirely from her marriage to a man who later became president.

Rather than defend herself, the First Lady spoke up for the students, saying that she understood their point and respected other
women's rights to make decisions different from hers. Then, in an
impressive public relations coup, she offered to bring along with her
to Wellesley Raisa Gorbachev, wife of Soviet Union President Mikhail
Gorbachev, who was scheduled to be in the United States at the time
to sign an important agreement on nuclear arms and chemical
weapons.

The Wellesley audience heard two women from quite different
backgrounds on June 1, 1990: Raisa Gorbachev, university professor,
and Barbara Bush, college dropout. The latter injected some wit in
her remarks by noting that "somewhere out in this audience may even
be someone who will one day follow in my footsteps and preside over
the White House as the president's spouse." She paused, then added,
"I wish him well."[126]

When feminists expressed disappointment over Barbara Bush's
traditional approach to the job, she tried to deflect them by keeping
quiet. The suspicion that she would have joined them, left to her own
reputation to defend, helped soften the criticism. In fact, she was
enormously popular with many segments of the public and often garnered an "approval rating" higher than that of her husband. *Good
Housekeeping* readers put her at the top of their "Most Admired" list for
four years in a row, and at the 1992 nominating convention, the
Republicans scheduled her speech during prime time on national
television. The convention had already broken one precedent by
listing the vice president's wife, attorney Marilyn Quayle, as a featured
speaker, and she had angered many in the audience by referring to
"women's essential nature" to be mothers and homemakers.

Much of the 1992 campaign centered on the country's economic
status. Although a recession appeared ended, the Republican candidate failed to make that message clear or credible, and many voters
who had supported him in 1988 cast their ballots for the Democrat or
the insurgent Texas billionaire Ross Perot. Even before the returns
came in, it was clear the president would lose. In fact, he garnered
only 38 percent of the popular vote, less than any incumbent since
William Howard Taft ran for a second term in 1912.

Barbara Bush did not seem entirely unhappy with the prospect of
leaving the White House. She had often said she wanted to get out of
politics while she was still vigorous enough to garden, and she
appeared to relish the privacy and freedom that her husband's exit
from public life promised. She had neither redefined the job of First
Lady nor been altered significantly by living in the White House.

Gardening, reading, and being with her grandchildren were sufficient to occupy her time and hopes. "Life inside the White House was great," she later wrote, "and believe it or not, it's great outside, too."[127] Still enormously popular with the public, she and George continued to top Gallup polls asking which couples Americans admired most.

When Barbara Bush relinquished the White House in early 1993, she closed a chapter in First Lady history. She and the trio of women who preceded her achieved a transition—their tenures looking as much backward to their predecessors as forward to the new century. All four had been born within a few years of each other (1918–1927), and they had matured at a time when daughters were less likely to go to college than their brothers. Of the four, only Nancy Reagan earned a college degree. All had worked at some time in their lives, but only one had a career of her own and that was clearly a stopgap measure until she married. Actress Nancy Reagan had never concealed from Hollywood the fact that her real goal in life was to have a family. Hers was small—two children—but the other three produced more: Bush gave birth to six, Ford and Carter each had four.

All the women had played important partnership roles in their husbands' political ascents, and in each case, the husband acknowledged his debt publicly. But much of the influence went undocumented and unquantified because it occurred off the record. Largely self-taught, the women learned quickly, and in the process they showed the potential in the job. But it remained for another generation of women to show what a well-educated, professionally qualified, forceful First Lady could do.

10

A New Generation in the
White House (1993–2017)

ON JANUARY 20, 1993, Hillary Rodham Clinton moved into the White House amid predictions that she would completely rewrite the job of First Lady. Headlines described a president's "First Partner" who is "breaking new ground."[1] One magazine searched the record of three administrations to fashion a composite that did her justice, finally concluding that she was a "presidential super spouse" who combined "the policy presence of an Eleanor Roosevelt [with] the sounding board of a Milton Eisenhower and the . . . generalship on hard decisions that Robert F. Kennedy offered during the Cuban missile crisis of 1962."[2] Within months, a popular magazine outlined not "The President's First One Hundred Days" but "A Hundred Days of Hillary."[3] The normally sedate *Atlantic* suggested that she was making "motherhood look good" on women's job résumés,[4] and the career-minded *Working Woman* evaluated the "ripple effect of the 'Billary' phenomenon" on "husband-wife business relationships" across the nation.[5] Television viewers of CNN's popular "Sonya Live" cheerfully offered their own opinions of how this presidential couple differed from their predecessors.[6]

The gap between George H. W. Bush's generation and that of Bill Clinton was bigger than is usual between one administration and the next, and for their wives the distance loomed even larger. Historians focusing on American women's lives may one day argue that the greatest watershed of all lay in those decades separating Barbara Bush's birth in 1925 and Hillary Rodham Clinton's in 1947. One year younger than Barbara's oldest child, Hillary had grown up in a very different world.

Hillary had not only graduated from college but had completed law school and then gone on to work her entire adult life. Barbara Bush dropped out of college after one year and never held a full-time job. The older woman's choices had been defined by her husband's jobs and by the needs of her children; the younger had begun a career first and then fit family around it. The contrast is underlined in their approach to their names. Most Americans find difficulty coming up with the maiden name of Barbara (Pierce) Bush, whereas few have trouble remembering that Hillary was born a Rodham.

It was not just that the two women had taken such remarkably different paths—in education, work, and domestic arrangements—but that so many of their contemporaries had made the same choices they had. Barbara Bush and Hillary Clinton were quintessential examples of women of their time and class. As the older woman, Bush may have had some friends whose careers resembled Clinton's but such a path would have been as much an anomaly as a Barbara-Bush-type among Hillary's contemporaries.

By the time the Clintons moved into the White House, young Americans showed the effect of changes in the 1970s and 1980s. In education, girls had evened out the odds, and by 1991, white females who graduated from high school were more likely to go on to college than were males.[7] Old quotas that had held down the numbers of women admitted to professional and graduate schools faded or disappeared, and by 1990, women collected a sizeable fraction of degrees granted: 34 percent of those in medicine; 31 percent in dentistry; 42 percent in law; 25 percent in theology; and more than half of the doctorates awarded in education, foreign languages, health sciences, literature, psychology, and public affairs.[8]

At work, the change was reflected in the numbers of women holding full-time jobs. When Barbara Bush's oldest child entered elementary school in 1952, it was the unusual mother in a two-parent household who went outside her home to work, especially when her children were very young. By the time Chelsea Clinton entered grade school, more than half of the nation's mothers with children her age held a job.[9]

A new generation of Americans grew accustomed to seeing women in places of power and influence: their actions covered on the front pages of important newspapers and their pictures in television programs of substance. First Ladies before 1993 had come of age when women in politics were rare and those who ventured to run for office found themselves denigrated as "hard," "unfeeling," and "unfeminine."

Dorothy Rodham believed that barriers against women in high government jobs would lift in her daughter's generation and she was right. Sandra Day O'Connor, the first woman to serve on the Supreme Court, was nominated by Republican President Ronald Reagan in 1981. Three years later the Democratic Party achieved a "first" of its own when it named Geraldine Ferraro of New York to run with Walter Mondale of Minnesota for the top two political jobs in the land. Female members of the president's cabinet ceased being a novelty, and the number of women legislators climbed slowly but steadily. By the time the 103rd Congress took seats in 1993, women claimed six places in the Senate and forty-eight in the House of Representatives. On the state level, they did even better, winning nearly twenty percent of the total posts. No wonder expectations ran high for Hillary.

Born on October 26, 1947, in a Chicago suburb, Park Ridge, Hillary Rodham Clinton had grown up in a comfortably middle-class home. Daughter of Hugh Rodham, who owned a small fabric store, and Dorothy Rodham, full-time wife and mother, she was the oldest of their three children (and the only girl), and played the classic role of the first-born who tries so hard to please. When her parents encouraged her to do everything that her brothers did, she took them seriously. "I was determined," Dorothy Rodham later told the *Washington Post*, "that just because she was a girl didn't mean she should be limited."[10]

On top of the parental grounding, Hillary ingested a strong dose of religious training that directed her toward many of her choices. As a youngster, she attended the Methodist church, whose founder John Wesley had taken as an important creed: "Do all the good you can, in all the ways you can, in all the places you can, at all the times you can, to all the people you can, as long as ever you can." In her case the admonition had been reinforced by other events at the time she came of age—in the 1960s—when talk of "what you can do for your country" and of the Peace Corps and community involvement drew many young people into public service. By the 1990s, when Americans came to know more of Hillary Rodham, such talk appeared dated, if not naïve and suspiciously self-serving, but two decades earlier, it had been common and often sprang from genuine conviction.

High school for Hillary included the chance to develop some of the skills and ideas that she would later transfer to the national arena. Class officer and organizer, she learned to speak in front of a student body of several hundred and when she graduated in 1965, classmates singled her out as the girl in her class most "likely to succeed,"[11] an accolade that signaled both affability and perseverance. Her political philosophy was still in the making because she combined what appears to have been genuine commitment to social progress with a hearty distaste for big government. As a high school senior, she backed Republican Barry Goldwater for president, and when she entered

Wellesley College in September 1965, she did so as a Goldwater Republican.

Four years at Wellesley changed her perspective, but it would be unfair to credit college alone with achieving that shift. By 1968 she was campaigning for Eugene McCarthy[12] as he challenged incumbent Lyndon Johnson for the Democratic nomination for president. McCarthy's run evolved out of the anti-war movement which, by March 1968, had helped drive Johnson out of the race, but other forces were at work challenging the old order of things. A fledgling feminist movement, a strong civil rights fight, and various other reforms aimed at improving schools and prisons and protecting the environment had encouraged many people to think differently about their lives and their government.

In college, Hillary Rodham honed the leadership skills she had developed in an Illinois high school and turned them to serve her new convictions. Majoring in political science, she had the opportunity to work out some of her ideas on exactly how societal change could come about, and increasingly she began to accept the idea that government should play a larger role. One of her professors wrote, in recommending her to law school, that he had "high hopes" for her. "She has the intellectual ability, personality, and character to make a remarkable contribution to American society."[13]

As the head of campus government, Hillary was chosen to speak for the student body at the Wellesley commencement exercises in June 1969. After the principal speaker, Massachusetts Senator Edward Brooke, gave the kind of speech typically heard on such occasions, full of optimism and generalities, Hillary delivered a strong reproach. She lashed out at those defending the status quo, with its "acquisitive and competitive corporate life," and encouraged searching for something better. Although many in the audience thought such remarks unseemly and inappropriate, *Life* published Hillary's picture in an article about graduation ceremonies across the nation.

Law school appeared the next logical step, and by the time Hillary applied in 1969, Yale stood high among possible choices. It had already achieved a reputation for turning out graduates geared to public service rather than profit alone, and it had begun accepting a sizeable number of female applicants.

It was in her first year at Yale that Hillary became acquainted with Yale alumna Marian Wright Edelman, an African American who would become an important mentor. Only eight years older than Hillary, Edelman had already compiled a remarkable résumé, including four years as an attorney for the NAACP in Mississippi and a role in founding the Washington Research Project, a public interest group in the nation's capital. Hillary quickly signed on to work at the Research Project during summer breaks, and her study of migrant workers' camps led directly to concern for children in those camps. Resolving to learn more about child development and legal issues involved in protecting children's health and safety, she located professors writing on the subject and signed on to assist them.

These pursuits outside the classroom tacked another year on to what would normally have been a three-year-law degree and put Hillary Rodham's graduation date in 1973, the same as Bill Clinton's although he had entered one year after her. Fourteen months older than Hillary, he had followed graduation from Georgetown with a Rhodes scholarship to Oxford, before returning to the United States to enter law school. The story of their meeting, in the Yale library, is not unique in the history of presidents and their wives. Lou Henry had first encountered young Herbert Hoover in the geology lab at Stanford University, and Lou, like Hillary, had gone on to earn the same degree as her husband earned.

But unlike the Hoovers who evidently decided to link their lives soon after they met, the Clintons made their decision more slowly. By the 1970s, women had more options than in Lou Hoover's days. While Bill returned to his native Arkansas, Hillary took a job in Washington working for the House Judiciary Committee investigating the intricacies of President Nixon's culpability in the Watergate break-in and its aftermath. One of three women on a legal team that totaled 41, Hillary came to the job with high recommendations and plenty of zeal, and she forged friendships there that she would take with her to the White House. The legal team brought impressive credentials, and Hillary later told Washington reporter Donnie Radcliffe that working on it had been a "great experience. . . . What a gift! I was twenty-six years old. I felt like I was walking around with my mouth open all the time."[14]

President Nixon's resignation in August 1974, abruptly ended the work of the investigative team, and Hillary made a momentous, but not irreversible, decision about her future. Although she later admitted she had been cautioned against the effect such a move would have on her career, she relocated to Bill's Arkansas. They did not marry until November 1975, but she had evidently made her decision a year earlier to fit her professional life around his. Had she contemplated a political career of her own, she would have been better advised to remain in the capital, return to her own state of

Illinois, or put down new roots in another state more amicable to the idea of women candidates. But like many of the women who became First Lady, she recognized that political work did not always include holding office in her own name.

As Bill Clinton moved single-mindedly into politics, Hillary Rodham taught at the state university's law school. When he won his first statewide election to attorney general and moved to the state capital, she gave up teaching and joined the Rose Law Firm in Little Rock, becoming the first woman hired by this prestigious old law firm. During her years at Rose, she forged close professional ties with people who would later assist in the campaign for president and then in running the Oval Office. Vincent Foster, a fellow attorney, served as Assistant White House Counsel until his death in the summer of 1993, and another attorney, Webster Hubbell, went to Washington as Associate Attorney General, the third highest rank in the Justice Department.[15]

Had she never married, Hillary Rodham could have consoled herself in her middle years that she had a remarkably successful career. Work on corporate boards and her legal practice earned her a comfortable six-figure income, thus putting her at the very top among American professional woman at the time. Popular with colleagues at work, she was twice named to the list of "100 Most Influential Lawyers in America."[16] Garry Wills, writing in the *New York Review of Books,* singled her out as "one of the more important scholar-activists of the last two decades."[17]

But like many other women of her generation, Hillary combined this success at work with a full family life—as wife and mother. The birth of Chelsea Victoria Clinton on February 27, 1980, evidently made only a tiny glitch in her mother's career path. Like other women who were her contemporaries, Hillary had learned to juggle the demands of household management and a stressful job, and although the events in her daily life were not those of every woman—hosting a reception at the Governor's Mansion and arguing an important case in court—the logistics were identical. Often it seemed she had to be in two places at the same time.

When Bill Clinton first announced he would try for the presidency in 1992, few observers foresaw any chance of his winning or showed much interest in his wife. President Bush's popularity stood at an all-time high at the end of the Kuwait war, and many Americans did not think or hope that he would be denied a second term.

Among the spouses of Democrats who challenged President Bush, Hillary Rodham Clinton (as her press releases announced her at the time) did not have a high profile. She had not campaigned in 1988 when so much attention went to candidates' spouses. The spotlight had actually turned on the women early in that race when Democrats in Polk County, Iowa, decided to sponsor a forum featuring candidates' wives twelve months before the nominating conventions took place. Invitations went out to the headquarters of all the contenders, and six wives agreed to appear. When they arrived in Des Moines, on July 26, 1987, they found hundreds of journalists, many armed with microphones and television cameras, and an auditorium full of interested listeners.

The forum, moderated by Attorney Ruth Harkin (whose husband served in the U.S. Senate), featured an impressive lineup of speakers: attorney Harriet Babbitt, wife of Arizona Governor Bruce Babbitt; attorney Jeanne Simon, spouse of Illinois Senator Paul Simon; author Tipper Gore, who had just written a book decrying sexually explicit lyrics in rock songs; educator Jill Biden, who had completed two master's degrees and vowed to continue teaching even if her husband won the presidency; Kitty Dukakis, whose list of professional activities and community service totaled four pages; and Jane Gephardt, spouse of Missouri Congressman Richard Gephardt and the only speaker to present herself as a traditional wife without a career of her own. Bill Clinton had dropped out of the race one week earlier or Hillary would have participated in this panel of six mothers who were also attorneys, authors, educators, and public advocates.

Hillary's first big opportunity for national attention came in early 1992, when she and her husband appeared on "60 Minutes" to respond to the claim made by Gennifer Flowers, an Arkansas woman, that she had had a twelve-year affair with Bill Clinton. Scheduled for January 26, 1992, following the Super Bowl, the broadcast was expected to attract 100 million viewers. This was not the first time Americans had seen wives of prominent politicos standing alongside their husbands in similar situations. Many of those watching had strong memories of Lee Hart's dejected appearance when she stood in front of cameras with her husband, Gary Hart, during his 1988 run for president and attempted to combat rumors of his own extramarital activities. Other viewers recalled Joan Kennedy's grim expression when she accompanied Ted Kennedy on public occasions after Chappaquiddick. But Hillary was the first to take the microphone on such an occasion and to do it on live TV.

Years of facing television cameras and of public speaking paid off for both Clintons. While he squirmed slightly, choosing his words carefully enough so as to admit "bringing pain" to his marriage without actually confessing what he had done, she charged ahead. In a final touch of defiance that he did not quite match, she challenged voters to consider what the Clintons represented and then if they did not like what they saw, "then heck, don't vote for him."[18]

The Clinton campaign hit other rough spots before Bill captured the nomination but Hillary's name had become a household word. She remained central to her husband's campaign, and when candidate Jerry Brown charged that she had gained professionally from her husband's governorship, she replied that she "could have stayed home and baked cookies" but had chosen not to. Her comment was picked up by the press and repeated out of context to convey the idea that she disparaged women who had no career outside their home and families. In fact, she had gone on to say that she had made her choices with the hope that she could ease the way for other women to have more options. But the "cookies" quote dogged her steps and tagged her, in opponents' eyes, as an enemy of traditional family values—a woman full of her own importance.[19]

Besides the charge of lacking domesticity, Hillary had to deal with her own weighty professional baggage. She had been packing it for twenty years. Since leaving Yale she had taken stands, worked on controversial issues, and acquired critics. Her work with the Legal Services Corporation, a federally funded nonpartisan attempt to provide legal aid to the nation's indigent, came in for special censure when word spread that it had provided money for less than mainstream causes, such as transsexual surgery and Native Americans' claims to ownership of a large chunk of Maine.

Even her work with the Children's Defense Fund came under attack, and her earlier writings on the legal rights of minors appeared, in some renditions, to argue that children had the right to sue their parents. A conservative journal dubbed Hillary "The Lady Macbeth of Little Rock,"[20] and the *New Yorker* ran a cartoon showing a woman asking a sales clerk for a "Nothing too Hillary" jacket.[21]

Moving into new territory without a model to follow, Hillary Rodham Clinton modified her role. She spoke out less, and at the Democratic convention, she gamely participated in a cookie bake-off, sponsored by *Family Circle,* that pitted her recipe for chocolate chip cookies against that of incumbent Barbara Bush. Then, as though to emphasize her domesticity, she permitted her twelve-year-old daughter, who had been shielded from public scrutiny, to appear before cameras and be featured in *People* magazine, thus underscoring Hillary's role as mother. The woman who aspired to First Ladyship chose softer, more feminine clothing and smiled a lot, so that when television cameras focused on her during her husband's acceptance speech at the convention, she appeared as fondly and demurely supportive as Nancy Reagan ever had.

The period between the November election and the January inauguration showed still more signs of her clout. After meeting with congressional leaders who journeyed to Little Rock to talk with the president-elect, he openly acknowledged that she had sat in all the discussions, "talked a lot and knew more than we did about some things."[22] Such a confession was without precedent, and it caused speculation abroad. Curious Japanese journalists puzzled about whether or not she would sit in on cabinet meetings and they queried First Lady watchers for their view of the odds. As though to encourage speculation about her role in the new administration, she participated in interviews with prospective appointees and put forward some names of her own drawn from her huge network of professional associates.

Although Hillary's participation in the inaugural festivities mirrored that of the most traditional First Ladies, and journalists showed great interest in the color of her daytime outfit and the cut of her evening gown, she soon made headlines of a different sort. She took an office in the West Wing of the White House, a few feet from the Oval Office. Since the entire West Wing measures only 60 by 90 and its three floors can accommodate fewer than two dozen offices, this access to the center of power appeared to signal an important symbolic move.[23] Her predecessors had contented themselves with space in the East Wing or the more distant Executive Office Building. Some of the most powerful First Ladies, including Nancy Reagan, set up no office for themselves outside the family residence.

As though to temper talk of too much clout in a First Lady, Hillary chose as her first in-depth interview to talk with Marian Burros, ex-food critic of the *New York Times*. When the nationally read newspaper ran the front page article on February 2, 1993, it included a photo of the new First Lady, glamorously clad in an off-the-shoulder black dress and leaning over a table set for a formal dinner in the State Dining Room. The article delved into her thoughts on menus, entertaining, and other traditionally domestic and "feminine" topics.[24] Soon other newspapers picked up on the domestic theme; they carried articles on how she had banned smoking in the executive mansion and encouraged the serving of wholesome foods, including broccoli, a vegetable that George Bush reportedly detested.

The new First Lady appointed a staff with excellent skills and long experience in Washington. Margaret Williams, chief of staff with a West Wing office near her boss, combined Capitol Hill expertise and graduate study in mass communications, but she had met Hillary while working as communications director for the Children's Defense Fund.[25] Williams's assistants brought many of her same strengths: political savvy, media insights, and long friendships with one or both of the Clintons.

Hillary would need additional staff for her most difficult assignment, which also exposed her to intense criticism and led to debate on what a president's spouse could do. During the campaign, Bill had made health care reform central to his agenda, and after his election, he moved quickly to deliver on that promise. Although Hillary, as the wife of an elected official, could receive no pay for her work, Bill named her head of the Task Force on Health Care Reform.

That decision quickly led to a series of events testing the status of a First Lady. After physicians were barred from Task Force hearings on the grounds that they did not qualify as "government officials," they responded that the First Lady was not a government official either.[26] A district federal court initially agreed with the physicians, and the presiding judge ordered the Task Force meetings open. But a federal appeals court reversed that decision on June 22, 1993, accepting the argument that there existed "a longstanding tradition of public service by First Ladies...who have acted (albeit in the background) as advisers and personal representatives of their husbands." Judge James L. Buckley wrote a dissenting opinion in which he pointed out that the president's wife was "greeted like a head of state, guarded by the Secret Service, and allowed to spend Federal money." But such perks did not make her a government employee, he argued, because "she has been neither appointed to nor confirmed in the position of First Lady, she has taken no oath of office and neither holds a statutory office nor performs statutory duties."[27]

Since the Task Force had completed its work and disbanded, the court's ruling had no immediate effect but criticism of Hillary Clinton's involvement was not so easily quelled. *Newsweek* magazine's cover queried "Who's in charge?" The First Lady made repeated trips to Capitol Hill to woo Congress into supporting her commission's findings, and in the fall of 1993, she broke all precedent by talking with five different congressional committees in the course of one week. Television news programs covered her talks, and newspapers and magazines printed "rave" reviews. Congresswoman Lynn Schenk of California relayed a message of admiration from her own mother who had not been so impressed since the days of Eleanor Roosevelt. Then, to an amused audience, Schenk noted: "My mother is not a woman who admires easily."

Such accolades diminished in the following months as new reports came out about the Clintons' financial dealings, involving Hillary more directly than Bill. Whitewater, a real estate venture a dozen years earlier, had gone bad, and now the Clintons were charged with acting improperly, if not illegally, to protect their partners in the aftermath. Aides to both the president and First Lady received subpoenas to talk about what they knew, and the president's chief counsel, Bernard Nussbaum, a former mentor of Hillary's, resigned. Reports that papers from the Whitewater dealings had been shredded added to the story. To further implicate Hillary, new evidence emerged that she had traded in futures commodities in 1979 and done it very profitably, converting a tiny $1,000 nest egg into a hefty $100,000 bankroll. And she had accomplished this remarkable feat in a very few months.

A flurry of interviews followed after Hillary admitted she had been perhaps "less understanding than I need to of both the press and the public's interest... [and their] right to know things about my husband and me."[28] She vowed to "rezone" herself to be more open and candid in the future.

But questions about Whitewater persisted, along with rumors about her role in the firing of White House travel office employees and in a cover-up associated with the suicide of her friend and colleague Vincent Foster.[29] Special Prosecutor Robert B. Fiske, named to investigate Whitewater dealings and report to Congress, took sworn testimony from both Clintons, speaking with the president for ninety minutes and the First Lady for sixty. Kenneth Starr, the independent counsel who replaced Fiske, subpoenaed Hillary to testify in front of a grand jury, the first time a president's wife had ever been required to make such an appearance. Suggestions from the Clintons and their advisers that a deposition taken from her in the White House would serve just as well—without exposing her to the indignity of having to go to a downtown Washington court house—were rejected, and she testified for four hours.

While the investigations continued (into 1998), Hillary found herself condemned in many quarters. William Safire, who had once written speeches for Richard Nixon, used his column in the *New York Times* to call her a "congenital liar."[30] She had already been blamed for the Democrats' debacle in the November 1994 election when the Republicans registered large gains, taking control of both houses of Congress and winning nearly all sixty of the seats that swung from one party to the other. It had been her brazen fight to reform health care and in other ways go beyond what a president's wife should do, her enemies charged, that voters didn't like. Additional information about her financial history added to the perception that she was both ambitious and greedy.

Hillary had already decided that much of the disapproval she encountered was beyond her control. She told biographer Gail Sheehy, "It's not me personally, they hate—it's the changes I represent." She attributed the anti-Hillary sentiments to "wounded men" who saw her as "the boss they never wanted to have...the daughter who they never wanted to turn out to be so independent."[31]

Nevertheless, she reverted to a more traditional First Lady mode, albeit in the activist mode of Lady Bird Johnson. She would remain a prominent part of the administration but in ways less likely to stir up controversy. In the syndicated weekly newspaper column she began writing in 1995 and in her speeches, she stuck to mainstream ideas, such as the need to improve reading test scores and make mammograms more accessible. Work progressed on her book, *It Takes a Village and Other Lessons Our Children Teach Us.*

The First Lady continued to travel widely, including a twelve-day trip to Asia, with stops in India, Pakistan, Nepal, Bangladesh, and Sri Lanka, but because she turned the trip into a mother-daughter outing with teenager Chelsea, she broke no new ground. When she spoke at the UN's Fourth World Conference on Women in Beijing in September 1995, she used a refrain of contemporary feminists for her title: "Women's rights are human rights."

When Bill Clinton won re-election easily in 1996, Hillary embarked on what might have been a tranquil, lame duck period. But it quickly turned into one of the most tumultuous periods in American history, with a president facing impeachment and a First Lady breaking new ground in politics.

Monica Lewinsky's name became a household phrase in January 1998 when Linda Tripp, a former White House aide, informed Independent Counsel Kenneth Starr that she possessed taped conversations documenting a sexual relationship between her one-time friend, Ms. Lewinsky, and the POTUS. As soon as national media relayed Tripp's account, the First Lady went on the popular *Today* show to defend her husband and label the story a creation of a "vast right-wing conspiracy" bent on destroying him.[32] The president tried to distance himself from Lewinsky by announcing that he had never had "a sexual relationship with that woman." Both statements would come back to haunt the president and First Lady. After Lewinsky presented physical evidence (a semen-stained dress) implicating him, Bill Clinton went on national television to admit he had not told the full truth. He also admitted misleading his wife.

For the remainder of 1998, the nation's attention stayed glued to the president and Monica. Sociologists offered their own explanations for "sexual addiction," and parents worried about how their young children were enlarging their vocabulary of sexual acts. On December 18, the U.S. House of Representatives voted for the second time in American history to impeach a president, and Bill Clinton faced trial for obstructing justice and committing perjury. Although the Senate returned a verdict of "not guilty" on both counts on February 12, 1999, the revelations of the previous few months had become part of the permanent public record.

Hillary's defense of her husband received both condemnation and praise. Some viewed her sympathetically as a woman who remained loyal to her husband although clearly suffering as the "wronged wife."[33] Others expressed dismay that anyone with her considerable resources, including a law degree and a powerful network, remained with a man whose infidelity humiliated her. Still others suggested she stayed in the marriage to satisfy her own gigantic personal ambition and to preserve her connections to the most powerful people in the nation.

Although Hillary refused to divulge publicly much about her feelings during those difficult months, she gradually began showing a new determination, a realization that her time had come. Her husband's second and final term would soon end, leaving both of these relatively young, energetic people to figure out how to spend the rest of their lives. Former First Ladies had typically retired beside their spouses, and only two widows, Eleanor Roosevelt and Jacqueline Kennedy, had embarked on careers of their own. None had run for office.

When rumors began circulating in late 1998 that Hillary might try for the U.S. Senate seat of Daniel Patrick Moynihan, who was retiring in 2000, many people were skeptical. She had never seemed to enjoy the flesh pressing of a campaign or the hectic schedule of a politician. Unlike Bill, she was a "policy person" rather than a "people person." But election to a potent, nationally visible platform—such as New York's seat in the U.S. Senate—would liberate her from her husband's shadow and give her the chance to achieve in her own name.

Since she had never resided in New York State, she had to combat charges of carpet bagging that had plagued Robert Kennedy in 1964. She started immediately crisscrossing the state on "listening tours" so she could talk directly with voters in small groups. She doggedly persisted in learning about economic conditions in upstate counties and ethnic conflicts in New York City. She memorized the state's official flora and fauna choices and read up on its authors and sports teams. When the Clintons announced they would be vacationing that summer in New York's Adirondacks, considerably less fashionable than Martha's Vineyard, where they had previously vacationed, it was taken as a sure sign that she was in the race.

Hillary Clinton thus initiated a new chapter in First Lady history— leading to charges of conflicting interests. How could she combine her White House duties while also running for office hundreds of miles away? Who was paying for all that travel around New York State?

The Clintons purchased a home in Chappaqua, just north of New York City, in late 1999, and Hillary began spending more time away from Washington. Daughter Chelsea, taking time off from her Stanford studies, sometimes filled in for her at White House functions, but mostly Hillary learned to divide her time, covering two fronts on the same day.

The presumed Republican opponent, New York City Mayor Rudolph Giuliani, dropped out of the race six months before the election, when he was diagnosed with prostate cancer, and Rick Lazio, a relatively unknown Long Island congressman, stepped in to replace him. Contributions poured in from across the country to help him mount a full campaign against a much better known candidate. Eventually this became one of the most costly senatorial races in history, with Clinton's campaign spending $29 million and Lazio's disbursing nearly $40 million, a record at that time for a losing candidate.[34]

When Hillary greeted her jubilant supporters at a victory celebration on November 7, she summed up the race as "Sixty-two counties, sixteen months, three debates, two opponents and six pantsuits."[35] In fact she had won handily, defeating Lazio by 12 percentage points.[36]

While Hillary concentrated on her own race, a quartette of remarkable women had their eyes on her First Lady job. Although the four wives of the men on the major parties' presidential tickets that year distanced themselves from her record, they had similar personal histories. Laura Bush and Lynne Cheney, whose husbands were on the Republican ticket, and Tipper Gore and Hadassah Lieberman, on the Democratic, were all well educated, with at least one graduate degree each. Cheney boasted a Ph.D. in English literature. Two had published books and all four had run enough charities and voluntary organizations to feel confident about undertaking an executive role. All four had spent enough time in the nation's power hub to feel comfortable in front of TV cameras. None appeared to suffer the "microphone fright" that paralyzed Mamie Eisenhower or the insecurities that dogged capital newcomer Rosalynn Carter.

As Hillary prepared to move out of the White House, she had to juggle two demanding roles, fulfilling all the duties of a lame duck

First Lady while serving as senator-elect from one of the nation's largest states. She entertained hundreds at 1600 Pennsylvania Avenue and published a book, *An Invitation to the White House,* replete with favorite family recipes, anecdotes about guests who had passed through, and photos of the mansion's interior.[37]

But she also tended to more substantive matters as part of her senator-elect duties. She attended briefing sessions, gave interviews on pressing national matters, and purchased a residence in Washington, D.C. When time came to sign a contract for her autobiography, she set another record for presidential spouses by drawing an $8 million advance.[38]

Not until nearly a month after Hillary's senate victory did Laura Bush know for sure that she would be moving into the White House. Her biography resembled her immediate predecessor more than that of her mother-in-law who had moved out of the White House eight years earlier. Almost a year older than Hillary Rodham Clinton, Laura Bush also boasted a work record of her own. But unlike Hillary she had waited until age thirty-one to marry and had then quit work to devote herself full time to running a household and assisting George W. Bush in his political and business career. Although she sometimes described how her agreement to marry him had included the promise that she would never have to give a political speech, no one quite believed her. When she first met George W. Bush, he was already preparing to run for Congress, and his father stood as a serious contender for the presidency. Anyone marrying into the Bush family in 1977 could expect to see a lot of politics.

The subject had rarely crossed Laura's mind for the first thirty years of her life. Raised in Midland, Texas, as the only child of housebuilder Harold Welch and his homemaker wife, Jenna Hawkins Welch, Laura had little direct exposure to political talk or campaigning. Like George W.'s parents, the Welches had settled in Midland after World War II, when a series of big oil strikes just south of town drew thousands of new settlers to the area. As the population jumped from fewer than 10,000 in 1940 to more than 62,000 in 1960,[39] Harold Welch saw a chance to prosper by filling the housing shortage; with his business partner, he built hundreds of new homes.[40] But George W.'s father increased his personal fortune far more dramatically by going into the oil business. With their elite Eastern connections (George W.'s grandfather had been Connecticut's U.S. Senator) and millionaire status, the Bushes did not meet the Welches, even though the two families lived only a few blocks apart in the 1950s. They attended different churches and, except very briefly, their children enrolled in different schools.[41]

Both Laura and George W. later remembered Midland as an ideal place to grow up in the 1950s—when residents felt no need to lock their doors and the school's athletic teams made the biggest news. Less than one hundred miles from the New Mexico border, Midland got its name from its location at the halfway point between Fort Worth and El Paso, the two extremes of the Texas and Pacific Railway. Whatever the hardships of the climate in western Texas, where summers could be hot, dusty, and dry, Laura developed a firm attachment to the area. In her preface to a book of poetry, *Whatever the Wind Delivers*, she wrote proudly that people from her part of the world "don't simply live on or off the land; they live with it—and thrive."[42]

Although neither Harold nor Jenna Welch ever graduated from college, they both held higher expectations for their daughter and began setting aside tuition money when she was in first grade. Jenna, an avid reader herself, fostered Laura's interest in the subject by reading to her when she was young and encouraging her to break the monotony of long rides by taking a book along. Not surprisingly, Laura decided to become a teacher while she was still very young, and later recalled that one of her earliest childhood memories was lining up her dolls and "teaching them." Too outgoing to be dubbed a bookworm, Laura also studied ballet and enrolled in Girl Scouts, but she had already settled on a career before graduating from Robert E. Lee High School in 1964.[43]

At age seventeen, she appeared the healthy, happy, all American girl—except for one ugly reminder that lives are rarely uncomplicated or neatly summed up. In November of her senior year, while driving near Midland, she went through a stop sign, struck a car driven by a classmate, Michael Douglas, and fatally injured him. For years Laura refused to discuss the incident, and when she finally confronted the subject during the 2000 presidential election, she admitted it was an extremely painful memory. "It was a horrible, horrible tragedy," she told one interviewer. "But at some point I had to accept that death is a part of life, and as tragic as losing Mike was, there was nothing anyone could do to change that. . . ."[44] Close friends insisted the accident had an enormous impact on her and permanently changed her views about personal responsibility. But at the time, neighbors in Midland refused to hold her responsible, and although they grieved, they attributed the death to some horrible "mishap" rather than to any fault of one of their most popular teenagers. Laura suffered no legal consequences and her driving privileges were not affected.[45]

Going 300 miles away from Midland to Southern Methodist University in Dallas, Laura evidently remained unaffected by the student unrest and anti-war movements associated with many campuses during the 1960s. This conservative, private university isolated its students in their own enclave away from Dallas's poverty and protest, and Laura remembered that smoking cigarettes and drinking beer were about the most rebellious activities that she and her friends ever engaged in. Her biographer later summed up Laura's college years as a time of playing bridge, listening to Beatles records, and shopping with her friends and their mothers.[46] After graduation in 1968, Laura accompanied an aunt, an uncle, and a cousin on a two-week trip to Europe, the only time she had yet ventured beyond American borders (except for a summer studying in Mexico when she was still in high school).[47]

Following her four college years, Laura moved frequently, changing jobs every year or so but always staying within Texas's borders. After a short stint teaching third grade in Dallas, she moved three hundred miles south to the John F. Kennedy Elementary School in Houston. "I particularly wanted to teach in a minority school," she later told an interviewer, and she credited those two years as opening her eyes to the inequalities in life—and a part of the world she had not seen in segregated Midland.[48] Many of her African-American students came from poor homes and she found herself shocked by the limitations on their lives—barriers she had not previously understood or noticed. Rather than turning to political action or economic reforms, Laura focused on literacy and books as a way to improve students' lives. Once again she moved, enrolling in the library-science program at the University of Texas at Austin where she earned a master's degree in 1972.

Up until that time, she had worked in elementary schools where she had few chances to meet young single men and, at age twenty-six, she decided to change that. "I thought by working in a big public library in downtown Houston, I might have a different social life," she told *USA Today*.[49] But after one year in Houston, she returned to Austin as a librarian in a heavily Hispanic elementary school. From Austin it was only a two-hundred-and-fifty-mile drive back to Midland to visit her parents, and it was on one of those weekend trips in the summer of 1977 that old friends invited her over to share a barbecue and to meet George W. Bush, aspiring candidate for congress.

Laura later said that she had resisted earlier attempts to be introduced to one of Midland's most eligible bachelors because she did not want to get involved with "someone real political." One meeting with George W. quickly changed her mind, and four months later, on November 5, 1977, she married him. "I don't know that it was love at first sight," she recalled, "[but] it was pretty close,"[50] Presidential historian Lewis Gould suggested that the timing of their meeting was propitious for both—"a married congressional candidate would have an advantage over a bachelor, and for Laura Welch her future husband promised more excitement than a school librarian's career would provide."[51]

Whatever the motivation for the match, Laura Welch brought to the spunky, athletic Bush clan a noticeably independent perspective. Her mother-in-law later recalled that the young librarian had amazed them all when, on first meeting George's outspoken grandmother, Dorothy Bush, Laura had asserted herself. Asked what she "did," Laura replied, "I read, I smoke and I admire."[52] (Laura later insisted that the story was apocryphal but Barbara Bush stood by it.) The steady, word-wise Miss Welch presented a striking contrast to the young George W., who already had a reputation for rebelliousness and malapropisms.

For the first fifteen years of her marriage, Laura fit her world into a pattern common among the wives of most successful CEO's. In 1978, George W. started his own small oil and gas company, and subsequent mergers and acquisitions increased his responsibilities considerably, along with his income. Bigger money resulted from his foray into the world of baseball. As managing partner of the Texas Rangers from 1989 to 1994, he earned a substantial salary, and eventually converted an investment of just over $600,000 into more than $10 million (helped by a new stadium paid for with tax dollars)."[53] This represented a new level of wealth for Laura, and managing the household and caring for twin daughters, Barbara and Jenna, born November 25, 1981, took up most of her time.

Some friends speculated that George W.'s success in the baseball business helped him escape the long shadow cast by his high-achieving father and changed his mind about running for office. After his one unsuccessful run for congress in 1978, he stayed clear of politics (except for serving as senior adviser to his father's 1988 presidential campaign.) By 1994, however, he was ready to test the waters himself and that year he won the governor's mansion in Texas. One other development helped make a political career possible. Around the time of his fortieth birthday, he determined to control his alcohol problem, and although he credited religious influences with helping him, friends also singled out his wife who had, they said, a remarkably steadying effect.[54] Laura attributed the change to "enormous discipline" which he also showed in other areas of his life, such as his physical exercise regimen.

Six years in the Texas governor's mansion provided a valuable apprenticeship for Laura, and she became very popular. The Texas Book Festival, which she started in 1996 to highlight the state's authors, turned into her most notable achievement after it helped raise hundreds of thousands of dollars for libraries to expand their holdings. She also promoted other educational programs such as "Ready to Read" for very young children, "Reach Out and Read," for older youngsters, and a magazine for parents, "Take Time for Kids." Austin's Habitat for Humanity, breast cancer awareness, and the problems of Alzheimer's sufferers all received some of her time, but her deepest commitment remained to reading programs and literacy campaigns. Popular across party lines, she impressed Texans with her warmth and genuine friendliness, and criticism of her was, according to one Texas historian, "virtually nonexistent."[55]

By the time Republicans met in July 2000 to name George W. Bush as their presidential nominee, his wife had become such a confident and popular speaker that she seemed the obvious choice to keynote the convention. In a speech carried live on national television, Laura impressed millions of Americans with her down-to-earth comments about teaching and her enthusiastic support of her husband's candidacy. She joked that a run for the White House was a "pretty drastic" antidote for the empty nest syndrome (their daughters were entering college that fall), and she gave examples of her family's genuine interest in education.[56] In the weeks that followed, she traveled thousands of miles and sat for dozens of interviews, many of them televised live. For a woman who insisted she had once vowed to stay clear of politics, this marked an important change, and it underlined how much Americans had come to expect a candidate's wife to play a public role.

Throughout her husband's long campaign for president, Laura Bush sometimes appeared alongside her mother-in-law (the first time a former First Lady ever campaigned for her son for the presidency) but she also asserted her own independence.[57] Whenever she was asked (and it happened often) to choose as her model either Barbara Bush or Hillary Clinton, she distanced herself a bit from both, promising, "I think I'll just be Laura Bush." In an interview with Barbara Walters, she eschewed the tag of "traditional First Lady" and insisted she would shape the job to suit herself.

In a pre-inaugural interview, she spoke out against reversing the 1973 Supreme Court decision *Roe v. Wade* guaranteeing women a right to abortion. "No, I don't think that it should be overturned," she told NBC news. Since that view seemed to contradict her husband's position on the subject, it made frontpage headlines.[58] She subsequently shied away from such statements, proving she could be flexible. When she named her staff, she dipped into her mother-in-law's talent pool and appointed people familiar with the capital to fill the delicate and politically sensitive jobs of social secretary and scheduler. For other posts, she chose women whom she had worked with in Texas.[59] One of the very few First Ladies who could claim familiarity with the 130-plus-room presidential mansion before moving in, she could truthfully quip, "I have slept in the Lincoln bedroom and the Queen's bedroom."[60]

Literacy took first place on her White House agenda. When Laura launched a national initiative called "Ready to Read, Ready to Learn," she directed much of her attention to the needs of pre-school children and to the parents who could assist them. She also put out a call to young college graduates, urging them to consider teaching as a career. Nine months into her tenure, on September 8, 2001, she opened the first National Book Festival, a joint production of the First Lady's office and the Library of Congress.[61] Unlike the book festival in Texas, this one did not raise money but sought to draw Americans to the world of books by offering a free day of storytelling sessions, tours of the Library of Congress, and conversations with popular authors from across the nation. The First Lady used the occasion to announce the formation of the Laura Bush Foundation for America's Libraries.[62]

Three days later, on the morning of September 11, Laura was on her way down Pennsylvania Avenue to meet with Senator Edward Kennedy's subcommittee on education when the first plane hit New York's World Trade Center. She would have become the fourth First Lady (after Eleanor Roosevelt, Rosalynn Carter, and Hillary Clinton) to testify before a congressional committee had her schedule not been so tragically altered. During the following terrible hours and days, she quietly encouraged calm and urged parents to take time to tell their children that they were safe. She encouraged families to spend more time together and gently listed her own thoughts on ways to make youngsters feel loved and secure. On September 23, the *New York Post* praised her for becoming "the First Mom, comforting and reassuring the entire nation."[63]

Even without the terror of September 11, Laura would have raised her popularity ratings. Americans who knew little about her and those strongly opposed to her husband's positions found themselves drawn into her fan club because of her genuine commitment to books. Prominent historians such as Pulitzer Prize–winning biographer David Levering Lewis and feminist writer Ursula Smith, who had outspokenly opposed the president's stance on the environment, foreign policy, and other matters, were dismayed when they received invitations from Laura Bush to speak at White House symposia on topics on which they had written. Both ended up accepting, however, and each came away from the East Room impressed with how she had managed to transform that most political of places into an arena for discussing ideas that reached beyond politics. Differences in political ideology receded in importance when symposium attendees shared admiration for the writers under discussion, such as Mark Twain and Eudora Welty. When queried on the subject, Laura Bush told *New York Times* reporter Elisabeth Bumiller, "There's nothing political about American literature. . . . Everyone can like American literature, no matter what your [political] party."[64]

Participants in the invitation-only events insisted that the two-hour discussions often moved outside what one would ordinarily expect to hear in the president's front room and delved into various authors' writings on prickly subjects such as race and class in America. The First Lady typically sat in the front row, ready to comment knowledgeably on the authors being discussed, even when their books seemed critical of the Texas oil world in which she had grown up. One invited author, Patricia Nelson Limerick, admitted that she had done "Mrs. Bush a terrible disservice" thinking she was so unacquainted with the writers and naïve about how deeply critical some of their writings about America were. Arnold Rampersad, the respected Stanford professor and biographer of Langston Hughes, also confessed that he had been surprised by the First Lady's genuine understanding of literature. After talking with her at one White House symposium, he concluded, ". . . it became very clear that she was seeing this world [of literature] from the inside, not the outside."[65]

When the First Lady's schedule took her away from schools and book talk, she spoke confidently on other subjects. In November 2001, she made history when she took the president's place on his regular weekly radio address and spoke out against the Taliban's oppression of women and children in Afghanistan.[66] Several of her predecessors, beginning with Lou Hoover in the 1930s, had used radio as a way to reach people, but this was the first time that a First Lady had stood in for the president in just this way.

"I am Laura Bush," she began, "and I'm delivering this week's radio address to kick off a worldwide effort to focus on the brutality against women and children by the al-Qaeda terrorist network and the regime it supports in Afghanistan, the Taliban." After noting that 70 percent of the Afghan people were malnourished and that one in four Afghan children would die before turning five, she listed the specifics of a repressive regime that did not permit children to fly kites or women to laugh out loud. To avoid charges that she misunderstood Afghan customs, she noted that "Muslims around the world" had already spoken out against the Taliban, and she encouraged listeners of all faiths to join them. "Fighting brutality against women and children is not the expression of a specific culture; it is the acceptance of our common humanity, a commitment shared by people of good will on every continent."[67]

This rousing call to action came less than a year after Laura Bush moved into the White House, but it foreshadowed an international bent that became clearer in the years that followed. In the next few months she gave five more speeches on Afghanistan, all of them urging help for that nation's women.[68] One communications scholar noted that the phrasing of her plea combined "maternal feminism" with "liberal feminism" by justifying women's participation in the public sphere through their maternal duties—such as overseeing their children's education and sewing school uniforms.[69] Rather than argue that Afghan women had the *same* rights as men, the American First Lady insisted they had rights, too, and that if allowed to exercise these rights, their entire communities would gain.

As for helping to motivate her to speak out about women's rights in another country, Laura Bush cited friends, relatives, and people she happened to meet who told her of their concern for Afghan women. She also received encouragement from presidential advisers, especially Karen Hughes. According to the *New York Times*, Hughes had suggested the First Lady and the president do a joint radio address on the subject on November 17, 2001, and he had replied, "What do you need me for?"[70]

In speaking out, Laura Bush illustrated once again how clearly the presidency had become a two-person career, one in which, as Karlyn Kohrs Campbell explained, the wife's functions may include "public performance" as well as "status maintenance and intellectual contributions."[71] In this case, Laura Bush's primary motive may have been to bolster morale in the war against terrorism, but in the process she brought up a feminist issue—equal rights for women.[72]

In doing so, she made it more difficult for First Lady scholars to place her on the various scales they had developed. Myra Gutin, a communications professor and longtime student of America's First Ladies, has argued that some presidents' wives in the twentieth century moved beyond being ceremonial hostesses to acting as emerging spokeswomen for their husbands; other First Ladies went even further and became independent activists and political surrogates.[73] In

Gutin's categorization, Laura Bush fell somewhere between the second and third roles—Bush was not entirely an independent voice of her own but was more than a ceremonial hostess like Pat Nixon. Laura's immediate predecessor, Hillary Clinton, had also spoken up for Afghan women's rights, but she did so as part of International Women's Day at the UN.[74]

Laura Bush's ambitious travel schedule underscored her commitment to Afghan women and to other international causes. Visiting seventy-five nations in eight years, she did not match Pat Nixon's record, but unlike Pat's ceremonial tours, these appearances promoted substantive health improvements. Press releases from Laura Bush's office noted that she visited ten of the fifteen countries identified by the President's Emergency Plan for AIDS Relief [PEPFAR] as focus countries in its fight against HIV/AIDS. She also called attention to the dangers of malaria by stopping in nations where it afflicted the population. To encourage women to take control of their health and get regular breast cancer screenings, she included this topic in speeches she gave in eight countries in Europe and the Middle East.[75]

But it was in Afghanistan that Laura Bush's efforts got the most attention. On her first visit in March 2005, she stayed only a few hours, visiting a teacher training institute at Kabul University where she spoke to several hundred women. Announcing a $20 million U.S. grant for new education projects, she performed a largely ceremonial role, albeit in a setting generally perceived as unsettled if not downright dangerous. But then she moved on to make observations that could not have pleased all that nation's leaders. "We are only a few years removed from the rule of terrorists," she reminded her audience, "when women were denied education and every basic human right."[76] Democracy was gaining in Afghanistan, she continued, but "the survival of a free society ultimately depends on the participation of all its citizens, both men and women" and this is possible only if women have "the most critical tool of all . . . education." On her last trip to that part of the world, in June 2008, the American First Lady made a point of meeting with Afghanistan's only female governor, Habiba Sarabi, of the Bamiyan province.[77] Back home, Laura Bush accepted honorary chairmanship of the U.S.-Afghan Women's Council, a group formed to improve health and education in Afghanistan.

Burma's oppressive government also got the First Lady's attention. On October 10, 2007, she published an opinion piece in the *Wall Street Journal*, "Stop the Terror in Burma," detailing the "shameful" abuses of that nation's military dictatorship. A few days later, the *New York Times* ran a front-page article, "First Lady Raising Her Profile without Changing Her Image," and dubbed her "the administration's leading voice on [Burma]."[78] A few months later, when a devastating cyclone put many of Burma's people in jeopardy, Laura Bush called a press conference and asked Burma's government to drop its entry restrictions so that international relief workers could distribute medical supplies and food to those in need.

In August 2008 she traveled to the Mae La refugee camp, the largest of several camps along the Thai-Burma border, where she listened to people on the run for their lives.[79] She visited a clinic and observed how its small staff tried to meet the medical needs of the thirty-five thousand men, women, and children camped there. Speaking out for Aung San Suu Kyi, the Burmese Nobel laureate who has been imprisoned for years, Laura Bush called on the ruling junta to release all political prisoners. She urged the international community to stop buying Burmese gemstones, because the profits went to the repressive leaders rather than to the people.

Like most First Ladies who got the chance, Laura Bush showed increased confidence in her second term. With no more campaigns to worry about, she felt freer to do as she liked. The first hint of change came in the choice of her inaugural gown. Michael Faircloth, an obscure Texan, had produced the first.[80] But in January 2005, Laura Bush appeared at the inaugural balls in a creation by the far more famous (and expensive) Oscar de la Renta. Then she caused a stir by firing Walter Scheb III, the White House chef for the previous eleven years, and replacing him with the first woman to hold that title—Cristeta Comerford.[81] To underscore her determination to make her second term different, she made significant changes in her staff.[82]

Signaling that she took her projects seriously, she turned for advice to experts, including some from the West Wing. Michael Green, of the Center for Strategic and International Studies, counseled her on projects in Asia. Laura's chief of staff during the second term, Anita McBride, boasted government experience reaching back to the Reagan years, including stints at the State Department and as Special Assistant to the President for White House Management. This impressive roster of skilled and experienced staff looked nothing like the string of social secretaries that had once worked for presidents' wives and still managed governors' mansions across the country.

The First Lady's commitment to literacy did not abate—and she continued to schedule book fairs to highlight that interest. She rescheduled her appearance in front of the Senate Education Committee, postponed by 9/11, so she could reiterate her enthusiasm for encouraging reading programs. But the author events at the White House, which had begun on such a promising note, succumbed to the growing criticism of her husband's foreign policy.

Just before the Iraq invasion, Laura Bush's office had announced that the February 12, 2003, symposium would focus on "Poetry and the American Voice." Almost as soon as invitations went out, word spread that some of the prospective guests meant to use the occasion to protest the administration's plan to invade Iraq, showing once again how a First Lady's initiatives are never viewed as entirely separate from her husband's policies. One of the invitees, Sam Hamill, editor of Copper Canyon Press and author of more than a dozen books of verse, explained that he felt "overcome by a kind of nausea" on opening his invitation.[83] Not only did he refuse to attend, he sent out e-mails urging other poets to join in putting together a book of antiwar poems to be presented to the First Lady.

According to one report, about three thousand five hundred poets around the world responded to Hamill's initiative. Some read their antiwar poems at rallies organized for that purpose; others sent their compositions to the website, www.poetsagainstthewar.org. Faced with this kind of publicity, the First Lady reiterated her view that everyone had a right to express an opinion but that there was nothing political about poetry; she then canceled the event without rescheduling it.

Laura Bush shrewdly found other ways to sidestep controversy. Unlike her mother-in-law—who spoke at Wellesley's commencement in 1990 despite student protests that a First Lady did not provide an acceptable role model—Laura pled "prior commitments" to avoid addressing Los Angeles graduates in 2002. When the protests first mounted, university officials stood by their invitation, insisting that Laura Bush's long-standing advocacy for education made her an appropriate choice for the commencement speech. But the First Lady decided that declining to appear would serve her husband better— she would deprive his critics of a national stage.

The U.S. invasion of Iraq in 2003 multiplied prospects for protest. Public opinion often focuses on the White House in times of calamity, when citizens across the country look to the president's wife to see what sacrifices and contributions she is making. Are her sons enlisting, as Eleanor Roosevelt's four sons did in World War II? Is she curtailing consumption, as Edith Wilson did in 1917? Does she appear too friendly to the enemy, as rumors suggested about Mary Lincoln during the Civil War? If the war loses favor, if its entire purpose gets questioned and its execution criticized, venom can run as visibly to the distaff side of the White House as to the president's office. While fleeing Washington in 1814, Dolley Madison was refused shelter by an irate boardinghouse keeper who blamed Dolley's husband for starting the war. Lady Bird Johnson learned to go to sleep to the sound of chants outside her window: "LBJ, LBJ, how many kids did you kill today?"

Antiwar sentiment never reached that intensity during the George W. Bush years, and Laura Bush's international travel, especially her trips to Muslim countries and parts of Africa where huge health problems existed, may have helped mute criticism. By putting humanitarian concerns alongside military intervention, she earned grudging respect from people who abhorred her husband's Iraq policy. Presidents' wives had been traveling outside the United States for more than a century, sometimes for pleasure (Edith Roosevelt in Cuba), as a ceremonial gesture (Edith Wilson at the Paris Peace talks), to represent the nation (Lady Bird Johnson at the funeral of King Paul of Greece), or to discuss substantive matters with foreign leaders (Rosalynn Carter in Central and South America). But some of Laura Bush's trips fell outside any of these categories—she sought to put a more humane face on U.S. foreign policy.

The length of the Iraq war increased objections to it and complicated her task. Although Saddam Hussein's statue crashed to the ground on April 10, 2003, and President Bush later declared the war won, Americans watched in dismay the continuing destruction and rising death toll in Iraq. When Iraq's new government failed to establish order as quickly as some had predicted, debates in the U.S. Congress grew louder about how to proceed. A majority of Americans had supported the president in the early stages of the war, but now they changed their minds, sending his popularity plummeting. By June 2005, one poll showed that 53 percent of Americans disapproved of the job the president was doing, the highest disapproval rating since he took office.[84] By May 2008, both CNN and the *New York Times* reported new polls showed the incumbent to be "the most unpopular president in history."[85]

Presidents' wives typically avoid low ratings by staying away from divisive issues such as war, sluggish economies, and universal health insurance to concentrate instead on such matters as White House restoration and education. An intelligent, voracious reader like Laura Bush knew this, and throughout her second term in the White House she stuck to an agenda unlikely to attract her husband's critics. Literacy continued to figure prominently in her schedule, but she avoided situations where she might meet protestors. Her office announced her visits to schools and libraries after they had occurred, and she scheduled few book events at the White House. She spoke up for the Preserve America and America's Treasures Act, a popular project and a favorite of legislators who wanted to bring funds to their home districts to restore art, buildings, and public records. Health issues continued to concern her, and she traveled around the country as ambassador for The Heart Truth, encouraging women to improve their chances for a long life by making healthier choices.

While tending her own image, she gave no hint of disagreeing with her husband's policies. Whenever asked about his legacy, she insisted he would be vindicated. This stance won her fans among those who prized a woman who "stood by her man." She already had proven a particularly effective money-raiser in her husband's reelection campaign, raising more than $5 million by the end of February 2004.[86]

In 2006, midway through her second term, CNN/USA/Gallup reported that Laura Bush enjoyed one of the highest approval ratings of any president's wife they had measured.[87] Nevertheless, while 82 percent of Americans liked what she was doing, only 43 percent felt the same way about her husband.

Some of her husband's harshest critics admitted they found little to fault in her, and they puzzled how husband and wife could appeal to such different camps. Novelist Curtis Sittenfeld, perhaps struck by reports that Laura had voted for Eugene McCarthy in 1968,[88] popularized the view that Laura held more liberal views than her husband did, and that, given the chance, she might reveal this. Sittenfeld's best-selling novel *American Wife*, which she admitted was "loosely inspired by the life of an American first lady," describes a thoughtful, spirited woman of liberal views who marries the fun-loving son of a politically connected Republican family and ends up living in the White House.[89] Even she seems puzzled by how it all happened. The fictional First Lady admits to voting for her husband's opponent in both 2000 and 2004 because she "believed sincerely that his opponent would do a better job." On the very last page of Sittenfeld's novel, as the First Lady considers the problems facing the nation and the president's role in them, she reminds the reader, "All I did is marry him. You are the ones who gave him power."

In various interviews, Sittenfeld revealed she admired Laura Bush for her down-to-earth attitudes, her work for so many good causes, and her seriousness and caring.[90] Partisan identification did not appear on the list. Indeed, Laura frequently reached across party lines. She explained away one of Michelle Obama's missteps during the 2008 campaign by saying Michelle was a newcomer to national politics and would soon learn to watch what she said. When asked about Hillary Clinton's strong run for the Democratic nomination that same year, the Republican First Lady had only praise for how Hillary had widened possibilities for all women.

By the time she left the White House, with a reported contract of $1.6 million for her memoir about living there, scholars viewed Laura Bush's record much less favorably than had Curtis Sittenfeld. In a poll released by the Siena Research Institute in December 2008, historians ranked Laura Bush #17 among post-1900 First Ladies, just above Pat Nixon, Ida McKinley, and Florence Harding.[91] In the longer list of thirty-eight women who had held the job since 1789, Laura did little better, coming in #23, well below Barbara Bush (#12) and Hillary Clinton (#4). Although above average in "background," "integrity" and "intelligence," she came out at the very bottom in the "own woman" category.

Eight years earlier, when asked which of her two predecessors she would emulate—her traditional mother-in-law or the activist-feminist Clinton—Laura had refused to choose, saying she would define the job in her own terms. And she had. By putting enormous effort into international travel and initiatives that sought to help women and others suffering from malaria and AIDS, she exposed the role of First Lady to an international spotlight. Standing by an unpopular president without looking weak or manipulated, she won fans in quarters unfriendly to her husband. All the while, she maintained her image of a caring, intelligent, down-to-earth person. But she realized she left the job of First Lady without doing all that she could have. In an interview with *People* magazine, she admitted, "Maybe if I have a regret, it's just that I didn't do more."[92]

Laura Bush's successor faced many of the same challenges. One was uniquely hers, and she knew it. As Michelle Obama watched her husband inaugurated as the 44th president of the United States on January 20, 2009, she understood she would undergo special scrutiny. Two centuries earlier, countless African Americans had worked to construct the mansion into which her family would move that afternoon. Dozens more had cleaned it, tended its gardens, and cooked for its many guests. However, the Obamas would be the first African Americans to occupy the master suite of the White House, to fill the private quarters with their mementos and with their friends, to leave their official portraits on the walls. Every president's family lives in a fishbowl. Hers would be watched more closely than most.

Michelle Obama also recognized the high expectations her husband faced. His presidential campaign had stressed the need for big changes—in health care, how the United States deployed its military, and how government worked. The current economic crisis, which he termed the worst since the Great Depression, underlined the urgency to find remedies that worked. Barack Obama had convinced a sufficient number of voters that he was the one to spearhead those changes, and now millions were waiting to see how quickly he delivered on his promises.

Neither of the Obamas was Washington-savvy, and she was a neophyte to both the capital and national politics. She had remained in Chicago with their two daughters when he took his seat in the U.S. Senate four years earlier. Unlike Hillary Clinton and Laura Bush, Michelle had never presided over a governor's mansion, and she lacked her predecessors' experience in both campaigning and winning. Her husband's entire elective history up to that point could be summarized in a single sentence, and her part in it was even shorter.

Nonetheless the new First Lady fully matched both Hillary and Laura in education, and that was due, in no small part, to her parents. Fraser Robinson III, a city water plant worker, and Marian Shields Robinson, a homemaker, had made sure their only daughter, Michelle LaVaughn, born January 17, 1964, and their only son, Craig, twenty-one months older, would have the very best education within reach. Rejecting the easy option to send both children to a nearby public high school, the Robinsons enrolled their tall, athletic son in a parochial school that boasted an excellent basketball program; for Michelle, they decided the newly opened Whitney M. Young Magnet School offered a quality education that more than compensated for the three-hour commute required. Among racially mixed classmates who came from all over the city, Michelle did well both academically and socially. She made the National Honor Society in her junior year and was elected treasurer of her senior class.

After graduation in 1981, Michelle followed Craig to Princeton, and, like him, she majored in sociology. Although one of the oldest colleges in America, Princeton had only begun to accept women as undergraduates in 1969. African Americans, first admitted after World War II, still comprised only about 10 percent of the student body. Even the sister of a basketball star could feel like an outsider, and Michelle saw herself as a "visitor on campus, as if I really don't belong."[93]

According to Liza Mundy, a *Washington Post* reporter who graduated three years ahead of Michelle, Princeton did not offer a friendly setting for African Americans in the early 1980s.[94] A small but vocal group of students made no secret of their opinion that admission standards had dropped to accommodate minorities, and the editor of a campus publication, *Prospect*, described "black culture" as pathologically violent and inferior to "white culture."[95]

Before Michelle had a chance to see how widespread those ideas were on campus, she encountered blatant racism in her freshman dorm. Her assigned roommate, a white coed from New Orleans, had no experience with interracial living, and when she called her mother to describe Michelle, the mother immediately began trying to get her daughter transferred. Princeton officials stood firm on the dorm assignment, but when a larger room became available, the roommate moved out. Michelle began searching for a spot on campus where she felt she fit in, and she soon became a regular at the Third World Center, a gathering place for students of color.

When it came time to choose a topic for her senior thesis, Michelle decided on "Princeton-Educated Blacks and the Black Community." Working under the direction of Professor Walter Wallace, one of only five tenured African Americans on the entire faculty, she set out to find how the college's African American alumni had changed their attitudes while at Princeton. Specifically, she wanted to learn if the Ivy League experience had made graduates more or less willing to help other African Americans who had not enjoyed the same privilege.

The eighty-nine respondents who answered her questionnaire provided too small a sample, she admitted, to draw many general conclusions. Indeed, the thesis tells more about the author than about those surveyed. As the twenty-one-year-old senior struggled with ideas about race and class, she realized that many of her non-black fellow students came from economic backgrounds much like hers, and they found themselves equally bewildered by classmates with large expense accounts, considerable international travel experience, and important family connections that promised easy access to successful careers.

In Michelle Robinson's case, race added a powerful component to the mix, raising what seemed to her an insurmountable barrier between her and white students. "My experiences at Princeton have made me far more aware of my Blackness than ever before," she wrote in her thesis, adding that it often seemed to her as if, to Whites at Princeton, she would "always be Black first and a student second."[96]

Although Michelle understood she and her white classmates shared identical career goals, she worried about how she could ever fit into a "White cultural and social structure" that kept her on its "periphery."[97] And if she achieved as much as she hoped, how would she reconcile her personal success with the obligation instilled by her parents to give back to the working-class community of Chicago's South Side where she grew up?

Following graduation from Princeton, Michelle Robinson entered Harvard Law School, and after receiving her J.D. in 1988, she headed back to Chicago and a job at the Sidley Austin law firm. At twenty-four, she was already collecting a larger salary than her father ever hoped to earn, and yet she continued to question whether it was the life she wanted. Michelle shortly decided to change course. She left Sidley Austin in 1991 to join the staff of Chicago Mayor Richard Daley. Then she moved on to hold various executive positions at the University of Chicago and its hospital.

It would be easy to attribute Michelle Robinson's career change to the influence of Barack Obama, whom she met when he came to work as a summer intern at Sidley Austin in 1989. His focus on community organizing offered a stark contrast to the views of many of her colleagues in corporate law, and as her relationship with Barack progressed, from mentor to fiancée and then marriage in October 1992, she was drawn into his world. But Michelle had already indicated her wish to "give back" to the community by participating in the Legal Aid Society while at Harvard, and then by working with Public Allies, a youth program, when she returned to Chicago.

When asked about her reasons for leaving Sidley Austin, she often pointed to the deaths of two persons close to her—her father in March 1991, and a college friend who died of cancer a few months earlier at age twenty-six. "All of a sudden," she later told a reporter, "I was on this path...sitting as a second-year associate at Sidley Austin and I hadn't really thought about how I got there." Her coworkers showed no special pleasure in their jobs, she noticed, "and the longer you stayed, the harder it was to get out. The golden handcuffs."[98]

Adjustments in her personal life took a little longer. Although the Obama marriage appeared happy and loving, both husband and wife struggled to balance career and family responsibilities. Neither claimed it was easy, and both admitted the bulk of their household's management fell to her, especially after he was elected to the Illinois State Senate in 1996 and had to spend several days a week in Springfield, two hundred miles away. Even earlier, when he was writing *Dreams from My Father* and teaching law, he had little energy left for mundane household matters. The birth of their daughter Malia in 1998, complicated scheduling even more and led to tough bargaining on how to handle childcare. In 2000, Barack's failed race for Congress soured Michelle on politics, and by the time daughter Natasha ("Sasha") was born in 2001, their marriage was reportedly "strained."[99]

According to journalist Richard Wolffe, author of the 2009 *Renegade: The Making of a President,* Michelle Robinson "had fallen in love with an idealistic young man who spoke about the difference between the world as it is and the world that can be.'"[100] But his political career had given him little chance to work toward his vision. In her view, politics seemed like a waste of energy, and holding elective office could do little to achieve the world he wanted. Much more likely to produce change, she believed, were non-elective jobs in public service.

Michelle found her own work at the University of Chicago immensely satisfying, and she admitted she took great pleasure solving "problems that have nothing to do with my husband and children."[101] Still, she felt frustrated and angry by conflicting demands on her time, and she perceived her husband's political aspirations as "selfishness and careerism."[102] Only when she decided to call on other resources—her mother and a good babysitter—to fill in when Barack could not be there, did she make peace with her situation. In a 2007 interview with Rebecca Johnson for *Vanity Fair,* she explained that she had spent a lot of time expecting her husband "to fix things but then I came to realize that he was there in the ways he could be. If he wasn't there, it didn't mean he wasn't a good father or didn't care.... Once I was OK with that, my marriage got better."[103]

Yet Michelle did not initially endorse Barack's entering the 2004 race for a U.S. Senate seat. His election would keep him in Washington, D.C., several days a week, leaving her with two little girls and a full-time job back in Chicago. Convinced of his competence and commitment, however, she reluctantly joined his campaign—an experience that helped prepare her for 2008.

Not yet attuned to the damage an off-the-cuff comment could do, Michelle accumulated critics during the presidential race. After she told an audience that she finally felt proud of her country "for the first time in my adult life," unfriendly media zeroed in on what they described as her "angry" attitude. The *National Review* put her picture on its cover and dubbed her "Mrs. Grievance."[104] In contrast to her husband's cool, unruffled demeanor, Michelle's exuberance gave her an unsettled look, and her frankness was sometimes interpreted as a chip on her shoulder.

Some voters had trouble reconciling her anger with what they saw as an enormously privileged life. The Obamas reported a family income (his Senate salary, her hospital salary, and the royalties from his books, both *Dreams from My Father* and *The Audacity of Hope,* published in 2006) of $4.2 million in 2007, which put them in the very top echelon of American households.[105] Michelle pointed out this was

a recent development, and, in fact, the bulk of their income that year
($3.9 million) came from book sales that were a result of his newly
acquired prominence. Because their earnings had been considerably
more modest in their earlier years together, Michelle explained that
both she and Barack had struggled—like many other Americans—to
pay off their student loans.

In other ways, Michelle Obama helped render her family "ordinary" and her husband just like other Americans. In her speech to the
Democratic convention in August 2008, she melded her own very
American family story, which included roots in South Carolina slavery,
with that of her husband's more exotic, international background.
With one parent from Kansas and one from Kenya, he had grown up
in Hawaii and Indonesia, raised by a single white mother and white
grandparents. Yet his wife insisted he had a lot in common with the
Robinsons in Chicago, who put a high value on hard work, held to the
promises they made, and recognized the importance of treating everyone, whether you agreed with them or not, with dignity and respect.
In the remaining weeks of the campaign, Michelle repeated this message on solo trips and alongside her husband.

In describing her own role, she would say, "I am a mother first,"
and she made a point of getting back home after no more than one
night away. Dubbing herself "Mom in chief," she moved decisions
affecting her daughters to the top of her to-do list as soon as the election results came in. Like any experienced professional, she kept an
eye on precedent while at the same time considering her family's
needs and preferences.

Although she initially considered remaining in Chicago until her
daughters completed the academic year, she decided it was more
important to keep the family under one roof, and she began looking
for schools around Washington.[106] Sidwell Friends, the school she
chose for fifth-grader Malia and Sasha, three years younger, was considerably smaller than the University of Chicago Lab School they were
leaving, and it had other advantages. On its list of alumni were many
children of top government leaders, including Chelsea Clinton, and
the grandchildren of incoming Vice President Biden, whom the
Obama daughters already knew, were currently enrolled.

To prepare the residential quarters of the White House for occu-
pancy on January 20, the incoming First Lady engaged interior deco-
rator Michael S. Smith in November. He would eventually redecorate
the Oval Office and update some of the public quarters, but his first
assignment was adapting the private areas to accommodate the young
Obama daughters as well as Michelle's seventy-one-year-old mother,

Marian Robinson. By moving to Washington, she could provide a reliable constant in the girls' lives and oversee their activities when their parents could not.

On the food front, the incoming First Lady had already signaled that she meant to use her new platform to encourage Americans to eat better. Among the food experts who sent her their recommendations, Alice Waters, the celebrity chef who championed using locally grown produce, suggested replacing the current White House chef, Cristeta Comerford, with someone more attuned to Michelle's preference for light, healthful menus. But Comerford stayed, and Sam Kass, who had worked for Michelle in Chicago, was enlisted to assist her.

Since Michelle lacked a network in Washington, she drew heavily on contacts made elsewhere, either in Chicago or during the 2008 campaign. Before Thanksgiving, she had named her top staff. Jackie Norris, an Iowan and early Obama supporter, took the demanding job of chief of staff, and Desirée Rogers, a Chicago businesswoman with a Harvard degree, was named social secretary, in charge of all official presidential entertaining.

By inauguration day, Michelle had a full staff in place. During her White House tenure, the number of those working on her staff would vary, from fifteen to twenty-four, about the size of her predecessors' staffs. Turnover was high, especially in the most stressful jobs, raising questions about how carefully they had been vetted and how fully their responsibilities were defined. Three different women served as Michelle's press secretary.[107] Her first chief of staff, Norris, lasted only a few months, to be replaced by Michelle's close friend and boss back in Chicago, Susan Sher. After less than a year, Sher turned the job over to attorney Tina Tchen who proved more durable, remaining until Michelle left the White House.

The other high-pressure job in the East Wing, social secretary, saw even more turnover. Desirée Rogers successfully oversaw scores of White House social events before November 2009, when two uninvited publicity seekers managed to get past security guards at a State dinner. Rogers got the blame and left a few months later. Her replacement, Democratic Party fundraiser Juliana Smoot, remained less than a year before Jeremy Bernard, the first male to hold the title, took over. His successful tenure of four years lasted until the younger Deesha Dyer replaced him, and she remained in charge of official White House entertaining until the Obamas moved out.

In her initial actions as First Lady, Michelle appeared ready to take stands, involve herself in policy matters, and promote her husband's agenda. She designated her first reception, on January 29, 2009, a salute to Lilly Ledbetter, whose name had become part of the Fair Pay Act, which President Obama signed that day. A recent Supreme Court decision had upheld Ledbetter's claim that employees needed more time to bring charges of unfair compensation, and the very first act that President Obama signed into law provided for that. The First Lady gave Ledbetter a glowing introduction to the nearly 200 guests, describing her as a woman who "knew unfairness when she saw it, and was willing to do something about it because it was the right thing to do, plain and simple."[108] In the following days Michelle visited government agencies to talk up the president's economic stimulus plan.

After seeing unfriendly headlines about a First Lady who caused "tongues [to] wag,"[109] Michelle changed tack and turned to traditionally domestic and sartorial matters. She used her public appearances to visit schools and dish out pasta in soup kitchens. When guests gathered for her first official dinner, she took them on a tour of the White House kitchen. To further groom a non-confrontational, bipartisan image of herself, she posed for *Vogue* and *Vanity Fair*, and when journalists sought interviews on substantial subjects, she was unavailable.

The two projects she had set for herself during the campaign—reducing childhood obesity and helping military families—fit neatly within this non-partisan parameter. She proceeded immediately on both fronts. In early March she made headlines by inviting fifth graders from a nearby school to help plant a vegetable garden on the White House lawn. After an initial meeting with military personnel at Fort Bragg, she teamed up with Jill Biden, the vice president's wife, to initiate programs that helped military families. One of the most effective, Joining Forces, aimed to match employers with returning vets and family members who needed jobs. By encouraging large firms to consider ex-military, Joining Forces enlarged employment possibilities for many and lessened the chances of financial hardship.

Although her popularity stood high her first year (a February poll indicated she was viewed more positively than any recent First Lady at this stage in her tenure), Michelle was not satisfied. Besides changing her chief of staff, she hired a full time speechwriter. Rather than promoting the president's controversial health care initiative, she encouraged individuals to come up with their own routes to better health—through exercise and putting fresh, unprocessed food on their tables. Although she occasionally mentioned the need to overhaul the nation's health care system, she focused on what individuals could do for themselves.[110] No testifying in front of congressional committees for her.

By early 2010, the First Lady's health initiative, dubbed "Let's Move," was fully organized with its own website (letsmove.gov) and fundraising apparatus. She appealed to corporations to contribute food, and she enlisted famous chefs to demonstrate how healthful meals could be both easy to prepare and tasty. Her well-toned arms, clearly visible in the sleeveless dresses she liked to wear, testified to her own dedication to exercise and physical fitness.

In reaching out to the broadest possible audience, Michelle Obama relied on social media, such as Twitter and the web, rather than TV interviews or one-on-one talks with print journalists. This was new ground for a First Lady, and Myra Gutin, historian and communications professor, deemed it a smart move, because it permitted "revising a message, deleting what she doesn't want to say. Her husband's a champion at it and she can be very effective."[111]

By the beginning of their second term in 2013, the Obamas had both significantly changed. Like most First Ladies, Michelle had gained confidence and become more accepting of her fishbowl existence. She had endeared herself to children by hugging them and appealed to older folks by revealing more about herself. She told amusing stories about her Princeton days and provided some poignant accounts of her own parenting quandaries. She seemed warmer than in 2009, more approachable, and likely to enjoy herself in public. A Siena Institute/C-SPAN poll in 2014 ranked her fifth among all First Ladies, nearly tying Abigail Adams in "Public Image."[112]

After gaining considerable publicity for a film clip she made for Carpool Karaoke, late-night host James Corden's routine, riding around the South Lawn of the White House while belting out "This Is for My Girls," Michelle explained to *Variety*,[113] "I have never been afraid to be a little silly and you can engage people that way. My view is, first you get them to laugh, then you get them to listen." In this case, she hoped the song underlined her new project to promote education for girls in places where they lacked the opportunity. She had scheduled the karaoke ride so that it aired just before she set off for Liberia, Morocco, and Spain to talk about women's education.

Michelle had fumbled a bit before coming to terms with the fact that a president's wife sent a message by where and how she and her family vacationed. The Obamas' 2009 trip to Ghana, Rome, and Moscow raised no serious objections. Nor did their stay at Martha's Vineyard. But the following summer proved a public relations nightmare. After an oil spill damaged the area around the Gulf of Mexico, the First Lady suggested Americans boost morale there by choosing it for their summer vacation. Then she took her own family to Arcadia

National Park in Maine. That same summer, Michelle arranged for friends to accompany her and daughter Sasha to southern Spain. Although all participants paid for lodging and flights, they did not pay enough to equal the actual costs, including security and operational expenses for the Air Force jet they used. Unfortunately, the trip coincided with a report on jobs lost in the United States, and a columnist for the *New York Daily News* dubbed Michelle "A modern-day Marie Antoinette."[114] Subsequent trips would be planned more carefully, and those to spots outside the United States (Europe, China, and Africa) included advocacy for a good cause or a visit to a military base.[115]

Michelle might have avoided some of her early errors had she relied on Washington insiders for advice, but she and the president had continued to turn to trusted Chicagoans for support. These were people they had known for years, who could be depended on not to take advantage of their relationship with the president and First Lady. Most remained stalwart backers for the two terms. Valerie Jarrett, a wealthy, well-connected lawyer and businesswoman who had hired Michelle back in 1991, moved to Washington in 2009 and remained there, ever available as confidante and advisor to both the president and First Lady.

Other longtime members of the Obamas' Chicago circle kept their day jobs in the Windy City while remaining on call, willing to fly to the capital on short notice to offer cheer and diversion. Martin Nesbitt, a real estate developer, and his wife, Anita Blanchard, an obstetrician who delivered both Malia and Sasha, were longtime friends who had shared vacations with the Obamas; Eric Whittaker and his wife, Cheryl Rucker, were both physicians who had stuck with Michelle and Barack through tough times and good. When the men got together, it could be for a pickup basketball game or some sports talk while their wives exchanged views on whatever came to mind, confident that what they said would not be quoted in the next day's paper.

The Obamas did not allot much time on their social calendar to members of Congress, though they did reach across the partisan aisle when it came to George and Laura Bush. Barack had been an early critic of his predecessor's war in Iraq, but there was no payback once Obama moved into the Oval Office himself.

Michelle developed her own rapport with Laura. As one of their prime post-presidency projects, the Bushes focused on health reforms in sub-Saharan Africa, and on a trip to Tanzania in July 2013, they reached out to the Obamas, who coincidentally were also in Africa. The men did not meet, but Laura invited Michelle to join her at Dar

Es Salaam for a forum on women's issues, including education, health, and jobs. Journalist Cokie Roberts, who moderated the discussion, observed that there had never been an event like this, with two presidents' wives from opposing parties working so easily together.

A year later, the Obama White House joined with the Bush Institute to sponsor a U.S.-Africa Summit in Washington, and one symposium focused on what spouses of world leaders could do to improve health and education in their own nations. Both Laura and Michelle participated.

Every First Lady receives many more invitations than she can possibly accept, and Michelle's determination to keep public appearances to three days a week meant she had to be selective. Each spring, at commencement time, her staff sifted through a myriad of pleas to come up with those that fit her priorities. In 2009, she spoke to only two graduating classes, one at a Washington, D.C., high school and the other at the University of California, Merced, whose students had wooed her for weeks. In the following years, she singled out those schools that resonated with her, such as the historically African American University of Arkansas at Pine Bluff, Oberlin College in Ohio (the first American college to admit both men and women, whites and blacks), and the City College of New York, long known for educating immigrants and minorities who became Nobel Prize winners and national leaders.

By the time she spoke at City College in early June 2016, the campaign to succeed her husband was well under way, and Donald J. Trump had become the presumptive head of the Republican ticket. To an audience of many immigrants and relatives of newcomers, Michelle denounced his plan to build a wall between the United States and Mexico, saying, "We don't build walls to keep people out." Then she attacked him more personally, disparaging "name calling" leaders who talk "anger and intolerance…who demonize and dehumanize entire groups of people."[116]

This was new territory for a First Lady. Presidents' wives had gone solo campaigning since the 1960s when Lady Bird Johnson showed its effectiveness, but they had stuck to the positive, emphasizing what their husbands could do. In 2016 Michelle's husband wasn't even in the race; yet she was going negative on the opposing party's candidate.

As the November election neared, she stepped up her appearances, outlining in her talks the outstanding qualifications of the Democratic candidate, Hillary Clinton, and admitting to her excitement about having a woman president. She reserved her toughest words for the Republican candidate. It took the airing of a tape of

Trump's 2006 interview with Billy Bush, full of boasts about groping women and kissing them without their consent, to unleash Michelle's full fury. When she spoke in New Hampshire on October 13, her sixth campaign talk in a month, it was with a quivering voice that she called the Trump interview "disgraceful...intolerable...it has shaken me to my core...I can't believe that I'm saying that a candidate for president of the United States has bragged about sexually assaulting women."[117]

Less than a month later, she would be sitting down with Donald and Melania Trump in the White House to talk about the transition.

11

The Ever-Changing Role of
First Lady

THE 2016 PRESIDENTIAL ELECTION yielded many firsts. Hillary Clinton, having launched a political career of her own while still First Lady, became the first woman to head a major party ticket. She campaigned vigorously against her Republican opponent and appeared the likely victor. When the results came in, she had won the popular vote but not a majority in the Electoral College, and Donald J. Trump became the first president to have neither served in the military nor held an elective office. His frequent tweets and verbal promises to rely on his own instincts rather than experts set the stage for another first—a media presidency of rapidly changing pronouncements and stands.

His wife, née Melanija Knavs, a naturalized American citizen, became the first presidential spouse to be perceived as foreign. Although Louisa Adams (1825–1829) is often described as nonnative, she was born in England to an American father, and her first language was English, making her far more familiar with the United States than the woman who followed her into the White House nearly a century later.

Although Melania Trump, at forty-six, was about the same age her predecessors had been at their husbands' inaugurations, she brought a different résumé. Twenty-four years younger than the president, she was his third wife and had little preparation for what has been called the most difficult unpaid job in the world. She seemed reluctant to take it. Rumors persisted that she had not expected a Trump win and wept when informed of it.[1]

Born in 1970 in Slovenia, then part of Communist Yugoslavia, Melania had grown up with only the scantiest exposure to her husband's native country—its language, geography, and history. She had dropped out of university after one year to pursue a modeling career, and after finding insufficient assignments in Europe she moved to New York in 1996. Under the guidance of Paolo Zampolli, a guru for many models, she confined herself to a very small stratum of Manhattan, sharing an apartment on Union Square with others in the same line of work and socializing almost exclusively on their turf.

Her 1998 meeting with entrepreneur Donald J. Trump widened that world, moving her uptown and exposing her to the city's elite entertainers, business tycoons, and philanthropists. These fleeting social encounters provided little chance to develop friendships of her own or enlarge her understanding of the United States beyond the Hudson River.

The biggest change in her life, as a result of her association with one of the city's most public figures, was a sharp increase in modeling jobs on both sides of the Atlantic. The British *Gentleman's Quarterly* cover in January 2000 showed her unclothed, lying on a fur rug, and wearing a pair of large diamond bracelets alongside handcuffs. This issue, which *Gentleman's Quarterly* dubbed its "Naked Supermodel Special," identified the model and clarified that the photo shoot occurred aboard an airplane ("Sex at 30,000 feet") but did not name the owner of the plane, Donald J. Trump. A few weeks later, when *Sports Illustrated* included bikini-clad Melania in its popular swimsuit issue, it showed her hugging an inflated plastic killer whale.

Details of just how much Melania earned during her first months in New York came under scrutiny after her husband, as a presidential candidate, proposed new limits on immigrants. Like many newcomers, she had originally entered with a tourist visa that did not permit her to work. A few weeks later, she obtained a more liberal H-1B visa that did allow employment. Although sometimes called the "Einstein visa," it was not reserved for geniuses, and thousands of chefs, athletes, and others whose abilities and expertise served their employers received H-1B visas.[2] Before obtaining the H-1B visa, however, according to one report during the 2016 campaign, she had taken ten modeling assignments for a total of more than $20,000.[3] Substantiating the number was difficult because records and personnel of the modeling agency that booked her were no longer available, and her former manager, Zampolli, offered no clarification. Her work status after 2001 was not in question because that was the year she received her green card that granted permanent residence and all the rights of a citizen except the right to vote.

Not yet a U.S. citizen when she married Donald J. Trump on January 22, 2005, thirty-four-year old Melania Knauss (as she spelled her name at the time) had nearly 500 guests at her lavish Palm Beach celebration. They came from the top echelon of entertainment (Billy Joel and Paul Anka); government (Hillary and Bill Clinton); and news media (Barbara Walters and Katie Couric). Yet the bride counted none of them among her close friends.

Had her husband proceeded to serve in Congress or other elective office, Melania would have been exposed to U.S. politics beyond what she learned during her naturalization process in 2006. Instead, he continued to gain his popularity and wealth from a real estate empire and from his frequent appearances on a widely viewed TV show, *The Apprentice*. Isolated in his rarefied world, his wife flew in private planes and divided her time among three luxurious residences: a gilded triplex in Trump Tower, Manhattan; sprawling quarters at his private golf club in Bedminster, New Jersey; and the 100-plus rooms of his Palm Beach retreat, Mar-a-Lago.

Had Melania Trump taken time to develop a trustworthy network of competent professionals from her university's faculty or the community of journalists and writers in her native country, she might have turned to them for guidance and support as her husband's political prospects grew. But she had left Slovenia at twenty-two without mentors, and she quickly truncated ties to the school friends and extended family who remained there. She accompanied Donald Trump on his sole visit to her country in 2002, when he stayed only a few hours to have dinner with her parents at a resort hotel on Lake Bled, and her subsequent solo visits were nearly as brief.

Her closest ties in America were to her immediate family, especially her sister, Ines, who had moved to New York to be near her and had been her sole bridesmaid. Their parents, Viktor and Amalija, who had made brief visits to their daughters in New York, extended those stays after the birth of grandson Barron William Trump in 2006. Viktor and Amalija eventually obtained green cards, making them legal residents, a fact much publicized after their son-in-law sought to end preferential treatment for family members, or what he called "chain migration."

Within that cocoon of parents and sister, Melania could continue speaking her native Slovenian; she could rely on them to introduce her son to the language. Since all three had limited education and even less familiarity than she with American culture, she had to figure most things out for herself. Assigning her a substantial role in the 2016 campaign would have been as unrealistic as asking Michelle Obama to give speeches for Barack if he ran for mayor of Melania's hometown.

Details of Melania Trump's early years are difficult to ferret out, partly because she has chosen not to share them and partly because Communist Yugoslavia kept a lid on what in the United States would be public records, including censuses and court cases. When Bojan Požar, a Slovenian journalist and talk show host, set out to write about her in 2015, he found many gaps in her record and blamed his Slovenian colleagues for their "lack of investigative research," which was, he wrote, "a true hallmark of post-communist" journalism in Slovenia.[4]

Požar, together with the economist and former politician Igor Omerza, dug into the sources available and reported their findings in *Melania Trump: The Inside Story,* published in early 2016 before her husband secured the Republican nomination. That book covers only the first thirty-six years of Melania's life (up to 2006) and concentrates on her time in Slovenia. Since the WhiteHouse.gov website under the Trump presidency omitted basic information about Melania, including the names of her parents and the schools she attended, Požar's book provides a starting point for filling in the missing information.

According to Požar, she was christened Melanija Knavs a few months after her birth on April 26, 1970. She and her sole sibling, Ines (born 1968), lived their earliest years in Unit Nine of a housing development, called Naselje Heroja Maroka, provided by the government-owned factory where their mother worked in Sevnica. Located about an hour's drive south of Ljubljana, which would become the capital of Slovenia when it gained independence in 1991, Sevnica offered a pleasant hillside setting for the Jutranjka textile factory, but much of the housing for its 5,000 inhabitants remained the dull, cinder block structures characteristic of Eastern Europe after World War II. The Knavs sisters attended an elementary school only a short walk from home, and although neither was an outstanding student, both showed talent in art and design. Melania began sewing her own clothes and altering those she bought to make them distinctive.[5]

Požar traces those sartorial interests directly to her mother's family. Born Amalija Ulčnik in 1945, in the small hillside town of Raka, a few miles away from Sevnica, Melania's mother had followed the example of an older sister, and after elementary school, enrolled for vocational training in clothing design and manufacture. Although a serious student and popular (her fourteen classmates elected her president) Amalija did not continue her training past the four years required for a diploma. Her older sister had pursued her studies, in order to qualify for a management position, but Amalija started working at nineteen as a cutter/pattern maker at Jutranjka. Amalija's father had remained a farmer and gained some local fame for producing a hybrid red onion, which he named "Raka" for his hometown.

Amalija also laid the foundation for her daughter's interest in personal beauty and fashion. Her neighbors observed that she paid considerable attention to her own appearance, chose her outfits carefully, and wore high heels when others sought the comfort of flats. When Jutranjka enlisted young girls as informal models for their latest children's fashions, Amalija arranged for Melanija to walk the runway.

While Amalija toiled at the same job until retiring in 1997 at the age of fifty-two, the man she married had a far more colorful employment record. Born on November 23, 1941, in tiny Jagnjenica, about twenty miles north of Amalija's hometown, Viktor Knavs (or Knaus, as his German language birth certificate listed him) soon moved with his family to the larger town of Radeče, where his adult relatives found work at the paper factory and he received his elementary education. Not much for books, he showed an early, avid interest in automobiles. After apprenticing in a car repair shop, he became a driver in the Yugoslav National Army. Other jobs at the wheels of flashy, big cars followed, including chauffeuring the mayor of Hrastnik and later, executives at the Jutranjka factory.

By the time Viktor Knavs and Amalija Ulčnik met, he had already fathered a son by another woman, although it is not clear when Amalija found out about this. Although Viktor initially denied any relationship to the young Denis Cigelnjak, the boy's mother sued and a court decree required Viktor to pay child support until Denis turned eighteen. The court decree did not require personal contact, and apparently there was none between Viktor and his biological son. His two daughters by Amalija insisted they never met their half-brother. When Julia Ioffe first revealed Denis Cigelnjak's story in an article in *Gentleman's Quarterly* in April 2016, Melania Trump initially denied the relationship and cited errors in Ioffe's reporting. She later admitted to knowing about Denis and attributed her earlier reaction to a language problem.

Ioffe's sources in Slovenia pointed out something else about Viktor Knavs—that he was "shockingly Trump like." A hefty, ebullient man, Viktor favored showy Mercedes vehicles and did not stay long in one place. Highly adaptable, he had been a member of the Communist Party when it controlled Yugoslavia but became a capitalist/entrepreneur when Slovenia converted to a republic. He opened his own cycle/moped shop, Knaus-Haus, and engaged in profitable real estate deals.

When the family's government-owned apartment became available for purchase in 1991, he bought it, then sold at a profit and built a freestanding house in Ribniki, the upscale section of Sevnica.[6]

At fifteen, when Melania qualified for entrance to the Secondary School for Design and Photography in Ljubljana, she effectively cut her ties to Sevnica and moved to the capital, where Viktor had purchased an apartment at Glinskova Ploscad 20. Ljubljana was not a world-class city, but with its population of 260,000 and picturesque cafes lining both sides of the river that ran through it, it offered much that Sevnica lacked. Melania's classes in a former monastery started early in the morning, and the course of study she chose in industrial design lasted four years.

That period as an unremarkable teen ended when Melania graduated from the School for Design at nineteen, the same age her mother had been when she took the job in the Jutranjka factory where she still worked. Her daughter had other ideas. After passing the competitive tests for entrance to Ljubljana's university, the Faculty of Architecture and Civil and Geodetic Engineering, she again chose to major in design. Before she completed a year there, she made a decision that changed her life.

Požar points to 1992 as a turning point in young Melania's life. At age twenty-two and unenthusiastic about her classes at the university, she entered a beauty contest and placed second. The resulting publicity emboldened her to try modeling. A local photographer, Stane Jerko, had already spotted her potential in 1987, when she was only seventeen and stood out for her tall (5'11") lithe figure and fresh, natural smile. Although she posed occasionally for Jerko, she was not yet ready to commit to a career in front of a camera, and his pictures of a relatively flat-chested, animated young woman bear little resemblance to the buxom sphinxlike figure Americans came to know later.

As Melania Knaus (the Knauss spelling came later) she set out to find modeling jobs, first in Europe (Vienna, Milan, and Paris) before signing with Zampolli and coming to New York. Colleagues reported she took her work very seriously. Not known as a party girl, she paid careful attention to the discipline required for success, watching her diet, getting adequate sleep, and exercising.

Melania's experience in front of a camera was her best preparation for 2016. Other spouses of candidates for high office frequently find themselves blindsided by ubiquitous photographers, eager to capture the candid shot, ready to record any fashion gaffe. Women new to politics often feel they have to hire wardrobe consultants and turn to hair stylists and makeup experts to keep them looking their best. For Melania, who had spent her entire adult life preparing for cameras, this was the easy part.

The speaking part was harder, and during her husband's long presidential campaign she took a very limited role. Explaining that she needed to stay in New York to look after her young son (who was coincidentally the same age as Michelle's older daughter during the 2008 campaign and three years older than Sasha), Melania appeared rarely at her husband's side during the primaries. In the campaign against Hillary, Melania rationed carefully her time on the road, going only to states where the race was especially tight, such as South Carolina, Wisconsin, and Pennsylvania. She kept her speeches extremely short and avoided controversy and policy matters, focusing instead on her husband's qualifications. She credited him as a "great communicator...great negotiator...great leader," and promised that he would "fight for you and for our country."[7]

Melania's modeling history became part of the campaign while her husband was still fighting for the nomination. An ad for one of his rivals, Ted Cruz, used the *Gentleman's Quarterly* photo of Melania on the fur rug, with the caption: "Meet Melania Trump. Your next first lady. Or you could support Ted Cruz on Tuesday."[8] Donald Trump blamed "Lyin' Ted Cruz" for circulating the picture and threatened to "spill the beans" on Mrs. Cruz. Even after candidate Cruz insisted that he had nothing to do with the ad—it had been prepared by the Super Pac "Make America Awesome" the two men continued to snipe at each other. Cruz called Trump a "sniveling coward," and Trump forwarded a message from one of his fans, showing glamorous Melania alongside a less glamorous Heidi Cruz, with the caption, "No need to spill the beans. The images are worth a thousand words."[9]

In spite of her reportedly limited enthusiasm for Donald's presidential aspirations, Melania agreed to follow what had become a tradition in recent nominating conventions and speak to the Republican delegates. Scheduled for an audience of 2,500 on July 18, Melania told reporters she had written her remarks herself. When the day arrived, everything seemed set for a dramatic appearance. Her husband introduced her in glowing terms, and she stepped to the microphone in stiletto heels and a stylish white sheath dress to talk about her own immigrant background and her thoughts on what America offered. Loud, prolonged applause at the end signaled a clear vote of approval.

Within hours, evidence came in that showed large chunks of the speech repeated exact phrases that Michelle Obama had used in 2008 at the Democratic nominating convention. Various explanations were offered for how Michelle's speech got recycled, and one Trump employee, Meredith McIver, eventually took responsibility, saying that Mrs. Trump had suggested some phrases and McIver had used them, without checking their provenance. What McIver did not need to say is clear: the Trump campaign team had not provided the vetting that any spouse needs in such a situation, especially a wife who comes without a cadre of advisers of her own.

Melania's low level of participation throughout the primaries and general election left the way open for the press to focus on Donald Trump's adult children from his first two marriages. Although all four appeared with him and gave endorsing speeches, Ivanka, a thirty-four-year old mother of three, took the biggest role and garnered the most attention. A successful entrepreneur herself, she defended her father's treatment of women employees and noted he promoted them to the highest ranks of his companies. One major newspaper saluted her with the headline: "Ivanka Trump Proves Savvy Surrogate for Her Father."[10]

Whenever Ivanka appeared on the same stage with her stepmother (who was eleven years her senior) the older woman always preceded her, but that did not prevent speculation that Ivanka would hold surrogate First Lady status if her father won. It was Ivanka, not Melania, who introduced him to the Republican Convention, and one newspaper printed the question that many people were thinking: "Ivanka Trump: A Real First Lady?"[11]

Nonetheless, it fell to Melania to come to Donald's defense in early October, when that recording of her husband's remarks to celebrity reporter Billy Bush for Access Hollywood, containing lewd boasts about his treatment of women and how his superstar status permitted him to "move" on them, surfaced.[12] Melania spoke with Anderson Cooper on CNN a few days later, telling him that the recording did not show "the man I know." As for the claims other women had made about his inappropriate behavior, she labeled them "lies."[13]

Two days after the Republican victory on November 8, Donald and Melania Trump flew to Washington for the traditional meeting between the outgoing presidential couple and their successors. For most incoming administrations, this marks an important impetus for action, the day when both incoming POTUS and FLOTUS start naming staff and outlining changes to come. The First Lady's agenda is obviously a small fraction of that of the president, but it is not inconsequential; it will affect his effectiveness and figure in his legacy.

Unlike her predecessors, who used the interim between election and inauguration to get a good start on the job, Melania Trump announced on November 21 that she would not be moving immediately to Washington, so that her son could remain in his Manhattan private school. Instead, she would continue to reside with him at Trump Tower and make occasional trips to the capital for official events. No previous First Lady had made such a choice, although others, including Julia Grant and Michelle Obama, had considered it.[14] For the inauguration on January 20 and peripheral events, Melania Trump appeared in Washington, but when the festivities ended, she returned to Manhattan.

Within weeks of the inauguration, the First Lady's absence from Washington became a subject of speculation. When Ivanka Trump accompanied her father on an official visit to Dover Air Force Base, a surrogate First Lady seemed plausible. Lady Bird Johnson and Hillary Clinton (among others) had enlisted daughters to stand in for them at receptions and ceremonial occasions, but only when illness or prior commitments precluded their own participation. In Melania's case no such explanation was noted.

As Melania remained in New York, without a fully operational staff in the East Wing, requests for White House tours were piling up, unanswered, and her approval rating in a Gallup poll in January stood at only 37 percent.

A small flurry of appointments followed in early February. Anna Cristina Niceta Lloyd, the new social secretary, came fully prepared to oversee the official entertaining on the new president's calendar. As an executive of the fashionable catering firm Design Cuisine, she had already worked on inaugural events for presidents of both political parties, including that of Trump. Melania picked Lindsay Reynolds, a former elementary school teacher with strong ties to the Republican Party, as her chief of staff, responsible for overseeing the East Wing. To redecorate the private residential quarters, the First Lady chose the relatively unknown Tham Kannalikham, a Laotian American who had most recently worked at Ralph Lauren Home in New York. Stephanie Wolkoff, a seasoned planner of celebrity events, volunteered to assist Melania from her New York City base, an arrangement that lasted until February 2018, when Wolkoff's account of spending for the inauguration festivities came under scrutiny.

Even after adding Stephanie Grisham, an experienced communications director, Melania did not have a staff anywhere near the number employed by her immediate predecessors, and they appeared more connected to the Trumps' society/fashion world than to politics/

government. The handling of one appointment, although not entirely in the First Lady's domain, underlined the administration's habit of bucking tradition. The chief usher, who supervises household employees and oversees the running of the executive mansion, typically remains through several presidents' tenures, serving without regard to changes in administration. But the Trumps replaced Angella Reid, who, as the first woman to hold the title, had been on the job since 2011, with Timothy Harleth, formerly of the Trump International Hotel in Washington.

Solo First Lady public appearances during 2017 were few, concentrated on children and women's issues and divided between Manhattan and Washington. In March she made a surprise visit to hospitalized children in New York and then spoke to female employees at the State Department about the need to combat abuse of women. She appeared at the annual Easter Egg Roll on the White House South Lawn in April but had yet to follow up on any substantial project of her own. Her view of the job at that point owed a lot to Bess Truman, who liked to escape Washington too and saw no need to hire a large staff and spearhead a cause of her own.

When Melania accompanied the president, enormous attention focused on her—especially what she wore and what it cost. Her much-photographed stiletto heels raised eyebrows as she embarked on a trip to hurricane-damaged Texas, but print media noted she had changed to sneakers by the time she landed. Concern about a First Lady's spending was nothing new. Michelle Obama's $540 Lanvin sneakers made headlines,[15] and Jacqueline Kennedy's designer wardrobe led to speculation about the family budget. But in Melania's case, debate over her clothing choices went beyond cost: Was it appropriate that she don a $51,500 jacket in Sicily, ancestral home of its designer, Stefano Gabbano, when she accompanied the president on his first trip abroad? Why did she cover her head to meet Pope Francis in the Vatican but go bare-headed in Israel?

At the time of that Mid-East/Europe trip in May 2017, Melania had not yet moved to Washington. That would come the following month, after Barron's academic year ended in New York and she could set about enrolling him at a private school within commuting distance of the White House. The decision to delay uniting the family fed speculation about her marriage and how close she and the president actually were; paparazzi stood ready with cameras to provide evidence. One video, showing Melania swatting away the president's hand after they landed in Tel Aviv, attracted millions of viewers on YouTube.

The subject of discord in the presidential household gained momentum in January 2018, about the time of the Trumps' twelfth wedding anniversary. The *Wall Street Journal* reported that Michael Cohen, the president's longtime personal attorney, had admitted using his own personal funds "to facilitate a payment of $130,000 to Ms. Stephanie Clifford"[16] in 2016. Other media identified Stephanie Clifford as the adult film star Stormy Daniels and explained why the president's lawyer might have paid her such a large sum just days before the election. The *New York Post* titled its story, "All the dirty details of Trump's alleged porn star affair."[17]

Clifford's story was not entirely new. In 2011 she had sold her account of an intimate relationship with Donald Trump to a tabloid magazine for $15,000, but the publisher had not run it, and in 2016, with the principal subject of her story a candidate for president, it was potentially worth much more. Since Cohen offered no reason for the payment, which came with a nondisclosure agreement for Clifford to sign, the conclusion seemed obvious that it had been made to keep her quiet. Common Cause and other watchdog groups immediately pounced on the exchange, asking why what was clearly a campaign contribution, since it was intended to hush up a potentially damaging story about one candidate, had not been reported.

Melania's reaction to the news had nothing to do with campaign financing—it was more personal. If Ms. Clifford's time line was accurate, the alleged encounter occurred in July 2006, more than a year after Melania had married Donald and three months after she gave birth to his son.

The First Lady's infrequent public appearances became even fewer, and CNN reported on January 23, 2018, that she had not been seen in public since the Stormy Daniels payoff story broke. Melania had accompanied her husband to Florida the weekend of January 12 but apparently skipped two important dinners he hosted. Although previously scheduled to go with the president to Davos, Switzerland, where he would speak to the World Economic Forum on January 26, the First Lady cancelled, with her communications director, Stephanie Grisham, referring vaguely to scheduling and logistical issues. Melania did show up at her husband's State of the Union address on January 30, but, contrary to tradition, she did not ride with him to the Capitol. Observers looking to her wardrobe for a clue on her thinking noted that her cream-colored pantsuit looked a lot like the white outfits favored by persons currently identifying with movements to empower women, such as #TimesUp and #MeToo.

The following month produced more evidence of Donald Trump's extramarital relationships and various moves to conceal them. The *New Yorker* published details of how Karen McDougal, a former Playmate of the Year (1998), had sold an account of her 2006 consensual affair with Trump to the *National Enquirer* during his presidential campaign. The story never ran, and Ronan Farrow, the *New Yorker* columnist, concluded it was common for tabloids to pay large sums for stories they intended to bury. A few weeks later, Stephanie Clifford moved to void the nondisclosure agreement she had signed, under a pseudonym, thus moving the matter of whether she could talk into the courts, and the president's personal attorney sought an injunction to keep her quiet.

This was not a good start to Melania's second year as First Lady. She had gained some sympathy, as the wronged wife, and her favorability rating had shot up in December 2017, when 57 percent of those polled described their opinion as positive. Even after adding a policy director, twenty-seven-year-old Reagan Thompson, to her team, Melania had yet to gain much traction on any specific project or cause of her own She continued to indicate an interest in children's issues and the nation's youth, and after the February 2018 school shooting in Parkland, Florida, that left seventeen dead, she defended the students who were calling for gun restrictions. She said she had been "heartened" by their protests: "They're our future and they deserve a voice."[18] She stopped short, however, of advocating new restrictions on gun ownership.

During the 2016 campaign, Melania had cited a need to curb cyber bullying, and after eight months as First Lady, she began speaking out on the subject. Her short speech at a UN lunch in September 2017 encouraged adults to take more responsibility for regulating social media, and in a meeting with junior high students in Detroit a month later, she urged them to be kinder and more compassionate in their relationships with others. In March 2018, she went a step further, inviting representatives from Facebook, Google, Amazon, and Twitter to a roundtable discussion at the White House. No concrete recommendations came out of that meeting, but it indicated Melania's continuing interest in the issue.

Ironically, while his wife was talking about the need for restraint, the president continued to tweet threats against world leaders, demean people who disagreed with him, and launch negatives at a long list of government officials and employees. Melania's predecessors had looked for a project to enhance their husbands' presidencies; she seemed geared to expose Donald's weakness and emphasize the thinness of his skin. She had reportedly encouraged him to stop tweeting, without success.

By mid-2018, with criticism of the president's policies and behavior growing and several of his former advisers coming under investigation for criminal activity, the First Lady began asserting an independent path for herself. It did not always parallel the president's and even, in some cases, ran contrary to his. She still appeared alongside her husband at ceremonial events, welcoming foreign leaders to the White House and marking national milestones with him. But as headlines blared evidence of his role in silencing accounts of his intimate relations with other women, she offered more than one hint that she had her own agenda, not always in sync with his. Rather than an East Wing operation supporting the president, hers appeared independently setting its own, very different course.

Increased emphasis on her anti-bullying initiative offered one sign of a changed approach. On May 7, 2018, at a much-publicized and heavily covered event in the Rose Garden, she announced that she was launching a campaign, Be Best, aimed at the nation's youth. Of its three parts, one addressed opioid abuse, and the other two zeroed in on social media and how to encourage young people to behave more responsibly and show kindness to others. The president sat in the audience that day and applauded her speech, even as others noted that his own use of social media ran contrary to her goals.

A week later, on May 14, the First Lady entered the hospital for treatment of a "benign kidney condition" and she stayed five days. After doctors acquainted with the procedure (but not treating her) weighed in on the subject, it became clear that the normal down time for such treatment was considerably less than the First Lady was taking. She did not appear in public again until June 4, when she and the president welcomed Gold Star families to a White House reception, no press permitted.

In an earlier time, First Ladies had been allowed considerable privacy in matters of health. Many did not reveal their illnesses, and others, like Florence Harding, falsified the information they gave to conceal the severity. In 1957, President Eisenhower's press secretary reported Mamie Eisenhower's hysterectomy as simply "a two hour operation."[19] By Melania Trump's White House tenure, Americans expected more frankness. The candor of both Betty Ford and Nancy Reagan about their mastectomies had helped quash the stigma of discussing such matters, and many women were encouraged to go for mammograms.

The refusal of Melania Trump's office to issue any clarification for her long time out of sight fueled rumors that she had actually been treated for something far more serious than "a benign kidney condition" or was using the time for recovery from plastic surgery, either for breast enhancement or wrinkle reduction. Foreign press took note of her "mysterious" disappearance.

As if to strike back at critics and assert herself, Melania Trump scheduled a trip of her own. On June 21, she flew to Texas to visit children who had been separated from their parents and held in detention facilities when their parents were deported to their home countries. The plight of these youngsters, numbering in the thousands, had captured international attention, and former First Lady Laura Bush joined the outcry against a policy of "zero tolerance" for persons who had entered the United States illegally. In an op-ed in the *Washington Post*, she noted that scores of the children were under the age of four, and separating them from their parents was "cruel...immoral. And it breaks my heart."[20]

By the time Melania scheduled her visit to the Texas detention centers, her husband had altered his "zero tolerance" stand, but it would take much longer for families already separated to be reunited. Her trip indicates she had not agreed with the policy in the first place, and the writing on the back of the jacket she wore when she left the White House offered more evidence of dissent. It read: "I really don't care. Do U?" Since the temperature peaked at 86 degrees that day in the nation's capital and was even warmer in Texas, the jacket served more as placard of protest than as garment for warmth. It was not the message of a happy camper.

Melania's next solo stop in the limelight occurred in early August when her office issued a statement at odds with the president's recent tweets. He had posted demeaning comments about two African Americans, CNN anchor Don Lemon and basketball superstar LeBron James, calling the first "the dumbest man on television" and implying equally limited intelligence of the second by tweeting, "He [Lemon] made LeBron look smart, which isn't easy to do." Lemon had recently interviewed James about the latter's project to help disadvantaged youth in his hometown of Akron, Ohio, and during their discussion, the president's name came up in a not entirely favorable context.

The president waited three days to strike back at Lemon and James, but Melania reacted more quickly to her husband's tweets. The very next day, her statement to the press endorsed the Akron project, saying, "It looks like LeBron James is working to do good things on behalf of our next generation."[21] Her predecessors had sometimes admitted to holding views at odds with their husbands or implied the same, notably Laura Bush on *Roe v. Wade* and Barbara Bush on gun control, but only when questioned on the subject. Melania Trump's statement was unsolicited and unprecedented in recent history.

As if to signal that the Knavs family would be contributing fractious notes to the Trump presidency frequently, Viktor and Amalija Knavs became U.S. citizens on August 9. Their green card status gave them all the rights of citizens except that of the vote, and as legal residents, they could continue to maintain a home in Slovenia and spend as much time as they wanted with their two daughters and one grandson in the United States. Yet they proceeded with a naturalization ceremony, which, although private and not attended by either daughter, was bound to attract enormous attention. The First Lady's parents had previously managed to keep low profiles, and their pictures rarely appeared in the media. Their trip to the Federal Building in Manhattan, where they took the citizenship oath, proved a bonanza for photographers, and the resulting images were widely circulated. Critics of the president's denunciation of family reunification as grounds for immigration had already pointed to the irony, that his own in-laws had benefitted from the policy by obtaining green cards. Their citizenship ceremony underlined the irony.

Melania had once said that she wanted to be a "very traditional first lady, like Betty Ford or Jackie Kennedy," but they had both left distinct marks on the job within weeks of taking it. Kennedy immediately announced plans to restore a shabby White House to its nineteenth-century grandeur, and Ford held her own press conference where she informed 150 reporters that she and her husband sometimes disagreed on important issues. Both gained accolades for their style, though their legacies rest on far more than what they wore.

Lady Bird Johnson, no slouch about activism, often said that every president's wife has the right to define the job for herself. Melania Trump appeared to be doing just that, taking it back in time, albeit via media tactics of the twenty-first century.

In the more than two centuries since Martha Washington struggled to define what a president's wife should do and be, dozens of women have experimented with different models.[22] Throughout the 1800s, few emerged as strong-minded, with views of their own, and even fewer left their imprint on a husband's administration. Some, including Abigail Fillmore and Eliza Johnson, remained in virtual hiding, while their daughters acted as surrogates.

Inspired by Eleanor Roosevelt's example and moved by new thinking on how a wife could enhance a president's legacy, the women in the White House became far more visible after 1960. The success of Lady Bird Johnson's solo campaigning encouraged Rosalynn Carter to go out on her own; Pat Nixon's popularity, as a result of thousands of miles of travel and countless public speeches, inspired her successors to take speech lessons and combat their stage fright. Nancy Reagan saw an immediate upswing in her approval rating after she announced her "Just Say No" initiative.

The trio of prominent First Ladies who followed them, serving over nearly a quarter century (1993–2017), illustrated how firmly attached the president's wife had become to her husband's administration. Hillary Clinton, Laura Bush, and Michelle Obama all hit the campaign trail for solo appearances and appealed to donors for support. In the White House they appointed and supervised large, highly qualified staffs. All three spearheaded significant projects of their own, and they traveled widely, including Africa and Asia, to promote women's causes. On leaving the White House, each signed a lucrative contract for a book about her part in her husband's presidency.

Melania Trump reverted to an earlier model. Well into her second year in the White House, she has remained private and minimally involved. Her tenure shows how open the job of First Lady remains to redefinition and change. If a woman becomes president, the role will be further altered. Should a future presidential spouse be an invalid or firmly committed to his/her own career or simply unwilling to serve, the job may well revert to the obscurity of the nineteenth century, similar to what most countries of the world deem appropriate.

Notes

Introduction

1. Edward T. James et al., *Notable American Women*, 3 vols. (Cambridge, 1971).

2. Popular volumes on First Ladies include Laura Holloway, *Ladies of the White House* (Philadelphia, 1881); Margaret Bassett, *Profiles and Portraits of American Presidents and Their Wives* (Freeport, 1969); Sol Barzman, *The First Ladies* (New York, 1970); Amy La Follette Jensen, *The White House* (New York, 1962); Bess Furman, *White House Profile* (New York, 1951); Esther Singleton, *The Story of the White House*, 2 vols. (New York, 1907); and Mary Ormsbee Whitton, *First First Ladies* (Freeport, 1948).

3. Mary Clemmer Ames, "A Woman's Letter from Washington," *The Independent*, March 15, 1877, p. 2.

4. *Frank Leslie's Illustrated Newspaper*, March 31, 1860.

5. Emily Edson Briggs, *The Olivia Letters* (New York, 1906), p. 173, reprints an 1870 column by Briggs.

6. William Howard Russell, *My Diary North and South* (Boston, 1863), p. 177.

7. Merriam Webster's *New International Dictionary* did not include the term until the second edition (1934) when it meant the "wife of the President of the United States, [or . . .] the woman he chooses to act as his official hostess." By the 1960s, the phrase had taken on some weight of its own and moved outside government. "Hostess" did not entirely disappear from the definition in Webster's *Third* (1961) or in *The American Heritage Dictionary* (1969), but now there was a second meaning: "the leading woman representative or practitioner of any art or profession [as in . . .] the first lady of the dance." *The Random House Dictionary* (1966) avoided "hostess" entirely, defining "first lady" as either the wife of an important government official or a woman who had achieved "foremost" status on her own, as in "first lady of the American theater."

Uncapitalized in the beginning, "first lady" had made its way slowly into the nation's lexicon. In the 1880s, Laura Holloway's book *Ladies of the White House* helped focus attention on the subjects, and in 1911, a hit play began to popularize the title. Charles Nirdlinger's "First Lady of the Land" took considerable liberty with history and had nothing to do with the wife of a president, but anyone unfamiliar with its plot could easily make the mistake of thinking it did. Subtitled, "When Mrs. Todd Kept a Boarding House," the play has as its heroine, Dolley Todd, who consents to marry James Madison only at the end of the fourth act—when Thomas Jefferson is still president. Ironically, it is not presiding over the White House that wins Dolley her "first lady" appellation but rather her down-to-earth casualness and her success in outwitting the snobbish wife of the British minister.

Another play, "First Lady," by Katharine Dayton and George S. Kaufman, appeared in 1935, and its plot involved competition among Washington women to make their husbands president. In exposing an unsavory side of the political process, this play (later movie) dealt more with human foibles than with life in the White House, but it helped move "first lady" into common usage.

8. George Reedy, *New York Times Book Review*, January 20, 1985, p. 1.

9. Peter Collier and David Horowitz, in *The Kennedys: An American Drama* (New York, 1984), p. 353, report that Jackie Kennedy pronounced the title more appropriate to a "saddle horse." Collier and Horowitz gave no source for this comment, and Jackie Kennedy did not grant interviews. Her White House social secretary, Letitia Baldrige, told the author that after a few months, Jackie Kennedy "gave up" on trying to stop her staff from using the term.

10. Hunter College Conference on Eleanor Roosevelt, New York, December 4, 1982, hereafter referred to as Hunter College Conference.

11. Hunter College Conference.

12. *New York Times*, December 12, 1974, section vi, p. 36.

13. *New York Times*, November 22, 1985, p. A14. Raisa Gorbachev also received considerable attention from foreign reporters covering the summit but, unlike Nancy Reagan, she remained a "photo opportunity" for "export only." Reporters in Moscow ignored her appearance at the summit.

14. Briggs, *Olivia Letters*, p. 211.

15. Donald Young, *American Roulette: The History and Dilemma of the Vice Presidency* (New York, 1965), p. 5. Unless the president dies, resigns, or is unable to carry on the duties of his office, the vice president remains a distant second in power, and political scientists continue to debate just what the job includes. Except for presiding over the Senate (and casting a vote in case of a tie), the vice president is assigned no other duties in the Constitution, and although he stands "one heart beat away from the presidency," by tradition he is not likely to be one of those who monitors the beating. During James Garfield's slow death in the summer of 1881, Vice President Chester Arthur was reluctant to show his face near the sickroom. He feared his concern might be interpreted as premature seizing of power, especially since the assassin had boasted of acting in the vice president's cause. A century later, George Bush, cognizant of the fact that taking an activist role could be interpreted in various ways, kept a low visibility during Ronald Reagan's surgery for wounds sustained in the attempted assassination in March 1981 and during the president's cancer surgery in July 1985.

Responsibility for defining the vice president's role lies partly with the chief executives, many of whom were reluctant to act, often for obvious reasons. In the nineteenth century, not every vice president established a year-round Washington residence, and most, therefore, were not on hand to participate in important discussions. Some lacked experience and ability, having acquired their jobs because of party efforts to balance the ticket. Others were very old and showed little vitality. Potential for rivalry between the chief executive and his second-in-command dictated prudence in assigning tasks.

The vice presidency became the subject of renewed discussion after the death of Franklin Roosevelt in 1945 just as the United States was preparing to conclude World War II by using the atomic bomb. Harry S. Truman, having served as vice president for only a few weeks, had not been privy to all the discussions of the power of the bomb or to other relevant information, and his predicament led to new efforts to define the job of presidential understudy. Eventually each president worked out his own arrangements, often—but not always—putting in writing just what he expected of his vice president if he himself had to undergo surgery or temporarily remove himself from the decision-making process. The twenty-fifth amendment to the Constitution (which became effective in February 1967) further clarified just how the vice president could become acting president.

16. Young, *American Roulette*, p. 5. Paul C. Light, *Vice Presidential Power* (Baltimore, 1984), shows how some vice presidents emphasized the potential power in the office.

17. Young, *American Roulette*, p. 134.

18. *New York Times*, July 13, 1986, p. E7.

19. Rufus Wilmot Griswold, *The Republican Court* (New York, 1854), p. 178.

20. *New York Times*, July 16, 1985, p. A11.

21. Allan Nevins, ed., *The Diary of John Quincy Adams* (New York, 1951), p. 337.

22. *Time* (August 28, 1964), p. 20.

23. At the 1986 convention of the Organization of American Historians, an entire session centered on a discussion of what is being called "women's political culture." Readers interested in following the arguments should consider the work of Kathryn Kish Sklar, Susan Ware, Mary Beth Norton, Jacquelyn Dowd Hall, J. Stanley Lemons, Mary Ryan, and Mari Jo Buhle, among others. They have considered the wide variety of women's political participation, whether separate from men's or not. The same historians have also looked at the American political process and American attitudes to see how they set the stage for women's leadership and effectiveness.

24. Mary Hoyt, speaking at conference, "Modern First Ladies: Private Lives and Public Duties," Gerald R. Ford Museum, Grand Rapids, Michigan, April 18–20, 1984, hereafter referred to as the Grand Rapids Conference.

Chapter 1

1. Stephen Decatur, *Private Affairs of George Washington* (Boston, 1933), p. 2.

2. *New York Times*, February 28, 1982, section 3, p. 19.

3. John C. Fitzpatrick, ed., *Writings of George Washington*, 39 vols. (Washington, D.C., 1939–1944), vol. 30, p. 363.

4. Douglas Southall Freeman, *George Washington*, 7 vols. (New York, 1948–1957), vol. 6. p. 186.

5. Freeman, *George Washington*, vol. 6, p. 398.

6. Doris Kearns, speaking at 92nd Street Y, New York, October 16, 1984.

7. For a full discussion of the problem, see chapter 11, "Presidential Wives and the Press," in earlier editions of this book.

8. Henry Cabot Lodge, ed., *The Works of Alexander Hamilton*, 9 vols. (New York, 1885–1886), vol. 8, pp. 83–95.

9. Freeman, *George Washington*, vol. 6, p. 207.

10. Freeman, *George Washington*, vol. 6, p. 187.

11. Freeman, *George Washington*, vol. 6, p. 207.

12. Decatur, *Private Affairs*, p. 44.

13. For reports of Martha Washington's first days in New York, see *Gazette of the United States*, May 30, 1789, p. 3; *Daily Advertiser*, June 15, 1789, p. 2.

14. Rufus Wilmot Griswold, *The Republican Court* (New York, 1854), p. 164.

15. Anne Hollingsworth Wharton, *Martha Washington* (New York, 1897), p. 197.

16. A major controversy has developed among historians concerning the fluidity of sex roles in colonial America. Mary Beth Norton argues forcefully in *Liberty's Daughters* (Boston, 1980) that earlier historians had exaggerated in describing an overlap between men's and women's tasks. George Washington's interest in household management is one

example, however, that had led Norton's predecessors to emphasize how much men and women exchanged tasks in the eighteenth century. See _George Washington as a Housekeeper_, ed. John C. Fitzpatrick (New York, 1924).

17. _Gazette of the United States_, May 6, 1789, p. 3, cited in Freeman, _George Washington_, vol. 6, p. 199.

18. Decatur, _Private Affairs_, p. 194.

19. Stewart Mitchell, ed., _New Letters of Abigail Adams_ (Boston, 1947), pp. 19–20.

20. Mitchell, _New Letters_, p. 20.

21. Decatur, _Private Affairs_, p. 117.

22. Freeman, _George Washington_, vol. 7, ed. John Alexander Carroll and Mary Wells Ashworth, p. 106.

23. James Thomas Flexner, _George Washington and the New Nation_ (Boston, 1969), p. 208.

24. L. H. Butterfield, ed., _Book of Abigail and John_ (Cambridge, 1975), p. 17.

25. Henry Adams, _Life of Albert Gallatin_ (Philadelphia, 1879), p. 185.

26. Page Smith, _John Adams_, 2 vols. (Garden City, 1962–1963), vol. 2, p. 908.

27. Mitchell, _New Letters_, p. 161.

28. Smith, _John Adams_, vol. 2, p. 937.

29. Janet Whitney, _Abigail Adams_ (Boston, 1947), p. 289.

30. Bradford Perkins, "A Diplomat's Wife in Philadelphia: Letters of Henrietta Liston, 1796–1800," _William and Mary Quarterly_, vol. 11 (October 1954), p. 593.

31. See Mitchell, _New Letters_, pp. 118–119, on Darby and Joan ballad. The text of the ballad is in _Gentleman's Magazine_, vol. 5 (1735), p. 153:

Old Darby with Joan by his side
You've often regarded wi' wonder
He's dropsical, she is sore-ey' d
Yet they're ever uneasy asunder
Together they totter about
Or sit in the sun at the door
And at night when old Darby's pot's out
His Joan will not smoak a whiff more. . . .

32. Smith, _John Adams_, vol. 2, p. 939.

33. Charles W. Akers, _Abigail Adams: An American Woman_ (Boston, 1980), p. 145.

34. Mitchell, _New Letters_, p. 91.

35. Mitchell, _New Letters_, p. 257.

36. Abigail Adams, _Letters of Mrs. Adams_ (Cambridge, 1840), p. 434.

37. Smith, _John Adams_, vol. 2, p. 1052.

38. Bess Furman, _White House Profile_ (New York, 1951), p. 36.

39. Katharine Anthony, _Dolly Madison: Her Life and Times_ (Garden City, 1949), p. 82.

40. Irving Brant, _James Madison_, 6 vols. (Indianapolis, 1941–1961), vol. 3, p. 406.

41. Margaret Bayard Smith, _The First Forty Years of Washington Society_ (New York, 1906), p. 58.

42. Gaillard Hunt, "The First Inaugural Ball," _Century_, vol. 64 (March 1905), p. 754.

43. Hunt, "First Inaugural Ball," p. 757.

44. Allan Nevins, ed., _The Diary of John Quincy Adams_ (New York, 1951), p. 58.

45. Nobel E. Cunningham, "The Diary of Frances Few, 1805–09," _Journal of Southern History_, vol. 29, no. 3 (1969), p. 349.

46. Gaillard Hunt, "Mrs. Madison's First Drawing Room," _Harper's Monthly Magazine_, vol. 121 (June 1910), p. 143.

47. Hunt, "Mrs. Madison's First Drawing Room," p. 143.

48. Allen C. Clark, *Life and Letters of Dolly Madison* (Washington, D.C., 1914), p. 114.

49. Josephine Seaton, *William Winston Seaton of the National Intelligencer* (Boston, 1871), p. 84.

50. Clark, *Life and Letters*, p. 143, quotes Elizabeth Fries Ellet, *Court Circles of the Republic* (Hartford, 1869).

51. Patricia Bell, "Dolly Madison: A Personality Profile," *American History Illustrated*, vol. 4 (1969), p. 17.

52. Cunningham, "Diary of Frances Few," pp. 351–352.

53. Cunningham, "Diary of Frances Few," p. 352.

54. Maud Wilder Goodwin, *Dolly Madison* (New York, 1896), p. 120.

55. Irving Brant, *James Madison*, vol. 5, p. 288.

56. Clark, *Life and Letters*, p. 124.

57. Dolly Madison, *Memoirs and Letters* (Boston, 1886), pp. 76ff.

58. Clark, *Life and Letters*, p. 147.

59. Seaton, *William Winston Seaton*, p. 84.

60. Elijah Mills, "Letters of Elijah Hunt Mills," *Massachusetts Historical Society Proceedings*, 1st series, vol. 19 (1881–1882), p. 18.

61. Maud Wilder Goodwin, *Dolly Madison* (New York, 1896), p. 101.

62. Seaton, *William Winston Seaton*, p. 113.

63. James Herring and J. P. Longacre, eds., *National Portrait Gallery of Distinguished Americans*, 4 vols. (Philadelphia, 1852–1867), vol. 3, p. 4.

64. Seaton, *William Winston Seaton*, p. 91.

65. Clark, *Life and Letters*, p. 123.

66. Harry Ammon, *James Monroe: The Quest for National Destiny* (New York, 1971), p. 401.

67. Seaton, *William Winston Seaton*, p. 89.

68. Seaton, *William Winston Seaton*, pp. 89ff.

69. Smith, *First Forty Years*, p. 141.

70. Elijah Mills, Letter of January 6, 1821.

71. George Ticknor, *Life, Letters and Journals of George Ticknor*, 3 vols. (Boston, 1876), vol. 1, p. 349.

72. Lucius Wilmerding, Jr., "James Monroe and the Furniture Fund," *New-York Historical Society Quarterly*, vol. 44, no. 2 (April 1960), pp. 133–150.

73. Nevins, ed., *Diary of John Quincy Adams*, p. 320.

74. Nevins, ed., *Diary of John Quincy Adams*, pp. 191–192.

75. Seaton, *William Winston Seaton*, p. 144.

76. Seaton, *William Winston Seaton*, p. 144.

77. Nevins, ed., *Diary of John Quincy Adams*, pp. 222–223.

78. Seaton, *William Winston Seaton*, p. 137.

79. Louisa Catherine Adams, "Diary," Adams Family Papers, microfilm reel 265, December 6, 1819 to January 8, 1824. The exact date of each entry in Louisa Adams's diary is not always clearly given.

80. Louisa Adams, "Diary," reel 265.

81. Nevins, ed., *Diary of John Quincy Adams*, p. 319 entry for March 31, 1824.

82. Louisa Adams, "Diary," reel 265.

83. Dolley Madison, *Memoirs and Letters*, p. 169. Elijah Mills wrote in one of his letters: "It is universal opinion that nothing has ever equalled [Louisa Adams's] party here, either in brilliancy of preparation or elegance of company."

84. Louisa Adams, "Diary," January 8, 1824, reel 265.

85. Louisa Adams, "Diary," December 13, 1820, reel 265.

86. Decatur, *Private Affairs of George Washington*, p. 46.

87. Griswold, *Republican Court*, p. 201: Decatur, *Private Affairs*, p. 66.

88. Louisa Adams, "Diary," November 24, 1820, reel 265.

89. George Morgan, *The Life of James Monroe* (New York, 1921), p. 421.

90. Ticknor, *Life, Letters and Journals*, vol. 1, p. 349.

91. Louisa Adams, "Diary," January 1, 1820, reel 265.

92. L. H. Butterfield, "Tending a Dragon-Killer," *Proceedings of the American Philosophical Society*, vol. 118, no. 2 (1974), p. 173.

93. Edward T. James et al., eds., *Notable American Women*, 3 vols. (Cambridge, 1971), vol. 1, p. 13.

94. Louisa Adams, "Diary," November 6, 1812, reel 264.

95. Louisa Adams, "Diary," February 7, 1814, reel 264.

96. Louisa Adams, "Diary," November 27, 1812, reel 264.

97. Louisa Adams, "Diary," August 14, 1812, reel 264.

98. Louisa Adams, "Diary," reel 265.

99. Louisa Adams, "Diary," reel 265.

100. Louisa Adams, "Diary," reel 265.

101. Wendy Martin, "Editorial on Abigail Adams," *Women's Studies*, vol. 3, no. 1 (1975), pp. 1–3.

102. Linda Kerber, "The Republican Mother: Women in the Enlightenment—An American Perspective," *American Quarterly*, vol. 28 (Summer 1976), p. 201. For a discussion of the Philadelphia organization, see Mary Beth Norton, *Liberty's Daughters* (Boston, 1980), p. 179.

103. L. H. Butterfield, ed., *Book of Abigail and John* (Cambridge, 1975), p. 127.

104. Norton, *Liberty's Daughters*, p. xv.

105. Norton, *Liberty's Daughters*, p. 242.

106. Judith Sargent Murray, "Constantia," *The Gleaner*, 3 vols. (Boston, 1798), vol. 3, p. 224.

107. *American Museum*, January 1787, p. 77.

108. Kerber, "Republican Mother," p. 199.

109. Judges 4:4–24.

110. Charles Parmer, "Close-up of the First Lady," *New York Times Magazine*, February 17, 1957, p. 32.

111. Parmer, "Close-up," p. 32.

112. Parmer, "Close-up," p. 12.

113. Mss. 1C9698a172 in Virginia Historical Society, Richmond, Virginia. Quoted by permission.

114. Parmer, "Close-up," p. 32.

115. Norton, *Liberty's Daughters*, p. 146.

116. Akers, *Abigail Adams*, p. 49. Norton makes the same point about women referring to crops as "mine." See *Liberty's Daughters*, p. 146.

117. Butterfield, *Book of Abigail and John*, p. 128. In addition to ordinary household problems, Abigail had to handle family emergencies during John's long absences. When dysentery hit Massachusetts in September 1775, most of her family fell ill, and before the epidemic ended, her brother-in-law, nephew, and mother had all succumbed to it. Raising five children meant that Abigail had to make many decisions on her own, and in the summer of 1776, while John was charting independence for the colonies in Philadelphia, she took her entire family to Boston to be inoculated against smallpox. The process still carried considerable risk, and the size of her brood meant the ordeal lasted all summer as one after the other was infected and then healed. Abigail's youngest

son, Charles, had to go through the vaccination process three times before it was successful. For a discussion of her family difficulties, 1775–1776, see Butterfield, *Book of Abigail and John*, p. 106, and Akers, *An American Woman*, p. 49.

118. Butterfield, *Book of Abigail and John*, p. 8.

119. Charles Frances Adams, *Familiar Letters of John Adams and His Wife, Abigail Adams* (1875; repr. Freeport, New York, 1970), p. xxiii.

120. Norton, *Liberty's Daughters*, p. 184, discusses Martha Jefferson's letter, which is located at the New-York Historical Society.

121. Esther Singleton, *The Story of the White House*, 2 vols. (New York, 1907; repr. New York, 1969), pp. 72–73.

122. Charles Flowers McCombs, "Imprisonment of Mme. Lafayette During the Terror," *New York Library Bookmen's Holiday: Notes and Studies in Tribute to Harry Miller Lydenberg* (New York, 1943), pp. 362–394.

123. McCombs, "Imprisonment of Mme. Lafayette," p. 371.

124. Stuart Gerry Brown, ed., *Autobiography of James Monroe* (Syracuse, 1959), p. 70.

125. Brown, ed., *Autobiography of James Monroe*, p. 70.

126. Louisa Adams's account of her journey from St. Petersburg to Paris was published in *Scribner's*, vol. 34, July–December, 1903, pp. 449–464. This appears to be a verbatim transcription of Louisa's account found on reel 268 of the Adams Family Papers.

127. *Scribner's*, p. 463.

128. Washington C. Ford, ed., *Writings of John Quincy Adams*, 7 vols. (New York, 1915), vol. 5, p. 299.

129. Abigail Adams, *Letters of Mrs. Adams*, p. 199.

130. Abigail Adams, *Letters of Mrs. Adams*, pp. 305–306.

131. Charles Frances Adams, *Familiar Letters*, p. xxiv.

132. Julian Boyd, ed., *Papers of Thomas Jefferson*, 12 vols. (Princeton, 1950–1955), vol. 12, p. 624.

133. Freeman, *George Washington*, vol. 7, p. 173.

134. Benjamin Rush, "Thoughts Upon Female Education," in Frederick Rudolph, ed., *Essays on Education in the Early Republic* (Cambridge, 1965), pp. 25–40.

Chapter 2

1. Margaret Bayard Smith, *The First Forty Years of Washington Society* (New York, 1905), p. 296.

2. The extent to which "Jacksonian democracy" was really democratic remains much debated. For some arguments, see Arthur Schlesinger, Jr., *The Age of Jackson* (Boston, 1945), and Edward Pessen, *The Log Cabin Myth* (New Haven, 1984).

3. Robert J. Hubbard, "Political and Social Life in Washington during the Administration of President Monroe," *Transaction*, vol. 9 (1903), p. 60.

4. Sarah Agnes Pryor, *Reminiscences of Peace and War* (New York, 1904), p. 9.

5. Pryor, *Reminiscences*, p. 9.

6. Katharine Helm, *Mary, Wife of Lincoln* (New York, 1928), p. 172. Helm was Mary Lincoln's niece and she noted that southern women, especially those from Virginia and Maryland, had for many years "held sway [in the capital and] represented a clique of wealth and social position." Although the author has attempted to examine as many primary materials and as many women's accounts as possible, most of the information on the years 1829–1869 comes from accounts of presidents, written by men, long after the subjects were dead. The magazine accounts may tell more about the writers than about the subjects.

7. Mary French Caldwell, *General Jackson's Lady* (Nashville, 1937), p. 423.

8. James Parton, *Life of Andrew Jackson*, 3 vols. (New York, 1860), vol. 3, p. 153.

9. Marquis James, *Andrew Jackson: Portrait of a President* (New York, 1937), p. 168.

10. Marquis James, *Andrew Jackson: Border Captain* (New York, 1933), p. 55.

11. Parton, *Life of Andrew Jackson*, vol. 1, p. 133.

12. James, *Andrew Jackson, Border Captain*, p. 30.

13. James, *Andrew Jackson, Portrait of a President*, p. 291.

14. Josephine Seaton, *William Winston Seaton of the National Intelligencer* (Boston, 1871), p. 132.

15. Parton, *Life of Andrew Jackson*, vol. 2, p. 650.

16. James, *Andrew Jackson, Border Captain*, p. 279.

17. James, *Andrew Jackson, Border Captain*, p. 280.

18. Moore Family Papers, Accession #303, p. 7, of a typescript copy of an undated manuscript, author and location unknown, as noted in letter of Kathleen Jacklin to author, June 3, 1986. The Moore Family Papers include 459 items and are located at the Cornell University Libraries, Ithaca, New York.

19. Caldwell, *General Jackson's Lady*, p. 397.

20. James, *Andrew Jackson, Portrait of a President*, p. 93.

21. Margaret Bassett, *Profiles and Portraits of American Presidents and Their Wives* (Freeport, 1969), p. 81.

22. David Hackett Fischer, *Growing Old in America* (New York, 1978), p. 8.

23. Fischer, *Growing Old*, p. 84.

24. Fischer, *Growing Old*, pp. 86–87.

25. Alison Lurie, *The Language of Clothes* (New York, 1981), pp. 62–65.

26. Henry David Thoreau, *Walden* (Boston, 1854), chapter 1, "Economy."

27. Alexis de Tocqueville, *Democracy in America*, 2 vols. (London, 1838), vol. 2, pp. 233–240.

28. Richard L. Rapson, ed., *Cult of Youth in Middle Class America* (Lexington, 1971), includes an article which reports on 260 books written by foreigners who visited the United States between 1845 and 1920.

29. For a fuller discussion, see Richard L. Rapson, ed., *Cult of Youth in Middle Class America*.

30. James, *Andrew Jackson, Portrait of a President*, p. 206.

31. James, *Andrew Jackson, Portrait of a President*, p. 316. The equally innocuous Sarah Yorke Jackson, who took Emily's place just months before Andrew's second term ended, had won the president's favor with her "sweet" disposition. See James, p. 292.

32. Esther Singleton, *The Story of the White House*, 2 vols. (New York, 1920; repr. New York, 1969), vol. 1, p. 265.

33. The Inman portrait, part of the White House Collection, is usually exhibited in the Red Room.

34. Lloyd C. Taylor, Jr., "Harriet Lane: Mirror of an Age," *Pennsylvania History*, vol. 30 (1963), pp. 213ff. Taylor gives no source on the dedication by the composer, Septimus Winner, and Winner's biographer, Charles Eugene Claghorn, does not mention the dedication to Harriet Lane.

35. Pryor, *Reminiscences*, p. 55.

36. Taylor, "Harriet Lane," p. 215.

37. Pryor, *Reminiscences*, p. 53.

38. Virginia Clay-Clopton, *A Belle of the Fifties* (New York, 1904), p. 114.

39. Pryor, *Reminiscences*, p. 39.

40. Pryor, *Reminiscences*, p. 53.

41. Taylor, "Harriet Lane," p. 219.

42. Taylor, "Harriet Lane," p. 218.

43. Edward T. James et al., eds., *Notable American Women*, 3 vols. (Cambridge, 1971), vol. 2, p. 281.

44. Taylor, "Harriet Lane," p. 215.

45. Taylor, "Harriet Lane," p. 219.

46. Taylor, "Harriet Lane," p. 213.

47. James Thomas Flexner, *George Washington and the New Nation* (Boston, 1969), p. 100.

48. Peter Shaw, *The Character of John Adams* (Chapel Hill, 1976), p. 258.

49. Maude Wilder Goodwin, *Dolly Madison* (New York, 1896), p. 109.

50. Freeman Cleaves, *Old Tippecanoe* (New York, 1939), p. 324.

51. Bess Furman, *White House Profile* (New York, 1951), p. 123.

52. Lyon Gardiner Tyler, *Letters and Times of the Tylers*, 2 vols. (Richmond, 1884–1885), vol. 2, p. 361.

53. Helen Stone Peterson, "First Lady at 22," *Virginia Cavalcade* (1961–1962), p. 14.

54. Elizabeth Tyler Coleman, *Priscilla Cooper Tyler and the American Scene* (University of Alabama, 1955), p. 102.

55. Peterson, "First Lady at 22," p. 15.

56. Coleman, *Priscilla Cooper Tyler*, p. 89.

57. Peterson, "First Lady at 22," p. 18.

58. Coleman, *Priscilla Cooper Tyler*, p. 104.

59. Jessie Benton Frémont, *Souvenirs of My Time* (Boston, 1887), pp. 99–100.

60. Frémont, *Souvenirs of My Time*, p. 99.

61. Holman Hamilton, *Zachary Taylor*, 2 vols. (Indianapolis, 1941–1961), vol. 2, p. 24.

62. Hamilton, *Zachary Taylor*, vol. 2, pp. 171–172.

63. Benjamin Perley Poore, *Perley's Reminiscences*, 2 vols. (Philadelphia, 1886), vol. 1, p. 357.

64. "A 'Pipe-Dream' Pipe Story," *Literary Digest*, vol. 86 (August 1, 1925), p. 40.

65. "A 'Pipe-Dream' Pipe Story," p. 40.

66. "A 'Pipe-Dream' Pipe Story," p. 42.

67. Laura Langford Holloway, *The Ladies of the White House* (Philadelphia, 1881), p. 208.

68. Mary Ormsbee Whitton, *First First Ladies* (1948, New York; repr. Freeport, 1969), p. 242.

69. Poore, *Perley's Reminiscences*, vol. 2, p. 385.

70. Whitton, *First First Ladies*, p. 242, reports that in 1840 when Millard was a U.S. Congressman from New York, his constituents invited Abigail to address them. The author has been unable to verify this and Whitton gives no source.

71. Whitton, *First First Ladies*, p. 243.

72. F. H. Severance, ed., *Millard Fillmore Papers*, 2 vols. (Buffalo, 1907), vol. 2, p. 493.

73. Letter to author from Elizabeth F. Abel, Stillwater Town Historian, Stillwater, New York, quotes letter from Millard Fillmore to Abigail Fillmore, April 1, 1850. Letter is in Library at State University of New York at Oswego.

74. Elizabeth Fries Ellett, *Court Circles of the Republic* (Hartford, 1869), p. 437.

75. Ellett, *Court Circles*, p. 242.

76. Severance, ed., *Fillmore Papers*, vol. 2, p. 491.

77. Severance, ed., *Fillmore Papers*, vol. 2, p. 492.

78. The recent interest in women's history has resulted in new debate over the impact of industrialization on women's lives. For one introduction to the issues, see chapter 1 of Thomas Dublin, *Women at Work: The Transformation of Work and Community in Lowell, Massachusetts, 1816–1860* (New York, 1979). See also chapter 3, "Industrial Wage Earners and the Domestic Ideology," in Alice Kessler-Harris, *Out to Work: A History of Wage-Earning Women in the United States* (New York, 1982). Articles which remain important in understanding the impact of industrialization on women's lives include: Barbara Welter, "The Cult of True Womanhood: 1820–1860," *American Quarterly* (Summer 1966), pp. 151–174; Mary Beth Norton, "The Paradox of Women's Sphere,' " in Carol Ruth Berkin and Mary Beth Norton, eds., *Women of America: A History* (Boston, 1979), pp. 139–149; and Gerda Lerner, "The Lady and the Mill Girl: Changes in the Status of Women in the Age of Jackson, 1800–1840," *Midcontinent American Studies Journal*, vol. 10 (Spring 1969), pp. 5–14.

79. Kathryn Kish Sklar, *Catharine Beecher: A Study in American Domesticity* (New York, 1973), pp. 204–205.

80. Barbara Berg, *The Remembered Gate: Origins of American Feminism* (New York, 1978), p. 112.

81. Carl Degler, *At Odds: Women and the Family in America From the Revolution to the Present* (New York, 1980), pp. 18off.

82. Sklar, *Catharine Beecher*, p. 204, concludes that Beecher's "basic assumption was that female debility was a sign of some fundamental opposition between the needs of women and many of the conditions of American society." See also Carroll Smith-Rosenberg, "The Hysterical Woman: Sex Roles and Role Conflict in Nineteenth-Century America," in *Disorderly Conduct,* edited by Carroll Smith-Rosenberg (New York, 1985), pp. 197–216.

83. Sklar, *Catharine Beecher,* p. 205.

84. Sklar, *Catharine Beecher,* p. 205.

85. Susan Sontag, *Illness as Metaphor* (New York, 1972), pp. 28ff.

86. Isabella Lucy Bird, *The Englishwoman in America* (1856; repr. Madison, 1966), p. 362.

87. Sontag, *Illness as Metaphor* p. 28.

88. Roy F. Nichols, *Franklin Pierce* (Philadelphia, 1931), p. 78.

89. Nichols, *Franklin Pierce,* p. 81.

90. Nichols, *Franklin Pierce,* p. 93.

91. Nichols, *Franklin Pierce,* p. 94.

92. Lloyd C. Taylor, Jr., "A Wife for Mr. Pierce," *New England Quarterly,* vol. 28 (September 1955), p. 342.

93. Taylor, "A Wife for Mr. Pierce," p. 343.

94. Anne M. Means, *Amherst and Our Family Tree* (Boston, 1921), p. 258.

95. Taylor, "A Wife for Mr. Pierce," p. 259.

96. Pryor, *Reminiscences,* pp. 16f.

97. Journal of Elihu Burritt, March 1854. New Britain Public Library, New Britain, Connecticut.

98. Means, *Amherst and Our Family,* p. 255.

99. Elihu Burritt's Journal, March 1854.

100. Margaret Gray Blanton, Unpublished Manuscript, "Tennessee Johnson's Eliza," University of Tennessee Library, Knoxville, Tennessee, p. 8.

101. Thomas A. Bailey, *The American Pageant* (Lexington, 1966), p. 493.

102. James et al., eds., *Notable American Women*, vol. 2, p. 277.

103. Blanton, "Tennessee Johnson's Eliza," p. 11.

104. Blanton, "Tennessee Johnson's Eliza," pp. 14–15.

105. Robert L. Winston, *Andrew Johnson: Plebeian and Patriot* (New York, 1928), p. 293.

106. Margaret Gray Blanton found a double meaning in what others have concluded was a humble apology.

107. Singleton, *Story of the White House,* vol. 2, p. 108.

108. Blanton, "Tennessee Johnson's Eliza," pp. 12–14.

109. Blanton, "Tennessee Johnson's Eliza," p. 18.

110. Margaret Gray Blanton, Letter to Milton Lomask, June 14, 1961, University of Tennessee Library.

111. Margaret Gray Blanton, Letter to Milton Lomask, June 14, 1961, University of Tennessee Library.

Chapter 3

1. Allan Nevins, ed., *The Diary of John Quincy Adams* (New York, 1951), p. 574.

2. Charles Sellers, *James K. Polk,* 2 vols. (Princeton, 1957), vol. 1, p. 93.

3. Adelaide L. Fries, *Historical Sketch of Salem Female Academy* (Salem, 1902), pp. 3–11.

4. Anson and Fanny Nelson, *Memorials of Sarah Childress Polk* (New York, 1892), p. 68.

5. Barbara Welter, Hunter College Conference, City University of New York, December 4, 1982.

6. Letter from Sarah Polk to James Polk, March 29, 1843, Polk Papers, Library of Congress.

7. Letter from Sarah Polk to James Polk, April 17, 1843, Polk Papers, Library of Congress.

8. Letter from Sarah Polk to James Polk, May 3, 1843, Polk Papers, Library of Congress.

9. Letter from Sarah Polk to James Polk, April 17, 1843, Polk Papers, Library of Congress.

10. Letter from Sarah Polk to James Polk, April 17, 1843, Polk Papers, Library of Congress.

11. Letter from Sarah Polk to James Polk, March 29, 1843, Polk Papers, Library of Congress.

12. Letter from Sarah Polk to James Polk, March 29, 1843, Polk Papers, Library of Congress.

13. Sarah Agnes Wallace, ed., "Letters of Mrs. James K. Polk," *Tennessee Historical Quarterly,* vol. 11 (June 1952), p. 181.

14. Sellers, *James K. Polk,* vol. 1, p. 340.

15. A. V. Brown to Sarah Polk, January 14, 1844, Polk Papers, Library of Congress.

16. Nelson and Nelson, *Memorials,* p. 79.

17. This particular comment by Ferraro aroused considerable comment. See, for example, the review of her book in the *New York Times,* October 30, 1985.

18. Nelson and Nelson, *Memorials,* p. 78.

19. Henry Dilwood Gilpin to Martin Van Buren, February 24, 1845, Van Buren Papers, Library of Congress.

20. Sellers, *James K. Polk,* vol. 2, p. 193.

21. Sellers, *James K. Polk,* vol. 1, p. 143.

22. Nelson and Nelson, *Memorials,* p. 68.

23. Nelson and Nelson, *Memorials,* p. 39.

24. Nelson and Nelson, *Memorials,* p. 79.

25. Sellers, *James K. Polk,* vol. 1, p. 250.

26. Nelson and Nelson, *Memorials*, p. 110.

27. Sellers, *James K. Polk*, vol. 2, p. 192.

28. Sellers, *James K. Polk*, vol. 2, p. 307.

29. Allan Nevins, ed., *Diary of a President* (New York, 1952), p. 358.

30. Jessie Benton Frémont, *Souvenirs of My Time* (New York, 1887), p. 103.

31. Sellers, *James K. Polk*, vol. 2, p. 308.

32. Nelson and Nelson, *Memorials*, p. 113.

33. Nelson and Nelson, *Memorials*, p. 112.

34. Nelson and Nelson, *Memorials*, p. 118.

35. For representative treatments, see Thomas A. Bailey, *The American Pageant*, 4th ed. (Lexington, 1971), pp. 306–308; John A. Garraty, *The American Nation*, 2d ed. (New York, 1971), p. 373.

36. Edward T. James et al., eds., *Notable American Women*, 3 vols. (Cambridge, 1971), vol. 3, p. 82.

37. Katharine Shelburne Trickey, "Young Hickory and Sarah," *Daughters of American Revolution Magazine*, vol. 108 (1974), p. 433.

38. *New York Herald*, cited in Aileen S. Kraditor, *Up From the Pedestal* (Chicago, 1968), p. 189.

39. Alfred Balch to Martin Van Buren, November 22, 1842, Polk Papers, Library of Congress.

40. Nevins, ed., *Diary of a President*, p. 352.

41. John Spencer Bassett, *The Southern Plantation Overseer* (New York, 1925), p. 268.

42. *Peterson's Magazine*, March 1849, p. 91.

43. *New York Times*, August 15, 1891, p. 5.

44. Clipping from *Mt. Vernon Banner,* undated, Polk Papers, Library of Congress, reel 63.

45. Nelson and Nelson, *Memorials*, p. 282.

46. The main catalogue at the New York Public Library lists thirty-two works on the subject of "Mary Todd Lincoln." In addition to biographical treatments, the entries include fiction, such as "The Trial of Mary Todd Lincoln" by James A. Rhodes and Dean Jauchius (1952), and dramas, such as "The Woman in Lincoln's Life" by Louis A. Warren (1946). Most of the works were published after her death.

47. Alfred Joseph Dumais, in "An Analysis of the Dramaturgical Use of History in the Writing of Two Full Length Plays about Mary Todd Lincoln" (Unpublished Ph.D. Dissertation, New York University, 1978), explores this problem.

48. Ruth Painter Randall, *Mary Lincoln: Biography of a Marriage* (Boston, 1953), p. 215.

49. Elizabeth Keckley, *Behind the Scenes* (New York, 1868), p. 96. Although there is considerable controversy about this book, it indicates the kind of material being published about Mary Lincoln in the 1860s. For one account of its being written, see Mark E. Neely, Jr., *The Abraham Lincoln Encyclopedia* (New York, 1982), p. 172.

50. Katharine Helm, *Mary, Wife of Lincoln* (New York, 1928), p. 17.

51. Helm, *Mary, Wife of Lincoln*, pp. 28–32.

52. Helm, *Mary, Wife of Lincoln*, p. 52.

53. Helm, *Mary, Wife of Lincoln* p. 32.

54. W. A. Evans, *Mrs. Abraham Lincoln* (New York, 1932), p. 35.

55. Helm, *Mary, Wife of Lincoln*, p. 44.

56. Ruth Painter Randall and Ishbel Ross have both written that Stephen Douglas courted Mary Lincoln, but Mark E. Neely, Jr., Director of the Louis A. Warren Lincoln

Library and Museum, Fort Wayne, Indiana, considers this "hearsay which . . . merits little serious consideration." Letter to author, October 2, 1985.

57. Alexander McClure, ed., *Lincoln's Yarns and Stories* (Chicago, n.d.), pp. 301–302.

58. Helm, *Mary, Wife of Lincoln,* emphasizes the intellectual side, while W. A. Evans, *Mrs. Abraham Lincoln,* shows Mary as manipulative, weak, and ill during the 1850s.

59. Julia Taft Bayne, *Tad Lincoln's Father* (Boston, 1931), p. 36.

60. For an account of the accusation supposedly made by Weed, see Neely, *Abraham Lincoln Encyclopedia,* p. 328.

61. Emanuel Hertz, *Abraham Lincoln: A New Portrait,* 2 vols. (New York, 1931), vol. 1, pp. 238–239, gave one account of Lincoln's appearance. Paul F. Boller, Jr., in *Presidential Anecdotes* (New York, 1981), p. 137, repeated the story although Mark E. Neely, Jr., had demonstrated that it could not have been true. See *Lincoln Lore* (January 1975).

62. Keckley, *Behind the Scenes,* p. 149.

63. Bess Furman, *White House Profile* (Indianapolis, 1951), pp. 173ff.

64. *Leslie's Weekly,* February 15, 1862, quotes a Washington newspaper.

65. *Leslie's Weekly,* February 22, 1862, p. 1.

66. Bayne, *Tad Lincoln's Father,* p. 49.

67. Bayne, *Tad Lincoln's Father,* p. 49.

68. Keckley, *Behind the Scenes,* p. 87.

69. John M. Simon, ed., *The Personal Memoirs of Julia Dent Grant* (New York, 1975), p. 146.

70. Keckley, *Behind the Scenes,* p. 149.

71. Furman, *White House Profile,* pp. 189–190. See also Neely, *Abraham Lincoln Encyclopedia,* p. 172.

72. Elizabeth Todd Grimsley, "Six Months at the White House," *Journal of Illinois State Historical Society,* vol. 10 (October–January, 1926–1927), p. 69.

73. William H. Crook, *Memories of the White House: The Home Life of Our Presidents from Lincoln to Roosevelt* (Boston, 1911), p. 17.

74. Grimsley, "Six Months," p. 55.

75. Grimsley, "Six Months," p. 48.

76. Randall, *Mary Lincoln,* p. 219.

77. Bayne, *Tad Lincoln's Father,* p. 7.

78. Bayne, *Tad Lincoln's Father,* p. 107.

79. Neely, *Abraham Lincoln Encyclopedia,* p. 184.

80. Handwritten memorandum to Judge David Davis, May 24, 1875, Chicago Historical Society. A witness described Mary Lincoln as behaving "like a lady" throughout the ordeal.

81. Rodney Ross, "Mary Todd Lincoln: Patient at Bellevue Place, Batavia," *Journal of Illinois State Historical Society,* vol. 63 (1970), pp. 8–9.

82. Ross, "Mary Todd Lincoln," p. 33.

83. Ross, "Mary Todd Lincoln," p. 14. Ross notes that Bradwell voiced contradictory assessments of Mary Lincoln's mental state.

84. Ross, "Mary Todd Lincoln," p. 14.

85. Sarah Bernhardt, *Memoirs of My Life* (New York, 1907), p. 370.

86. Henry Steele Commager, *New York Times,* February 12, 1985, p. A14. For a later and considerably more favorable view of Mary Todd Lincoln, see Doris Kearns Goodwin, *Team of Rivals: The Political Genius of Abraham Lincoln* (New York, 2005).

87. *New York Times,* March 5, 1869, p. 3.

88. Simon, ed., *Personal Memoirs,* p. 128.

89. Jesse R. Grant, *In the Days of My Father* (New York, 1925), p. 97.

90. Simon, ed., *Personal Memoirs*, p. 183.

91. Simon, ed., *Personal Memoirs*, p. 173.

92. Simon, ed., *Personal Memoirs*, p. 186.

93. Louis T. Palmer, *General U. S. Grant's Tour Around the World* (Hartford, 1879), gives a full account of the journey.

94. Joseph Nathan Kane, *Facts About the Presidents*, 4th ed. (New York, 1981), p. 128.

95. Simon, ed., *Personal Memoirs*, p. 182.

96. Simon, ed., *Personal Memoirs*, p. 186.

97. Simon, ed., *Personal Memoirs*, p. 199.

98. Simon, ed., *Personal Memoirs*, p. 199.

99. Simon, ed., *Personal Memoirs*, p. 184.

100. Simon, ed., *Personal Memoirs*, p. 174.

101. See chapter 11, "Presidential Wives and the Press," from earlier editions of this book.

Chapter 4

1. Emily Apt Geer, *First Lady: The Life of Lucy Webb Hayes* (Kent State University, 1984), p. 137.

2. Carl Degler, *At Odds: Women and the Family in America from the Revolution to the Present* (New York, 1980), p. 152. Mary Beth Norton, *Liberty's Daughters* (Boston, 1980), p. 241, notes that the trend had begun earlier.

3. Barbara Harris, *Beyond Her Sphere: Women and the Professions in American History* (Westport, 1978), p. 112.

4. Edward T. James et al., eds., *Notable American Women*, 3 vols. (Cambridge, 1971), vol. 3, pp. 450–451.

5. James B. Pond, *Eccentricities of Genius* (New York, 1900), p. 155.

6. Mary A. Livermore, *The Story of My Life* (Hartford, 1897), pp. 483–484.

7. Mary I. Wood, *The History of the General Federation of Women's Clubs* (Norwood, Massachusetts, 1912), p. 27.

8. Frances Willard, *Home Protection Manual* (New York, 1879), p. 6.

9. William Rhinelander Steward, *The Philanthropic Work of Josephine Shaw Lowell* (New York, 1911), p. 52.

10. Mary Clemmer Ames, "A Woman's Letter from Washington," *The Independent*, March 15, 1877, p. 2.

11. Geer, *First Lady*, p. 4.

12. Geer, *First Lady*, p. 98.

13. Emily Apt Geer, "Lucy Webb Hayes and Her Influence Upon Her Era," *Hayes Historical Journal*, vol. 1 (1976), p. 25.

14. Geer, "Lucy Webb Hayes and Her Influence," p. 25.

15. Geer, *First Lady*, p. 168.

16. On Lucy's uncle, see Richard A. Manuel, "Matthew Scott Cook: A Register of the Papers," Western Reserve Historical Society, Ms. no. 2129. Rutherford's sister Fanny, who had been a strong feminist influence on Lucy, died in 1856 about the time Rutherford ran for his first elective office.

17. Geer, *First Lady*, pp. 35–36.

18. Harry Barnard, *Rutherford B. Hayes and His America* (Indianapolis, 1954), p. 214.

19. Geer, *First Lady*, p. 64.

20. Charles Richard Williams, *The Life of Rutherford Birchard Hayes*, 2 vols. (Boston, 1914), vol. 1, p. 208.

21. Margarita Spalding Gerry, "Rutherford B. Hayes in the White House," *Century*, vol. 77 (March 1909), p. 648.

22. Geer, *First Lady*, pp. 57–59.

23. Geer, *First Lady*, p. 86.

24. Rutherford B. Hayes, *Diary and Letters of Rutherford B. Hayes*, ed. Charles Richard Williams, 5, vols. (Columbus, Ohio, 1922–1926), entry for February 4, 1866.

25. Geer, *First Lady*, pp. 95–97.

26. Emily Apt Geer, "Lucy Webb Hayes and Her Family," *Ohio History*, vol. 77 (1968), p. 49.

27. Geer, "Lucy Webb Hayes and Her Family," p. 47.

28. Geer, "Lucy Webb Hayes and Her Influence," p. 27.

29. Geer, "Lucy Webb Hayes and Her Influence," p. 27.

30. Since March 4 fell on Sunday, a private inauguration had taken place at the White House on Saturday evening, March 3. For details, see Webb Hayes and Watt P. Marchman, "First Days of the Hayes Administration," *Hayes Historical Journal*, vol. 1 (1977), pp. 231–262.

31. Williams, *Life of Rutherford B. Hayes*, vol. 2, p. 299.

32. Williams, *Life of Rutherford B. Hayes*, vol. 2, p. 307.

33. Geer, "Lucy Webb Hayes and Her Family," p. 56.

34. William Henry Crook, *Memories of the White House* (Boston, 1911), p. 112.

35. Laurel Thatcher Ulrich, *Good Wives* (New York, 1980), p. 3.

36. Williams, *Life of Rutherford B. Hayes*, vol. 2, p. 300.

37. Marcus Cunliffe, *American Presidents and the Presidency* (New York, 1968), p. 201.

38. Williams, *Life of Rutherford B. Hayes*, vol. 2, p. 316.

39. Hayes, *Diary and Letters*, May 28, 1879.

40. Henry James, *The Henry James Reader*, ed. Leon Edel (New York, 1965), p. 484.

41. Henry Adams, *Democracy* (1880; repr. Gloucester, Massachusetts, 1965), p. 107. Henry Adams's authorship was not acknowledged until the 1920s although he wrote *Democracy* in 1878.

42. Barnard, *Rutherford B. Hayes*, p. 171.

43. Barnard, *Rutherford B. Hayes*, p. 170.

44. Hayes, *Diary and Letters*, February 28, 1879.

45. Hayes, *Diary and Letters*, January 16, 1881.

46. Geer, *First Lady*, p. 184.

47. Emily Apt Geer to author, December 1, 1985. Geer kindly shared her conclusions with the author and quoted Rutherford B. Hayes's letter of December 13, 1883. This occurred after the Hayes administration ended, but Lucy's endorsement would have been valuable to Willard.

48. Ben Perley Poore, *Perly's Reminiscences*, 2 vols. (Philadelphia, 1886), vol. 2, p. 350.

49. H. J. Eckenrode, *Rutherford B. Hayes: Statesman of Reunion* (New York, 1930), p. 46, concluded that Lucy took the rap for her husband.

50. Mrs. John Davis, *Lucy Webb Hayes, A Memorial Sketch* (Cincinnati, 1890), p. 37. Emphasis added.

51. "Nellie Bly Visits Spiegel Grove," *Hayes Historical Journal*, vol. 1 (1976), p. 144.

52. Bess Furman, *White House Profile* (Indianapolis, 1951), p. 224.

53. Beverly Beeton, "The Hayes Administration and The Woman Question," *Hayes Historical Journal*, vol. 2 (1978), p. 52.

54. Elizabeth Davis to Mrs. Rutherford B. Hayes, December 9, 1878. Letter in Elizabeth Davis Collection, Latter Day Saints Church Archives, Salt Lake City. The salutation on the letter was "Dear Lady," and Elizabeth Davis wrote: "Having been informed through friends of the goodness of your heart and your sympathetic nature toward those of your sex, who appeal to you for aid, I determined to approach you by letter in behalf of myself and sisters, who like yourself have availed themselves of the privileges, granted us by the glorious Constitution of our country, viz. the 'right to worship God, according to the dictates of our own conscience.'" The writer then asked Lucy to help protect "plural or Celestial order of Marriage." Quoted by permission of the Latter Day Saints Church Archives.

55. Laura Langford Holloway, *The Ladies of the White House* (Philadelphia, 1881), p. 629. Originally published in 1869, this book was enlarged to include the Hayes and Garfield administrations and republished in 1881.

56. Holloway, *Ladies of the White House,* p. 662.

57. Harry J. Brown, ed., *Diary of James A. Garfield,* 4 vols. (East Lansing, 1967–1981), vol. 1, p. 160.

58. Garfield, *Diary and Letters,* vol. 1, p. 234.

59. Garfield, *Diary and Letters,* vol. 1, p. 271.

60. James A. Garfield Papers, Library of Congress; microfilm reel 5 contains letters from November 16, 1853 to November 23, 1862.

61. Lucretia Rudolph to James Garfield, August 19, 1858, James A. Garfield Papers, Library of Congress.

62. Lucretia Garfield to James Garfield, March 18, 1860, James A. Garfield Papers, Library of Congress.

63. Lucretia Garfield to James Garfield, March 18, 1860, James A. Garfield Papers, Library of Congress.

64. James Garfield to Lucretia Garfield, December 26, 1862, James A. Garfield Papers, Library of Congress.

65. Margaret Bassett, *Profiles and Portraits of American Presidents and Their Wives* (Freeport, 1969), p. 195.

66. Theodore Clarke Smith, *James Abram Garfield: Life and Letters,* 2 vols. (New Haven, 1925), vol. 2, p. 755. For an entirely different explanation of why the Garfields became more compatible, see Margaret Leech and Harry J. Brown, *The Garfield Orbit* (New York, 1978), p. 121.

67. Allan Peskin, *Garfield* (Kent State, 1978), p. 347.

68. Peskin, *Garfield,* p. 348.

69. Peskin, *Garfield,* p. 348.

70. *Biographical Sketches of James A. Garfield and Chester Arthur,* published by the Republican Party, 1880, p. 6.

71. Smith, *James A. Garfield,* vol. 2, p. 1187.

72. Albeit P. Marble, "Directions to Teachers on the Exercises Commemorative of Garfield" (Worcester, 1881).

73. James et al., eds., *Notable American Women,* vol. 2, p. 18.

74. Lady Bird Johnson, *A White House Diary* (New York, 1970), p. 6.

75. Brown, ed., *Diary of James A. Garfield,* vol. 4, p. 635. Lucretia's White House diary is published at the end of vol. 4.

76. Brown, ed., *Diary of James A. Garfield,* vol. 4, 630.

77. Brown, ed., *Diary of James A. Garfield,* vol. 4, p. 636.

78. James Garfield to Elizabeth Stanton, January 9, 1872, James A. Garfield Papers, Library of Congress.

79. James Garfield to "Brother Erret," January 18, 1872, James A. Garfield Papers, Library of Congress.

80. Brown, ed., *Diary of James A. Garfield*, vol. 3, p. 64.

81. Brown, ed., *Diary of James A. Garfield*, vol. 3, p. 64.

82. Brown, ed., *Diary of James A. Garfield*, vol. 3. p. 64.

83. See introduction to James A. Garfield Papers, microfilm ed., Library of Congress. Series 3 includes letters between Lucretia and James.

84. Sarah Agnes Pryor, *Reminiscences of Peace and War* (New York, 1904), p. 83.

85. Giraud Chester, *Embattled Maiden* (New York, 1951), p. 40. See Betty Boyd Caroli, "Women Speak Out on Reform," in *The Rhetoric of Protest and Reform, 1878–1898*, ed. Paul H. Boase (Athens, Ohio, 1980), pp. 214–217.

86. Chester, *Embattled Maiden*, p. 154.

87. Amy La Follette Jensen, *The White House and Its Thirty-Three Families* (New York, 1958), p. 129.

88. Jensen, *White House*, p. 128.

89. *New York Times*, November 27, 1918, p. 13; A Sermon Preached to the Colonial Dames of the State of New York at Grace Church (New York City) on January 26, 1919 by Charles Lewis Slattery, D.D.

90. *New York Times*, January 10, 1886, p. 1, and February 20, 1886, p. 1.

91. *New York Times*, August 17, 1885, p. 3.

92. Furman, *White House Profile*, p. 240.

93. Furman, *White House Profile*, p. 245.

94. Frances Cleveland did not receive a high rating from historians in the 1980s (see Appendix II), but her popularity extended through the 1920s. See *Good Housekeeping* (February, 1932), p. 18.

95. Furman, *White House Profile*, p. 242.

96. Furman, *White House Profile*, p. 242.

97. Allan Nevins, *Grover Cleveland* (New York, 1932), p. 312.

98. Nevins, *Grover Cleveland*, p. 308.

99. Robert McElroy, *Grover Cleveland*, 2 vols. (New York, 1923), vol. 1, p. 286.

100. *New York Times*, October 30, 1917.

101. Harriet McIntire Foster, *Mrs. Benjamin Harrison* (Indianapolis, 1908), p. 14.

102. Frank G. Carpenter, *Carp's Washington* (New York, 1960), p. 301.

103. James et al., *Notable American Women*, vol. 2, pp. 145–146.

104. Jensen, *White House*, p. 139.

105. Jensen, *White House*, p. 139.

106. Emily Holt, "Household Economy," *Good Housekeeping*, vol. 36 (June 1903), p. 546.

107. Ophia Smith, "Caroline Scott Harrison," *National Historical Magazine*, vol. 75 (April, 1941), p. 4; Olive Flower, *History of Oxford College for Women* (Miami, 1949), p. 258.

108. "After College," *Good Housekeeping* (June 1903), p. 508.

109. Review of *Woman Who Toils* in *Good Housekeeping* (June 1903), p. 510.

110. *Ladies' Home Journal* (March 1887), p. 13.

111. *Good Housekeeping* (June 1903), p. 509. Barbara Welter has documented that domesticity formed part of the "cult of true womanhood" in the antebellum period. (See *American Quarterly*, Summer 1966, pp. 151–174.) Presidents' wives had not yet become prominent national figures.

112. Carpenter, *Carp's Washington*, p. 302. Caroline Harrison also had the assistance of several women relatives. After her death, one of them, her niece, Mary Dimmick, married Benjamin Harrison.

113. Alan M. Chesney, *The Johns Hopkins Hospital,* 3 vols. (Baltimore, 1943–1963), vol. 1, pp. 193–196.

114. Bassett, *Profiles and Portraits,* p. 235.

115. Joseph Hartzell, *Sketch of Mrs. William McKinley* (Washington, D.C., 1896), p. 1.

116. *New York Times,* May 27, 1907, p. 1.

117. Margaret Leech, *In the Days of McKinley* (New York, 1959), p. 15.

118. Leech, *In the Days of McKinley,* p. 15.

119. For two very different accounts of Ida's behavior and the explanation for it, see Leech, *In the Days of McKinley,* and Wayne Morgan, *William McKinley and His America* (Syracuse, 1963).

120. John A. Kasson, "Impressions of President McKinley," *Century* (December 1901), p. 268.

121. "The Good Natured Presidency," *Nation,* vol. 72 (March 7, 1901), p. 188. For a considerably more positive view of the McKinley presidency, see Lewis L. Gould, *The Presidency of William McKinley* (Lawrence, KS, 1980). Gould concludes that William McKinley was "the first modern president" because he formalized relations with the press, brought experts and academics into government, and traveled a great deal.

122. Leech, *In the Days of McKinley,* p. 456.

123. Ellen Maury Slayden, *Washington Wife: Journal of Ellen Maury Slayden from 1897–1919* (New York, 1962), p. 8. Slayden's entry is for May 6, 1897, near the beginning of the first McKinley administration.

124. Bassett, *Profiles and Portraits,* p. 238.

125. William Jennings Bryan, *Memoirs* (Chicago, 1925), p. 302.

126. *Washington Post,* March 20, 1892. Cited in Paxton Hibben, *The Peerless Leader* (New York, 1929), p. 138.

127. Hibben, *Peerless Leader,* p. 129.

128. Louis Koenig, *Bryan: A Political Biography* (New York, 1971), p. 236.

129. Barbara Sicherman et al., eds., *Notable American Women: The Modern Period* (Cambridge, 1980), p. 138. Ruth Bryan is listed as Ruth Bryan Owen Rohde.

130. Bryan, *Memoirs,* p. 451.

131. Paolo E. Coletta, "Won, 1880—One 1884: The Courtship of William Jennings Bryan and Mary Elizabeth Baird," *Illinois State Historical Society Journal,* vol. 50 (Autumn 1957), p. 236.

132. Coletta, "Won," p. 240.

133. Koenig, *Bryan,* p. 95.

134. *Harper's Bazaar,* vol. 33 (August 11, 1900), pp. 954–956.

135. Frances Wright Saunders, *Ellen Axson Wilson: First Lady Between Two Worlds* (Chapel Hill, 1985), p. 214.

136. Koenig, *Bryan,* p. 596.

137. Sicherman et al., *Notable American Women,* pp. 591–592.

Chapter 5

1. Alice Roosevelt Longworth, *Crowded Hours: Reminiscences of Alice Roosevelt Longworth* (New York, 1933), p. 158.

2. Helen Herron Taft, *Recollections of Full Years* (New York, 1914), p. 351.

3. Amy La Follette Jensen, *The White House and Its Thirty-Three Families* (New York, 1958). Pages 190 and 194 show two contrasting portraits.

4. Carleton Putnam, *Theodore Roosevelt,* 2 vols. (New York, 1958), vol. 1, pp. 170–171; Henry F. Pringle, *The Life and Times of William Howard Taft,* 2 vols. (New York, 1939), vol. 1, p. 107.

5. Hermann Hagedorn, *The Roosevelt Family of Sagamore Hill* (New York, 1955), p. 10.

6. Hagedorn, *Roosevelt Family*, p. 82.

7. Jacob A. Riis, "Mrs. Roosevelt and Her Children," *Ladies' Home Journal*, vol. 19 (August 1902), p. 5.

8. Riis, "Mrs. Roosevelt and Her Children," p. 6.

9. *McClure's* (July 1905); *Harper's Bazaar* (May 1901); *Harper's Weekly* (March 9, 1901); *Review of Reviews* (July 1904).

10. *Harper's Weekly* (March 9, 1901); *Review of Reviews* (July 1904); *Harper's Bazaar* (May 1904); *Current Literature* (September 1907); *Ladies' Home Journal* (August 1902).

11. Mabel Potter Daggett, "Mrs. Roosevelt: The Woman in the Background," *Delineator* (March 1909), p. 394.

12. Jensen, *White House*, pp. 185–187.

13. Archibald W. Butt, *The Letters of Archie Butt*, ed. Lawrence F. Abbott (Garden City, NY, 1924), p. 53.

14. Lady Bird Johnson, *A White House Diary* (New York, 1970), p, 263.

15. Taft, *Recollections*, p. 281.

16. *Harper's Bazaar* (February 1908), p. 158.

17. Butt, *Letters*, p. 299, reports that Edith delegated to Butt the task of conveying the message to the woman named.

18. Jensen, *White House*, p, 191.

19. Helen McCarthy, "Why Mrs. Roosevelt Has Not Broken Down," *Ladies' Home Journal* (October 25, 1908), p. 25.

20. Sylvia Jukes Morris, *Edith Roosevelt: Portrait of a First Lady* (New York, 1980), p. 277.

21. Butt, *Letters*, p. 238.

22. Butt, *Letters*, p. 127.

23. Morris, *Edith Roosevelt*, p. 172.

24. Butt, *Letters*, p. 83.

25. Edward T. James et al., *Notable American Women*, 3 vols. (Cambridge, 1970), vol. 3, p. 193.

26. Mrs. Theodore Roosevelt, Jr., *Day Before Yesterday: Reminiscences of Mrs. Theodore Roosevelt, Jr.* (Garden City, 1959), p. 301.

27. Edith Kermit Roosevelt and Kermit Roosevelt, *American Backlogs: The Story of Gertrude Tyler and Her Family, 1660–1860* (New York, 1928).

28. Mrs. Theodore Roosevelt, Sr., Mrs. Kermit Roosevelt, Richard Derby, and Kermit Roosevelt, *Cleared for Strange Ports* (New York, 1927), p. 5.

29. Diary of Helen Herron, *Papers of William Howard Taft*, Library of Congress, Series II, reel 609, vol. 16, entry for September 3, 1883. Referred to hereafter as diary of Helen Herron.

30. Diary of Helen Herron, September 3, 1883.

31. Diary of Helen Herron, October 6, 1883.

32. Diary of Helen Herron, September 5, 1879. For more about the options open to young Nellie Herron, see Carl Sferrazza Anthony, *Nellie Taft: The Unconventional First Lady of the Ragtime Era* (New York, 2005), 33–58.

33. Taft, *Recollections*, p. 10.

34. Taft, *Recollections*, p. 10.

35. Papers of William H. Taft, Library of Congress. William's first letter to Helen is in Series II (1879–1885), reel 609, dated April 19, 1882 and addressed to "My dear Miss Herron."

36. Letter of April 29, 1884, Papers of William H. Taft.

37. Letter of October 11, 1884, Papers of William H. Taft.

38. Letter of June 17, 1885, Papers of William H. Taft.

39. Taft, *Recollections*, p. 20.

40. George E. Mowry, *Theodore Roosevelt and the Progressive Era* (New York, 1958), p. 234.

41. Judith Icke Anderson, *William Howard Taft: An Intimate Biography* (New York, 1981), p. 48.

42. Henry F. Pringle, *Life and Times of William Howard Taft*, 2 vols. (New York, 1939), vol. 1, p. 160.

43. Taft, *Recollections*, p. 30.

44. Taft, *Recollections*, p. 33.

45. For a full discussion of how Helen Taft used her White House years to showcase American music and performers, see Lewis L. Gould, *Helen Taft: Our Musical First Lady* (Lawrence, KS, 2010).

46. Taft, *Recollections*, p. 233.

47. Anderson, *William H. Taft*, p. 85.

48. Taft, *Recollections*, p. 280.

49. Henry F. Pringle, *Theodore Roosevelt, A Biography* (New York, 1931), p. 259.

50. Pringle, *Life and Times of William Howard Taft*, vol. 1, p. 315. Helen Taft skips the details of her appointment with the president (although it is documented in many other places), but she makes no secret of her disdain for the "fixed groove" of judicial life. See *Recollections*, p. 263.

51. Anderson, *William Howard Taft*, p. 111.

52. Taft, *Recollections*, p. 324.

53. Butt, *Letters*, p. 362.

54. Irwin Hood Hoover, *Forty-Two Years in the While House* (Boston, 1934), p. 40.

55. Taft, *Recollections*, p. 331.

56. Taft, *Recollections*, p. 332.

57. Lillian Rogers Parks and Frances S. Leighton, *It Was Fun Working at the White House* (New York, 1969), p. 26. Lillian Parks reports her mother's recollection of inauguration day in 1909, but it should be noted that the book was published well after Richard Nixon's famous comment about not being "kicked around." However, Irwin Hoover, *Forty-Two Years in the White House,* was published well ahead of Nixon (1934), and on p. 45, Hoover gives a similar report of Taft's statement.

58. *New York Times,* May 18, 1909, p. 1; July 30, 1909, p. 1.

59. Anderson, *William Howard Taft*, p. 166.

60. Pringle, *William Howard Taft*, vol. 2, p. 603.

61. George Griswold Hill, "The Wife of the New President," *Ladies' Home Journal* (March 1909), p. 6.

62. Taft, *Recollections*, p. 365.

63. Butt, *Letters*, p. 362.

64. Butt, *Letters*, p. 623.

65. Taft, *Recollections*, p. 349.

66. Elizabeth Jaffray, *Secrets of the White House* (New York, 1927), p. 7.

67. Ellen Maury Slayden, *Washington Wife: Journal of Ellen Maury Slayden, 1897–1919* (New York, 1962), pp. 156–157.

68. Pringle, *Life and Times of William Howard Taft*, vol. 2, p. 1076, cites a letter from a Washington jeweler who advised against changing the monogram because the piece would be ruined.

69. Papers of William H. Taft, July 8, 1895, Series II, reel 24.

70. Stanley Kutler, biographical entry for Helen Herron Taft in *Notable American Women*, vol. 3, p. 420.

71. Anderson, *William Howard Taft*, pp. 161–164.

72. George Griswold Hill, "The Wife of the New President," *Ladies' Home Journal* (March 1907), p. 7.

73. Butt, *Letters*, p. 234.

74. Theodore Roosevelt, *An Autobiography* (New York, 1924), p. 357.

75. Archibald Butt, *Taft and Roosevelt* (New York, 1930), p. 436.

76. Pringle, *Life and Times of William Howard Taft*, vol. 2, p. 622.

77. Eleanor Wilson McAdoo, *The Woodrow Wilsons* (New York, 1937), p. 50.

78. Frances Wright Saunders, *Ellen Axson Wilson: First Lady Between Two Worlds* (Chapel Hill, 1985), p. 18.

79. Saunders, *Ellen Axson Wilson*, p. 15.

80. Arthur Link, biographical entry for Ellen Axson Wilson in *Notable American Women*, vol. 3, p. 627.

81. The League had originated in a student rebellion against the National Academy of Design and although the League quickly achieved a reputation as a serious place to study, it lacked the prestige of the Academy. See Michael E. Landgren, *Years of Art* (New York, 1940), *passim*.

82. On admission of women to study at art schools in the United States, see Charlotte Streiffer Rubinstein, *American Women Artists: From Early Indian Times To the Present* (Boston, 1982), p. 441.

83. Ellen Axson lived only three blocks from the League's studios at 38 West Fourteenth Street. The student body numbered 500, and the faculty included, by the year she left, George De Forest Brush and Thomas Eakins. See Landgren, *Years of Art*, p. 46.

84. Eleanor Wilson McAddo, *The Priceless Gift* (New York, 1962), p. 88.

85. McAdoo, *Priceless Gift*, p. 122.

86. McAdoo, *Priceless Gift*, p. 122.

87. McAdoo, *Priceless Gift*, p. 122.

88. Rubinstein, *American Women Artists*, p. 89.

89. Cornelia Crow Carr, *Harriet Hosmer: Letters and Memories* (New York, 1912), p. 35. I am indebted to Enid Bell, the sculptor, for information on Harriet Hosmer and other women artists of the nineteenth century.

90. Saunders, *Ellen Axson Wilson*, p. 79.

91. McAdoo, *Priceless Gift*, p. 81. See *Papers of Woodrow Wilson*, vol. 3, p. 494, for text of letter of October 31, 1884.

92. Arthur S. Link et al., eds., *The Papers of Woodrow Wilson*, 53 vols. (Princeton, 1966–1986), vol. 3, p. 494, gives text of letter of November 28, 1884.

93. John A. Garraty, *Woodrow Wilson* (New York, 1956), p. 16.

94. Carl F. Price, *Wesleyan's First Century* (Middleton, 1932), pp. 161–162.

95. Saunders, *Ellen Axson Wilson*, p. 70.

96. Saunders, *Ellen Axson Wilson*, p. 89.

97. McAdoo, *Priceless Gift*, p. 181.

98. Saunders, *Ellen Axson Wilson*, *passim*, esp. p. 147.

99. Saunders, *Ellen Axson Wilson*, p. 110.

100. Saunders, *Ellen Axson Wilson*, pp. 188, 201–202.

101. Saunders, *Ellen Axson Wilson*, p. 201.

102. McAdoo, *Priceless Gift*, p. 256. Frances Wright Saunders, in letters to the author, pointed out that Woodrow would not have approved of coeducational schools for his daughters and that Goucher did have a Phi Beta Kappa chapter.

103. Hester E. Hosford, "New Ladies of the White House," *The Independent,* vol. 73 (November 21, 1912), pp. 1159–1165.

104. Slayden, *Washington Wife,* pp. 224–225.

105. *Ladies' Home Journal,* vol. 30 (May 1913), pp. 18–19.

106. Mabel Potter Daggett, "Woodrow Wilson's Wife," *Good Housekeeping,* vol. 56 (March 1913), pp. 316–323.

107. "New Mistress of the White House," *Current Opinion* (March 1913), pp. 195–196

108. Daggett, "Woodrow Wilson's Wife," p. 320.

109. Frances McGregor Gordon, "The Tact of Mrs. Woodrow Wilson," *Collier's,* vol. 50 (March 8, 1913), p. 13, gives a contemporary account. For historians' evaluations, see Saunders, *Ellen Axson Wilson,* pp. 214–215. Bryan's motives at the 1912 Democratic convention remain the subject of much speculation. See George E. Mowry, "Election of 1912," Arthur M. Schlesinger, Jr., et al., eds., *History of American Presidential Elections,* 4 vols. (New York, 1971), vol. 3, pp. 2150–2151.

110. Daggett, "Woodrow Wilson's Wife," p. 322.

111. Mrs. Ernest P. Bicknell, "The Home-Maker of the White House," *Survey,* vol. 33 (October 3, 1914), p. 19.

112. Parks and Leighton, *It Was Fun,* p. 36.

113. Arthur S. Link, *Wilson: The New Freedom* (Princeton, 1956), pp. 247–249.

114. Bicknell, "Home-Maker," p. 20.

115. McAdoo, *Woodrow Wilsons,* p. 201.

116. McAdoo, *Woodrow Wilsons,* p. 201.

117. *New York Times,* August 7, 1914, p. 1; September 15, 1914, p. 10.

118. McAdoo, *Woodrow Wilsons,* p. 247. No president since John Adams had addressed Congress in person.

119. Edith Bolling Wilson, *My Memoir* (New York, 1939), p. 38. This autobiography has been judged unreliable in many areas, and Edith herself gave contradictory accounts of events, as, for example, her first meeting with Woodrow.

120. Wilson, *My Memoir,* p. 33.

121. Wilson, *My Memoir,* p. 18.

122. Arthur S. Link, biographical entry for Edith Boiling Galt Wilson, in Sicherman et al., eds., *Notable American Women: The Modern Period,* p. 740.

123. Papers of Woodrow Wilson, Library of Congress, reel 71.

124. Wilson, *My Memoir,* p. 146.

125. Jaffray, *Secrets of the White House,* p. 58.

126. *New York Times,* March 5, 1913, p. 8.

127. Wilson, *My Memoir,* p. 125.

128. *New York Times,* July 10, 1977, p. 42.

129. Alden Hatch, *Edith Bolling Wilson: First Lady Extraordinary* (New York, 1961), p. 80.

130. *New York Times,* January 10, 1918, p. 1; Sally Hunter Graham, "Woodrow Wilson, Alice Paul, and the Woman Suffrage Movement," *Political Science Quarterly,* vol. 98 (Winter 1983–84), pp. 665–679, presents evidence showing a gradual shift in the president's position.

131. *New York Times,* January 9, 1918, p. 12.

132. Charles A. Selden, "Mrs. Woodrow Wilson: Wife and Secretary Who Kept the President Alive During the World's Greatest Crisis," *Ladies' Home Journal* (October 1921), p. 20.

133. Dudley Harmon, "What is Mrs. Wilson Doing?" *Ladies' Home Journal* (July 1918), p. 22.

134. Florence Jaffray Harriman, *From Pinafores to Politics* (New York, 1923), p. 325.

135. Selden, "Mrs. Woodrow Wilson," p. 156.

136. Wilson, *My Memoir,* p. 289.

137. Jaffray, *Secrets of the White House,* p. 71.

138. Gene Smith, *When the Cheering Stopped* (New York, 1964), p. 112.

139. Robert J. Bender, "Signed—Edith Bolling Wilson," *Collier's,* vol. 65 (March 1920), p. 5.

140. Wilson, *My Memoir,* p. 299.

141. Barbara Klaw, "Lady Bird Johnson Remembers," *American Heritage* (December 1980), p. 7.

142. Edith James, Mabel E. Deutrich, and Virginia C. Purdy, "Edith Bolling Wilson: A Documentary View," in Mabel E. Deutrich and Virginia C. Purdy, eds., *Clio Was a Woman: Studies in the History of American Women* (Washington, D.C., 1980), p. 238.

143. Judith Weaver, "Edith Bolling Wilson as First Lady: A Study in the Power of Personalities," *Presidential Studies Quarterly* (Winter 1985), p. 51.

144. Wilson, *My Memoir,* p. 297. According to Edith, she had suggested that Woodrow consider a compromise with senators who opposed him, and he had replied: "Little girl, don't you desert me; that I cannot stand."

145. Weaver, "Edith Bolling Wilson," p, 70.

146. On December 11, 1975, the National Broadcasting Company included in a publicity release this summary of Edith Wilson: "During an era when women had not yet been given the right to vote, Mrs. Wilson virtually took over the reins of the White House when her husband collapsed." Cited in Deutrich and Purdy, *Clio Was a Woman,* pp. 239–240.

147. Hatch, *Edith Bolling Wilson;* Ishbel Ross, *Power With Grace* (New York, 1975).

148. Gregg Phifer, "Edith Bolling Wilson: Gatekeeper Extraordinary," *Speech Monographs,* vol. 38 (1971), pp. 277–289.

149. Robert J. Maddox, "Mrs. Wilson and the Presidency," *American History Illustrated,* vol. 7 (1973), pp. 36–44.

Chapter 6

1. Frederick Lewis Allen, *Only Yesterday: An Informal History of the 1920s* (New York, 1931). See especially chapter 5, "The Revolution in Manners and Morals." Although the Allen book is now old, its view of the 1920s continues to dominate in general textbooks. For more recent works on how outdated Allen's view of the 1920s has become, particularly in regard to women's history, see J. Stanley Lemons, *The Woman Question* (Urbana, 1973). Important articles on American women in the 1920s include James R. McGovern, "The American Woman's Pre-World War I Freedom in Manners and Morals," *Journal of American History,* vol. 55 (September 1968), in which changes in women's manners and morals are traced to the first decade of the twentieth century, and Estelle Freedman, "The New Woman: Changing Views of Women in the 1920s," *Journal of American History,* vol. 61 (September 1974), in which the author provides a historiographical framework for studying women from the 1920s to the 1970s.

2. William H. Chafe, *The American Woman: Her Changing Social, Economic, and Political Roles* (New York, 1972), p. 50.

3. Chafe, *American Woman,* p. 30.

4. Chafe, *American Woman,* p. 58.

5. Ruby A. Black, "The White House Day," *Household* (February 1930), p. 12.

6. Anne O'Hagan, "The Woman We Send to the White House," *Delineator* (November 1920), p. 7.

7. Lois W. Banner, *Women in Modern America* (New York, 1974), pp. 160–167.

8. *Good Housekeeping,* vol. 90 (April 1930), p. 24.

9. The Harding Memorial in Marion, Ohio, has a large collection of Florence Harding's clothes, and I am grateful to Herbert S. Gary for showing them to me and for sharing his knowledge of the Hardings.

10. Barbara Sicherman et al., eds., *Notable American Women: The Modern Period* (Cambridge, 1980), p. 163.

11. U.S. Census Bureau, *Statistical Abstract* (Washington, D.C., 1931), p. 91. In 1900, eighty-one divorces were granted in the United States for every one thousand marriages. By 1925, this figure had increased to 148 (per one thousand marriages) and to 163 in 1929.

12. *New York Times,* July 16, 1957, p. 25.

13. In a campaign biography, Roger W. Babson, *Cox: The Man* (New York, 1920) carefully explains the details of the Cox divorce and assigns blame to neither party. James Cox's parents had separated when he was a teenager; James's first wife, whose maiden name was coincidentally "Harding," had remarried in 1914 before James reportedly met his second wife. The candidates in the 1920 election must have set something of a record for the number of marital splits that had occurred in their immediate families: Warren Harding's father had been divorced from his second wife, Eudora Adella Kelley Luvisi Harding, in 1916.

14. O'Hagan, "Woman We Send to the White House," p. 7.

15. Edward T. James et al., eds., *Notable American Women,* 3 vols. (Cambridge, 1971), vol. 2, p. 132. Carl Sferrazza Anthony, *Florence Harding: The First Lady, the Jazz Age, and the Death of America's Most Scandalous President* (New York, 1998), xvii, calls the marriage to DeWolfe "a sham. They were never married."

16. Samuel Hopkins Adams, *Incredible Era: Life and Times of Warren Gamaliel Harding* (Boston, 1939), p. 19.

17. Nan Britten, *The President's Daughter* (New York, 1927), and Carrie Phillips's letters. See note 29 below.

18. Adams, *Incredible Era,* p. 25. See also Andrew Sinclair, *The Available Man: The Life Behind the Masks of Warren G. Harding* (Chicago, 1961), p. 297, for a different interpretation—one that gives less importance to Florence's business acumen.

19. Britten, *President's Daughter,* page 74. It is hardly necessary to note that Warren might not have been completely honest in what he told Nan about his wife or his relationship with her.

20. Francis Russell, *The Shadow of Blooming Grove* (New York, 1968), p. 162.

21. *Good Housekeeping* (February 1931), p. 18.

22. Harry M. Daugherty and Thomas Dixon, *The Inside Story of the Harding Tragedy* (New York, 1932), p. 170.

23. Alice Roosevelt Longworth, *Crowded Hours* (New York, 1933), pp. 324–325.

24. Evalyn Walsh McLean, *Father Struck It Rich* (Boston, 1936), p. 239.

25. McLean, *Father Struck It Rich,* p. 251.

26. McLean, *Father Struck It Rich,* p. vii.

27. McLean, *Father Struck It Rich,* p, 217.

28. McLean, *Father Struck It Rich,* p. 220.

29. See *New York Times,* July 10, 1964, p. 1; "250 Letters from Harding to Ohio Merchant's Wife Found." The letters between Warren Harding and Carrie Phillips are the property of the Library of Congress and closed to researchers, but one historian, who claimed to have seen them briefly, discussed their contents in *American Heritage* (February 1965), pp. 25–31.

30. Judith Exner, *My Story* (New York, 1977), esp. pp. 220–221 and 244–245.

31. Kay Summersby Morgan, *Past Forgetting: My Love Affair with Dwight David Eisenhower* (New York, 1976). Nan Britten's claim of intimacy with Warren Harding has generally been accepted as credible, although some evidence suggests that mumps, which he had as a teenager, had left him sterile and that he could not have been the father of Britten's child. In that case, Florence's failure to have a child by Warren would not have been a matter of her choice or the result of the "tiny white pills."

32. *New York Times*, June 13, 1920, p. 7.

33. Adams, *Incredible Era*, pp. 125–126.

34. Robert K, Murray, *The Harding Era* (Minneapolis, 1969), p. 64.

35. McLean, *Father Struck It Rich*, p. 254.

36. Longworth, *Crowded Hours*, p. 324.

37. Edith Wilson, *My Memoir* (New York, 1939), p. 318; Beatrice Fairfax, *Ladies Then and Now* (New York, 1944), p. 204.

38. Ishbel Ross, *Ladies of the Press* (New York, 1936), p. 312.

39. Murray, *Harding Era*, p, 418.

40. *New York Times*, June 13, 1920, p. 7.

41. Murray, *Harding Era*, p. 418.

42. Russell, *Shadow of Blooming Grove*, p. 399. Although Florence Harding was photographed frequently, pictures of her with her grandchildren are not easily located—if they exist at all.

43. John D. Hicks, biographical entry for Florence Harding in *Notable American Women*, vol. 2, p. 132.

44. O'Hagan, "Woman We Send to the White House," p. 7.

45. Russell, *Shadow of Blooming Grove*, p. 428.

46. Photograph in collection at Harding Memorial, Marion, Ohio.

47. Letter of February 7, 1922, Harding Papers, reel 242, Ohio Historical Society, Columbus, Ohio. Florence Harding's Papers are on reels 242–247, with her letters on 242–243 and clippings about her on the subsequent reels.

48. Lillian Rogers Parks and Frances Spatz Leighton, *My Thirty Years Backstairs at the White House* (New York, 1961), p. 162.

49. Florence Kling Harding to Mary E. Lee, Letter of January 5, 1922, Harding Papers.

50. Florence Kling Harding to Evalyn Walsh McLean, Letter of July 28, 1922, Harding Papers.

51. Sinclair, *Available Man*, pp. 285–286.

52. An entire book on the subject was later published, detailing how Florence poisoned Warren to save him from the shame that exposure of corruption in his administration would bring. See *The Strange Death of President Harding: From the Diaries of Gaston B. Means as Told to May Dixon Thacker* (New York, 1930)

53. Adams, *Incredible Era*, p. 8.

54. Thomas A, Bailey, *The American Pageant*, 4th ed. (Lexington, Massachusetts, 1971), p. 806.

55. "Warren Harding's 4,000 Mile Funeral," *Literary Digest*, vol. 78 (August 25, 1923).

56. McLean, *Father Struck It Rich*, p. 274.

57. Daugherty and Dixon, *Inside Story*, p. 174.

58. *New York Times*, November 22, 1924, p. 3.

59. Nicholas Murray Butler, *Across the Busy Years*, 2 vols. (New York, 1939–40), vol. 1, pp. 355–356.

60. *Good Housekeeping* (February 1932), p. 18.

61. Grace Coolidge, "The Real Calvin Coolidge," *Good Housekeeping* (February 1935), p. 181. This is the first of a series of articles (all with the same title) published over several months by Grace Coolidge. The articles include quotations from their friends and Grace's recollections.

62. Grace Coolidge, "The Real Calvin Coolidge," *Good Housekeeping* (June 1935), p. 42.

63. Coolidge, *Good Housekeeping* (February 1935), p. 186. For an interpretation that gives Grace Coolidge more credit, see Robert H. Ferrell, *Grace Coolidge: The People's Lady in Silent Cal's White House* (Lawrence, KS, 2009).

64. Florence Jaffray Harriman, *From Pinafores to Politics* (New York, 1923), p. 347.

65. Coolidge, *Good Housekeeping* (March 1935), p. 217.

66. Paul A. Burns, "Profile of First Lady," *The New Yorker* (May 15, 1926), p. 17.

67. Anne Hard, "First Lady of the Land," *Pictorial Review* (September 1926), p. 7.

68. Ishbel Ross, *Grace Coolidge and Her Era: The Story of a President's Wife* (New York, 1962), p. 264.

69. Coolidge, *Good Housekeeping* (February 1935), p. 184.

70. Margaret Bassett, *Profiles and Portraits of American Presidents and Their Wives* (Freeport, 1969), p. 310.

71. Coolidge, *Good Housekeeping* (March 1935), p. 214.

72. Coolidge, *Good Housekeeping* (February 1935). p. 184.

73. Al Fortunato to author, March 7, 1986.

74. Coolidge, *Good Housekeeping* (March 1935), p. 22.

75. Coolidge, *Good Housekeeping* (March 1935), p. 22.

76. Coolidge, *Good Housekeeping* (March 1935), p. 217.

77. Mary Randolph, "Presidents and First Ladies," *Ladies' Home Journal* (June 1936), p. 166.

78. Coolidge, *Good Housekeeping* (April 1935), p. 41.

79. Anne Hard, "First Lady," *Pictorial Review* (September 1926), p. 7.

80. Randolph, "Presidents and First Ladies," p. 16.

81. Coolidge, *Good Housekeeping* (March 1935), p. 225.

82. Irwin Hood Hoover, *Forty-Two Years in the White House* (Boston, 1934), p. 290.

83. Letter of July 25, 1985 to author from Lawrence E. Wikander, Curator of the Calvin Coolidge Memorial Room, Forbes Library, Northampton, Massachusetts.

84. Ross, *Grace Coolidge*, p. 87.

85. Amy La Follette Jensen, *The White House and Its Thirty-Three Families* (New York, 1958), p. 227.

86. Coolidge, *Good Housekeeping* (March 1935), p. 227.

87. Ross, *Grace Coolidge*, p. 257.

88. *Outlook* (January 14, 1931), p. 50.

89. *New York Times*, July 9, 1957, p. 1.

90. Coolidge, *Good Housekeeping* (March 1935), p. 224.

91. On different interpretations of the Hoover presidency, see Murray N. Rothbard, "The Hoover Myth," in James Weinstein and David Eakins, eds., *For a New America* (New York, 1970).

92. William A. Williams, review of *The Shattered Dream* by Gene Smith, *The New York Review of Books*, November 5, 1970, p. 7.

93. William H. Crawford, "Helping Their Husbands to Great Office," *Ladies' Home Journal* (September 1921), p. 17.

94. Joan Hoff-Wilson, *Herbert Hoover: Forgotten Progressive* (Boston, 1975), p. 18.

95. Herbert Hoover, "Memoirs," *Collier's* (February 24, 1951), p. 22.

96. This is Herbert Hoover's recollection of his earnings, but Joan Hoff-Wilson, *Herbert Hoover*, p. 14, points out that he frequently exaggerated his success.

97. Herbert Hoover, *Memoirs*, 3 vols. (New York, 1951–1952), vol. 1, p. 36.

98. Hoover, *Memoirs*, vol. 1, pp. 50–55.

99. Frederick Palmer, "Mrs. Hoover Knows," *Ladies' Home Journal* (March 1929), p. 6.

100. "Hoover's Silent Partner," *Literary Digest* (September 8, 1917), p. 55.

101. Hoover, *Memoirs*, vol. 1, p. 99.

102. *The American Historical Review*, prestigious journal of the American Historical Association, reviewed the Hoovers' work in its April 1914 issue, pp. 597–599. The reviewer called the translation "a noteworthy monument of patient and intelligible scholarship. . . . This work required both literary and technical training—a combination rarely found in one person, but furnished in this case by the partnership of husband and wife, both Stanford graduates, and the latter specifically familiar with the Latin language and with editorial work."

103. *New York Times*, March 10, 1914, p. 11.

104. Hoover, *Memoirs*, vol. 1, p. 153.

105. Hoover, *Memoirs*, vol. 1, p. 155.

106. Hoover, *Memoirs*, vol. 1, p. 156.

107. Helen B. Pryor, *Lou Henry Hoover: Gallant First Lady* (New York, 1969), p. 98. For an interpretation written after Lou Hoover's papers were opened in 1985, see Nancy Beck Young, *Lou Henry Hoover: Activist First Lady* (Lawrence, KS, 2004).

108. Pryor, *Lou Henry Hoover*, p. 100.

109. Pryor, *Lou Henry Hoover*, p. 93.

110. Pryor, *Lou Henry Hoover*, p. 104.

111. "Dining With the Hoovers," *Ladies' Home Journal* (March 1918), p, 38.

112. Pryor, *Lou Henry Hoover*, p. 112.

113. Hoover, *Memoirs*, vol. 1, pp. 273–274.

114. Hoover, *Memoirs*, vol. 2, p. 188. The point has been made elsewhere that the visits might have stopped during the war even without the influence of Lou Hoover. Many women, including the wife of the assistant secretary of the navy, Franklin D. Roosevelt, objected to spending their time on social visits.

115. Hoff-Wilson, *Herbert Hoover*, p, 20.

116. *New York Times*, April 20, 1923, p. 14.

117. Hoff-Wilson, *Herbert Hoover*, p. 19.

118. Alice Kessler-Harris, *Out To Work: A History of Wage-Earning Women in the United States* (New York, 1982), p. 229.

119. Matthew and Hannah Josephson, *Al Smith: Hero of the Cities* (Boston, 1969). p. 368.

120. Richard O'Connor, *The First Hurrah: A Biography of Al Smith* (New York, 1970), p. 166.

121. Josephson, *Al Smith*, p. 388.

122. Frederick L. Collins, "Mrs. Hoover's Washington," *Woman's Home Companion* (March 1929), p. 66.

123. Mary Roberts Rinehart, "A New First Lady Becomes Hostess for a Nation," *World's Work* (March 1929), p. 34.

124. Hoover, "Memoirs," *Collier's* (March 10, 1951), p. 33.

125. Dare Stark, "Heirlooms in the White House," *Woman's Home Companion* (March 1932), pp. 17–18.

126. Parks and Leighton, *Thirty Years*, p. 52.

127. Parks and Leighton, *Thirty Years,* p. 80.

128. Ava Long (with Mildred Harrington), "Presidents at Home," *Ladies' Home Journal* (September 1933), p. 8.

129. Irwin Hood Hoover, *Forty-Two Years in the White House* (Boston, 1934).

130. Myra Greenberg Gutin, "The President's Partner: The First Lady as Public Communicator, 1920–1976" (Unpublished Ph.D. Dissertation, University of Michigan, 1983), p. 156.

131. Hoover, "Memoirs," *Collier's* (February 17, 1951), p. 13.

132. Letter to author, July 23, 1985, from Dale C. Mayer, archivist and supervisor of the Lou Henry Hoover project at the Herbert Hoover Library, West Branch, Iowa.

133. *New York Times,* November 6, 1931, p. 4.

134. Gutin, "President's Partner," p. 166.

135. *New York Times,* June 23, 1929, p. 16.

136. Gutin, "President's Partner," p. 160, cites an interview with Thomas Thalkin, former curator at the Herbert Hoover Library. Dale C. Mayer, supervisor of the Lou Henry Hoover project at the library, substantiated the point in a letter to the author, July 23, 1985.

137. Gutin, "President's Partner," p. 173. Joy Scimé, who is completing at SUNY Buffalo a doctoral dissertation on the federal government's regulations on married women working in the 1930s, concluded that Herbert Hoover listened to members of the National Woman's Party in deciding to issue the 1932 Executive Order. Scimé found no evidence of Lou Hoover's influence. The order did little to advance the cause of women's equal right to work—in fact, it worked to their detriment, as Scimé has pointed out. Prior to 1932, Civil Service appointments were made "without regard to sex unless sex is specified in the request." Since a request for either a man or woman was usually included in the job description, the appointment was made from the appropriate list of those who had taken the Civil Service examination. (The exam had been open to both men and women since 1919.) What the National Woman's Party (and presumably President Hoover) had not foreseen was the disadvantage that women faced when placed on a single list that included men. Because veterans automatically received extra points on their examination scores and since few women had military experience to qualify them for the extra points, men got the jobs. Franklin Roosevelt, with the encouragement of the League of Women Voters, reinstated the dual list.

138. Karen Keesling and Suzanne Cavanaugh, "Women Presidential Appointees Serving or Having Served in Full-Time Positions Requiring Senate Confirmation, 1912–1977," Congressional Research Service, Library of Congress, March 23, 1978.

139. Gutin, "President's Partner," p. 160.

140. Mildred Adams, "The First Lady Rules a Broad Realm," *New York Times,* November 30, 1930, section 5, p. 9.

141. Pryor, *Lou Henry Hoover,* p. 180. See *Journal of Negro History,* vol. 65 (1980), pp. 6–17, for a political interpretation of this event.

142. Collins, "Mrs. Hoover's Washington," p. 32.

143. Bess Furman, *Washington By-Line* (New York, 1949), p. 57.

144. *New York Times,* March 24, 1931, p. 20.

145. *New York Times,* November 6, 1932, p. 34; *New York Times,* November 28, 1932, p. 3.

146. Alice Longworth, "Some Reminiscences," *Ladies' Home Journal* (February 1936), p. 8.

147. *New York Times,* February 26, 1944, p. 9.

Chapter 7

1. Lorena Hickok, *Eleanor Roosevelt, Reluctant First Lady* (New York, 1962), p. 4.

2. Eleanor Roosevelt, "Today's Girl—Tomorrow's Job," *Woman's Home Companion* (June 1932), p. 11.

3. Joseph P. Lash, "Eleanor Roosevelt's Role in Women's History," Mabel E. Deutrich and Virginia C. Purdy, eds., *Clio Was a Woman* (Washington, D.C., 1976), pp. 243–253.

4. Roosevelt, "Today's Girl," p. 11.

5. Joseph P. Lash, *Eleanor and Franklin* (New York, 1971), p. 122.

6. Eleanor Roosevelt, *Autobiography* (New York, 1960), p. 55.

7. Roosevelt, *Autobiography*, p. 68. See Blanche Wiesen Cook, *Eleanor Roosevelt: 1884–1933* (New York, 1992).

8. Joseph P. Lash, *Love, Eleanor: Eleanor Roosevelt and Her Friends* (Garden City, 1982), p. 67.

9. Lash, *Love, Eleanor*, p. 67.

10. Roosevelt, *Autobiography*, p. 192.

11. Roosevelt, *Autobiography*, p. 150; Hickok, *Eleanor Roosevelt*, p. 13.

12. Roosevelt, *Autobiography*, p. 104.

13. Roosevelt, *Autobiography*, p. 112. A great deal of attention has focused on Eleanor's network of women friends. See Elisabeth Israels Perry, "Training for Public Life," in *Without Precedent*, ed. Joan Hoff-Wilson and Marjorie Lightman (Bloomington, 1984), pp. 28–45. Also see Susan Ware, *Beyond Suffrage* (Cambridge, 1981) for a discussion of women's networks in the 1930s.

14. Lash, *Love, Eleanor*, p. 103.

15. M. K. Wisehart, "What Is a Wife's Job Today?" *Good Housekeeping* (August 1930), p. 34.

16. Hickok, *Eleanor Roosevelt*, p. 2. For one view of the relationship between Eleanor and Lorena Hickok, see Doris Faber, *The Life of Lorena Hickok* (New York, 1980).

17. Lash, *Love, Eleanor*, p. 278.

18. Lash, *Love, Eleanor*, p. 441.

19. Lash, *Love, Eleanor*, p. 283.

20. Lash, *Love, Eleanor*, p. 161.

21. Maurine Beasley, ed., *The White House Press Conferences of Eleanor Roosevelt* (New York, 1983), p. 170.

22. Hickok, *Eleanor Roosevelt*, p. 5. In 1959, after Eleanor Roosevelt had left Washington, she agreed to advertise margarine on television because, she said, the $35,000 remuneration would buy many CARE packages. See Bernard Asbell, ed., *Mother and Daughter* (New York, 1982), p. 329.

23. Hickock, *Eleanor Roosevelt*, p. 5.

24. George Gallup, *Gallup Poll*, 3 vols. (New York, 1972), vol. 1, p. 39.

25. Hickok, *Eleanor Roosevelt*, pp. 75–78.

26. Gerald D. Nash, *The Great Depression and World War II: Organizing America* (New York, 1979), p. 75.

27. For a fuller discussion of Eleanor Roosevelt's relation with the press, see chapter 11, "Presidential Wives and the Press," from previous editions of this book.

28. Beasley, *Press Conferences*, p. 107.

29. Nash, *Great Depression*, p. 76.

30. Susan Ware, *Holding Their Own: American Women in the 1930s* (Boston, 1982), pp. 40–41. For several important essays on Eleanor's efforts to help women, see Joan Hoff-Wilson and Marjorie Lightman, eds., *Without Precedent* (Bloomington, 1984).

31. Paul C. Taylor, biographical entry for Mary Williams Dewson, in Barbara Sicherman et al., eds., *Notable American Women: The Modern Period* (Cambridge, 1980), p. 190.

32. Lois Banner, *American Beauty* (New York, 1983), p. 189.

33. Beasley, *Press Conferences*, p. 128.

34. Lash, *Eleanor and Franklin*, p. 471.

35. Lash, *Eleanor and Franklin*, p. 470.

36. Jerre Mangione to author. Jerre Mangione has also described his visits to the White House in *Ethnic At Large* (New York, 1978), pp. 353–365.

37. Lash, *Love, Eleanor*, p. 157.

38. Lash, *Love, Eleanor*, p. 170.

39. Lash, *Love, Eleanor*, p. 180.

40. Lash, *Love, Eleanor*, p. 159.

41. Lash, *Love, Eleanor*, p. 189.

42. James Roosevelt, *My Parents* (Chicago, 1976), p. 170.

43. Asbell, ed., *Mother and Daughter*, p. 177.

44. Lash, *Love, Eleanor*, p. 331.

45. Lash, *Love Eleanor*, p. 223.

46. Roosevelt, *Autobiography*, p. 192.

47. Lash, *Love, Eleanor*, p. 223.

48. Ware, *Holding Their Own*, p. 91, quotes from an unpublished manuscript at the Schlesinger Library.

49. Beasley, *Press Conferences*, p. 90.

50. Dorothy Bromley, "The Future of Eleanor Roosevelt," *Harper's* (January 1940), pp. 130ff.

51. *Time* (March 6, 1939), p. 11.

52. Robert Day, *The New Yorker* (June 3, 1933), p. 15.

53. Hickok, *Eleanor Roosevelt*, p. 3.

54. Beasley, *Press Conferences*, p. 101.

55. Roosevelt, *Autobiography*, p. 178.

56. Roosevelt, *Autobiography*, p. 209.

57. Bromley, "Future of Eleanor Roosevelt," p. 131.

58. Raymond Clapper, "10 Most Powerful People in Washington," *Readers' Digest* (May 1941), p. 45. *Good Housekeeping* editors in 1980 rated Eleanor's influence with the president much lower. See Appendix V.

59. Roosevelt, *Autobiography*, p. 256.

60. Beasley, *Press Conferences*, p. x.

61. Eleanor Roosevelt, "Flying Is Fun," *Collier's* (April 22, 1939), p. 15.

62. Kathleen McLaughlin, "First Lady's View of First Lady's Role," *New York Times*, January 21, 1940, p. 3.

63. Eleanor Roosevelt, "Women in Politics," *Good Housekeeping* (April 1940), p. 45.

64. Susan Becker, *Origins of the Equal Rights Amendment: Feminism Between the Wars* (Westport, 1981), pp. 216–217.

65. Ware, *Holding Their Own*, p. 90.

66. Joanna Schneider Zangrando and Robert L. Zangrando, "ER and Black Civil Rights," in Joan Hoff-Wilson and Marjorie Lightman, eds., *Without Precedent: The Life and Career of Eleanor Roosevelt* (Bloomington, 1984), p. 99.

67. Eleanor Roosevelt, "24 Hours," *Ladies' Home Journal* (October 1940), p. 20.

68. Modern First Ladies Conference, Grand Rapids, Michigan, April 18–20, 1984.

69. Lash, *Love, Eleanor*, p. 167.

70. Lash, *Love, Eleanor,* p. 193.

71. Lash, *Love, Eleanor,* p. 399.

72. Eleanor Roosevelt to Jacqueline Kennedy, December 1, 1960, in Letters of Eleanor Roosevelt, Hyde Park.

73. Asbell, *Mother and Daughter,* p. 189.

74. William H. Chafe, biographical entry for Eleanor Roosevelt in Sicherman et al., eds., *Notable American Women: The Modern Period,* p. 600.

75. Lash, *Eleanor and Franklin,* p. 97.

76. Lash, *Love, Eleanor,* p. 399.

77. Bess Furman, *Washington By-Line* (New York, 1949), p. 324.

78. Lilian Rixey, "Bess Truman and Her Town," *Life* (July 11, 1949), p. 88.

79. Helen Worden Erskine, 'The Riddle of Mrs. Truman," *Collier's* (February 9, 1949), p. 14.

80. Margaret Truman, *Souvenir: Margaret Truman's Own Story* (New York, 1956), p. 13. For more on the enigma of Bess Truman, see Margaret Truman, *Bess W. Truman* (New York, 1986).

81. Jhan Robbins, *Bess and Harry: An American Love Story* (New York, 1980), p. 80, cites Oral History Project interview, Columbia University. On the announcement of the cancellation, see *New York Times,* May 7, 1945, p. 30.

82. Lillian Rogers Parks and Frances Spatz Leighton, *It Was Fun Working at the White House* (New York, 1969), p. 14.

83. For the public report, see "First Lady Swings Bottle Unbroken," *New York Times,* May 31, 1945, p. 22. For repercussions in the Truman household, see Margaret Truman, *Souvenir,* p. 107.

84. Margaret Truman pointed out that her mother began to fly after 1953, and that almost all her trips after that date were by air, *Bess W. Truman,* p. 401.

85. *New York Times,* October 30, 1947, p. 27.

86. Truman, *Bess W. Truman,* p. 271; Parks and Leighton, *It Was Fun,* p. 19.

87. *New York Times,* July 23, 1944, p. 29. Truman, *Bess W. Truman,* p. 87, notes her mother's family's connections to politics and how they helped Harry in the early years.

88. *New York Times,* July 27, 1944, p. 11.

89. Robert H. Ferrell, ed., *Dear Bess: The Letters from Harry to Bess Truman, 1910–1959* (New York, 1983), p. vii.

90. Ferrell, *Dear Bess,* p. 465.

91. Ferrell, *Dear Bess,* p. 521.

92. Marianne Means, "What 3 Presidents Say About Their Wives," *Good Housekeeping* (August 1963), p. 184. Margaret Truman later wrote that her mother "obviously knew about the atomic bomb" but that Harry did not discuss its use with her. See *Bess W. Truman,* p. 270.

93. Ferrell, *Dear Bess,* p. 554.

94. Furman, *Washington By-Line,* p. 336.

95. Rixey, "Bess Truman," *Life* (July 11, 1949), p. 88.

96. Robbins, *Bess and Harry,* pp. 17–21.

97. Truman, *Bess W. Truman,* p. 387, writes that the story of the suicide was not told during Bess's lifetime, but Jhan Robbins wrote about it in *Bess and Harry,* p. 22.

98. Ferrell, *Dear Bess,* p. 143.

99. Robbins, *Bess and Harry,* p. 31.

100. Erskine, "Riddle of Mrs. Truman," p. 14.

101. Robbins, *Bess and Harry,* p. 38.

102. *Newsweek* (January 7, 1946), p. 26.

103. Bess Furman, "The Independent Lady from Independence," *New York Times,* June 9, 1946, p. 20.

104. Erskine, "Riddle of Mrs. Truman," p. 14.

105. *New York Times,* October 30, 1947, p. 27.

106. *New York Times,* January 19, 1947, section VI, p. 43.

107. *Time* (November 10, 1947), p. 24.

108. *Newsweek* (January 7, 1946), p. 26.

109. *Time* (June 3, 1946), p. 45.

110. *New York Times,* February 28, 1946, p. 21.

111. J. B. West, *Upstairs at the White House: My Life with the First Ladies* (New York, 1973), p. 75.

112. *Newsweek* (February 4, 1946), p. 25.

113. *New York Times,* January 25, 1946, p. 20.

114. *New York Times,* July 22, 1944, p. 10.

115. Lillian Parks, *My 30 Years Backstairs at the White House* (New York, 1961), p. 311.

116. Parks and Leighton, *It Was Fun,* p. 139.

117. Liz Carpenter at Modern First Ladies conference, Gerald R. Ford Museum, Grand Rapids, Michigan, April 18–20, 1984.

118. Robbins, *Bess and Harry,* p. 2.

119. Means, "What 3 Presidents Say," p. 182.

120. *New York Times,* October 30, 1946, p. 29.

121. *New York Times,* July 16, 1946, p. 26.

122. Jonathan Daniels, "The Lady from Independence," *McCall's* (April 1949), p. 86.

123. *Time* (March 23, 1953), p. 19.

124. Parks, *My 30 Years,* p. 312.

125. *New York Times,* November 2, 1979, p. 1.

126. *Collier's* (October 4, 1952), p. 48.

127. Lenore Hailparn, "What Is She Like? Our New First Lady?" *Independent Woman* (January 1953), p. 2.

128. *New York Times,* October 17, 1945, p. 44.

129. Kay Summersby Morgan, *Past Forgetting* (New York, 1976), p. 201.

130. Dwight D. Eisenhower, *Letters to Mamie,* ed. John S. D. Eisenhower (Garden City, 1978).

131. Merle Miller, *Plain Speaking: An Oral Biography of Harry S. Truman* (New York, 1973), pp. 339–340.

132. Morgan, *Past Forgetting,* p. 14.

133. Steve Neal, *The Eisenhowers: Reluctant Dynasty* (New York, 1978), p. 177.

134. Lester and Irene David, *Ike and Mamie* (New York, 1981), pp. 125–128.

135. Ruth Montgomery, "An Intimate Portrait of Our Vivacious First Lady After One Year in the White House," *Look* (February 23, 1954), p. 31.

136. *Time* (March 23, 1953), p. 19.

137. *U. S. News and World Report* (August 21, 1953), p. 52.

138. Montgomery, "An Intimate Portrait," p. 31.

139. *Time* (March 23, 1953), p. 19. See also Marilyn Irvin Holt, *Mamie Doud Eisenhower: The General's First Lady* (Lawrence, KS, 2007).

140. Dwight D. Eisenhower, *Mandate for Change* (Garden City, 1963), p. 264.

141. Letter of Mrs. Edward J. Birmingham, February 1954, in Chicago Historical Society.

142. *Life* (October 20, 1958), p. 60.

143. Means, "What 3 Presidents Say," p. 193.

144. Parks and Leighton, *It Was Fun*, p. 174.

145. Parks, *My 30 Years*, p. 33.

146. West, *Upstairs at the White House*, pp. 130–131.

147. Alden Hatch, *Red Carpet for Mamie* (New York, 1954), p. 251.

148. Helen Worden, "The American Story of Mrs. Eisenhower," *Coronet* (August 1951), pp. 56–62.

149. Nanette Kutner, "The Story of Mamie," *Woman's Home Companion* (July 1953). p. 25.

150. Photographs appear in *Life* (January 26, 1953) pp. 77–78.

151. *New York Times*, December 17, 1952, p. 38.

152. *New York Times*, November 22, 1952, p. 20.

153. David, *Ike and Mamie*, p. 211.

154. Helen Worden Erskine, "Call Me Mamie," *Collier's* (October 4, 1952), p. 46.

155. Photograph in *Life* (October 20, 1958), p. 60.

156. "They Love Mamie in Augusta," *McCall's* (September 1953), p. 32.

157. Kutner, "Story of Mamie," p. 46.

158. *New York Times*, November 9, 1952, p. 64.

159. Helen Worden, "The American Story of Mrs. Eisenhower," *Coronet* (August 1951), p. 56.

160. *New York Times*, March 15, 1959, p. 62.

161. "How Would You Raise a First Lady?" *Better Homes and Gardens* (June 1955). p. 1.

162. Obituary of Mrs. John S. Doud, *New York Times*, September 30, 1960, p. 27.

163. "How Would You Raise a First Lady?" p. 178.

164. West, *Upstairs at the White House*, pp. 129–130.

165. Parks, *My Thirty Years*, p. 321.

166. *New York Times*, November 2, 1979, p. 1.

167. Lauris Norstad Interview, cited in Stephen E. Ambrose, *Eisenhower*, 2 vols. (New York, 1983), vol. 1, p. 532.

168. David, *Ike and Mamie*, p. 264.

169. Stephen E. Ambrose, *Eisenhower*, vol. 1, pp. 74–75. For photographs of Mamie and her first-born, see Dwight D. Eisenhower, *In Review: Pictures I've Kept* (Garden City, 1969).

170. Ambrose, *Eisenhower*, vol. 1, p. 104.

171. Ambrose, *Eisenhower*, vol. 1, p. 439.

172. *New York Times*, March 9, 1955, p. 17.

173. *New York Times*, March 11, 1955, p. 6.

174. "White House Duties Putting Strain on Mamie's Health," *U.S. News and World Report* (March 25, 1955), p. 40.

175. *New York Times*, September 25, 1955, p. 1.

176. *New York Times*, March 1, 1956, p. 14.

177. *New York Times*, August 7, 1957, p. 1.

178. Lash, *Love, Eleanor*, p. 131.

179. Mamie Eisenhower, "Vote for My Husband or for Governor Stevenson, But Please Vote," *Good Housekeeping* (November 1952), p. 13.

180. Esther Stineman, *American Political Women: Contemporary and Historical Profiles* (Littleton, Colorado, 1980), *passim*. On Nixon's speech, see *National Business Woman* (March 1957), p. 14.

181. Rosalynn Carter, *First Lady from Plains* (Boston, 1984), p. 292.

Chapter 8

1. *Newsweek* (February 22, 1960), p, 29.

2. Marilyn Bender, "The Woman Who Wins High Fashion's Vote Is Jacqueline," *New York Times,* July 15, 1960, p. 17.

3. *New York Times,* October 30, 1960, section VI, p. 10.

4. Lester David, *The Lonely Lady of San Clemente* (New York, 1978), p. 117.

5. David, *Lonely Lady,* p. 118, recounts a slightly different version, but the point is the same.

6. John H. Davis, *The Bouviers: Portrait of an American Family* (New York, 1969), p. 307.

7. Davis, *Bouviers,* p. 313.

8. *New York Times,* November 23, 1960, p. 14.

9. Letitia Baldrige, *Of Diamonds and Diplomats* (Boston, 1968), p. 162. The number is large for 1960 and included part-timers.

10. *The New Yorker* (January 14, 1961), pp. 77–78.

11. Bess Furman, "First Lady and Art Experts Plan Decor," *New York Times,* January 25, 1961, p. 37.

12. *New York Times,* June 12, 1961, p. 59.

13. Edith Gaines, "At Home: Building the White House Collection," *Art and Antiques* (July–August 1981), pp. 76–83.

14. Public Law 87–286 was approved September 22, 1961.

15. Jack Gould, *New York Times,* February 15, 1962, p. 1.

16. *New York Times,* January 20, 1962, p. 14.

17. Davis, *Bouviers,* p. 326.

18. Katie Louchheim, *By the Political Sea* (Garden City, 1970), p. 222.

19. Margaret Mead, "A New Kind of First Lady," *Redbook* (February, 1962), p. 8.

20. Sam Houston Johnson, *My Brother Lyndon* (New York, 1969), p. 108.

21. Pierre Salinger, *With Kennedy* (New York, 1966), p. 305.

22. Siena Research Institute, "First Ladies Poll." See Appendix IV. Jackie Kennedy's popularity plunged after her marriage in 1968 to Aristotle Onassis, a Greek shipping magnate. She gradually recaptured the press's praise in the 1970s as she held down a job in a major publishing house and appeared to have raised her two children with less scandal and unfavorable publicity than Robert Kennedy's children faced.

23. Marianne Means, "What 3 Presidents Say about Their Wives," *Good Housekeeping* (August 1963), p. 197.

24. Eunice Kennedy Shriver was the exception among John Kennedy's sisters—she was graduated from Berkeley.

25. Among the more vivid accounts of Joseph P. Kennedy's life, see Peter Collier and David Horowitz, *The Kennedys: An American Drama* (New York, 1984), pp. 1–172.

26. Patricia Zelman, *Women, Work, and National Policy: The Kennedy-Johnson Years* (Ann Arbor, 1980), p. 26.

27. Zelman, *Women, Work and National Policy,* pp. 26–27.

28. Nan Dickerson, *Among Those Present: A Reporter's View of Twenty-Five Years in Washington* (New York, 1976), p. 63.

29. Herbert Parmet, *Jack* (New York, 1980), p. 304, cites oral history of Lady Barbara Ward at Kennedy Library.

30. Zelman, *Women, Work and National Policy,* pp. 23–25. Cynthia E. Harrison, "A 'New Frontier' for Women," *Journal of American History,* vol. 67, no. 3 (1980), pp. 630–646.

31. Davis, *The Bouviers,* p. 316.

32. Lady Bird Johnson, *A White House Diary* (New York, 1970), p. 12.

33. Abigail McCarthy, *Private Faces, Public Places* (New York, 1972), p. 303.

34. Michael Gillette, *Lady Bird Johnson: An Oral History*, (New York: Oxford University Press), p. 8.

35. Merle Miller, *Lyndon: An Oral Biography* (New York, 1980), p. 61.

36. *Good Housekeeping* (October 1968), p. 98.

37. Dickerson, *Among Those Present*, p. 98.

38. Barbara Klaw, "Lady Bird Johnson Remembers," *American Heritage* (December 1980), p. 13. This is a verbatim interview.

39. Dickerson, *Among Those Present*, p. 98.

40. Marie Smith, *The President's Lady* (New York, 1964), p. 38.

41. Klaw, "Lady Bird Remembers," p. 13.

42. Miller, *Lyndon*, p. 52.

43. Elizabeth Janeway, "The First Lady: A Professional at Getting Things Done," *Ladies' Home Journal* (April 1964), p. 64.

44. Miller, *Lyndon*, p. 62.

45. Miller, *Lyndon*, p. 63.

46. Klaw, "Lady Bird Remembers," p. 8.

47. *Time* (November 29, 1963), p. 33.

48. Robert Caro, *The Path to Power* (New York, 1982), p. 408.

49. Miller, *Lyndon*, p. 73.

50. Miriam Amanda Wallace Ferguson was elected Governor of Texas in 1924 after her husband, who had opposed woman's suffrage, was impeached and convicted. See Sicherman et al., eds., *Notable American Women: The Modern Period*, pp. 230–231.

51. Anne Morrow Lindbergh, "As I See Our First Lady," *Look* (May 19, 1964), p. 105.

52. Janeway, "The First Lady," *Ladies' Home Journal* (April 1964), p. 119. For Lady Bird's recollections of this period, see "A National Tribute to Lady Bird Johnson on the Occasion of her 65th Birthday," Lyndon Baines Johnson Library, Austin, Texas.

53. Miller, *Lyndon*, p. 110.

54. Henry Brandon, "A Talk With the First Lady," *New York Times,* September 10, 1967, section VI, p. 47.

55. Miller, *Lyndon*, p. 369.

56. Caro, *Path to Power*, p. xxiii, quotes attorneys who claimed that Lyndon Johnson continued during his presidency to make decisions about his holdings, "down to the most minute details."

57. Klaw, "Lady Bird Remembers," p. 6.

58. Luci Johnson Turpin, Grand Rapids Conference, April 18–20, 1984.

59. Klaw, "Lady Bird Remembers," p. 13.

60. Caro, *Path to Power*, p. 302.

61. Klaw, "Lady Bird Remembers," p. 13.

62. Brandon, *New York Times*, September 10, 1967, section VI, p. 47.

63. Klaw, "Lady Bird Remembers," p. 13.

64. Marjorie Hunter, "Public Servant Without Pay: The First Lady," *New York Times*, December 15, 1963, section VI, p. 10.

65. Klaw, "Lady Bird Remembers," p. 7.

66. Dickerson, *Among Those Present*, p. 37.

67. Klaw, "Lady Bird Remembers," p. 16.

68. Marvella Bayh, *Marvella* (New York, 1979), p. 90.

69. Dickerson, *Among Those Present*, p. 53.

70. Marie Smith, *The President's Lady* (New York, 1964), p. 124.

71. Katie Louchheim, *By the Political Sea* (Garden City, 1970), p. 135.

72. Blake Clarke, "Lyndon Johnson's Lady Bird," *Reader's Digest* (November 1963), p. 109.

73. Eric Goldman, *Tragedy of LBJ* (New York, 1963), p. 367.

74. Klaw, "Lady Bird Remembers," p. 17.

75. Liz Carpenter, *Ruffles and Flourishes* (Garden City, 1969), p. 143. Perhaps Lady Bird's enthusiastic campaigning helps explain her special role in Lyndon's 1965 inauguration—she became, at his suggestion, the first wife to hold the Bible for the swearing in.

76. Carpenter, *Ruffles and Flourishes*, pp. 144f.

77. Klaw, "Lady Bird Remembers," p. 8.

78. Luci Johnson Turpin and Lynda Johnson Robb, Grand Rapids Conference, April 18–20, 1984.

79. Klaw, "Lady Bird Remembers," p. 6.

80. "Beautification Summary: the Committee for a More Beautiful Capital," Lyndon Baines Johnson Library, Austin, Texas. The same library also has oral history of Sharon Francis who worked on the beautification program.

81. Miller, *Lyndon*, p. 400.

82. Johnson, *A White House Diary*, p. 271.

83. Carpenter, *Ruffles and Flourishes*, p. 239. For a discussion of Lady Bird's role in beautification, see Lewis L. Gould, *Lady Bird Johnson: Our Environmental First Lady* (Lawrence, KS, 1988).

84. Johnson, *A White House Diary*, p. 325. The cartoon, by Bill Mauldin, appeared in the *Chicago Sun Times*.

85. Letter to author from Nancy Smith, archivist at Lyndon Baines Johnson Library, July 17, 1984.

86. *New York Times*, January 19, 1968, p. 1, gives an account of the lunch.

87. Nancy Smith to author, July 17, 1984.

88. Goldman, *Tragedy of LBJ*, p. 361.

89. Meg Greenfield, "The Lady in the East Wing," *Reporter* (July 15, 1965), p. 29.

90. Greenfield, "Lady in the East Wing," p. 28.

91. *New York Times*, January 12, 1969, section IV, p. 12.

92. *Life* (December 13, 1968), p. 22B.

93. Siena Research Institute, "First Ladies Poll," Appendix II.

94. Klaw, "Lady Bird Remembers," p. 7.

95. *New York Times*, August 9, 1968, p. 21.

96. *New York Times*, September 24, 1969, p. 19.

97. *New York Times*, January 21, 1970, p. 94.

98. *New York Times*, March 2, 1971, p. 25.

99. Helen Dudar, review of Lester David's book, *The Lonely Lady of San Clemente*, *New York Times Book Review*, November 12, 1978, p. 20.

100. Nan Robertson, "A Starring Role Is Not for Mrs. Nixon," *New York Times*, January 26, 1970, p. 1.

101. David, *Lonely Lady*, p, 19.

102. David, *Lonely Lady*, p. 19.

103. Judith Viorst, "Pat Nixon Is the Ultimate Good Sport," *New York Times Magazine*, September 13, 1970, p. 25.

104. David, *Lonely Lady*, p. 40.

105. David, *Lonely Lady*, p. 40.

106. Earl Mazo, *Nixon: A Political Portrait* (New York, 1968), p. 22.

107. Mazo, *Nixon*, p. 27.

108. David, *Lonely Lady*, p. 61.

109. Viorst, "Pat Nixon," *New York Times Magazine*, September 13, 1970, p. 25.

110. David, *Lonely Lady*, p. 79.

111. David, *Lonely Lady*, pp. 79–80.

112. Richard Nixon, *Six Crises* (Garden City, 1962), p. 137.

113. Several versions of this "pledge" exist, including Mazo, *Nixon*, p. 127.

114. Robert S. Pierpoint, *At The White House* (New York, 1981), pp. 184–185.

115. David, *Lonely Lady*, p. 88.

116. Jane Howard, "The 38th First Lady Not a Robot At All," *New York Times Magazine*, December 8, 1974, p. 36.

117. "The Ordeal of Political Wives," *Time* (October 7, 1974), p. 15.

118. *Time* (October 7, 1974), p. 15.

119. Jessamyn West, "Pat Nixon: An Intimate View," *Good Housekeeping* (February 1971), p. 66.

120. Flora Rheta Schreiber, "Pat Nixon Reveals for the First Time. . . . " *Good Housekeeping* (July 1968), p. 62.

121. Viorst, "Pat Nixon," *New York Times Magazine*, September 13, 1970, p. 25.

122. Robertson, "A Starring Role," *New York Times*, January 26, 1970, p. 1.

123. In gathering information for this book, the author contacted each of the presidential libraries (and various historical societies for presidents before 1929). Each responded generously, but Richard Nixon's New York office (he had no presidential library) replied in two sentences: one wished the author luck and the other was, "I am sorry to say that we do not have any of the information you need in this office." Letter to author from John H. Taylor, Administrative Assistant, Office of Richard Nixon, August 1, 1984. However, Julie Nixon Eisenhower replied graciously to requests for insights into her mother's record as First Lady; and Helen McCain Smith furnished considerable documentation and offered her own recollections.

124. David, *Lonely Lady*, pp. 82–83.

125. Schreiber, "Pat Nixon," *Good Housekeeping* (July 1968), p. 62.

126. John Erhlichman, *Witness to Power: The Nixon Years* (New York 1982), p. 81.

127. David, *Lonely Lady*, p. 164. Smith assured the author that she had been accurately quoted in David's book.

128. David, *Lonely Lady*, p. 166.

129. Ehrlichman, *Witness to Power*, p. 103.

130. Dudar, *New York Times Book Review*, November 12, 1978, p. 20.

131. Veteran Washington reporter to author, Grand Rapids Conference, April 18–20, 1984.

132. David, *Lonely Lady*, p. 165.

133. Helen McCain Smith to author, July 30, 1986. Smith graciously supplied the author with records to document her account of Pat Nixon's White House activities.

134. Richard Nixon, *Memoirs* (New York, 1978), p. 535.

135. Washington resident and observer of many First Ladies to author, Grand Rapids Conference, April 18–20, 1984.

136. Bob Woodward and Carl Bernstein, *The Final Days* (New York, 1976), pp. 164–166.

137. Julie N. Eisenhower, Letter to author, April 8, 1986.

138. *New York Times*, September 21, 1972, p. 41.

139. David, *Lonely Lady*, p. 163.

140. David, *Lonely Lady*, pp. 163–164.

141. West, "Pat Nixon," *Good Housekeeping* (February 1971), p. 66.

142. Gerald Ford, *A Time To Heal* (New York, 1979), p. 39.

143. Seymour Hersh, "Nixon, Ford, Haig, and the Nixon Pardon," *Atlantic Monthly* (August 1983), p. 64.

144. Dudar, *New York Times Book Review*, November 12, 1978, p. 20.

145. Letitia Baldrige to author, August 6, 1985.

146. Julie N. Eisenhower's prominence in defending her father during the Watergate investigations can be included in her role as a campaigner—she was, once again, showing her father's fitness to hold national elective office.

147. Helen McCain Smith to author, July 31, 1986. See also Julie Nixon Eisenhower, *Pat Nixon* (New York, 1986), p. 321.

Chapter 9

1. *New York Times*, July 16, 1985, p. 1.

2. Seymour Hersh, "Nixon, Ford, Haig, and the Nixon Pardon," *Atlantic Monthly* (August 1983), p. 62.

3. Myra Greenberg Gutin, "The President's Partner: The First Lady as Public Communicator, 1920–1976" (Unpublished Ph.D. Dissertation, University of Michigan, 1983), p. 540.

4. Betty Ford (with Chris Chase), *The Times of My Life* (New York, 1978), p. 55.

5. Myra MacPherson, "Betty Ford: The Untold Story," *McCall's* (July 1978), p. 22.

6. Marvella Bayh, *Marvella* (New York, 1979), p. 93.

7. Ellen Proxmire, *One Foot in Washington: The Perilous Life of a Senator's Wife* (Washington, D.C., 1963).

8. Abigail McCarthy, *Private Faces, Public Places* (New York, 1972), p. 302.

9. Jean Libman Block, "The Betty Ford Nobody Knows," *Good Housekeeping* (May 1974), p. 88.

10. Block, *Good Housekeeping* (May 1974), p. 88.

11. Ford, *Times of My Life*, p. 66.

12. Ford, *Times of My Life*, p. 205.

13. Gutin, "President's Partner," p. 536.

14. Rosalynn Carter, *First Lady from Plains* (Boston, 1984), p. 100.

15. Helen Thomas, *Dateline: White House* (New York, 1975), p. 273.

16. Carter, *First Lady*, p. 100.

17. *New York Times*, September 5, 1974, p. 25.

18. *New York Times*, September 8, 1974, p. 21.

19. *New York Times*, December 8, 1974, section VI, p. 36.

20. Lenore Hershey, "The New Pat Nixon," *Ladies' Home Journal* (February 1972), p. 89.

21. Sheila Rabb Weidenfeld, *First Lady's Lady: With the Fords at the White House* (New York, 1979), pp. 86–87. For a full history of the Equal Rights Amendment, see Joan Hoff-Wilson, ed., *Rights of Passage* (Bloomington, 1986).

22. Betty Ford, Grand Rapids Conference, April 18–20, 1984.

23. *New York Times*, February 15, 1975, p. 31.

24. *New York Times*, February 15, 1975, p. 15.

25. *New York Times*, February 20, 1975, p. 31.

26. *New York Times*, February 20, 1975, p. 32.

27. Sheila Rabb Weidenfeld takes considerable credit for easing Betty Ford's anxieties about her role, but she does not indicate that any serious consideration was given to changing course. See *First Lady's Lady*, p. 92.

28. Karen Keesling and Suzanne Cavanagh, "Women Presidential Appointees Serving or Having Served in Full-Time Positions Requiring Senate Confirmation, 1912–1977," Congressional Research Service, Library of Congress, Washington, D.C., March 23, 1978.

29. *New York Times*, August 10, 1974, p. 19. Rebekah Harkness, the philanthropist and dance enthusiast, was quoted immediately on Gerald Ford's inauguration: "I feel confident that because [of Betty Ford's past] she will work for the betterment of the arts and dance."

30. Jane Howard, "The 38th First Lady Not a Robot at All," *New York Times Magazine*, December 8, 1974, p. 36. Betty consulted with experts, according to Howard, because she "didn't want to get [information] second hand from men—or comment just on the beautiful walls." On the attention given to Betty Ford's dancing in China, see John J. O'Connor, "Coverage of Ford in China: Was It Journalism?" *New York Times*, December 8, 1975, p. 63.

31. *New York Times*, October 10, 1975, p. 39.

32. Weidenfeld, *First Lady's Lady*, pp. 86–87.

33. *New York Times*, September 5, 1974, p. 25.

34. *New York Times*, January 14, 1977, p. 21.

35. *New York Times*, December 17, 1974, p. 43.

36. Lewis Gould, "Modern First Ladies in Historical Perspective," *Presidential Studies Quarterly* (Summer 1985), p. 536.

37. Abigail McCarthy, "Hers," *New York Times*, November 30, 1978, p. C2. McCarthy noted that the book is about southerners "who are poor, isolated, and driven" but the women in the book often emerge as business partners because of "close knit families and domestic help."

38. Rosalynn Carter to author, June 19, 1984.

39. Carter, *First Lady*, p. 10.

40. Carter, *First Lady*, p. 17.

41. Carter, *First Lady*, p. 15.

42. Carter, *First Lady*, p. 27.

43. Rosalynn Carter to author, June 19, 1984.

44. Carter, *First Lady*, p. 29.

45. Carter, *First Lady*, p. 44.

46. Carter, *First Lady*, pp. 44–45. Betty Glad, *Jimmy Carter: In Search of the Great White House* (New York, 1980), p. 138, demonstrates that the Carters were less consistent in their anti-segregationist stance than Rosalynn indicates.

47. Carter, *First Lady*, p. 49.

48. Carter, *First Lady*, p. 105.

49. Rosalynn Carter to author, June 19, 1984.

50. See Edna Langford and Linda Maddox, *Rosalynn: Friend and First Lady* (Old Tappan, NJ, 1980), pp. 50–53 for an account of this trip from the viewpoint of Langford, whose daughter had married Rosalynn's son.

51. Carter, *First Lady*, p. 117.

52. Carter, *First Lady*, p. 117.

53. On Rosalynn Carter's White House staff, see *New York Times*, January 11, 1977, p. 20; *New York Times*, December 31, 1979, p. D2; Scott Kaufman, *Rosalynn Carter: Equal Partner in the White House* (Lawrence, KS, 2007) p. 36.

54. *Newsweek* (June 13, 1977), p. 17.

55. Carter, *First Lady*, p. 188.

56. *New York Times*, July 20, 1977, section III, p. 2.

57. Meg Greenfield, "Mrs. President," *Newsweek* (June 20, 1977), p. 100.

58. *Newsweek* (June 13, 1977), p. 17.

59. Rosalynn Carter to author, June 19, 1984.

60. Carter, *First Lady*, pp. 278–279.

61. Marjorie Hunter, "Mrs. Carter in Capitol Debut," *New York Times*, February 8, 1979, p. 1.

62. *New York Times*, February 3, 1979, p. 2; and February 8, 1979, p. 1.

63. Carter, *First Lady*, p. 279.

64. Carter, *First Lady*, p. 279.

65. Letter of Madeline MacBean (later Edwards), Personal Assistant to Rosalynn Carter, to author, July 23, 1984.

66. *Newsweek* (June 13, 1977), p. 17.

67. William Shannon, "The Other Carter Is Running," *New York Times*, September 15, 1976, p, 45.

68. *New York Times*, August 13, 1978, p. 79.

69. Cyrus Vance, *Hard Choices* (New York, 1983), p. 218.

70. Carter, *First Lady*, p. 239.

71. Carter, *First Lady*, p. 243.

72. Carter, *First Lady*, p. 245.

73. Carter, *First Lady*, p. 265.

74. *New York Times Book Review*, April 15, 1984, p. 7.

75. *New York Times*, June 11, 1976, p. 1.

76. Rosalynn Carter to author, June 19, 1984.

77. Abigail McCarthy, "Hers," *New York Times*, November 30, 1978, p. C2.

78. Carter, *First Lady*, pp. 289–290.

79. Carter, *First Lady*, p. 340.

80. Siena Research Institute, "First Ladies Poll." See Appendices II and IV.

81. Carter, *First Lady*, pp. 290–292.

82. Walter Shapiro, "Madeleine Lee, Meet Nancy Reagan," *Washington Monthly* (March 1981), p. 49.

83. Betty Friedan, *The Feminine Mystique* (New York, 1963). Friedan did not, of course, compose her book in a vacuum—she had, no doubt, been influenced by authors such as Simone de Beauvoir, whose book *The Second Sex* appeared in English in 1953.

84. Marabel Morgan, *The Total Woman* (Old Tappan, NJ, 1973).

85. Gloria Steinem, "Finally a Total Woman in the White House," *Ms.* (March 1981), p. 13.

86. Nancy Reagan (with Bill Libby), *Nancy* (New York, 1980), p. 122.

87. Lawrence Leamer, *Make-Believe: The Story of Nancy and Ronald Reagan* (New York, 1981), p. 64.

88. Lou Cannon, *Reagan* (New York, 1982), p. 142.

89. Cannon, *Reagan*, p. 146.

90. Siena Research Institute, "First Ladies Poll." See Appendix IV of poll conducted in 1982. Nancy did best on the item "value to the President," ranking eighth out of 17.

91. Leamer, *Make-Believe*, pp. 290–291.

92. Leamer, *Make-Believe*, p. 291. Also see Ronnie Dugger, *On Reagan: The Man and His Presidency* (New York, 1983), p. 122.

93. NBC documentary on Nancy Reagan, June 24, 1985.

94. Leamer, *Make-Believe*, pp. 346–347.

95. Siena Research Institute, "First Ladies Poll." It should be emphasized that this poll was taken during Nancy's first year in the White House.

96. Alfred Descheidt designed a "Queen Nancy" postcard in late 1981. See *New York Times*, February 28, 1982, section III, p. 19.

97. NBC documentary on Nancy Reagan, June 24, 1985, showed Nancy Reagan continuing to talk about designer clothing but limiting herself to off-camera remarks.

98. Leamer, *Make-Believe*, p. 359, supplies the lyrics of Nancy's song on secondhand clothes.

99. *New York Times*, April 25, 1985, p. 1; April 26, 1985, p. B6.

100. *New York Times*, March 26, 1985, p. A20.

101. NBC documentary on Nancy Reagan, June 24, 1985, showed several White House staffers making these judgments.

102. *New York Times*, July 16, 1985, p. 1.

103. *New York Times*, July 17, 1985, p. 1; MacNeil/Lehrer NewsHour, July 15, 1985.

104. *New York Times*, July 21, 1985, p. 22.

105. *New York Times*, July 13, 1986, p. E7.

106. *New York Times*, February 28, 1986, p. A12.

107. Donald T. Regan, *For the Record: From Wall Street to Washington* (New York, 1988), p. 72.

108. Nancy Reagan, *My Turn: The Memoirs of Nancy Reagan* (New York, 1989), p. 316.

109. *New York Times*, December 15, 1988, p. B20.

110. *New York Times*, July 12, 1986, p. A6.

111. Donnie Radcliffe, *Simply Barbara Bush: A Portrait of America's Candid First Lady* (New York, 1989), p. 73.

112. Radcliffe, *Simply Barbara Bush*, pp. 84–85.

113. Radcliffe, *Simply Barbara Bush*, p. 87.

114. The others: Eliza Johnson, Mamie Eisenhower, and Rosalynn Carter.

115. Radcliffe, *Simply Barbara Bush*, p. 105.

116. Radcliffe, *Simply Barbara Bush*, p. 113.

117. Radcliffe, *Simply Barbara Bush*, p. 120.

118. Radcliffe, *Simply Barbara Bush*, pp. 127–128.

119. *U.S. News & World Report* (May 28, 1990), p. 24.

120. *Vogue* (November 1988), p. 444.

121. Radcliffe, *Simply Barbara Bush*, p. 1.

122. On March 30, 1989, several newspapers, including the *New York Times* and the *Atlanta Journal and Constitution*, published interviews in which she described her symptoms and medication.

123. *Ebony* (October 1990), p. 76.

124. *Washington Post*, November 19, 1990, p. B1.

125. Radcliffe, *Simply Barbara Bush*, pp. 54–55. For the view that Barbara Bush had shown a sarcastic streak as a child, see Myra G. Gutin, *Barbara Bush: Presidential Matriarch* (Lawrence, KS, 2008), p. 2.

126. *New York Times*, June 2, 1990, p. A1.

127. To Author, September 23, 1993.

Chapter 10

1. *National Journal* (June 19, 1993), p. 1472.

2. *National Journal* (February 6, 1993), p. 358.

3. *Vanity Fair* (June 1993), p. 108.

4. *Atlantic* (June 1993), p. 22.

5. *Working Woman* (May 1993), p. 13.

6. May 17, 1993.

7. U.S. Department of Commerce, *Statistical Abstract of the U.S., 1993*, 12th ed. (Washington, DC, 1993), p. 173.

8. *Statistical Abstract 1993*, p. 184.

9. According to *Statistical Abstract 1993*, p. 400, 56.8 percent of married women with children under six years of age were employed in 1987.

10. Quoted in Judith Warner, *Hillary Clinton: The Inside Story* (New York, 1993), p. 13.

11. Warner, *Hillary Clinton*, p. 24.

12. Radcliffe, *Hillary Rodham Clinton*, p. 67.

13. Radcliffe, *Hillary Rodham Clinton*, p. 79.

14. Radcliffe, *Hillary Rodham Clinton*, p. 120.

15. *New York Times*, March 15, 1994, p. 1. Some of these early professional ties embarrassed Hillary later, and Hubbell resigned in March 1994, amid charges of misconduct at Rose.

16. Patricia O'Brien, "The First Lady with a Career?" *Working Woman* (August 1992), p. 44.

17. Garry Wills, "Clinton's Case," *New York Review of Books* (March 5, 1992), p. 3.

18. Quoted in Radcliffe, *Hillary Rodham Clinton*, p. 231.

19. No one pointed out that Sarah Polk had been criticized in the 1844 campaign for not being interested enough in domestic details. See chapter 3.

20. Daniel Wattenberg, "The Lady Macbeth of Little Rock," *American Spectator* (August 1992), p 25.

21. Maureen Dowd, *New York Times*, May 18, 1992, p. A15.

22. *New York Times*, November 17, 1992, p. A18.

23. For security reasons, diagrams of the West Wing are not often published, but in 1985, the *New York Times* showed office assignments at that time. See Betty Boyd Caroli, *Inside the White House* (New York, 1992), p. 98.

24. Marian Burros, "Hillary Clinton's New Home: Broccoli's In, Smoking's Out," *New York Times*, February 2, 1993, p. 1.

25. *National Journal* (June 19, 1993), pp. 1475–1476.

26. A 1972 law required that federal advisory committee meetings be open to the public, except for those advisory committees made up entirely of federal officials that are exempt. Hillary Rodham Clinton's legal team argued that for the purposes of the 1972 law, she "is a Federal official or employee as First Lady." See *New York Times*, May 1, 1993, p. 8.

27. *New York Times*, June 23, 1993, p. A1

28. *New York Times*, April 23, 1994, p. 12.

29. For a list of the many books and articles on the subject, see the website: www.firstladies.org.

30. *New York Times*, January 8, 1996.

31. Gail Sheehy's interview with Hillary Clinton, conducted in January 1995, is reported in Sheehy's book, *Hillary's Choice* (New York, 1999) p. 256.

32. *Today*, interview with Matt Lauer, January 27, 1998.

33. For a summary of how her favorable ratings rose in 1998, see *New York Times*, September 27, 2000.

34. *New York Times*, September 8, 2001.

35. *New York Times*, November 8, 2000.

36. *New York Times*, November 12, 2000.

37. Hillary Rodham Clinton, *An Invitation to the White House: At Home With History* (New York, 2000). The dust jacket noted that the author's proceeds had been assigned

to the White House Historical Association and that a portion of the publisher's profits would be donated to the National Park Foundation.

38. Before she had completed two years in the Senate, Hillary was already being mentioned as a possible candidate for president, and in 2008, she mounted a strong campaign to head the Democratic ticket. When she lost out to Barack Obama and he went on to win the presidency, she accepted a place in his cabinet, as Secretary of State. That designation had become something of a female position, with women serving eight of the preceding twelve years. (Madeleine Albright, 1997–2001 and Condoleezza Rice, 2005–2009). As Secretary of State, Hillary would travel widely and cultivate the ties and the background to make a run for president in 2016.

39. Population information on Midland was kindly supplied by Nancy Oldham and Donna Cervantes. See Midland's website: www.co.midland.tx.us.

40. Antonia Felix, *Laura: America's First Lady, First Mother* (New York, 2002) p. 16.

41. Christopher Andersen, *George and Laura: Portrait of an American Marriage* (New York, 2002), p, 81, quotes a "friend of Laura's": "It is really odd, considering Midland's small size and how remote it was that the Welches and the Bushes didn't know each other back then."

42. Walt McDonald (Texas Poet Laureate in 2001), *Whatever the Wind Delivers: Celebrating West Texas and the Near Southwest* (Lubbock, TX, 1999).

43. For more information on Laura Welch's youth, see list of articles on www.firstladies .org.

44. See *Oprah* magazine, May 2001 as quoted in Felix, *Laura: America's First Lady*, pp. 29–30.

45. For a fuller discussion of the accident, see Lewis L. Gould, "Laura Welch Bush," in Lewis L. Gould, ed., *American First Ladies: Their Lives and Their Legacy* (New York, 2001) pp. 440, 445. In the bibliographical essay, Gould cites a 1963 headline in the *Midland Reporter-Telegram*: "Lee High School Senior Dies in Traffic Mishap."

46. Felix, *Laura: America's First Lady*, p. 39.

47. Felix, *Laura: America's First Lady*, pp. 26, 40.

48. Felix, *Laura: America's First Lady*, pp. 40–41.

49. *USA Today*, March 22, 2001.

50. Felix, *Laura: America's First Lady*, p. 69.

51. Gould, "Laura Welch Bush," p. 441.

52. This often-told story varies slightly with the telling, but the central point does not change—that Laura Welch stood up to the older woman and felt no need to apologize for preferring reading to competitive sports. Accounts of Barbara Bush's reaction to the interchange also vary but in one account, she described the elderly Dorothy Bush as so surprised she "darn near collapsed." See Andersen, *George and Laura*, p. 124.

53. Andersen, *George and Laura*, p. 160, reports that George W. Bush was being paid $200,000 annually by 1989. For accounts of the sale of the baseball club in 1998, see Andersen, p. 194.

54. For various perspectives on Laura's influence on George's decision to stop drinking, see Andersen, *George and Laura*, pp. 149ff. Andersen quotes "one friend" as saying, "His marriage was falling apart, and he cared about his girls. That's what turned him around" (p. 150).

55. Gould, "Laura Welch Bush," p. 443.

56. Elizabeth Palmer, "Laura Bush: Convention Speaker," *Congressional Quarterly Weekly*, July 29, 2000. Excerpts from the speech appear in the *New York Times*, August. 1, 2000.

57. *New York Times*, October 19, 2000.

58. *New York Times*, January 19, 2001.

59. *New York Times*, January 9, 2001.

60. *International Herald Tribune*, December 19, 2000.

61. For details of the book festival, see Elaine Sciolino, "First Lady Opens a Festival To Promote National Literacy," *New York Times*, September 7, 2001.

62. Less than a year later, the Foundation had raised $5 million. See *AP Online*, June 4, 2002.

63. Other headlines pointed to a changed role for the First Lady. See Faye Fiore, "A First Lady's Metamorphosis," *Los Angeles Times*, October 10, 2001; Nina Burleigh, "A New Life for Laura Bush," *US Weekly*, October 15, 2001.

64. *New York Times*, October 7, 2002.

65. *New York Times*, October 7, 2002.

66. For one example of coverage of this event, see Bob Kemper, "In Solo Radio Address, Laura Bush Opens Worldwide Effort to Spotlight Taliban's Policies Against Women," *Chicago Tribune*, November 17, 2001.

67. For the transcription of Laura Bush's radio address, see the website for the George W. Bush White House archives.

68. Laura Bush's United Nations speech on March 8, 2002, is available online.

69. Tasha Dubriwny, "First Ladies and Feminism: Laura Bush as Advocate for Women's and Children's Rights," *Women's Studies in Communication* (2005), p. 95.

70. Sheryl Gay Stolbert, "First Lady Raising Her Profile without Changing Her Image," *New York Times*, October 15, 2007.

71. Karlyn Kohrs Campbell, "The Rhetorical Presidency: A Two-Person Career," in Martin J. Medhurst, ed., *Beyond the Rhetorical Presidency* (College Station, 1996), p. 180.

72. Dubriwny, "First Ladies and Feminism," p. 84.

73. Myra Greenberg Gutin first put forth this categorization in her doctoral dissertation, "The President's Partner: The First Lady as Public Communicator, 1920–1976" (Unpublished Ph.D. Dissertation, University of Michigan, 1983). Her book *The President's Partner: The First Lady in the Twentieth Century* (Westport, 1989) drew on this dissertation. Later she published "Using All Available Means of Persuasion: The Twentieth-Century First Lady as Public Communicator," *Social Science Journal* (2000), pp. 563–75.

74. Hillary Clinton, United Nations International Women's Day Speech on Women's Rights, March 4, 1999, is available online from the Clinton White House archives.

75. "Mrs. Laura Bush's Leadership: First Lady's Work Advances President Bush's Agenda at Home and Abroad," fact sheet from Laura Bush's office.

76. Carlotta Gall, "Laura Bush Carries Pet Causes to Afghans," *New York Times*, March 31, 2005, p. A10.

77. "Mrs. Laura Bush's Leadership" fact sheet.

78. Stolbert, "First Lady Raising Her Profile."

79. "Mrs. Laura Bush's Leadership" fact sheet.

80. Emily Eakin, "Mrs. Bush, It's Not about Fashion," *New York Times*, January 20, 2001, p. B9.

81. Kelly Wallace, "First Lady Shakes Up White House Staff," available on the CNN website. Also see Elisabeth Bumiller, "All Quiet in the West Wing, but More Change in the East," *New York Times*, March 27, 2006.

82. Bumiller, "All Quiet in the West Wing."

83. Katha Pollitt, "Poetry Makes Nothing Happen? Ask Laura Bush," *The Nation,* February 6, 2003.

84. Poll results, June 27, 2005, available on CNN website.

85. Poll results, May 1, 2008, available on CNN website.

86. Elisabeth Bumiller, "A First Lady Fiercely Loyal and Quietly Effective," *New York Times,* February 7, 2004.

87. Poll results available online.

88. "Talk of the Town," *New Yorker,* June 6, 2005, p. 31.

89. Curtis Sittenfeld, *American Wife: A Novel* (New York, 2008).

90. Curtis Sittenfeld, "The Compassionate Conservative," *New York Times,* November 2, 2008, Sunday Opinion, p. 11.

91. The author is indebted to Prof. Douglas Lonnstrom for sharing early results of this survey. For more poll results, see Appendix VII and the website of the Siena Research Institute.

92. Sandra Sobieraj Westfall, "I Didn't Realize the Impact the First Lady Can Have," *People,* January 19, 2009, p. 66.

93. Michelle LaVaughn Robinson, "Princeton-Educated Blacks and the Black Community," is available online.

94. Liza Mundy, *Michelle: A Biography,* p. 65.

95. Mundy, *Michelle: A Biography,* p. 66.

96. Robinson, "Princeton-Educated Blacks," p. 2.

97. Robinson, "Princeton-Educated Blacks," p. 2.

98. Richard Wolffe, *Renegade: The Making of a President,* pp. 35–36.

99. Wolffe, *Renegade,* p. 52.

100. Wolffe, *Renegade,* p. 60.

101. Rebecca Johnson, "The Natural," *Vanity Fair,* September 2007, p. 781.

102. Wolffe, *Renegade,* p. 52

103. Johnson, "The Natural," p. 777.

104. *National Review,* April 2008.

105. Jeff Zeleny, "Book Sales Lifted Obamas' Income in 2007 to a Total of $4.2 Million," *New York Times,* April 17, 2008.

106. Jodi Kantor, "Michelle Obama and the Evolution of a First Lady," *New York Times,* January 6, 2012.

107. The initial press secretary, Katie McCormick Lelyveld, who had joined the Obama team after being impressed by a speech she heard Michelle give in 2007, lasted until May 2011, when, at thirty-two, she decided to return to Chicago. An even younger woman, Hannah August, a graduate of University of Pennsylvania with some experience in communications management, replaced Lelyveld and stayed until January 6, 2014, when twenty-six-year-old Joanna "Jojo" Rosholm took over. A known quantity, since she had already worked more than three years in the Obama White House, Rosholm stayed until January 2017, describing her time there as "a dream."

108. Ben Meyerson, "Michelle Obama Salutes Lilly Ledbetter at White House," *Los Angeles Times,* January 29, 2009.

109. *New York Times,* February 8, 2009.

110. *New York Times,* September 18, 2009.

111. Myra Gutin, interview with author, July 23, 2010.

112. Siena College Research Institute/C-SPAN Study of the First Ladies of the United States, 2014. See Appendix VIII.

113. Text of interview is available online. For video of ride, see YouYube.

114. *New York Times*, August 6, 2010.
115. *New York Times*, March 25, 2016.
116. *New York Times*, David W. Chen, June 3, 2016.
117. Julie Hirschfeld, "Voice Shaking, Michelle Obama Calls Trump Comments on Women 'Intolerable'." *New York Times*, October 13, 2016.

Chapter 11

1. Michael Wolff, *Fire and Fury*, p. 18.
2. *New York Times*, March 4, 2018.
3. Article in *Guardian*, November 5, 2016.
4. Bojan Požar, *Melania Trump: The Inside Story* (Ljubljana, Slovenia: Zalozba Ombo, 2016), p. 11.
5. Požar, p. 122.
6. Požar, p. 128.
7. *New York Times*, April 16, 2016
8. *New York Times*, March 24, 2016.
9. *New York Times*, March 24, 2016.
10. *New York Times*, April 13, 2016. Ten days later, on April 23, the same newspaper underlined Ivanka's role in her father's political and business life: "In Campaign and Company, Ivanka Trump Has Central Role."
11. *New York Times*, July 21, 2016
12. *New York Times*, October 9, 2016
13. *New York Times*, October 17, 2016.
14. Several First Ladies delayed their arrival in the capital but blamed extenuating circumstances such as their own illness or that of a close relative. See sections on Martha Washington, Abigail Adams, and Anna Symmes Harrison.
15. *New York Daily News*, April 30, 2009.
16. *Wall Street Journal*, January 12, 2018.
17. *New York Post*, January 19, 2018.
18. *New York Times*, February 26, 2018.
19. *New York Times*, August 7, 1957.
20. *Washington Post*, June 17, 2018.
21. Alex Horton and T. J. Ortenzi, "Melania Trump issues statement in support of LeBron James after president insults him," *Washington Post*, August 4, 2018.
22. In the second decade of the twenty-first century, new scholarship on American First Ladies continues to offer additional insights and interpretations. For examples of books that focus on marriages and family relationships, see Flora Fraser, *The Washingtons: George and Martha: "Join'd by Friendship, Crown'd by Love"* (2015); Will Swift, *Pat and Dick: The Nixons, An Intimate Portrait of a Marriage* (2014); Betty Boyd Caroli, *Lady Bird and Lyndon: The Hidden Story of a Marriage that Made a President* (2015); Diane Jacobs, *"Dear Abigail: The Intimate Lives and Revolutionary Ideas of Abigail Adams and Her Two Remarkable Sisters* (2014); Lewis L. Gould, ed., *My Dearest Nellie: The Letters of William Howard Taft to Helen Herron Taft, 1909–1912* (2011).

For books that reexamine how the women fit into their times, see: Jeanne E. Abrams, *First Ladies of the Republic: Martha Washington, Abigail Adams, Dolley Madison and the Creation of an Iconic American Role* (2018); Marie Jenkins Schwartz, *Ties That Bound: Founding First Ladies and Slaves* (2017); Margery M. Heffron, *Louisa Catherine: The Other Mrs. Adams* (2014); Louisa Thomas, *Louisa: The Extraordinary Life of Mrs. Adams* (2016); Annette Dunlap, *Frank: The Story of Frances Folsom Cleveland, America's Youngest First Lady* (2009); Lewis L. Gould, *Helen Taft: Our Musical First Lady* (2010); Kristie Miller, *Ellen and Edith: Woodrow Wilson's First Ladies* (2010).

Appendices

	Year Married*	Years as First Lady**
Martha Dandridge Custis Washington (1731–1802)	1759	1789–1797
Abigail Smith Adams (1744–1818)	1764	1797–1801
Dolley Payne Todd Madison (1768–1849)	1794	1809–1817
Elizabeth Kortright Monroe (ca. 1763–1830)[1]	1786	1817–1825
Louisa Catherine Johnson Adams (1775–1852)	1797	1825–1829
Anna Symmes Harrison (1775–1864)	1795	1841[2]
Letitia Christian Tyler (1790–1842)	1813	1841–1842[3]
Julia Gardiner Tyler (1820–1889)	1844	1844–1845[4]
Sarah Childress Polk (1803–1891)	1824	1845–1849
Margaret Mackall Smith Taylor (1788–1852)	1810	1849–1850[5]
Abigail Powers Fillmore (1798–1853)	1826	1850–1853
Jane Means Appleton Pierce (1806–1863)	1834	1853–1857
Mary Todd Lincoln (1818–1882)	1842	1861–1865[6]
Eliza McCardle Johnson (1810–1876)	1827	1865–1869
Julia Dent Grant (1826–1902)	1848	1869–1877
Lucy Webb Hayes (1831–1889)	1852	1877–1881
Lucretia Rudolph Garfield (1832–1918)	1858	1881[7]
Frances Folsom Cleveland (1864–1947)	1886[8]	1886–1889
		1893–1897
Caroline Scott Harrison (1832–1892)	1853	1889–1892[9]
Ida Saxton McKinley (1847–1907)	1871	1897–1901[10]
Edith Carow Roosevelt (1861–1948)	1886	1901–1909
Helen Herron Taft (1861–1943)	1886	1909–1913
Ellen Axson Wilson (1860–1914)	1885	1913–1914[11]
Edith Bolling Galt Wilson (1872–1961)	1915	1915–1921[12]
Florence Kling Harding (1860–1924)	1891	1921–1923[13]
Grace Goodhue Coolidge (1879–1957)	1905	1923–1929
Lou Henry Hoover (1874–1944)	1899	1929–1933
Eleanor Roosevelt Roosevelt (1884–1962)	1905	1933–1945[14]
Bess Wallace Truman (1885–1982)	1919	1945–1953
Mamie Doud Eisenhower (1896–1979)	1916	1953–1961
Jacqueline Bouvier Kennedy (1929–1994)	1953	1961–1963[15]

I. *Presidents' Wives Who Served as First Lady (Continued)*

	Year Married*	Years as First Lady**
Lady Bird Taylor Johnson (1912–2007)	1934	1963–1969
Patricia Ryan Nixon (1912–1993)	1940	1969–1974[16]
Betty Bloomer Warren Ford (1918–2011)	1948	1974–1977
Rosalynn Smith Carter (1927–)	1946	1977–1981
Nancy Davis Reagan (1921–2016)	1952	1981–1989
Barbara Pierce Bush (1925–2018)	1945	1989–1993
Hillary Rodham Clinton (1947–)	1975	1993–2001
Laura Welch Bush (1946–)	1977	2001–2009
Michelle Robinson Obama (1964–)	1992	2009–2017
Melania Knauss Trump (1970–)	2005	2017–

*Date is that of marriage to man who became President. In some cases an earlier (or later) marriage also occurred.

**Terms of First Ladies coincide with the presidential term and run from one inauguration to another except as noted. Until 1937, Presidents assumed the office March 4.

1. Actual birthdate is disputed.

2. William Henry Harrison died one month after taking office, before Anna had arrived in Washington.

3. Letitia Tyler died September 10, 1842.

4. Julia Gardiner married President John Tyler on June 26, 1844, only a few months before his presidential term ended.

5. Zachary Taylor died in office on July 9, 1850.

6. Abraham Lincoln was assassinated on April 15, 1865.

7. James Garfield died September 19, 1881 after having been shot on July 2.

8. Frances Folsom married President Grover Gleveland on June 2, 1886, after he had taken office in March, 1885. He was defeated for a second consecutive term but was reelected in 1892 and served from 1893 to 1897.

9. Caroline Harrison died in the Executive Mansion, October 25, 1892.

10. William McKinley was assassinated on September 14, 1901, just months after beginning his second term.

11. Ellen Wilson died in the White House on August 6, 1914.

12. Edith Galt married President Woodrow Wilson on December 18, 1915.

13. Warren Harding died in office on August 2, 1923.

14. Franklin Delano Roosevelt died in office on April 12, 1945.

15. John F. Kennedy was assassinated on November 22, 1963.

16. Richard Nixon resigned from the presidency on August 9, 1974.

II. *Historians' Ranking of First Ladies in 1982*

First Lady's Rank	President's Rank		Score
1	1	Eleanor Roosevelt	93.3
2	10	Abigail Adams	84.6
3	14	Lady Bird Johnson	77.5
4	9	Dolley Madison	75.4
5	33	Rosalynn Carter	73.8
6	23	Betty Ford	73.4
7	6	Edith Wilson	71.8
8	8	Jacqueline Kennedy	69.5
9	4	Martha Washington	67.5
10	5	Edith Roosevelt	65.4
11	27	Lou Hoover	63.5
12	22	Lucy Hayes	63.1
13	18	Frances Cleveland	62.3
14	17	Louisa Adams	62.0
15	7	Bess Truman	61.7
16	6	Ellen Wilson	61.5
17	30	Grace Coolidge	61.3
18	2	Martha Jefferson Randolph (daughter of widower Thomas Jefferson)*	61.0
19	20	Helen Taft	61.0
20	36	Julia Grant	60.7
21	38	Eliza Johnson	60.7
22	12	Sarah Polk	60.5
23	26	Anna Harrison	60.1
24	15	Elizabeth Monroe	60.1
25	24	Mary Arthur McElroy (sister of Chester Arthur)	60.1
26	13	Emily Donelson (niece of Andrew Jackson)	60.0
27	34	Julia Tyler	59.9
28	32	Abigail Fillmore	59.8
29	37	Harriet Lane (niece of bachelor James Buchanan)	59.8
30	25	Lucretia Garfield	59.8
31	11	Mamie Eisenhower	59.7
32	38	Martha Patterson (daughter of Andrew Johnson)	59.6
33	29	Margaret Taylor	59.4
34	31	Caroline Harrison	59.4
35	34	Letitia Tyler	59.3
36	21	Angelica Van Buren (daughter-in-law of Martin Van Buren)	59.3
37	28	Pat Nixon	58.5
38	35	Jane Pierce	57.6
39	16	Nancy Reagan	57.4
40	19	Ida McKinley	57.0

II. Historians' Ranking of First Ladies in 1982 (Continued)

First Lady's Rank	President's Rank		Score
41	39	Florence Harding	55.8
42	3	Mary Lincoln	52.9

This poll was conducted in 1982 by Professors Thomas Kelly and Douglas Lonnstrom, Directors of the Siena Research Institute, Siena College, Loudonville, New York. History professors in 102 colleges were asked to rate the First Ladies. In another poll, conducted by the Siena Research Institute in 1981, political scientists and historians were asked to rank presidents on a different scale. (See results in Appendix III.) The list above merges the results of the two polls, with scores rounded to the nearest tenth of 1 percent. It should be emphasized that both polls were conducted early in the first Reagan administration. No explanation was given for including some of the women who served as First Lady although not married to a president, such as Mary Arthur McElroy, Chester Arthur's sister, and excluding others, such as Rose Cleveland, Grover Gleveland's sister. The author is grateful to the Siena Research Institute for sharing this data.

* In the Tyler and Wilson administrations, the first wife of the respective presidents died and both men remarried while in office. In the Andrew Johnson presidency, both his wife and daughter served as First Lady. As a result, the total of First Ladies outnumbers that of presidents.

III. *Professors' Ranking of Presidents in 1981*

Rank		Score
1	Franklin D. Roosevelt	85.0
2	Thomas Jefferson	82.7
3	Abraham Lincoln	81.0
4	George Washington	80.3
5	Theodore Roosevelt	79.5
6	Woodrow Wilson	76.8
7	Harry Truman	71.1
8	John Kennedy	70.7
9	James Madison	70.0
10	John Adams	68.6
11	Dwight Eisenhower	68.4
12	James Polk	67.9
13	Andrew Jackson	67.7
14	Lyndon Johnson	67.6
15	James Monroe	67.3
16	Ronald Reagan	65.7
17	John Q. Adams	65.6
18	Grover Cleveland	65.0
19	William McKinley	63.5
20	William Taft	62.9
21	Martin Van Buren	61.5
22	Rutherford B. Hayes	59.5
23	Gerald Ford	59.3
24	Chester B. Arthur	59.2
25	James Garfield	59.1
26	William Henry Harrison	58.0
27	Herbert Hoover	57.7
28	Richard Nixon	57.5
29	Zachary Taylor	57.3
30	Calvin Coolidge	57.0
31	Benjamin Harrison	57.0
32	Millard Fillmore	56.7
33	Jimmy Carter	56.1
34	John Tyler	56.1
35	Franklin Pierce	54.6
36	Ulysses S. Grant	52.4
37	James Buchanan	51.5
38	Andrew Johnson	49.2
39	Warren Harding	48.7

Results of a poll conducted in 1981 by Professors Thomas Kelly and Douglas Lonnstrom, Directors of the Siena Research Institute, Loudonville, New York. Political scientists and historians were asked to rank presidents on twenty different qualities or characteristics: background, party leadership, communication ability, relationship with congress, court appointments, handling of the U.S. economy, luck, ability to compromise, willingness to take risks, executive appointments, overall ability, imagination, domestic accomplishments, integrity, executive ability, foreign policy accomplishments, leadership ability, intelligence, avoidance of crucial mistakes, ranker's overall view. The author is grateful to the Siena Research Institute for permission to cite these results here.

This is only one of many rankings of United States Presidents. For a review of literature on the subject, see David C. Nice, "The Influence of War and Party System Aging on the Ranking of Presidents," *Western Political Quarterly*, vol. 37 (September 1984), pp. 443–455.

IV. Historians' Ranking of Twentieth-Century First Ladies in 1982

Rank		Score	Background	Value to country	Integrity	Leadership	Intelligence	"Own Woman"	Accomplishments	Courage	Public Image	Value to President
1	Eleanor Roosevelt	93.3	1	1	1	1	1	1	1	1	1	2
2	Lady Bird Johnson	77.5	3	2	5	2	2	3	2	3	3	3
3	Rosalynn Carter	73.8	7	4	3	3	3	4	4	5	5	1
4	Betty Ford	73.4	9	5	2	5	5	2	5	2	4	5
5	Edith Wilson	71.8	5	3	8	4	4	5	3	4	11	4
6	Jacqueline Kennedy	69.5	2	6	17	6	6	6	6	6	2	7
7	Edith Roosevelt	65.4	4	7	7	7	8	9	7	8	7	9
8	Lou Hoover	63.5	6	8	6	9	7	8	8	10	12	12
9	Bess Truman	61.7	16	10	4	17	13	13	13	9	9	6
10	Ellen Wilson	61.5	8	9	11	10	9	11	11	11	13	13
11	Grace Coolidge	61.3	12	11	10	11	11	12	10	13	8	14
12	Helen Taft	61.0	10	12	13	8	10	7	9	12	14	15
13	Mamie Eisenhower	59.7	13	13	9	15	17	16	14	14	6	10
14	Pat Nixon	58.5	15	15	12	16	12	17	16	7	10	11
15	Nancy Reagan	57.4	11	17	15	14	14	15	17	15	17	8
16	Ida McKinley	57.0	14	14	14	13	15	14	12	16	15	16
17	Florence Harding	55.8	17	16	16	12	16	10	15	17	16	17

Results of poll conducted in 1982 by Professors Thomas Kelly and Douglas Lonnstrom, Directors of the Siena Research Institute, Siena College, Loudonville, New York. History professors in 102 colleges were asked to rate First Ladies. The professors came from 57 northern colleges and 45 southern colleges. It should be emphasized that the poll was conducted early in the first Reagan administration. The author is grateful to the Siena Research Institute for sharing this data.

V. Good Housekeeping's *Ranking of Twentieth-Century First Ladies (1980)*

Ratings on Individual Characteristics

Rank		Score	Host-ess	Cam-paigner	Leader in Causes	Interest in Politics	Femin-ist	Tradi-tional-ist	Improv-ing the White House	Influ-ence on Presi-dent	Helpful-ness to Presi-dent	Out-spoken-ness	Cha-risma	Inspira-tion to Women
1	Lady Bird Johnson	92	8	10	9	10	6	4	8	9	10	2	9	7
2	Eleanor Roosevelt	89	8	10	10	10	10	0	0	5	8	10	10	8
3	Rosalynn Carter	88	7	10	8	10	10	0	2	10	10	7	8	6
4	Lou Hoover	83	10	3	9	8	8	2	8	5	10	5	7	8
5	Jacqueline Kennedy	79	8	6	0	0	4	6	10	7	6	4	10	8
6	Betty Ford	73	8	2	6	4	7	3	2	6	8	10	9	8
7	Helen Taft	69	6	9	2	10	5	2	2	9	9	2	7	6
8	Pat Nixon	63	10	8	0	0	0	9	10	4	8	0	6	8
9	Bess Truman	60	2	7	0	10	0	10	4	7	10	0	6	4
9	Florence Harding	60	6	5	0	10	0	8	6	8	10	2	5	0
11	Edith Roosevelt	54	8	0	1	0	0	10	9	0	8	0	8	10
12	Edith Wilson	53	1	8	0	8	6	0	0	10	8	0	6	6
13	Grace Coolidge	52	10	0	0	0	0	10	7	0	6	2	9	8
13	Mamie Eisenhower	52	10	8	0	0	0	10	3	0	8	0	8	5
15	Ellen Wilson	48	4	3	0	4	0	7	5	0	7	0	6	2

Good Housekeeping editors evaluated the records of fifteen twentieth-century First Ladies and published the results in the July 1980 issue, p. 120. It should be noted that this ranking occurred before Ronald Reagan was elected, so Nancy Reagan is not included. Ida McKinley, whose husband was assassinated in September 1901, is also excluded, although technically she was a twentieth-century First Lady.

Although the *Good Housekeeping* overall ranking does not differ greatly from the historians' ranking (see Appendix IV), the characteristics on which the women were judged are quite different and sometimes contradictory (e.g., traditionalist and feminist). *Good Housekeeping* editors pointed out that their evaluations were not intended to pit the record of one woman against that of another but merely to "call attention to the manner in which each has responded to the challenge of her unpaid job."

VI. *Historians' Ranking of First Ladies in 2008*

First Lady Rank	President's Rank	Name	Overall Score
1	1	Eleanor Roosevelt	93.71
2	12	Abigail Adams	84.31
3	14	Jackie Kennedy	82.88
4	18	Hillary Clinton	79.67
5	15	Lady Bird Johnson	76.37
6	9	Dolley Madison	75.85
7	28	Betty Ford	74.35
8	25	Rosalynn Carter	72.71
9	4	Martha Washington	72.21
10	6	Edith Wilson	69.31
11	3	Edith Roosevelt	68.19
12	22	Barbara Bush	66.29
13	6	Ellen Wilson	65.62
14	31	Lou Hoover	65.17
15	16	Nancy Reagan	65.13
16	7	Bess Truman	65.08
17	29	Grace Coolidge	63.65
18	27	Lucy Hayes	63.10
19	10	Mamie Eisenhower	62.88
20	20	Frances Cleveland	62.52
21	17	Louisa Adams	62.19
22	21	Helen Taft	61.90
23	23	Laura Bush	61.69
24	35	Julia Grant	61.65
25	26	Pat Nixon	61.50
26	11	Sarah Polk	61.38
27	33	Lucretia Garfield	60.90
28	37	Julia Tyler	60.75
29	8	Elizabeth Monroe	60.35
30	32	Caroline Harrison	60.29
31	19	Ida McKinley	60.25
32	38	Abigail Fillmore	59.77
33	42	Eliza Johnson	59.67
34	34	Margaret Taylor	59.54
35	37	Letitia Tyler	59.10
36	2	Mary Lincoln	58.75
37	40	Florence Harding	58.63
38	39	Jane Pierce	58.13

Omitted from this list are presidents who served without a First Lady: widowers Jefferson, Jackson, Van Buren, and Arthur; bachelor Buchanan. Woodrow Wilson's first wife, Ellen, died in 1914 and he married Edith in 1915. John Tyler's first wife, Letitia, died in 1842 and he married Julia in 1844. William Henry Harrison's wife had not yet arrived in the capital city when her husband died so she is omitted from the rankings.

This Siena Institute ranking for presidents was done in 2001; and it was done for First Ladies in 2008. Therefore, Laura Bush's ranking was done at the end of eight years while her husband's was after only one year, before his popularity dropped.

The author is grateful to the Siena Research Institute, Siena College, Loudonville, New York, for sharing the results of multiple surveys. For more information and updates, see the website of the Siena College Research Institute.

VII. Siena College Research Institute Poll: Historians' Ranking (2008) of First Ladies Who Served from 1900 to 2009

Name	Rank	Overall Score	Background	Value to County	Integrity	Leadership	Intelligence	"Own Woman"	Accomplishments	Courage	Public Image	Value to President
Eleanor Roosevelt	1	93.71	1	1	1	1	1	1	1	1	2	1
Jackie Kennedy	2	82.88	2	2	3 (TIE)	3	3	3	3 (TIE)	2	1	2
Hillary Clinton	3	79.67	3	4	16	2	3	2	2	3	15	4
Lady Bird Johnson	4	76.37	4	3	3 (TIE)	4	4 (TIE)	5	3 (TIE)	5	3	6
Betty Ford	5	74.35	7 (TIE)	5	5	5	6	4	5	4	4	7
Rosalynn Carter	6	72.71	9	6	2	7	4 (TIE)	7	6	7	5	5
Edith Wilson	7	69.31	7 (TIE)	7	15	6	7	6	7	6	17	8
Edith Roosevelt	8	68.19	5	8	7	8	8	8	8	9	8	12
Barbara Bush	9	66.29	6	11	8	12 (TIE)	9	10	15	15	6	10
Ellen Wilson	10	65.62	11	13	12	9	10	9	10	11	14	14
Lou Hoover	11	65.17	10	9	11	10	11	9	9	13	12 (TIE)	16
Nancy Reagan	12	65.13	14	17	19	12 (TIE)	12	12 (TIE)	14	10	7	3
Bess Truman	13	65.08	17	10	6	15	13	14	12	12	11	9
Grace Coolidge	14	63.65	15	14	13	11	14	12 (TIE)	11	14	12 (TIE)	17
Mamie Eisenhower	15	62.88	12	12	9	18	18	18	16	16	9	13
Helen Taft	16	61.9	16	15	17 (TIE)	14	17	15	13	17	18	18
Laura Bush	17	61.69	13	18	10	20	16	20	20	20	10	11
Pat Nixon	18	61.5	18	16	14	19	15	19	19	8	16	15
Ida McKinley	19	60.25	19	19	17 (TIE)	17	19	17	17	18	19	19
Florence Harding	20	58.63	20	20	20	16	20	16	18	19	20	20

VIII. Siena College Research Institute/C-SPAN
Study of the First Ladies of the United States 2014

2014	Background	Rank Background	Value to Country	Rank Value to Country	Integrity	Rank Integrity	Leadership	Rank Leadership	White House Steward	Rank White House Steward	Own Woman	Rank Own Woman	Accomplishments	Rank Accomplishments	Courage	Rank Courage	Public Image	Rank Public Image	Value to President	Rank Value to President	Mean	Mean Rank
Eleanor Roosevelt	4.14	82.89	4.31	86.28	4.17	83.47	4.32	86.36	3.63	72.64	4.41	88.18	4.31	86.12	4.31	86.12	4.21	84.13	4.23	84.63	4.20	84.08
Abigal Adams	4.07	81.32	4.17	83.39	4.21	84.30	4.07	81.32	3.66	73.22	4.29	85.87	3.93	78.51	4.22	84.38	3.94	78.76	4.43	88.60	4.10	81.97
Jacqueline Kennedy	4.04	80.74	4.04	80.83	3.48	69.59	3.60	72.07	4.25	84.96	3.61	72.23	3.69	73.80	4.12	82.31	4.45	88.93	3.93	78.51	3.92	78.40
Dolley Madison	3.64	72.73	4.03	80.66	3.79	75.87	3.84	76.78	4.09	81.82	3.85	77.02	3.73	74.55	4.05	80.91	4.08	81.57	4.07	81.40	3.92	78.33
Michelle Obama	3.82	76.45	3.76	75.21	3.73	74.63	3.78	75.54	3.55	70.99	4.05	80.91	3.64	72.73	3.70	73.97	3.92	78.43	4.02	80.33	3.80	75.92
Hillary Clinton	3.88	77.52	3.83	76.61	3.17	63.39	3.93	78.68	3.24	64.71	4.26	85.12	4.00	79.92	3.81	76.12	3.33	66.69	3.94	78.84	3.74	74.76
Lady Bird Johnson	3.62	72.48	3.78	75.62	3.71	74.21	3.67	73.47	3.67	73.31	3.62	72.31	3.72	74.46	3.63	72.56	3.67	73.39	3.80	76.03	3.69	73.79
Betty Ford	3.31	66.12	3.59	71.74	3.74	74.79	3.62	72.40	3.28	65.54	3.88	77.52	3.64	72.73	3.98	79.59	3.70	74.05	3.73	74.55	3.65	72.90
Martha Washington	3.68	73.55	3.91	78.26	3.73	74.55	3.23	64.63	3.18	63.64	3.30	65.95	3.17	63.39	3.60	71.90	3.96	79.17	4.01	80.17	3.58	71.52
Rosalynn Carter	3.24	64.79	3.38	67.69	3.78	75.62	3.44	68.84	3.31	66.20	3.56	71.24	3.38	67.69	3.39	67.85	3.40	67.93	3.84	76.78	3.47	69.46
Barbara Bush	3.45	69.01	3.27	65.37	3.42	68.35	3.16	63.22	3.30	65.95	3.39	67.85	3.03	60.66	3.26	65.21	3.52	70.33	3.59	71.82	3.34	66.78
Laura Bush	3.30	65.95	3.22	64.38	3.63	72.56	3.10	61.98	3.40	68.10	3.07	61.32	3.15	63.06	3.21	64.30	3.57	71.40	3.68	73.64	3.33	66.67
Edith Roosevelt	3.45	68.93	3.26	65.29	3.38	67.60	3.19	63.72	3.38	67.60	3.29	65.79	3.14	62.89	3.24	64.88	3.34	66.86	3.45	69.09	3.31	66.26
Edith Wilson	3.16	63.14	3.22	64.38	2.98	59.67	3.38	67.60	3.21	64.13	3.57	71.40	3.28	65.62	3.45	69.09	3.00	59.92	3.76	75.12	3.30	66.01

Nancy Reagan	3.23	64.63	3.11	62.15	2.97	59.42	3.24	64.71	3.46	69.17	3.34	66.86	3.06	61.24	3.35	66.94	3.21	64.30	3.93	78.60	3.29	65.80
Bess Truman	3.21	64.21	3.15	62.98	3.47	69.42	2.90	57.93	3.21	64.30	3.26	65.21	2.92	58.35	3.21	64.13	3.19	63.72	3.62	72.31	3.21	64.26
Lou Hoover	3.25	65.04	3.10	61.90	3.24	64.79	3.13	62.56	3.11	62.23	3.27	65.45	3.19	63.88	3.17	63.39	2.98	59.67	3.21	64.30	3.17	63.32
Louisa Adams	3.31	66.28	3.11	62.23	3.26	65.12	3.07	61.40	3.13	62.56	3.15	63.06	3.06	61.16	3.20	64.05	3.07	61.40	3.24	64.71	3.16	63.20
Ellen Wilson	3.19	63.80	3.07	61.32	3.13	62.56	3.15	62.98	3.12	62.48	3.21	64.13	3.11	62.23	3.21	64.21	3.08	61.65	3.31	66.28	3.16	63.17
Lucy Hayes	3.17	63.31	3.12	62.40	3.22	64.46	3.14	62.89	3.17	63.39	3.18	63.55	3.09	61.74	3.16	63.14	3.13	62.56	3.21	64.21	3.16	63.17
Grace Coolidge	3.18	63.64	3.12	62.31	3.26	65.12	3.03	60.58	3.14	62.89	3.07	61.49	3.05	60.99	3.13	62.56	3.21	64.21	3.26	65.29	3.15	62.91
Julia Grant	3.15	62.98	3.12	62.31	3.16	63.22	3.05	60.99	3.14	62.89	3.17	63.47	3.02	60.50	3.14	62.89	3.13	62.56	3.31	66.28	3.14	62.81
Sarah Polk	3.15	62.98	3.10	61.98	3.19	63.80	3.13	62.56	3.07	61.49	3.17	63.31	3.07	61.49	3.12	62.31	3.05	60.99	3.26	65.29	3.13	62.62
Mamie Eisenhower	3.20	64.05	3.17	63.31	3.28	65.54	2.89	57.77	3.18	63.64	2.90	58.10	2.82	56.36	3.11	62.23	3.40	68.10	3.29	65.87	3.12	62.50
Helen Taft	3.19	63.88	3.08	61.65	3.11	62.23	3.07	61.32	3.10	61.90	3.22	64.38	3.07	61.49	3.10	61.90	3.03	60.58	3.22	64.38	3.12	62.37
Frances Cleveland	3.11	62.23	3.13	62.56	3.11	62.23	3.04	60.83	3.12	62.40	3.10	61.90	3.05	61.07	3.04	60.83	3.24	64.79	3.20	64.05	3.11	62.29
Julia Tyler	3.14	62.89	2.95	59.09	3.02	60.41	2.98	59.59	3.02	60.33	3.07	61.32	2.98	59.50	3.03	60.58	3.03	60.58	3.12	62.31	3.03	60.66
Lucretia Garfield	3.06	61.16	2.98	59.59	3.09	61.82	2.97	59.34	3.00	59.92	3.01	60.17	2.95	59.09	3.09	61.74	3.03	60.58	3.08	61.65	3.03	60.50
Caroline Harrison	3.04	60.74	3.01	60.17	3.05	60.99	3.04	60.74	3.09	61.74	3.03	60.58	3.00	60.08	3.00	60.08	2.97	59.34	3.01	60.25	3.02	60.47
Elizabeth Monroe	3.17	63.31	2.98	59.50	3.14	62.73	2.92	58.43	3.02	60.41	3.01	60.17	2.95	59.01	3.07	61.40	2.93	58.51	3.05	60.99	3.02	60.45
Mary Lincoln	3.40	68.02	2.98	59.50	2.97	59.42	2.79	55.70	3.07	61.49	3.31	66.12	2.83	56.69	3.31	66.28	2.49	49.75	3.05	61.07	3.02	60.40
Abigail Fillmore	3.03	60.58	2.97	59.34	3.07	61.32	2.95	59.01	3.02	60.41	2.99	59.75	2.97	59.42	3.00	59.92	2.92	58.43	3.05	61.07	3.00	59.93
Pat Nixon	3.10	62.07	2.95	59.01	3.19	63.80	2.71	54.21	3.09	61.82	2.72	54.46	2.72	54.38	3.20	63.97	2.94	58.84	3.12	62.40	2.97	59.50
Ida McKinley	3.07	61.32	2.90	57.93	3.04	60.74	2.87	57.44	2.89	57.77	2.89	57.85	2.88	57.60	3.05	60.91	2.94	58.76	3.07	61.32	2.96	59.17
Margaret Taylor	2.96	59.17	2.90	57.93	3.02	60.33	2.86	57.27	2.89	57.77	2.96	59.26	2.90	57.93	2.99	59.83	2.88	57.69	2.96	59.26	2.93	58.64
Florence Harding	2.99	59.83	2.85	57.02	2.82	56.36	2.86	57.27	3.16	63.14	2.86	56.17	3.01	60.17	2.83	56.53			2.95	59.09	2.93	58.50
Letitia Tyler	3.05	61.07	2.82	56.45	3.02	60.41	2.85	57.02	2.94	57.77	2.85	56.94	2.86	56.94	2.98	59.50	2.86	57.11	2.93	58.51	2.92	58.36
Eliza Johnson	2.93	58.68	2.85	56.94	2.98	59.67	2.81	56.20	2.93	57.44	2.83	58.51	2.83	56.61	2.97	59.42	2.82	56.45	3.06	61.24	2.91	58.12
Jane Pierce	2.98	59.67	2.72	54.38	2.94	58.84	2.74	54.71	2.85	55.54	2.75	57.02	2.75	54.96	2.90	57.93	2.75	55.04	2.79	55.79	2.82	56.39

Index